Crime in Canadian Society

Crime in Canadian Society

SIXTH EDITION

Robert A. Silverman

Queen's University

•

James J. Teevan

University of Western Ontario

•

Vincent F. Sacco

Queen's University

HARCOURT
BRACE
CANADA

Harcourt Brace & Company, Canada

Toronto Montreal Fort Worth New York Orlando
Philadelphia San Diego London Sydney Tokyo

Canadian Cataloguing in Publication Data

Main entry under title:

Crime in Canadian society

6th ed.
ISBN 0-7747-3627-5

1. Crime — Canada.   I. Silverman, Robert A., 1943–   .   II. Teevan, James J., 1942–   .   III. Sacco, Vincent F., 1948–   .

HV6807.C75 1999   364.971   C98-932751-5

New Editions Editor: Megan Mueller
Developmental Editor: Lise Dupont
Supervising Editor: Liz Radojkovic
Production Editor: Shana Hayes
Production Co-ordinator: Sue-Ann Becker/Cheryl Tiongson
Copy Editor: Tilman Lewis
Cover Design: Sonya V. Thursby, Opus House Incorporated
Interior Design: Sonya V. Thursby, Opus House Incorporated
Typesetting and Assembly: IBEX Graphic Communications Inc.
Printing and Binding: Transcontinental Printing Inc.

Cover Art: Yvonne McKague Housser, *Summer Night, Toronto*, 1949. Oil on masonite, 49.7 x 64.8 cm. Macdonald Institute purchase, 1956. University of Guelph Collection/Macdonald Stewart Art Centre, Guelph, Ontario. Reproduced with permission of the Macdonald Stewart Art Centre.

Harcourt Brace & Company Canada, Ltd.
55 Horner Avenue, Toronto, ON, Canada M8Z 4X6

Customer Service
Toll-Free Tel.: 1-800-387-7278
Toll-Free Fax: 1-800-665-7307

This book was printed in Canada.

1 2 3 4 5   03 02 01 00 99

To some extent the first edition of this book was modelled on an American book of readings for introductory criminology classes titled *The Sociology of Crime and Delinquency* edited by Marvin E. Wolfgang, Leonard Savitz, and Norman Johnson. On April 12, 1998, Marvin Wolfgang died at age 73. According to the *British Journal of Criminology* he was the "most influential criminologist in the English-speaking world." Every criminologist and criminology student is indebted to Marvin Wolfgang for his contributions to the discipline and to the endeavour of training the next generation. We note his passing with sadness.

For our wives and our teachers.

PREFACE

When people ask us what our academic specialty or discipline is and we answer "criminology," the inevitable response is "that sounds really interesting." The truth is, it is interesting especially from the point of view of discovery that comes from serious attention and scholarship. On a regular basis we (and the other criminologists in the world) get to think about, study, and attempt to understand why some of our fellow human beings steal from one another, kill each other, and generally violate laws that most of us, most of the time, obey. We want to share with readers a sample of the stimulating contributions by Canadian criminologists to our discipline.

Much has changed in Canadian criminology since the first edition of *Crime in Canadian Society* was published in 1975. We have seen the field blossom and Canadian researchers take their place with the major contributors to the discipline. An analysis of the tables of contents of the five preceding editions tells the story of Canadian criminology — at least to some extent.

That first edition had both American and Canadian contributions, and we had to search hard to include articles that covered all of the main sub-areas of criminology. We had an easier time with subsequent editions. In fact, with each subsequent edition, we have had an increasingly large number of good research articles from which to choose. In the last fifteen years Canadian criminology has become a kind of full service industry. Canadian criminologists have made contributions to theory, measurement of crime, and empirical tests of theory that have had international impact.

Like its predecessors, this edition is designed to introduce students to the field of criminology from a specific perspective. Our orientation is, for the most part, empirical, meaning that we are interested in work that links theoretical insights to research. Much criminological work in Canada involves a more philosophical/ideological approach. We leave it to other books to introduce students to that way of exploring the criminological enterprise. The organization of the book is more or less the same as in the previous editions, but there have been revisions to the essays that introduce each section and to the articles — some have been updated and others appear for the first time. In spite of the changes, the focus of the book remains sociological, looking to the role of society for the causes of crime, and it will probably fit best into criminology courses in which that approach dominates.

The introductions to the first three sections familiarize students with the major topics in criminology: the law, measurement of crime, and theories of crime. The readings are chosen to illustrate the points made in the introductions, as students are offered a chance to read the results of original Canadian research. The topics span the range of crime from spousal homicide to corporate crime. They also reflect criminology's concern with gender, age, and social class in the analysis of crime and delinquency.

Definitions of crime and delinquency are the subject of the first part of the book. Students will learn that defining crime is not as easy as it seems. Controversy and conflict in attempts to define crime and criminality result in a variety of definitions of crime, all of which serious students should be aware. Along with the introduction, the readings illustrate how different orientations lead to different definitions. Examples of recent changes in the law are also discussed in this section.

Part 2 is about measuring crime — trying to find out how much of each type of crime is occurring in Canada. This too is not as easy a task as it may seem. Through the introduction and readings, students are shown the problems with current data collection techniques, and are introduced to alternative measures of crime and to a relatively new system that was initiated by Statistics Canada in the late 1980s. The readings show how different measurement techniques produce different information. In earlier editions we included an appendix that showed crime statistics from Canada. In this edition the appendix has been replaced by an overview of crime in Canada presented in the first article in this section.

Part 3 introduces the student to contemporary explanations of crime causation. The major theories currently being discussed by sociologists are presented. The readings include original theory generated in Canada (power-control theory) as well as research showing the application and testing of particular theories in a Canadian context.

Part 4 examines "Crimes and Criminals: Selected Research." The title fits the array of research presented in this section. In the last edition, we asked several experts in the field to report either their own research or write an overview of the research of others on particular topics. We have asked them to update those articles as they proved to be very popular with readers. Contained in this section are pieces about issues of gender and crime, violence against women, corporate crime, organized crime, aboriginal involvement in crime, and the controversial topic of ethnicity, immigration, and crime.

Our goal in compiling this book has been to update our overview of Canadian criminology. It presents data on some very contemporary topics as well as some more traditional approaches to the field. As noted, this edition and its precursors

represent a particular orientation to criminology — we do not try to cover everything in depth, but we believe we manage to present a fair overview of the field as it exists.

We hope that the student/reader will gain a great deal from the book and that it will stimulate further exploration of this challenging discipline. We certainly hope you find the field as fascinating as we do.

ACKNOWLEDGEMENTS

Many people participated directly and indirectly in making this revision possible. We rely completely on the generosity of our colleagues in allowing us to make use of their work. When we called for papers, we received a large number of potential contributions that we had to examine to find those that would best fit our readers' needs. This was a daunting task, as we have had to omit many articles that readers would find interesting and that illustrate the points we want to make. Some of the work we received was fascinating but the topics were too complex or too specific for use in this introductory work. We feel that the advent of more and more of that type of article is a very good sign regarding the direction of Canadian criminology.

We are also grateful to those authors who agreed (on short notice) to revise the pieces they had done for the fifth edition of this book. (Wood and Griffiths, Gordon and Nelson, Beare, and Keane have all updated and revised their important overview articles.)

Harcourt Brace conducted a survey of users of our last edition. We have tried to revise on the basis of the comments that came from those surveys. For the most part our approach seems to be meeting the needs of a group of teachers and students interested in an empirical approach to the study of crime and delinquency. At Harcourt Brace the project was begun by Megan Mueller, who had worked on our last edition. Megan decided to have a baby girl and she put us into the very capable hands of Lise Dupont to take the project to completion. During the production stage, Shana Hayes was our very capable guide who brings you the book in your hands. We are grateful to all of them for help and encouragement.

Queen's University and the University of Western Ontario Departments of Sociology provided the facilities and environment necessary to complete our work. We also utilized the Criminology Library at the University of Toronto while searching for specific articles. That library is a gem and those who get to use it are fortunate.

Vince Sacco would like to thank his friends and colleagues at Queen's University for their support and advice. Bob Silverman relied entirely on the good will and understanding of his staff in the Faculty of Arts and Science office as they arranged his schedule so that work could be done on the book. Lynda MacDonald, the ultimate secretary/assistant, made sure that the needed days remained free. She is particularly skilful in keeping those in upper administration, who conspire to make demands on Silverman's time, at bay. At the very end of the project, Nancy Cutway's expertise with WordPerfect saved the day.

Tracey Peter was the research assistant on the book. Her technical abilities more than met the tasks that were assigned, and having her help at various stages took a good deal of pressure off the editors. She was a great asset.

We also owe special thanks to Ron Gillis, who arranged our day at the University of Toronto during which we made final selections for inclusion in the book. Also, through John Turner at Statistics Canada we obtained one critical article as soon as it became available.

Our wives, Elaine, Bonnie, and Tiia have provided the same level of support and encouragement as they have through all of the editions of the book. Katherin and Daniel Sacco have matured to the point where their father can no longer use them as an excuse for not getting work done.

ROBERT A. SILVERMAN
JAMES J. TEEVAN, JR.
VINCENT F. SACCO

August 1998

CONTRIBUTORS

DONALD A. ANDREWS
Department of Psychology
Carleton University

STEPHEN W. BARON
Department of Sociology
University of Windsor

MARGARET BEARE
Nathanson Centre for the Study
of Organized Crime and Corruption
York University

LUCIA BENAQUISTO
Department of Sociology
McGill University

NEIL BOYD
School of Criminology
Simon Fraser University

PETER J. CARRINGTON
Department of Sociology
University of Waterloo

MARIA CRAWFORD
Women We Honour Action Committee

MYRNA DAWSON
Department of Sociology
University of Toronto

DOREEN DUCHESNE
Canadian Centre for Justice Statistics
Statistics Canada

ROSEMARY GARTNER
Centre of Criminology
University of Toronto

ROBERT M. GORDON
School of Criminology
Simon Fraser University

CURT T. GRIFFITHS
School of Criminology
Simon Fraser University

JOHN HAGAN
Department of Sociology
University of Toronto

TIMOTHY F. HARTNAGEL
Department of Sociology
University of Alberta

HOLLY JOHNSON
Canadian Centre for Justice Statistics
Statistics Canada

CARL KEANE
Department of Sociology
Queen's University

LESLIE W. KENNEDY
School of Criminal Justice
Rutgers University

REBECCA KONG
Canadian Centre for Justice Statistics
Statistics Canada

TERESA C. LAGRANGE
Department of Sociology
Cleveland State University

ROSS MACMILLAN
Department of Sociology
University of Minnesota

JACQUELYN NELSON
Ministry of the Attorney General
of British Columbia

VINCENT F. SACCO
Department of Sociology
Queen's University

ROBERT A. SILVERMAN
Department of Sociology
Queen's University

LINDA SIMOURD
Simourd Consulting

JAMES J. TEEVAN
Department of Sociology
University of Western Ontario

ERIN VAN BRUNSCHOT
Department of Sociology
University of Calgary

DAVID VEITCH
Edmonton Police Service

DARRYL S. WOOD
Justice Centre
University of Alaska, Anchorage

CONTENTS

Definitions of Crime and Delinquency

Introduction

Most people think they know what crime is. Crime is, after all, a "hot" topic. The mass media often report on the sorry state of Canada, telling us how much crime and violence there is here. Citizens discuss their fears of becoming crime victims and then take protective measures, especially those who live in large cities (cf. Hagan, 1992; Sacco & Johnson, 1990). Crime is cocktail conversation. Crime is the subject of social surveys. Crime is a political issue. But what exactly is crime? Crime is, in fact, different things to different people. Sorting out the various definitions of crime and examining the formation of criminal law is the subject of this section of the book.

LAY DEFINITIONS OF CRIME

Generally, the legal bureaucracy and the average citizen agree on the acts that should be called crimes. Murder is a crime, as are shoplifting, arson, robbery, fraud, and break and enter. In some instances, however, citizens define acts as criminal when legally they are not. This is apparent in casual conversation when individuals refer to general social ills as crimes. The closing of hospitals, the decreased value of the dollar, and the disrespect of youth, none of which is a *legally* defined crime, may thus be defined as crimes by some people. Even more serious examples, such as emotional neglect of children or elderly parents, are generally not criminal matters. For most people, this process of making crime roughly equal to what they consider bad in their society is not an important error (indeed, many are aware that it is wrong), and is certainly quite acceptable in

an informal context. For a scientific study of crime, however, the inclusion of the bad or immoral, but not illegal, would make the boundaries of criminology vague and its content almost limitless. For these and other reasons, most criminologists reject such popular definitions of crime.

On the other hand, there are many instances in which crimes legally have occurred but the individuals involved — victim, offender, or both — do not define the act as criminal. Sometimes this is due to ignorance of the law; for instance, the general public is often unaware of the broad extent of the criminal law and has a narrower definition of crime than is legally the case. It is a *Criminal Code* offence, for example, to give trading stamps to purchasers of goods in Canada (section 427), or even to *offer* to transport someone to a common bawdy house (section 211), but few Canadians would be aware of these crimes.

In other instances, it is more disagreement than ignorance, as when people say that what occurred is "no big deal," that no real crime occurred. Until the modern feminist movement, much spousal abuse fell into this category (cf. Backhouse, 1991). In practice, the definition of acts as crimes or not often depends on the perceptions of the actors involved, how they define the behaviours that have occurred. For example, when one individual strikes another without consent, a criminal assault may have occurred. But suppose it was in fun, as a result of a playful struggle? Most people experience an assault in fun at some time in their lives. The pushing and shoving of children, considered to be a normal part of growing up, is just one example. Among adults as well, and not only when playing hockey and other sports, one finds the equivalents of pushing and shoving matches, little of which is defined as criminal. Even if the force used is excessive and injures one of the participants, the injury is often defined as accidental. The context is thus crucial.

Similarly, some assaults may be considered a part of daily life, and not a crime, by some segments of our society. Hitting an individual, for example, may be viewed as a legitimate way of settling a dispute in some subcultures in Canada today. If both parties agree to this solution, then neither will define the act involved as criminal and neither will call the police.

Suppose, however, that only one of the participants thinks this way or someone is hit, not by a friend or acquaintance, but by a stranger. In such cases, the "victim" may indeed define the event as a crime and call the police. In this instance, an assault as defined by the *Criminal Code of Canada* (section 265) may have been committed, not because the action was different, but because it was *defined* differently. The attacker may even be arrested and prosecuted. Thus the same use of force may or may not be a crime depending upon the context and upon the actors', especially the victims', perceptions of the situation.

A SOCIOLOGICAL DEFINITION

For sociologists, crimes are a part of a more general category called *deviance* (see Sacco, 1992) and involve the violation of *norms* — social rules that tell people what to do and what not to do in various situations. These rules are passed on to children in any society in a process called socialization and may vary both over time and across different societies. For example, in traditional Inuit culture, infanticide and abandoning the elderly to starve to death were not condemned, but were accepted as means to protect a limited food supply (cf. Edgerton, 1985). In the rest of Canada, strict norms would have prohibited such behaviour. While some societies do not permit the eating of pork, for

others beef is not allowed; while most groups prohibit cannibalism, some societies have allowed the practice. The point of these examples is that definitions of deviance are specific to time, place, and circumstances.

Deviance also generally involves, besides the violation of a norm, the possibility of punishment. One measure of how strongly a society feels about its various norms is the punishment or sanction it applies to those who violate them. Since norms range from the important and binding (thou shalt not kill) to the less important and optional (a person should not remain seated when being introduced to another), one would expect different types of reaction to those who violate them. But breaking even the most minor norm usually results in some type of reaction, insignificant though it be in terms of punishment. For example, walking down a street has many behavioural requirements that most of us rarely think of as norms. As you approach a stranger coming toward you, you are expected to avert your eyes at a certain point. If you do not, you have violated a norm, and the reaction to the violation may be anything — from no reaction, to the other individual looking at you, to the verbal challenge, "What are you staring at?" These less severely sanctioned norms are called *folkways; mores* are those norms whose infractions carry more serious punishments. Violations of mores are seen as more threatening to society — most crimes are violations of mores. But while most criminal laws (for example, those prohibiting sexual assault and theft) are mores, not all mores are laws. For a large part of our society, mores include the permanence of marriage, heterosexuality, and eventually having children. Divorce, homosexuality, and childlessness are not, however, crimes in Canada.

While there have been many attempts to summarize the sociological notion of crime, one of the best is still Gillin's (1945, p. 9) classic statement that crime is

> . . . an act that has been shown to be actually harmful to society, or that is *believed* to be socially harmful by a group of people that has the power

to enforce its belief and that places such an act under the ban of positive penalties.

Gillin's definition includes the ideas that the harm involved can be a constructed (believed) harm and that power determines what will be defined as criminal. That last point is the subject of the next section.

CONFLICT VERSUS CONSENSUS DEFINITIONS

Durkheim, one of the founders of sociology, argued that a crime is a violation of a widely held norm or value, an act that attacks what he called the *collective conscience* of a society (1964, p. 79). In this view the criminal law arises out of consensus, out of commonly agreed upon norms and values. Thus, since all or most people would agree that murder, arson, and theft are serious threats to individuals, these acts are defined as crimes. Further, everyone is outraged by such crimes because they weaken and attack the very basis of society.

For conflict theorists, on the other hand, the law is a tool, part of the superstructure of institutions created by the ruling class to serve itself. The law, instead of arising from consensus and providing justice for all, is in reality a weapon of oppression. Conflict theorists disagree among themselves on the role played by the capitalist class in this process, whether it shares its power with other power groups (sometimes called *moral entrepreneurs*) or by and large controls by itself the enactment of laws (cf. Turk, 1993), but they do agree that conflict and power determine the law, not consensus (cf. Young & Matthews, 1992).

Very few sociologists take either of the these two extreme positions. Underneath consensus there is always some disagreement or conflict. For example, does euthanasia, abortion, or killing in wartime constitute murder? Inside conflict there is always some consensus and negotiation, for without some co-operation there would be anarchy and lawlessness (cf. Kent, 1990). In addition, there are other more moderate positions on the sources of laws. Some sociologists, for example, have pointed to the role, not just of capitalists, but of the media, especially the publicity given to shocking crimes, and the politics of election years as having important effects on criminal legislation (McGarrell & Castellano, 1991).

This discussion is relevant to the definition of crime, since more conservative consensus and more radical conflict theorists might come to quite different definitions. Whereas conservatives would define acts that violate the *Criminal Code of Canada* as crimes, for conflict theorists, some of the building blocks of capitalism should be defined as crimes: for example, the relentless pursuit of profit, the practice of speculation, and the encouragement of overconsumption. Hence, from a conflict perspective, some of the "real" crimes have not been defined as such; they are not illegal because their victims do not control the law and thus the definition of what constitutes a crime. Thus the concept of ruling-class crimes, legal acts that "should" be illegal, provides us with another potential definition of crime.

In a less dramatic argument, conflict criminologists criticize criminology's traditional focus on the crimes of the powerless and its relative inattention to the crimes of the powerful (e.g., white-collar crime; see Keane in Part 4 of this volume) and ask whether the media deliberately underplay their reporting of corporate crime, directing public fear to muggers rather than polluters. Comack-Antony (1980) presented a chart that compares and contrasts the ways that radical (conflict) criminology and liberal (consensus) criminology define crime (cf. Burtch, 1992). The chart, slightly modified and reproduced in Table P1.1, illustrates well how one's perspective affects definitions of crime. Before examining it, think about one final example of the point we are making, sometimes called the *social construction* of crime. Is terrorism a crime only if it is unsuccessful? In framing your answer, think about the difference between the storming of the Bastille and the reign of terror or of the Boston Tea Party and Louis Riel.

Table P1.1
Liberal and Radical Perspectives in Defining Crime

Liberal Criminology	Radical Criminology
DEFINITION OF CRIME: legalistic approach: crime as behaviour	legalistic approach: crime as a definition of behaviour made by officials of the State
leads to an examination of the characteristics and life experiences of the criminal actor; general acceptance of the State	leads to an examination of political authority and questioning of the State
emphasis on cultural variables as they relate to explanations of crime, e.g., how failure in school can lead to crime	emphasis on structural variables as they relate to explanations of crime, e.g., how the whole economic system causes crime
ROLE OF CRIMINOLOGISTS: criminologists as "expert advisers" to "enlightened leaders"	commitment to Praxis, to the *application* by scientists of their results to improve society
social research used to provide information for the smooth and efficient running of the State system	social research used to determine the means by which desired change can be implemented and inequalities between individuals and groups diminished
IMAGE OF CRIME AND CRIMINALS: crime as a universal phenomenon caused by the inadequacies of human beings; deterministic (controlled by heredity and environment) image of people	crime as a universal phenomenon due to the conflictual nature of society; human behaviour seen as intentional and goal-oriented (more free will)
PRESCRIPTIONS FOR CHANGE: adherence to the rehabilitative ideal; emphasis on changing the nature of individual offenders	stresses political nature of crime; emphasis on changing the structural components of society
adjustment of individuals to the needs of the system	adjustment of the system to the needs of individuals

SOURCE: Adapted from Comack-Antony, A.E. (1980). Radical Criminology. In Robert A. Silverman and James Teevan (eds.) *Crime in Canadian Society* (2nd ed.) 246–247. Toronto: Butterworths.

THE LEGAL DEFINITION

Most classic criminology texts agree that criminal law and thus the legal definition of crime is marked by four ideals: politicality, specificity, uniformity, and penal sanction. Politicality means that only governments, and in Canada this means the federal government, can make criminal laws; specificity, that the laws are quite precise in their wording, telling exactly what is forbidden (*proscribed*) or demanded (*prescribed*); uniformity, that the laws apply equally to all; and penal sanction, that violators are threatened with a penalty and punishment. A crime is then any act or omission in violation of that criminal law. Omission offences include section 129b: "Everyone who (b) omits, without reasonable excuse, to assist a public officer or peace officer in the execution of duty in arresting a person or in preserving the peace, after having reasonable notice of a requirement to do so . . . is guilty of . . ."

Legally, then, a crime is a specific act or omission forbidden to all Canadians by Parliament and punishable for all who break that law. The Law Reform Commission of Canada (1974, p. 1–4) added the following points. (1) Not all acts against the law are crimes. Civil wrongs, called *torts* (for example, wrongful dismissal from a job), are not crimes. Criminal acts are proceeded against by *prosecution* and may result in *punishment*, while civil actions proceed by *suit* and may result in *compensation*. (2) Although under the *British North America Act* (now the *Constitution Act*, 1982) only the federal government can make a criminal law, the provinces can create provincial *offences* that, while technically not crimes, are treated like crimes. Examples of such legislation include traffic offences and enforced closing of stores on legal holidays. Crimes are thought of as more serious than such provincial offences because (a) they are seen to involve greater harm to individuals, (b) they are more often a violation of fundamental rules, like mores, and (c) "they are wrongs that any person *as a person* could commit. Offences are more specialized [wrongs] that people commit when playing certain special roles." For example, individuals disobey speed limits as drivers; they generally commit murders or thefts as individuals (1974, p. 3).

Despite the distinctions between crimes and offences, the consequences to individuals prosecuted for committing any of the many acts prohibited by provincial and municipal legislation and named "offences" may be similar (or even worse) than the consequences for committing a crime. For violators, then, there may be only a technical difference between a federal *crime* and a provincial *offence*. Thus, for some purposes, the important components of a legal definition of crime are that it is a violation of a law made by any political body, is deemed to be a state rather than a personal matter, and involves threats of punishment rather than compensation.

In a still more technical and legal sense, for an act or omission to be considered a crime, several other conditions are necessary. First, the act must have been legally forbidden before the act was undertaken; that is, the act or omission must be in violation of an already existing law that forbids or

commands the act. This means that an act or omission, no matter how ugly, mean, or distasteful, is not a crime if no law exists against it. The main rationale behind this principle is that it would be unfair to punish persons who, when they acted, did so in good faith thinking they were obeying the law. An *ex post facto* (after the fact) law thus cannot designate as criminal an act legal at the time it was committed, and the general ideal of *nullum crimen sine lege, nulla poena sine lege*, that is, no crime without law, no punishment without law, is still an important principle of Canadian jurisprudence. For example, in 1991 the Canadian Supreme Court refused to allow the extradition of two FLQ members to the United States to stand trial for the 1968 hijacking of a plane to Cuba because in 1968 hijacking was not an offence in Canada's *Criminal Code*. That offence was created in 1972. An implication of this principle is that laws must be quite specific and not vague, again applying the logic that the public should know exactly what it legally can and cannot do. Vaguely worded laws would make attempts to obey the law problematic, as people would not be sure if their behaviour would or would not result in penal sanction.

Second, there must be an *actus reus* or act. Merely thinking about or planning to violate the law is generally not a crime, with the exception of the crime of conspiracy (conspiracy to commit offences, *Criminal Code*, section 465). Actually there have never been many conspiracy charges laid in Canada; thus it is fairly safe to say that an *actus reus* is a requirement for a legal definition of crime.

Mens rea or criminal intent is a third requirement for a crime. Intentions are not the same as motives (which are the reasons why individuals commit crimes), but instead involve determination and purpose — that individuals intend the consequences of their acts. This means that they know what they are doing, for example, they are not insane, and mean to do what they are doing, for example, the acts were not accidental.

Finally, two additional requirements for the legal definition of a crime are that there should be a causal connection between the *actus reus* and any harm or outcome, and that the *mens rea* and *actus reus* must relate to the same act. These are general rules, ignored in certain circumstances, and sometimes a matter of dispute. For discussion of some of these and similar issues, see the article by Boyd in this section of the book.

DEFINITIONS MADE BY POLICE, PROSECUTORS, AND JUDGES

After Parliament makes the criminal law, the agents of the Canadian criminal justice system, from the police, to Crown prosecutors, to judges, must enforce it, and all may exercise considerable discretion in deciding whether an act or omission is a crime and, if so, which specific crime it is (cf. Kennedy, 1990). For example, suppose one man attacks another and hurts him, and the victim calls the police. Under a strict and static notion of law enforcement and crime, section 267 (assault with a weapon or causing bodily harm) of the *Criminal Code* would be enforced by the police: "Every one who, in committing an assault, . . . causes bodily harm to the complainant, is guilty of an indictable offence and is liable to imprisonment for a term not exceeding ten years. . . ." The Crown would then prosecute the defendant using the available evidence, the accused would be found guilty, and the convicted criminal would be given a sentence of up to ten years.

However there are alternatives to this scenario: (1) the police arrive and the victim indicates that while he did call them, he is not willing to testify against the offender in court. His motives are private, but could include an unwillingness to see the assaulter, often a friend or a relative, sent to trial or even an unwillingness to take time off from work to appear in court as a complainant. The police in most cases will not pursue the incident because they know that they will have insufficient evidence without the testimony of the victim. According to all public records, then, no crime of assault has taken place. The legal code does not indicate that the police have such discretion, but under these conditions it is in fact normal practice. (2) The victim is

abusive to the police, and in anger they decide not to record the crime. In fact, the police take many variables into consideration in deciding to write up less serious cases: how busy they are, the type of complainant, and so on. (3) The police do arrest the alleged attacker and charge him with unlawfully causing bodily harm. The Crown is ready to proceed when the defence attorney suggests a deal. If the charge is reduced to assault, punishable by a summary (less serious) conviction (*Criminal Code*, section 266b), the accused will plead guilty. Otherwise, he will plead not guilty to the original charge and insist on a trial. To speed things through the overburdened criminal justice process, the Crown agrees. (4) The police arrest the individual and the Crown proceeds with the case. The defendant pleads not guilty and is able to convince a judge that he in fact did not intend to injure the victim (recall the discussion of *mens rea*). The judge finds the defendant not guilty. Officially, then, no crime of assault causing bodily harm took place.

The combinations of events in the criminal justice system that can occur to redefine an act, compared to the behaviours that actually happened, are thus numerous. In Part 2 of this book, we discuss how these decisions affect official crime statistics. The subject is introduced here to point out that agents of social control must interpret and enforce the law, and the way in which they do so is a part of the process of defining crime (Evans & Himmelfarb, 1996).

CHANGING LAWS CHANGE DEFINITIONS

Many people think of the law as being relatively static. Lawyers know this is not so. The *Criminal Code* is frequently amended by Parliament. Minor changes are routinely made and are based on a "fine-tuning" of legislation or on recent court interpretations. More important changes take more time and reflect broader social movements. For example, while the public and the mass media both refer to the crime of rape, or forcible sexual intercourse, "rape" is not a crime in Canada. The sections of the *Criminal Code* dealing with rape were repealed and replaced in a process begun in 1980, partly as a result of the modern feminist movement. These activities are now found under the general heading of assault and are specified as sexual assault (section 271); sexual assault with a weapon, threats to a third party, or causing bodily harm (section 272); or aggravated sexual assault (section 273). The sexual aspect has been downplayed — even penetration is no longer a requirement in the definition of the crime — and the physical harm emphasized. Changing the crime to assault shifted the focus away from the end sought (sexual activity) to the force used, and thus sexual assault joined a slap to the face, a punch to the stomach, or a kick to the groin as assaults to the body. So dramatic was the change in definition that in fact the term "rape" does not even appear in the index to Carswell's latest *Pocket Criminal Code*. Thus, while many Canadians (including some journalists) call the event previously described a rape, legally, in Canada, no crime of "rape" exists.

On the other hand, in 1994 in the *R. v. Bernard* case the Supreme Court of Canada made a change with regard to intoxication as a mitigating factor in crimes such as sexual assault. Previously, drunkenness, no matter how severe, could not be used as a defence in such cases. The Supreme Court decided that "offenders" can be acquitted of sexual assault "because they were so drunk they did not know what they were doing." But the Court also said this defence would only be used in the "rarest" of cases — where the perpetrator was so drunk he was acting like an "automaton." Thus the law reflects the priorities of different power groups, sometimes the victims and sometimes the accused.

Changes with larger implications occur even less often. The passage of the *Charter of Rights and Freedoms* (1982) led to many procedural changes (making our criminal justice system more like its U.S. counterpart) and to some substantive changes in the criminal law as well. The *Charter's* protection of free speech led to nullification of parts of the promotion of racial hatred sections of the *Criminal Code* and to modifications to the obscenity law.

The most recent major change, however, was the introduction in 1985 of the *Young Offenders Act* (YOA), which replaced the 1970 revision of the *Juvenile Delinquents Act* (originally 1908). The philosophy and effects of the YOA are well documented (cf. Carrington & Moyer, 1994; Corrado, Bala, Linden, & LeBlanc, 1992). It combined a justice model (those accused of delinquency should have the same rights as adults accused of crime although be treated somewhat differently) with a crime control model (society must be protected) and largely replaced the welfare model of the JDA (in which the court acted as a wise and judicious parent but often ignored legal safeguards).

Right from the beginning the changes were controversial (cf. Bala, 1997). Some felt that the welfare model philosophy of the old system was superior to the new act. With the introduction of the YOA, youths basically gained the protection of due process (legal safeguards such as right to counsel), but lost some of the informal treatment previously routinely provided under the old act. Some civil libertarians were especially concerned that the new system led to more frequent and longer custody for youths than had occurred under the old act (cf. Clark & Fleming, 1993; Doob & Meen, 1993). At the other end of the spectrum, many, especially among the public, felt that the new age limits provided by the act (12 to 17 instead of the previous lower limit of age 7) allowed younger children (up to age 11) to "get away with murder" (not to mention sexual assault, robbery, and arson). Children 11 years of age or younger were defined as incapable of having the *mens rea* necessary for crime — a view challenged when people heard of the 11-year-old who sexually assaulted a girl and then taunted the police with his underage status. Perhaps the greatest public concern surrounded the maximum sentences for those age 12 to 17 who commit serious violent crimes, such as the 1994 drive-by shooting of a British man in Ottawa. Many felt that the maximum sentences are too short for some violent crimes and that society deserves greater protection from some young offenders, including trying them in adult court.

·····················

Public pressure was successful. In February 1995 the House of Commons passed Bill C-37 (An Act to amend the Young Offenders Act and the Criminal Code), which dealt with some of the concerns of the public. While the Bill did not change the age range of young offenders it did increase penalties, especially for the most serious crimes. When the *Young Offenders Act* was initially introduced the maximum penalty for any crime was three years. This was later raised to five years for some crimes, and a juvenile convicted (in youth court) of first-degree murder could be sentenced to a penalty of ten years. It also visited the issue of transfer to adult court. In the case of murder, attempted murder, manslaughter, or aggravated sexual assault by 16- or 17-year-olds, they would henceforth be dealt with by ordinary (i.e., adult) court unless they could make a successful application to have the case heard in youth court. Hence, the onus was on the teenagers to prove that they should have the privilege of being heard in youth court.

The changes did not go far enough for many, so as this is being written Parliament is considering further changes. To convince a fearful public that they are not just tinkering, a new name has been suggested, the Youth Criminal Justice Act. Again, those under age 12 are spared, despite strong pressure to lower the minimum age to 10, but 14- and 15-year-olds convicted of the most serious crimes like murder, aggravated sexual assault, and so on will join 16- and 17-year-olds in being vulnerable to longer sentences. In fact all repeat violent offenders aged 14 to 17 will also be punishable by longer sentences and having their names published upon conviction. These changes reflect that protecting society is the main goal of the criminal law but also that prevention and rehabilitation, including community-based sentences, are important aspects too.

CONCLUSIONS

In summary, there are several definitions of crime from which to choose: (1) acts that violate norms; (2) acts that violate *legal* norms; (3) acts that the participants define as violations of *legal* norms;

(4) acts that agents of the Canadian criminal justice system interpret as violations of legal norms; (5) acts for which *mens rea* and *actus reus* have been demonstrated; and (6) acts that from a conflict perspective are the "real" crimes. Each definition may be appropriate under different circumstances. Also remember that whichever definition is chosen, the actual acts defined as criminal are not universal. They are specific to a given time and society.

Different definitions may not be that important in themselves. The crucial point to consider is that different definitions will lead to different criminal statistics (Part 2 of this volume) and yield different theories about the causes of crime (Part 3). Readers of criminological research (as in Part 4) should thus pay close attention to the definition of crime being used by the researchers. Such scrutiny will help to evaluate the adequacy of their conclusions.

THE READINGS

"Media Constructions of Crime" by Vincent F. Sacco is the first piece presented. Its thesis is that the media define the larger crime picture by telling society which crimes are most problematic and how it should deal with them. Contrast this viewpoint with the other three articles in which legal definitions of crime are featured. Neil Boyd's "Canadian Criminal Law" introduces students to some of the fundamentals of the subject. Doreen Duchesne's "Street Prostitution in Canada" briefly talks about recent legislative developments in the laws of soliciting and their effect on who is charged in these transactions. Finally, a more specific point concerning allowable defences is made by Robert A. Silverman and Leslie W. Kennedy in "The Battered Wife Defence." Future criminologists who prefer only strict legal definitions of crime will find all three of these discussions most useful.

REFERENCES

Backhouse, C. (1991). *Petticoats and prejudice: Women and law in nineteenth-century Canada.* Toronto: Butterworths.

Bala, N. (1997). *Young offenders law*. Concord, ON: Irwin.

Burtch, B. (1992). *The sociology of law: Critical approaches to social control*. Toronto: Harcourt Brace Jovanovich.

Carrington, P., & Moyer, S. (1994). Trends in youth crime and police response, pre- and post-YOA. *Canadian Journal of Criminology, 36*, 1–28.

Clark, B., & Fleming, T. (1993). Implementing the *Young Offenders Act* in Ontario: Issues of principles, programmes and power. *Howard Journal of Criminal Justice, 32*, 114–126.

Comack-Antony, A. E. (1980). Radical criminology. In R.A. Silverman & J. Teevan (Eds.), *Crime in Canadian society* (2nd ed.). Toronto: Butterworths.

Corrado, R., Bala, N., Linden, R., & LeBlanc, M. (Eds.). (1992). *Juvenile justice in Canada*. Toronto: Butterworths.

Doob, A., & Meen, J. (1993). An exploration of changes in dispositions for young offenders in Toronto. *Canadian Journal of Criminology, 35*, 19–29.

Durkheim, E. (1964). *The rules of sociological method*. New York: Free Press.

Edgerton, R. B. (1985). *Rules, exceptions, and social order*. Berkeley, CA: University of California Press.

Evans, J., & Himmelfarb, A. (1996). Counting crime. In R. Linden (Ed.), *Criminology: A Canadian perspective*. (3rd ed.) Toronto: Harcourt Brace Jovanovich.

Gillin, J. (1945). *Criminology and penology* (3rd ed.). New York: Appleton-Century-Crofts.

Hagan, J. (1992). Class fortification against crime in Canada. *Canadian Review of Sociology and Anthropology, 29*, 126–139.

Kennedy, L. W. (1990). *On the borders of crime*. New York: Longman.

Kent, S. (1990). Deviance, labelling, and normative strategies in "The Canadian new religion/counter-cult" debate. *Canadian Journal of Sociology, 15*, 393–416.

Law Reform Commission of Canada. (1974). *The meaning of guilt: Strict liability*. Ottawa: Information Canada.

McGarrell, E., & Castellano, T. (1991). An integrative conflict model of the criminal law formation process. *Journal of Research in Crime and Delinquency, 28*, 174–196.

Rodrigues, G. P. (1998). *Pocket Criminal Code 1999*. Toronto: Carswell.

Sacco, V. (1992). *Deviance: Conformity and control in Canadian society*. Scarborough: Prentice-Hall.

Sacco, V. F., & Johnson, H. (1990). *Patterns of criminal victimization in Canada*. Ottawa: Minister of Supply and Services Canada.

Turk, A. T. (1993). A proposed resolution of key issues in the political sociology of law. In F. Adler & W. Laufer (Eds.), *New directions in criminological theory, vol. 4*. New Brunswick, NJ: Transaction.

Young, J., & Matthews, R. (1992). *Rethinking criminology: The realist debate*. London: Sage.

CHAPTER

1

Media Constructions of Crime

INTRODUCTION

Crime, like an economic recession, a lack of afford-able housing, or inadequate health care, is experi-enced as both a private trouble and a public issue. Quite obviously, for victims, a criminal offense and the resulting loss or injury present problems of a highly personal nature. For victims and non-victims alike, however, the "plague of drugs," the "epidemic of random violence," and other aspects of the crime problem are matters for intense public discussion and political debate.

While the distinction between private troubles and public issues is an important one, these dimen-sions are not independent. Citizens' personal trou-bles with crime provide the building blocks out of which public issues are constructed. On the other hand, the warnings of danger implicit in public pronouncements about the seriousness and perva-siveness of crime problems may be a source of private trouble if they increase the fear of crime among those who have routine exposure to such pronouncements.

Central to the interplay between individuals' private troubles with crime and the social issue of crime are the mass media. The news media, in par-ticular, provide an important forum in which pri-vate troubles are selectively gathered up, invested with a broader meaning, and made available for public consumption. The dynamic character of

these processes and the consequences that they have for public understanding of crime and its solution invite close scrutiny.

FROM PRIVATE TROUBLE . . .

Numerous studies of media content have docu-mented the fact that crime reports are a durable news commodity. While news about crime figures prominently in all types of media, important differ-ences exist between print and electronic media, between more elite and more popular media, and among media markets. Because of this variability, estimates of the proportion of total news that is devoted to crime coverage range from 5 to 25 per-cent (Surette, 1992: 62).

News about crime is most frequently news about the occurrence or processing of private trou-ble in the form of specific criminal events. Analyses of media content, however, demonstrate that the news provides a map of the world of criminal events that differs in many ways from the one pro-vided by official crime statistics. Variations in the volume of news about crime seem to bear little rela-tionship to variations in the actual volume of crime between places or over time (Skogan and Maxfield, 1981). Whereas crime statistics indicate that most crime is nonviolent, media reports suggest, in the aggregate, that the opposite is true (Schlesinger et al., 1991). While crime news tends to provide only

Adapted from Media Constructions of Crime, by Vincent F. Sacco (May 1995). *Annals of the American Academy of Political and Social Science, 539*, p. 141–154. Reprinted with permission of Sage Publications, Inc. and the author. Copyright © 1999 by Sage Publications.

sparse details about victims and offenders, what is provided is frequently at odds with the official picture. Both offenders and victims, for instance, appear less youthful in media reports than they do in statistical records (Gordon and Riger, 1989: 70).

In addition, news content does not reflect and frequently even reverses the relationship that, according to much social scientific evidence, exists between minority group membership and criminal offending (Lotz, 1991: 114) with minorities underrepresented in the media compared to official data. With respect to gender, however, both crime statistics and crime news portray offending as predominantly a male activity (Bortner, 1984). Finally, news reports also distort the relationship between crime and legal control. In the news, the police appear to be more effective in apprehending offenders than police data would suggest they are (Marsh, 1991).

The images of crime, the criminal, and the victim that do appear with patterned regularity in print and broadcast news emerge quite logically from the organizational processes of news production. For example, news stories are most useful to news organizations when they are gathered easily from credible sources; for this reason, policing agencies have become the principal suppliers of these stories (Ericson, 1989). In addition, the public view of the police as apolitical crime experts gives police-generated crime authority and objectivity. The major exception of course is corporate crime, which is covered with greater difficulty. Generally, corporate crimes are more complex and more difficult to personalize, and well-established source-reporter relationships do not exist for corporate crime as they do for personal crimes.

Ease of access to authoritative news is not the only advantage that police-generated crime stories offer, since such stories are consistent with several other professional values that structure the news production process. Much of what we call news consists of reports of specific incidents that have occurred since the publication of the previous day's newspaper or the airing of the previous night's newscast. As discrete incidents that occur at particular times and places, individual crimes conform closely to this requirement of periodicity.

Stories about individual crimes — with their characteristic portrayals of villains and victims — also have dramatic value. The dramatic potential is heightened when the victim or offender is a celebrity, when the incident is of a very serious nature, or when the circumstances of the offense are atypical. In addition, the routine crime story is a rather uncomplicated matter, and it is unnecessary for news workers to assume that readers or viewers require an extensive background in order to appreciate the story. The lack of factual complexity associated with the ordinary individual crime story generally means that it can be easily written and edited by news workers whose professional activities are consistently regulated by rigid deadlines.

The elastic character of the crime news supply offers a further advantage. On any given day, particularly in large metropolitan areas, there is an almost limitless supply of crimes that could be the object of media attention. However, from day to day, or from week to week, the demand of the news agency for crime news may vary due to other events that are seen to demand coverage. Depending on the size of the news hole, crime coverage may be expanded or contracted in compensatory fashion. A study by Sherizen (1978: 221) of crime news in Chicago newspapers found, for instance, that crime reports were often located on the obituary pages so that layout difficulties resulting from the inability to plan these pages could be overcome through the use of crime news filler.

Over the last several years, a number of changes in local and national media environments have altered the nature and extent of crime coverage. The growth of cable stations, for instance, has increased the carrying capacity for news generally and for crime news specifically. More stories can be covered, and those that are judged to be particularly newsworthy can be covered in greater detail. The live television coverage of court proceedings — as in the case of the Menendez brothers, Lorena Bobbit, or O.J. Simpson — has become commonplace. The increasing sophistication of news gathering, surveillance, and home video technologies has meant that it is no longer unusual to capture thefts, robberies, or even homicides on tape. One consequence of the diffusion of these technologies has been to raise to national prominence stories with no real national significance. Crime stories that would have been a purely local affair in an earlier period now attract much wider attention because a videotape of the incident is available for broadcast.

The last two decades have also witnessed a redefinition of what can be considered an appropriate subject for news reporting. Changes in mores relating to public discussion of sex and violence have allowed respectable media outlets to report crimes that would have previously been seen as taboo and to do so at a level of detail that would once have been considered lurid. At the same time, the politicization of crimes such as sexual assault and domestic violence has broadened the range of crime stories that, it can be argued, legitimately require coverage (Soothill and Walby, 1991: 6).

Programmatic developments in commercial broadcast media have magnified the impact of these changes. The proliferation of news magazines, daytime talk shows, docudramas, and various other forms of infotainment has ushered in a programming cycle that is heavily dependent on crime news and victim accounts. The frequent reliance of many of these programs on dramatic reenactments of real events and their mixing of factual reports with rumor and speculation blur the basic distinctions that analysts of crime content have traditionally drawn between news and entertainment media (Newman, 1990).

...TO PUBLIC ISSUES

Public issues grow up around private troubles when the experiences of individuals are understood as exemplifying a larger social problem, and the news media play a vital role in the construction of such problems (Best, 1989a; Gusfield, 1989; Schneider, 1985). Most notably, professional judgments of newsworthiness and the selective use of news sources allow some groups, rather than others, the oppor-

tunity to express a view about what is and what is not a problem and how any such problem should be managed. By implication, the relationships that link the police to news agencies serve law enforcement as well as media interests. The police role as the dominant gatekeeper means that crime news is often police news and that the advancement of a police perspective on crime and its solution is facilitated (Ericson, 1989). It has been argued that this results in the adoption of an uncritical posture with respect to the police view of crime and the measures necessary to control it (Ericson, 1991). More generally, the frame of reference offered by a government bureaucracy or other recognized authority with respect to crime problems may only infrequently be called into question and, as a consequence, competing perspectives may become marginalized.

This tendency may be no less true of in-depth issue coverage than of routine news reporting. Brownstein (1991) maintains that during the 1980s, there was relatively little reporting that took issue with the official version of the drug problem constructed by government experts. In a similar way, Jenkins (1994: 212–13) has noted how experts of the Federal Bureau of Investigation were able to present themselves as the authorities on the subject of serial murder and how they made themselves available to journalists who reciprocated with favorable coverage of the agency.

It would be incorrect, however, to suggest that news media are merely the passive conveyors of the claims about problems offered up by government bureaucracies, political candidates, or other self-interested groups, since any such claims must be transformed to meet the requirements of the medium in question. In an analysis of television network news coverage of threats to children, Best argued that "inevitably, network news stories distort the problems they explore" in large part because news conventions impose severe constraints on how stories are covered (1989b: 277).

Stories must be told in a few minutes, frequently by reporters who may have little more than a surface familiarity with the complexities of the problem at hand. Moreover, the topic must be viewed as serious enough and as visual enough to be chosen over competing issues. Best found, in the case of child victimization, that the stories used frightening and dramatic examples to typify the problem and that they emphasized the existence of a consensus among knowledgeable experts regarding its scope and seriousness. In other instances, news media may more actively engage in problem construction. Investigative reporting, or the coverage of an event judged to be especially newsworthy, may contribute to the establishment of a media agenda that finds expression in the reporting of further stories or in more detailed features. A study by Protess and his colleagues (1985) revealed how one Chicago newspaper set its own media agenda after an extensive investigative series on rape. The researchers found that, while the series did not appear to have a substantial impact on the perceptions of policymakers or the general public, there were significant changes in the extent and depth of rape coverage after the series ended, even though police reports of rape were unchanged. In a related way, during the summer of 1994, the O.J. Simpson case provided an opportunity for sidebar stories relating to the prevalence and causes of domestic violence, the inadequacy of justice system responses, and pending federal and state legislation. Such coverage contextualized the original incident in a way that helped construct the social issue of violence against women at the same time that it legitimated continuing, detailed attention to the original story.

The Content of Crime Problems

Media constructions of crime problems address both the frequency and the substance of private trouble with crime. Rhetoric regarding both of these dimensions serves to impress on readers and viewers the gravity of particular crime problems and the need to confront them in particular ways.

Large numbers of problems provide convincing evidence that problems exist. This is perhaps most evident in the case of crime waves, when it is argued that crime is becoming more frequent. A study by Gorelick, for instance, of an anti-crime campaign

sponsored by a New York daily newspaper found that crime in the city was frequently described as a "mushrooming cloud," a "floodtide," a "spreading cancer," or in similar terms (1989: 429). Sometimes these claims about the numbers of people affected have greater specificity in that some particular segment of the population is claimed to be experiencing rapidly increasing risks of offending or victimization (Cook and Skogan, 1990).

Yet, with respect to many crime waves, it is the belief that crime is increasing, rather than crime itself, that is really on the rise (Baker et al., 1983). A recent example of a journalistic construction of rapidly rising crime is provided by Orcutt and Turner (1993). Their analysis focused on the way in which graphic artists in the national print media transformed survey data, which showed modest yearly changes in drug use, into evidence of a "coke plague." While the numbers were real, their graphical presentation in the weekly periodical under study was misleading. The dynamics of competitive journalism created a media feeding frenzy that found news workers "snatching at shocking numbers" and "smothering reports of stable or decreasing use under more ominous headlines" (1993: 203).

Claims about statistical frequency are not restricted to reports about how the numbers are increasing, however. With respect to the problem of violence against women, for instance, it is argued that the numbers have always been very high but that the failure to police such incidents, the stigma associated with victimization, and an institutional unwillingness to believe the accounts of victims have resulted in statistical counts that dramatically underestimate the problem. Thus, whether or not the numbers are going up is defined as less salient than the observation that they have always been higher than we have thought.

According to Gilbert (1994), outrageous claims about the prevalence of problems sometimes make their way into news reports in part because of journalists' general inability to evaluate the data supplied to them. Too often, they lack the technical sophistication to critically assess claims about the frequency of crime or victimization in an independent fashion. Instead, they collect and validate information by talking to experts who are expected to offer informed opinions. However, in the case of emergent problems, it is often the problem advocate, interested in advancing a particular point of view, who may be among the first to collect and publicize empirical evidence. As a result, the estimates yielded by advocacy research may be the only ones available at the earliest stages of problem development. Jenkins has argued that the emergence of serial murder as a social issue in the early 1980s was spurred by "epidemic estimates" that placed the number of serial murder victims at between 20 and 25 percent of American homicides (1994: 22). While such numbers continue to circulate through popular and journalistic accounts, more reasoned analysis suggests that the number of serial murder victims is closer to 2 percent of American homicides.

The emergence of crime problems is related not only to claims about the frequency of criminal events but also to claims about their character. Exactly what types of events such incidents are thought to be and who is thought to be typically involved in them matter as much as does the rate at which they are thought to occur.

Any particular social problem can be framed in many ways, and these various frames imply different causal attributions and prospective solutions (Gusfield, 1989; Schneider, 1985). Because they are able to legitimate some views and to marginalize others, the news media are an important part of this framing process. Depending on the sources accessed or the type of coverage, rape can be framed as a sex crime or as a crime of violence; the "drug problem" as a product of pushers who hook their victims or as an example of the overreach of criminal law; and violence on the part of youths as a condition necessitating either swift punishment or comprehensive community development.

In a related way, the social distributional character of victimization is frequently ignored by news coverage that stresses the random character of victimization. While the best social science literature indicates that the risks of crime, like the risks of

other misfortunes, are not equally shared, media images often convey a different message. According to Brownstein (1991: 95), for instance, much of the coverage of the drug issue in New York City between 1986 and 1990 emphasized the random character of drug violence even though police statistics indicated that the risks of such violence were extremely low. Themes relating to randomness serve the interests of both news workers and others who seek to frame crime problems. News stories about random crimes have great dramatic value, as the media frenzies that surround serial murders illustrate. Moreover, the advocates to whom news workers have access during the early stages of problem development often stress the random nature of a particular form of victimization, since problems must be seen as more urgent when everyone is threatened.

While much routine crime reporting can be understood as maintaining established crime problem frames, new problems are always being discovered as old problem paradigms expand or as novel elements come together with established news themes. The discovery of new problems provides a journalistic opportunity to tell a story that has not been told before, but such stories are told most effectively when they resonate with existing cultural themes. In the 1970s, the problem of crime against the elderly brought together in one package an already familiar concern about crime in the streets and victims' rights with an emerging concern about the aging population (Cook and Skogan, 1990). The problem of satanic crime, which received extensive media coverage in the 1980s, combined familiar news themes relating to religious cults, child abuse and juvenile crime (Crouch and Damphousse, 1992; Jenkins and Maier-Katkin, 1992). Media attention to date rape and stalking extends earlier news themes relating to violence against women.

The transition from private troubles to public issues is not always a linear process, since media interest in particular crime problems can vary in intensity or decline over time. The 1987 shootings on California freeways never became a well-established problem, despite a strong start (Best, 1991). In the case of crimes against the elderly, Cook and Skogan (1990) observe that, while the issue achieved a prominent position on media and other agendas during the early 1970s, by the decade's end, it had declined precipitously. On the other hand, Fishman has argued that as long as police departments are the routine sources of crime news, the media will reinforce a climate of opinion that keeps the attention of the police focused on "crime in the streets." He concludes that, while social problems may come and go, "law-and-order news is here to stay" (1981: 389).

...AND BACK AGAIN?

There can be little doubt that media consumers have broad and regular exposure to crime news (Garofalo, 1981). What are the consequences of this exposure? One potential consequence that has generated considerable interest relates to the deleterious effects that media attention to crime problems may have on audience members' fear of victimization. On the surface, arguments about such effects seem plausible. Public fear of crime is pervasive, and it outstrips measured levels of victimization. By implication, public anxieties would appear to be rooted in vicarious rather than direct experiences, and since messages about crime are so prevalent in the media, it seems reasonable to conclude that much public fear originates in media coverage of crime problems. At issue is whether experience with media treatments of crime as a public issue contributes to fear as a personal trouble. There is a large body of empirical evidence that bears on the relationship between audience exposure to mass media and fear of crime. In the aggregate, however, the findings are equivocal regarding the strength of such a relationship or even whether such a relationship exists (Carlson, 1985; Sparks, 1992; Sacco, 1982).

Some of the inconsistency in this respect is methodological in nature. Considerable variation exists regarding the ways in which crime news, crime news exposure, and fear of crime have been operationalized in the research literature (Sparks

and Ogles, 1990). In addition, since people not only read or watch crime news but also talk about it with friends and neighbors, measured variations in media exposure are not necessarily indicative of exposure to crime news (Doob, 1982). Nor is it reasonable to assume for research purposes that people are always able to keep clear and report to researchers what is learned in which information channel (Gordon and Riger, 1989). Even when such methodological limitations are taken into account, however, the research indicates that the effects of media exposure on fear of crime are less significant than any naive hypothesis would suggest.

Several factors explain this apparent paradox. To begin with, it would be inappropriate to assume that audience members respond passively to the warnings of danger issued by omnipotent news media. Instead, as Williams and Dickinson note, news consumers are actively involved in investing the news with meaning (1993: 34). Audience members bring to the reading and viewing experience their own predispositions, which influence what crime news means for them. These predispositions may include personal experiences with crime or violence (Schlesinger et al., 1992: 165), perceptions of the credibility of news media (O'Keefe, 1984), or the extent of prior concern about personal safety (Sacco, 1982). In the context of cross-sectional research, these predispositions suggest the possibility that the correlation between media usage and fear of crime may be more indicative of selective exposure than of media influence (Williams and Dickinson, 1993: 51; Zillmann and Wakshlag, 1987).

While people avidly read and watch crime news, it is unclear that in so doing they extract lessons relating to their own safety. Such lessons, it appears, are more effectively learned in other contexts. The relevant research indicates that the news about crime that travels through interpersonal channels may be more likely to induce fear than is the news that travels through mass channels (Skogan and Maxfield, 1981; Tyler, 1984). To learn about crime by talking to one's neighbors is to learn about victims whose experiences cannot be easily dismissed because they are nameless or faceless or live somewhere else.

By contrast, the typical media crime story is stripped of much of its emotional character and is likely to involve victims about whom the viewer or reader has no personal knowledge. In addition, the average news story may provide readers and viewers with so little information about the victim, the setting in which the crime occurred, or other circumstances of commission that it may be irrelevant to any assessment of personal victimization risks (Gordon and Riger, 1989: 75; Tyler, 1984: 34). Most crime news is non-local and therefore far removed from judgments that must be made regarding the safety of the immediate environment. Not surprisingly, there is research that suggests that increased fear is, in fact, related to crime news exposure when local random violent crimes are reported in prominent fashion (Heath, 1984; Liska and Baccaglini, 1990). On the other hand, coverage of non-local violence may decrease fear by allowing the audience to feel safer by comparison. Taken together, these findings are consistent with a more general body of research that indicates that people may be less dependent on news media when they seek information about matters close to home (Palmgreen and Clarke, 1977).

Overall, it would appear that as crime news relates to matters of personal safety, consumers appear to exercise a healthy dose of skepticism (Katz, 1987: 60). As Dennis Howitt observes, newspaper readers do not necessarily think that crime rates are going up just because the number of column inches devoted to crime increases (1982: 125–26). They are more likely to put what is learned from the media in the context of what they learn from other sources, and they may be well aware when media are behaving in a highly sensationalist manner (Williams and Dickinson, 1993).

CONCLUSION

If the news business is concerned with the production of crime problems, then the private troubles of criminal offenders and crime victims are the raw materials. These troubles are not simply reported on, however, since they are fundamentally transformed by the news-gathering process. Screened through a law enforcement filter, contextualized by advocacy claims and culturally resonant news themes, and shaped and molded by the conventions and requirements of commercial media, these private troubles become public issues.

While news media coverage of crime may not have a powerful influence on the concern for personal safety, this should not obscure other, perhaps more significant effects.

Such effects are not narrowly attitudinal or behavioral but are broadly ideological. Some critics argue that the police perspective implicit in so much crime news reporting dramatically restricts the parameters of discussion and debate about the problem of crime. As a consequence, the causes of offending are individualized and the relationships that link crime to broader social forces are left largely unexplored (Gorelick, 1989; Humphries, 1981).

Correspondingly, traditional law-and-order responses are reaffirmed as the most efficient way to manage crime problems. A study of media coverage of attacks against women in Toronto found that explanations of the phenomenon tended to focus attention on the ways in which victims placed themselves in conditions of risk, on offender pathology, and on the need for a more coercive criminal justice response (Voumvakis and Ericson, 1984). The authors note that while these terms of reference were not unreasonable, the attention they received left little room for alternative interpretations of the problem, particularly those interpretations that link the victimization of women to structures of gender inequality.

When crime problems are successfully constructed, a consensus emerges regarding what kinds of public issues private troubles represent (Gusfield, 1989: 434–36). Yet the development of such a consensus — regarding what the problems are, who is responsible for them, and how they should be resolved — should not be understood in conspiratorial terms. While both news workers and their sources are interested in offering a convincing and credible construction of reality for many in the media, the construction of these problems is not a matter of activism but just another day at the office (Hilgartner and Bosk, 1988).

DISCUSSION QUESTIONS

1. Sacco often talks about the media generally. How would comparing radio, television, newspapers, and other forms affect some of his arguments? For example, would certain media instill more fear of crime than others? Take a widely reported crime in your area and compare how the different media reported it.

2. How do local and national media differ in their coverage of crime?

3. There was no mention of the Internet in the article. How would you integrate it into Sacco's arguments?

4. How far should the media go in uncovering crime? Is that their role? Since they rely on advertisers for revenue, will they ever be free to fully examine the white collar criminality of that major source of income? If they will not, who can?

REFERENCES

Baker, M. H., et al. (1983). The impact of a crime wave: Perceptions, fear, and confidence in the police. *Law and Society Review, 17,* 317–334.

Best, J. (Ed.). (1989a). *Images of issues: Typifying social problems.* Hawthorne, NY.: Aldine de Gruyter.

Best, J. (Ed.). (1989b). Secondary claims-making: Claims about threats to children on the network news. *Perspectives on Social Problems, 1,* 277.

Best, J. (Ed.). (1991). Road warriors on hair-trigger highways: Cultural resources and the media's construction of the 1987 freeway shootings problem. *Sociological Inquiry, 61,* 327–345.

Bortner, M. A. (1984). Media images and public attitudes toward crime and justice. In R. Surette (Ed.), *Justice and the media* (pp. 15–30). Springfield, IL: Charles C. Thomas.

Brownstein, H. H. (1991). The media and the construction of random drug violence. *Social Justice, 18,* 85–103.

Carlson, J. M. (1985). *Prime time law enforcement: Crime show viewing and attitudes toward the criminal justice system.* New York: Praeger.

Cook, F. L., & Skogan, W. G. (1990). Agenda setting and the rise and fall of policy issues: The case of criminal victimization of the elderly. *Government and Policy, 8,* 395–415.

Crouch, B. M., & Damphousse, K. R. (1992). Newspapers and the anti-satanism movement: A content analysis. *Sociological Spectrum, 12,* 1–20.

Doob, A. N. (1982). The role of mass media in creating exaggerated levels of fear of being the victim of a violent crime. In Peter Stringer (Ed.), *Confronting social issues: Applications of social psychology* (pp. 145–159). Toronto: Academic Press.

Ericson, R. V. (1989). Patrolling the facts: Secrecy and publicity in police work. *British Journal of Sociology, 40,* 205–226.

Ericson, R. V. (1991). Mass media, crime, law and justice. *British Journal of Sociology, 31,* 219–249.

Fishman, M. (1981). Police news: Constructing an image of crime. *Urban Life, 9,* 371–394.

Garofalo, J. (1981). Crime and the mass media: A selective review of research. *Journal of Research in Crime and Delinquency, 18,* 319–350.

Gilbert, N. (1994). Miscounting social ills. *Society, 31,* 24–25.

Gordon, M. T., & Riger, S. (1989). *The female fear.* New York: Free Press.

Gorelick, S. M. (1989). Join our war: The construction of ideology in a newspaper crimefighting campaign. *Crime and Delinquency, 35,* 421–436.

Gusfield, J. R. (1989). Constructing the ownership of social problems: Fun and profit in the welfare state. *Social Problems, 36,* 431–441.

Heath, L. (1984). Impact of newspaper crime reports on fear of crime: Multi-methodological investigation. *Journal of Personality and Social Psychology, 47,* 263–276.

Hilgartner, S., & Bosk, C. L. (1988). The rise and fall of social problems: A public arenas model. *American Journal of Sociology, 94,* 57.

Howitt, D. (1982). *The mass media and social problems.* Oxford: Pergamon.

Humphries, D. (1981). Serious crime, news coverage and ideology: A content analysis of crime coverage in a metropolitan newspaper. *Crime and Delinquency, 27,* 191–205.

Jenkins, P. (1994). *Using murder: The social construction of serial homicide.* Hawthorne, NY: Aldine de Gruyter.

Jenkins, P., & Maier-Katkin, D. (1992). Satanism: Myth and reality in a contemporary moral panic. *Journal of Crime, Law and Social Change, 17,* 53–76.

Katz, J. (1987). What makes crime news. *Media, Culture and Society, 9,* 60.

Liska, A. E., & Baccaglini, W. (1990). Feeling safe by comparison: Crime in the newspapers. *Social Problems, 37,* 360–374.

Lotz, R. E. (1991). *Crime and the American press.* New York: Praeger.

Marsh, H. L. (1991). A comparative analysis of crime coverage in newspapers in the United States and other countries from 1960 to 1989: A review of the literature. *Journal of Criminal Justice, 19,* 67–80.

Newman, G. R. (1990). Popular culture and criminal justice: A preliminary analysis. *Journal of Criminal Justice, 18,* 261–274.

O'Keefe, G. J. (1984). Public views on crime: Television exposure and media credibility. In R. Bostrom (Ed.), *Communication Yearbook 8* (pp. 514–535). Beverly Hills, CA: Sage.

Orcutt, J. D., & Turner, J. B. (1993). Shocking numbers and graphic accounts: Quantified images of drug problems in the print media. *Social Problems, 40,* 190–206.

Palmgreen, P., & Clarke, P. (1977). Agenda-setting with local and national issues. *Communication Research, 4,* 435–452.

Protess, D. L., et al. (1985). Uncovering rape: The watchdog press and the limits of agenda setting. *Public Opinion Quarterly, 49,* 19–37.

Sacco, V. F. (1982). The effects of mass media on perceptions of crime: A reanalysis of the issues. *Pacific Sociological Review, 25,* 475–493.

Schlesinger, P., Tumber, H., & Murdock, G. (1991). The media of politics, crime and criminal justice. *British Journal of Sociology, 42,* 397–420.

Schlesinger, P., et al. (1992). *Women viewing violence.* London: BFI.

Schneider, J. W. (1985). Social problems theory: The constructionist view. *Annual Review of Sociology, 11,* 209–229.

Sherizen, S. (1978). Social creation of crime news: All the news fitted to print. In Charles Winick (Ed.), *Deviance and mass media* (pp. 213–224). Beverly Hills, CA: Sage.

Skogan, W. G., & Maxfield, M. G. (1981). *Coping with crime: Individual and neighborhood reactions.* Beverly Hills, CA: Sage.

Soothill, K., & Walby, S. (1991). *Sex crime in the news.* London: Routledge.

Sparks, G. G., & Ogles, R. M. (1990). The difference between fear of victimization and the probability of being victimized: Implications for cultivation. *Journal of Broadcasting and Electronic Media, 34,* 351–358.

Sparks, R. (1992). *Television and the drama of crime.* Buckingham, England: Open University Press.

Surette, R. (1992). *Media, crime and criminal justice.* Pacific Grove, CA: Brooks/Cole.

Tyler, T. R. (1984). Assessing the risk of crime victimization: The integration of personal victimization experience and socially transmitted information. *Journal of Social Issues, 40,* 27–38.

Voumvakis, S. E., & Ericson, R. V. (1984). *News accounts of attacks on women: A comparison of three Toronto newspapers.* Toronto: University of Toronto, Centre of Criminology.

Williams, P., & Dickinson, J. (1993). Fear of crime: Read all about it: The relationship between newspaper reporting and fear of crime. *British Journal of Sociology, 33,* 34.

Zillmann, D., & Wakshlag, J. (1987). Fear of victimization and the appeal of crime drama. In D. Zillman & J. Bryant (Eds.), *Selective Exposure to Communication* (pp. 141–156). Hillsdale, NJ: Lawrence Erlbaum.

Canadian Criminal Law

NEIL BOYD

*So criminal law must be an instrument of last resort.
Society's ultimate weapon must stay sheathed as long as
possible. The watchword is restraint — restraint
applying to the scope of criminal law, to the meaning
of criminal guilt, to the use of the criminal trial and to
the criminal sentence.*

— The Law Reform Commission of Canada, 1976

INTRODUCTION

We must always remind ourselves that the criminal
law is the most coercive and intrusive form of public law. The task of those who create, enforce, and
administer it is to ask continually about the circumstances in which this force should be used. As
Winston Churchill once observed, the state of a
civilized society can be divined from the manner in
which it responds to its criminals.

The purpose of the criminal law is to punish
certain acts that have been declared in law to be
threats to the established social order. Crime can be
conceptualized as falling into one of three categories:
offences against persons; property offences; and
offences considered to be evil in themselves, irrespective of whether harm befalls another person or the
property of another person. Examples of the first category of crime are straightforward enough: culpable
homicide, sexual assault, robbery, assault, attempted

murder, and the like. Crimes against property are
also easily determined: theft, fraud, income tax evasion, insider trading, forgery, and so on. Offences
considered to be punishable irrespective of their
immediate impact on others include soliciting for
prostitution, pornography, the use and distribution
of narcotics, and certain gaming activities.

In pre-state societies, there was no criminal law as
such. Killings and other serious assaults were reacted
to in a myriad of ways: revenge executions, compensation from one tribe or clan to another, and concili-
ation between individuals or collectives. In Canada,
a criminal code did not exist until as late as 1892,
when the federal government adopted the British
reform code written by Sir James Fitzjames Stephens.

Criminal law, unlike tort law, is concerned with
public wrongs. The state or the collective has determined that certain kinds of conduct must be
responded to with various penalties, in order to deter
those who might be inclined to engage in these activities, and also in order to express community outrage
and/or concern about a particular act. The historical
distinction between criminal and tort law creates an
inevitable tension. A citizen notion of justice is likely
to be compensation for an inflicted harm, but the
criminal law makes the state's interest in conviction
and punishment the objective of prosecution. For
victims of crime, the criminal law is typically less
personal and less emotionally satisfying than the

compensatory imperative of tort. The victim receives no tangible benefit from the penalty imposed, be it a suspended sentence, discharge, fine, probation order, community service order, or imprisonment.

Another way of expressing the intent of the criminal law is to say it defines what the state regards as intolerable deviance. Over time, the definitions of deviance and the associated penalties have changed markedly, particularly with respect to crimes defined as evil in themselves, the victimless offences listed earlier.

While most legal scholars and the Canadian public agree that the designation of crimes against persons and property can be morally justified, debate continues about the appropriateness of using the criminal law to control such matters as the commercialization of sex, the public health risks involved in the use and distribution of certain drugs, and the potential economic exploitation involved in certain forms of gambling. But debate also continues about what constitutes crimes against persons and property. Sociologists Herman and Julia Schwendinger (1975: 132–37) have addressed the moral criteria employed in defining crime:

> . . . Isn't it time to raise serious questions about the assumptions underlying the definitions of the field of criminology, when a man who steals a paltry sum can be called a criminal while agents of the State can, with impunity, legally reward men who destroy food so that price levels can be maintained whilst a sizeable portion of the population suffers from malnutrition?

A more cautious assessment of the problem of defining what constitutes crime has been advanced by sociologist Steven Box (1981: 9):

> Deviant behaviour is behaviour which is proscribed by those who have the institutionalized power, and occasionally the consensual authority, to create rules; it is behaviour which places its perpetrator at risk of being punished by those who have the institutionalized power, and occasionally the consensual authority, to do something to those who do not keep to the rules.

MENS REA AND ACTUS REUS: PREREQUISITES FOR CONVICTION

The definitions of crime fluctuate with changes in the social, political, and economic order. But the basic conceptual elements of a crime remain, at least in theory, consistent over time. The concepts of *mens rea* and *actus reus* have their origins in the development of the criminal law of England. In order to be convicted of a criminal offence, an individual must have committed an *actus reus,* an evil act, and must simultaneously possess *mens rea,* an evil mind or intention. It is only the coincidence of *mens rea* and *actus reus* that can lead to criminal conviction.

In many contexts, the connection between the two concepts is straightforward. Take the theft of a chocolate bar. The *actus reus* is the taking of the bar from a store without giving payment; the *mens rea* is the intention to do so. However, if a person was forced at gunpoint to steal the bar or was two years old, there would clearly be no intention to commit the offence. If, in another example, the police were to discover marijuana in a person's luggage, they could fairly presume *actus reus* — commission of the act of possession of marijuana. But if the possessor had no knowledge of the presence of the marijuana, and the court believed this to be true, there would be no *mens rea* — no intent to possess the narcotic.

How does one find a coincidence of *mens rea* and *actus reus* in the commission of the offence of murder? Consider the following excerpt from the Supreme Court of Canada's judgement in *R. v. Cooper.* The Newfoundland Court of Appeal had allowed an appeal by the accused from his conviction for second-degree murder; the Crown was appealing that ruling.

> Cory, J.: At issue, on this appeal, is the nature of the intent required to found a conviction for murder pursuant to s.212(a)(ii) of the *Criminal Code,* R.S.C. 1970, c.C-34 (now R.S.C. 1985, c.C-46, s.229(a)(ii)).
> [Section 229(a)(ii) is part of section 229(a), one of three legal definitions of murder. Section 229(a)(ii) reads:

Culpable homicide is murder
(a) where the person who causes the death of a human being
(i) means to cause his death, or
(ii) means to cause him bodily harm that he knows is likely to cause his death, and is reckless whether death ensues or not.]

FACTUAL BACKGROUND

The respondent Lyndon Cooper and the deceased Deborah Careen lived in Labrador City, Newfoundland. At one time, they had been friends and lovers. On January 30, 1988, they met at a gathering place known as the K-Bar in Labrador City. Although by this time the respondent was living with somebody else, they spent the evening together at the bar. There is no doubt that they consumed a considerable amount of alcohol. Eventually, Cooper, the deceased and a mutual friend left the bar in a taxi. After they dropped off the friend they continued in the cab to the residence of another of Cooper's friends, where he borrowed a Jeep. Cooper then drove the deceased to the secluded parking-lot of a power station.

At the parking lot the respondent testified that he and the deceased engaged in some form of consensual sexual activity. He said that they began to argue at one point and that the deceased struck him. At this he became angry. He hit the deceased and grabbed her by the throat with both hands and shook her. He stated that this occurred in the front seat of the Jeep. He then said that he could recall nothing else until he woke in the back seat and found the body of the deceased beside him. He had no recollection of causing her death. He pushed her body out of the Jeep and drove away. Later during the drive to his home he found one of her shoes in the vehicle and threw it out the window into the snow.

The expert evidence established that the deceased had in fact been struck twice. However, these blows could not have killed her. Rather, death was caused by "a classic pattern of one-handed manual strangulation." That same evidence confirmed that death by strangulation can

occur as quickly as 30 seconds after contact with the throat and that a drunken victim is likely to die from asphyxiation more quickly than a sober one. Nonetheless, the presence of petechial haemorrhages on the neck of the deceased and the finding that the hyoid bone in her throat was not fractured suggested to the expert that death occurred rather more slowly, probably after two minutes of pressure.

The position of the defence was that the respondent was so drunk that he blacked out shortly after he started shaking her with both hands. Thus, it was said that the respondent did not have (i) the required intent to commit murder, or (ii) alternatively, did not foresee that holding someone by the neck was likely to cause death. . . .

What degree of concurrency is required between the wrongful act and the requisite *mens rea?*

There can be no doubt that under the classical approach to criminal law it is the intent of the accused that makes the wrongful act illegal. It is that intent which brings the accused within the sphere of blameworthiness and justifies the penalty or punishment which is imposed upon him for the infraction of the criminal law. The essential aspect of *mens rea* and the absolute necessity that it be present in the case of murder was emphasized by Lamer, J. (as he then was) in *R. v. Vaillancourt* (1987) 39 C.C.C. (3d) 118. . . . At p. 133 he stated: "It may well be that, as a general rule, the principles of fundamental justice require proof of a subjective *mens rea* with respect to the prohibited act, in order to avoid punishing the 'morally innocent.'. . ."

However, not only must the guilty mind, intent or *mens rea* be present, it must also be concurrent with the impugned act. Professor D. Stuart has referred to this as "the simultaneous principle": see *Canadian Criminal Law 2nd ed.* (1987), p. 305. This principle has been stressed in a number of cases. For example, in *R. v. Droste* (1979) 49 C.C.C. (2d) 52, 18 C.R. (3d) 64 (Ont. C.A.), the accused had intended to murder his wife by pouring gasoline over the interior of the car and setting fire to it while she was within it. Before he could light the gasoline the car crashed into a bridge and ignited prematurely. As a result, both his children were killed rather than his wife. He was charged with their murder and convicted. On appeal Arnup, J.A., speaking for the Court of Appeal in directing a new trial, stated at pp. 53–54:

. . . the trial judge did not instruct the jury of the necessity of the Crown showing that at the time of the occurrence at the bridge, the appellant, intending to kill his wife, had done an act with that intention, and in the course of doing so his children were killed. In short, he did not tell them that the *mens rea* and the *actus reus* must be concurrent. *(Emphasis added)*

. . . There is, then, the classic rule that at some point the *actus reus* and the *mens rea* or intent must coincide. Further, I would agree with the conclusion of James, J. that an act *(actus reus)* which may be innocent or no more than careless at the outset can become criminal at a later stage when the accused acquires knowledge of the nature of the act and still refuses to change his course of action. . . .

Yet, with respect, I do not think that it is always necessary that requisite *mens rea* (the guilty mind, intent or awareness) should continue throughout the commission of the wrongful act. There is no question that in order to obtain a conviction the Crown must demonstrate that the accused intended to cause bodily harm that he knew was ultimately so dangerous and serious that it was likely to result in the death of the victim. But that intent need not persist throughout the entire act of strangulation. When Cooper testified that he seized the victim by the neck, it was open to the jury to infer that by those actions he intended to cause her bodily harm that he knew that [*sic*] was likely to cause her death. Since breathing is essential to life, it would be reasonable to infer the accused knew that strangulation was likely to result in death. I would stress that the jury was, of course, not required to make such an inference but, on the evidence presented, it was open to them to do so.

Did the accused possess such a mental state after he started strangling the victim? Here death occurred between 30 seconds and two minutes after he grabbed her by the neck. It could be reasonably inferred by the jury, that when the accused grabbed the victim by the neck and shook her that there was, at that moment, the necessary coincidence of the wrongful act of strangulation and the requisite intent to do bodily harm that the accused knew was likely to cause her death. Cooper was aware of these acts before he "blacked out." Thus although the jury was under no compulsion to do so, it was nonetheless open to them to infer that he knew that he was causing bodily harm and knew that it was so dangerous to the victim that it was likely to cause her death. It was sufficient that the intent and the act of strangulation coincided at some point. It was not necessary that the requisite intent continue throughout the entire two minutes required to cause the death of the victim. . . .

In the result, I would set aside the order of the Court of Appeal directing a new trial and restore the conviction.

Appeal allowed; conviction restored.

Lamer, C.J.C. (dissenting): . . . It is crucial to a correct charge under s.212(a)(ii) that the jury understand that there must be intention to cause bodily harm which the accused knows is likely to cause death. Intention to cause bodily harm, without knowledge that such is likely to cause death, is not sufficient. Given the position of the defence in this case, a clear understanding of this aspect was essential to a fair trial. . . .

I do not raise this point to question whether the accused here intended to cause bodily harm. That was conceded in the argument before us. I raise it rather to emphasize that the intention to cause bodily harm by no means leads inexorably to the conclusion that the accused knew that the bodily harm was likely to cause death. It is, of course, this second aspect which is essential to a finding of guilt of murder under s.212(a)(ii). Particularly with respect to an action such as grabbing by the neck, there may be a point at the outset when there is no intention to cause death and no knowledge that the action is likely to cause death. But there comes a point in time when the wrongful conduct becomes likely to cause death. It is, in my view, at that moment or thereafter, that the accused must have a conscious awareness of the likelihood of death. This awareness need not, however, continue until death ensues.

Cooper intended to choke the deceased and cause her bodily harm. Under s.212(a)(i), it was open to the jury to infer from his conduct and on all of the evidence that in doing so he intended to kill her. To be found guilty under s.212(a)(ii), however, he must have been aware of the fact that he persisted in choking her long enough for it to become likely that death would ensue.

This instruction, given the particular facts of this case and the nature of the defence presented by the accused, had to be given. Additionally, the jury should have been instructed to consider the evidence of drunkenness in relation to this awareness. In my respectful view, upon a reading of the whole charge, this was not done adequately.

I would dismiss the appeal.

The differing judgements of Justice Cory and Chief Justice Lamer raise questions about the *mens rea* required to substantiate a conviction for murder. Justice Cory argues that "it could be reasonably inferred by the jury that . . . there was . . . the necessary coincidence of the wrongful act of strangulation and the requisite intent to do bodily harm that the accused knew was likely to cause her death." Chief Justice Lamer argues, on the contrary, that it is not clear that Cooper was "aware of the fact that he persisted in choking her long enough for it to become likely that death would ensue." The difference between the two positions hinges on the inferences that one is willing to draw with respect to intention. Chief Justice Lamer asserts that any conviction for murder requires proof of subjective knowledge of the likelihood of death; it is not sufficient to base criminal conviction under s.229(a)(ii) upon an inference of knowledge of likelihood of death, in the absence of supporting evidence.

The question of whether criminal conviction for murder should be premised upon objective or subjective intention is one that will continue to be debated within criminal law. In essence, the distinction is between what a reasonable person would be expected to intend, and what the accused actually did intend. The American jurist Oliver Wendell Holmes set out the following proposition in 1863 (cited in Stuart and Delisle, 1986: 254–55):

If the known present state of things is such that the act done will very certainly cause death, and the probability is a matter of common knowledge, one who does the act, knowing the present state of things, is guilty of murder, and the law will not inquire whether he did actually foresee the consequences or not. The test of foresight is not what this very criminal foresaw, but what a man of reasonable prudence would have foreseen.

But consider the comments of Justice Dickson in *R. v. City of Sault Ste. Marie*, in direct opposition to Holmes's sentiments (cited in Stuart and Delisle, 1986: 288):

Where the offence is criminal, the Crown must establish a mental element, namely, that the accused who committed the prohibited act did so intentionally or recklessly, with knowledge of the facts constituting the offence, or with wilful blindness toward them. Mere negligence is excluded from the concept of the mental element required for conviction. Within the context of a criminal prosecution a person who fails to make such enquiries as a reasonable and prudent person would make, or who fails to know facts he should have known, is innocent in the eyes of the law.

There are many criminal offences for which the requisite *mens rea* is a subjective intention to commit the given offence, but is founded on "recklessness" or "advertent negligence" rather than a direct intent. Consider the following excerpt from the Supreme Court's decision in *R. v. Hundal,* a case concerned with the criminal offence of dangerous driving causing death.

Cory, J.: At issue on this appeal is whether there is a subjective element in the requisite *mens rea* which must be established by the Crown in order to prove the offence of dangerous driving. . . .

The relevant portions of s.233 read as follows:

233 (1) Every one commits an offence who operates
(a) a motor vehicle on a street, road, highway or other public place in a manner that is dangerous to the public, having regard to all the circumstances, including the nature, condition and use of such place and the amount of traffic that at the time is or might reasonably be expected to be on such place; . . .

(4) Every one who commits an offence under subsection (1) and thereby causes the death of any other person is guilty of an indictable offence and is liable to impris-onment for a term not exceeding fourteen years. . . .

The appellant contends that the prison sentence which may be imposed for a breach of s.233 (now s.249) makes it evident that an accused cannot be convicted without proof beyond a reasonable doubt of a subjective mental element of an intention to drive dangerously. Certainly every crime requires proof of an act or failure to act, coupled with an element of fault which is termed the *mens rea*. This court has made it clear that s.7 of the *Canadian Charter of Rights and Freedoms* prohibits the imposition of imprisonment in the absence of proof of that element of fault. . . .

Depending on the provisions of the particular section and the context in which it appears, the constitutional requirement of *mens rea* may be satisfied in different ways. The offence can require proof of a positive state of mind such as intent, recklessness or wilful blindness. Alternatively, the *mens rea* or element of fault can be satisfied by proof of negligence whereby the conduct of the accused is measured on the basis of an objective standard without establishing the subjective mental state of the particular accused. In the appropriate context, negligence can be an acceptable basis of liability which meets the fault requirement of s.7 of the *Charter*. . . .

. . . [T]he wording of the section itself which refers to the operation of a motor vehicle "in a manner that is dangerous to the public, having regard to all the circumstances" suggests that an objective standard is required. The "manner of driving" can only be compared to a standard of reasonable conduct. That standard can be readily judged and assessed by all who would be members of juries.

Thus, it is clear that the basis of liability for dangerous driving is negligence. The question to be asked is not what the accused subjectively intended but rather whether, viewed objectively, the accused exercised the appropriate standard of care. It is not overly difficult to determine when a driver has fallen markedly below the acceptable standard of care. There can be no doubt that the concept of negligence is well understood and readily recognized by most Canadians. Negligent driving can be thought of as a continuum that progresses, or regresses, from momentary lack of attention giving rise to civil responsibility through careless driving under a provincial Highway Traffic Act to dangerous driving under the *Criminal Code*.

. . . The trial judge carefully examined the circumstances of the accident. He took into account the busy downtown traffic, the weather conditions, and the mechanical condition of the accused's vehicle. He concluded, in my view very properly, that the appellant's manner of driving represented a gross departure from the standard of a reasonably prudent driver. No explanation was offered by the accused that could excuse his conduct. There is no reason for interfering with the trial judge's finding of fact and application of the law.

In the result, the appeal must be dismissed.

It is fair to conclude from Justice Cory's reasoning that the very nature of *mens rea* changes as one moves from offence to offence.

Mens Rea and Parties to an Offence

There is one final issue with regard to *mens rea* that should be discussed: parties to an offence. Under section 21 of the *Criminal Code*, parties to an offence may be held as criminally responsible as the person or persons who actually commit the crime.

> 21. (1) Every one is a party to an offence who
> (a) actually commits it;
> (b) does or omits to do anything for the purpose of aiding any person to commit it; or
> (c) abets any person in committing it.
>
> (2) Where two or more persons form an intention in common to carry out an unlawful purpose and to assist each other therein and any one of them, in carrying out the common purpose, commits an offence, each of them who knew or ought to have known that the commission of the offence would be a probable consequence of carrying out the common purpose is a party to that offence.

In most circumstances, the meaning of this section of the *Code* can be readily understood. If a person provides a gun for the purpose of a crime, drives the getaway car, or keeps a lookout for the police, that person will be held to be as guilty of the crime as the person who pulls the trigger or robs the bank.

What of the following instance, however? Stan is walking down the street and sees his friend Fred beating Jim, whom Stan knows and doesn't particularly like. If he simply walks by and allows Fred to continue the beating, is he a party to the offence? What if he smiles at Fred? What if he shouts encouragement to him? What if Stan volunteers to hold Jim down? In short, at what point does Stan violate section 21 of the *Code* by doing or omitting to do anything for the purpose of aiding another person to commit an offence? Mewett and Manning (1978: 43) provide a framework, if not a definitive answer, for this conundrum:

> As a general proposition, some act of aiding or abetting must occur over and above mere presence. . . . In the case of *Coney* the court . . . held that the mere presence of persons at a prize fight, unexplained, is not in itself conclusive proof of the intent to encourage the fight, but where the accused bet on the fight or shouted encouragement to the fighters, then that would amount to aiding and abetting.

Thus, while mere voluntary presence, in itself, does not amount to aiding or abetting, presence together with some form of participation might.

DEFENCES TO AND MITIGATIONS OF CRIMINAL OFFENCES

There are many circumstances in which people charged with criminal offences will be able to escape responsibility, or some degree of responsibility, for their crime. They may have inflicted harm in self-defence; they may have been enticed by the police to commit a crime (usually related to illegal drugs or prostitution); they may have been forced at gunpoint to help rob a bank; they may have been mistaken about a woman's consent to sexual relations; or they may have been too intoxicated or too emotionally or mentally disturbed to understand or appreciate the alleged offence.

These "excuses" for crime are highly controversial and are often criticized for supporting unjust societal assumptions. Is it reasonable, for example, that the voluntary consumption of alcohol should diminish an accused's responsibility for the offence of murder? Is it reasonable for a man who sexually assaults a woman to argue that he was mistaken about the woman's consent — that in his world, women "like it rough"? In these contexts — murder and sexual assault — the state of the criminal law often reflects the values of a culture that forgives men their trespasses and lends support to excessive use of alcohol.

The Defence of Drunkenness

Consider the following excerpt from the judgement of the British Columbia Court of Appeal in *R. v. Tom*, an appeal by the accused, Darryl Tom, from his conviction for assault with intent to resist arrest.

> Wood, J.A.: The events leading to the charges in this case took place on the Pinchie Reserve, some 30 miles from Fort St. James, in northern British Columbia. At 9:20 p.m., on the night of June 29, 1990, Constables Darryl Lock and Douglas Cope of the Fort St. James R.C.M.P detachment received

a radio communication while on patrol, requesting their attendance at the reserve as back-up for an ambulance crew on its way there in response to a report that someone had received a head injury.

Both officers were in uniform and they were in a marked police vehicle. . . . On their arrival they saw the appellant Mr. Tom sitting on the steps of the house next door to the residence to which they had been dispatched.

A brief investigation led the officers to believe that Tom had been causing a disturbance and smashing furniture in that residence. They decided to speak with him. By this time he was no longer sitting where he had been seen. The officers drove around the reserve looking for him. Within a few minutes they saw him running toward them being chased by Randy Monk who was carrying a baseball bat. The officers stopped and Constable Lock stepped out of the police vehicle to intervene. At this point Tom veered off the road toward a lake. Constable Lock took up the chase, and Monk apparently decided to retire.

Constable Lock chased Tom down to the edge of the lake and along the beach. Eventually Tom stopped and turned around. The officers described him as swaying back and forth, very glassy-eyed, and having a very strong odour of liquor emanating from his person. Tom spoke, but his speech was so slurred the constable could not understand what he said. In the words of the officer:

He appeared intoxicated to me, just from the — the visual signs that he was showing; his — he had the slurred speech, his balance was very unsteady, the strong odour of liquor from his person was very, very noticeable.

Constable Lock advised Tom that he was under arrest for being intoxicated in a public place contrary to s.43 of the Liquor Control and Licensing Act. . . . He was told of his right to remain silent and asked if he understood. He made no response. He was advised of his right to retain and instruct counsel without delay, and given particulars on the availability of legal aid, following which he was again asked if he understood. He made no response. Constable Lock asked him if he wanted to call a

lawyer. Again there was no response. Throughout all of this Tom maintained eye contact with the officer, but gave no other sign of comprehension.

Constable Lock took hold of Tom's arm from behind and began to walk him back toward the village. Tom, who was very unsteady in his balance, was barely able to walk and the officer found it difficult to support his weight on the rough terrain which they had to negotiate. When they reached the main road, he lowered Tom to the ground while they waited for Constable Cope to return with the police vehicle. He was standing some five feet away when Tom, who knew him by name, said: "Darryl [Lock], give me your gun, I want to shoot them." The officer responded: "Darryl [Tom], don't talk like that."

Moments later, as the police vehicle came into view, Tom stood up, grabbed a rock and swung it at Constable Lock, hitting him on the head. A short chase ensued, Tom fell and the constable fell on top of him before passing out.

Within moments Constable Cope arrived on the scene. He assisted Constable Lock to the police vehicle. Tom was placed in a prisoner's cage in the back of that vehicle. Half-way to town they met the ambulance which had set out in response to the original complaint. Constable Lock was transferred to it and rushed to hospital. Constable Cope carried on with his prisoner . . .

(The trial judge convicted Tom of assault causing bodily harm, and assaulting a police officer. His decision follows.)

The defendant relies upon the Supreme Court of Canada decision in R. v. Bernard *. . . and only quoting from the headnote, the decision of Madam Justice Wilson with whom Madam Justice L'Heureux-Dubé concurred. The Madam says that:*

"Evidence of intoxication may go to the trier of facts in general intent offences only if it is evidence of extreme intoxication involving an absence of awareness akin to a state of insanity or automatism. Only in such a case is the evidence capable of raising a reasonable doubt as to the existence of the minimal intent required for the offence."

Mr. Justices McIntyre and Beetz (also quoting from the headnote) state that: "The defence of intoxication, however, has no application in offences of general intent."

Now, in my view, it is a fine line between the two (the decision of McIntyre and Beetz and that of Wilson and L'Heureux-Dubé). But there may well be a small distinction there. And if I were to adopt the reasoning of Madam Justice Wilson, that is that there must be evidence of intoxication involving the "absence of awareness," can I find on the evidence an absence of awareness? In my view the answer is no. Looking at the evidence of Vern Tom or Randy Monk, both who knew the accused for a long time, said that he was drunk, but he was able to carry on a conversation with them. To them he appeared oriented as to time and place. Constable Lock also spoke with the defendant and the defendant spoke to him. The evidence is that the defendant and Lock knew each other prior to the incidents of June 29, 1990. The defendant spoke to Constable Lock and calls him by his first name. It seems to me that that is evidence of recognition and awareness.

The only evidence of lack of awareness is to be found in the evidence of the defendant and basically he says: "I don't recall." Well, that does not, in my mind, show lack of awareness, it just means that he does not remember what he was doing that evening because of the voluntary consumption of alcohol.

So, in my view, the defence of mens rea *does not succeed because there is no lack of awareness or absence of awareness; it is just that he was so drunk that he does not now remember But it was clear to the people who were dealing with him that he was oriented as to time and place.*

The British Columbia Court of Appeal disagreed, directing acquittals on all charges connected with this incident, as the conviction "was based on a mistaken view of the evidence."

To begin with, he [Wood, J.A.] was, apparently, of the view that both Vern Tom and Randy Monk had offered in testimony the opinion that the appellant was "oriented as to time and place." Neither offered any such opinion. Both did say that

the appellant spoke to them before the police arrived, but their evidence only established that they could understand what he was saying, not that what he said made any sense or seemed coherent. The fact that an accused can speak and be understood is, by itself, probative of very little when the issue is whether there is, through intoxication, a lack of awareness akin to a state of insanity or automatism. One does not need the assistance of expert evidence to know that many who are unfortunate enough to find themselves in either state are nonetheless perfectly capable of articulating words. More important to the inquiry is whether what they have to say can support a reasonable inference, one way or the other, as to their cognitive awareness. Here, there was no evidence of what was said by the appellant, in his "conversations" with either Randy Monk or Vern Tom, which would assist the court in drawing such an inference.

Secondly, in his reasons the trial judge stated that the "only" evidence of "lack of awareness" was that of the appellant himself, who simply said he could not remember. I agree with the trial judge's conclusion that, by itself, the appellant's inability to remember would not be much evidence of a lack of awareness, of the sort under consideration, at the time the events in question were unfolding. But his conclusion that there was no other evidence from which such an inference could reasonably be drawn was, with respect, in error. The evidence of the two constables was that their attempts to communicate to the appellant the fact of his arrest, and the rights which he had as a consequence, ended with each separately reaching the conclusion he did not comprehend what they were saying. Furthermore, the behaviour of the appellant, both before and after he was placed under arrest, was sufficiently bizarre to lead to the conclusion there was something at least abnormal about his cognitive function.

The *Tom* case, in canvassing the decision of the trial judge and that of the British Columbia Court of Appeal, sets out quite different positions with respect to the defence of drunkenness, or at least to its applicability to this specific set of facts. Should drunkenness continue to be a defence to a criminal charge, albeit in very restricted circumstances? Or should drunkenness be irrelevant to the determination of guilt and have potential applicability only to the sentence to be imposed?

The Defence of Mistake of Fact

It is impossible in this paper to detail the law relating to all the defences to and mitigations of criminal charges: intoxication, insanity, self-defence, duress, entrapment, and mistake. Consider, however, the ambit of the defence of mistake of fact. If a man has an honest but mistaken belief that a woman has consented to sexual activity, should this preclude a conviction for sexual assault? What can you conclude from the following excerpts of fact in *Pappajohn v. R* and *Sansregret v. R.* — should either accused be able to avail himself of the defence of honest but mistaken belief in consent, with the *mens rea* of the crime negated by this belief?

McIntyre, J.: . . . The complainant [in *Pappajohn v. R.*] was a real estate saleswoman employed by a well-known and well-established real estate firm in Vancouver. She was successful in her work. The appellant is a businessman who was anxious to sell his home in Vancouver, and he had listed it for sale with the real estate firm with which the complainant was associated. She was to be responsible for the matter on her firm's behalf. On 4th August 1976 at about 1:00 p.m. she met the appellant by appointment at a downtown restaurant for lunch. The purpose of the meeting was to discuss the house sale. The lunch lasted until about 4:00 or 4:30 p.m. During this time a good deal of liquor was consumed by both parties. The occasion became convivial, the proprietor of the restaurant and his wife joined the party and estimates of the amount of alcohol consumed varied in retrospect, as one would expect. It does seem clear, however, that, while each of the parties concerned had a substantial amount to drink, each seemed capable of functioning normally.

At about 4:00 p.m. or shortly thereafter they left the restaurant. The appellant drove the complainant's car while she sat in the front passenger seat. They went to the appellant's house, the one which was listed for sale, to further consider questions arising in that connection. Up to the time of arrival at the home, at about 4:30 or 5:00 p.m., there is no significant variation in their accounts of events. From the moment of arrival, however, there is a complete divergence. She related a story of rape completely against her will and over her protests and struggles. He spoke of an amorous interlude involving no more than a bit of coy objection on her part and several acts of intercourse with her consent. Whatever occurred in the house, there is no doubt that at about 7:30 p.m. the complainant ran out of the house naked with a man's bow tie around her neck and her hands tightly tied behind her back with a bathrobe sash. She arrived at the door of a house nearby and demanded entry and protection. The occupant of the house, a priest, admitted her. She was in an upset state and exhibited great fear and emotional stress. The police were called, and these proceedings followed. . . .

Dickson, J.: There is circumstantial evidence supportive of a plea of belief in consent: (1) Her necklace and car keys were found in the living room. (2) She confirmed his testimony that her blouse was neatly hung in the clothes closet. (3) Other items of folded clothing were found at the foot of the bed. (4) None of her clothes were damaged in the slightest way. (5) She was in the house for a number of hours. (6) By her version, when she entered the house the appellant said he was going to break her. She made no attempt to leave. (7) She did not leave while he undressed. (8) There was no evidence of struggle. (9) She suffered no physical injuries, aside from three scratches. . . .

McIntyre, J.: The appellant [in *Sansregret v. R.*], a man in his early 20s, and the complainant, a woman of 31 years, had lived together in the complainant's house for about a year before the events of 15th October 1982. Their relationship had been one of contention and discord with violence on the part of the appellant: "slappings" or "roughing up" in his description, "blows" in hers. The appellant had left the house for short periods and in September 1982 the complainant decided to end the affair. She told the appellant to leave and he did.

On 23rd September 1982, some days after his dismissal, the appellant broke into the house at about 4:30 a.m. He was "raging" at her and furious because of his expulsion. He terrorized her with a file-like instrument with which he was armed. She was fearful of what might occur, and in order to calm him down she held out some hope of a reconciliation and they had intercourse. A report was made to the police of this incident, the complainant asserting she had been raped, but no proceedings were taken. The appellant's probation officer became involved and there was evidence that he had asked the complainant not to press the matter, presumably because it would interfere with the appellant's probation.

On 15th October 1982, again at about 4:30 a.m., the appellant broke into the complainant's house through a basement window. She was alone, and awakened by the entry she seized the bedroom telephone in an effort to call the police. The appellant picked up a butcher knife in the kitchen and came into the bedroom. He was furious and violent. He accused her of having another boyfriend; pulled the cord of the telephone out of the jack and threw it into the living room; threatened her with the knife and ordered her to take off her nightdress and made her stand in the kitchen doorway, naked save for a jacket over her shoulders, so he could be sure where she was while he repaired the window to conceal his entry from the police, should they arrive. He struck her on the mouth with sufficient force to draw blood, and on three occasions rammed the knife blade into the wall with great force, once very close to her. He told her that if the police came he would put the knife through her, and added that if he had found her with a boyfriend he would have killed them both. At one point he tied her hands behind her back with a scarf. The complainant said she was in fear for her life and sanity.

By about 5:30 a.m., after an hour of such behaviour by the appellant, she tried to calm him down. She pretended that there was some hope of a reconciliation if the appellant would settle down and get a job. This had the desired effect. He calmed down and after some conversation he joined her on the bed and they had intercourse. The complainant swore that her consent to the intercourse was solely for the purpose of calming him down, to protect herself from further violence. This, she said, was something she had learned from earlier experience with him. In her evidence she said:

I didn't consent at any time.

I was very afraid. My whole body was trembling. I was sure I would have a nervous breakdown. I came very, very close to losing my mind. All I knew was I had to keep this man calm or he would kill me.

At about 6:45 a.m., after further conversation with the appellant, she got dressed and prepared to leave for work. She had a business appointment at 8:00 a.m. She drove the appellant to a location which he chose, and in the course of the journey he returned her keys and some money that he had taken from her purse upon his arrival in the early morning. Upon dropping him off she drove immediately to her mother's home, where she made a complaint of rape. The police were called and the appellant was arrested that evening.

In both *Pappajohn* and *Sansregret*, the Canadian judiciary was divided about the defence of mistaken belief in consent. In *Pappajohn,* Supreme Court Justice Dickson concluded, "It does not follow that, by simply disbelieving the appellant on consent, in fact, the jury thereby found that there was no belief in consent and that the appellant could not reasonably have believed in consent." In other words, the appellant may not have been believed by the jury, but the jury may have been mistaken. And in *Sansregret*, the trial judge concluded:

....

. . . [H]is honest belief finds support in the testimony of the complainant. She knows him and, in her opinion, notwithstanding all the objective facts to the contrary, he did believe that everything was back to normal between them by the time of the sexual encounter. His subsequent behaviour as well attests to that fact.

I do not like the conclusion which this leads me to. There was no real consent. There was submission as a result of a very real and justifiable fear. No one in his right mind could have believed that the complainant's dramatic about-face stemmed from anything other than fear. But the accused did. He saw what he wanted to see, heard what he wanted to hear, believed what he wanted to believe.

Both cases were resolved in the Supreme Court of Canada, and in both instances the accused was convicted. The defence of honest mistake of fact remains as a legal possibility, but it seems clear that it is not to be a purely subjective test of the accused's intention; wholly unreasonable beliefs, however honestly held, are not likely to be viewed as negating the *mens rea* required for conviction.

CONCLUSIONS

The criminal law, like all forms of law, is, for better or worse, a barometer of the culture in which we live. In closing, we should recall a point made at the outset of this paper: the task of those who create, enforce, and administer this law is to ask continually of the circumstances in which such force should be used. To paraphrase Churchill, how we define and respond to our criminals will tell us a lot about ourselves.

DISCUSSION QUESTIONS

1. What purposes are served by enforcing *Criminal Code* and *Controlled Drugs Substances Act* provisions relating to trade in drugs or the trade in sexual services? Are these businesses too exploitive to be capable of public-health regulation? What is the nature of the exploitation in each instance? Can drug distribution and prostitution be seen as similar to other forms of commerce that are not criminalized?

2. Which test of intention for murder is more compelling: subjective or objective? Do you agree or disagree with Chief Justice Lamer's argument that, for murder charges, "it is crucial . . . that the jury understand there must be intention to cause bodily harm which the accused knows is likely to cause death. Intention to cause bodily harm, without knowledge that such is likely to cause death, is not sufficient."?

3. Do you agree or disagree with Churchill's observation that the strength of a civilization is to be seen in the way it responds to criminals?

REFERENCES

Box, S. (1981). *Deviance, reality and society* (2nd ed.). London: Holt, Rinehart and Winston.

Mewett, A. W., & Manning, M. (1978). *Criminal law.* Toronto: Butterworths.

Ruby, C. C. (1987). *Sentencing* (3rd ed.). Toronto: Butterworths.

Schwendinger, H., & Schwendinger, J. (1975). Defenders of order or guardians of human rights? In L. Taylor, P. Walton, & J. Young (Eds.), *Critical criminology.* London: Routledge and Kegan Paul.

Stuart, D., & Delisle, R. (1986). *Learning Canadian criminal law* (2nd ed.). Toronto: Carswell.

Cases Cited

R. v. Cooper [1993] 78 C.C.C. (3d) 289.

R. v. Hundal [1993] 79 C.C.C. (3d) 97.

R. v. Tom [1993] 79 C.C.C. (3d) 84.

Pappajohn v. R. [1980] 2 S.C.R. 120.

Sansregret v. R. [1985] 1 S.R.C. 570.

Street Prostitution in Canada

DOREEN DUCHESNE

INTRODUCTION

Many people do not realise that prostitution — the exchange of money for sex — is not illegal in Canada. However, it is unlawful to engage in peripheral activities, such as publicly communicating with another person for the purpose of buying or selling sexual services, or living on the avails of the prostitution of another individual.

Street prostitution is a controversial issue, with legal, social, health, and economic implications. It is also closely linked to other criminal activities. Since the act of prostitution has traditionally been considered voluntary, it has often been perceived as a victimless crime. Yet the life of a street prostitute is frequently characterized by exploitation, violence, substance abuse, and disease.

A different perspective is presented by ordinary citizens faced with street prostitution in their communities. Indeed, many of them feel that they are the victims, since the trade usually brings added traffic, loitering, noise, and drugs. In some neighbourhoods, inhabitants are mistaken for prostitutes or clients, while children playing outside are exposed to discarded condoms and needles.

RECENT LEGISLATIVE DEVELOPMENTS

Until the early 1970s, prostitution was treated as a "status" offence associated with vagrancy; that is, a prostitute found in a public place who could not provide a satisfactory reason for being there could be arrested. In contrast, the soliciting law, introduced in 1972, focused on behaviour by prohibiting individuals from soliciting others in a public place for prostitution. Enforcement of this legislation was problematic, however. "Public place" was not adequately defined, many types of sexual activity were not covered, and it was not clear whether it also applied to male prostitutes and clients. Furthermore, solicitation had to be "pressing and persistent," a condition of arrest that was open to various interpretations. The law remained ineffective, despite a 1983 amendment that noted its application to prostitutes of either sex and defined "public place."

Because of these problems, the federal government established the Fraser Committee in the early 1980s to assess the adequacy of the laws related to prostitution and pornography (SPE, 1985), and the Badgley Committee to report on the efficacy of the current legislation in protecting children from sexual abuse, including juvenile prostitution (COM, 1984). Recommendations were set forth, including the decriminalization of adult solicitation, and the creation of new offences to protect children and deter procurers (i.e., pimps).

Following these consultations, the "communicating" law replaced the soliciting law in December 1985, and two years later additional legislation imposed strong penalties for persons living on the

Adapted from Street Prostitution in Canada, by Doreen Duchesne (February 1997). *Juristat 17* (2), Statistics Canada Catalogue 85-002-XPE. Reprinted with permission of Statistics Canada.

avails of juvenile prostitutes, or purchasing their services. The purpose of the communicating law, which remains in force today, is to maintain public order by making prostitution less visible, and therefore less of a nuisance, to the general public. Although the law does not make the act of prostitution itself a crime, it is illegal to communicate with another person in public to buy or sell sexual services. The legislation applies to both prostitutes and clients of either sex.

A number of criticisms have since been levelled at the communicating law. Although prostitution remains legal, there are no clear guidelines on where it can take place. As a result, enforcement is difficult and costly (to arrest a prostitute or customer, police must generally pose as one or the other) and erratic, as many prostitutes fear testifying against their pimps. An evaluation by the Department of Justice (1989) deemed the legislation ineffective in terms of reducing street prostitution and the aggravation experienced by members of the community.

Since early 1995 there have been ongoing consultations among the ministries responsible for justice at the federal, provincial, and territorial levels and key stakeholders, with a view towards further reform of the prostitution-related sections of the Criminal Code (FED, 1995b). Issues being reviewed include devising better strategies for dealing with juvenile prostitution; expanding social services aimed at prevention and intervention; imposing more severe penalties for pimps and clients; facilitating law enforcement; empowering municipalities to deal with the problem; licensing the sex trade; creating zones of tolerance; and adopting new measures to curb the activities of clients.

POLICE ENFORCEMENT PRACTICES VARY

In 1995, police in all provinces and territories reported 7165 prostitution-related incidents (i.e., involving one or more communicating, procuring, or bawdy-house violations). Although the number of incidents that year was 29% higher than in 1994, this increase was preceded by steep declines

---

Box 3.1

Prostitution in the Criminal Code

Communicating offences

The communicating law, found in section 213 of the Criminal Code, states the following:

Offence in relation to prostitution

(1) Every person who in a public place or in any place open to public view

  (a) stops or attempts to stop any motor vehicle,

  (b) impedes the free flow of pedestrian or vehicular traffic or ingress to or egress from premises adjacent to that place, or

  (c) stops or attempts to stop any person or in any manner communicates or attempts to communicate with any person for the purpose of engaging in prostitution or of obtaining the sexual services of a prostitute is guilty of an offence punishable on summary conviction.

(2) In this section, "public place" includes any place to which the public have access as of right or by invitation, express or implied, and any motor vehicle located in a public place or in any place open to public view.

In addition, section 197 has been interpreted such that "the 'practice of prostitution' does not require ... physical contact between the customer and the performer. Prostitution merely requires proof that the woman offered her body for lewdness or for the purposes of the commission of an unlawful act in return for payment."

The maximum penalty for being convicted of this summary offence is a fine of $2000 and/or six months of imprisonment.

Bawdy-house offences

Keeping a common bawdy-house, or transporting a person to bawdy-house (sections 210 and 211)

In summary, a person keeping a common bawdy-house (i.e., a place kept, occupied, or frequented for purposes of prostitution or indecent acts) may be imprisoned for up to two years. An individual occupying or found unlawfully in a bawdy-

(continued)

Box 3.1 *(continued)*

house, or taking someone there, or in control of such a place and allowing prostitution-related activities to occur, may be imprisoned up to six months and/or fined up to $2000.

Procuring offences

Procuring (section 212)
This offence encompasses a variety of crimes. To summarize, a person may be imprisoned up to ten years for the following activities: procuring or soliciting another to engage in prostitution; enticing a person who is not a prostitute to a place for prostitution; concealing someone in a bawdy-house; procuring a person to enter or leave Canada for prostitution; encouraging or forcing someone to prostitute for gain; enticing an individual to take drugs or alcohol (or administering such) to enable anyone to carry out sexual activities with that individual; or living on income earned through another's prostitution activities. If the person is living on the income of a prostitute under 18, the maximum prison sentence is 14 years.

A procuring violation is also committed when a client purchases or attempts to purchase the sexual services of a person under 18; the maximum penalty for this offence is five years in jail.

Convicted procurers may also be fined. There is no maximum amount specified in the Criminal Code.

Since the communicating law has been in force, the focus of arrests has been on street prostitutes and their clients. For example, in 1995 the vast majority of prostitution incidents involved communicating (92%), distantly followed by procuring (5%), and bawdy-house incidents (3%). In contrast, only 22% of the incidents recorded in 1985 were for soliciting, while over half (58%) were related to bawdy-house activities, and 19% were for procuring.

Indeed over half (55%) of the 1994–1995 increase in prostitution incidents noted earlier can be traced to a substantial rise in the number of communicating incidents reported from just the Vancouver Census Metropolitan Area (from 341 to 1211). As a result of this "crackdown," Vancouver accounted for 17% of all prostitution-related incidents reported nationally in 1995, compared with only 7% the previous year. But, as previously mentioned, year-to-year fluctuations are common. For example, the total number of prostitution incidents in Canada dropped sharply in 1993, largely due to fewer communicating incidents in Vancouver; an even steeper decline occurred in 1994, mostly in Toronto, Edmonton and Calgary.

Most of the 7646 persons charged in a prostitution-related incident in 1995 were accused of communicating (6710). Just over half (55%) of those charged with a communicating offence were female. Although the data do not indicate whether the person charged was a prostitute or client, it is generally recognized that most prostitutes are female and almost all clients are male. Females also predominated among those accused of a bawdy-house offence (64%), while seven in ten persons charged with procuring were male.

Since December 1985, when the communicating law replaced the soliciting law, there has been a shift towards more males being charged. Specifically, males accounted for just over one-third (36%) of all persons charged with soliciting between 1977 and 1985; in comparison, almost half (47%) of those charged with communicating during the 1986 to 1995 period were male. This increase may reflect changes in enforcement practices, in that some police agencies are charging

between 1992 and 1994. Furthermore, the number of incidents in 1995 remained one-third lower than the peak recorded in 1988, the third year following the implementation of the communicating law. Such fluctuations are common and usually reflect changes in the enforcement of the communicating law, rather than criminal prevalence; for example, public complaints or media coverage can lead to a few large crackdowns, which temporarily inflate statistics.

more men in an effort to hold customers more accountable for their participation in the sex trade; also, since 1985, the law in force has clearly applied to clients as well as prostitutes. In contrast, from 1986 onwards, a higher percentage of accused procurers have been female (36%), compared with 25% of procurers charged between 1977 and 1985. In both periods, 6 in 10 persons charged with a bawdy-house offence were female.

YOUTHS TEND TO BE HANDLED DIFFERENTLY

The lack of maturity possessed by adolescent and child prostitutes adds to their victimization by procurers and clients, who are usually adults. Serious and lasting harm to these children, mental as well as physical, has been extensively documented. Social agencies and legislative measures have been focusing more on prevention, protection, and redirection, through the creation and application of provincial child welfare legislation and municipal welfare programs.

Criminal legislation may also be applied to help redirect youths away from prostitution. For example, a juvenile may be arrested and offered the option of participating in an Alternative Measures program, whereby he or she admits responsibility for the offence committed and voluntarily engages in some form of remedial action, such as obtaining counselling or performing community service; in exchange, court proceedings and a possible criminal record are avoided. Youths who end up in court and are convicted may be given probation. Although more severe than a fine, probation can be used to keep youths off the street by requiring them to live in specified locations, avoid areas where they normally work, and report to probation officers on a regular basis.

CONCLUDING REMARKS

Prostitution evokes strong and wide-ranging reactions and opinions. Some individuals abhor the exploitation and violence associated with the trade, while others resent the damage inflicted on their neighbourhoods. A number of these people want stronger laws enacted and less leniency shown by the courts.

At the other end of the spectrum, there are those who feel that prostitutes have a right to exercise their profession freely. Other persons favour legalizing the trade to enable prostitutes to work at home or in brothels, subject to provincial regulation and municipal zoning and licensing.

In between lie suggestions to simply reduce the visibility of street prostitution through greater enforcement of the current law. Some proposals aim to contain the activity in clearly defined districts (e.g., outside residential neighbourhoods), through negotiation among sex trade workers, police officials, local politicians, and affected citizens.

Other options target prevention or intervention through counselling, medical services, education, and job training. Activities are also directed at hindering or deterring clients; for example, police in some cities have published the names of customers, impounded their automobiles, set up traffic barriers, or introduced programs such as the john school.

The variety of approaches taken to deal with the problems associated with prostitution reflect the urgency felt by many stakeholders for solutions. Innovative strategies aimed at prevention as well as enforcement are being developed, and many affected communities are expending significant efforts grappling with these matters. Through such activities, an increasing number of Canadians are becoming aware of the issues involved and the need to address them.

DISCUSSION QUESTIONS

1. How is prostitution like other "victimless crimes" and how is it different?
2. Are increased traffic, loitering, noise, and drugs enough to be able to call the neighbours of prostitutes victims as Duchesne says? Could we not just use existing legislation against these problems without criminalizing soliciting?

3. What would the implications be of legalizing use of marijuana but not its sale? Compare with the legal status of prostitution in Canada.

4. What role did the modern feminist movement have in the changes to the prostitution legislation?

REFERENCES

[COM] Committee on Sexual Offences Against Children and Youths. (1984). *Sexual offences against children* (Vol. 2). Ottawa: Minister of Supply and Services Canada.

Department of Justice Canada. (1985). *Discussion paper. The report of the committee on sexual offences against children and youths and the report of the special committee on pornography and prostitution.* Ottawa: Minister of Supply and Services Canada.

Department of Justice Canada. (1989). *Street prostitution: Assessing the impact of the law — Synthesis report.* Cat. no. J23-7/1-1989E (JUS-P-544E). Ottawa: Department of Justice Canada.

[FED] Federal-Provincial-Territorial Working Group on Prostitution. (1995a). Dealing with prostitution in Canada: A consultation paper.

Federal-Provincial-Territorial Working Group on Prostitution. (1995b). Results of the national consultation on prostitution in selected jurisdictions — Interim report.

Moyer, S., & Carrington, P. J. (1989). Street prostitution: Assessing the impact of the law — Toronto. Cat. no. J23-7/4-1989E (JUS-P-548E). Ottawa: Department of Justice Canada.

[SPE] Special Committee on Pornography and Prostitution. (1985). *Pornography and prostitution in Canada: Report of the special committee on pornography and prostitution* (Vol. 1 and Vol. 2). Ottawa: Minister of Supply and Services Canada.

Wolff, L., & Geissel, D. (1993). Street prostitution in Canada. *Juristat.* Cat. no. 85-002, 13(4). Ottawa: Statistics Canada, Canadian Centre for Justice Statistics.

The Battered Wife Defence

ROBERT A. SILVERMAN
LESLIE W. KENNEDY

INTRODUCTION

Cipparone (1987) indicates that the traditional legal standard justifying the use of deadly force in self-defence against another is a reasonable belief that (1) the victim was faced with an imminent threat of death or serious bodily harm and (2) deadly force was necessary to avoid or prevent such harm. In Canada, the parts of the *Criminal Code* most relevant are section 34(2) and section 37. Section 34(2) states that

> everyone who is unlawfully assaulted and who causes death or grievous bodily harm in repelling the assault is justified if
> (a) he causes it under reasonable apprehension of death or grievous bodily harm from the violence with which the assault was originally made or which the assailant pursues his purposes; and
> (b) he believes, on reasonable grounds, that he cannot otherwise preserve himself from death or grievous bodily harm.

Section 37 states that if attacked one should use no more force than is necessary to prevent the assault or the repetition of it.

Normally in a self-defence situation, then, the threat to an individual is immediate. Thus the Canadian Supreme Court, when it accepted the battered wife defence, in effect modified the doctrine of

self-defence, extending it to a fear for life, not immediately but in the near future, based on past behaviour of the homicide victim. In so doing it accepted the argument that a battered wife, even in a period of relative calm, could feel unable to walk out of her untenable situation and thus perceive that she had no alternative but to kill her abusing spouse.

THE SUPREME COURT OF CANADA: *LAVALLEE V. R.*

The key decision concerning the battered wife syndrome defence was handed down by the Supreme Court on May 3, 1990, in the case of *Lavallee v. R.*; its implications will be far-reaching indeed. The case had gone to there on appeal by Ms. Lavallee against prosecution attempts to secure a new trial and overturn her acquittal for killing her common-law husband. The appeal included the issue of the utility of expert evidence in assisting a jury confronted with a plea of self-defence to a murder charge by a wife who had been battered by the deceased.

In describing the decision and its likely aftermath, we begin with a portion of the police transcripts that describe, in Lyn Lavallee's words, the actual murder event.

> Me and Wendy argued as usual and I ran in the house after Kevin pushed me. I was scared. I was really scared. I locked the door. Herb was down-

Adapted from *Deadly Deeds: Murder in Canada*, by Robert A. Silverman and Leslie W. Kennedy (1994). Toronto: Nelson, p. 149–155. Reprinted with permission of ITP Nelson and the authors.

stairs with Joanne and I called for her but I was crying and when I called him I said, "Herb, come up here please." Herb came up to the top of the stairs and I told him that Kevin was going to hit me, actually beat me again. Herb said he knew and that if I was his old lady things would be different; he gave me a hug. Okay, we are friends, there's nothing between us. He said, "Yeah, I know" and he went outside to talk to Kevin leaving the door unlocked. I went upstairs and hid in my closet from Kevin I was so scared. . . . My window was open and I could hear Kevin asking questions about what I was doing and what I was saying. Next thing I know he was coming up the stairs for me. He came into my bedroom and said, "Wench, where are you?" and he turned on my light and he said, "Your purse is on the floor" and he kicked it. Okay, then he turned and he saw me in the closet. He wanted me to come out but I didn't want to come out because I was scared. I was so scared. [The officer who took the statement then testified that the appellant started to cry at this point and stopped after a minute or two.] He grabbed me by the arm right there. There's a bruise on my face also where he slapped me. He didn't slap me right then, first he yelled at me then he pushed me and I pushed him back and he hit me twice on the right hand side of my head. I was scared. All I thought about was all the other times he used to beat me. I was scared, I was shaking as usual. The rest is a blank, all I remember is he gave me the gun and a shot was fired through my screen. This is all so fast. And then the guns were in another room and he loaded it, the second shot, and gave it to me. And I was going to shoot myself. I pointed it to myself, I was so upset. Okay, and then he went and I was sitting on the bed and he started going like this with his finger [the appellant made a shaking motion with an index finger] and said something like "You're my old lady and you do as you're told" or something like that. He said, "Wait till everybody leaves, you'll get it then" and he said something to the effect of, "Either you kill me or I'll get you." That was what it was. He kind of smiled and then he

turned around. I shot him but I aimed out. I thought I aimed above him and a piece of his head went that way (*R. v. Lavallee*, 1990: 337–38).

It is clear that the relationship between Lyn Lavallee and the victim, Kevin Rust, was volatile and punctuated by frequent arguments and violence. They would go through periods of fighting in which the defendant would receive bruises and even fractures. She once explained to her family physician that she received these injuries from falling from a horse. (It is fairly typical of battered women to attempt to hide the real source of their injuries.) Further, after many of the fights, Rust would shower her with flowers and other gifts to try to make up. After a period of calm, the beatings would begin again. The violence was severe.

In the original Manitoba case, the expert testimony was provided by psychiatrist Dr. Fred Shane. Shane's opinion was that the appellant had been terrorized by Rust to the point of feeling trapped, vulnerable, worthless, and unable to escape the relationship despite the violence. The continuing pattern of abuse put her life in danger. Shane felt that Lyn Lavallee sincerely believed she would be killed that night if she did not kill Kevin Rust first. The doctor's opinion was based on four hours of formal interviews with the appellant, a police report of the incident (including the appellant's statement), hospital reports documenting eight of her visits to the emergency departments between 1983 and 1985, and an interview with her mother.

The judge in the lower court had admitted Shane's evidence. The Crown's argument against the use of Shane's testimony was based on two grounds. First, it argued that because none of the information that Shane used to form his opinion was "proved in evidence," his expert opinion should not be allowed to be placed in evidence. Neither Lyn Lavallee nor her mother testified, which led the prosecution to argue that the interviews with both her and her mother constituted hearsay and were therefore inadmissible. Second, the prosecution argued that the jury should be able to make up its own mind about issues of admissible evidence, and that the expert testimony was unnecessary and superfluous.

In writing for the Supreme Court, Justice Wilson says:

> Expert evidence on the psychological effect of battering on wives and common-law partners must, it seems to me, be both relevant and necessary in the context of the present case. How can the mental state of the appellant be appreciated without it? The average member of the public (or of the jury) can be forgiven for asking: Why would a woman put up with this kind of treatment? Why would she continue to live with such a man? How could she love a partner who beat her to the point of requiring hospitalization? We would expect the woman to pack her bags and go. Where is her self-respect? Why does she not cut loose and make a new life for herself? Such is the reaction of the average person confronted with the so-called "battered wife syndrome." We need help to understand it and help is available from trained professionals (*R. v. Lavallee*, 1990: 349).

Justice Wilson, in this opinion, also confronts the issue of the "reasonable man." Claims made by the feminist movement that the law reflects a male orientation are substantiated by this case (see Comack, 1991). What would a reasonable man do in Lyn Lavallee's circumstances? It is hard to say because a reasonable man virtually never has to confront such an issue. We can instead ask what a reasonable *person* would do when we take into account the variables of gender, physical stature, and psychological state.

Does the defendant have a reasonable apprehension of death? The Supreme Court decision refers to an earlier Canadian case that used the battered wife syndrome as a defence against murder. This case, known as *R. v. Whynot* (1983), involved a defendant who shot her husband while he was passed out in his truck. The deceased had administered regular beatings to his wife and others in the family. On the night in question the deceased had threatened to kill the woman's son. The Nova Scotia Court of Appeal held, in essence, that it is inherently unreasonable to fear death or grievous bodily harm unless and until the physical assault is actually in progress (*R. v. Whynot*, 1983: 353). According to the Justice Wilson decision, however, "expert testimony can cast doubt on these assumptions as they are applied in the context of a battered wife's efforts to repel an assault." It is likely that both sections 34 and 37 of the *Criminal Code* will have to be reinterpreted as a result of this decision.

Justice Wilson explains the behaviours involved in this case in terms of the stages predicted in the Walker Cycle Theory of Violence (Walker, 1979). We have in Lyn Lavallee an individual who was beaten, who felt she could not leave the relationship, who genuinely loved the person beating her, and who, finally, felt she would be killed if she did not immediately take action. This is the interpretation of the defence psychologist, which, if admissible, suggests that Lavallee had reasonable grounds to believe her life was in imminent danger, even though the assault was not in progress. She felt incapable of escape. On the subject of admissibility, Justice Wilson says:

> I think the question the jury must ask itself is whether, given the history, circumstances and perceptions of the appellant, her belief that she could not preserve herself from being killed by Rust that night except by killing him first was reasonable. To the extent that expert evidence can assist the jury in making that determination, I would find such testimony to be both relevant and necessary (*R. v. Lavallee*, 1990: 362).

Justice Wilson cautions, however, that battered women may kill their partners for reasons other than self-defence. The mere fact that the appellant is a battered woman does not necessarily entitle her to an acquittal. The focus must be not on the woman but on what she did and whether it was justifiable. Thus the interpretation by the Supreme Court, while it expands the defences to homicide offered under the *Criminal Code*, does not give carte blanche to women to kill their battering husbands.

CONCLUSIONS

The Supreme Court has held that the battered wife defence is a legal defence in Canada. A defence can be based on the facts of the case combined with expert testimony concerning the psychological state of the victim. Expert testimony can be based on interviews that, prior to the Supreme Court decision, would have been considered hearsay. While we do not know the frequency with which battered wives kill their husbands, we can expect and predict that the number of such cases utilizing the battered woman syndrome as a defence will increase in the near future.

DISCUSSION QUESTIONS

1. To be non-sexist, the topic should be the battered person defence. Discuss.
2. Does the defence not make the wife into the judge and jury in this situation? Who presents the arguments of the deceased?
3. Our country does not allow capital punishment. Is this relevant in this discussion?

REFERENCES

Cipparone, R. C. (1987). The defense of battered women who kill. *University of Pennsylvania Law Review, 135,* 427–452.

Comack, E. (1991). Legal recognition of the "battered wife syndrome": A victory for women? Paper presented at the Annual Meeting of the American Society of Criminology. San Francisco. November.

Walker, L. (1979). *The battered woman.* New York: Harper and Row.

Cases Cited

R. v. Lavallee [1990] 1 S.C.R. 853.

R. v. Whynot [1983] 37 C.R. (3d) 198, 9 C.C.C. (3d) 449, 61 N.S.R. (2d) 33, 133 A.P.R. 33 (CA).

Measuring Crime and Delinquency

Introduction

Canadian criminologists, statisticians, and government employees of various kinds spend a good deal of time worrying about how much crime occurs in our society. Why worry about it? After all, we can find out about crime by just reading the newspapers. Or can we? The fact is that the amount of crime reported in those newspaper reports does not represent the actual amount of crime occurring in Canada. The ways in which criminologists have attempted to better estimate how much crime there really is in Canada is the theme of this section of the book.

In Canada, and in most other countries, crime statistics are used for a variety of purposes. They are used in decisions involving funding of police and related agencies. They can be used in the deployment of police. They are used by politicians on the election trail and can result in significant changes in the composition of a government. And, from an academic point of view, they are used to both generate and attempt to confirm explanations of criminal activity. In effect, ". . . crime statistics help establish the basic social facts of crime. For example, how does the crime rate vary by age, sex, race and income level of offenders and/or victims?" (O'Brien, 1985).

Since crime statistics serve such important purposes, it is critical that we know exactly what they represent. As you will learn, crime statistics generally represent the number of crimes recorded by some official agency (e.g., Statistics Canada). But even those agencies underrepresent the amount of crime occurring. For instance, if a crime is committed and no one reports it, or the police do not find

out about it, then that event is not calculated in crime statistics. Most of the rest of this section is devoted to explaining how crime statistics are generated, and what they mean.

CRIME FUNNEL

Crime statistics for Canada (and elsewhere) can be represented as a funnel, with information about the number of crimes decreasing as one moves through that funnel. Figure P2.1 illustrates that not all actual crime is detected, not all detected crime is reported, not all reported crime is recorded, not all recorded crime results in arrests, not everyone arrested is brought to trial, not everyone tried is convicted, and not everyone convicted is sentenced. For instance, there were about 2.6 million crimes recorded in 1996 (fourth down the funnel) but there were only 37 000 individuals in federal prisons and provincial jails (the bottom of the funnel) and, of course, they were not all put into prison in the same year — far fewer would have *entered* prison in 1996. While the numbers are not exactly comparable, the difference between them should give you an idea of the vast range in the crime funnel.

At the top of the funnel is the *actual crime rate*, the total number of crimes committed by all individuals in any given place and period of time, for example, in Canada during 2000. The total number of crimes is unknown — for a variety of reasons outlined below — but it is at least theoretically knowable. As things currently stand, however, we have only several approximations of *actual crime*.

Figure P2.1
Theoretical Funnel of Crime

the number of crimes decreases as one moves down through the funnel	actual crime	knowable
	crime detected	knowable
	crime reported	knowable
	crime recorded	official police statistics
	arrests	official police statistics
	trials	official court statistics
	convictions	official court statistics
	dispositions (fine, probation, institutionalization)	official court statistics

Early criminologists recognized that the "actual" crime rate was unknown. They assumed, however, that *official crime rates* calculated from data gathered by the criminal justice system were good substitutes and reflected reasonably well the actual crime rate. Thus they assumed that the direction (either up or down), the magnitude (either large or small), and the speed (either slow or quick) of changes observed in the official statistics were similar to the direction, magnitude, and speed of changes in the actual crime rate. The more criminologists learned about reporting and official recording of crime, the less they accepted these assumptions. For instance, criminologists learned that recorded crime statistics respond to forces in society that have little to do with the actual crime rate. Sometimes, pressure to "clean up" an area or type of crime results in an increase in police resources deployed, which in turn causes an increase in the crime rate as more police are able to arrest more offenders. The actual crime rate has not changed, only the enforcement of the law has changed. More specifically, as police have become more sensitive to issues of family violence and society less tolerant of this behaviour, the number of incidents reported have risen (Statistics Canada, Daily, May 28, 1998).

All three elements at the top of the funnel, actual crime, crime detected, and crime reported, are concepts for which only incomplete data exist. Later in this introduction we shall discuss attempts to estimate those concepts using victimization and self-report data. For now, before proceeding with our discussion of official police data on crime, crime recorded (see the first article in this section for an example of how real crime statistics are presented), a few important concepts must be introduced.

CRIME RATES

Common sense says that there would be more crimes in a population of one million than in a population of one thousand. There would also be more births, deaths, and marriages. It follows, then, that any change in population will have an effect on any increase or decrease in the number of crimes recorded. Maybe our crime problem appears to be growing because Canada is growing. For this reason, crime rates, are calculated to take into account population size. Crime rates tend to be stated in terms of the number of crimes occurring for every 100 000 people in the defined population.

Crude crime rates are based on official statistics and take total population size into account. They are calculated as follows:

$$\frac{\text{Number of crimes recorded by police in a particular year}}{\text{Estimated population for the year}} \times 100\ 000 = \text{Crude crime rate}$$

For example, in 1997 there were 2 530 354 violations of the Canadian *Criminal Code* recorded by

Statistics Canada. The estimated population for that year was 30 285 800. The crude crime rate in Canada for *Criminal Code* violations in 1997 is therefore 8355 per 100 000 population (Kong, this volume).

$$\frac{2\ 530\ 354}{30\ 285\ 800} \times 100\ 000 = 8355 \text{ } Criminal\ Code \text{ violations per 100 000 people living in Canada}$$

Most criminologists would argue, however, that age-specific crime rates are more desirable than the crude rate (see, for example, Lee, 1984; Maxim, 1985) because the crude crime rate may be affected by changes in the age compositions of Canada. For example, since people between the ages of 14 and 30 commit most of the officially recorded crimes in Canada, if there are proportionately more people in that age group in particular years compared to previous years, perhaps due to the maturing of a "baby-boom," then the overall crime rate may increase while the age-specific rates would remain unchanged for those years. Thus, rates that take into account shifts in age composition, perhaps due to increasing or decreasing birth rates, are preferable to avoid these misinterpretations. For instance, the proportion of the population in Canada between the ages of 18 and 24 has consistently risen since the mid-1970s (Canadian Centre for Justice Statistics, 1998) so we might expect higher crime rates. On the other hand, when the proportion of those in the highest crime commission ages drops, the overall crime rate may well decline.

Finally, some believe, since males commit a disproportionate amount of crime in most countries, including Canada, that crime rates should be sex-specific too. Since the proportion of males in Canada has been relatively constant recently, this is probably not important for our discussion of accurate crime statistics. Still, it could be important for other purposes — for example, for historical studies, as over time the proportion of males has fluctuated in Canada.

It should be noted that the formula illustrated above can be used to generate other types of crime rates. For instance, by using the number of "victim incidents reported" (discussed later in this introduction) instead of "crimes reported to the police," victimization rates are computed.

Changes in either the numerator (number of crimes) or denominator (the population) of the equation will affect the crime rate, as will any errors in either figure. For example, there are cases where the denominator has been found to be incorrect. A study of Native Americans showed that an assumption of very high crime rates for this group was based on faulty counting of the Native American population. In effect, the Native American population was undercounted, resulting in a higher crime rate (i.e., the division was by a number smaller than the accurate number). When a more accurate census was used in the denominator, the crime rate dropped (Silverman, 1996). In other instances, the numerator is incorrect, for instance, when the public do not report crime to the police — often because they do not think the police can do anything about it.

Further, when laws change the definition of crime, there are corresponding changes to the numerator (the number of crimes) of the equation. For instance, in 1985 Bill C-49 broadened the definition of solicitation (a component of prostitution) resulting in a rise of approximately 800 percent in reported prostitution incidents (Canadian Centre for Justice Statistics, 1998). Similarly, when laws changed concerning the age at which young offenders could be charged, there were some interesting effects on the rates of juvenile-perpetrated homicide (Silverman, 1990).

POLICE DATA ON CRIME

A statistic about crime is one that is recorded in a place from which it can be retrieved. Official statistics in Canada are generated by Statistics Canada through reports received from police departments. In the simplest sense, we only officially know about crime if the information is written down and available to be disseminated. The process that results in an official crime statistic starts with the police, who first become aware of crime either through their own observations or through public reports. In a classic U.S. study, Black and Reiss (1967) estimated that 84 percent of crimes reported to police are citizen-discovered, while only 14 percent are police-discovered. Citizens do not report all crimes of which they are aware. The Statistics Canada General Social Survey (1994) found that only 52 percent of victimizations across Canada were reported to the police in 1993. The other 48 percent were never reported — hence, never recorded in official statistics. The police, in turn, have some discretion as to what types of crimes they will "discover," and these decisions also will affect criminal statistics (Ericson, 1981). Grosman (1975), for example, in a study of a Canadian prairie police department, found that chiefs of police can affect crime rates just by the allocation of personnel to such areas as traffic or drugs. Any increase in the number of police assigned, other things being equal, will increase the official crime rates for those crimes, at least initially, since there will be more police to react to and record those crimes. In fact, "increased levels of per capita police strength precede increased crime rates" (Koenig, 1993, p. iii). Put very simply, the more police, the more crimes "discovered."

Sometimes the structure of policing can itself result in losses in reported crime. For instance, in a large western Canadian city, community policing has been replacing centralized policing for some years, and recent statistics have shown a decrease in calls for service to police. The police believe that this is a result of community policing making their officers more responsive to the needs of the public. To a limited extent they are correct, but they are also observing an unanticipated consequence of community policing. When a call (especially for a minor crime) comes into the central police station, those on duty will often tell callers that there is a community police station in their neighbourhood and they should go there to report the incident. For some reason, many reports are lost between the initial call and the community police station (see the article by Kennedy and Veitch in this section). That is, people who make the initial call to the central

---

Box P2.1

An Example of Why Crimes Do Not Get Reported

Recently, one of the editors was the victim of a "theft from auto" while visiting Montreal. The item stolen was a cell phone. Given the insurance deductible (higher than the value of the phone), there was no point to reporting the crime from the point of view of insurance claims. But the editor, trying to be a good citizen and aware of crime statistics, decided to report. A call to the police elicited the response that these are not taken over the phone and one had to go to the police station. The closest station was in an area unfamiliar to the victim and somewhat grungy, at that. The report was taken but the event (excluding driving time) took about 40 minutes — and there is, of course, no hope of getting the item back. We would argue that this system discourages crime reporting and suppresses crime statistics for a great deal of minor theft.

---

police station do *not* pursue the call to the community police station. Essentially, they drop the matter. Hence, many of these minor crimes simply do not become police statistics.

Even in communities without community policing, communications officers are the first to exercise discretion in responding to crime and thereby to affect crime statistics. If there are many calls coming in at once, such officers decide which sound the most serious, thus which will get attention and ultimately which will be recorded in official statistics. Major crimes are probably responded to and recorded, but minor crimes are especially vulnerable to such discretion. Sometimes, however, even for major crimes, there is some unofficial discretion. One frequent example is the crime of assault, especially if a drunk person calls in to complain about another drunk person's physical abuse and the communications officer, faced with several calls, fails to dispatch a car to the scene (Burris and Jaffe, 1983). The case of wife battering provides an opposite example. As the social sensitivity to that event has changed, discretion has decreased and arrest rates have risen (Sherman and Cohen, 1989; Statistics Canada, Daily, May 28, 1998).

Police discretion continues on the beat (Ericson, 1981; Sewell, 1985). All police officers have the option of continuing or not continuing the criminal justice process. Such discretion may not be officially sanctioned, but it occurs many times, every day, across the country. Officers consider a variety of factors before deciding whether to intervene in criminal incidents. First of all, they consider how serious the crime is, but officers also may consider the likelihood of successful prosecution, and even how close they are to the end of a shift. All of their decisions have important effects on crime statistics.

The police on the beat also exercise discretion in citizen-initiated crime reports. Wishes of the complainant for leniency, characteristics of the victim, and the seriousness of the offence are examples of factors that determine whether the crime is recorded. A citizen who wishes not to be involved in court proceedings may not wish to prosecute. While this is not, in fact, strictly the victims' choice when the criminal law has been violated, the wishes of victims are most important, for without their testimony there can be no conviction. While the police could proceed with the offence on their own, they may be hesitant to do so without the co-operation of a primary witness. Black (1970) found that those victims who are not respectful to the police are less likely to have their complaints recorded than are the most courteous victims, and the police pay slightly greater attention to complaints from white-collar than from blue-collar victims. Murder, arson, robberies, and other serious crimes probably do not suffer from these biases and are probably recorded as reported, but assaults and most less serious crimes may be less diligently recorded. More important for users of criminal statistics, this process of police discretion does not operate uniformly for all victims, for all types of crime, nor for all places.

In an attempt to develop a system to enhance the quality of Uniform Crime Reporting (UCR) data, the Canadian Centre for Justice Statistics (CCJS) undertook a study of procedures used in Calgary and Edmonton to generate crime statistics (1990). In 1988, Edmonton's crime rate for *Criminal Code* offences was 69 percent higher than Calgary's. The study was an attempt to discover if Edmonton's higher crime rate was real or was a result of reporting and recording differences. It was hypothesized that part of the difference in crime rates in the two cities was due to differences in the structure, organization, and operation of the information systems in the two police departments. This hypothesis was confirmed in a number of ways. First, in each city, there were a number of crimes that disappeared from the system of record-keeping after the stage of the initial phone call (from the public) about a crime. But the proportion missing was almost twice as high in Calgary (9.9 percent) as in Edmonton (5.5 percent). The second part of the study traced the link between records kept in the communications area and those found in the records section. Calgary lost close to 11 percent of its cases in this route, while Edmonton lost only 1 percent. Combining the results of these two studies, Calgary loses close to 20 percent of its cases, while Edmonton loses only 6 percent. A third study examined loss of specific offences and concluded that there is a good deal of variability in the reporting of specific offences between the two cities, but again, Calgary loses far more in the system than does Edmonton. It should be noted that the rules for reporting crime are uniform across the country, so it is obvious that there is some slippage in the *use* of the rules.

One final source of differences in the two crime rates is the population base. Crime rates are based on city populations excluding suburbs. When the study was done, about 15 300 people lived in the Calgary suburbs (2.3 percent of the city population), while in Edmonton there were 128 600 suburbanites (22 percent of the city population). It makes sense to base crime rates on populations including the suburbs (metropolitan area) because it is likely that some crimes in the city are perpetrated by suburbanites and some suburban crimes are committed by city-dwellers. If crime rates were based on metropolitan rates (inclusion of the suburban population and crime), Edmonton's crime rate would be reduced by about 8.2 percent, while there would be only a negligible decrease in Calgary's rate. In terms presented earlier with regard to crime rates, we have increased the denominator (the number of people in the population) by a greater amount than we have increased the numerator (the numbers of crimes), resulting in a lower crime rate.

The final conclusion of the researchers is that the loss of cases in Calgary and the exclusion of the larger Edmonton suburbs in calculating rates accounts for one-half of the difference in crime rates in the two cities. However, even when these sources of difference are considered, Edmonton still has a *Criminal Code* crime rate 32 percent higher than Calgary's. The difference may be real or it may be the result of other factors not identified or measured in the CCJS study.

No doubt Calgary and Edmonton are not unique in these differences. Similar differences probably occur in many other places across the country. It would thus seem that intercity and interregional comparisons (which are constantly made in the national and local press) are risky (see also Hackler and Paranjape, 1983). On the other hand, the trends generated in any *one* city may be a reliable estimate of police activity for that city, at least in the short run. Further, annual city statistics are likely a reasonable indicator of *trends* within that city.

After police discretion has reduced the total number of crimes recorded, those that remain are sent for compilation to the Canadian Centre for Justice Statistics, a unit within Statistics Canada. The numbers forwarded to that body by the police are probably fairly close to those entered by local police into their own records. The exact methods used by the police for reporting those totals of officially recorded offences to Statistics Canada are presented in the next section. Some of the crimes initially recorded and forwarded by the police can later be discounted — a small proportion of recorded *Criminal Code* violations (usually less than 5 percent) are later listed by the police as *unfounded*, which means the police believe that

those crimes did not happen or were not attempted (Statistics Canada, 1994). It is important to know how these decisions are made, as they may also affect actual crime data.

This discussion of how information on crimes is lost is not meant to be complete, but instead is intended to give the reader an idea of some of the ways in which information about crime is omitted from the official records. The point to be remembered is that some of the crimes that the police are or could be aware of are not recorded in the official documents. Crime recorded will always be a smaller figure than crime reported. This decreases the official crime rates, since the Statistics Canada data include only the smaller number.

The loss of information continues at each stage in the criminal justice process subsequent to the police stage. As the "crime funnel" shows, there are fewer people counted as the criminal justice process continues from police intervention to arrest, to court and final disposition of the case. Not all of this information is collected systematically, and certainly not all of it is available to the public. In this section, therefore, we are concerned mainly with police statistics, for they are most often used as the measure of crime in society. As the noted criminologist Thorsten Sellin (1932) pointed out, they are the official data closest to the commission of the criminal act.

GENERATING OFFICIAL STATISTICS: CANADIAN UNIFORM CRIME REPORTING, 1961–1988

Police record crimes according to a set of rules that are contained in a Uniform Crime Reporting Manual. Statistics Canada and the Canadian Association of Chiefs of Police are responsible for the rules for recording crime in Canada, and those rules remained fairly constant (with only minor changes) between 1962 and 1988. A major criticism of this system, which remains in use (see below),[1] is the limited data that it collects (Statistics Canada, 1990). Police departments enter their data on standardized forms that summarize their monthly crime data and these are forwarded to Statistics Canada for compilation. Those crime statistics are known as the Canadian Uniform Crime Reports.

Since 1982, this task has been handled by the Canadian Centre for Justice Statistics. It publishes *Canadian Crime Statistics*, annual books that display the crime data, and *Juristat* (see the article in this section by Kong for an example), a series of reports that analyze current crime statistics. *Canadian Crime Statistics* presents information about crimes reported, persons charged, offences cleared, and crime rates for the country as a whole and for regions, provinces, and urban areas (as well as some other data). The annual volume also offers a discussion of the rules used to report crime and some of the limitations of the data generated. Some of the rules used to generate the data result in interpretation problems, however, and these are discussed below.

Official Statistics, 1961–1988: Some Problems

First, attempted offences are counted in the same category as completed offences. The only exception to this rule is attempted murder, which is counted separately from completed murder. For some purposes, it would be beneficial to count attempted and completed acts separately. Certainly, the courts and the *Criminal Code* view them separately and usually cut the maximum punishment for an attempt to one-half that for a completed act.

Second, the definition of what constitutes an offence varies with the type of crime. For *crimes against the person,* one offence is counted per victim, while in the case of *crimes against property* one offence is counted for every "distinct or separate operation." A distinct operation is one that involves the "same time, location and circumstances." The difficulties that result from this distinction are numerous. For instance, if an offender enters a room and physically assaults three persons, three crimes are counted. If, on the other hand, an offender enters a room and steals the belongings of

three people at the same time, then according to the official statistics one crime is counted. If there is a rationale for this inconsistency in the method of counting personal and property offences, Statistics Canada does not provide it.

Within the category of property offences, there are other problems of enumeration, not the least of which is that robbery is not counted as a crime against the person. Below are definitions used by Statistics Canada in describing the methods of counting robbery, break and enter, and theft.

Robbery — Count one offence for each distinct operation carried out or attempted: e.g., if three persons in a store are held up and the store is robbed, score a single offence of robbery. If four persons rob one, or one person robs four at the same time and location only one robbery is scored.

Breaking and Entering — When a building contains several independently occupied residences such as apartments, suites, hotel rooms, or offices, each one entered would be scored. When a building has one occupant, for example, a warehouse, store, shop, etc., and is broken into, score only one offence. Score one offence for any number of box cars broken into when grouped in one location. Grouped in one location means the same spur or siding.

Theft — Property stolen from a number of persons located in one place constitutes one offence for scoring purposes (1986: 7-2–7-3).

The inconsistency that occurs is evident when robbery is compared with the other two offences. If four people live in four different apartments in the same building and each has property stolen from his or her apartment in break and enters, then four offences are counted in the official statistics. However, if these four people happen to be gathered in the lobby of that apartment building and are robbed of their possessions, then only one offence is counted in the official statistics. The rationale offered by Statistics Canada is that robbery often involves many victims, and counting all of them as individual incidents (as for other crimes of violence) would result in overstating the rate of robbery (Canadian Centre for Justice Statistics, 1994). This may in fact be true, but one would not be overstating the rate of robbery victimization.

Third, the instructions from Statistics Canada concerning multiple offences direct that "where several offences occur in one incident, score the more serious offence" (1986). Two problems arise from this method of counting. The first involves the process by which the most serious offence is determined.

> Seriousness of the offences is determined by the maximum penalty allowed by law, or the offence that is considered the most serious by the police when the penalties are the same; or the offence which appears first in the offence classification (Statistics Canada, 1977, p. 11).

However, according to the reporting rules governing the older method (Canadian Centre for Justice Statistics, 1994, p. 8), ". . . violent offences always take precedence over non-violent offences." Hence, if a break and enter and an assault occur in the same incident, the event is counted as an assault. It is possible that this particular method of determining seriousness may not always reflect the feelings of the community concerning the seriousness of the offences (see Akman and Normandeau, 1967; Sellin and Wolfgang, 1963; Atkinson, 1998).

A further problem that results from this method of counting involves loss of information. In a hypothetical case, a hitchhiker flags down a car on the highway. The car, which contains a man and a woman, stops on the shoulder of the highway. The hitchhiker shoots the man, killing him, sexually assaults the woman, takes their money and credit cards, and drives off in the car. In the official statistics, that multiple crime would likely be counted as one homicide and one sexual assault or, perhaps, only one homicide. Information would be lost concerning the robbery, auto theft, and a weapons offence. (Note that while the statistics do not

record those crimes, this loss has no effect on the prosecution of the case. The offender, if caught, would likely be prosecuted for murder, sexual assault, robbery, a weapons offence, and auto theft).

Finally, the issue of "crimes cleared" continues to result in problems. Clearing a crime is essentially a housekeeping measure used by police. Crimes are cleared or "closed" by apprehending a suspect and laying a charge, or if the police have enough evidence to lay a charge even if the suspect has not been apprehended (cleared by charge), or by some other means (cleared otherwise). In either case, the case is considered "solved." The first category is relatively straightforward, but the "otherwise" category incorporates a wide variety of occurrences including, for instance, the case of a known offender who has diplomatic immunity and hence cannot be arrested, and the case of offenders who kill someone and then commit suicide and hence cannot be arrested. Both of the examples would be "cleared otherwise." The problem is that the category does not seem to be used in a consistent manner. In some Canadian police departments, when known burglars are arrested police may ask about other offences they have committed. Often burglars cannot remember the specifics of the cases in which they have been involved, but the police will use the apprehension of the burglar to clear "otherwise" a great many active cases, even though they are not certain that this particular burglar was actually involved in those specific break and enter offences. This is not the purpose for which the "cleared otherwise" category was designed, and not all police departments use it in this way. But as long as it is used this way, the cleared categories are not very useful for comparative purposes.

GENERATING OFFICIAL STATISTICS: CANADIAN UNIFORM CRIME REPORTING AFTER 1988[2]

The statistics generated and published by Statistics Canada between 1962 and 1988 are based on police reports that summarize crime in police districts on a monthly basis. The information generated by the police and used by Statistics Canada are therefore aggregated statistics. Statistics from grouped data, however, are less useful for analytic purposes than information based on characteristics of individual crimes.

Recognizing these problems, the law enforcement program of the Canadian Centre for Justice Statistics, with the involvement of the Police Information and Statistics Committee of the Canadian Association of Chiefs of Police, undertook the task of developing a revised uniform crime reporting survey that would more fully satisfy the information needs of the criminal justice community (Statistics Canada, 1990).

The new system is designed to overcome some of the faults evident in the old Uniform Crime Reporting system. Among other things, it is meant to generate more information for analysis. After being discussed at many levels of the criminal justice community, the new system was ready for testing in March 1986. By 1988, the first police departments were actually using the system, and by 1992, 30 percent of eligible departments were reporting to Statistics Canada using the revised UCR. In 1998, about 48 percent of eligible departments were reporting. It will not be possible to reach full coverage until the RCMP reporting system is changed in a way that is consistent with the new scheme. Until that time both the new and the old UCR will be used. As the revised UCR is compatible with the older system, most recent published reports contain information from both systems.

By basing the new system on existing computer technology, the respondent burden — the amount of work that the police expend in collecting these data — remains manageable. The Canadian Centre for Justice Statistics captures police information about crime directly from the police computer. This requires that all systems be compatible to the extent that interface programs can be used to capture the same data from each participating police department. It also requires that all participating police departments utilize computer technology to record and store information about crime.

The new system is *incident-based* rather than *summary*. That is, the unit of analysis is the crime incident rather than an aggregate of monthly crime data. Because data are available on an individual basis and more data are being collected, it is easier to analyze trends and to test theoretical propositions. The following elements have been added to the Uniform Crime Reporting content:

1. Information on victims: age, sex, victim/accused relationship, level of injury, type of weapon causing injury, drug and/or alcohol use.
2. Information on the accused: age, sex, type of charges laid or recommended, drug and/or alcohol use.
3. Information on the circumstances of the incident: type of violation (or crime), target of violation, types of property stolen, dollar value of property affected, dollar value of drugs confiscated, type of weapon present, date, time, and type of location of the incident.

It is clear that these types of data will be useful to local law enforcement agencies for purposes of management, operational evaluation, program development and evaluation, and crime analysis. Also important, the additional data are critical for theory testing by the academic community.

In the 1990s, the potential for the collection of information regarding race of offenders and victims became controversial. Some argue that such information might reveal patterns of crime among members of specific groups that will lead to crime prevention and thus should be collected. On the other side are those who, for political or ethical reasons, oppose the collection of racial information (see for examples of the controversy: Bowling, 1990; several articles in the *Canadian Journal of Criminology*, vol. 36, no. 2, 1994; Wortley, 1994).

The new system yields other improvements over the old system as well. There is no longer any issue concerning different methods of counting crimes against the person and crimes against property. Crime rates should be more easily calculated and more accurate. Data on age and sex of victims and offenders (where available) make easier estimation of age- and sex-specific rates. Problems involving a multiple offence rule (that is, count the most serious crime when more than one crime occurs in the same incident) have not been completely cleared up, but there is additional information on the lesser offences in a multiple incident. It is likely that multiple offences constitute a rather small proportion of crime and probably do not affect overall crime rates very dramatically.

The new system does not, in itself, address problems directly related to intercity or interregional comparisons (discussed with regard to the Edmonton/Calgary situation above). The uniformity of the data elements generated by the new system will likely reduce, but certainly not eliminate, problems between jurisdictions. Differing styles of policing in different cities will still contribute to consistent differences between cities. Further, the new system does not affect levels of reporting by citizens. As a result, the new UCR only gets us a little closer to the universe of crime as compared to the old UCR.

Clearly, the new system improves the quality of data being utilized in Canada. It is likely that Canada will be the first country to have such a system fully in place early in the new millennium. The first article in this section uses both types of data, as do the more recent Statistics Canada reports on crime (e.g., Statistics Canada, 1994).

In conclusion, crime statistics collected and published by Statistics Canada are the only statistics collected on a national and annual basis in the country. Thus, for many purposes, they must be used by default as our measure of the volume and patterns of crime. However, their deficiencies must be kept in mind. If used with caution they can provide a useful social indicator of crime as defined by the law and of police activity in Canada. Moreover, the vast changes made to the data collection techniques after 1988 have improved Canadian crime statistics a great deal. We hope that, at very least, readers of this chapter will read newspaper accounts of crime trends with a much more educated eye to what they really mean.

OTHER SOURCES OF DATA ON CRIME

Given the problems of police data, some criminologists have suggested that we go back up the crime funnel from recorded crime to reported crime. That is, data should be collected by criminologists at the police level itself, perhaps by sitting in police stations and police cars, walking beats, and recording all crime of which they become aware. This, of course, is a very large-scale, clumsy, and virtually impossible operation, at least at a national level. (An example of the kinds of information available by going directly to police files is found in the article by Erin Van Brunschot in this section.)

Two alternative ways of measuring crime have been explored by criminologists in some detail. One method involves asking people if they have been crime victims (victimization studies), while the other involves asking individuals what crimes they have committed (hidden delinquency or self-report crime studies). We shall begin with the latter, as it was developed chronologically first by criminologists.

Self-Report Studies

A dissatisfaction with official measures of crime led criminologists to look for other ways to determine the actual amount of crime in society. In self-report studies, individuals are asked about their own law-violating behaviour. Initial studies using the self-report technique were done in the 1930s and 1940s in the United States, and they became very popular in the 1950s and 1960s, beginning with a study conducted by Short and Nye (1958).

In hidden delinquency/crime research, respondents are asked if they have committed specific delinquencies or crimes in a given time period. Think of yourself. Have you done any of the following acts: Have you ever taken something from a store without paying for it? Have you ever driven a vehicle while even mildly intoxicated? Have you ever used marijuana or other illegal drugs? Have you ever damaged public property? Have you ever taken anything from anyone by force? Have you ever taken office supplies for personal use? Have you ever taken goods into Canada without declaring them? Have you ever pushed, hit, or threatened someone in anger?

If you answered yes to any of these questions, then you probably violated a criminal law. Hundreds of similar questions could be used to demonstrate that, at some time in your life, you have probably committed at least several acts that are punishable by law. And probably you have committed a crime serious enough to be punishable by a jail or reformatory term. If the police did not become aware of your actions, then your behaviour is part of hidden delinquency or the "dark number" of crime.

Studies using self-report methods generally conclude that most people have committed some crimes and delinquencies, some of them serious, of which the police are unaware. In fact, most crime and delinquency does not result in police apprehension and punishment. Again, police statistics generally underestimate the amount of crime in society.

Self-report techniques are still very much alive in criminology but *not* for estimating the real volume of crime in society, partly because of their serious methodological difficulties (Nettler, 1984; O'Brien, 1985). Probably the most obvious problems involve respondents' memory, and lying by either concealing or enhancing crime involvement. The early studies rarely controlled for these issues. Looking at the positive side, for some kinds of criminal behaviour, self-report studies provide the only way of obtaining any information. Despite the methodological flaws, the technique can provide valuable insights. In fact, the original self-report technique is being used in some of the most important delinquency research being undertaken in North America (e.g., Thornberry et al., 1994).

In sum, while hidden delinquency studies have added to our knowledge about the extent of delinquency and crime, methodological problems have handicapped their ultimate usefulness in measuring crime (Lab and Allen, 1984; O'Brien, 1985; Nettler, 1984). Criminologists continue to seek better measures of the actual amount of crime in society. For many, victimization studies, described in the next section, are a better method of data collection. While self-report techniques have been abandoned as a method to reveal the volume of crime in society, for purposes of exploring the causes of crime and delinquency they serve a valuable function because they reveal offender information that is otherwise unavailable. (To see an example of how self-report information is used to test theoretical propositions, see LaGrange and Silverman, Chapter 15 in this volume).

Victimization Studies

Victimization surveys ask respondents whether or not they have been victims of crime in a given period of time, and may explore the circumstances of the crimes and whether or not the individuals have informed the police about the incident. These studies generally reveal that, even when people know they have been victimized, much crime is not reported to the police, and thus crime detected is a much larger figure than either crime reported or crime recorded (the official data). The results of early victimization studies were first reported in 1967 in the United States (Biderman et al., 1967; Ennis, 1967). Since that time, a great deal of money has been poured into U.S. victimization studies, and the level of sophistication has correspondingly improved. The U.S. National Crime Victimization Survey, the largest of its type in the world, collects data every six months on 60 000 households representing about 135 000 persons over 12 years of age. This commitment to victimization studies no doubt reflects both the resources available in the United States and the seriousness of its crime problem.

Canada has taken advantage of the U.S. developments, and in early 1982 the Ministry of the Solicitor General of Canada, with the assistance of Statistics Canada, conducted a victimization survey in seven major cities — Greater Vancouver, Edmonton, Winnipeg, Toronto, Montreal, Halifax–Dartmouth, and St. John's. The survey collected information about reported and unreported crime during 1981, the risk of victimization, the impact of crime, public perceptions of crime and the criminal justice system, and victims' perceptions of their experiences (Solicitor General, 1983). In 1985, a follow-up victimization survey was conducted in Edmonton by the Solicitor General of Canada.

The 1982 study found that "for the year 1981, there were more than 700 000 personal victimizations of people over 16 (sexual assault, robbery, assault, and theft of personal property) and almost 900 000 household victimizations (break and enter, motor vehicle theft, theft of household property and vandalism) in the seven cities surveyed . . . Fewer than 42% of these had been reported to the police" (Solicitor General, 1983). The point made earlier concerning the incompleteness of police statistics is well documented in these findings (even though these figures are not directly comparable to any set of police statistics that could be generated; see also Skogan, 1984).

A more recent source on victimization in Canada is the Statistics Canada General Social Survey. In the 1988 survey and again in 1993, a national sample of approximately 10 000 persons 15 years of age or older were interviewed by telephone, providing the most up-to-date information on victimization for Canada. In fact, because this survey involved the entire Canadian population (over age 15) it reflects victimization in Canada better than the 1982 survey, which involved only seven urban areas. Findings from this survey are discussed in the next section. It is worth noting that the next General Social Survey involving victimization will be undertaken around the time that this book goes to press. We suggest that readers look for reports from that survey in newspapers and at the Statistics Canada Web site — www.statcan.ca.

Victimization surveys are not without methodological flaws. Respondents may forget crimes or they may bring significant events (such as crimes) forward in time (telescoping) (Nettler, 1984; O'Brien, 1985; Skogan, 1984). In this case, the crime actually happened before the period in question, with the result that the data for the survey will be inflated and inappropriate for any time comparisons. Further, the respondent's notions of being victimized may not correspond to a legal definition

---

Box P2.2

Selected Findings from Early Canadian Victimization Studies

◆ Of all crimes, motor vehicle theft is the crime most likely to be reported (70 percent), while theft of personal property is least likely (29 percent).

◆ Reporting increases as injury or financial loss increases.

◆ The closer to home violence occurs, the more likely a violent crime will be reported.

◆ Women and older people are more likely to report their victimization than men and youth (although women and older people suffer less victimization overall).

◆ Income variations are not related to reporting — the rich and the poor are equally likely to report being victimized.

◆ The most common reasons for not reporting crimes are that the crime was "too minor," that "the police could not do anything about it," or that reporting it was "too inconvenient" (Solicitor General, 1983, Bulletin 1).

---

of crime. Worse, Levine (1976) argued that some respondents may invent crime to please the interviewers, and the interviewers may invent crime to please their employers. Indeed, some methodological investigations of victimization surveys reveal that responses on these surveys may be quite inaccurate. For example, Schneider (1977) was unable to locate any record for about one-third of the crimes that her respondents indicated they had reported to the police. In another example, Koss (1992) suggests that sexual assault may be underdetected not only because of the nature of the crime, but because of methodological problems in trying to get respondents to admit victimization.

One final problem with victimization surveys is that they ask about a limited number of crimes. In fact, they leave out certain types of crime completely. For rather obvious reasons, murder is never one of the crimes on the list. But also, crimes against businesses and crimes that are consensual (e.g., illicit drug purchases) are missed. By leaving out important crimes, those who develop these surveys operationally define victimization in a way that is different from official definitions of criminality. The result of these differences may be a lack of comparability between victimization surveys and other types of crime data (Biderman and Lynch, 1991; Ogrodnik and Trainor, 1997).

While there are methodological flaws in victimization surveys, they do reveal that the majority of crimes committed in Canada are not known to the police. Further, they reveal the correlates of crime reporting, that is, they tell who is and who is not likely to report a crime. They are by no means a perfect measure, but they do help to fill in gaps in police statistics.

Comparing the Uniform Crime Reports and the General Social Survey

There is a common assumption that various sources of information about crime should yield similar data. After all, they measure exactly the same phenomena, over the same period of time, and within the same geographical area. Essentially, this assumption is incorrect.

Victimization rates were comparable in the 1988 and 1993 General Social Surveys; that is, the rate of victimization in Canada did not change much in a five-year period. During that same time, the Uniform Crime Reports show rising crime rates (Ogrodnik and Trainor, 1997; Gartner and Doob, 1994). Why is there a difference?

In spite of the stability of victimization rates, Ogrodnik and Trainor (1997) report that 46 percent of Canadians believed that crime had increased. There is a troubling gap between the public's perception and the reality of crime in Canada — at least in terms of victimization data. The public's notion of rising crime rates comes primarily from newspaper reports about the Uniform Crime Reports, media reports of individual crimes, and a spillover of news and entertainment from the United States. The public rarely hears of reports of GSS victimization results, partly because these studies are undertaken periodically, not annually, and partly because the results are rarely as dramatic as those of other sources.

It is useful to attempt to understand why the two data sources produce different results and how each represents crime in Canada. Earlier, we pointed out both the methods by which the UCR data and the GSS data are generated, and noted the sources of error in the two kinds of study. Table P2.1 reviews, in a concise manner, the methods, scope, and sources of error in each type of study.

Ogrodnik and Trainor (1997) performed an interesting comparison between the two data sets.[3] The major findings from their study are summarized in Table P2.2.

The summary offered by these researchers is worth reproducing (Ogrodnik and Trainor, 1997: 8).

One advantage of victimization surveys is that information is gathered directly from respondents, including their experiences as victims, associated socio-economic risk factors and the after-effects of crime. This type of information is valuable to researchers in measuring the impact of crime, a dimension of information unavailable from a survey based solely on administrative data. As well, victim surveys offer greater flexibility in that descriptive details can be collected on relatively rare but serious criminal events (e.g., stalking). The scope of the surveys can also be expanded to include crimes that are believed to be under-reported in police administrative systems (e.g., hate-motivated crimes, elder abuse).

The UCR has the major advantage over victim surveys with respect to coverage and volume. The database allows for the analysis of crime data by small geographic area (municipalities) and over time (since 1962). In comparison, the GSS sample size (ten thousand persons) allows fairly extensive analysis at the national level, but only limited analysis at the provincial level. . . .

Joint publication of victimization and police-reported crime data with a clear statement of their

Table P2.1

Differences between the Uniform Crime Reports and General Social Survey

UCR	GSS
DATA COLLECTION METHODS:	
Administrative police records	Personal reports from individual citizens
Census	Sample survey
100% coverage of all police agencies	Sample of approximately 10 000 persons using random digit dialling sampling technique
Data submitted on paper or in machine-readable format	Computer assisted telephone interviews (CATI) excludes households without telephones
National in scope	Excludes Yukon and Northwest Territories
Continuous historical file: 1962 onwards	Periodic survey: 1988, 1993, next survey anticipated in the year 2000
All recorded criminal incidents regardless of victims' age	Target population: persons aged 15 and over, excluding full-time residents of institutions
Counts only those incidents reported to and recorded by police	Collects crimes reported and not reported to police
SCOPE AND DEFINITIONS:	
Primary unit of count is the criminal incident	Primary unit of count is criminal victimization (at personal and household levels)
Nearly 100 crime categories	Eight crime categories
"Most serious offence" rule results in an undercount of less serious crimes	Statistics are usually reported on a "most serious offence" basis, but counts for every crime type are possible, depending on statistical reliability
Includes attempts	Includes attempts
SOURCES OF ERROR:	
Reporting by the public	Sampling error
Processing error, edit failure, non-responding police department	Non-sampling error related to the following: coverage, respondent error (e.g., recall error), non-response, coding, edit and imputation, estimation
Police discretion, changes in policy and procedures	
Legislative change	

SOURCE: Adapted from Ogrodnik, L. & Trainor, C. (1997). An Overview of the Differences between Police-Reported and Victim-Reported Crime, 1997, Cat. no. 85-542-XPE. Ottawa: Ministry of Industry. Statistics Canada: Canadian Centre for Justice Statistics.

....

Table P2.2

Comparative Analysis of Police-Reported (UCR) and Victim-Reported (GSS) Crime Rates[a]

1. Sexual Assault

GSS DEFINITION	Sexually assaulted, molested, or attempt to sexually assault or molest
UCR CATEGORY	Sexual assault (level 1) Sexual assault with weapon (level 2) Aggravated sexual assault (level 3) Other sexual offences Attempts
ADJUSTMENTS	To the UCR: combine all sexual assault offences and other sexual offences reported or known to police (including unfounded incidents) to approximate the GSS category of sexual assault and molestation; adjust UCR data using UCR2[b] data to estimate the number of persons aged 15 and older; exclude the two territories and calculate a rate per 1000 GSS population.
RESULTS	Rate (per 1000 population) of offences reported to police GSS:UCR Ratio, 1993 = 1.8:1 (This ratio means that for every 18 sexual assaults were reported in the GSS, ten sexual assaults were reported in the UCR.)

2. Robbery

GSS DEFINITION	Something taken, or there was an attempt, and the person who committed the act had a weapon, or there was an attack or threat of force
UCR CATEGORY	Robbery with firearm Robbery with other offensive weapons Other robbery Attempts
ADJUSTMENTS	To the UCR: exclude the two territories and calculate a rate per 1000 GSS population. (Because the UCR does not record the actual number of victims in an incident, the UCR2 was used to calculate the average number of victims per robbery incident. A factor of 1.2 persons per UCR robbery was used in both 1987 and 1993.) Actual or attempted robbery of a business was not to be reported by GSS respondents. The aggregate UCR does not distinguish between business robberies and other robberies. UCR2 estimates for 1995 show that 49% of robberies occurred in a commercial or corporate location.
RESULTS	Rate (per 1000 population) of offences reported to police GSS:UCR Ratio, 1993 = 2.7:1 GSS:UCR Ratio, 1988 = 3.0:1

(continued)

Table P2.2 *(continued)*

3. Assault

GSS DEFINITION	A weapon was present or there was an attack (ranging from being hit, slapped, grabbed, or knocked down, to being shot or beaten up) or threat of an attack
UCR CATEGORY	Assault (level 1) Assault with weapon, causing bodily harm (level 2) Aggravated assault (level 3) Unlawfully causing bodily harm Other assaults Attempts
ADJUSTMENTS	To the UCR: combine the UCR assault categories to roughly equate the GSS category; exclude the two territories and calculate a rate per 1000 GSS population.
RESULTS	Rate (per 1000 population) of offences reported to police GSS:UCR Ratio, 1993 = 1.8:1 GSS:UCR Ratio, 1988 = 2.3:1

4. Break and Enter

GSS DEFINITION	The person had no right to be there and actually got in; or the person tried to get in; or not known if actually got in, and there is evidence of force, or knowledge of how a person tried to get in
UCR CATEGORY	Residential break and enter Other break and enter Attempts
ADJUSTMENTS	To the UCR: exclude business break and enter incidents; exclude the two territories and calculate the rate per 1000 GSS population.
RESULTS	Rate (per 1000 population) of offences reported to police GSS:UCR Ratio, 1993 = 1.2:1 GSS:UCR Ratio, 1988 = 1.3:1

5. Motor Vehicle Theft

GSS DEFINITION	Theft of car, truck, van, motorcycle, moped, other motor vehicle; attempted theft of motor vehicle
UCR CATEGORY	Motor vehicle theft — Automobiles Trucks Motorcycles Other Attempts
ADJUSTMENTS	To the UCR: combine all UCR motor vehicle theft categories to roughly equate the GSS category; exclude the two territories and calculate the rate per 1000 population.

(continued)

Table P2.2 *(continued)*

	To the GSS: Use only actual or attempted motor vehicle thefts; exclude actual or attempted theft of motor vehicle parts.
RESULTS	Rate (per 1000 population) of offences reported to police GSS:UCR Ratio, 1993 = 1:1.5 GSS:UCR Ratio, 1988 = 1:1.4
	Possible explanations for the higher rates of motor vehicle theft reported to the UCR than the GSS include the following:
	1) The UCR includes motor vehicle thefts from car dealerships, while the GSS only includes motor vehicle thefts from households. In addition, GSS respondents are asked to exclude company owned vehicles.
	2) The GSS treats motor vehicle theft as a household crime and assumes that anyone living in a household would report a motor vehicle theft regardless of whether or not they owned the vehicle. However, if some respondents' perception is that the vehicle is personal property rather than household property, they may not report the incident, thus underestimating the number of vehicle thefts.

NOTES:

[a] Results are based on a rudimentary analysis and are subject to high sampling variability.

[b] The UCR2 (Revised UCR), introduced in 1988, collects detailed information on up to four separate violations committed during an incident. Coverage is limited, however (approximately 46% of the volume of all reported crime in 1995).

SOURCE: Adapted from Ogrodnik, L. & Trainor, C. (1997). An Overview of the Differences between Police-Reported and Victim-Reported Crime, 1997, Cat. no. 85-542-XPE. Ottawa: Ministry of Industry. Statistics Canada: Canadian Centre for Justice Statistics.

appropriate uses contributes towards informing the public about the full nature and extent of crime. Data from GSS victimization surveys can be used to contextualize information from the UCR. Alternatively, the two data sources can be used to test alternative hypotheses related to criminal activity. Neither administrative statistics nor victimization surveys alone can provide comprehensive information about crime. Each is useful for addressing specific issues.

SUMMARY

No perfect method of counting crime has yet been invented. The Canadian Uniform Crime Reports for 1961 to 1988 had some serious faults but were probably reliable as indicators of gross trends in seri-

ous Canadian crime. The new system of Uniform Crime Reporting offers a much richer data set and eliminates many of the problems inherent in the first UCR. Self-report crime studies have methodological problems that make them inappropriate for determining the volume of crime in any global sense but, when used with appropriate caution, they offer the only feasible way to get enough detail about offenders to test criminological theory. Finally, victimization surveys seem to offer more valid and reliable data than the other two methods in terms of volume of crime. However, here too caution must be used in interpreting these data, and we must not forget that the data are not directly comparable to police statistics.

In all social science, because of imperfect data, multiple measures are preferred for measuring any social phenomena. Hence, the student is advised to examine patterns generated by all sources of crime data and to do so with a critical eye. Caution must be the operant word.

After reading about the problems with these sources of data, the student may well ask why it is so important to collect fully accurate crime data. The answer is quite simple. These data (particularly official statistics) are used to decide how much and what type of effort to put into any "fight against crime." For instance, they are used to make policy decisions involving resources to be devoted to policing and crime prevention. Thus, incorrect data can mislead us into over-, under-, and inappropriately reacting to a perceived crime threat, perhaps resulting in unnecessary restrictions of civil liberties, insufficient levels of protection, or wasted financial resources. Because of these policy implications, it is crucial that crime data be as accurate as possible. For social scientists, these data are used to test various hypotheses about crime causation (see Part 3 of this book). If the data are inaccurate, then erroneous conclusions may be drawn about the causes of crime in Canada. While hypothesis testing does not lead directly to policy making, it often influences it.

In concluding this introduction to Part 2, one final caution is in order. In Part 1, we alerted you to the many definitions of crime; after reading this section you should be aware of several measures of crime. When you read reports about "crime" in this book and elsewhere, carefully examine both the definition and the measure of crime being used before you draw any conclusions.

THE READINGS

The first article in this section is a slightly edited version of the Statistics Canada *Juristat* that reports the patterns of crime in Canada using both aggregate and incident-based reporting. In other words, this article shows you exactly the kinds of data that the earlier part of this chapter focussed on. As you read it, try to remember which data are generated by each part of the UCR program.

Leslie Kennedy and David Veitch discover that crime is going down in Edmonton, and they try to determine the reasons for the decline. Kennedy and Veitch eliminate many of the causes of fluctuations of crime rates, and ultimately they find that the crime rate is declining because of a decline in the reporting of property crime, administrative decisions, and a shift toward community policing with an emphasis on problem solving and crime prevention. The article illustrates well the complexities involved in trying to figure out what a crime rate really means.

Peter Carrington examines patterns of youth crime over a twenty-year period. His analysis examines the effects of the *Young Offenders Act* on the generation of youth crime statistics. When the new *Young Offenders Act* took over from the earlier *Juvenile Delinquents Act*, there was speculation that the change might affect reporting of crime rates or police behaviour with regard to young offenders. He shows that the advent of the *Young Offenders Act* appears to have resulted in a change in police charging of apprehended youth in some provinces. In essence the use of police discretion was reduced after the advent of the new act, at least in some jurisdictions.

Holly Johnson's article introduces readers to the Violence Against Women survey, which is a victimization study. This survey is concerned with particular female victimization. The article examines the methodological problems and implications of such a survey and contains some provocative results. It provides evidence, for example, of widespread violence against women in Canada. Three in ten women who have ever been married or lived with a man in a common-law relationship have experienced violence by a marital partner, and almost four in ten women have been sexually assaulted. A great many women have been victimized more than once.

Rosemary Gartner and Ross Macmillan use the data generated by the Violence Against Women survey to examine the effect of victim-offender relationship on reporting crimes of violence against women. They show how a crime victim's relationship with her offender affects her behaviour with regard to reporting crime, and they find that criminal justice knowledge of violence against women is systematically biased. Further, while all types of violence against women are underreported, intimate violence is the least likely to be reported to the police, independent of type and severity of violence and victim characteristics. This article illustrates how a good data set can result in insightful research that has some clear policy implications.

The final article in the section is by Erin Van Brunschot. It reveals that the level of detail that we desire and need to study crime is often not available in official or unofficial data sources. Sometimes, it is only possible to generate that level of richness in a data set by listening to accounts of the crime from those who were there. In this case, Van Brunschot lets us hear the victims' accounts of what happened during an assault as revealed in police reports.

NOTES

1. When we did the fifth edition of this book we thought that it would be the last time that we discussed these original Uniform Crime Reports. However, as the new system has not completely replaced the old, readers should be introduced to both.
2. The substance of this section is generated from materials provided by the Canadian Centre for Justice Statistics. These materials are not cited, as most are unpublished documents.
3. In order to make the data sets comparable, Ogrodnik and Trainor had to make several adjustments, including the following:
   ♦ Crimes mentioned by GSS respondents that were not reported to the police were excluded from the GSS counts.
   ♦ UCR data for the Yukon and Northwest Territories were omitted from the UCR counts.
   ♦ Police reports of "unfounded" incidents were included in the UCR count.
   ♦ UCR-based rates of offences reported to police were converted to conform to GSS rates for both persons and households (1997: 7).

REFERENCES

Akman, D., & Normandeau, A. (1967). The measurement of crime and delinquency in Canada: A replication study. *British Journal of Criminology, 7,* 129–149.

Atkinson, J. (1998). Neutralization among male and female fraud offenders. Ph.D. dissertation, Psychology Department, Queen's University.

Biderman, A. D., Johnson, L. A., McIntyre, J., & Weir, A. W. (1967). Report on a pilot study in the District of Columbia on victimization and attitudes towards law enforcement. In United States President's Commission on Law Enforcement and the Administration of Justice, *Field Survey I.* Washington, DC: U.S. Government Printing Office.

Biderman, A. D., & Lynch, J. P. (1991). *Understanding crime incidence statistics: Why the UCR diverges from the NCA.* New York: Springer-Verlag.

Black, D. J., & Reiss, A. J. (1967). Patterns of behavior in police and citizen transactions. In President's Commission on Law Enforcement and the Administration of Justice, *Studies in Crime and Law Enforcement in Major Metropolitan Areas, Field Surveys III, vol. 2.* Washington, DC: U.S. Government Printing Office.

Black, D. (1970). Production of crime rates. *American Sociological Review, 35,* 733–747.

Bowling, B. (1990). Conceptual and methodological problems in measuring "race" differences in delinquency: A reply to Marianne Junger. *British Journal of Criminology, 30*(4), 483–492.

Burris, C., & Jaffe, P. (1983). Wife abuse as a crime: The impact of police laying charges. *Canadian Journal of Criminology, 25,* 309–318.

Canadian Centre for Justice Statistics. (1990). The development of data quality assessment procedures for the Uniform Crime Reporting Survey: A case study of Calgary-Edmonton. Ottawa: Canadian Centre for Justice Statistics.

Canadian Centre for Justice Statistics. (1994). *Canadian crime statistics 1994.* Ottawa: Minister of Industry, Science and Technology.

Canadian Centre for Justice Statistics. (1998). *A graphical overview of crime and the administration of criminal justice in Canada, 1996.* Cat. no. 85F0018XPE. Ottawa: Minister of Industry.

Ennis, P. H. (1967). Criminal victimization in the United States: A report of a national survey. In

President's Commission on Law Enforcement and the Administration of Justice, *Field Survey II*. Washington, DC: U.S. Government Printing Office.

Ericson, R. (1981). *Making crime: A study of detective work*. Toronto: Butterworths.

Gartner, R., & Doob, A. (1994). Trends in criminal victimization 1988–1993. *Juristat, 14*(13). Ottawa: Canadian Centre for Justice Statistics.

Grosman, B. (1975). *Police command*. Toronto: Macmillan.

Hackler, J., & Paranjape, W. (1983). Juvenile justice statistics: Mythmaking or measure of system response. *Canadian Journal of Criminology, 25,* 209–226.

Hartnagel, T. F. (1978). The effect of age and sex composition of provincial populations on provincial crime rates. *Canadian Journal of Criminology, 20,* 28–33.

Kennedy, L.W., & Forde, D. (1990). Routine activities and crime: An analysis of victimization in Canada. *Criminology, 28,* 137–152.

Koenig, D. J. (1993). *Do police cause crime? Police activity, police strength and crime rates*. Ottawa: The Canadian Police College.

Koss, M. P. (1992). The underdetection of rape: Methodological choices influence incidence estimates. *Journal of Social Issues, 48*(1), 61–75.

Lab, S. P., & Allen, R. B. (1984). Self-report and official measures: A further examination of the validity issue. *Journal of Criminal Justice, 12*(15), 445–455.

Lee, G. W. (1984). Are crime rates increasing? A study of the impact of demographic shifts on crime rates in Canada. *Canadian Journal of Criminology, 26,* 29–42.

Levine, J. (1976). The potential for crime over reporting in criminal victimization surveys. *Criminology, 14,* 307–330.

Maxim, P. (1985). Cohort size and juvenile delinquency: A test of the Easterlin hypothesis. *Social Forces, 63*(3), 661–681.

Nettler, G. (1984). *Explaining crime* (3rd ed.). New York: McGraw-Hill.

Nielsen, M. (1979). RCMP policing: A question of style. Unpublished M.A. Thesis, University of Alberta, Edmonton.

O'Brien, R. M. (1985). *Crime and victimization data*. Beverly Hills: Sage.

Ogrodnik, L., & Trainor, C. (1997). *An overview of the differences between police-reported and victim-reported crime, 1997*. Cat. no. 85-542-XPE. Ottawa: Ministry of Industry. Statistics Canada: Canadian Centre for Justice Statistics.

Schneider, A. L. (1977). *The Portland forward record's check of crime victims: Final report*. Eugene, OR: Institute for Policy Analysis.

Schneider, A. L., & Sumi, D. (1981). Patterns of forgetting and telescoping: An analysis of LEAA survey victimization data. *Criminology, 19*(3), 400–410.

Sellin, T. (1932). The basis of a crime index. *Journal of Criminal Law and Criminology, 23,* 335–356.

Sellin, T., & Wolfgang, M. E. (1964). *The measurement of delinquency*. New York: John Wiley and Sons.

Sewell, J. (1985). *Police: Urban policing in Canada*. Toronto: James Lorimer.

Sherman, L., & Cohen, E. (1989). The impact of research on legal policy: The Minneapolis domestic violence experiment. *Law and Society Review, 23*(1), 117–144.

Short, J., & Nye, F. (1958). Extent of unrecorded juvenile delinquency: Tentative conclusions. *Journal of Criminal Law, Criminology and Police Science, 49,* 296–302.

Silverman, R. A. (1977). Criminal statistics: A comparison of two cities. *Report to the Solicitor-General of Alberta*. Mimeographed.

Silverman, R. A. (1980) Measuring crime: A tale of two cities. In R. A. Silverman & J. J. Teevan, *Crime and Canadian society* (2nd ed.). Toronto: Butterworths.

Silverman, R. A. (1990). Trends in youth homicide: Some unanticipated consequences of a change in the law. *Canadian Journal of Criminology, 32*(4), 651–656.

Silverman, R. A. (1996) Patterns of Native American criminality. In M. Nielsen & R. A. Silverman (Eds.), *Native Americans, crime, and justice*. Boulder, CO: Westview.

Skogan, W. G. (1981). *Issues in the measurement of victimization*. Washington, DC: U.S. Government Printing Office.

Skogan, W. G. (1984). Reporting crimes to the police: The status of world research. *Journal of Research in Crime and Delinquency, 21,* 113–137.

Solicitor General of Canada:

(1983). Bulletin 1: Victims of crime.

(1984). Bulletin 2: Reported and unreported crimes.

(1984). Bulletin 3: Crime prevention: Awareness and practice.

(1985). Bulletin 4: Female victims of crime.

(1985). Bulletin 5: Cost of crime to victims.

(1985). Bulletin 6: Criminal victimization of elderly Canadians.

(1986). Bulletin 7: Household property crimes.

(1987). Bulletin 8: Patterns in violent crime.

(1988). Bulletin 9: Patterns in property crime.

(1988). Bulletin 10: Multiple victimization.

Statistics Canada. (1977). *Crime and traffic enforcement statistics.* Ottawa: Government of Canada.

Statistics Canada. (1986). *Canadian crime statistics, 1985.* Ottawa: Minister of Supply and Services

Statistics Canada. (1990). The future of crime statistics from the UCR survey. *Juristat, 10*(10). July.

Statistics Canada. (1994). *The 1993 general social survey: Tables in victimization.* Statistics Canada Cat. no. 12F0042XPE, December.

Statistics Canada. (1997). Crime statistics 1996. *Juristat, 17*(8), catalogue 85-002-XPE.

Statistics Canada. Daily. Ottawa: www.statcan.ca
    June 19, 1998. Violence committed by strangers.

June 4, 1998. A profile of inmates in adult correctional facilities, October 1996.

May 28, 1998. Family violence: A statistical profile, 1996.

July 30, 1997. Crime in Canada, 1996.

July 30, 1997. Homicide in Canada, 1996.

Thornberry, T. P., Lizotte, A., Krohn, M., Farnworth, M., & Joon Jang, S. (1994). Delinquent peers, beliefs, and delinquent behavior: A longitudinal test of interactional theory. *Criminology, 32*(1), 47–84.

Wilson, J. Q. (1968). *Varieties of police behavior: The management of law and order in eight communities.* Cambridge, MA: Harvard University Press.

Wortley, S. (1994). The collection and use of statistics on race and crime: An issues and options paper. Toronto: Commission on Systematic Racism in the Ontario Criminal Justice System.

Canadian Crime Statistics

REBECCA KONG

INTRODUCTION

Every year since 1962, Canada's police agencies have reported criminal incidents that come to their attention to the Uniform Crime Reporting (UCR) survey. This report is an examination of the 1997 reported crime. Data are presented within the context of both short and long term trends.

Analyses in this report focus on trends in violent crime, property crime, impaired driving offences, drug offences and youth crime. Crime rates are examined at the national, provincial/territorial and major metropolitan levels. The trend in Canada's crime rate is put into perspective by comparing it with crime trends in other industrialized countries. The Canadian Centre for Justice Statistics gratefully acknowledges the assistance of Canada's police agencies and of the Canadian Association of Chiefs of Police in making this report possible.

Interpreting Police-Reported Crime Data

Data on incidents that come to the attention of police are captured and forwarded to the Canadian Centre for Justice Statistics (CCJS) according to a nationally approved set of common scoring rules and definitions. The reader should note, however, that many factors could influence official crime statistics. These include reporting by the public to the police; reporting by police to the CCJS; and the impact of new initiatives such as changes in legislation, policies or enforcement practices.

REPORTING TO POLICE

It can be argued that official crime statistics merely reflect Canadians' willingness to report criminal activity to police. There are many reasons why victims may not report these incidents to police. Estimates of unreported crime are available from victimization surveys, such as the 1993 General Social Survey (GSS)[1] and the 1995 International Criminal Victimization Survey (ICVS).[2] Mirroring the trends in police-reported data, results from victimization surveys show recent decreases in criminal victimization among Canadians. Overall, victimization rates in Canada fell 11% between 1991 and 1995 compared to a 14% decrease in the police-reported crime rate.

While under-reporting to police can negatively affect official crime statistics, the opposite is also true: as the tolerance for certain crimes lowers, reporting to police will increase, driving crime statistics upward. For example, increased education in the areas of family violence, sexual assault and youth crime have lowered society's tolerance for these behaviours which, in turn, may encourage victims and witnesses to report to police.

Adapted from Canadian Crime Statistics, 1997, by Rebecca Kong (July 1998). *Juristat*, *18*(11), Statistics Canada Catalogue 85-002-XPE. Reprinted with permission of Statistics Canada.

REPORTING BY POLICE TO THE CCJS

Crimes reported to the CCJS by police agencies are subjected to numerous quality control procedures, both on-site at the police agency and at the CCJS. The CCJS and police agencies work together on an ongoing basis to detect and resolve any difficulties in the reporting or transmission of data.

In addition, concerns have been raised that tighter budgets are diminishing the ability of some police agencies to respond to, and document, all incidents reported to them, a situation that may also result in a loss of UCR coverage. While it has been suggested that this may have contributed to the recent declines in the crime rate, these decreases have applied equally to serious crimes (those which are less prone to non-recording by police) and to less serious crimes. Moreover, a comparison of trends among police agencies shows that agencies across all provinces/territories have been experiencing decreases in crime.

CHANGES IN LEGISLATION, POLICIES AND PRACTICES

Changes in legislation, policies and police enforcement practices may also have an impact on police-reported statistics. For instance, where an amendment to the *Criminal Code* creates a new offence or broadens the definition of an existing one, the number of incidents reported to police will likely increase.

For certain crimes, the rise and fall of statistics is driven largely by police enforcement. Crimes such as prostitution, drug offences and impaired driving are most often identified through police enforcement, or "proactive" policing, and are rarely reported by the public. Therefore, police enforcement efforts, such as special operations to target prostitution, the drug trade and impaired driving will affect official crime statistics.

Some police agencies attribute recent declines in local crime rates to community-based policing or to new strategies initiated to reduce certain crimes. The concept of community-based policing revolves around the idea that police should move toward a proactive approach, including working with indi-

---

Box 5.1

Key Terminology and Definitions

Throughout this report, the terms "crime" and "crime rate" refer to total police-reported *Criminal Code* "actual" incidents, excluding traffic crime, unless noted otherwise. "Actual" incidents are those which have been substantiated through police investigation. It is also important to note that, for incidents involving multiple offences, only the most serious offence in the incident is counted. Unless otherwise stated, violent crime counts reflect the number of victims in the incidents, whereas non-violent crime counts reflect the number of incidents or occurrences of crime. Crime rates are based on 100 000 population. Please refer to the methodology section for further details on the UCR survey.

---

viduals and businesses in the community to address community problems and concerns. Critics, however, suggest that rates of reporting to police may decrease as some community-based policing programs require complainants to appear in person at the community police centres to file a report. On the other hand, focusing on community problems may result in improved police responses to minor violations or in increased reporting by members of the community, both of which can increase a police agency's crime statistics. While community-based policing can have an impact on police-reported crime statistics, the direction and size of the impact are difficult to assess. Aside from community policing, some police agencies attribute declines in certain crimes to improved case management and new approaches to resolving and preventing crime.

1997 CRIME TRENDS

Lowest Crime Rate since 1980

Of the 2.5 million *Criminal* Code incidents (excluding traffic incidents) reported in 1997, 12%

were violent crimes, 58% were property crimes, and 30% were other *Criminal Code* crimes (e.g., mischief, prostitution, arson, bail violations, disturbing the peace). In addition, there were approximately 155 000 *Criminal Code* traffic incidents (mostly impaired driving), 67 000 drug incidents, and 35 000 other federal statute incidents (e.g., *Excise Act, Immigration Act, Canada Shipping Act)* reported. In total, there were 2.8 million federal statute incidents reported to police (Table 5.1).

After peaking in the early 1990s, Canada's crime rate has been falling steadily. In 1997, the police-reported crime rate dropped for the sixth consecutive year (-5%) (Table 5.2). Over these six years, the crime rate has decreased by 19%, making the 1997 rate the lowest since 1980 (Figure 5.1). Compared to 20 years ago, however, the 1997 crime rate is 20% higher, and it is up almost 120% from 30 years ago. Over the last few decades, amendments to Canada's definition of criminal behaviour and changes in our tolerance for certain crimes may have influenced reporting to police.

Crime Rate Down across Majority of Provinces and Census Metropolitan Areas

There is considerable regional variation in the distribution of reported crime across Canada. Historically, crime rates in the Atlantic provinces and Quebec have been lower than those in Ontario, which in turn have been lower than rates in the Western provinces. Since 1993, however, this pattern has changed, with Alberta reporting much lower crime rates than its neighbouring provinces (Figures 5.2a, 5.2b). Crime rates in the Northwest Territories and the Yukon Territory are usually higher than those in the provinces (Table 5.3).

In 1997, provincial crime rates ranged from a low of 5571 incidents per 100 000 population in Newfoundland to 12 870 per 100 000 in British Columbia (Table 5.3). Except for Saskatchewan (+4%) and Alberta (+1.8%), all other provinces followed the national trend of a declining crime rate in 1997. The crime rate in Saskatchewan has been

increasing since 1994. The growth in Alberta for 1997, on the other hand, followed five years of declines, three of which were large declines. Prince Edward Island reported the largest provincial decrease in 1997 (–10%). Ontario, which accounts for almost four-tenths of Canada's population, reported a drop of 9%.

Declining crime rates were also the norm in most of the census metropolitan areas (CMAs).[3] Rates grew in only 4 of the 25 CMAs: Chicoutimi-Jonquière (+5%), Saskatoon (+4%), Edmonton (+2%) and Trois-Rivières (+1.7%). The largest decreases were reported in Ottawa (–15%),[4] Saint John (New Brunswick) (–13%), Vancouver (–12%) and Quebec (–12%). Rates also fell in the nation's two largest CMAs: Toronto (–8%) and Montreal (–6%) (Table 5.4). Compared to five years ago, crime rates in most CMAs have fallen. In 1997, Quebec continued to report the lowest crime rate, while Regina reported the highest.

Crime Also Falling in the U.S. and in England and Wales

Other countries have also experienced recent declines in their crime rates. The Federal Bureau of Investigation reported that the indexed crime[5] rate in the United States had dropped 4% in 1997, including a 5% decrease in violent crime and a 4% decline in property crime. Decreases were reported for all indexed offences including murder (–9%), robbery (–9%), motor vehicle theft (–5%) and burglary (–3%). Moreover, the crime rate in England and Wales has fallen annually since 1992, including a 9% decrease in 1997.

While the Crime Rate Is Down, So Is the Number of Young People in Canada

The field of criminology holds a wealth of research on factors that can influence the level of crime in society. For instance, studies of criminal behaviour suggest that young people are at higher risk of engaging in criminal activity and that the prevalence of offending increases to a peak in teenage

Table 5.1
Federal Statute Incidents Reported to Police, by Most Serious Offence, Canada, 1993–1997

	1993		1994		1995ʳ		1996ʳ		1997		Percent change in rate 1996-97[1]
	Number	Rate*	Number	Rate*	Number	Rate*	Number	Rate*	Number	Rate*	
Population ('000)	28 895.7		29 264.7		29 616.5		29 959.5		30 285.8		
Homicide	630	2	596	2	588	2	635	2	581	2	−9.5
Attempted murder	984	3	922	3	939	3	878	3	861	3	−3.0
Assaults — Total (levels 1, 2, 3)	223 754	774	222 300	760	217 618	735	219 919	734	222 210	734	—
Level 1	181 807	629	181 577	620	178 934	604	181 545	606	182 946	604	−0.3
Level 2 — Weapon	38 767	134	37 725	129	35 921	121	35 626	119	36 618	121	1.7
Level 3 — Aggravated	3 180	11	2 998	10	2 763	9	2 748	9	2 646	9	−4.7
Other assaults	14 749	51	14 264	49	13 462	45	12 171	41	11 778	39	−4.3
Sexual assaults — Total (levels 1, 2, 3,)	34 754	120	31 706	108	28 234	95	27 026	90	27 063	89	−0.9
Level 1	33 536	116	30 572	104	27 278	92	26 076	87	26 186	86	−0.7
Level 2 — Weapon	860	3	769	3	659	2	653	2	605	2	−8.3
Level 3 — Aggravated	358	1	365	1	297	1	297	1	272	1	−9.4
Other sexual offences	4 171	14	3 818	13	3 494	12	3 343	11	3 672	12	8.7
Abduction	1 204	4	1 129	4	1 035	3	977	3	982	3	−0.6
Robbery — Total	29 955	104	29 010	99	30 332	102	31 797	106	29 590	98	−7.9
Firearms	8 038	28	7 361	25	6 692	23	6 737	22	5 478	18	−19.6
Other Weapons	9 720	34	9 386	32	10 127	34	10 543	35	9 933	33	−6.8
No Weapons	12 197	42	12 263	42	13 513	46	14 517	48	14 179	47	−3.4
Violent crime — Total	310 201	1 074	303 745	1 038	295 702	998	296 746	990	296 737	980	−1.1

(continued)

Table 5.1 (continued)

	1993 Number	1993 Rate*	1994 Number	1994 Rate*	1995ʳ Number	1995ʳ Rate*	1996ʳ Number	1996ʳ Rate*	1997 Number	1997 Rate*	Percent change in rate 1996–97[1]
Break & enter — Total	406 421	1 407	387 867	1 325	390 784	1 319	397 057	1 325	373 355	1 233	−7.0
Business	115 757	401	110 480	378	108 749	367	110 196	368	100 652	332	−9.6
Residential	239 322	828	227 199	776	235 129	794	242 639	810	233 844	772	−4.7
Other	51 342	178	50 188	171	46 906	158	44 222	148	38 859	128	−13.1
Motor vehicle theft	156 685	542	159 469	545	161 696	546	180 123	601	177 286	585	−2.6
Theft over $5000 ($1000 prior to 1995)	117 765	408	116 396	398	42 080	142	27 075	90	24 026	79	−12.2
Theft $5000 and under ($1000 prior to 1995)	774 293	2 608	727 414	2 486	820 908	2 772	823 732	2 749	758 025	2 503	−9.0
Possession of stolen goods	30 827	107	30 130	103	31 293	106	31 772	106	29 544	98	−8.0
Fraud	113 046	391	103 243	353	103 964	351	102 052	341	96 694	319	−6.3
Property crime — Total	1 599 037	5 534	1 524 519	5 209	1 550 725	5 236	1 561 811	5 213	1 458 930	4 817	−7.6
Mischief	415 508	1 438	396 904	1 356	380 041	1 283	365 830	1 221	341 687	1 128	−7.6
Gaming and betting	704	2	421	1	568	2	766	3	421	1	−45.6
Bail violation	66 271	229	65 952	225	66 939	226	68 949	230	68 920	228	−1.1
Disturbing the peace	54 492	189	51 213	175	51 401	174	54 563	182	57 594	190	4.4
Offensive weapons	18 584	64	18 898	65	17 571	59	16 400	55	16 079	53	−3.0
Prostitution	8 517	29	5 575	19	7 170	24	6 397	21	5 812	19	−10.1
Arson	12 470	43	13 509	46	13 156	44	12 830	43	12 799	42	−1.3
Other	249 842	865	265 473	907	256 381	866	260 601	870	271 375	896	3.0

(continued)

Table 5.1 (continued)

	1993 Number	1993 Rate*	1994 Number	1994 Rate*	1995ʳ Number	1995ʳ Rate*	1996ʳ Number	1996ʳ Rate*	1997 Number	1997 Rate*	Percent change in rate 1996–97[1]
Other Criminal Code — Total	826 388	2 860	817 945	2 795	793 227	2 678	786 336	2 625	774 687	2 558	−2.5
CRIMINAL CODE WITHOUT TRAFFIC — TOTAL	2 735 626	9 467	2 646 209	9 042	2 639 654	8 913	2 644 893	8 828	2 530 354	8 355	−5.4
Impaired driving — Total[2]	117 574	407	107 768	368	102 285	345	96 280	321	90 099	297	−7.4
Fail to stop/remain	60 066	208	60 138	205	54 180	183	49 896	167	49 954	165	−1.0
Other C.C. traffic	20 185	70	18 529	63	17 419	59	16 286	54	15 274	50	−7.2
Criminal Code Traffic — Total	197 825	685	186 435	637	173 884	587	162 462	542	155 327	513	−5.4
CRIMINAL CODE — TOTAL	2 933 451	10 152	2 832 644	9 679	2 813 538	9 500	2 807 355	9 371	2 685 681	8 868	−5.4
DRUGS	56 817	197	60 153	206	61 613	208	65 729	219	66 521	220	0.1
OTHER FEDERAL STATUTES	48 282	167	40 525	138	36 121	122	34 274	114	35 207	116	1.6
TOTAL FEDERAL STATUTES	3 038 550	10 516	2 933 322	10 023	2 911 272	9 830	2 907 358	9 704	2 787 409	9 203	−5.2

[1] Percent change based on unrounded rates.

[2] Includes impaired operation of a vehicle causing death, causing bodily harm, alcohol rate over 80 mg, failure/refusal to provide a breath/blood sample.

* Rates are calculated based on 100 000 population. The population estimates are provided by Statistics Canada, Census and Demographic Statistics, Demography Division. Populations as of July 1st: final postcensal estimates for 1993 to 1995; updated postcensal estimates for 1996 and 1997.

ʳ Revised. After the release of 1996 data in July 1997, an error was discovered that had resulted in an under-counting of 1996 crime for Toronto and 1995 and 1996 crime for Winnipeg. These errors were corrected and the data in this *Juristat* reflect the corrections. Please refer to the methodology section for more details.

— amount too small to be expressed.

SOURCE: *Uniform Crime Reporting Survey*, Canadian Centre for Justice Statistics, Statistics Canada.

Table 5.2
Rates of Criminal Code Incidents, Canada, 1986–1997[1]

	1987	1988	1989	1990	1991	1992	1993	1994	1995[r]	1996[r]	1997
Population ('000)	26 549.7	26 894.8	27 379.3	27 790.6	28 111.0	28 532.5	28 895.7	29 264.7	29 616.5	29 959.5	30 285.8
Violent crime rate	826	865	908	970	1 056	1 078	1 074	1 038	998	990	980
Year-to-year % change*	5.7	4.7	5.0	6.8	8.9	2.0	-0.4	-3.3	-3.8	-0.8	-1.1
Property crime rate	5 531	5 419	5 271	5 593	6 153	5 870	5 534	5 209	5 236	5 213	4 817
Year-to-year % change*	0.1	-2.0	-2.7	6.1	9.8	-4.4	-5.7	-5.9	0.5	-0.4	-7.6
Other Criminal Code rate	2 565	2 603	2 682	2 891	3 114	3 034	2 860	2 795	2 678	2 625	2 558
Year-to-year % change*	7.7	1.5	3.0	7.8	7.7	-2.6	-5.7	-2.3	-4.2	-2.0	-2.6
Total Criminal Code rate excluding traffic offences	8 923	8 887	8 860	9 454	10 313	9 982	9 467	9 042	8 913	8 828	8 355
Year-to-year % change*	2.6	-0.4	-0.3	6.7	9.1	-3.2	-5.2	-4.5	-1.4	-1.0	-5.4

[1] Rates are calculated on the basis of 100 000 population. The population estimates are provided by Statistics Canada, Census and Demographic Statistics, Demography Division. Populations as of July 1st: revised intercensal estimates from 1986 to 1990, final postcensal estimates for 1991 to 1995, updated postcensal estimates for 1996 and 1997.

* Percent change based on unrounded rates.

[r] Revised. After the release of 1996 data in July 1997, an error was discovered that had resulted in an under-counting of 1996 crime for Toronto and 1995 and 1996 crime for Winnipeg. These errors were corrected and the data in this *Juristat* reflect the corrections. Please refer to the methodology section for more details.

SOURCE: *Uniform Crime Reporting Survey*, Canadian Centre for Justice Statistics, Statistics Canada.

Figure 5.1
Crime Rate, Canada, 1962–1997

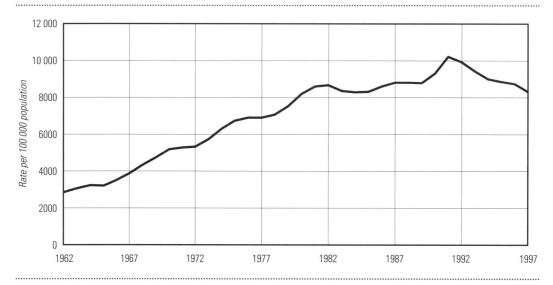

SOURCE: *Uniform Crime Reporting Survey*, Canadian Centre for Justice Statistics, Statistics Canada.

years and then decreases during one's twenties.[6] While Canada's crime rate has declined in recent years (i.e., 1992 to 1997), the number of persons aged 15 to 24 in the population has remained at a low point. From 1986 to 1991, the number of young people in this age group dropped steadily from 4.5 million to 4.1 million, a level at which it remains today. In addition, Canada's population is ageing. Compared to 1986, the population aged 55 and older has grown from 5.1 million to 6.5 million and is projected to continue growing, possibly reaching 8.1 million by the year 2006.[7]

VIOLENT CRIME

Violent Crime Continues to Drop, Yet . . .

Violent criminal incidents (296 737 in 1997) include homicide, attempted murder, assault, sexual assault, other sexual offences, abduction and robbery (Figure 5.3). Violent crimes comprised 12% of *Criminal Code* offences in 1997, an increase from 9% a decade ago.

The violent crime rate declined by 1.1% in 1997, marking the fifth consecutive annual decrease (Table 5.2, Figure 5.4). Prior to these declines, the violent crime rate increased for 15 straight years. Much of this increase is directly attributable to a large increase in the rate of common assaults (level 1), the least serious form of assault, which accounts for six in ten violent crimes. Compared to 1987, the 1997 violent crime rate is 19% higher. If the category of common assault is excluded from total violent crime, the increase drops to only 4%.

Among the provinces, Manitoba, Saskatchewan and British Columbia reported the highest rates of violent crime and Quebec the lowest (Figure 5.2a), a pattern consistent with previous years. The rate of violent crime grew only in Saskatchewan (+15%), Alberta (+6%) and Manitoba (+1.6%) in 1997 (Table 5.3). Growth in Saskatchewan was fueled by increases in the CMAs of Regina (+29%) and Saskatoon (+7%). Similarly, the increase in Alberta is a reflection of increases in the CMAs of Calgary (+8%) and Edmonton (+4%). The only other CMA to experience a notable increase in violent

Figure 5.2a
Violent Crime, Canada and the Provinces, 1997

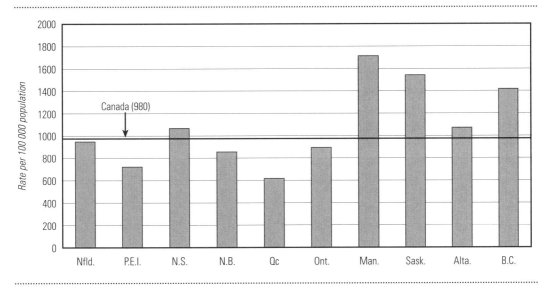

SOURCE: *Uniform Crime Reporting Survey*, Canadian Centre for Justice Statistics, Statistics Canada.

Figure 5.2b
Property Crime, Canada and the Provinces, 1997

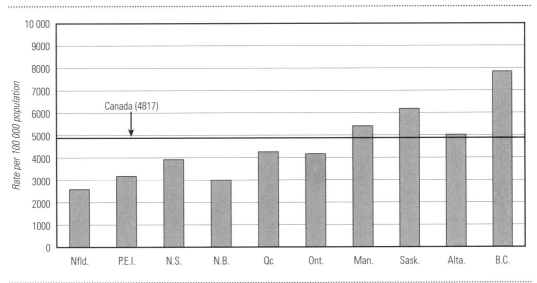

SOURCE: *Uniform Crime Reporting Survey*, Canadian Centre for Justice Statistics, Statistics Canada.

Table 5.3
Selected Criminal Code Incidents,[1] Canada and the Provinces/Territories, 1997

	Nfld.	P.E.I.	N.S.	N.B.	Qc	Ont.[2]	Man.[2]	Sask.	Alta.	B.C.	Yukon	N.W.T.	Canada[2]
Population, 1997	562 198	137 148	946 824	761 117	7 430 997	11 421 648	1 142 169	1 021 696	2 841 328	3 921 546	31 607	67 478	30 285 800
Homicide													
number	6	—	24	8	132	178	30	25	60	114	1	3	581
rate	1.1	—	2.5	1.1	1.8	1.6	2.6	2.4	2.1	2.9	3.2	4.4	1.9
% change in rate*	-13.2	-100.0	32.6	-11.2	-14.7	-6.1	-33.6	-22.2	11.0	-10.6	...	-25.8	-9.5
Sexual assault (1,2,3)													
number	863	142	1 167	933	3 302	9 021	1 533	1 699	3 071	4 636	113	583	27 063
rate	154	104	123	123	44	79	134	166	108	118	358	864	89
% change in rate*	9.2	-15.3	0.8	-5.5	-0.2	-5.7	-1.1	14.6	-0.8	-1.3	26.1	32.6	-0.9
Assault (1,2,3)													
number	4 125	779	8 088	5 044	30 342	77 630	14 882	11 801	23 099	42 817	833	2 770	222 210
rate	734	568	854	663	408	680	1 303	1 155	813	1 092	2635	4 105	734
% change in rate*	-1.6	-14.0	-4.6	-4.6	-3.9	-2.3	1.0	16.0	8.6	-0.2	-2.6	2.5	—
Robbery													
number	68	17	425	145	8 224	9 272	2 136	971	2 333	5 931	27	41	29 590
rate	12	12	45	19	111	81	187	95	82	151	85	61	98
% change in rate*	32.5	-0.4	-2.4	-28.2	-16.4	-6.5	6.2	20.4	-2.3	-7.8	78.8	9.6	-7.9
Violent crime — Total													
number	5 370	996	10 153	6 529	45 964	101 910	19 571	15 751	30 432	55 298	1 053	3 710	296 737
rate	955	726	1 072	858	619	892	1 713	1 542	1 071	1 410	3 332	5 498	980
% change in rate*	-1.6	-11.4	-4.3	-5.7	-6.7	-2.8	1.6	15.5	5.9	-1.1	4.6	9.6	-1.1
Break & enter													
number	3 867	895	9 193	6 108	104 092	108 066	16 837	18 791	31 144	71 942	773	1 647	373 355
rate	688	653	971	803	1 401	946	1 474	1 839	1 096	1 835	2 446	2 441	1 233
% change in rate*	-7.2	-18.5	-4.0	-11.3	-2.7	-11.7	0.3	1.5	-3.0	-10.3	1.0	-16.8	-7.0
Motor vehicle theft													
number	506	265	2 588	1 526	49 426	55 937	11 297	6 999	15 508	32 659	214	391	177 286
rate	90	193	270	200	665	490	989	685	546	833	677	579	585
% change in rate*	-7.3	26.9	5.6	2.2	2.4	-5.6	9.9	7.6	6.5	-14.2	13.1	-13.3	-2.6

(continued)

Table 5.3 (continued)

	Nfld.	P.E.I.	N.S.	N.B.	Qc	Ont.²	Man.²	Sask.	Alta.	B.C.	Yukon	N.W.T.	Canada²
Other Theft													
number	8 200	2 670	21 568	12 113	143 560	268 484	29 076	30 307	80 502	182 289	1 407	1 875	782 051
rate	1 459	1 947	2 278	1 591	1 932	2 351	2 546	2 966	2 833	4 648	4 452	2 779	2 582
% change in rate*	-5.5	-6.4	-0.7	-10.0	-8.3	-11.8	-13.8	-4.7	-0.1	-10.6	-5.8	-17.4	-9.1
Property crime — Total													
number	14 378	4 357	37 530	23 053	317 681	478 882	62 139	63 524	143 011	307 482	2 624	4 269	1 458 930
rate	2 557	3 177	3 964	3 029	4 275	4 193	5 440	6 218	5 033	7 841	8 302	6 327	4 817
% change in rate*	-5.6	-10.2	-1.5	-8.6	-4.7	-11.0	-5.5	-1.7	-1.0	-10.5	-0.3	-14.5	-7.6
Offensive weapons													
number	135	65	476	334	1 039	6 422	1 202	823	2 030	3 322	56	175	16 079
rate	24	47	50	44	14	56	105	81	71	85	177	259	53
% change in rate*	-18.1	40.8	-4.6	-2.4	-19.4	-5.4	-4.7	5.6	-3.6	6.8	-7.3	5.6	-3.0
Mischief													
number	4 723	1 638	12 788	6 355	58 700	112 022	21 879	16 985	38 906	63 295	1 004	3 392	341 687
rate	840	1 194	1 351	835	790	981	1 916	1 662	1 369	1 614	3 177	5 027	1 128
% change in rate*	-11.9	-13.5	-1.4	-18.0	-8.5	-12.3	-2.1	2.3	9.2	-12.1	9.0	22.0	-7.6
Other Criminal Code — Total													
number	11 572	3 967	30 013	17 723	128 507	257 114	43 333	44 571	85 871	141 923	3 029	7 064	774 687
rate	2 058	2 892	3 170	2 329	1 729	2 251	3 794	4 362	3 022	3 619	9 583	10 469	2 558
% change in rate*	-8.9	-8.7	-1.7	-6.3	-2.5	-5.9	-0.7	7.9	5.3	-4.1	12.0	5.6	-2.5
CRIMINAL CODE — TOTAL													
number	31 320	9 320	77 696	47 305	492 152	837 906	125 043	123 846	259 314	504 703	6 706	15 043	2 530 354
rate	5 571	6 796	8 206	6 215	6 623	7 336	10 948	12 122	9 127	12 870	21 217	22 293	8 355
% change in rate*	-6.2	-9.7	-2.0	-7.4	-4.3	-8.5	-2.8	3.6	1.8	-7.8	5.7	-0.2	-5.4

[1] Excludes traffic crimes.

[2] After the release of 1996 data in July 1997, an error was discovered that had resulted in an under-counting of 1996 crime for Toronto and 1995 and 1996 crime for Winnipeg. These errors were corrected and the data in this *Juristat* reflect the corrections. Please refer to the methodology section for more details.

– nil or zero

… figures not appropriate or applicable

* In comparison to the 1996 rate. Rates are calculated on the basis of 100 000 population. The population estimates are provided by Statistics Canada, Census and Demographic Statistics, Demography Division. Populations as of July 1st: Updated postcensal estimates for 1996 and 1997.

— amount too small to be expressed

SOURCE: *Uniform Crime Reporting Survey*, Canadian Centre for Justice Statistics, Statistics Canada.

Table 5.4

Selected Criminal Code Incidents for Major Census Metropolitan Areas, 1997[1]

	Toronto[2]	Montreal	Vancouver	Edmonton	Calgary	Ottawa-Hull (Ont. part)	Québec	Winnipeg[2]	Hamilton
Population, 1997	4 511 966	3 384 233	1 927 998	899 466	885 130	788 788	700 197	677 291	663 587
Homicide									
number	77	72	49	27	9	9	9	20	11
rate	1.7	2.1	2.5	3.0	1.0	1.1	1.3	3.0	1.7
% change in rate*	-4.0	0.7	-14.2	33.8	-27.8	-19.4	-40.2	-28.6	7.8
Sexual assault (1,2,3)									
number	2 583	1 554	1 579	920	583	565	306	541	601
rate	57	46	84	102	66	72	44	80	91
% change in rate*	-1.3	4.9	-0.1	-2.3	-0.9	-15.7	2.3	5.6	-9.4
Assault (1,2,3)									
number	28 509	16 705	17 339	6 125	5 401	4 945	2 327	6 845	6 141
rate	632	494	939	681	610	627	332	1 011	925
% change in rate*	-5.7	-2.6	0.3	8.1	10.2	-9.1	-4.8	-3.9	-1.0
Robbery									
number	5 915	6 305	4 632	1 075	1 028	987	630	1 995	502
rate	131	186	240	120	116	125	90	295	76
% change in rate*	-6.4	-18.8	-7.9	-8.7	9.9	1.9	-17.0	6.2	-6.3
Violent crime — Total									
number	38 439	26 450	24 262	8 632	7 371	6 795	3 529	9 864	7 447
rate	852	782	1 258	960	833	861	504	1 456	1 122
% change in rate*	-1.4	-7.0	-4.7	4.0	8.0	-5.9	-6.1	-1.6	-1.8

(continued)

Table 5.4 *(continued)*

	Toronto[2]	Montreal	Vancouver	Edmonton	Calgary	Ottawa-Hull (Ont. part)	Québec	Winnipeg[2]	Hamilton
Break & enter									
number	34 144	51 289	42 233	10 783	9 903	9 791	8 963	10 063	6 533
rate	757	1 516	2 191	1 199	1 119	1 241	1 280	1 486	984
% change in rate*	–8.2	0.8	–12.4	–0.7	–8.3	–15.2	–16.9	–2.9	–4.1
Motor vehicle theft									
number	20 703	32 145	21 922	4 818	6 581	6 131	2 822	9 158	6 350
rate	459	950	1 137	536	744	777	403	1 352	957
% change in rate*	–10.6	2.3	–19.2	–2.5	11.7	–7.4	–7.6	8.3	3.1
Other theft									
number	106 715	80 577	103 301	25 948	26 562	21 074	12 988	19 040	14 765
rate	2 365	2 381	5 358	2 885	3 001	2 672	1 855	2 811	2 225
% change in rate*	–9.1	–8.6	–12.0	0.1	–1.4	–18.5	–13.7	–19.0	–14.3
Property crime — Total									
number	177 400	173 487	175 058	46 753	46 217	39 676	26 365	40 448	29 239
rate	3 932	5 126	9 080	5 198	5 221	5 030	3 765	5 972	4 406
% change in rate*	–9.1	–4.3	–13.1	–0.5	–3.3	–15.8	–14.2	–9.0	–8.6
Offensive weapons									
number	1 606	369	1 222	458	289	380	61	505	228
rate	36	11	63	51	33	48	9	75	34
% change in rate*	–2.7	–22.9	–2.7	4.8	–11.7	6.6	–32.5	–4.8	2.5
Mischief									
number	33 602	28 751	25 559	11 424	9 413	7 879	5 880	11 764	5 891
rate	745	953	1 326	1 270	1 063	999	840	1 737	888
% change in rate*	–14.3	–0.2	–20.0	11.3	5.9	–21.2	–7.4	–6.6	–12.6

(continued)

Table 5.4 (continued)

	Toronto[2]	Montreal	Vancouver	Edmonton	Calgary	Ottawa-Hull (Ont. part)	Québec	Winnipeg[2]	Hamilton
Other Criminal Code — Total									
number	79 647	54 945	51 883	24 094	15 419	16 815	9 765	19 317	13 801
rate	1 765	1 624	2 691	2 679	1 742	2 132	1 395	2 852	2 080
% change in rate*	−7.2	−9.5	−11.5	7.5	2.7	−16.6	−5.6	−0.9	−3.2
CRIMINAL CODE — TOTAL excluding Traffic									
number	295 486	254 882	251 203	79 479	69 007	63 286	39 659	69 629	50 487
rate	6 549	7 531	13 029	8 836	7 796	8 023	5 664	10 281	7 608
% change in rate*	−7.6	−5.8	−12.0	2.3	−0.9	−15.1	−11.5	−5.9	−6.2

[1] Comparable data for all police services are available upon request. Rates are calculated based on 100 000 populations. The estimates are based on populations from Statistics Canada, Census and Demographic Statistics, Demography Division. The intercensal estimates match the jurisdictional boundaries of the police department.

[2] After the release of 1996 data in July 1997, an error was discovered that resulted in the under-counting of 1996 crimes for Winnipeg and Toronto. This error has been corrected and the data in this *Juristat* reflect the corrections. Please refer to the methodology section for more details.

* Compared to the 1996 rate. Percent change based on unrounded rates.

SOURCE: *Uniform Crime Reporting Survey*, Canadian Centre for Justice Statistics, Statistics Canada.

Figure 5.3

Violent Crime Categories, Canada, 1997

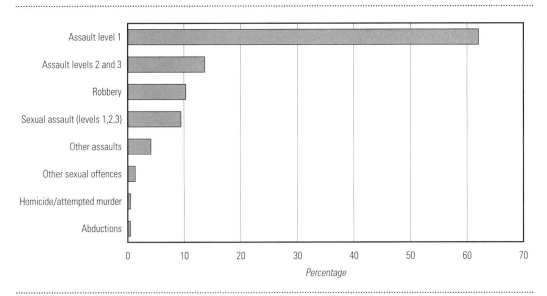

SOURCE: *Uniform Crime Reporting Survey*, Canadian Centre for Justice Statistics, Statistics Canada.

Figure 5.4

Violent, Property, and Other Criminal Code Incidents, Canada, 1987–1997

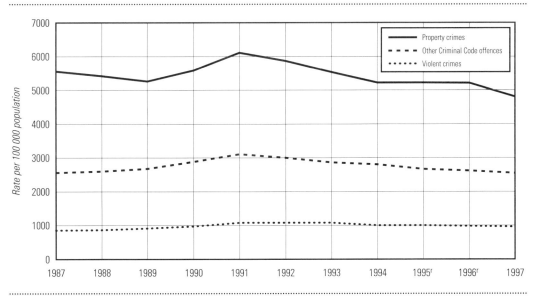

ʳ Revised

SOURCE: *Uniform Crime Reporting Survey*, Canadian Centre for Justice Statistics, Statistics Canada.

crime was Saint John (+10%), although the rate for New Brunswick declined. Violent crime rates decreased in 16 of the 25 CMAs, with the largest drop reported in Chicoutimi-Jonquière (–14%).

Thunder Bay reported the highest rate of violent crime (1810 incidents per 100 000 population), followed by Regina (1638), Winnipeg (1456), Saskatoon (1397), and Victoria (1385). The rates were lowest in Sherbrooke (410) and Trois-Rivières (488).

. . . Some Canadians Remain Fearful and Concerned

Despite the recent drops in violent crime in most of the country, some Canadians remain fearful. Findings from the 1995 International Crime Victimization Survey show that 25% of Canadians reported feeling "a bit unsafe" or "very unsafe" when walking alone in their neighbourhood after dark. This is up from the 20% who expressed these feelings in the 1991 ICVS. However, as the rate of crime varies across the provinces, so too may the levels of fear and concern about crime.

Homicides Continue to Decline

Homicide includes first- and second-degree murder, manslaughter and infanticide. In 1997, there were 581 homicides and 861 attempted murders (Table 5.1). Together these crimes continue to account for less than 1% of reported violent incidents. The homicide rate has generally been declining since the mid-1970s and is at the lowest point since 1969. In 1997, this trend continued with a 9% drop in the rate (54 fewer homicides than in 1996). The rate of attempted murders (2.8 per 100 000) also fell in 1997 (–3%), generally following the trend in the rate of murder (Figure 5.5).

The homicide rate dropped in 14 of the 25 CMAs. Rates were highest in Saskatoon (3.59 incidents per 100 000 population), Halifax (3.15) and Edmonton (3.00), and were lowest in Chicoutimi-Jonquière (no homicides), Kitchener (0.69) and London (0.71).

The number of homicides committed with a firearm decreased 10% from the previous year. Consistent with the trend since 1979, firearm homicides accounted for one-third (33%) of all homicides in 1997. Other methods used to commit homicide included stabbing (29%), beating (20%), strangulation/suffocation (9%), smoke inhalation/burns (5%) and poisoning (1%).

As has been the case in the past, the large majority of victims knew their killers. Of the homicides where an accused was identified, 44% of the victims were killed by an acquaintance, 42% by a spouse or other family member, and 13% by a stranger.

Robberies Down after Increasing Two Years in a Row

The 29 590 robberies in 1997 accounted for one in ten violent crimes. After increasing two years in a row, the rate of robbery decreased 8% in 1997 (Table 5.1). Despite decreases in the early 1990s, the rate of robbery has been generally increasing during the last 10 years, up 10% from 1987 (Figure 5.6).

Fewer robberies now involve firearms. The rate for this type of robbery has generally been falling since 1991, including a 20% decrease in 1997. Over these six years, the rate has dropped by 41%. Robberies involving weapons other than firearms (e.g., knives) have shown the largest rate increases in the last decade, even though the rate dropped in 1997 (–7%). Compared to 10 years ago, the rate is over 50% higher, increasing an average of 5% annually. Robberies with no weapons decreased in 1997 (–3%) after two years of growth. Over four in ten robberies involved no weapons.

The rate of robbery grew in only 8 of the 25 CMAs. Rates of robbery were highest in Winnipeg (295 incidents per 100 000 population) and Vancouver (240), and lowest in St. John's (Newfoundland) (22), Saint John (New Brunswick) (22) and Chicoutimi-Jonquière (32).

Compared to other violent crimes, robbery is more likely to involve youths. In 1997, 38% of

Figure 5.5

Homicide and Attempted Murder Incidents, Canada, 1987–1997

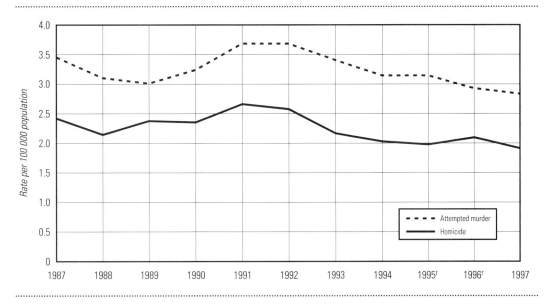

SOURCE: *Uniform Crime Reporting Survey*, Canadian Centre for Justice Statistics, Statistics Canada.

Figure 5.6

Robbery Incidents, Canada, 1987–1997

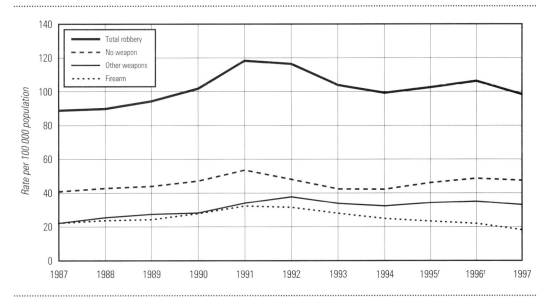

r Revised

SOURCE: *Uniform Crime Reporting Survey*, Canadian Centre for Justice Statistics, Statistics Canada.

Box 5.2

1997 UCRII (Incident-Based) Data File

The revised UCR survey captures detailed information on individual criminal incidents reported to police, including characteristics of victims, accused persons and the incidents. The survey presently collects data from 179 police agencies in six provinces. These data represent 48% of the national volume of actual *Criminal Code* crimes. *The reader is cautioned that these data are not nationally representative*: respondents from Quebec account for 41% of the sample and those from Ontario account for a further 33%. Outside of Quebec, these data are largely an urban sample. Please refer to the methodology section for more information. All calculations exclude records where the variable under study is reported as unknown, unless otherwise mentioned.

persons charged with robbery were youths compared with only 15% of persons charged with other violent crimes.

Sexual Assaults Drop for the Fourth Straight Year

Sexual assaults accounted for almost one in ten violent crimes in 1997. Sexual assault is classified into one of three levels according to the seriousness of the incident: level 1 sexual assault (the category of least physical injury to the victim); level 2 sexual assault (with a weapon, threats to use weapon, or causing bodily harm); and level 3 aggravated sexual assault (wounds, maims, disfigures or endangers life of victim). In 1997, the rate for each level of sexual assault decreased (Table 5.1).

There were 27 063 reported incidents of sexual assault in 1997, most of which (97%) were classified by police as level 1. In 1997, the rate of total sexual assaults decreased 0.9% (Table 5.1). Although this marked the fourth consecutive

decline it was not much smaller than decreases reported in previous years. While the 1997 rate was 26% lower than five years ago, it was still 6% higher than a decade ago.

Rates of sexual assault decreased in 14 of the 25 CMAs. The rate of sexual assault was highest in Saint John (New Brunswick) (198 incidents per 100 000 population) and St. John's (Newfoundland) (162), and was lowest in Sherbrooke (34) and Trois-Rivières (36).

According to a sample of police departments, the vast majority of victims of sexual assault were female (84%). Female victims were most frequently victimized by a casual acquaintance (33%), followed by a family member including a spouse/ex-spouse (27%) and a stranger (23%). Victims of sexual assault tended to be quite young, with almost 60% of victims younger than 18 years old. The median[8] age for females was 17 years. Male victims tended to be much younger (median age of 11 years) and were also most frequently victimized by a casual acquaintance (e.g., a neighbour) (42%), a family member (29%) or a stranger (13%). Young girls (12 and under) had most frequently been sexually assaulted by a family member (49%), while boys of the same age were equally attacked by a casual acquaintance (39%) and a family member (39%).[9]

Assaults Stable after Three Years of Decline

The most frequently reported category of violent crime is assault. The *Criminal Code* defines several categories of assault: common assault (level 1), assault with a weapon or causing bodily harm (level 2), aggravated assault (level 3) and other assaults (i.e., assault on peace officer, unlawfully causing bodily harm, discharge of firearm with intent and other assaults). Common assault accounts for almost eight in ten assaults and six in ten reported violent incidents. It includes behaviours such as pushing, slapping, punching, face-to-face verbal threats and threats by an act or gesture.

In 1997, police recorded 222 210 incidents of assault levels 1, 2 and 3 (Table 5.1). After decreasing three years in a row, the rate of assaults remained unchanged in 1997. This stability was due to little change in the rate of common assault (–0.3%) and a small increase in assault with a weapon (+1.7%). Aggravated assault continued to decrease, failing for the sixth year in a row (–5%).

The rate of assault (levels 1, 2, 3) dropped in 15 of the 25 CMAs. Despite showing a drop of 7% in 1997, Thunder Bay reported the highest rate (1517 incidents per 100 000 population), followed by Regina (1195). Rates were lowest in Sherbrooke (284) and Trois-Rivières (310).

Unlike sexual assaults, victims of assault were as likely to be male as female. Females, however, accounted for more victims of common assault (53%) and males accounted for more victims of assault with a weapon and aggravated assault (66%). Overall, the median age of victims of assault was 28 years; males were somewhat younger than females (26 years compared to 29 years). Females had most often been assaulted by a spouse (43%) or an acquaintance(18%). Among male victims, their assailants had most often been strangers (39%), followed by acquaintances (34%). Children under 18 years assaulted by parents accounted for 3% of all assault victims. However, the secrecy surrounding child abuse and the powerlessness of young children means that these incidents often go unreported to police.

Sample of Police Agencies Shows Presence of Weapons in Violent Crime Declining

Between 1993 and 1997, the presence of weapons in violent incidents decreased. While firearms were present in 6.8% of violent incidents reported by a sample of 61 police forces in 1993, by 1997 they were present in only 5.1%. The presence of clubs/blunt instruments declined from 7.6% to 6.5%, and the presence of knives decreased from 9.6% to 9.1%.

PROPERTY CRIME

Property Crime Rate Continues to Drop

Property incidents involve unlawful acts with the intent of gaining property but do not involve the use or threat of violence. Theft, breaking and entering, fraud and possession of stolen goods are examples of property crimes. In 1997, there were approximately 1.5 million property crime incidents. The property crime rate has generally been decreasing since 1991, including an 8% drop in 1997. The 1997 rate was 18% lower than the rate recorded five years ago and 13% lower than ten years ago (Table 5.2).

Rates of property crime dropped in all ten provinces in 1997. Ontario (–11%), British Columbia (–11%) and Prince Edward Island (–10%) experienced the largest declines, with Alberta (–1.0%), Nova Scotia (–1.5%) and Saskatchewan (–1.7%) reporting the smallest decreases (Table 5.3). Despite decreasing in 1997, British Columbia's property crime rate continues to rank the highest among the provinces (Figure 5.2b). Newfoundland reported the lowest rate.

Of the 25 CMAs, all but four reported declines, with Saint John (New Brunswick) showing the greatest drop (–18%). Declines of 10% or more were experienced by Ottawa (–16%), Quebec (–14%), Vancouver (–13%), Sudbury (–11%), Windsor (–11%) and Victoria (–10%). Rates increased only in Chicoutimi-Jonquière (+10%), Halifax (+1.6%) and Trois-Rivières (+1.2%); the rate for Saskatoon remained stable (–0.1%). Regina reported the highest rate of property crime, despite a decrease in 1997, and Saint John (New Brunswick) reported the lowest.

Rate of Breaking and Entering Continues to Fall

In total, there were 373 355 reported incidents of breaking and entering (B&E) in 1997, representing one-quarter of property crimes (Table 5.1). In general the B&E rate has been falling since 1991 (Figure 5.7), including a 7% decrease in 1997.

Figure 5.7

Breaking and Entering Incidents, Canada, 1987–1997

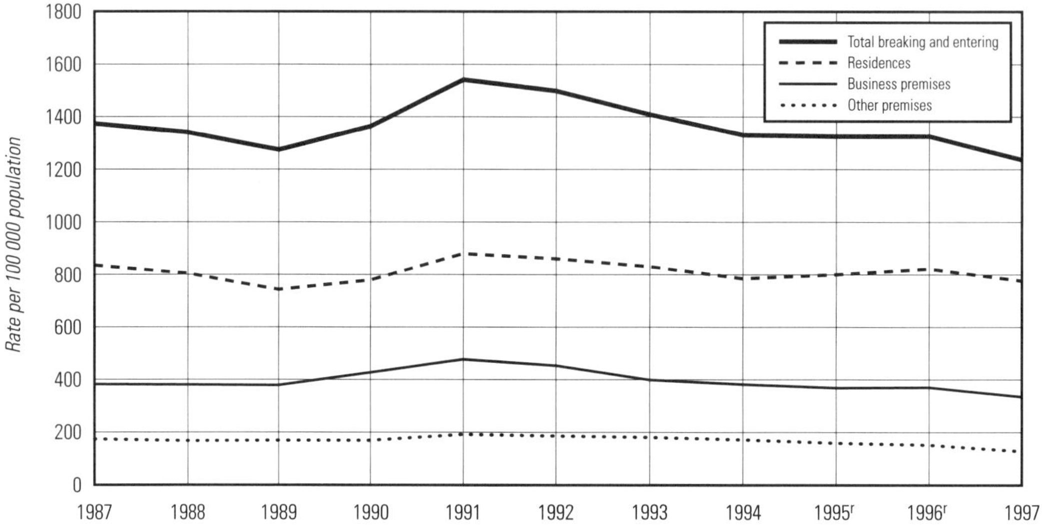

ᵣ Revised

SOURCE: *Uniform Crime Reporting Survey*, Canadian Centre for Justice Statistics, Statistics Canada.

Four in ten persons charged with this offence were youths (Table 5.5).[10]

The majority of B&Es in 1997 occurred at private residences (63%) as opposed to commercial establishments or businesses (27%), or other places (e.g., shed, storage facilities) (10%). After increasing two years in a row, the rate of residential B&E dropped in 1997 (–5%). The police-reported rate for business B&E (–10%) and other types of B&E (–13%) also declined, continuing their downward trend.

The rate of B&E increased in only 4 of the 25 CMAs in 1997: Chicoutimi-Jonquière (+22%), Trois-Rivières (+15%), Halifax (+2%) and Montreal (+0.8%). In 1997, rates were highest in Regina (2834 incidents per 100 000 population) and Vancouver (2191), and lowest in Toronto (757) and Saint John (New Brunswick) (769).

According to the Insurance Information Centre of Canada,[11] the average claim by home-owners and tenants for losses through B&E amounted to $5034 in 1996 (the most recent year for which data are available) and the average claim for commercial businesses amounted to $5162. In total, property losses associated with B&Es cost the insurance industry about $398 million in 1996.

Theft of Motor Vehicles Declines for the First Time in Over a Decade

Motor vehicle theft accounted for roughly one in eight property crimes in 1997 (177 286 incidents). After steady growth for over a decade, the rate of motor vehicle theft finally decreased in 1997 (–3%). The current rate, however, is still much higher than five (+14%) and ten (+79%) years ago.[12] In particular, there has been a large increase in the number of "trucks" stolen in recent years, which includes mini-vans and sport-utility vehicles. This is not surprising given that the number of mini-vans and sport-utility vehicles on the road increased 84% between 1992 and 1996.[13]

Table 5.5

Persons Charged by Age and Sex, Selected Incidents, 1997

	Sex		Age		Median Age[1]		
	Males %	**Females %**	**Adults %**	**Youth (12–17 yrs) %**	**Males**	**Females**	**Total**
Homicides[2]	84	16	88	12	29	28	29
Attempted murder	89	11	91	9	29	27	28
Assaults	83	17	86	14	30	27	30
Sexual assaults (levels 1, 2, 3)	98	2	84	16	33	22	33
Other sexual offences	96	4	86	14	37	28	36
Abduction	58	42	97	3	33	32	32
Robbery	88	12	62	38	21	16	21
Violent crime — Total	85	15	84	16	29	26	29
Break & enter	92	8	60	40	20	19	20
Motor vehicle theft	90	10	57	43	19	17	19
Fraud	69	31	93	7	29	29	29
Theft over $5000	80	20	80	20	22	30	23
Theft $5000 and under	69	31	71	29	25	28	26
Property crime — Total	77	23	71	29	23	27	23
Mischief	88	12	66	34	20	25	21
Arson	88	12	57	43	19	34	19
Prostitution	44	56	96	4	34	28	31
Offensive weapons	92	8	79	21	27	25	26
Criminal Code — Total	81	19	77	23	26	27	26
Impaired driving[3]	89	11	…	…	35	35	35
Cocaine — Possession	83	17	96	4	30	30	30
Cocaine — Trafficking	83	17	96	4	30	29	30
Cannabis — Possession	89	11	82	18	22	24	22
Cannabis — Trafficking	85	15	85	15	26	26	26

[1] These data are based on the 1997 Uniform Crime Reporting Incident-based Research File — CCJS, representing 48% of the national volume of crime.

[2] These data are based on the Homicide Survey, CCJS.

[3] Includes impaired operation of a vehicle causing death, causing bodily harm, alcohol rate over 80 mg, failure/refusal to provide a breath/blood sample.

… Figures not available.

SOURCE: *Uniform Crime Reporting Survey*, Canadian Centre for Justice Statistics, Statistics Canada.

Despite a decrease at the national level, the rate of motor vehicle theft grew in almost half of the 25 CMAs. Regina reported the highest rate (1479 per 100 000 population), followed by Winnipeg (1352). The lowest rates were reported by St. John's (Newfoundland) (134) and Saint John (New Brunswick) (149).

Theft of vehicles and their components cost the Canadian insurance industry approximately $600 million in 1996 (the most recent year for which data are available) compared to $500 million in 1995.[14]

As with incidents of breaking and entering, motor vehicle theft is generally described as a youth crime. In 1997, 43% of persons charged with motor vehicle theft were youths aged 12 to 17 years compared to only 22% of persons charged with all other *Criminal Code* offences (Table 5.5).

Thefts Account for One-Third of All Crimes

In 1997, the 782 051 incidents of theft (excluding motor vehicle thefts and B&Es) accounted for one-third of all *Criminal Code* incidents and over one-half of property crimes. The 1997 theft rate was 9% lower than the previous year (Table 5.1) and has generally been declining since 1991.

Of all thefts, 40% were thefts from motor vehicles, 13% were shoplifting, 9% were bicycle thefts, and 37% were "other" types of theft. Decreases were reported for all types of theft in 1997. Relative to other offences, a high proportion (31%) of persons charged with "theft $5000 and under" are female, most of whom were charged with shoplifting (Table 5.5).

OTHER *CRIMINAL CODE* INCIDENTS

The 744 687 *Criminal Code* crimes that are not in the violent or property crime categories are reported under the category "other *Criminal Code*" (Figure 5.8). These crimes account for three in ten *Criminal Code* incidents and include such crimes as mischief, weapons offences, prostitution, arson, bail violations and disturbing the peace.

Offensive Weapons Crimes Decrease

Offensive weapons crimes include possession/use of prohibited and restricted weapons, possession of a weapon for the purpose of committing a crime, and careless use of a firearm. Prohibited weapons are those which are illegal to possess. These include spring-loaded knives, nunchaku sticks, fully automatic firearms, and sawed-off shotguns or rifles. Restricted weapons, such as handguns, are those which may be owned under certain conditions (e.g., lawful use and registration with the police). Non-restricted weapons may be possessed legally. In the case of rifles and shotguns, however, individuals are required to hold a valid firearms acquisition certificate (FAC) to acquire such guns.[15]

The 16 079 offensive weapons crimes reported by police in 1997 accounted for less than 1% of *Criminal Code* incidents. The rate of these incidents declined for the third consecutive year (–3%) (Table 5.1).

Arson Down, But Still Higher Than a Decade Ago

Police reported 12 799 incidents of arson in 1997 (Table 5.1). From 1989 to 1992, the rate of arson jumped by 70%. Since then, the rate has remained relatively stable, failing an average of 1.6% annually, including a 1.3% drop in 1997. The most common targets for arson in 1997 were motor vehicles (28%), residences (25%), non-commercial enterprises (24%) and commercial or corporate places (15%). Four in ten persons charged with arson were youths (Table 5.5).

The Rate of Mischief Offences Continues to Decline

In 1997, the 341 687 mischief incidents reported by police accounted for 14% of total *Criminal Code* crimes and over four in ten of "other" *Criminal Code* incidents (Table 5.1). The general decline in the rate of mischief incidents continued in 1997 with an 8% decrease. The most common targets of

Figure 5.8

Other Criminal Code Categories, Canada, 1997

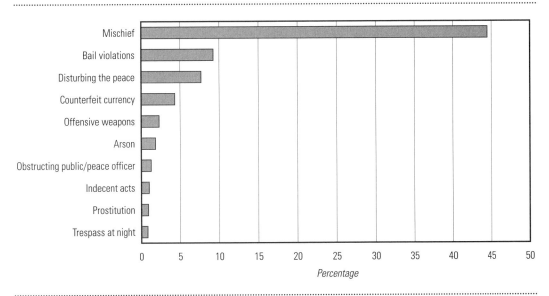

SOURCE: *Uniform Crime Reporting Survey*, Canadian Centre for Justice Statistics, Statistics Canada.

mischief were motor vehicles (66%). Consistent with previous years, youths aged 12 to 17 years comprised one-third of persons charged with this offence in 1997 (Table 5.5).

Prostitution-Related Incidents Drop

Most prostitution-related crimes involve communicating with a person for the purpose of engaging in prostitution (including both prostitutes and clients) or stopping a vehicle for the same purpose. The rate of prostitution incidents reported by police dropped by 10% in 1997 (Table 5.1). Despite an increase in 1995, the rate of prostitution incidents during the 1990s has generally been decreasing. Of the different types of prostitution offences, those involving bawdy houses are the only ones to have consistently increased since 1993, including a 54% jump in the rate in 1997. This most recent growth is largely due to an increase in the province of Quebec. The reporting of prostitution incidents is highly sensitive to police enforce-

ment practices. The reader is cautioned that these practices may vary over time and across provinces and municipalities.

In 1997, 5884 persons were charged with prostitution-related crimes, 56% of whom were female. Although some males charged were living from the avails of prostitution or were themselves prostitutes, it can be assumed that the majority of them were clients. Only 4% of persons charged in prostitution incidents in 1997 were youths. Child prostitution is a serious concern for Canadians, and young people who come to the attention of police are often diverted to social services in lieu of being charged.[16] Therefore, it is important to note that UCR counts do not reflect the actual extent of child prostitution.

CRIMINAL CODE TRAFFIC INCIDENTS

Police reported 155 327 incidents involving *Criminal Code* traffic crimes in 1997, resulting in a rate 5% below that of 1996 (Table 5.1). Impaired driving accounted for 58% of these incidents in 1997, failure to stop and/or remain at the scene of an accident accounted for 32%, and dangerous driving and driving while prohibited comprised the remaining 10%.

Impaired Driving Incidents Continue to Decline

Impaired driving offences include impaired operation of a motor vehicle, boat or aircraft, driving with over 0.08% alcohol in the bloodstream, and failing to provide a breath and/or blood sample when requested by a police officer. In 1997, police charged 72 139 persons with impaired driving, a decline of 10% below 1996, and a continuation of the long-term trend of declining rates. As with drug and prostitution offences, changes in statistics on impaired driving can be influenced by police enforcement.[17]

DRUGS

Little Change in Rate of Drug Offences

As of 1997, all drug incidents involve offences under the new *Controlled Drugs and Substances Act* (CDSA). Cannabis offences accounted for seven in ten of the 66 521 drug-related incidents reported in 1997. Almost nine in ten persons charged with drug offences were adults.

After increasing three years in a row, the rate of drug-related incidents remained virtually unchanged in 1997 (+0.1%) (Table 5.1). After growing steadily since 1991 with an average annual increase of 6%, the rate of cannabis offences also remained virtually unchanged in 1997 (+0.3%), a stability which affected the overall rate of drug crimes (Figure 5.9). Consistent with the general downward trend since 1992, the rate of cocaine offences dropped again in 1997 (−1.6%). After a fairly large increase in 1996 (+8%), the rate of offences involving other drugs (e.g., heroin, amphetamines, barbiturates) grew just 1.0% in 1997.

Historically, the majority of drug incidents involve "possession" (62% in 1997), and most possession incidents involve cannabis. As with prosti-

---

Box 5.3

New Legislation Regulating Drugs: *The Controlled Drugs and Substances Act*

Prior to 1997, the regulation of drugs fell under two separate federal statutes: the *Narcotics Control Act*, which dealt with illicit drugs such as cannabis, cocaine and heroin, and the *Food and Drug Act*, which dealt with controlled and restricted drugs such as amphetamines, LSD and various prescription drugs. On May 14, 1997, a new act entitled the *Controlled Drugs and Substances Act* (CDSA) was proclaimed into force, replacing the two previous acts. The CDSA consolidates certain parts of the two previous acts, modernizing and enhancing Canada's drug abuse control policy. Another focus of the CDSA is to fulfil Canada's international obligations under several international protocols on drugs.

---

tution and impaired driving, trends in drug-related crimes are subject to police enforcement activities.

YOUTH CRIME

Decrease in Rate of Youths Charged Mostly Due to Fall in Charges for Non-Violent Crime

Fueled by a decrease in charges for non-violent crimes, the overall rate of youths charged with *Criminal Code* offences dropped 7% in 1997 (Table 5.6). In total, 111 736 youths aged 12 to 17 years were charged with *Criminal Code* offences in 1997. Over half (53%) of these youths were charged with property crimes, while 20% were charged with violent crimes. The remaining youths were charged with other *Criminal Code* offences, such as mischief and offences against the administration of justice. This distribution has changed since a decade ago, when 69% of youths were charged with property crimes and 9% with violent crimes. Increases in youths charged with common (level 1) assault and

Figure 5.9

Drug Incidents, Canada, 1987–1997

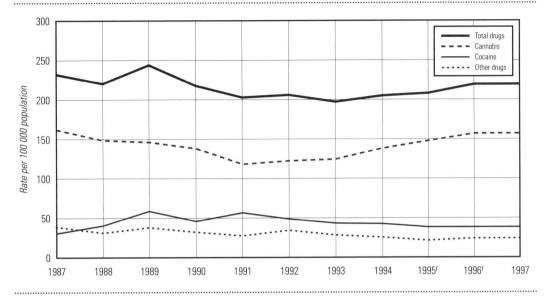

ʳ Revised

SOURCE: *Uniform Crime Reporting Survey*, Canadian Centre for Justice Statistics, Statistics Canada.

decreases in charges for theft and breaking and entering account for much of this shift (Table 5.6).

Rate of Youths Charged with Violent Crime Declines for Second Year in a Row

In 1997, the rate of youths charged with violent crime declined (−2%) for the second year in a row (Figure 5.10, Table 5.6). Compared to five years ago, the 1997 rate is 5% higher, and over twice that of a decade ago. This increase cannot simply be attributed to an increase in the rate of youths charged with common (level 1) assault.

In 1997, the rate of youths charged increased for homicide (+9%) and "other" types of assault (e.g., assault against police officer)(+7%). Rates changed very little for youths charged with robbery (−0.2%). The rate of youths charged with sexual assault decreased for the fourth year in a row (−7%) and the rate for those charged with assault (levels 1, 2, 3) dropped for the second year in a row (−3%).

In 1997, 54 youths aged 12 to 17 years stood accused of homicide, five more compared to 1996. Between 1986 and 1996, an average of 49 youths were accused of homicide each year.

In recent years, concern has been raised about increasing violence among females, particularly young females. Over the last 10 years, the rate of female youths charged with violent crimes has increased much faster (+179%) than that for male youths (+85%). In 1997, the rate of male youths charged with violent crime dropped 4%, while the rate for female youths increased by 5%. However, the rate of female youths charged with violent crime (472 per 100 000 population) is still considerably lower than that for male youth (1328).

Rate of Youths Charged with Property Crimes Continues to Fall

In terms of property crimes, the rate of youths charged declined (−12%) for the sixth consecutive

Box 5.4

Measuring Youth Crime

Young persons in conflict with the law may or may not be formally charged. The decision to proceed with the laying of a charge is influenced by many factors, one of which is the eligibility of the youth for an alternative measures program. As outlined in the *Young Offenders Act*, the objective of alternative measures (AM) is to avoid court proceedings for young persons, provided certain conditions are met. Generally, referrals to AM programs are made before charges are laid and are reserved for first-time offenders. In addition, when dealing with first-time offenders involved in minor incidents, police may choose to deal with a youth informally by giving him or her a warning or discussing the incident with the youth's parents.

As a result, charge rates are influenced by the extent to which AM is used, whether AM is used at the pre- or post-charge stage, and the extent to which youths are dealt with informally. Consequently, there are limitations to using the youth charge rate as an indicator of the prevalence of youth crime, particularly with respect to measuring relatively minor offences committed by first-time offenders. However, data on youths not charged (i.e., AM or dealt with informally) are available from many jurisdictions and show that the rate of youths *not* charged has also been declining since 1991. This suggests that the decrease in youths charged is not simply a reflection of increased use of alternative measures.

year (Figure 5.10, Table 5.6). The rate of youths charged dropped for all property offences including thefts (−13%), breaking and entering (−9%) and motor vehicle theft (−8%).

Youths charged with other *Criminal Code* offences also decreased (−2%) in 1997 (Figure 5.10, Table 5.6). While the rate of youths charged dropped for most of these offences such as weapons offences (−5%) and mischief (−8%), rates increased

for youths charged with arson (+9%) and counterfeiting currency (+50%). The rate of adults charged with counterfeiting currency also experienced a large increase in 1997 (+68%).

Persons Accused of Property Crimes Are Younger Than Those Accused of Violent Crime

While persons accused[18] of property crimes are likely to be young, the age range of persons accused of violent crimes is much wider. While more than four in ten persons accused of property crimes were aged 13 to 20 years (Figure 5.11a), this age group accounted for less than one-quarter of persons accused of violent crimes (Figure 5.11b). The median age of persons accused of property crimes was 21 years, compared to 29 years for those charged with violent offences.[19]

METHODOLOGY

The Uniform Crime Reporting Survey

The Uniform Crime Reporting (UCR) Survey was developed by Statistics Canada with the co-operation and assistance of the Canadian Association of Chiefs of Police. The aggregate UCR survey, which became operational in 1962, collects crime and traffic statistics reported by all police agencies in Canada. UCR survey data reflect reported crime that has been substantiated through police investigation.

Currently, there are two levels of detail collected by the UCR survey:

AGGREGATE UCR SURVEY
The aggregate-based UCR survey records the number of incidents reported to the police. It includes the number of reported offences and the number of actual offences (excluding those that are unfounded), the number of offences cleared by charge, and the number of persons charged by sex and by an adult/youth breakdown. It does not include victim characteristics. Unless otherwise

Table 5.6
Youths Charged in Selected Criminal Code Incidents, Canada, 1987–1997[1]

	1987	1988	1989	1990	1991	1992	1993	1994	1995ʳ	1996ʳ	1997
Population (aged 12–17)	2 260 900	2 249 500	2 245 800	2 260 100	2 284 800	2 315 700	2 341 300	2 360 800	2 386 900	2 417 500	2 445 400
Homicide											
number	36	47	47	47	48	58	36	58	68	49	54
rate	1.6	2.1	2.1	2.1	2.1	2.5	1.5	2.5	2.8	2.0	2.2
% change in rate*	-13.8	31.2	0.2	-0.6	-1.0	19.2	-38.6	59.8	16.0	-28.9	8.9
Assaults (1,2,3)											
number	6 891	7 679	9 245	10 797	12 815	13 584	14 981	15 363	15 898	15 945	15 696
rate	305	341	412	478	561	587	640	651	666	660	642
% change in rate*	13.2	12.0	20.6	16.0	17.4	4.6	9.1	1.7	2.4	-1.0	-2.7
Sexual assaults (1,2,3)											
number	1 220	1 247	1 478	1 609	1 906	2 074	2 132	1 896	1 586	1 581	1 494
rate	54	55	66	71	83	90	91	80	66	65	61
% change in rate*	15.8	2.7	18.7	8.2	17.2	7.4	1.7	-11.8	-17.3	-1.6	-6.6
Robbery											
number	1 204	1 544	1 950	2 055	2 746	2 966	2 996	3 006	3 535	3 741	3 778
rate	53	69	87	91	120	128	128	127	148	155	154
% change in rate*	-7.1	28.9	26.5	4.7	32.2	6.6	-0.1	-0.5	16.3	4.5	-0.2
Violent crime — Total											
number	10 165	11 437	13 780	15 690	18 919	20 028	21 477	21 629	22 441	22 521	22 252
rate	450	508	614	694	828	865	917	916	940	932	910
% change in rate*	10.2	13.1	20.7	13.1	19.3	4.4	6.1	-0.1	2.6	-0.9	-2.3

(continued)

Table 5.6 *(continued)*

	1987	1988	1989	1990	1991	1992	1993	1994	1995ʳ	1996ʳ	1997
Break & enter											
number	25 321	23 894	22 155	24 066	26 901	24 747	21 947	19 992	18 654	18 532	17 143
rate	1 120	1 062	987	1 065	1 177	1 069	937	847	782	767	701
% change in rate*	-7.0	-5.2	-7.1	7.9	10.6	-9.2	-12.3	-9.7	-7.7	-1.9	-8.6
Motor vehicle theft											
number	5 865	6 436	7 330	7 945	8 768	8 122	8 211	7 476	6 875	7 011	6 503
rate	259	286	326	352	384	351	351	317	288	290	266
% change in rate*	-4.4	10.3	14.1	7.7	9.2	-8.6	—	-9.7	-9.0	0.7	-8.3
Theft											
number	36 397	36 368	38 897	42 514	45 221	39 648	35 301	32 228	33 762	32 473	28 537
rate	1 610	1 617	1 732	1 881	1 979	1 712	1 508	1 365	1 414	1 343	1 167
% change in rate*	-4.1	0.4	7.1	8.6	5.2	-13.5	-11.9	-9.5	3.6	-5.0	-13.1
Property crime — Total											
number	74 769	74 316	76 317	83 741	91 656	83 603	74 981	68 907	68 105	66 702	59 532
rate	3 307	3 304	3 398	3 705	4 012	3 610	3 203	2 919	2 853	2 759	2 434
% change in rate*	-4.7	-0.1	2.9	9.0	8.3	-10.0	-11.3	-8.9	-2.2	-3.3	-11.8
Mischief											
number	7 832	8 643	8 491	8 647	9 725	9 066	8 214	7 687	7 745	7 695	7 150
rate	346	384	378	383	426	392	351	326	324	318	292
% change in rate*	0.2	10.9	-1.6	1.2	11.3	-8.0	-10.4	-7.2	-0.3	-1.9	-8.1
Offensive weapons											
number	1 416	1 514	1 702	1 809	2 020	1 906	1 932	1 963	1 693	1 551	1 488
rate	63	67	76	80	88	82	83	83	71	64	61
% change in rate*	-3.2	7.5	12.6	5.6	10.5	-6.9	0.3	0.8	-14.7	-9.5	-5.2

(continued)

Table 5.6 *(continued)*

	1987	1988	1989	1990	1991	1992	1993	1994	1995ʳ	1996ʳ	1997
Other Criminal Code											
— Total											
number	22 764	24 136	25 865	27 118	31 741	31 651	30 429	29 089	30 117	30 187	29 952
rate	1 007	1 073	1 152	1 200	1 389	1 367	1 300	1 232	1 262	1 249	1 225
% change in rate*	9.6	6.6	7.3	4.2	15.8	−1.6	−4.9	−5.2	2.4	−1.0	−1.9
CRIMINAL CODE											
— TOTAL											
number	107 698	109 889	115 962	126 549	142 316	135 282	126 887	119 625	120 663	119 410	111 736
rate	4 764	4 885	5 164	5 599	6 229	5 842	5 420	5 067	5 055	4 939	4 569
% change in rate*	−0.7	2.6	5.7	8.4	11.2	−6.2	−7.2	−6.5	−0.2	−2.3	−7.5

[1] Rates are calculated on the basis of 100 000 youths. The population estimates are provided by Statistics Canada, Census and Demographic Statistics, Demography Division. Populations as of July 1st; revised intercensal estimates from 1987 to 1990, final postcensal estimates for 1991 to 1995, updated postcensal estimates for 1996 and 1997.

[2] These date are based on the Homicide Survey, CCJS.

* Percent change based on unrounded rates.

ʳ Revised. After the release of 1996 data in July 1997, an error was discovered that had resulted in an under-counting of 1996 crime (and persons charged) for Toronto and of 1995 and 1996 for Winnipeg. These errors were corrected and the data in this *Juristat* reflect the corrections. Please refer to the methodology section for more details.

— numbers too small to be expressed

SOURCE: *Uniform Crime Reporting Survey*, Canadian Centre for Justice Statistics, Statistics Canada.

Table 5.7

	Youths charged	Adults charged
Selected Offences		
Total violent	20%	30%
Assaults	15%	26%
Robbery	3%	2%
Total property	53%	38%
Theft	26%	19%
Break & enter	15%	7%
Theft motor vehicle	6%	2%
Total other Criminal Code	27%	32%
Mischief	6%	4%
TOTAL *CRIMINAL CODE*	100%	100%

mentioned, all analysis in this report is based on aggregate survey counts.

The aggregate UCR survey classifies incidents according to the most serious offence in the incident (generally the offence that carries the longest maximum sentence under the *Criminal Code of Canada*). In categorizing incidents, violent offences always take precedence over non-violent offences. As a result, less serious offences are under-represented by the UCR survey.

Figure 5.10
Rate of Youths Charged, 1987–1997

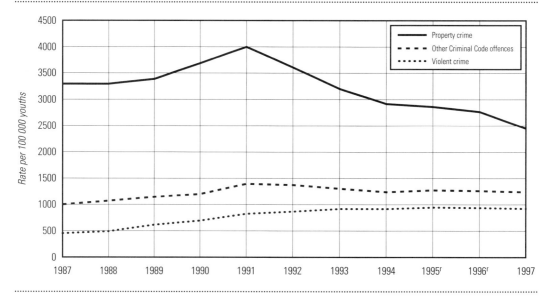

^r Revised

SOURCE: *Uniform Crime Reporting Survey*, Canadian Centre for Justice Statistics, Statistics Canada.

Figure 5.11a

Persons Accused of Property Crimes by Age, 1997

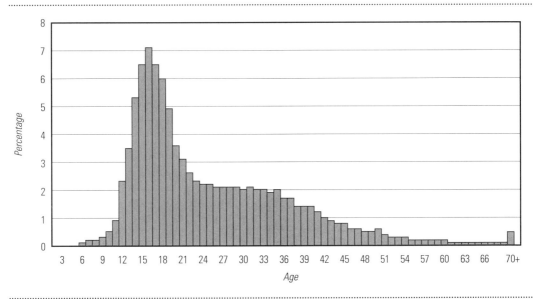

SOURCE: Non-random sample of 179 police agencies representing 48% of the national volume of crime. The data are not nationally representative.

The aggregate UCR survey scores violent incidents (except robbery) differently from other types of crime. For violent crime, a separate incident is recorded for each victim (i.e., if one person assaults three people, then three incidents are recorded; but if three people assault one person, only one incident is recorded). Robbery, however, is counted as if it were a non-violent crime in order to avoid inflating the number of victims (e.g., persons in a bank during a robbery). For non-violent crimes, one incident (categorized according to the most serious offence) is counted for every distinct or separate occurrence.

REVISED UCR SURVEY (UCRII INCIDENT-BASED RESEARCH FILE)

The revised micro-data survey captures detailed information on individual criminal incidents reported to police, including characteristics of victims, accused persons and the incidents. In 1997, detailed data were collected from 179

departments in six provinces through the Revised UCR Survey. These data represent 48% of the national volume of actual *Criminal Code* crimes. The incidents contained in the 1997 Research File are distributed as follows: 41% from Quebec, 33% from Ontario, 11% from Alberta, 8% from British Columbia, 6% from Saskatchewan, and 1% from New Brunswick. Other than Quebec, the data are primarily from urban police departments. The reader is cautioned that these data are not nationally representative. Continuity with the aggregate survey data is maintained by a conversion of the incident-based data to aggregate counts at year end.

In this report, the crime rate excludes traffic violations as these data have proven to be volatile over time. This volatility is the result of changes in police procedures that allow for traffic violations to be scored under either a provincial statute or the *Criminal Code* (e.g., failure to stop or remain at an accident).

Figure 5.11b

Persons Accused of Violent Crime by Age, 1997

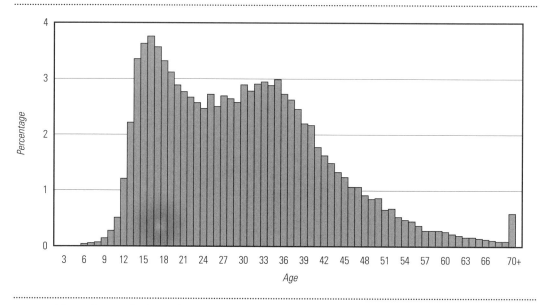

SOURCE: Non-random sample of 179 police agencies representing 48% of the national volume of crime. The data are not nationally representative.

NOTES

1. The General Social Survey is conducted by Statistics Canada. See "Trends in Criminal Victimization, 1988/1993" by Rosemary Gartner and Anthony Doob in *Juristat* (Cat. no. 85-002, Vol. 14, no. 13).

2. For further information, refer to "Criminal Victimization: An International Perspective," by Sandra Besserer, *Juristat* (Cat. no. 85-002XPE/F, Vol. 18, no. 6). See the methodology section at the end of this report for a brief description of the survey.

3. A CMA refers to a large urban core (over 100 000 population) together with adjacent urban and rural areas that have a high degree of economic and social integration. The areas that police forces serve may differ in their mix of urban/suburban populations, making the comparability of crime rates among these forces difficult. This lack of comparability is addressed by analyzing crime rates by CMA. Usually, more than one police force is responsible for enforcing the law within the boundaries of a CMA.

4. "Ottawa" in this report refers to the Ontario portion of the Ottawa-Hull CMA.

5. The U.S. Crime Index is composed of the violent crimes of murder, non-negligent manslaughter, forcible rape, robbery and aggravated assault (not common assault), and the property crimes of burglary, larceny theft, motor vehicle theft and arson.

6. For instance, Gottfredson and Hirschi, *A General Theory of Crime* (Stanford: Stanford University Press, 1990); and Farrington, David P., "The Explanation and Prevention of Youthful Offending" in David J. Hawkins (Ed.), *Delinquency and Crime: Current Theories* (Cambridge University, 1996), p. 74.

7. Statistics Canada. *Population Projections for Canada, Provinces and Territories, 1993–2016* (Cat. no. 91-520), December 1994.

8. The median value is the one in the middle when a set of values is arranged in order from highest to lowest.

9. For further information, refer to "Children as Victims of Violent Crime" by Robin Fitzgerald, *Juristat* (Cat. no. 85-002 XPE/F, Vol. 17, no. 11).

10. For further information, refer to "Breaking and Entering in Canada, 1996," by Rebecca Kong, *Juristat* (Cat. no. 85-002 XPE/F, Vol. 18, no. 5).

11. Members of the Insurance Information Centre of Canada represent about 80% of the total insurance industry.

12. For further information, refer to "Motor Vehicle Theft in Canada — 1996," by Julie Sauve, *Juristat* (Cat. no. 85-002 XPE/F, Vol. 18, no. 1).

13. Vehicle Information Centre of Canada. 1997. "How Cars Measure Up, 1995-1996."

14. Vehicle Information Centre of Canada.

15. Please refer to the *Criminal Code of Canada* for exact definitions and conditions.

16. For more information, see "Street Prostitution in Canada," by Doreen Duchesne, *Juristat* (Cat. no. 85-002-XPE/F, Vol. 17, no. 2). Chapter 3 in this volume.

17. For further information, see "Impaired Driving in Canada, 1996," by Sylvain Tremblay, *Juristat* (Cat. no. 85-002 XPE/F, Vol. 17, no. 12).

18. Persons accused refer to those involved in incidents "cleared by charge" and "cleared otherwise."

19. These median ages will differ from those presented in Table 5.5 as they are based on all accused, not just persons charged.

DISCUSSION QUESTIONS

1. How does legislation affect crime statistics? Explain and give examples.

2. Describe the pattern of Canadian crime from 1986 to 1997. How does it vary by major crime type (violence, property, other crimes)?

3. There is great public concern about youth crime. On the basis of the statistics, is the concern reasonable? Justify your response.

Why Are Crime Rates Going Down in Edmonton?[1]

LESLIE W. KENNEDY
DAVID VEITCH

INTRODUCTION

Patterns in crime rates in the last two decades have been subject to much criminological investigation, analysis, and speculation. As Martin and Ogrodnik (1996) indicate, the number of Criminal Code offences (excluding traffic) reported in 1994 for Canada is over five times greater than that reported in 1962. Even after adjusting for a 160% increase in the Canadian population, the crime rate in 1994 was still almost three-and-one-half times greater than in 1962. The largest single year-over-year decline (–5.3%) in the crime rate since UCR crime reporting began occurred in 1993. This drop followed a smaller decline (–3%) in 1992. The drop has been repeated (–4.8%) in 1994.

There has been a great deal of public discussion about the drop in rates of crime but no detailed analysis concerning why this drop has occurred. Are the factors that led to increases in the levels of crime the same as those that are driving them down? Is the decline a function of changes in social behaviour by high risk groups, changes in police practice, or a product of both? Could it be that these drops are statistical aberrations, hiding actual increases in crime, as has been claimed by some critics (Grainger 1996: 23)? We will examine the experience with the decline in crime rates using population and police data from the city of Edmonton.

THE STUDY

The data reported here, covering 1984 to 1994, are provided by the Edmonton Police Service (EPS). We will examine dispatch data generated through the communications division responsible for 911 and calls for service. In addition, we will look at data collected through an annual survey of Edmonton citizens (District Area Survey or DAS) conducted by the Organisational Studies Unit of the EPS since 1990. The DAS is designed to focus on issues such as public attitudes towards police performance, public concerns over safety and security, fear of crime, victimisation, and confidence in the police. The survey uses a random sample of telephone numbers with eligible respondents 18 years and older. The surveys are conducted on a yearly rotation, with samples in the first year drawn from the total city (n = 460); in the second year from police divisions (n = 1200); and in the third year from police districts (n = 4600). The rotation is repeated in subsequent years. In addition, we draw data from reports on social and economic change prepared by the City of Edmonton and Statistics Canada and on property crime loss collected by the Insurance Bureau of Canada.

ANALYSIS AND RESULTS

Crime Rate Changes

Looking at Figure 6.1, we see that from 1989 to 1991 crimes against persons rose 21%. Since 1992, crimes against persons dropped 32%, from its peak in 1991. Similarly, property-related offences increased by 16% from 1989 to 1991 (see Figure 6.2). Since 1992, the number of property offences dropped 39%. Correspondingly, clearance rates for these two crime categories also improved since 1991, up 12.8% for crimes against persons (Figure 6.1) and 22.8% for property occurrences (Figure 6.2). In addition to crime trends, Figures 6.1 and 6.2 show clearance rate changes over the time period under study. Clearance rate has been used as a measure of how well police "solve crime," so increases in these numbers are seen as evidence of increased police effectiveness.

According to the Insurance Bureau of Canada, residential break and enters for Edmonton peaked in 1991 at 6152 claims and then decreased 500% (to 2994) by 1994. During this same period, glass and vandalism claims also declined over 50%. Theft claims were down from 3037 in 1991 to 1194 in 1994, a drop of 60%. We might conclude that these decreases are due to the increase in deductibles discouraging victims from reporting these crimes, but in fact deductibles were raised only in 1994. These drops appear tied to increased security and better guardianship, a phenomenon witnessed across the country. In Edmonton, this pattern coincides with changes in ways that people access the police and in administrative changes in handling complaints, including proactive prevention that comes with community policing. We will discuss these changes below.

Social Change

In looking at demographic characteristics of Edmonton during the time period in which we are

Figure 6.1

Violent Occurrences and Clearance Rates, 1984–1994

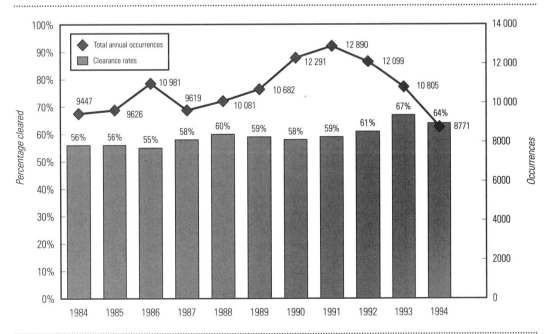

Figure 6.2

Property-Related Occurrences and Clearance Rates, 1984–1994

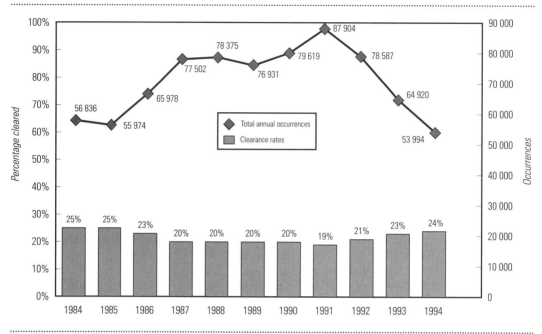

interested, we see limited evidence of major shifts in at-risk populations. Reports from the civic census show the number of males aged 15 to 24 years in 1991 as 47 543. This number in 1992 was 46 516; in 1995 this number is estimated to be 44 819 (City of Edmonton Civic Census). While there is a small drop in numbers from 1991, this seems insignificant compared to the large drop in crime rates. Further, the unemployment rate in Edmonton has stayed very steady with rates of 9.5% (1991), 11% (1992), 11.2% (1993), and 10.6% (1994). Net migration to the city has also been quite low (in 1993 it was 2600) when compared to the rapid growth that the city experienced in the boom times of the late 1970s and early 1980s (up to 7000 to 8000 people per annum). Socio-demographic characteristics have not changed in the city over the time period in question to the extent that crime rates have.

We need to consider a related factor which has some importance in affecting economic conditions

of the city. After Ralph Klein was elected premier in 1993, his government immediately set about reviewing social welfare payments criteria. In fact, there was a drop in the Edmonton Social Services case load from 32 074 in 1993 to 22 939 in 1994 and 21 148 in 1995. Part of this drop could have meant people left the city, although the low interprovincial net migration figures do not support this view. It could be argued that all of the 11 000 social service recipients moved away from Alberta during this time to be replaced by higher income migrants but this seems very unlikely. In addition, not all of these individuals fit the at-risk characterisation of the young and unemployed. What we do know is that many people who were dropped off the welfare roll continued to find support from government by returning to school, while others found jobs.

In addition, if social service clients are more at risk for crime (a questionable assumption, given the wide variety of reasons for people turning to the government for help), a decrease in social support

Table 6.1

Selected Communication Performance Measures, 1991–1994

	% Change 1991–94	1991	1992	1993	1994
911 police	−30%	84 431	83 139	72 041	58 960
Calls answered	−46%	400 878	280 499	247 367	216 594
Abandoned calls	−51%	102 234	65 309	40 369	50 285
ASA (Average speed of answer)	−33%	81.4 sec.	49.0 sec.	33.0 sec.	54.9 sec.
Total calls	−46%	485 309	363 638	319 408	264 477
Dispatched calls	−29%	171 880	141 684	133 539	122 739

seems more likely to result, in the short term at least, in a rise in crime — not a drop. Finally, even if there were subsequently a substantial movement of at-risk individuals, this would have occurred in 1994, 2 years after the beginning of the drop in reported crime.

Legal and Police Administrative Changes

During the time under study, the EPS force strength stayed fairly constant. Further, there have been no major changes in the law during the time period under consideration to which we can attribute these changes in crime rates, despite a great deal of recent public discussion of the need to revise the Young Offenders Act and to impose stricter gun laws.

Of major concern to the EPS prior to 1992 was the rising number of calls for service (CFS), including 911 and complaint calls. The 911 calls are emergency requests for immediate police response. Examples of these types of calls include serious injury accidents, alarms, and in progress criminal occurrences. (A small percentage of 911 calls are not pure emergency requests.) Complaint line calls are service-related, involving other types of activity, such as investigating mischief. Responding to these calls is not as urgent as for emergency calls and, therefore, these receive a lower response priority. Prior to 1992, the high volume of complaint calls led to many going unanswered. The number of calls to the communications centre, combining both 911 and the complaint line, peaked in 1991

at 485 309 (see Table 6.1). Over 100 000 callers hung up before their call was answered, as it took an average of 81 seconds to answer a non-emergency call in 1991. It is possible that the actual number of crime occurrences was actually higher than reported due to congestion in the system, with complainants simply giving up in their attempts to report these crimes. Often, calls for service (CFS) waited in dispatch queue for hours before an officer arrived to deal with the incident. Over 60% of the CFS were classed as service-related. It is these calls which take a disproportionate amount of officer time to investigate and are more amenable to problem-solving initiatives.

To redress the problems of an overloaded system, the EPS decentralised the reporting process. The four divisional stations were restructured to handle calls directly. Twelve community stations were located, through a workload analysis, across the city (Bevan 1991). Community station hours of operation were set at 9:00 AM to 9:00 PM, six days a week, and at 10:00 AM to 6:00 PM on Sundays. In addition, seven storefront (Neighbourhood Foot Patrol) offices were in operation. Dispatch evaluators at central communications were directed to consider alternatives to dispatching a patrol unit. If the complaint met certain criteria (e.g., the caller was the victim of a property crime), he or she was encouraged to come into a community station to report. Also, community officers obtained pagers and answering machines to increase contact with the public, further diverting calls away from central communications.

Figure 6.3

EPS Service Workload, 1991–1993

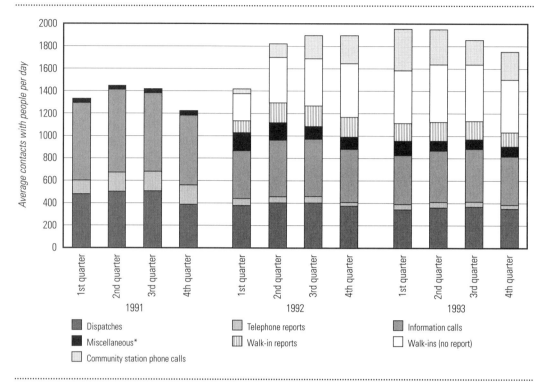

Dispatches
Miscellaneous*
Community station phone calls
Telephone reports
Walk-in reports
Information calls
Walk-ins (no report)

* Miscellaneous includes referrals, delayed response, and collisions reported at stations.

Total calls for both 911 and the complaint line dropped 46% from 1991 to 1994 (Table 6.1). Total 911 calls alone dropped 30%. Abandoned calls or hang-ups dropped by 51%, while the average speed of answering (ASA) calls improved by almost 30 seconds in 1994 over the average in 1991. These measures all have an impact on one another. Fewer calls mean faster answering, resulting, in turn, in fewer hang-ups. It should be noted, however, that the public did not stop reporting to the police. Since 1992, an average of over 200 000 people have visited the different reporting outlets (see Figure 6.3). This does not include those individuals coming to community stations, or contacting their assigned officer via pager, cellular phone, answering machine, or fax.[2] The drop in calls for service to the communication centre was offset by

an actual increase in overall service workloads due to citizens going to community stations to report their complaints.

The objective of improving response times was only partially achieved. Priority 1 (emergency) response times have improved slightly since 1991 (by 2 minutes); priority 2 (highs), which peaked in 1992, improved by 12 minutes by 1995; and priority 3 (service calls) showed the greatest improvement, reaching a high of 195 minutes in 1991 and dropping to a more acceptable level of 116 minutes for the same month in 1995. The concern that calls are lost through congestion is reduced through quick response times.

Organisational restructuring accompanied these changes. Specialised investigative units were amalgamated. The Auto Theft Unit was combined with the Youth Unit. The rationale for this was that over 75% of stolen autos involve youths who "take a vehicle without the owner's consent" (a.k.a. joy riding). The vehicle theft rate has dropped since then (e.g., the drop in theft of vehicles from Nov. 1994 to Nov. 1995 has been 5480 to 4533), while the recovery and clearance rates since combining the two units have improved.

PREVENTION, PROBLEM-SOLVING, AND COMMUNITY POLICING

Providing more reporting outlets changed the flow of information for police. In addition, the restructuring of the EPS included a new emphasis away from a rapid response to a problem-solving approach. The public were expected to take their non-emergency service concerns to the community reporting outlets. The community station was offered as a viable alternative to dispatching a car. Encouraged, as well, was MDT (Mobile Data Terminal) self-assignment of calls. Policy and procedure manuals were taken from officers and put into the divisional offices to reduce reliance upon preset responses. These manuals were rewritten to encourage decision-making at the lowest level. Decentralisation was achieved by providing alternative methods to contact the community neighbourhood assigned officer. How much effect did this emphasis on proactive policing, encouraged by diverting calls to the community level, have on crime reporting and problem-solving?

In the EPS, at the present time, only "concluded" problem-solving initiatives are submitted for inclusion in the central data base. This has become a dilemma because many problems are not "concluded." Often, they develop into an ongoing project, such as a program to help neighbours mediate conflicts. An audit of the problem-solving data base created by EPS reveals approximately 100 problems catalogued. This is misleading because numerous innovative projects have been implemented but members would rather "attack the problem" than write it up for distribution. There is obviously a need for better information about how

"crimes" become "problems." This information is not currently available in the EPS.

It might be argued that the crime rate is dropping not because of the community policing initiative, but because of non-recording by police. A crime is only a crime if the police record it, for example, an assault can become a "sick or injured" man or a theft can become trouble with person (which is not a crime category). If this were true, then a large increase should be noticed in UCR defined "other offences" or "non-offence" categories. During the post-1992 period in Edmonton, there was a decrease in both of these categories: "other offences" decreased 44.7%. In 1995, "non-offences" was down 7.8% over the 1990–1994 average.[3]

Finally, what of the "dark figure of crime," i.e., incidents that are not reported to the police? Data drawn from the District Area Survey (DAS) show that victimisation stays at a constant 22% average over the time period before and after the implementation of community policing. If non-recording was an issue, the percentage of victimisation to the total number of reported crimes (which has decreased) should be up considerably. Rather, it stays constant as it goes down with the downward trend in the levels of reported crime. We must look at these victimisation numbers carefully, though: the survey does not canvas a large number of respondents and so may not provide a sufficiently sensitive measure of changes in victimisation (particularly the more serious and less frequent occurrences). In addition, the less serious crimes of assault and property crime that the police now treat as problems may remain crimes in the mind of the respondents. The parallel trends of police-reported crime with victim reports, though, is an interesting finding and needs further analysis.

DISCUSSION

Reporting levels have stayed high (despite the diversion of complaints to community stations), while crime rates have dropped. Overall, the drop in crime rates in Edmonton appears unrelated to changes in laws or in the socio-demographic character of the city. Rather, these changes appear to rest, at least partially, on the dramatic drop in the reporting of property crime. This decline appears to be due to increases in private security and new crime prevention practices, including proactive policing which seeks to solve problems rather than simply reply to calls for service. Police have targeted problem areas and are encouraged to deal with the root causes of crime rather than simply taking a report. Initiatives encouraging diversion of complaints also means that community involvement with police changes the nature of how complaints are defined (i.e., they become problems rather than crimes) both by the police and by the complainant. In addition, police who do respond to complaints use more discretion; complaints brought to community stations, where cars are not dispatched to the scene of the incident, are even less likely to result in arrests; problem-solving approaches lower the numbers of disorder crimes and increase crime prevention; and at-risk groups are easier for community-based programs and projects to track and deter. These changes in police behaviour are reflected not only in the lower levels of reported crime but also in the lower reports of victimisation.

CONCLUSION

Future crime rate trends are hard to predict. We are so unaccustomed to downward trends in crime reporting that we are not sure where the lower threshold for this may be. Even with its initiatives in community policing, the EPS (as do most Canadian police forces) still relies on rapid response in handling more serious crime. How much we move downward is clearly a function of further innovations in creating new ways of accessing the police and ways in which the police deal with the problems in the communities in which they work. We need more research in different locations on the multiple reasons for crime rate declines with an emphasis on establishing the relative importance of police initiatives and changes in social behaviour in driving these numbers down.

The EPS and other police agencies should also be encouraged to collect more information about the nature of problems that are being addressed by their members and the relationship between these initiatives and crime occurrences. To understand these issues more clearly, we need more accurate and sensitive measures of the results of the community policing programs that are sweeping across North American policing. It is clear that conventional approaches to the study of crime rates will need to be supplemented by more qualitative assessments of how these numbers are influenced by police practice and how this, in turn, influences how the public comes to define the crime problem. New measures of effectiveness and efficiency need to be developed to match the new style of proactive policing.

NOTES

1. The authors would like to thank Joe Pendleton, Kim Don, and members of the Edmonton Police Service for assistance in the preparation of data charts and in providing constructive feedback on the manuscript.
2. Often complainants will take a report home to fill out and then send it back to the officer through the fax.
3. "Other" offences and "non-offences" are UCR groupings of incidents, which contain non-crime and strictly service or order maintenance involvement by police.

DISCUSSION QUESTIONS

1. What are the general societal forces that might be affecting the crime rate in Edmonton?
2. What do Kennedy and Veitch show is the most likely reason for crime to be declining in Edmonton? Is the decline real or an artifact of some other events? (Be specific).
3. Discuss the way in which this research was conducted. That is, how did Kennedy and Veitch go about examining the crime situation in Edmonton?

REFERENCES

Bevan, J. (1991). Workload analysis: Community breakdown of crime occurrences. Unpublished paper. Edmonton Police Services.

Black, D. (1980). *The manners and customs of the police.* New York: Academic Press.

Blau, J. R., & Blau, P. M. (1982). The cost of inequality: Metropolitan structure and violent crime. *American Sociological Review, 4* (February), 114–129.

Brantingham, P. L., & Brantingham, P. J. (1990). Situational crime prevention in practice. *Canadian Journal of Criminologyi, 32*(1), 17–40.

Canadian Centre for Justice Statistics. (1990). *The development of data quality assessment procedures for the Uniform Crime Reporting Survey: A case study of Calgary-Edmonton.* Ottawa: Statistics Canada.

Cantor, D., & Land, K. C. (1985). Unemployment and crime rates in the post-World War II United States: A theoretical and empirical analysis. *American Sociological Review, 50*(3), 317–332.

City of Edmonton. (1995). *Civic census.* Edmonton: Department of Organizational Analysis.

Felson, M. (1994). *Crime and everyday life.* Newbury Park, CA: Pine Forge Press.

Goldstein, H. (1990). *Problem oriented policing.* New York: McGraw-Hill.

Gove, W. R., Hughes, M., & Geerken, M. (1985). Are uniform crime reports a valid indicator of the index crimes? An affirmative answer with minor qualifications. *Criminology, 23*(3), 451–501.

Grainger, R. (1996). Data and methodology in the area of criminal justice. In L. W. Kennedy & V. Sacco (Eds.), *Crime counts.* Toronto: Nelson.

Kennedy, L. W. (1991). Evaluating community policing. *Canadian Police College Journal, 15*(4), 275–290.

Kingsley, R. (1996). Assault. In L. W. Kennedy & V. Sacco, *Crime counts.* Toronto: Nelson.

Koenig, D. J. (1991). *Do police cause crime? Police activity, police strength and crime rates.* Ottawa: Canadian Police College.

Koenig, D. J. (1996). Do police cause crime? In R. Silverman, J. Teevan, & V. Sacco, *Crime in Canadian society* (5th ed.). Toronto: Harcourt Brace & Company, Canada.

Krahn, H., & Kennedy, L. W. (1986). Producing personal safety: The effects of crime rates, police force size, and fear of crime. *Criminology 23*(4), 607–710.

Martin, M., & Ogrodnik, L. (1996). Canadian crime trends. In L. W. Kennedy & V. Sacco (Eds.), *Crime counts.* Toronto: Nelson.

Normandeau, A., & Leighton, B. (1990). *A vision of the future of policing in Canada: Police-challenge 2000.* Ottawa: Solicitor General of Canada.

Quinney, R. (1975). *Criminology.* Boston: Little Brown.

Rosenbaum, D. P. (1994). *The challenge of community policing: Testing the promise.* Newbury Park. CA: Sage.

Sacco, V., & Johnson, H. (1990). *Patterns of criminal victimisation in Canada.* Ottawa: Ministry of Supply and Services.

Sacco, V., & Kennedy, L. W. (1994). *The criminal event.* Toronto: Nelson.

Schissel, B. (1992). The influence of economic factors and social control policy on crime rate changes in Canada, 1962–1988. *Canadian Journal of Sociology, 17*(4), 405–428.

Silverman, R. (1980). A tale of two cities. In R. Silverman & J. Teevan, *Crime in Canadian society.* Toronto: Butterworths.

Time. (1996). Finally, the US is winning the war against crime: Here's why. *147*(3), 18–26.

Weisel, D., & Eck, J. (1994). Toward a practical approach to organizational change: Community policing initiatives in six cities. In D. P. Rosenbaum (Ed.), *The challenge of community policing: Testing the promises.* Thousand Oaks, CA: Sage.

Williams, K. R., & Flewelling, R. L. (1988). The social production of criminal homicide: A comparative study of disaggregated rates in American cities. *American Sociological Review, 53,* 421–431.

Wycoff, M. A., & Skogan, W. (1993). *Community policing in Madison: Quality from the inside out (an evaluation of implementation and impact).* Washington: National Institute of Justice.

7

Trends in Youth Crime in Canada

PETER J. CARRINGTON

INTRODUCTION

In 1991, police-reported youth crime in Canada reached the highest level ever recorded. This peak followed increases in five of the six years since the *Young Offenders Act* came into force in 1985. Not surprisingly, the long climb from 1985 to 1991 in the level of youth crime, immediately following the inception of the YOA, aroused considerable adverse comment in the media, and contributed to public disenchantment with the YOA (Corrado and Markwart 1992: 160–163; Bala 1994: 248–251; Hylton 1994: 236–239; Task Force on Youth Justice 1996: 14–19). By 1996, the rate of youth crime had returned to the same level as in 1983, prior to the YOA, after falling for four of the five years since 1991; this decrease seems to have received less public attention.

Although scholarly commentators did not attribute the rise in youth crime to the YOA, the rise did occasion debate about the extent to which its level exceeded that under the *Juvenile Delinquents Act*. More than a decade has now elapsed since the YOA came into effect. At the time of writing (August, 1998), the federal government is once more considering changes to the YOA in response to public concern about youth crime. This is therefore an opportune time to review the fluctuations in youth crime over the past twenty years, and to assess the change, if any, in its post-YOA level, and

the extent to which any change that has occurred is due to the YOA.

PREVIOUS RESEARCH

Has the Level of Youth Crime in Canada Increased since 1984?

Carrington and Moyer (1994: 8-11) compared quarterly data from the Uniform Crime Reporting (UCR) Survey on rates of young persons apprehended and charged for the periods 1980–84 (under the JDA) and 1985–90 (under the YOA), and concluded that the average per capita rate of police-reported youth crime (young persons apprehended) during 1985–90 was the same as during 1980–84, but that the average rate of young persons *charged* was 21 percent higher in the post-YOA period. They also noted that there was no upward or downward trend in either rate during 1980–84, but that there appeared to be slight upward trends, which were not statistically significant, in both rates during 1985–90, especially during 1989–90.

Corrado and Markwart (1994: 350–51) concluded from analysis of annual UCR data on young persons charged with *Criminal Code* offences from 1986 to 1992 that there was a "relatively modest 25 percent increase" over the period. Comparing annual UCR data for 1986–92 with 1980–83,

Adapted from Trends in Youth Crime in Canada, 1977–1996, by Peter Carrington (1999). *Canadian Journal of Criminology*, 41(1), p. 1–32 Copyright by the Canadian Criminal Justice Association. Reproduced by permission of the *Canadian Journal of Criminology*.

Carrington (1995: 63–64) found a statistically non-significant increase of 5 percent in the per capita rate of young persons apprehended, and an increase of 29 percent in the rate of young persons charged. He also reported an apparent upward trend in both rates from 1986 to 1992, which he said required further data for confirmation.

In summary, there is agreement that the per capita rate of young persons charged has increased significantly since the inception of the YOA, but disagreement as to the size and interpretation of the change, if any, in the per capita rate of young persons apprehended.

What Has Caused the Increase, If Any, in Youth Crime? Is It the YOA?

After comparing the 1985–90 period with 1980–84, Carrington and Moyer (1994) concluded that the observed increase in the per capita rate of young persons charged with offences reflected a change in the police propensity to charge young persons, rather than in the criminal behaviour of young persons, since the average rate of young persons *apprehended* by police did not change. Furthermore, they speculated that this change in police propensity to charge young persons might be statistical rather than "real": that is, that it might reflect a change in statistical categories rather than in police behaviour. After examining this phenomenon on a province-by-province basis, they suggested that the observed post-YOA increase in police charging could be due to a possibly pre-existing practice of charging 16 and 17 year old suspects in higher proportions than 12 to 15 year olds. When these 16 and 17 year olds were added, in many provinces, to the youth justice system and therefore the statistics on youth crime by the Uniform Maximum Age provision of the YOA, the average per capita rate of young persons charged would increase: more "young persons" per capita would be charged (although no more people would actually be charged) due to the legal redefinition of 16 and 17 year olds as "young persons." However, Carrington (1998) analysed age-specific data for Ontario and Saskatchewan and concluded that a substantial part — between one-half and all — of the observed increase in police charging of young offenders in at least those two provinces is not a statistical artifact, and reflects a change in actual police behaviour.

None of these writers attributes the observed changes in youth crime since 1985 to the effect of the YOA on the criminal behaviour of young persons. DuWors (1997) and Kong (1997) note that peaks in the early nineteen-nineties in overall police-reported crime in Canada are mirrored by similar trends in other countries. As Markwart and Corrado put it,

> . . . the international evidence seems quite clear that crime control changes in law alone will not have any significant effect on youth crime rates, changes to which, of course, arise as a result of far broader social factors . . . (1995: 84).

THE PRESENT STUDY

The logic of this study is that of the interrupted time series experiment. It attempts to detect the effects, if any, of the YOA on youth crime by comparing the level and direction of time series of crime data before and after the legislation came into effect. This "natural experiment" has serious weaknesses as a design for establishing cause-and-effect (Cook and Campbell 1979). In order to attribute any observed changes to the YOA, it is necessary to rule out other possible causes and to establish a plausible conceptual connection with the YOA. This can never be done with certainty. Nevertheless, we believe that a *prima facie* case for an effect of the YOA can be made on the basis of evidence of sudden changes occurring immediately after 1985 which cannot be attributed to other events. More gradual changes during the period are more likely to be due to the "broader social factors" referred to in the quotation above.

The analyses presented here are based on annual UCR data on young persons apprehended and charged during 1977 to 1996, omitting 1984–85 because of problems in the data for those years. Data from the UCR Survey, however, cannot be taken at face value as an indicator of the level of youth crime, as they are limited to criminal activity known to police and considered by police to be worth recording. Furthermore, counts of young persons implicated and charged in connection with criminal incidents, which are used in the present study, are necessarily limited to incidents which have been "cleared": that is, incidents in which the offender(s) have been identified, or "apprehended," by police. Thus, the very substantial number of incidents that are known to and recorded by police, but not cleared, are omitted: in 1996, for example, only about 38 percent of incidents known to police in Canada were cleared.

The UCR Survey reports counts of both "young persons charged" and "young persons not charged." Counts of "young persons charged" are probably a very accurate indicator of the *charging* of young persons, since the laying of charges is an official act which must be carefully recorded as the first step in court process. However, as an indicator of the amount of youth crime, it has the major disadvantage of omitting the substantial number of persons — especially young persons — who are apprehended but not charged: that is, levels of "young persons charged" reflect both criminal activity by young persons (and its detection and recording by police) and the exercise of police discretion to charge or to deal with the apprehended youth by other means, such as a warning or notification of parents. Thus, changes in numbers of young persons charged may confuse changes in youth crime with changes in police charging practices. The analyses presented below show that the use of "young persons charged" as an indicator of youth crime (which is a common practice) would lead to seriously erroneous conclusions concerning changes in the level of youth crime after the YOA came into effect. Therefore, in this study, "young persons charged" is interpreted as precisely that: an indicator of the charging of young persons by police.

For an indicator of changes over time in the amount of youth crime, this study uses UCR data

on "young persons apprehended" — that is, the sum of police-reported "young persons charged" and "young persons not charged." Numbers of young persons apprehended are a more valid indicator of changes in the level of youth crime than numbers of young persons charged, since they are not filtered by the decision to charge; but they are less reliable — that is, consistent — because the criteria for classifying a person as "[apprehended but] not charged" are much less precise than for "charged," and vary considerably among police forces reporting to the UCR (Hackler and Paranjape 1983). Data on young persons apprehended also systematically underestimate the amount of youth crime known to the police, because police tend to under-report minor incidents involving young persons (Doob and Chan 1982).

In order to make meaningful comparisons of levels of crime over time or across jurisdictions, population-standardized rates such as the rate per 100 000 population must be used. This is a difficult problem in the comparison of youth crime during the periods under the JDA and the YOA, because the populations defined as "juveniles" under the JDA and as "young persons" under the YOA differ. The age jurisdiction of the YOA is 12 to 17 years inclusive, everywhere in Canada. However, the age jurisdiction of the juvenile courts under the JDA varied by province: 7 to 17 years inclusive in Quebec and Manitoba, 7 to 16 years in Newfoundland and British Columbia, and 7 to 15 years in the other provinces and the territories.

One obvious approach to defining youth crime and the corresponding populations would be to use the legal definitions given above: that is, to compare the number of persons apprehended or charged by police who were aged 7 to 15 (or 16 or 17, depending on the province) during the JDA period with the number aged 12 to 17 during the YOA period. This results in the technically correct but rather spurious conclusion that there was a huge jump in youth crime after the YOA came into effect: the jump in the population-standardized rate is due to the inclusion of the very low crime rates of 7 to 11 year olds in the rates for the JDA period, and the inclusion of the relatively high crime rates of 16 and 17 year olds in the rates for the YOA period.[1]

ANALYSIS AND RESULTS

Young Persons Apprehended by Police

As Figure 7.1 shows, the per capita rate of youth apprehended by police increased rapidly during the late nineteen-seventies, which were the last years of a rising trend in officially recorded crime in Canada extending from the nineteen-sixties (Brantingham 1991: 399). From 1980 to 1988, youth crime remained at about the same level, then it rose to a peak in 1991, and fell back almost to its former level by 1996. During the period of stable rates under the JDA — 1980 to 1983 — the average annual rate of juveniles apprehended was approximately 7891 per 100 000. During 1986–96, the average annual rate of young persons (aged 12 to 17) apprehended was 8413 per 100 000 — a statistically significant increase of 522 per 100 000, or 7 percent, over the annual rate under the JDA.

Thus, the rate of police-reported youth crime was a little higher during the first decade under the YOA than during the last few years under the JDA. Was this increase due to the YOA itself? If the YOA had affected rates of youth crime, we would expect to see one or both of the following phenomena: a jump in level after 1984–85, or a rising trend after 1984–85 that had not existed previously. Changes such as these would indicate that something had happened that affected the rate of youth crime around 1984–85, and if other causes could be ruled out, the changes could be attributed to the YOA.

In fact, there was no jump after 1985, as can be seen from Figure 7.1. There was a slight change in the trend over time. During 1980–83, the trend was an annual increase of 25 per 100 000, but this was not statistically significant — that is, it could represent random fluctuations, rather than a "real" trend. During 1986–96, the rising trend increased to 46 per 100 000, but it remained statistically non-significant. Thus, we cannot be confident that any real change in trend took place after 1986. The

Figure 7.1

Rates per 100 000 of Juveniles/Young Persons Apprehended and Charged by Police, Canada, 1977–1996

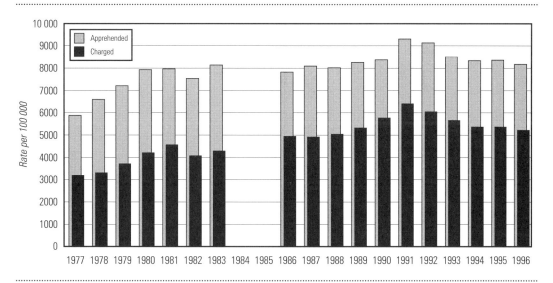

SOURCE: Based on tabulations supplied by Canadian Centre for Justice Statistics.

Table 7.1
Changes over Time in Rates per 100 000 of Young Persons Apprehended by Police, by Province, 1980 to 1996

Region/province	% of young offenders	Ages added by the YOA	JDA 1980–83 (adjusted)	YOA 1986–96	Mean level — Difference between mean levels	Mean level — Difference (as % of JDA rate)	Jump after 1985?	Trend — JDA 1980–83 (adjusted)	Trend — YOA 1986–96
CANADA	100.0		7 891	8 413	+522	+7%	no	+25	+46
ATLANTIC	6.9								
Newfoundland		17	5 885	6 329	+444	+8%	no	+469	+105*
P.E.I.		16–17	4 651	6 675	+2 024**	+44%	no	+727*	+181
Nova Scotia		16–17	5 016	7 021	+2 005***	+40%	no	+270**	+164*
New Brunswick		16–17	3 553	6 226	+2 673***	+75%	yes	+191	+173***
QUEBEC	17.5	—	6 062	4 955	–1 107**	–18%	drop	+164	+94**
ONTARIO	35.6	16–17	9 486	8 487	–999**	–11%	drop	+267	–76
SASKATCHEWAN	5.9	16–17	9 020	13 950	+4 930***	+55%	yes	–661	+84
WEST	33.0								
Manitoba		—	9 256	10 763	+1 507*	+16%	no	–33	+164
Alberta		16–17	7 753	11 051	+3 298**	+43%	no	+237	+125
B.C.		17	9 234	11 702	+2 468***	+27%	yes	–13	+103
NORTH	1.1								
Yukon		16–17	23 018	20 701	–2 317	–10%	no	–2 839	–194
N.W.T		16–17	31 571	23 228	–8 343**	–26%	no	+1 040	–946**

NOTE: Significance levels: * $p < .05$; ** $p < .01$; *** $p < .001$.
SOURCE: Adapted from tabulations supplied by Canadian Centre for Justice Statistics; the adjustment for 1980–83 is explained in the text.

Figure 7.2

Rates per 100 000 of Juveniles/Young Persons Apprehended, by Region, 1977–1996

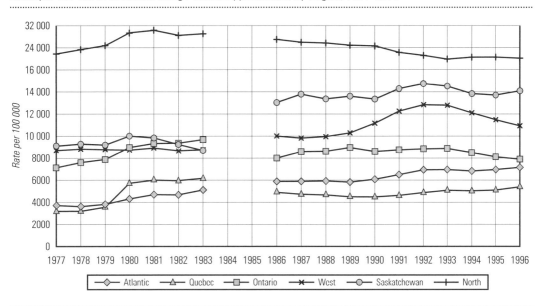

Notes: *Rates are modified 3-year moving averages. The upper part of the Y-axis scale is not linear.*
SOURCE: Based on tabulations supplied by Canadian Centre for Justice Statistics.

only noteworthy change in the level of youth crime that took place after 1984–85 was the "hump" in the early nineteen-nineties, and this is highly unlikely to have been caused by the YOA, since it occurred several years later, and was mirrored by similar "humps" in crime in other countries, that could not be related to the YOA.

Another way of looking for changes in youth crime due to the YOA is to examine data for individual provinces and territories, since some underwent large changes in age jurisdiction, due to the addition of 16 and 17 year olds, and others underwent smaller or no change in age jurisdiction. It is in the provinces and territories that added 16 and 17 year olds that we would most expect to see changes in the rate of youth crime following 1984–85 (cf. Carrington and Moyer 1994).

The results of this examination are shown in Figure 7.2 and Table 7.1. Figure 7.2 has been simplified by aggregating the provinces and territories

having similar levels and trends, based on detailed analysis (not shown in this edited version), and by smoothing with 3 year moving averages.

In the four Atlantic provinces, there appears to have been a rising trend in youth crime during the entire period, 1977–96, with a temporary peak in the early nineteen-nineties. This is suggested in Table 7.1 by positive trend parameters for both the JDA and YOA periods, and higher average levels during 1986–96 than during 1980–83. New Brunswick is the only province in which there was a (small) jump after 1984–85. Thus, the rate of police-reported youth crime in the Atlantic provinces was much higher during 1986–96 than during 1977–83, but this appears to be due to a pre-existing trend, not to the YOA.

In Quebec, the rate of youth crime was significantly *lower* during 1986–96 than during 1980–83. This decrease was due to a sudden drop, not to a falling trend: in fact, there was a slight *rising* trend during both periods (Table 7.1). We would speculate that this drop in official youth crime reflects not a sudden change in actual youth crime, but rather a change made by the Quebec government in 1984 in the screening procedure for young offenders (LeBlanc and Beaumont 1992) which could have affected the numbers of young persons reported to the UCR as apprehended offenders.

There was also a substantial drop in Ontario in police-reported youth crime in 1986, and little trend thereafter. As a result, the average rate of youth crime in Ontario was 999 per 100 000 *lower* during 1986–96 than during 1980–83: a statistically significant decrease of 11 percent. Perhaps some or all of this was due to the YOA, but we are unable to say how.

In Manitoba, Alberta, and British Columbia, rates of police-reported youth crime were fairly stable from 1980 to 1983, then rose steadily from 1988 to peaks in the early nineteen-nineties, from which they declined through 1996. In British Columbia, there was a jump in 1986. The large "hump" in youth crime rates during 1986–96 (Figure 7.2), and the post-1985 jump in British Columbia, resulted in average rates for the period that were significantly (16 to 27 percent) higher than during 1980–83. With the possible exception of the jump in 1986 in British Columbia, the timing of these phenomena suggests that they are not related to the YOA.

Saskatchewan is shown separately in Figure 7.2, because of the unique, and spectacular, one-time jump in its rate of official youth crime after 1986, which (along with a very small, and statistically non-significant, upward trend during 1986–96) resulted in an average rate during 1986–96 that was 55 percent higher than during 1980–83, and the highest among the ten provinces. Since this coincided with the introduction of the YOA, it may well have been related to it; however, we are unable to determine from these data to what extent this sudden increase of more than 50 percent reflects a change in the criminal behaviour of young persons, and to what extent it reflects a

change in police enforcement activity and reporting practices.

Beginning at very high levels, both the Yukon and the Northwest Territories experienced somewhat erratic downward trends in police-reported youth crime from 1980 to 1996, and no jump after 1984–85. (The non-significant positive trend value of 1040 for 1980–83 for the Northwest Territories is due to an anomalous high value for 1983: the rates for 1980–82 decline consistently.)

This survey of trends over two decades in police-reported youth crime in the provinces and territories confirms once again the diversity of patterns of criminal behaviour in Canada. With the exception of Quebec, regional youth crime rates rise from east to west and are far higher in the territories. Saskatchewan and British Columbia are the only provinces in which there was a substantial increase in recorded youth crime immediately after the YOA was introduced (the increases in 1986 in Nova Scotia and Manitoba appear to be part of a trend that existed prior to 1984). Ontario and Quebec experienced *drops* in police-reported youth crime immediately after 1984–85; this could have been due to changes in the *Youth Protection Act* in Quebec, and may have been related somehow to the introduction of the YOA in Ontario. In the other provinces and territories, there were rising or falling trends, or both, that appear to be unrelated to the YOA.

Young Persons Charged by Police

Figure 7.1 shows that the rate per 100 000 of young persons charged (the "charge rate") tracked the rate of young persons apprehended fairly consistently over the period 1977 to 1996, with one important exception: there was a jump in charging in 1986 that did not occur in apprehensions of young persons. As a result of this jump, the average charge rate during 1986–96 was 27 percent higher than during 1980–83, compared with the 7 percent increase in young persons apprehended. There was practically no rising or falling trend in the charge rate, either before or after 1984–85.

Figure 7.3

Rates per 100 000 of Juveniles/Young Persons Charged, by Region, 1977–1996

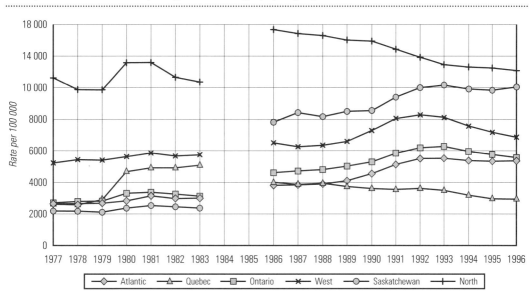

Notes: *Rates are modified 3-year moving averages. The upper part of the Y-axis scale is not linear.*
SOURCE: Based on tabulations supplied by Canadian Centre for Justice Statistics.

Since the rate of young persons apprehended increased by only 7 percent after 1985, most of the 27 percent increase in the charge rate was due to an increase in the proportion of apprehended young persons who were charged (the "charge ratio"), and a corresponding reduction in the use by police of informal means — that is, in police discretion (cf. Carrington and Moyer 1994).

It seems likely that this jump in charging of apprehended youth was due to the YOA, since it occurred immediately after the YOA came into effect, and the charge ratio was stable over the rest of the two decades examined (except for the temporary peak in the early nineteen-nineties, which is characteristic of many indicators of crime and police activity). The following section examines changes in charging of young persons by province, to see if the changes were more pronounced in the eight provinces and territories which experienced the greatest expansion of their youth justice systems

due to the addition of 16 and 17 year olds, as Carrington and Moyer (1994) suggested.

Table 7.2 shows the average level and trends in rates of young persons charged, by province. In Figure 7.3, these data are aggregated into regions with similar levels and trends, and are smoothed using 3 year moving averages. Table 7.3 shows similar information for charge ratios.

Quebec is the only province in which fewer young persons per capita were charged after 1984–85 than during 1980–83. There was an immediate drop after 1985, similar to the drop in the rate of apprehensions, but then the charge rate declined slowly through 1996; whereas the rate of apprehensions rose slightly in Quebec during 1986–96. This divergence in the rates of apprehensions and charging is reflected in a strong downward trend in the charge ratio — the proportion of apprehended youth who were charged — from 80 percent in 1986 to 51 percent in 1996 (Table 7.3).

Table 7.2

Changes over Time in Rates per 100 000 of Young Persons Charged by Police, by Province, 1980 to 1996

Province	Ages added by the YOA	JDA 1980–83 (adjusted)	YOA 1986–96	Mean level		Jump after 1985?	Trend	
				Difference between mean levels	Difference (as % of JDA rate)		JDA 1980–83 (adjusted)	YOA 1986–96
Canada		4 302	5 483	+1 181***	+27%	yes	−22	+46
Quebec	—	4 930	3 375	−1 555***	−32%	drop	+127	−112***
Manitoba	—	6 987	8 429	+1 442**	+21%	no	−80	+210*
Newfoundland	17	3 520	4 687	+1 167*	+33%	no	−41	+226*
B.C.	17	5 832	6 466	+634*	+11%	no	+6	−45
P.E.I.	16–17	2 084	4 391	+2 307**	+111%	no	+149	+109
Nova Scotia	16–17	2 646	5 379	+2 733***	+103%	yes	−36	+184**
New Brunswick	16–17	2 539	4 391	+1 852***	+73%	yes	−59	+145***
Ontario	16–17	3 105	5 450	+2 345***	+76%	yes	−153	+94
Saskatchewan	16–17	2 306	9 290	+6 984***	+303%	yes	−117	+236**
Alberta	16–17	4 358	7 366	+3 008***	+69%	small	−24	+120
Yukon	16–17	11 616	12 986	+1 370	+12%	no	−1 856	+266
N.W.T.	16–17	11 063	14 486	+3 423	+31%	yes	−788	−883***

NOTE: Significance levels: * p < .05; ** p < .01; *** p < .001.

SOURCE: Adapted from tabulations supplied by Canadian Centre for Justice Statistics; the adjustment for 1980–83 is explained in the text.

Table 7.3

Changes over Time in Proportions of Apprehended Youth Who Were Charged by Police, by Province, 1977 to 1996

Province	Ages added by the YOA	Mean level					Trend	
		JDA 1977–83 %	YOA 1986–96 %	Difference between mean levels	Difference (as % of JDA level)	Jump after 1985?	JDA 1977–83 %	YOA 1986–96 %
Canada		53.5	65.1	+11.6***	+22%	yes	+0.3	+0.2
Quebec	—	80.9	68.8	−12.1**	−15%	no	+0.2	−3.5***
Manitoba	—	77.2	78.1	+0.9	+1%	no	−1.2*	+0.8*
New Brunswick	16–17	74.8	70.5	−4.3	−6%	no	−2.8*	+0.4
Newfoundland	17	65.8	73.5	+7.7	+12%	no	−3.9*	+2.5*
British Columbia	17	55.1	55.3	+0.2	+0%	no	+2.9*	−.09***
P.E.I.	16–17	44.2	65.3	+21.1***	+48%	yes	+0.3	−0.1
Nova Scotia	16–17	58.6	76.5	+17.9**	+31%	yes	−3.8**	+0.9*
Ontario	16–17	34.0	64.4	+30.4***	+89%	yes	−1.2*	+1.7**
Saskatchewan	16–17	24.3	66.5	+42.2***	+174%	yes	+0.7	+1.3***
Alberta	16–17	56.1	66.4	+10.3*	+18%	small	−1.8	+0.5
Yukon	16–17	46.2	63.1	+16.9***	+37%	no	+1.1	+1.8*
N.W.T.	16–17	36.9	61.9	+25.0***	+68%	yes	−2.4*	−1.3*
Coefficient of variation		0.33	0.10					

NOTE: Significance levels: * p < .05; ** p < .01; *** p < .001.

SOURCE: Adapted from tabulations supplied by Canadian Centre for Justice Statistics; the adjustment for 1977–83 is explained in the text.

Quebec moved from being the province having the highest proportion of apprehended youth charged during 1980 to 1988, to having the lowest proportion charged, and by far the lowest per capita rate of young persons charged, by 1996. Since these trends are unique to Quebec, it seems likely that they are due to its unique system for diversion of young offenders, which was implemented in 1979 by the provincial *Youth Protection Act*, rather than to the YOA (cf. LeBlanc and Beaumont 1988, 1992).

The other provinces and territories all experienced increases after 1985 in rates of young persons charged: in the range of 10 to 30 percent in British Columbia, Newfoundland, Manitoba, the Yukon, and the Northwest Territories, and 70 to 110 percent in the other provinces, except Saskatchewan, in which the rate of young persons charged tripled after 1985. Saskatchewan moved from having the second-lowest rate of youth charged in the country during 1980–83 to having the highest rate, except for the territories, during 1987–96. This spectacular increase was due both to the large increase in the rate of young persons apprehended and to the large increase after 1985 in the proportions of these apprehended youth who were charged: from around 25 percent in 1977–83 to 60 to 70 percent in 1986–96 (Table 7.3). Both of these increases were mainly in the form of large jumps in 1986, but there were also upward trends after 1986.

Ontario also experienced a large increase — about 75 percent — after 1985 in the rate of young persons charged, due to a jump from about 3000 per 100 000 in the early nineteen-eighties to about 4500 in 1986, rising to 5000–6000 per 100 000 in the early nineteen-nineties. This was not due to an increase in apprehensions — which actually declined during the period — but to a jump in the proportion of these apprehended youth who were charged, from about 30 percent in 1983 to about 55 percent in 1986, followed by a steady increase to about 70 percent in the early nineteen-nineties.

Indeed, one of the most striking aspects of the transition from the JDA to the YOA in five of the eight provinces and territories that had a maximum age of 15 years under the JDA, and therefore added

16 and 17 year olds under the Uniform Maximum Age provision of the YOA, is the sudden transition in 1986 from charging relatively low proportions of apprehended youth — that is, high use of police discretion — to charging high proportions. This has resulted in greater national homogeneity in police charging practices. This sudden change was particularly pronounced in Saskatchewan and Ontario, but also occurred in Prince Edward Island, Nova Scotia, and the Northwest Territories (Table 7.3). The timing suggests the influence of the YOA. Previous research suggests that the increase in proportions charged in Ontario and Saskatchewan applied over the entire YOA age range (12 to 17 years inclusive), and was therefore not simply due to the addition of 16 and 17 year olds to the jurisdiction of the youth justice system (Carrington 1998).

In Prince Edward Island and Nova Scotia, this increase in charge ratios, combined with the rising trends in both the rate of apprehensions and charge ratios, resulted in rising trends after 1986 in the rates of young persons charged, and in average rates of young persons charged that were twice as high as during 1980–83 (Table 7.2). In the Northwest Territories, the large jump in charge ratio in 1986 was offset to some extent by a decrease in the rate of apprehensions (Table 7.1), resulting in a moderate, statistically non-significant, increase in the rate of young persons charged (Table 7.2).

On the other hand, the higher average charge ratios for 1986–96 in Alberta and the Yukon are due to rising trends rather than large jumps in 1986, and may be unrelated to the YOA.

In New Brunswick and Manitoba, there were fairly stable, high proportions of apprehended youth charged throughout 1977–96 (Table 7.3), so the rate of young persons charged followed the rate of apprehensions.

In Newfoundland, the charge ratio decreased steeply during 1977–83, rose sharply from 1988 to 1993, then fell. Similarly, the rate of young persons charged rose from a rather low level of about 3200 per 100 000 in 1986 to a peak of about 6000 in 1991, then fell to about 5300 in 1996. In British

Columbia — the other province in which 17 year olds were added to the youth justice system by the YOA — the charge ratio and the rate of young persons charged increased from 1977 to 1983, then decreased from 1986 to 1996. In neither province was there a significant change in level in 1986, and it is difficult to know to what extent the changes in charging in these provinces might have been affected by the YOA.

DISCUSSION

This paper has shown that there is no basis in fact for public concern about increased levels of youth crime or the supposed failure of the YOA to control youth crime. Apart from a temporary peak in the early nineteen-nineties, the level of police-reported youth crime in Canada has changed very little since 1980. The average per capita rate of police-reported youth crime was 7 percent higher during the first eleven years under the YOA than during the last four years under the JDA. This increase does not appear to be due to the YOA, since it did not occur immediately after 1985, but is largely accounted for by a temporary "hump" in youth crime during the early nineteen-nineties, mainly in the Western provinces. There were jumps in police-reported youth crime in Saskatchewan and British Columbia immediately after 1985, which may have been due to the YOA, possibly because of changes in police recording practices rather than the criminal behaviour of young persons. On the other hand, police-reported youth crime was *lower* under the YOA than during 1980–83 in Quebec and Ontario. Although the drop in Quebec was probably at least partly due to the unique provincial youth diversion system, which predated the YOA by five years, we cannot account for the drop in 1986 in Ontario.

However, the average rate of young persons *charged* by police was 27 percent higher during 1986–96 than 1980–83. Unlike the rate of young persons apprehended, the charge rate jumped immediately after the YOA came into effect. Before and after this, the charge rate followed the rate of apprehensions quite closely.

The jump in 1986 in young persons charged reflects a jump in the proportion of identified young offenders who were charged — that is, a sudden drop in police diversion of young offenders. This sudden change in the charge ratio, a time series that is otherwise quite stable, suggests the effect of a discrete event: presumably the YOA. The jump in police charging was especially pronounced in Saskatchewan and Ontario, but also occurred in Prince Edward Island, Nova Scotia, and the Northwest Territories. All of these jurisdictions were characterized, prior to the YOA, by the charging of relatively low proportions of apprehended youth — that is, by the use of relatively high levels of police discretion. On the other hand, Quebec — which had the highest proportion of apprehended youth charged prior to the YOA — experienced a continuous decline in the charge ratio after 1988. The charging of apprehended youth in the other six jurisdictions appears not to have been affected by the YOA.

During the decade after the YOA came into effect, the rate of police-reported youth crime in Canada has increased slightly, but probably not because of the YOA. It has decreased in Ontario, Quebec, and the Yukon, and increased elsewhere. However, the YOA does appear to have caused a substantial increase in the rate of young persons charged in Canada, by causing an increase in the proportion of apprehended youth who are charged — that is, a reduction in the use of police discretion — in some jurisdictions. In other jurisdictions, the rate of young persons charged has also increased, but apparently not because of the YOA. Quebec is the only province in which the rate of young persons charged has declined since 1985.

In its Declaration of Principle, the YOA recognizes the right to the "least possible interference" in the lives of young persons accused of crimes. It encourages the use of informal processing in preference to formal proceedings against young persons. However, Quebec is the only province in which formal charging of apprehended young persons has decreased under the YOA. It is difficult to see how the increase in the laying of charges against young persons in Ontario, Saskatchewan, Prince Edward Island, Nova Scotia, and the Northwest Territories is consistent with the intent of the YOA. The federal government is currently considering changes to the YOA that may encourage more use of police discretion and other innovative alternatives to formal charging. The findings reported in this paper suggest that such measures are needed.

NOTE

1. Editor's note: Omitted here are the technical aspects of how this problem was corrected.

DISCUSSION QUESTIONS

1. Discuss the patterns of youth crime in Canada from 1977 to 1996.
2. How does the advent of the *Young Offenders Act* affect the youth crime rate in Canada? Are all provinces affected in the same way?
3. How is Quebec different from the rest of the country with regard to trends in youth crime? What is the reason for the difference?
4. According to Carrington, does the *Young Offenders Act* result in "the least possible interference" in the lives of young persons accused of crime? What facts help to answer this question?

REFERENCES

Bala, N. (1994). What's wrong with YOA bashing? What's wrong with the YOA? Recognizing the limits of the law. *Canadian Journal of Criminology, 36*(3), 247–270.

Bala, N., & Corrado, R. R. (1985). *Juvenile justice in Canada: A comparative study.* Technical Report TRS No. 5. Ottawa: Solicitor General Canada.

Bala, N., & Mahoney, D. (1994). *Responding to criminal behaviour of children under 12: An analysis of Canadian law & practice.* Ottawa: Department of Justice Canada.

Brantingham, P. J. (1991). Patterns in Canadian crime. In M. A. Jackson & C. T. Griffiths (Eds.), *Canadian criminology.* Toronto: Harcourt Brace Jovanovich, Canada.

Canadian Centre for Justice Statistics. (1994). *Canadian crime statistics 1993.* Ottawa: Canadian Centre for Justice Statistics, Statistics Canada.

Canadian Centre for Justice Statistics. (1995). *Canadian crime statistics 1994.* Ottawa: Canadian Centre for Justice Statistics, Statistics Canada.

Canadian Centre for Justice Statistics. (1996). *Canadian crime statistics 1995.* Ottawa: Canadian Centre for Justice Statistics, Statistics Canada.

Carrington, P. J. (1995). Has violent youth crime increased? Comment on Corrado and Markwart. *Canadian Journal of Criminology, 37*(1), 61–73.

Carrington, P. J. (1996). *Age and youth crime in Canada.* Working Document No. 1996-1e. Ottawa: Department of Justice Canada.

Carrington, P. J. (1998). Changes in police charging of young offenders in Ontario and Saskatchewan after 1984. *Canadian Journal of Criminology, 40*(2), 153–164.

Carrington, P. J., & Moyer, S. (1994). Trends in youth crime and police response, pre- and post-YOA. *Canadian Journal of Criminology, 36*(1), 1–28.

Clark, B. M., & O'Reilly-Fleming, T. (1994). Out of the carceral straightjacket: Under twelves and the law. *Canadian Journal of Criminology, 36*(3), 305–327.

Cook, T. D., & Campbell, D. T. (1979). *Quasi-experimentation.* Boston: Houghton Mifflin.

Corrado, R. R., & Markwart, A. (1992). The evolution and implementation of a new era of juvenile justice in Canada. In R. R. Corrado, N. Bala, R. Linden, & M. LeBlanc (Eds.), *Juvenile justice in Canada.* Toronto: Butterworths.

Corrado, R. R., & Markwart, A. (1994). The need to reform the YOA in response to violent young offenders: Confusion, reality or myth? *Canadian Journal of Criminology, 36*(3), 343–378.

Doob, A. N., & Chan, J. B. L. (1982). Factors affecting police decisions to take juveniles to court. *Canadian Journal of Criminology, 24*, 25–37.

DuWors, R. (1992). *Report on the involvement of children under 12 in criminal behaviour.* Ottawa: Canadian Centre for Justice Statistics, Statistics Canada.

DuWors, R. (1997). The justice data factfinder. *Juristat, 17*(13). Ottawa: Canadian Centre for Justice Statistics, Statistics Canada.

Hackler, J., & Paranjape, W. (1983). Juvenile justice statistics: Mythmaking or measure of system response. *Canadian Journal of Criminology, 25*, 209–226.

Hornick, J. P., Caputo, T., Hastings, R., Knoll, P. J., Bertrand, L. D., Paetsch, J. J., Stroeder, L., & Maguire, A. O. (1996). *A police reference manual on crime prevention and diversion with youth.* Ottawa: Solicitor General Canada.

Hylton, J. H. (1994). Get tough or get smart? Options for Canada's youth justice system in the twenty-first century. *Canadian Journal of Criminology, 36*(3), 229–246.

Kong, R. (1997). Canadian crime statistics, 1996. *Juristat, 17*(8). Ottawa: Canadian Centre for Justice Statistics, Statistics Canada.

LeBlanc, M., & Beaumont, H. (1988). The Quebec perspective on the Young Offenders Act: Implementation before adoption. In J. Hudson, J. P. Hornick, & B. A. Burrows (Eds.), *Justice and the young offender in Canada.* Toronto: Wall and Thompson.

LeBlanc, M., & Beaumont, H. (1992). The effectiveness of juvenile justice in Quebec: A natural experiment in implementing formal diversion and a justice model. In R. R. Corrado, N. Bala, R. Linden, & M. LeBlanc (Eds.), *Juvenile justice in Canada.* Toronto: Butterworths.

Markwart, A., & Corrado, R. R. (1995). A response to Carrington. *Canadian Journal of Criminology, 37*(1), 74–87.

Moyer, S. (1996). *A profile of the juvenile justice system in Canada.* Report to the Federal-Provincial-Territorial Task Force on Youth Justice. Ottawa: Department of Justice Canada.

Scanlon, R. L. (1986). Canadian crime trends. In R. A. Silverman & J. J. Teevan, Jr. (Eds.), *Crime in Canadian society (3rd ed).* Toronto: Butterworths.

Schissel, B. (1993). *Social dimensions of Canadian youth justice.* Toronto: Oxford University Press.

Silverman, R. A. (1990). Trends in Canadian youth homicide: Some unanticipated consequences of a change to the law. *Canadian Journal of Criminology, 32,* 651–656.

Task Force on Youth Justice. (1996). *A review of the Young Offenders Act and the youth justice system in Canada.* Report of the Federal-Provincial-Territorial Task Force on Youth Justice. Ottawa: Department of Justice Canada.

Violence against Women: A Special Topic Survey

HOLLY JOHNSON

INTRODUCTION

Victimization surveys were initially designed to address the need for information about the "dark figure" of crimes not reported to the police and to provide a source of crime statistics that complement the longstanding Uniform Crime Reporting survey of police-reported data. Canada has a history of crime victimization surveys dating back to the late 1970s. However, it gradually became apparent that, while they are proficient at measuring property offences and perceptions of crime, these surveys were not designed to measure the more sensitive kinds of victimizations that primarily affect women, such as wife assault and sexual violence. In attempting to measure a wide variety of crimes, these omnibus surveys did not allow for detailed analysis of all types of violence and threats to women, the emotional and physical consequences, the decisions women make to use support services and their satisfaction with these services, and other detailed information that is necessary to the development of public policy around this issue. Thus, the federal Department of Health commissioned the Violence Against Women survey in recognition of the lack of reliable statistical data on which to test theories and develop policies and programs to address violence against women. Canada's first national survey on male violence against women was conducted by Statistics Canada early in 1993 to address these needs.

The design of this survey evolved out of the tradition of victimization surveys, whereby a random sample of the population is interviewed about their perceptions of crime and their experiences of victimization, and their responses are weighted to represent the population at large. A total of 12 300 women 18 years of age and over across the ten provinces were interviewed for this survey. Random selection helps ensure that those who respond are statistically representative of everyone in the population and that the results can be generalized to the population at large. The Violence Against Women survey differs, however, from traditional victimization surveys, such as Canada's General Social Survey (GSS), the National Crime Survey in the United States, and the British Crime Survey, in important ways. Drawing on his experience with two telephone surveys of women in Toronto, Smith (1994) articulates a number of strategies designed to improve the accuracy of survey data on sensitive subjects such as wife assault and sexual assault. "Violence" in crime surveys is typically defined in legalistic terms through a single question embedded among a series of other crimes. Non-traditional surveys, on the other hand, tend to use broader definitions that "take women's subjective experiences seriously." Smith advocates, for example, the use of multiple measures at different points in the survey to offer many opportunities to respondents to divulge a previously forgotten incident or one that may be painful to recall. He also

Written for this volume. Adapted from the article that appeared in the fifth edition of *Crime in Canadian Society*.

recommends giving greater attention to building rapport between respondents and interviewers through open-ended questions that allow respondents to speak in their own words, and through the careful selection of interviewers.

Smith also criticizes traditional crime victimization surveys for a narrow emphasis on annual victimization rates. The GSS asks respondents about incidents that took place during the twelve months preceding the interview. While twelve-month rates avoid problems of memory recall and are useful for tracking trends over time, they can obscure the scope of the problem. Eighty percent of violent incidents reported to the Violence Against Women survey occurred *before* the twelve months leading up to the survey. Arbitrarily assigning one year as the cutoff point for victim or non-victim status may skew the analysis of correlations and consequences of victimization. Many women designated non-victims may continue to suffer serious consequences of a previous victimization, and the comparison of their responses with those of recent victims may produce misleading results.

Careful testing of survey questions, multiple measures, selection and training of interviewers, and lifetime victimization rates were all incorporated into the design of the survey. In addition, the approach that was developed was particularly sensitive to the constraints that apply to surveying women about their experiences of violence over the telephone in a household setting, including respondent burden, the sensitivity of the information being sought, and the difficulty of responding to questions while the abuser may be present in the home. In discussions with women who had been victims of violence, the survey designers felt strongly that the appropriate approach would take account of the many realities of the women responding, and should be flexible, sensitive, and offer options as to when and where the women would participate.

One unique aspect of the Violence Against Women survey was the extensive consultation process undertaken during the design and development phases. Advice and recommendations on the

methodology and content of the survey were sought through ongoing discussions with a wide variety of experts, academics, government representatives, the police community, shelter workers, counsellors and advocates for battered women, as well as victims of violence seeking support in shelters and sexual assault counselling groups. These groups were instrumental in helping to design question wording that is sensitive, and that respondents can understand as reflective of their experiences. This was accomplished through lengthy discussions over the content of the questionnaire and issues to be addressed, focus group testing of question wording, one-on-one interviews with drafts of the questionnaire, and two large field tests.

A common concern among survey researchers is one of biased results if a large proportion of respondents refuse to participate in the survey or refuse to answer specific questions. There are a number of reasons why a woman may not wish to reveal her experiences to an interviewer over the telephone: she may feel her experience is too personal or painful to discuss; she may be embarrassed or ashamed about it; she may fear further violence from her abuser should he find out; or, she may have forgotten about it if it was minor or happened a long time ago (Smith, 1994). A survey of this nature asks the women responding to disclose the most intimate and perhaps the most troubling details of their lives to a stranger over the telephone. Even more important, from an ethical point of view, researchers must never lose sight of the possibility that with every telephone call the respondent could be living with an abusive man and that her safety could be jeopardized should he learn of the content of the survey. The selection and training of interviewers are critical factors in enabling a relationship of trust to develop between interviewers and respondents, a climate in which respondents feel safe and comfortable enough to discuss their experiences. Another important aspect of the approach developed for this survey, from the point of view of respondents' safety, was to provide options as to when and where they would participate. At the outset of the interview, every woman was provided with a toll-free telephone number that she could use to call back to resume the interview in the event that she had to hang up suddenly. A great many women took advantage of this option. A total of 1000 calls were received on the toll-free line over the five-month period of interviewing, and 150 were women wanting to continue an uncompleted interview that they had had to interrupt or were calling to add additional information to a completed interview. This kind of interest and commitment to the interview process indicates an exceptional level of emotional commitment that this line of questioning can provoke and to which survey researchers must respond. Over one-half of all calls were from women wanting to verify the legitimacy of the survey, many at the point of sensitive questions about violence in their lives. One-quarter wanted more information about the sponsorship of the survey and how they could obtain the results. Many women called to express their appreciation for the opportunity to be involved in the survey and commended the government for taking the issue seriously (see Johnson and Sacco, 1995; and Johnson, 1996 for a more in-depth discussion of the development of this survey).

This chapter presents the results of the Violence Against Women survey as they relate to the prevalence of violence and emotional abuse by marital partners and sexual violence by men other than spouses. But this survey goes beyond quantifying women's experiences of criminal violence. The importance of this survey ties in its ability to put women's experiences of violence into a broader context, taking into account parallels among violence inside and outside the home, threats to women's feelings of security that they experience through sexual harassment, women's fear of victimization, and how women manage threats to their safety in their everyday lives. It allows an elaboration of our understanding of violence against women and the impact it has on their lives. Much recent scholarship recognizes the links between women's experiences of all types of violence and threats to women's personal security in the public and private spheres (Kelly, 1988; Stanko, 1990; DeKeseredy and MacLean,

1990). Criminal violence is only one dimension of a much broader problem manifest in the day-to-day lives of all women. To address only one type of violence, for example, wife assault or specific forms of sexual assault, is to ignore the wider social context in which women routinely feel threatened by male violence. It is to disregard the very real connections between the violence in women's lives by intimates, men they know and trust, perhaps a work colleague, a doctor, or a relative, and men they fear as strangers. Frightening and potentially volatile situations, such as being followed or leered at, with the implied threat of sexual violence, are very threatening experiences that cause women to feel fearful and insecure. These factors play a central role in shaping women's perceptions of their safety, and yet most traditional crime victimization surveys or family violence surveys do not consider them an important component of women's victimization. Some writers have described this range of violent and intimidating behaviours as a "continuum" of violence in women's lives because of the similar effects of these experiences on the female victim (Kelly, 1988; Stanko, 1990). It is this continuum that this survey is attempting to address.

CONSTRUCTING DEFINITIONS OF VIOLENCE

The broad objectives of this survey were to provide reliable statistical information about the extent and the nature of violence against women and women's fear of violence. Definitions of violence against women used in statistical surveys vary widely. They include psychological and emotional abuse, financial abuse, and sexual coercion, as well as physical and sexual assault as legally defined (DeKeseredy and Kelly, 1993; Koss and Gidycz, 1985). The prevalence of "violence" was estimated by this survey using questions based on legal definitions of physical and sexual assault as contained in the Canadian Criminal Code. These strict definitions were necessary in view of the fact that respondents would be asked a series of questions about the actions they took to get help, including reporting to the police, whether the incident resulted in an offender appearing in court, and their satisfaction with the action taken by the police and the courts.

The range of behaviours considered a sexual assault under Canadian law include unwanted sexual touching up to violent sexual attacks with severe injury to the victim. Physical assaults range from face-to-face threat of imminent attack up to and including attacks with serious injury. Sexual violence outside marriage was measured through responses to two questions:

SEXUAL ATTACK ◆ Has a male stranger (date or boyfriend or other man known to you) ever forced you or attempted to force you into any sexual activity by threatening you, holding you down or hurting you in some way?

UNWANTED SEXUAL TOUCHING ◆ Has a male stranger (other man known to you) ever touched you against your will in any sexual way, such as unwanted touching, grabbing, kissing or fondling?

Physical violence by men other than marital partners was measured through the following two questions:

PHYSICAL ATTACK ◆ Now I'm going to ask you some questions about physical attacks you may have had since the age of 16. By this I mean any use of force such as being hit, slapped, kicked or grabbed to being beaten, knifed or shot. Has a male stranger (date or boyfriend or other man known to you) ever physically attacked you?

THREATS OF ATTACK ◆ The next few questions are about face-to-face threats you may have experienced. By threats I mean any time you have been threatened with physical harm since you were 16. Has a male stranger (date or boyfriend or other man known to you) ever threatened to harm you? Did you believe he would do it?

Incidents that involved both sexual and physical attack were counted only once as a sexual assault.

Women were not asked about unwanted sexual touching in dating and marital relationships. While technically these behaviours are legally considered to be crimes, in the testing of the questionnaire the majority of respondents found this concept to be ambiguous and confusing and there was a concern among the survey designers that the responses to these questions would be of questionable validity.

Ten questions were used to measure violence by a marital partner (including legally married and common-law partners), taking account of Smith's advice to offer many opportunities for disclosure in order to overcome hesitancy on the part of the woman responding. Development of these items began with the violence items listed in the Conflict Tactics Scale (CTS) (Straus, 1990). These items were then tested in focus groups of abused women, and two pilot tests were undertaken with random samples of women. A number of modifications were made throughout the testing phase in response to ambiguity in the question wording. The original CTS item "threatened to hit or throw something at you" was altered to read "threatened to hit you with his fist or anything else that could hurt you." Similarly, the item "threw something at you" has been clarified to read "thrown anything at you that could hurt you." The item "hit you with something" now reads "hit you with something that could hurt you." These modifications were made following field testing in which some respondents were clearly confused about whether to include incidents in which they were threatened or hit in a playful way with harmless objects that could not possibly hurt them. The addition of an item on forced sexual activity recognizes the reality of sexual violence in marriage.[1] (The complete list of items is contained in Table 8.2.)

THE PREVALENCE OF VIOLENCE AGAINST WOMEN

According to the Violence Against Women survey, 51 percent of Canadian women have experienced at least one incident of physical or sexual assault since the age of 18 (Table 8.1). Ten percent were victims

Table 8.1

Number and Percentage of Women 18 Years of Age and Over Who Have Been Physically or Sexually Assaulted, by Relationship of Perpetrator

Relationship	Number	Percent
Total	5377	51
Spouse or ex-spouse	2652	29[1]
Date-boyfriend	1724	16
Other known man	2461	23
Stranger	2456	23

[1]Based on the number of women who have ever been married or lived with a man in a common-law relationship.

Numbers expressed in thousands.

Figures do not add to totals because of multiple response.

of violence in the one-year period preceding the survey. Women are at greater risk of violence by men they know than by strangers. Almost one-half of all women (45 percent) have been victimized by men known to them (spouses, dates, boyfriends, family, acquaintances, etc.) while 23 percent have experienced violence by a stranger. These percentages add to more than 51 percent because of the very high number of women who reported violence by both strangers and known men.

Almost four women in ten (39 percent) have been victims of sexual assault (5 percent in a one-year period). One in four women reported unwanted sexual touching, and the same proportion reported a violent sexual attack. A much smaller proportion, 17 percent, have been physically threatened or assaulted by men other than spouses (1 percent in the previous year).

The percentage of women who have been assaulted by a spouse or live-in partner is 29 percent (the one-year rate is 3 percent). Overall, rates of violence in previous marriages were estimated to be 48 percent compared to 15 percent in marriages that were current at the time of the interview. There is a continued risk of violence to women from *ex-partners* despite a divorce or separation. In fact, 19 percent of women assaulted by a previous partner said the man was violent during a period of separation, and in one-third of these cases the violence became more severe during that time.

As Table 8.2 illustrates, the most common forms of violence inflicted on women by marital partners were pushing, grabbing, and shoving; followed by threats of hitting; slapping; throwing something at them; kicking, biting, and hitting with fists. While the percentage of women who have been beaten up, choked, sexually assaulted, or had a gun or knife used against them are all less than 10 percent, in each of these categories, between 400 000 and 800 000 Canadian women have been affected.

Not only do Canadian women report significant levels of violence, a majority of those who have been physically or sexually assaulted have been victimized more than once. The greatest risk of repeat victimization is in the area of sexual violence. Sixty percent of women who have been sexually assaulted by someone other than a spouse reported more than one such incident, and 26 percent were assaulted *four times or more*. Four in ten women who have been violently sexually attacked, and six in ten who reported unwanted sexual touching, said it happened to them more than once.

Women are at risk of sexual violence in a variety of locations and situations. Almost one-half of all sexual assaults (46 percent) occurred in a private place such as the woman's home, the man's home, someone else's home, or in a car. For some, sexual assault is an occupational hazard (10 percent occurred at the woman's place of work) and not an

Table 8.2

Number and Percentage of Ever-Married Women 18 Years and Over Who Reported Violence by a Marital Partner,[1] by Type of Assault

Type of Assault	Number	Percent
Total	2652	29
1. Threatened to hit her with his fist or anything else that could hurt her	1688	19
2. Thrown anything at her that could hurt her	1018	11
3. Pushed, grabbed, or shoved her	2221	25
4. Slapped her	1359	15
5. Kicked, bit, or hit her with his fist	955	11
6. Hit her with something that could hurt her	508	6
7. Beat her up	794	9
8. Choked her	607	7
9. Threatened to or used a gun or knife on her	417	5
10. Forced her into any sexual activity when she did not want to by threatening her, holding her down, or hurting her in some way	729	8

[1]Includes common-law partners.

Numbers expressed in thousands.

Figures do not add to totals because of multiple response.

uncommon risk of being on the street, at a bar or dance, and using public buildings.

In the majority of cases, wife assault is characterized by this survey as ongoing or repeated acts of violence, in which incidents recur and increase in severity over time. Although pushing, grabbing, and shoving was the most commonly reported type of violence, only 5 percent of women said this was the only thing that happened to them, and only 4 percent said they were just threatened. The majority of abused women said they were assaulted on more than one occasion, and one-third were assaulted more than ten times. Men from previous marital relationships were more violent than others. Ten percent of women reporting violence by a current partner said it happened more than ten times, compared to 41 percent of women who were assaulted by a previous partner.

EMOTIONAL ABUSE BY MARITAL PARTNERS

Research shows that a great deal of violence against wives occurs in the context of the man's possessive-

ness, jealousy, and his demands or criticisms over her domestic performance (Dobash and Dobash, 1984; Dobash et al., 1996; Hart, 1988; Walker, 1979). The man's obsessiveness about his wife and his desire to control her have also been cited as precursors to wife killings (Daly and Wilson, 1988; Wilson and Daly, 1992, 1994; Walker, 1979). Emotionally abusive behaviour, therefore, is important contextual information about wife battering. Emotional abuse was measured in this survey through responses to statements about the partner's efforts to jealous guard the woman's contact with other men, to late her from outside support, to control her w abouts, or to degrade her through name-calli put-downs. The percentage of ever-married reporting emotional abuse by a spouse is b the percentage reporting violence: 35 their partner has done one or more of them compared to 29 percent wh physical or sexual violence. Emo used in conjunction with violence violent men: three-quarters of assaulted by a spouse were als A much smaller proporti reported no physical violence by a marital partner were nonetheless emotionally abused.

Obsessive and controlling behaviours feature prominently in serious battering relationships. Emotional abuse is present in the majority of violent relationships, but the frequency of emotionally abusive and controlling behaviours on the part of violent men increases dramatically as the seriousness of the battering increases (Wilson, Johnson, and Daly, 1995). In cases of severe violence by an ex-spouse, emotionally abusive and controlling behaviours were used by 95 percent of abusers. Severe violence was defined as being beaten up or worse or receiving injuries that required medical attention.

For a controlling and abusive man, his partner's pregnancy may represent to him a threat to his exclusive control over her and to her exclusive attention and affection toward him. Overall, 21 percent of women physically or sexually assaulted by a spouse were assaulted during pregnancy. Violence during pregnancy was four times more frequent among women who experienced the most severe forms of violence than among others victimized less severely (33 percent as compared to 8 percent). These findings add important empirical support to theories that explain wife assault as a function of gender relations, male dominance and power, and control in marital relationships.

CORRELATES OF VIOLENT VICTIMIZATION

Sample surveys like the Violence Against Women survey lend themselves to an analysis of the distribution of violent victimization within the population. In other words, it allows us to describe who is at greatest risk of being victimized according to certain social characteristics of Canadian women and men.

Women learn about sexual violence and threats to their safety at a young age. Young women 18 to 24 years of age experienced rates of sexual assault twice that of women in the next age group (25 to 34) and had rates of wife assault that were three times higher. Although characteristics of perpetrators are not shown, the same distinct age effect is evident in men who are violent toward their wives. The rate of wife assault in newer marriages, that is, relationships of two years or less, was almost three times the national average. In addition, there is a fourfold difference in rates of violence reported by women in common-law relationships compared to women in legal marriages.

Other personal characteristics that are associated with age also show up as strong predictors of risk of sexual assault. For example, single women and those with some postsecondary education (the largest proportion of whom are in the youngest age group) report the highest rates of sexual assault. In the case of wife assault, a woman's education has no bearing on her risk, although her partner's education does seem to have an effect: men without a high school education assaulted their wives at twice the rate of men with a university degree. Men who were out of work in the year prior to the survey committed assaults against their wives at twice the rate of employed men.

Contrary to common stereotypes of battered women, household income is not as strong a factor in wife assault as some others (see Lupri, Grandin, and Brinkerhoff, 1994). Women living in households with incomes under $15 000 have rates of wife assault that are twice the national average; however, rates for women in high-income households ($60 000 and over) are the same as rates for women in the middle-income range. Rates of sexual assault also decline slightly as the woman's household income increases, but not markedly.

Witnessing violence in childhood and alcohol abuse are two commonly cited risk factors for wife assault that were found by this survey to be important. Men who witnessed their mothers being abused were up to three times as likely to be violent against their own wives as men who grew up in non-violent homes. Women, too, who were exposed to wife battering were twice as likely to be victims of violence as women from non-violent environments. Rates of violence were five times higher for men who were heavy drinkers compared to non-drinkers, and two to four times higher than for infrequent or moderate drinkers. In addition, the level of the violence inflicted on their wives by men exposed to violence in childhood, and those who are heavy drinkers, tended to be more serious and more frequent.

Rates of violent victimization vary depending on the geographic area in which a woman lives. Women living in urban areas have somewhat higher rates of wife assault and sexual violence; women living in British Columbia and Alberta report the highest provincial rates and Newfoundland women the lowest. It not clear to what extent these provincial differences may be attributed to cultural differences and the willingness or reluctance of the women responding to report their experiences to an interviewer, or whether these are genuine indicators of real differences in the levels of violence against women. The general east-west pattern with rising rates in the western provinces is consistent with police statistics and theories that the greater migration into British Columbia and Alberta results in fewer social controls in these provinces and subsequent increases in criminal activity. Newfoundland, on the other hand, is a province with much higher out-migration and lower in-migration than others, which may produce greater social cohesion and controls against behaving violently. These provincial patterns, together with the relatively weak relationship between wife assault and household income, must cause us to question certain assumptions about the links between poverty and abuse, since Newfoundland, one of the most economically depressed areas of the country, has the lowest rates of violence against women.

Multi-variate analysis allows us to separate out the effects of these individual correlates of violence and to better understand which are the most important. When all these variables are entered into a logistic regression equation, the most important predictor of assaults on wives become verbal abuse and put-downs. Also important are sexual jealousy, efforts to limit her autonomy and contacts with others, the age of the couple, his education, living in a common-law relationship, being in a relationship of short duration, early exposure to violence, and situations where the woman is employed but the man is not. Variables that lose predictive power include household income and heavy drinking.

CONCLUSIONS

The Violence Against Women survey provides empirical evidence about violence against women in Canadian society. Three in ten women who have ever been married or lived with a man in a common-law relationship have experienced violence by a marital partner, and almost four in ten women have been sexually assaulted. A great many women have been victimized more than once.

Violence and the threat of violence are lessons learned early in life. Young women have the highest rates of sexual assault, and young women in new marriages are at greatest risk of violence from their equally young male partners. Common-law marital status elevates the risk of wife assault. The highest rates of wife assault are reported to have occurred in relationships that have ended, quite often from estranged spouses. Emotionally abusive and controlling behaviour is common in men who assault their wives, especially as the severity of the violence escalates.

Some writers would argue that "lifestyle" and "routine activities" are central to developing an explanation of how personal characteristics affect rates of violent victimization. Adherents of this position maintain that victimization rates reflect differences in exposure to risk that result from occupational and leisure activities. To the extent that lifestyle puts people in dangerous places, or out on the street late at night, their risk of victimization will increase. Crime victimization surveys have shown that young people have fewer family responsibilities and a more active lifestyle than older people that allows them to engage in evening activities outside the home. In the context of the lifestyle/routine activities perspective, the higher victimization rates of young women would be explained by the greater likelihood that these women are unmarried, free from family responsibilities, and active in evening activities that put them in close proximity to offenders.

There are problems in attempting to apply the lifestyle/routine activities approach to violent victimization of women, however. As the Violence Against Women survey indicates, women face a greater risk of violence in familiar places by men they know. While lifestyle and routine activities may play a role in stranger attacks, or in understanding sexual assault as an occupational hazard for some women, they cannot account for the very high rate of violence involving intimates. Clearly, a different perspective is necessary to explain the causes of wife assault and dating violence, since the greatest risk factor, according to lifestyle/routine activities, is to be married, dating, or living with a man. This is the "activity" that puts women in close proximity to an offender and at risk of violence. Similarly, in a significant proportion of cases of sexual assault, the risky activity is dating, or having a father, a colleague, or a neighbour. The victim-blaming focus of this perspective when applied to situations of sexual violence and wife assault helps perpetuate negative stereotypes about women who "ask for it" by their appearance or style of dress or who stay with a violent man because somehow they enjoy it. What is needed for a clearer understanding of why so many men use violence in their relationships with women is a focus on the offender and on societal factors that legitimate male dominance over women in so many aspects of life. For example, what is the role of emotional abuse in battering relationships, and how does it keep women from leaving the men who abuse them? What assumptions do men make about the "availability" of young women in particular as acceptable targets for sexual violence? How have the criminal justice system and other helping systems reinforced cultural messages that violence against women will be tolerated? These are the questions and the orientation necessary to tackle the important research issues and policy decisions ahead in the area of violence against women.

NOTE

1. The manner in which the Conflict Tactics Scale is typically introduced to respondents, as a list of ways of settling differences, is problematic: it is potentially very confusing to respondents and not appropriate for orienting them toward thinking about violence they have suffered at the hands of their partners. While some respondents may think about experiences of violence as ways of settling differences, a great many may not, which must cause us to question the reliability and validity of a scale to measure violence that was, in fact, designed to address ways of resolving conflict. There is substantial evidence that many acts of aggression by men against their wives are not precipitated by an argument or disagreement between them, and it is questionable whether respondents would think them appropriate to include. The Violence Against Women survey represents a significant departure from other surveys employing the CTS in that it has an extensive lead-up to questions about spousal violence through detailed questions about fear of violence in public places, precautionary behaviour, sexual harassment, and sexual and physical violence by strangers, dates and boyfriends, and other known men. This survey is concerned not with ways of settling disagreements but with violence against women, and this context will have been established at this point.

Traditional usage of the CTS asks respondents to quantify each violent act or blow, a seemingly impossible task for victims of repeated or ongoing violence. Emphasis throughout the Violence Against Women survey is on the number of different occasions of marital violence, the types of violent acts, and the level of injury and emotional upset suffered by the victim, and not on counting each threat or blow.

DISCUSSION QUESTIONS

1. Discuss the ways in which the Violence Against Women survey differs from other victimization surveys.

2. What proportion of women are victims of violence in Canada? Discuss the most common circumstances under which violence against women takes place.

3. Discuss victim and offender characteristics when violence against women occurs.

4. Discuss the circumstances under which sexual assault takes place.

REFERENCES

Daly, M., & Wilson, M. (1988). *Homicide.* New York: Aldine de Gruyter.

Dekeseredy, W., & Kelly, K. (1993). The incidence and prevalence of woman abuse in Canadian university and college dating relationships. *Canadian Journal of Sociology, 18*(2), 137–159.

Dekeseredy, W., & MacLean, B. (1990). Researching women abuse in Canada: A realist critique of the conflict tactics scale. *Canadian Review of Social Policy, 25,* 19–27.

Dobash, R., & Dobash, R. (1984). The nature and antecedents of violent events. *British Journal of Criminology, 24,* 269–288.

Dobash, R., Dobash, R., Cavanaugh, K., & Lewis, R. (1996). *Research evaluation programmes for violent men.* Edinburgh: Scottish Office.

Hart, B. (1988). Beyond the "duty to warn": A therapist's "duty to protect" battered women and children. In K. Yllo & M. Bograd (Eds.), *Feminist perspectives on wife abuse.* Beverly Hills: Sage.

Johnson, H. (1996). *Dangerous domains: Violence against women in Canada.* Toronto: Nelson Canada.

Johnson, H., & Sacco, V. (1995). Researching violence against women: Statistics Canada's national survey. *Canadian Journal of Criminology, 37*(3), 281–304.

Kelly, L. (1988). *Surviving sexual violence.* Minneapolis: University of Minnesota Press.

Koss, M., & Gidycz, C. (1985). Sexual experiences survey: Reliability and validity. *Journal of Consulting and Clinical Psychology, 53,* 422–423.

Lupri, E., Grandin, E., & Brinkerhoff, M. (1994). Socioeconomic status and male violence in the Canadian home: A reexamination. *The Canadian Journal of Sociology, 19*(1), 47–73.

Smith, M. (1994). Enhancing the quality of survey data on violence against women: A feminist approach. *Gender and Society, 8*(1), 109–127.

Stanko, E. (1990). *Everyday violence: How men and women experience sexual and physical danger.* London: Pandora.

Straus, M. (1990). Measuring intrafamily conflict and violence: The conflict tactics (CTS) scales. In M. Straus & R. Gelles (Eds.), *Physical violence in American families: Risk factors and adaptions to violence in 8,145 Families.* New Brunswick, NJ: Transaction.

Walker, L. (1979). *The battered woman.* New York: Harper Perennial.

Wilson, M., & Daly, M. (1992). Who kills whom in spouse killings? On the exceptional sex ratio of spousal homicides in the United States. *Criminology, 30*(2), 189–215.

Wilson, M., & Daly, M. (1994). Spousal homicide. *Juristat, 14*(8).

Wilson, M., Johnson, H., & Daly, M. (1995). Lethal and nonlethal violence against wives. *Canadian Journal of Criminology, 37*(3), 331–361.

Victim-Offender Relationship and Reporting Crimes of Violence against Women

ROSEMARY GARTNER
ROSS MACMILLAN

INTRODUCTION

In the mid-1970s, a wide-ranging movement to increase public awareness of violence against women emerged in Canada and several other countries. Among this movement's continuing concerns has been the extent to which violence against women fails to come to the attention of legal officials. Feminist activists and researchers have argued that, because women are most likely to be victimized by people they know well and because people victimized by those they know well are less likely to inform authorities, official information on violence against women inevitably underestimates its prevalence and misrepresents its character.

Coincidentally, two developments within the social sciences, one empirical and one theoretical, raised similar questions about gaps in legal awareness of different types of violent behaviours. The empirical development was made possible by victimization surveys, which were initiated in the late 1960s by social scientists concerned with the "dark figure of crime" or that portion of crime not known to criminal justice officials. These surveys provided the first empirical basis for determining whether some types of victimization are less likely than others to be subject to legal intervention. Subsequently, a major theoretical development in the sociology of law (Black 1976) furnished a concep-

tual framework for expecting the relationship between parties involved in violent conflicts to affect whether and what kinds of legal reactions would ensue.

And so, the question of whether legal awareness of violent behaviour varies by the relationship between victim and offender arose simultaneously, albeit for different reasons, in both public and academic arenas. Nevertheless, the concordance between the claims of the violence against women movement and the predictions of Black's theory has yet to find consistent support in the empirical evidence. To date, data from victimization surveys have not shown unequivocally that non-stranger or intimate violence is less likely than stranger violence to come to the attention of legal officials.

In this paper, we examine whether the relationship between female victims of violence and their offenders affects the likelihood of legal awareness of the violence. What distinguishes our examination of this question from previous work is the empirical basis for our analysis: Statistics Canada's Violence Against Women Survey, the most comprehensive survey data set on violence against women currently available. In the sections that follow, we review first the conceptual bases for the claim that non-stranger violence is less subject to legal intervention and, then, the empirical evidence relevant to this claim. We then discuss the limitations of the

Adapted from The Effect of Victim-Offender Relationship on Reporting Crimes of Violence Against Women, by Rosemary Gartner and Ross Macmillan (1995). *Canadian Journal of Criminology*, *37*(3), p. 393–429. Copyright by the Canadian Criminal Justice Association. Reproduced by permission of the *Canadian Journal of Criminology*.

empirical evidence and highlight the characteristics of the VAW Survey that make it uniquely suited to addressing the question. The next section presents a series of analyses that estimate the effects of victim-offender relationship on police knowledge of acts of violence against women. In our conclusion, we discuss the theoretical and practical implications of these findings.

VICTIM-OFFENDER RELATIONSHIP AND DECISIONS TO SEEK LEGAL INTERVENTION

Conceptual Perspectives

A SOCIOLOGICAL FRAMEWORK

Law is not automatically invoked whenever a crime occurs or interpersonal violence erupts. The decision to resort to law, as opposed to using other forms of social control or doing nothing, depends on a variety of factors. In his theory of the behaviour of law, Donald Black (1976) identifies a series of social structural characteristics that, he argues, determine when, how much, and what style of law is used. One of these characteristics is morphology, or "the distribution of people in relation to one another" (Black 1976: 37). Morphology consists of people's networks of interaction, the intimacy of their relationships, and their integration with others. Law is most common where interaction, intimacy, and integration are scarce. Strangers frequently use law to solve their disputes, whereas those who know each other tend not to resort to law. According to Black, this is because other, less formal and less costly forms of social control are more likely to be available to those who know each other.

In subsequent work, Black (1979, 1984) and others (Horwitz 1990) have elaborated on this positive relationship between law and relational distance. Those who know each other should prefer other forms of social control to law for several reasons. Where people interact on a regular basis, where they have close ties to each other, and where they desire the relationship to continue they usually choose more informal means to solve disputes or

deal with harmful behaviours. For example, family members, friends, and neighbours are often called on to intervene in or mediate disputes between people within their networks. In such familiar groups, shared moral sensibilities can be invoked to bring deviants into line. In these settings, not only is law unnecessary, it is also avoided because of its costs. Compared to informal controls, law is more adversarial and punitive; it disrupts close ties, brings private troubles to public attention, and may encourage further vengeful deviance by the punished party.

Anthropological studies of disputes among family and friends provide Black and Horwitz numerous illustrations of these points. Such disputes rarely reach legal attention, according to the framework developed by Black, firstly because they are not defined by the disputants and their networks as either serious enough or appropriate for legal intervention (Black 1980). As Horwitz (1990: 30) states, "offenses that intimates commit do not engender the same degree of moral outrage" as offenses non-intimates commit. People also tend to define their intimate disputes as private matters to be dealt with outside of the public arena of law (Horwitz 1990: 150–151). These definitions of intimate disputes as both less serious and private are shared by outsiders, as well. Legal and other state officials have traditionally avoided involvement in conflicts between family members or close friends (Black 1976: 42; Horwitz 1990: 28–29).

Black's framework is intended as highly general and applicable to the behaviour of all law in a variety of contexts. On the more limited question of when crime victims will contact police, a number of accounts consistent with Black's formulation have been constructed. In these accounts, the victim is a rational decision-maker who calculates the costs and benefits of informing the police (Block 1974; Skogan 1984). For victims who know their offenders, the costs will often include damage to the relationship, potential reprisal by the offender, and public awareness of their private troubles. But even before these costs are calculated, the victim's decision will be influenced — and most strongly influenced —

by the seriousness of the crime. And a substantial amount of research on perceptions of crime seriousness indicates, as Black predicts, that crimes by strangers are perceived by the general public as more serious than crimes by known offenders (Sellin and Wolfgang 1964; MacKinnon 1983).

A FEMINIST FRAMEWORK

Feminist examinations of the systematic under-reporting of violence by non-strangers point to many of the same processes identified in these sociological analyses. Where feminist work differs is in its development of a political analysis in which to situate these processes. Feminist perspectives are at odds with Black's assumption that the behaviour of law can be studied apart from the motivations or interests of individuals and without reference to the purpose, value, or impact of law. Feminist perspectives are also at odds with what are seen as de-gendered and de-contextualized rational choice models of victim decision-making. So, while feminist analysts see the same types of processes working to discourage victims of intimate violence from seeking legal protection, they understand these processes as played out within and structured by relations of domination and subordination — the same relations that encourage or allow male violence toward women.

From a feminist framework, the decreasing chances of legal intervention with increasing intimacy of victims and offenders results from two general processes. First, victims of intimate violence are less likely to define their victimizations as criminal acts. This tendency is not, however, a natural and inherent quality of intimate relations and the conflicts that arise within them, as is implied in some sociological analyses. Rather, it results from a specific construction of knowledge about intimate relations and a more general construction of reality, both of which are male dominated[1] (MacKinnon 1983). Thus, women and men come to view violence by intimates as less serious than violence by strangers, but not because stranger violence is inherently more serious.[2] Women and men come to view intimate relationships as private and (at

least some types of) legal intervention into them as an accusation of failure, a source of embarrassment and shame, and a cause of breakdowns in those relationships. However, even though the belief that violence by strangers is what law exists to control derives not from some innate features of law or interpersonal relations, its acceptance reinforces offenders in their use of violence in intimate settings and victims in their reluctance to invoke the law against intimates who attack them.

Of course, many victims of intimate violence do consider seeking legal intervention — either because they do not believe law is an inappropriate response to intimate violence or because they experience frequent and/or serious violence. In this case, a second process operates to discourage legal help-seeking, according to a feminist perspective. Here, the victim as rational decision-maker re-appears, but her judgements about the costs and benefits of legal intervention are shaped by perceptions of institutional reactions to violence against women, and especially to intimate violence by male partners or relatives. These costs and benefits reflect gender differences in power, not simply inevitable and gender-neutral costs of resorting to the law. Feminist analysts argue that women choose not to call the police because they know (from their own or others' experiences) that they may not be taken seriously, may be blamed for their victimization, may incur the wrath of their victimizer, family, or friends, may not be able to control the legal process once it decides to treat the incident as a "real crime," may lose their home and children, and, ultimately, may not be protected from further violence (Dobash and Dobash 1992; Hanmer, Radford, and Stanko 1989).

In some very important respects, then, the sociological and the feminist frameworks for understanding the effect of the victim-offender relationship on decisions to seek legal intervention differ sharply. The basic prediction derived from them is, however, the same: the more intimate the relationship between a victim of violence and her offender, the less likely the criminal justice system will learn about the violence. Despite this bipartisan consensus over the predicted effects of the victim-offender relationship, the empirical evidence has been far from consistent.

DATA AND METHODS

The Violence Against Women Survey

Statistics Canada's Violence Against Women Survey has several features which make it uniquely suited to examining whether the relationship between a victim and her offender affects a woman's willingness to inform the police. As described by Johnson and Sacco (1995), unlike other victimization surveys, the VAW Survey was designed specifically to elicit information on the full range of violence women experience in all types of relationships. Women reporting incidents of victimization were asked a series of detailed questions about the characteristics of the incident, the effects of the victimization on them, and the actions they took as a consequence of their victimization. Answers to these questions provide data that fulfil most of the prerequisites identified above.

The data we use in our analysis are taken from the sections of the Survey that asked about violence, abuse, and threats by strangers, dates or boyfriends, other known men (Sections C and D), and current and former marital or common-law partners (Sections J and L); and from victimization reports providing detailed information on non-spousal (Section V) and spousal victimization (Section W). The types of non-intimate experiences asked about are sexual assaults (including unwanted sexual activity involving violence or threats of violence, and unwanted sexual touching), physical assaults, and face-to-face threats of physical harm. For intimate violence, an expanded set of questions reflect all types of violence asked in regard to non-intimate violence, except that there were no questions about unwanted sexual by touching by intimates.

Our sample consists of women who acknowledged at least one victimization since the age of 16. Although many of these women reported more than one victimization, detailed data were collected on only one randomly selected incident. Ours is

not, then, a sample of incidents but a sample of victims who provided information (such as whether the police learned of the victimization) on one of what may have been several victimizations they experienced. As the vast majority of our analyses employ non-linear regression, the data are used in an unweighted form.

VARIABLES AND MEASUREMENT

In our analysis, we distinguish among five different types of victim-offender relationship: (1) spouses and ex-spouses (including legal and common-law), (2) dates and boyfriends, (3) relatives, (4) men known through work, friendship, or other means,[3] and (5) strangers. These are more fine-grained categories than the stranger/non-stranger distinction common in much previous research and will allow us to examine variations in reporting to police across categories of known offenders.

To measure police awareness of the violence, we use responses to the question "Did the police ever find out about the incident?" This is a broader question than that typically asked in victimization surveys, which refers to whether the victim reported the incident to the police. It allows for the possibility that third parties or the police themselves may have initiated the legal intervention.[4]

Our interest is in estimating the effect of victim-offender relationship on reporting, independent of characteristics of the incident that might be associated with both. To control for these factors, we include measures of the type and the seriousness of the incident, both of which influence reporting to police, according to previous research (Gove et al. 1985; Lizotte 1985; Skogan 1984). To measure type of incident, we distinguish between physical assaults, sexual assaults, threats, and sexual touching against the victim's will. To control for seriousness of the incident, we include measures of physical injury, psychological impact, theft of property, and weapon use. Physical injury is measured by a six-category scale, in which 1 indicates no physical injury and 6 indicates serious physical injury, such as miscarriage or internal injuries. Psychological impact is measured as a dichotomy, in which 0 indicates no negative consequences and 1 indicates respondents reported one or more negative consequences.[5] Weapon use and theft also are measured as dichotomies.

Ideally, we should control for characteristics of the victim and offender that might be associated with the likelihood of the police learning of the victimization. In some research, victims' income, education, employment status, and marital status[6] have been found to influence reporting to the police, though the effects are not consistent in size or direction across studies (Braithwaite and Biles 1980; Gottfredson and Hindelang 1979; Kennedy 1988; Lizotte 1985; Skogan 1984). However, the VAW Survey measured these characteristics at the time of the interview, but not for the time at which the victimization occurred, which may have been several years or even decades earlier. Therefore, apart from the analysis of victimization and reporting in the year prior to the interview, our analyses cannot control for characteristics of the victims. There is one exception to this: we can control for victim's age at the time of victimization in all of our analyses. Victims' age has been consistently associated with reporting to police in previous research. Older people appear to be more likely to report victimizations to the police (Sacco and Johnson 1990; Skogan 1984; Hindelang 1976). We measure age as a 12-category ordinal variable, with an age range of five years in all but the youngest (ages 18–24) and oldest (ages 75 and older) categories.

PROCEDURES AND ESTIMATION TECHNIQUES

We begin our analysis by cross-tabulating the five victim-offender relationship types with police knowledge of the incident for the total time period and for three different time periods. This analysis parallels the types of bivariate analyses common in the research on reporting to police. Our subsequent analyses of the effects of victim-offender relationship on reporting are multivariate. Because the dependent variable is dichotomous (police either learned about the incident or did not), we use logistic regres-

sion to estimate these models. From the results of the logistic regressions, we derive estimates of the probability that police learned of a victimization for different configurations of predictor variables.

RESULTS OF THE ANALYSES

Descriptive Statistics

Descriptive statistics on victim-offender relationship, type of victimization, seriousness of victimization, and whether the police learned of the incident are presented in Table 9.1. The percentage of cases in each of the victim-offender relationship categories is determined, in part, by the design of the VAW Survey and does not reflect actual percentages of women in the sample experiencing victimizations from each type of relationship.[7] In this sample, about one-third of the victimization experiences we analyze were committed by spouses or ex-spouses and about one-quarter were committed by strangers. The remaining 43% were victimizations by boyfriends or dates, relatives, and other known men. The victimizations included almost equal percentages of sexual assaults, physical assaults, and sexual touching, with threats constituting only a small minority of the incidents. A substantial minority of these victimizations resulted in some form of physical injury or psychological harm. In only a small percentage of incidents was a weapon used or property taken.

Police learned of these victimizations relatively rarely, only about 15% of the time. This figure is, in fact, an over-estimate of police knowledge of victimizations, because of the way in which spousal victimizations and police knowledge of them were measured. Recall that victims of spousal violence spoke generally about their victimization, rather than providing information on a specific incident. In other words, they were not asked if the police learned of a particular incident of spousal violence, but rather if the police ever learned of violence by the victim's spouse or ex-spouse. Most victims of spousal assault (63%), however, reported having been victimized more than once and 30% reported

Table 9.1

Respondents Reporting Any Victimization since Age 16, Violence Against Women Survey (N = 6023)

Characteristics of victimizations	Percentage	N
VICTIM-OFFENDER RELATIONSHIP		
Spouse, ex-spouse	31	1867
Date or boyfriend	17	1024
Relative	5	301
Work, friend, other	21	1265
Stranger	26	1566
TYPE OF VIOLENCE		
Sexual assault	29	1747
Touched against will	30	1807
Threatened	9	542
Physical assault	31	1867
SERIOUSNESS OF INCIDENT		
Physical injury scale (0–6)[a]	21 (1.34)	1291
Psychological harm	39	2349
Weapon used	4	241
Theft of property	2	120
POLICE LEARNED OF VICTIMIZATION	15	897

[a] Figure in parentheses represents the mean on the physical injury scale.

four or more victimizations by their spouses. An affirmative response could mean the police learned of only one of many incidents of spousal violence. For spousal violence, then, the denominator for calculating the percentage known to police is women who experienced spousal violence, not incidents of spousal violence. It is not strictly comparable to the figures for other types of victim-offender relationships, which are calculated on the basis of a single incident for each woman. The effect of this difference in the calculation of spousal victimizations known to police and other victimizations known to the police can be seen in Table 9.2.

Multivariate Results

The goal of the multivariate analyses is to determine if the bivariate relationships we observed

Table 9.2

Proportion of Victimizations Known to Police by Victim-Offender Relationship

Victim-offender relationship	All incidents: Percent known to police
Spouse	23.7 (442)
Date/boyfriend	9.2 (96)
Relative	11.5 (36)
Work/other	5.5 (69)
Stranger	17.8 (268)

Table 9.3

Logistic Regression Equations for Victimizations Known to Police, All Incidents (N = 5919)

Variable	Equation 1	Equation 2	Equation 3	Equation 4
Age group	.0187 (.0030)***	.0092 (.0033)***	.0096 (.0033)***	.0104 (.0036)***
Spouse		.2991 (.0905)***	−.4997 (.1105)***	−.3477 (.1247)***
Date/boyfriend		−.7223 (.1272)***	−1.4766 (.1356)***	−1.4095 (.1485)***
Relative		−.4923 (.1898)***	−.7344 (.1978)***	−.7334 (.2147)***
Work/other		−1.3157 (.1414)***	−1.0780 (.1476)***	−.9605 (.1559)***
Sexual assault			−.1241 (.0956)	−.0888 (.1006)
Touched against will			−2.2172(.1644)***	−1.6263 (.1725)***
Threatened			.1120 (.1301)	.7254 (.1447)***
Psychological impact				.5914 (0817)***
Physical injury				.4546 (.0322)***
Theft of property				1.6646 (.2161)***
Weapon used				1.3678 (.1718)***
Intercept	−2.2726 (.0995)***	−1.7820 (.1135)***	−.9729 (.1396)***	−2.3951 (.1665)***
Model chi–square	37.927***	256.7840***	556.9880***	1039.1670***
Improvement		218.857***	300.204***	482.179***
Pseudo–R^2	0.01	0.05	0.12	0.20

NOTE: Standard errors of the logistic regression coefficients appear in parentheses.

* p < .10 ** p < .05 *** p < .01

between victim-offender relationship and reporting to police can be accounted for by characteristics of the victimization or of the victim.

The results of this analysis are shown in Table 9.3. Equation 1 indicates that victimizations of older women were significantly more likely to become known to the police, a finding consistent with prior research. Equation 2 estimates the effects of different types of victim-offender relationships on reporting to police, controlling for this age effect. As the bivariate analysis in Table 9.2 would lead us to expect, each type of known-offender victimization, except spouse victimizations, was significantly less likely than stranger victimizations to become known to the police. Victimizations by spouses, in contrast, appear to be significantly more likely than victimizations by strangers to become known to police when characteristics of the victimization are not taken into account. Although the

effects of all the variables in Equation 2 are highly significant, the pseudo-R^2 indicates that only a small proportion of the variance in police knowledge of victimization is explained by this relatively simple model.[8]

The remaining two equations estimate the effects of victim-offender relationship controlling for characteristics of the victimization. Equation 3, which adds the dummy variables for type of victimization, shows that sexual assaults and threats are about as likely as physical assaults (the excluded category) to become known to the police, whereas touching against the victim's will is significantly less likely to become known to the police. Introducing these variables significantly improves the model's fit and increases the explained variance. Most important for our purposes, when controlling for the type of incident, all four types of known-offender victimizations are now significantly less likely than stranger victimizations to become known to the police. In other words, the positive coefficient for spouse victimizations in Equation 2 is solely due to the fact that spouse victimizations are more likely to be physical assaults and physical assaults tend to come to police attention more often than other types of victimization. Once we control for type of incident, we find the expected negative and significant effect of victimization by spouses.

The final equation (Equation 4) introduces our measures of the seriousness of the victimization. As expected, the coefficient for each measure of seriousness is positive and highly significant, indicating that incidents that involve physical and psychological harm, economic loss, or the use of a weapon are much more likely to become known to the police. At the same time, controlling for these characteristics does not alter the effects of victim-offender relationship. In other words, the lower probabilities of known-offender victimizations becoming known to the police cannot be explained by differences in their seriousness or type from stranger victimizations. The final equation, which significantly improves the fit of the model, explains approximately 15% of the variance in the dependent variable.

Consistent with the predictions of sociological perspectives and feminist perspectives, then, we find that police are much less likely to be informed when women are victimized by intimates and other known men than when women are victimized by strangers.

CONCLUSION

Summary of Findings

This study has demonstrated that criminal justice knowledge of violence against women is systematically biased. While all such violence is underreported to police, violence by known offenders is much less likely to come to the attention of authorities than is violence by strangers. This finding is consistent with expectations derived from both sociological and feminist perspectives on the behaviour of law.

The study also found evidence suggestive of a change in this pattern over time. While intimate violence (i.e., violence by spouses and dates) was significantly less likely than stranger violence to be reported in all time periods, in recent years, differences in the reporting of violence by strangers and violence by less intimate known offenders (e.g., coworkers, friends, and relatives) appear to have diminished. This finding, too, is consistent with the aims of many feminist activists and with the predictions of some sociologists of law. One of the goals of many feminist activists has been to criminalize a fuller range of violence against women, especially violence by men known to their victims. If our tentative finding is correct, it suggests their efforts may have achieved a first step in this direction by reducing the differences in criminal justice system awareness of stranger and non-stranger violence.

A reduced reluctance to bring violence between people who know each other to legal attention would also fit with the expectations of sociologists of law working within Donald Black's (1976) theoretical framework. According to this framework, "growing individualism, declining interdependence, and the expansion of organization foreshadow basic changes in social control systems" (Horwitz 1990: 242). These social changes are reflected in changing definitions of intimacy. Relations between friends, family, and intimate partners have become "more like contractual agreements between sovereign individuals" (Horwitz 1990: 153); similarly, women have become less dependent on their husbands as egalitarianism in marital relationships has increased. Consequently, when violence by men known to their victims occurs, victims and their supporters should now feel less hesitant to seek legal intervention (Black 1980: 124–128). This is what our analysis suggests may have happened over the last several years in Canada.

Reasons for Not Informing Police

One limitation of our study is that our analysis does not link the patterns of (and potential changes in) under-reporting we describe to the processes by which victims and others decide whether to contact police. Without a detailed analysis of why respondents did or did not contact legal authorities, we cannot say whether their decisions actually reflect the processes outlined in feminist and sociological perspectives. The VAW Survey did ask women who did not inform the police why they chose not to do so and we examined the distributions of these responses for different victim-offender relationships. This very simple comparison did not, however, reveal strong and consistent differences in the reasons victims of intimate and stranger violence did not report. For example, contrary to the expectations of feminist and sociological perspectives, victims of spouse violence were not substantially more likely than victims of stranger violence to say they did not report because they were ashamed (7% of stranger victims and 6% of spouse victims), thought they would not be believed (4% of stranger victims and 2% of spouse victims), wanted to keep the matter private (7% of stranger victims and 9% of spouse victims), did not want the offender arrested (1% of stranger victims and 3% of spouse victims), or did not want to get involved with the police and court system (6% of stranger victims and 7% of spouse victims). For victims of both spouse and stranger victimizations, the major reasons given for non-reporting were that the incident was too minor (51% of stranger victims and 55% of spouse victims), they did not want any help (10% of both groups), or the police could not do anything about the incident (12% of stranger victims and 7% of spouse victims).[9]

Our examination of these reasons is admittedly too crude for drawing definitive conclusions. More sophisticated analysis would be needed to determine if there are systematic, significant differences in reasons for not reporting by victim-offender relationship, but such an analysis is beyond the scope of this paper. Ideally, such analysis would draw on more detailed information on the various decisions about help-seeking women make after being victimized. Too often, the decision to contact police has been studied in isolation from the numerous ways in which people react to violence. And too often, a decision not to contact police is assumed to mean that the victim failed to take positive action to end the violence. But we know from some research that many women devise ingenious strategies when faced with violence by men they know, strategies that often accomplish the women's goals without invoking legal action (Bowker 1983; Gordon 1988; Hoff 1990). It is important for future research to devise methods to understand the processes by which women make these choices, rather than relying solely on methods that reduce these choices to discrete, easily categorized, and often unrealistically simplified outcomes.

Implications for Criminological Research

Our study reinforces admonitions expressed by many criminologists about analyzing data from victimization surveys and official sources. Both conventional victimization surveys and official statistics on crime undercount violence by known offenders to a greater degree than violence by strangers. Victimization surveys, as they have typically been conducted, therefore are not the panacea for biases in official statistics they were initially envisaged to be. Consequently, results of research based on existing large-scale victimization surveys need to be evaluated and interpreted in light of this systematic undercounting of some types of violence and crime. Research based on official statistics should also consider the possibility that changes in the official rate of certain crimes may reflect changes in victims' willingness to report crimes by persons known to them.

At the same time, the success of the VAW Survey at capturing a fuller range of violence by known offenders offers hope to researchers pessimistic about the future of large-scale victimization surveys. Such surveys can be designed and implemented to provide knowledge about many forms of violence that previously remained hidden not from just legal officials, but from researchers as well.

NOTES

1. From a feminist perspective, Black's (1976: 9) assertion that "the seriousness of a deviant act is defined by the quantity of social control to which it is subject" begs the question of what or who determines the quantity of social control and, hence, the seriousness of a deviant act.

2. Indeed, studies show that female victims of intimate violence report as much or more trauma as female victims of stranger or acquaintance violence (Lurigio and Resick 1990; Maguire and Corbett 1987; Russell 1990; Shields and Hanneke 1987).

3. This category includes a varied range of relationships, including doctors, clergy, landlords, teachers, students, neighbours, and other acquaintances.

4. For case of presentation, we sometimes use the term "reported to police" when referring to our measure. Readers should keep in mind that the measure encompasses various ways in which the police might have learned about the incident.

5. The types of negative psychological impacts reported included depression, anxiety attacks, guilt, lowered self-esteem, sleeping problems, and problems relating to men. We considered measuring psychological impact with factor scores, but a factor analysis of responses did not yield a meaningful factor structure. We also constructed a measure that added the number of different negative impacts reported by respondents. This and the dichotomous measure performed similarly in all of our analyses.

6. Victim's race has also been found to influence reporting to police in some research, though the effects are not consistent. Because the VAW Survey does not include a measure of race or ethnicity, we cannot control for it in any of our analyses.

7. A large number of women reported multiple victimizations by both strangers and known offenders. However, in the survey they were asked detailed questions about only one of these victimizations, which was chosen randomly from among the incidents they reported.

8. The pseudo-R^2 is calculated using the formula: $R^2 = L.R. / (N + L.R.)$, where L.R. is the likelihood ratio value for the equation and N is the sample size.

9. Of course, if feminist claims about male-dominated knowledge construction are correct, the reasons women give for not reporting to the police cannot be taken as evidence challenging (at least some) feminist explanations for the greater under-reporting of more intimate violence.

DISCUSSION QUESTIONS

1. This article argues that criminal justice knowledge of violence against women is biased. Explain.

2. Discuss the variables that affect the reporting of violence against women to the police.

3. Compare and contrast the feminist and the sociological frameworks for examining the effect of victim-offender relationship.

4. This article and Chapter 8 use the special survey on violence against women for their data source. Using these articles and the introduction to this section discuss the value of special victimization surveys.

REFERENCES

Black, D. (1976). *The behavior of law*. New York: Academic Press.

Black, D. (1979). Common sense in the sociology of law. *American Sociological Review, 44*, 18–27.

Black, D. (1980). *The manners and customs of the police*. New York: Academic Press.

Black, D. (1984). Social control as a dependent variable. In D. Black (Ed.), *Toward a general theory of social control*. New York: Academic Press.

Block, R. (1974). Why notify the police? The victim's decision to notify the police of an assault. *Criminology, 11*, 555–569.

Bowker, L. (1983). *Beating wife-beating*. Lexington, MA: D.C. Heath.

Braithwaite, J., & Biles, D. (1980). Empirical verification and Black's Behavior of Law. *American Sociological Review, 45*, 334–338.

Currie, D. (1990). Battered women and the state: From the failure of theory to the theory of failure. *Journal of Human Justice, 1*, 77–96.

Dobash, R. E., & Dobash, R. P. (1992). *Women, violence, and social change*. London: Routledge.

Fineman, M. A. (1994). Preface. In M. A. Fineman & R. Mykitiuk (Eds.), *The public nature of private violence*. New York: Routledge.

Gottfredson, M. R., & Hindelang, M. J. (1979). A study of The Behavior of Law. *American Sociological Review, 44*, 3–18.

Gordon, L. (1988). *Heroes of their own lives: The politics and history of family violence in America*. New York: Viking.

Gove, W. R., Hughes, M., & Geerken, M. (1985). Are UCRs a valid indicator of the index crimes? An affirmative answer with minor qualifications. *Criminology, 23*, 451–501.

Hanmer, J., Radford. J., & Stanko, E. A. (1989). *Women, policing, and male violence*. London: Routledge.

Harlow, C. W. (1991). *Female victims of violent crime*. Washington, DC: Bureau of Justice Statistics, U.S. Department of Justice.

Hindelang, M. J. (1976). *Criminal victimization in eight American cities*. Cambridge, MA: Ballinger.

Hindelang, M. J., & Gottfredson, M. R. (1976). The victim's decision not to invoke the criminal justice process. In William McDonald (Ed.), *Criminal justice and the victim*. Beverly Hills: Sage.

Hoff, L. A. (1990). *Battered women as survivors*. London: Routledge.

Horwitz, A. V. (1990). *The logic of social control*. New York: Plenum.

Jensen, G. F., & Karpos, M. (1993). Managing rape: Exploratory research on the behavior of rape statistics. *Criminology, 31*, 363–387.

Kennedy, L. (1988). Going it alone: Unreported crime and individual self-help. *Journal of Criminal Justice, 16*, 403–412.

Kincaid, P. J. (1982). *The omitted reality: Husband-wife violence in Ontario and policy implications for education*. Maple, ON: Learners Press.

Lizotte, A. (1985). The uniqueness of rape: Reporting assaultive violence to police. *Crime and Delinquency, 31*, 169–190.

Lurigio, A. J., & Resick, P. (1990). Healing the psychological wounds of criminal victimization: Predicting post-crime distress and recovery. In A. J. Lurigio, W. G. Skogan, & R. C. Davis (Eds.), *Victims of crime: Problems, policies, and programs*. Newbury Park, CA: Sage.

MacKinnon, C. (1983). Feminism, Marxism, method, and the state: Toward a feminist jurisprudence. *Signs: Journal of Women in Culture and Society, 8*, 635–658.

MacLeod, L. (1987). Battered but not beaten: Preventing wife battering in Canada. Ottawa: Canadian Advisory Council on the Status of Women.

Maguire, M., & Corbett, C. (1987). *The effects of crime and the work of victim support schemes*. Aldershot: Gower.

Mahoney, M. R. (1994). Victimization or oppression? Women's lives, violence, and agency. In M. A. Fineman and R. Mykitiuk (Eds.), *The public nature of private violence*. New York: Routledge.

Rouse, L. P., Breen, R., & Howell, M. (1988). Abuse in intimate relationships: A comparison of married and dating college students. *Journal of Interpersonal Violence, 3*, 414–429.

Russell, D. E. H. (1990). *Rape in marriage*. Bloomington: Indiana University Press.

Sacco, V. F., & Johnson, H. (1990). *Patterns of criminal victimization in Canada*. Ottawa: Statistics Canada.

Sacco, V. F., & Johnson, H. (1995). Researching violence against women: Statistics Canada national survey. *Canadian Journal of Criminology, 37*(3), 281–429.

Schneider, E. (1994). The violence of privacy. In M. A. Fineman & R. Mykitiuk (Eds.), *The public nature of private violence*. New York: Routledge.

Sellin, T., & Wolfgang, M. E. (1964). *The measurement of delinquency*. New York: Wiley.

Sherman, L. W. (1992). *Policing domestic violence: Experiments and dilemmas*. New York: Free Press.

Shields, N., & Hanneke, C. (1987). Comparing the psychological impact of marital and stranger rape. Paper presented at the National Council for Family Violence and Researchers, Durham, New Hampshire.

Silverman, R. A. (1992). Street crime. In V. F. Sacco (Ed.), *Deviance: Conformity and control in Canadian society*. Scarborough: Prentice-Hall.

Skogan, W. (1984). Reporting crimes to the police: The status of world research. *Journal of Research in Crime and Delinquency, 21*, 113–137.

Smart, C. (1989). *Feminism and the power of law*. London: Routledge.

Stanko, E. (1988). Hidden violence against women. In M. Maguire & J. Pointing (Eds.), *Victims of crime: A new deal?* Milton Keynes: Open University Press.

Williams, L. (1984). The classic rape: When do victims report? *Social Problems, 31*, 459–467.

Worrall, A., & Pease, K. (1986). Personal crimes against women: Evidence from the 1982 British Crime Survey. *The Howard Journal, 25*, 118–124.

Assault Stories

ERIN VAN BRUNSCHOT

Editor's Note: The following is an excerpt from a larger study of assault (Van Brunschot, 1997). We have eliminated most of the theoretical context for these "stories." The study is based on police data, and while these have limitations, they also provide rich detail on events that make up criminal statistics. This approach is included so that readers can compare this level of detail with the information from official sources discussed earlier. The larger study is currently being prepared for journal publication.

INTRODUCTION

The increased interest in violence in recent years has focused attention on its extreme forms, on homicide, rape, and aggravated assault, crimes considered to be the most harmful and threatening to the public. They attract a great deal of attention from the media and from academic researchers, yet we know from official statistics and from victim surveys that these extreme forms of harm constitute a small proportion of the overall violence occurring in society. The majority of violent crime is of a less serious nature, involving minor assault and threatening behavior. These crimes of assault have not received the same attention as the more serious crimes even though we know from homicide research that many murders begin as minor altercations, arguments, and assaults (Kennedy, 1990). Looking for the keys to understanding violence, then, requires that we pay closer attention to assault.

ELABORATING ROUTINE ACTIVITIES THEORY TO EXPLAIN ASSAULT

In explaining how individuals become involved in assaultive exchanges, routine activities theory provides an excellent starting point when it makes the intuitive point that lifestyles of individuals leave them more or less vulnerable to involvement in criminal activity (Hindelang, Gottfredson, and Garofalo, 1978). Although routine activities theory has tended primarily to be a theory of victimization (in assuming a motivated offender), it also, as we later demonstrate, serves equally well as a starting point for a routine activities approach to offending. Routine activities theory incorporates dimensions of time and space by suggesting that the routinized activities of individuals either increase or decrease the probability of the convergence of three necessary components of criminal activity — a vulnerable victim, a motivated offender and lack of suitable guardianship (Cohen and Felson, 1979). Individuals are more likely to be perceived as vulnerable victims by motivated offenders depending upon their routine daily activities. Similarly, individuals may or may not be motivated to offend depending upon whether they regularly come into contact with vulnerable victims.

Routine activities theory suggests that the occurrence of criminal activity may be more or less likely depending on the spatial and temporal

Written for this volume.

convergence of elements in the daily paths to which participants in crime adhere. We conduct ourselves in routine ways, not only by way of our time-tabled activities, but also by way of modes of conduct and interpretation that we use within a range of situations that we have either previously encountered, or might reasonably expect to encounter, throughout the course of our days.

In the analysis that follows, we illustrate our model by examining police files of assault cases. As Barley (1986) suggests, we first elucidate the links between action and structure through a series of encoding which begins by considering the actions of individuals involved in specific assault cases. We then reduce these actions to "generic scripts" (Barley, 1986) or routine practices. Routine practices in the context of assault are identified by considering Luckenbill and Doyle's (1989) situated transactions. These authors suggest that there are specific behaviors that cause individuals to become upset with one another and that individuals employ routine methods of dealing with these upsetting behaviors. As per Barley's (1986) suggestion that routines accompany various phases or stages of interaction, we consider the routines implicit in a situated transaction analysis of conflict leading to assault.

The second part of our strategy involves an examination of how it is that individuals interpret and account for their involvement in assault. It is at this stage that we identify accounts that bolster and support interpretations of involvement as consisting of victims and offenders. Within the context of conflict, behavior tends to be interpreted as conforming to the social categories of either victim or offender. Individuals interpret their participation in events informally labelled as "conflict," and formally labelled as "criminal," by accounting for their behavior in these terms. We refer to these strategies as "routine accountability." Within the context of a formally labelled situation, individuals use routine accounting devices that support their interpretation of events and the roles they played within that event as victims or offenders. Within the context of conflict, we suggest that individuals "do" conflict

according to the implicit categories of conflict in routine ways, both from the context of the present (routine practice) and from the context of the future (routine accountability). The identification of routines transgresses the boundaries of the immediate situation, and serves the purpose of locating the general (i.e., social categories of offender and victim) within the specific.

Prior to illustrating the means by which action and structure are linked through routine practices and routine accountability, we first consider how the data for the present study were gathered.

THE STUDY

The research reported here is based on findings from a study of assault conducted in a mid-sized Canadian city using police files. The data allow for the investigation of assault from one source which is also comprehensive in the perspectives found within assault situations — including victim, offender and bystander. In the Canadian context, assaults are categorized by police into three Criminal Code sections: aggravated assault (Level Three), assault causing bodily harm (Level Two) and common assault (Level One). For the city under consideration, approximately 200 aggravated assaults, 2000 Level Two assaults, and 4500 common assaults were recorded for the calendar year 1993. Random samples of each of the lower levels of assault are included for consideration and all aggravated assault cases are included in the analysis. The total sample size is 745.

FINDINGS

Routine Practices

Luckenbill's early (1977) work on homicide as a situated transaction fits well with our focus on routine, as he suggests that not only are there specific stages to conflict, but also that there are standardized, routine responses within these stages. Luckenbill and Doyle (1989) suggest that there are three stages to conflict leading to violence: naming, claiming and aggressing. In their analysis of the naming, claiming and aggressing sequence, Kennedy and Forde (1998) define naming as the degree of upset that an individual feels in response to a particular action perpetrated by an interacting other (or others). Unlike Kennedy and Forde's research, which employed scenarios, the data available to us here prevent assessing the "degree of upset" an individual felt in response to a particular action. We cannot tell the degree of upset from an individual's actions or words, although we might assume that an individual who punched in response to some initiating action was more upset than an individual who demanded an apology. Rather than degree of upset, however, the significance of these behaviors for our purposes is that they changed the interaction from one of a non-conflict to a conflict situation.

We investigate routine practices by first considering the behaviors that served to ignite conflict and draw forth a particular routine practice. Luckenbill (1977) suggests that there are six actions that serve to upset: verbal insults; direct verbal expressions; refusals to cooperate/comply; refusals to conciliate relationships/misunderstandings; refusals to comply with sexual requests; and physical or non-verbal gestures. We apply these categories to our investigation of assault to illustrate that despite the variety of conditions under which assaults occur, as well as the more limited initiating actions which precede assault, individuals respond in more limited, routine ways. The routine practices described below are differentially invoked depending on the features of the context to which the interactants attend. Similar situations may produce very different responses depending upon the salience of certain contextual features for those involved. Not only, for example, does physical location influence routine responses, but so too does the relationship of the parties involved and the number of bystanders, which may serve either to reduce or aggravate the upset felt by the offended party. Below, we divide our analysis into six sections, each of which represent an "upsetting behavior," to consider the ways in which routine practices are used to counter these behaviors across a variety of contexts.

Each of the 745 assault incidents was examined to determine specifically what happened — what each participant said and did while in each other's physical presence. It was determined that adequate information existed to code 395 of the 745 cases. Of the 395, 287 cases are examples of "Luckenbill cases" with the transaction initiated by an action of the victim. Seventy-nine (of 395) cases were offender-initiated, while the remaining 29 cases were those in which the assault event was tangential to another criminal event, such as robbery, theft or break and enter, and were excluded from this analysis. Wherever possible, we make use of verbatim witness statements (including grammatical and spelling errors) to illustrate context, upsetting/initiating acts and routine practices.

It is important to emphasize that this study is intended to illustrate, rather than test, the means by which action and structure are linked through routine practices to behavioral cues (upsetting behaviors) that appear to initiate and precede subsequent conflict. Our undertaking here is illustrative primarily because of the fact that we consider only events in which assault is indeed the outcome of routine responses to upsetting behaviors. The nature of police data is such that only cases resulting in a crime (in our case, assault) are included.

(1) VERBAL INSULTS

As per Luckenbill's (1977) operationalization of verbal insults, this category is broad, in that it contains a range of remarks interpreted as offensive by the eventual offender in the transaction. These remarks include insults directed toward the offended party's self, family or friends, "to verbal tirades which disparaged the overall character of the offender" (Luckenbill, 1977: 179), to allegations of spreading rumors. The routine practice with which an insult is countered depends upon the context or domain in which it occurs. In the following example, the assault took place in a parking lot of a bank in a downtown area. The offending individual asked the accused to move his truck so that he could get into his vehicle. The two parties are strangers and there appears to be no one else in the immediate general vicinity.

. . . He got out of the truck looking frustrated and I thanked him and said you Don't have to Be a Asshole about it. He stopped appx. 1 ft from his truck and said Did you call me a asshole. I said yes, Don't Be a Asshole about this, as I couldn't get in. He said don't call me a asshole, I said well ok, But Don't Be a Asshole and what's your problem and Don't Be a Asshole. Then he struck me. [#42975, complainant]

The offended party reacts to the stranger calling him an "asshole," and a routine practice is invoked. In this case, the offended party advises the complainant to stop calling him names. Whether compliance at this point on the part of the complainant would have averted the complainant from actually being struck is speculative, although suggestive. Instead, the complainant does not comply and the accused hits him.

The next example suggests a different routine practice associated with a verbal insult and takes place in a much different realm, the home. The offender and complainant are daughter and mother, respectively. The daughter also reacts to her mother's comments (and hitting), but rather than asking her to stop, as in the previous case, she goes to the kitchen and gets a knife.

I left my brother to look after my kids, but he left shortly after I did. When I got home in the morning, my mom was crazy, she was yelling that she was going to send my kids to the welfare, she is always saying that. She said I was an unfit mother. She started hitting me in face. She pushed me too far. I went and got one of my knifes and I stabbed her. I didn't mean to hurt my mom. [#40842, accused]

(2) DIRECT VERBAL EXPRESSIONS

Direct verbal expressions include both verbal statements and requests which cause a party to take offense. Unlike the above insults or derogatory remarks which involve a personal attribute of the offended party, these verbal expressions focus more on generalized activities that another may be engaging in. The following example is a definitive Luckenbill assault. First, a witness asks the offended party to turn around, the offended party responds, and then the complainant asks the offended party what his problem is. In response to the witness, the offended party responds with a verbal comment, and then responds by leaving the premises — a physical gesture.

. . . Within the next 20 min. he had been staring at us and bothering us so I turned to him and said "would you mind turning around because he was annoying us". Then he came back with "Fuck you all I came in here was for a beer and listen to the music so fuck off!" My boyfriend CO turned to him and said "Do you have a problem?" Then the guy in question finished his beer and left. The next thing I know the other guy came back and hit CO in the head with 3/4″ pipe and took off out the door. My friend ran out after him over to the next apartment block while CO started having convulsions and started to black out. [#3081, witness]

In the following example, the complainants (2) had been drinking with their friends at a bar, celebrating a friend's birthday. The complainant suggests that he was drunk, as were his friends.

After a few minutes we turned to face the [bar]. Upon turning I notice a group of 5 to 6 people standing to our Left. Next I noticed one of the members of this group stepped past us starring without looking away once. As he completed his walk he stood to our right about 10′ away. I then said, "what are you staring at?" "Do you have a problem?" Which he replied, "The only problem I have is I'm staring at a couple of Losers." At this point I was struck from behind. [#59736, complainant]

Although the accused was the party initially staring in both of the above instances, the complainant's offending actions appear to have initiated the conflict, as the complainant's actions changed the nature of the interaction which was peaceful up to that point, staring or not. The response to the complainant's direct verbal expression is a verbal comment in kind but with little opportunity for reciprocation, as the comment is immediately followed by physical contact.

(3) REFUSAL TO COOPERATE/COMPLY

The largest category consists of the offending party's refusal to cooperate or comply with a request, demand or suggestion of the offended party. This category is obviously broad, and as one might expect, the demand or suggestion the offending party is refusing to comply or cooperate with varies greatly both between and within contexts. In the first example below, the offended and offending party are both on-shift cab drivers who are strangers to each other. It is late afternoon, and the precipitating event occurs on the street, which for cab-drivers, is a work domain.

> . . . about 4:45 I was droping a customer at [address] while i droping or offloading my customer at service road, the above mentioned address a car stopped behind me while he was horning to loud. After he understand that I am not pay any attention, he came out from his car came to my cab, and started insulting and dropped his drinks on me. [#43378]

The request, indicated by the horn blowing, was for the offending party to move. The offending party did not comply with the request; therefore the offended party invoked a routine consisting of verbal insults, accompanied by the physical action of dropping his drink upon the offending party.

> On or about 5:00 PM today, I came home with my mother. Shortly after my brother [accused] came home and demanded eighty cents from my mother. She refused and he proceeded to roll pennies. He was six cents short, but I refused to give him it. He then went into my room and just grabbed pennies off of my dresser. Both my mother and I demanded he put it back, because he does nothing to deserve it. He put up a struggle

when I tried to physically take it form him. He layed on my bed and started to kick me. [#59818, complainant]

The next example is of an assault that takes place within the confines of a correctional institution. The offended and offending parties appear to be acquaintances, as suggested by the complainant's ability to identify his assailant(s) by name.

> . . . I was in my cell which was [##]. I was just about to walk out of my cell and two guys pushed me back in. One of the guys, [Accused1], told me they were collecting for a debt that I owed. [Accused1] told me that I owed a "bail of weed" (pouch of tobacco) to [name]. I said, "heh, I gave him one last canteen". [Accused1] said that was bullshit. [Accused1] punched me in the head. After I got punched in the head I sat down on the bottom bunk and they both grabbed each of my legs and pulled me onto the floor. They then started to kick and punch me. I kept telling them to stop and they said that they would stop when they got a bales worth. [#127159, complainant]

The complainant refused to comply with the request that he pay the debt owed to a third party. The accused, acting on behalf of the person to whom money is owed, verbally commented on the complainant's assessment of the debt, "bullshit," and then proceeded to assault the offending party.

(4) REFUSAL TO CONCILIATE RELATIONSHIP/ MISUNDERSTANDING

Refusals to conciliate relationships or misunderstandings consisted primarily of the offending party refusing to listen to, or comply with, the offended party's assessment of a relationship or situation. The nature of the initiating event implies an existing relationship among offenders, thus eliminating assault events involving strangers. The following example is one derived from a couple in an intimate relationship (which included spousal, common-law or estranged couples), all of whom invoked the same routine practice — physically or

gesturally responding to the offending party —
often by way of physically following the party.

> I was at home at [address] when AC, my comon-
> law husband was there and he got upset because I
> want him to move and that I took him off my
> social services . . . and he got mader when I told
> him that I was not going to give him any money
> from my cheque, and that he would have to apply
> again for himself. So I walked out he came after
> me. When I was going to my Dad's house he fol-
> lowed me in. I told him to leave he started to call
> me names and then he pushed me . . . [#57192,
> complainant]

(5) REFUSAL TO COMPLY WITH SEXUAL REQUEST

Sexual requests may be either physical or verbal as
the following cases illustrate. Again, the context in
which these rejections or refusals occur varies
widely. In the first example, the relationship
between the accused and complainant is customer
and prostitute — the two are strangers. The transaction occurred at night and there are no witnesses.

> The complainant had taken a date to her apart-
> ment (the complainant is a prostitute). The two
> had agreed that the transaction would be 20 min-
> utes for $60. When the complainant had
> finished, the suspect wanted more time. The
> complainant got dressed, then left her suite,
> leaving the suspect behind. The suspect followed
> her into the parking lot of her building. The sus-
> pect then grabbed the complainant by her jacket,
> punched her in the nose and pushed her to the
> ground. [#53284]

The offending act is the complainant's refusal to
give her customer more time as he demanded. In
response to the complainant's getting dressed and
leaving, the offended party follows, invoking a routine consisting of a physical response.

In another situation, the complainant and
accused are acquaintances, and the complainant
had agreed to give the accused a ride home.

> The complainant and suspect sat in the front seat
> while the boyfriend, a witness, sat in the back seat
> of the complainant's car. The complainant arrived
> at the designated street address and told the sus-
> pect to get out. The suspect then reached over and
> grabbed the complainant's breasts. The com-
> plainant pushed him away and then the suspect
> grabbed the complainant by the hair and punched
> her in the head. [#54640]

The complainant rejected the accused's sexual
advances, and his response to her rejection was to
physically grab her and proceed with the assault.

(6) PHYSICAL OR NON-VERBAL GESTURE

Precipitating events consisting of physical or non-
verbal gestures are most easily identified. Here,
offending acts are just that — actions or behaviors
to which a party takes offense, ranging from a
poised middle finger, to a lingering gaze, to the
unwarranted use of property. The contexts in
which these actions may occur are many, as are the
relationships between parties, the location in which
they occur and the number of bystanders found
within the immediate area. In the first example,
taking place on the street, the accused responds to
the initiating action by verbally abusing the offending party. No physical altercation occurs, other
than the phlegm landing on the complainant's face,
culminating in the eventual threat by the offended
party toward the complainant.

> . . . A brown van [license plate #]? swerved around
> me honking his horn and waving his hands, he
> then cut off my vehicle and proceed in and out of
> lanes untill he came to a stop in the center [of
> street] . . . I pulled up beside the van in the right
> hand lane. The driver in the van then started to
> yell and scream about my driving, calling me a
> fucking asshole. I realied after several seconds of
> profanity that given his driving habit's he would
> be mistaken if he felt I cared about his opinion.
> With that the driver [physical description] leaning
> across the passenger a blond women and spit out
> the window hit my face. I replied, oh that's nice.

He said listen you yuppy faggot if you say another word I will get out of my van and beat the fucking shit out of you. [#86132, complainant]

In a different, however public, context, physically offensive moves are met with other routine practices. Take, for example, jostling in a bar, which is responded to by threatening the offending party.

I [victim] and [witness] on friday night . . . went into the [bar] and walking around and accidently bumped into another person he said fuck you asshole, watch it or I will beat the shit out of you. I said to the stranger fuck you, turned my head and attempted to walk away. He grabbed me and put me in a headlock and dragged me outside. He punched me I fell down then he kicked me in the head. I managed to get up and I punched him to defend myself. I stepped outside and said to him that he kicks like a girl would do. The man came towards me punched me in the head and continude punching even when I asked him to stop and tried to walk away. I felt at that point that I had better try my best to defend myself or get hurt real bad. [#70932, complainant]

The following examples of physical gestures, or suspected physical action, address infidelity, whereby the offending party is believed to have engaged in sexual activity deemed illegitimate by the offended party. In the first example, the involved parties are partners in an intimate relationship. In the second example, the offended party suspects the complainant of having slept with his ex-girlfriend. The routine practices range from physically holding the offending party down while demanding an explanation (first example), to challenging the offending party to fight.

I was in the middle of a deep sleep when I heard [accused's] voice yelling at me about 2 telephone numbers scribbled in a cigarette package. he was holding me down hitting me in the face repeatedly, I wasn't aware of what was going on, I tried to

defend myself as he kept hitting me very hard and called me a cheap bitch. [#8275, complainant]

. . . When there was a knock at the door. I answered the door and saw AC (Psyco) standing there he started to blame me for sleeping with his ex-girlfriend. I told him I didn't want to hear anymore about it, so I pushed him down the stairs then he wanted to fight me one on one so we rolled around the grasses for a little while, that's when I noticed the knife in AC's right hand that when I ran into the house and told WI "that son of a bitch wanted to stab me". That was when WI noticed that he did stab me. [#80089, complainant]

DISCUSSION

The above examples illustrate six initiating actions that invoke routine practices. The interpretation of initiating actions, however, varies depending upon the actor's identification of specific situational features, and his or her attendance to these features. While there is regularity or pattern to both the initiating actions and responses to these actions, in the form of routine practices, specific features of the context will determine which routine practice is employed, as well as which initiating action serves to upset. The above examples illustrate Luckenbill's (1977) suggestion that offensive behaviors are met with seven routine practices. Specifically, routine practices consist of, first, demanding an apology or explanation; second, demanding that the offended party leave or "get out of here"; and third, demanding that the other stop or discontinue whatever it is that he or she is doing that is offending the upset individual. Examples include, "stop calling me that," "let go of that," etc. Fourth is threatening the offending party with harm, warning the individual, or challenging the other to a fight. "If you don't stop doing that, I'm going to break your neck," "I told you not to call me that," and "let's take this outside" are examples. Fifth is demanding that the initiator back down, or comply with the demands of the offended party: "Take that back," etc. Sixth is verbally challenging the other: "are you some kind of smart-ass?" or "do you want to get your lights punched out?" Finally, an individual may gesturally or physically respond. These reactions include "giving the finger," shoving, or retrieving a weapon.

DISCUSSION QUESTIONS

1. Show how behavioral routines can lead to violence. Use specific examples.
2. What can we learn from this kind of data that is different from what we learn from the official sources of crime data discussed earlier? Is it valuable?
3. Discuss the six initiating actions that invoke routine practices.

REFERENCES

Barley, S. R. (1986). Technology as an occasion for structuring: Evidence from observations of CT scanners and the social order of radiology departments. *Administrative Science Quarterly, 31*, 78–108.

Cohen, L., & Felson, M. (1979). Social change and crime rate trends. *American Sociological Review, 44*, 588–608.

Hindelang, M. J., Gottfredson, M. R., & Garofalo, J. (1978). *Victims of personal crime: An empirical foundation for a theory of personal victimization.* Cambridge, MA: Ballinger.

Kennedy, L. W. (1990). *On the borders of crime.* New York: Longman.

Kennedy, L. W., & Forde, D. R. (1998). Social roots of violence: A routine conflict approach. Forthcoming manuscript.

Luckenbill, D. F. (1977). Criminal homicide as a situated transaction. *Social Problems, 25*, 176–186.

Luckenbill, D. F., & Doyle, D. P. (1989). Structural position and violence: Developing a cultural explanation. *Criminology, 27*(3), 419–436.

Savitz, L. D., Kumar, K. S., & Zahn, M. A. (1991). Quantifying Luckenbill. *Deviant Behavior, 12*, 19–29.

Van Brunschot, E. (1997). Ph.D. Dissertation, University of Alberta.

Theories of Crime and Delinquency

Introduction

One of the central objectives of any social science — including criminology — is explanation. In other words, we are interested not only in describing the realities of crime and delinquency that we observe but also in making sense out of them. Why are men so much more likely than women to engage in violent criminal conduct? Why are bars high risk locations for crimes? Why did crime rates climb so dramatically in the 1960s? Why are rates of property crime so much higher in big cities than in small towns?

The frameworks that are employed to answer such questions are referred to as "theories." In short, theories are explanations. They are generalizations intended to explain the relationships between classes or categories of events. To attempt to explain why people who are in late adolescence or early adulthood are more likely to commit crime than people who are older or younger is to theorize. In this section, we review the major theories that criminologists have used to understand the relationship between crime and society.

As will become clear, criminology is characterized by a vast theoretical repertoire. However, most contemporary theoretical thought in criminology can be said to emerge out of and reflect two major intellectual trends, each of which is a legacy of a previous century. The first, which arose in the eighteenth century, is known as "classical" thought. The second, which arose in the nineteenth century, is known as "positivist" thought. Before we proceed to a review of contemporary theory, it might be useful to discuss these ideas in somewhat more detail.

THE CLASSICAL AND POSITIVIST SCHOOLS

What has come to be known as "classical thought" originated in the writings of eighteenth-century philosophers — most notably Cesare Beccaria in Italy and Jeremy Bentham in England. Although both men wrote as social critics interested in the reform of the corrupt and harsh justice systems of their time, their writings may be interpreted as suggesting early explanations of crime and offenders.

The essential point of classical thought is that crime can be understood as an expression of free will and rationality. In other words, in answer to the question, "why do people commit crime?" Beccaria or Bentham would have answered, "because they believe that there is more pleasure than pain associated with doing so." In short, people commit crime not because something makes them, not because they are compelled to behave criminally but because in general, they operate on the basis of a "rational hedonism." Unlike later observers who would see the "causes" of crime in the influence of a range of biological, psychological, or social influences, the classical writers stressed an understanding of crime as a human volitional process.

As will become clear, the idea of the offender as a rational actor who chooses criminal behaviour in order to maximize pleasure still has currency. Perhaps most notably, contemporary attempts to explain crime with respect to the ability (or inability) of the law to deter criminal conduct derive directly from the writings of classical thinkers.

Between the classical period and the middle of the nineteenth century, a revolution in thinking occurred. Most generally this revolution was rooted in the development of the scientific enterprise and the growing sense that the methods and tools of science could be applied to a wide range of human problems. The positivist writers who came to the fore in the late decades of the nineteenth century were distinguished by their insistence that it was possible to think about crime and its causes in scientific terms. Thus, rather than argue, as the classical writers had, that crime reflected free will and choice, they attempted to understand the factors that *caused* crime.

The most influential of the nineteenth century positivists was the Italian physician named Lombroso (1876), who with his colleagues advocated biological theories of criminality, based upon and closely following Darwin's theory of evolution. Lombroso and his colleagues believed that many criminals are *atavists,* humans with animal-like traits who are lower on the evolutionary scale than non-criminals and thus more susceptible to crime. These individuals, it was argued, could be recognized by visible physical signs, such as excessive length of arms, or ears of unusual size. Unfortunately, these "born criminals," who were thought to account for about one-third of the entire criminal population, could not be helped, according to Lombroso, as they were born that way and thus their behaviour was biologically determined. Other categories of Lombroso's typology include the *insane* (idiots, imbeciles, and hysterical women!), the *criminaloid* (for whom situational factors play a part in precipitating crime), the *habitual criminal* (for whom crime is a way of life), and finally the *passionate criminal* (whose crime, such as murder, is committed in a fit of passion and is thus not likely to be repeated).

Lombroso's research methods were crude, and his findings were later found to be incorrect. Problems with his physical measurements and his inadequate use of a control group of non-criminals for comparison purposes (he examined only criminals) proved to be Lombroso's downfall (Goring, 1913).

On the other hand, Lombroso tried to be objective and deterministic, unlike adherents of the then popular free-will doctrine, and advocated the study of interrelated rather than single causes (Vold & Bernard, 1986).

Of course, biological theories are still being advanced, and there is a biological chain stretching from Lombroso to the present day (Katz & Chambliss, 1995). However, the key point here is that the essential premises of the positivist writers — that it is meaningful to speak of the "causes" of crime and that the relationship between crime and its causes can be understood through the application of the scientific method — characterize not only the way that biologists approach crime but also the way many other types of scholars do. Psychologists, for instance, are interested in the ways in which the tendency to commit crime reflect the influence of individual-level cognitive process. Still, because the approach involves the attempt to use science to understand the causes of crime, it could be characterized as positivist.

More relevant to the review that follows, sociological explanations of crime causation have as their basis cultural or social determinism, rather than biological determinism. In other words, they seek to understand how crime is made more likely by particular kinds of social arrangements, cultural environments, or patterns of interaction.

CONTEMPORARY THEORIES OF CRIME

At present, most of the explanations of crime are sociological, in that they seek the social causes of crime. This is because most criminologists have been trained as sociologists. Reflecting this bias, most of the theories discussed in this book are also sociological. A review of the most influential sociological theories of crime and delinquency must be preceded by two cautions. First, any attempt to summarize several decades of sociological thought on the causes of crime requires the sacrifice of the subtleties of many of these arguments. The reader should be aware that more detailed reviews of the relevant theoretical and research literature are readily available (Hagan, 1994; Vold, Bernard, & Snipes, 1998). Second, the classification scheme employed below is somewhat arbitrary, and many of the theorists would place themselves in more than one theoretical tradition.

Ecological Theories

Ecological theories attempt to understand the causes of crime in reference to environmental characteristics that make crime more or less likely. Such theories do not ask why some individuals tend to commit crimes, but rather what social conditions make it likely that many people will. In general, ecological approaches are directed toward an understanding of why some communities (neighbourhoods or cities) have higher rates of crime than other communities.

The suggestion that an understanding of the structure of communities is important to an understanding of differences in levels of crime may be traced to the work of several sociologists who were affiliated with the University of Chicago in the first several decades of this century. On the basis of his observations of the city of Chicago, Burgess (1923) suggested that modern cities exhibit a pattern of five concentric circles or zones, from the centre out, with each area reflecting distinctive living arrangements. Zone one is the central downtown business core of the city, zone two the downtrodden slum area of transition waiting to be annexed to the business core, zone three the working-class homes, zone four the middle-class residential area, and zone five the commuter suburbs. Shaw and McKay (1942) then applied this concentric-zone model to the study of delinquency. They found that as one moves toward the city core and away from the suburbs, one finds not only increasing rates of delinquency but also increasing rates of crime, truancy, mental disorder, infant mortality, and tuberculosis.

Furthermore, Shaw and McKay found that these forms of social pathology were unrelated to changes in ethnic population or population composition. They argued that regardless of which ethnic group

inhabits the transitional run-down area, the social pathology rates are high and they stay proportionately the same in zone-by-zone comparisons. This implies that factors associated with the zones, such as denial of economic opportunity, ethnic segregation, and physical deterioration, rather than the specific characteristics of the people living there, are associated with the relative incidence of social problems such as crime and delinquency.

For Shaw and McKay and others whose research followed the Chicago tradition, the concentration of crime in inner-city urban neighbourhoods is best explained with reference to the high levels of "social disorganization" that may be said to characterize such areas. Although the term social disorganization has been defined and used in a number of different ways, it generally refers to the breakdown of the formal and informal mechanisms that are normally thought to regulate behaviour and thus to discourage juvenile as well as adult criminal conduct. Specifically, it may be argued that the greater degree of poverty, family dissolution, ethnic heterogeneity, and other associated conditions prevents the effective exercise of community control and in turn leads to higher delinquency rates.

The work of Shaw and McKay stimulated considerable debate among subsequent generations of sociologists. Much of this empirical research and theoretical thinking criticized their initial efforts. Some writers argued, for instance, that the claim that high-delinquency areas were socially disorganized reflected nothing more than the biases of the Chicago sociologists and their unwillingness or inability to recognize that such areas were not disorganized but rather were organized differently from the middle-class communities with which they were more familiar (Mills, 1943; Whyte, 1955). A second problem identified by critics concerns the fact that although ecological theory can be used as a predictive model of gross rates of crime and delinquency in terms of their general location in a metropolis, it is not as useful in predicting *individual* crime and delinquency — that is, which individuals in the area will become criminal. Third, empirical attempts to replicate the findings of Shaw and McKay have frequently been unsuccessful (Lander, 1954). Finally, it may be argued that many of the ecological studies that employed official crime data have been unable to determine whether there are more or different *reactions* to crime in some areas, rather than more actual crime (see, for example, O'Brien, 1985). More will be said about this in the discussion of labelling below.

Despite such criticisms, ecological approaches to the study of crime and delinquency have undergone a resurgence of interest in recent years (Bursik & Grasmick, 1993). This resurgence has been spurred by the development of more powerful techniques for data analysis and by the availability of alternative data sources (such as victimization surveys). While this recent work finds its origins in the pioneering efforts of Shaw and McKay and other Chicago sociologists, it represents a more sophisticated approach to understanding the relationship between levels of crimes and the dynamics of community life.

Robert Sampson (1995), for instance, has reformulated arguments about social disorganization in terms that emphasize the importance of "social capital" (Coleman, 1990). Social capital is created whenever the relationships among people allow them to accomplish what they could not accomplish in the absence of such relationships. In this way, social capital can be understood as a social good that is embodied within the structure of social networks. Given such a conceptualization, it follows that one of the primary features of socially disorganized areas is a lack of social capital. For Sampson, the theoretical task of the social ecologist is to identify the features of communities that make social capital available or unavailable to residents.

Of perhaps greatest importance in this regard, according to Sampson, is the degree of *closure* (or connectedness) associated with social networks. In communities in which the relationships among adults are characterized by large numbers of mutual expectations and obligations, social networks are better able to facilitate the control and supervision of adolescents. Closure implies that the influence of adults can extend beyond their own households and to children other than their own. When the adults in a community are connected to each other, they have the opportunity to observe the child in a variety of different settings, to compare notes about the child's behaviour and to provide consistent feedback about community standards of behaviour.

A modification and elaboration of the social disorganization model has also been provided by Bursik and Grasmick (1993). They argued that communities control crime through the effective utilization of three types of control. "Private control" refers to the types of constraints that operate through the family and other intimate relationships. "Parochial control" is exercised by neighbours and local stores and businesses. Finally, "public control" involves the ability of the local community to secure public goods and services (for example, policing services) allocated by agencies outside of the neighbourhood. They maintain that factors such as socioeconomic composition, residential mobility, and racial (or ethnic) heterogeneity influence the ability of local communities to mobilize these controls.

In a different way, Sherman, Gartin, and Buerger (1989) have argued that much ecological research has tended to restrict itself to the study of relatively large aggregates (cities or neighbourhoods) and in so doing has obscured important distinctions among places that constitute such aggregates. They stressed instead the study of "hot spots" of crime (street addresses and intersections), which allow finer distinctions to be made with respect to the manner in which crime is distributed across the urban landscape. Using data on more than 300 000 calls to police in the city of Minneapolis over a one-year period, Sherman and his colleagues found that relatively few hot spots produced most of the calls to police. Thus, 50 percent of the calls involved only 3 percent of the 115 000 addresses and intersections. Such findings raise important questions about the importance that researchers have traditionally attached to larger ecological units.

Aside from some notable exceptions, Canadian researchers have traditionally not been particularly attentive to ecological approaches to crime and delinquency. Recently, however, analyses by Doob,

Grossman, and Auger (1994) of the relationship between social disorganization and aboriginal homicides and by Hartnagel of the relationship between geographic mobility and provincial crime rates (Chapter 12, this volume) may signal a renewed interest in this perspective.

Strain Theories

Strain theories locate the causes of criminal conduct in the attempts that people make to solve problems that society presents to them. Merton's (1938) theory of anomie is probably the version of strain theory that has gained the most attention.

Material success is the main goal of North American society, according to Merton, and almost everyone is expected to try to be successful. The capitalist economy in which we live, however, is based on inequalities, and thus not everyone is able to obtain that material success. (Changing or lowering one's goals or aspirations is not recognized as a desirable option. Merton calls individuals who lower their goals "ritualists," and those who "drop out" "retreatists" — neither of which concerns us here.) Hence, persons lacking legitimate means to success may feel pressured to use illegitimate means to achieve the goals society says they should be achieving. Borrowing from the famous French sociologist Emile Durkheim, Merton uses the term *anomie* to describe this discrepancy between the goals of a society and access to the legitimate means to obtain them. The more anomie that exists in a society, the greater the pressure toward crime.

Merton added that lower-class individuals are more often denied legitimate means; thus most feel the pressure of anomie and more frequently become criminal offenders, or "innovators," in Merton's terminology. Such an image of the class distribution of crime is consistent with images provided by the media and official statistics.

Critics of Merton, however, have pointed to the great amount of upper-class or white-collar crime, which anomie theory is less successful in explaining. They argue that many people with access to legitimate means are also criminal, while most lower-class individuals with curtailed access to legitimate means do not engage in serious criminal activity but instead lower their goals, becoming "ritualists." Many writers, such as Tittle (1983), question the relationship between social class and crime; others, like Agnew (1984), argue that low, not high, aspirations may be related to deviance.

The theory also does not provide us with guidance regarding why individuals differ in their choice of deviant adaptations. In other words, why do some people lower their aspirations and use legitimate means, while others refuse to lower their aspirations and thus adopt illegitimate means (Cloward & Ohlin, 1960; Jackson, 1984)? Moreover, the utility of the theory may be limited to the explanation of "instrumental crimes" that involve some type of material goal; it may be less useful in explaining expressive-emotional crimes, for example, a murder in the heat of passion, or a barroom assault. Finally, like most traditional accounts of crime and deviance, Merton's anomie theory would seem to have relatively little to say about the occurrence of female crime or delinquency (Pfohl, 1985). Traditionally, women have had less access to the legitimate means of goal attainment but have also been less rather than more criminal.

In an important reformulation of strain theory, Cohen (1955) argued that many working-class male adolescents cannot achieve according to middle-class standards, and find it especially difficult to do well in the middle-class–dominated school system. These boys then tend to gravitate toward one another, and together attempt to develop new norms and standards by which they can succeed. Sensing failure and contempt, they create new criteria for success that are directly opposite to middle-class standards, but that are achievable (Cohen, 1955, p. 65–66). These new norms take the form of a rejecting counter-culture, then antisocial behaviour, and, ultimately, gang delinquency. Essentially these boys are of the type Merton called innovators — individuals who lack conventional means to achieve common success goals.

Cloward and Ohlin (1960) developed a theory of delinquency and opportunity that suggested an important refinement of Merton's original argument. They argued that while the strain toward anomie may encourage criminality, it does not determine the type of criminal conduct in which anomic individuals become involved. This will depend upon the illegitimate opportunities available to them. In substantive terms, Cloward and Ohlin focussed upon the study of lower-class urban juvenile gangs and argued that these youth become delinquent because they experience "a marked discrepancy between culturally induced aspirations . . . and the possibilities of achieving them by legitimate means" (1960, p. 78). Because lower-class youth cannot achieve as easily as middle-class youth, they may become alienated from the dominant society. They then may externalize the blame for their failure onto that society and seek a group solution to their perceived problems. Delinquent acts occur after this alienation develops. Cloward and Ohlin saw these acts as far more rational than Cohen did. In their opinion, the acts serve as solutions to the anomie problem faced by the youth. Such solutions are found in groups organized around specific delinquent activities, and in these groups ideologies and rules of behaviour take shape.

Concerning opportunity, Cloward and Ohlin hypothesized two opportunity structures for attaining society's success goals. One is legitimate; delinquents aspire to this, but cannot realize it. The other opportunity structure is illegitimate; it offers illegal means for attaining success. There are three possible delinquent subcultures: the *criminal*, the *conflict*, and the *retreatist*.

The criminal gang flourishes where younger adults and youths of all ages mix, and where petty criminals freely interact with non-criminal individuals. Youths in this situation have the opportunity to learn criminal activity from others who are slightly older than themselves. They also have adult role models to emulate, for example, successful pimps or gamblers. The major activities of the criminal juvenile gang involve offences such as theft and extortion.

In areas where youths do not mix with older people and/or there are no criminal adult role models, the type of delinquent group that develops is known as the conflict gang. These gangs develop in disorganized slums, and behaviour is centred on fighting and gang wars.

The third subculture is called the retreatist subculture (cf. Merton, 1957). Possessing neither the conventional nor the criminal means, the individuals attracted to this subculture are, in essence, double failures. Their activity revolves around some kind of illicit consumption, such as drug taking. There is often some theft involved as well, since theft may be necessary to maintain drug habits.

The major contribution of Cloward and Ohlin's theory to criminology has been to direct attention to the role played by illegitimate means in criminogenic processes. Although the theory has not been fully supported empirically (for example, see Agnew, 1984), it is also worth noting that some aspects of the theory have proved useful in the examination of the neglected topic of female criminality (Adler, 1975). Steffensmeier (1983), for example, described how women are denied equal opportunity in crime.

As Downes and Rock (1995, p. 116) noted, it is probably correct in the present period to characterize strain theory as "distinctly out of fashion." Its dominance as an explanation of crime was successfully challenged in the 1960s by a number of competing accounts including labelling, conflict, and control theories. Still, interest in the development and refinement of the strain argument continues to exist.

Robert Agnew (1992) has offered a revised version of strain theory that is intended as a much more general account of the relationship between social strain and juvenile crime. According to Agnew, the type of strain described by Merton (which involves the actual or anticipated failure to achieve socially valued goals) is only one type of strain. A more comprehensive theory must recognize two other forms of strain that promote criminal conduct. One of these involves strain that results when individuals are presented with negatively valued conditions that they are unable to avoid or escape. So, for instance, an adolescent may be unable to escape an abusive home life. The second form of strain may arise as a result of being forced to move to a new city (and therefore being forced to leave behind old friends) or when a parent is lost through death or family dissolution. A test of this general theory by Agnew and White (1992) found that the effects of strain on delinquency are strongest when individuals have delinquent friends or (to a less important degree) when they lack a sense of self-efficacy (i.e., when they feel less able to control events in their lives). A recent test of the relationship between strain and delinquency among a sample of "high risk" street youth by Baron and Hartnagel (1997) also lends partial support to Agnew's general theory. The study focusses upon one particular type of strain — occupational strain — and examines the hypothesis that the ways youth respond to strain reflect the nature of the attributions they make with respect to predicaments in which they find themselves. When youth blame others for their unemployment they are more likely to feel angry and to respond in delinquent ways. Conversely, when they blame themselves, they are more likely to feel guilty and to engage in drug or alcohol use as a way of coping with strain. Hartnagel and Baron suggest that several other factors are likely to condition the ways in which youth respond to strain.

Cultural Theories

Cultural theorists argue that people become criminals because their socialization experiences expose them to beliefs, values, and norms that permit or encourage such conduct. These sources of crime are thus seen to reside in the cultural environments that individuals inhabit rather than in the individuals themselves.

Edwin Sutherland provided criminology with perhaps the most influential version of cultural theory. His theory of *differential association* maintains that one learns criminality in the same manner that one learns any other behaviour. For Sutherland, society could be characterized as being in a state of "differential social organization" such that there

exist groups that carry and transmit conventional conformist values and groups that carry and transmit criminal values. As individuals associate with one of these groups rather than the other, they will come to see the world through the cultural lenses the group provides. Thus people become criminal because they learn to be criminal through association with others who transmit cultural values and beliefs supportive of criminality. For Sutherland, then, one learns to be criminal in essentially the same manner that one learns any other occupational, recreational, or cultural activity. This position may not sound radical today, but when initially formulated, Sutherland's theory had to compete with the previous biological theories, which argued that criminality is not learned but innate. Sutherland's theory gained wide popularity, and the differential association hypothesis was expanded and refined as several editions of his book *Principles of Criminology* were published (Sutherland, 1939; Sutherland & Cressey, 1978).

On the whole, differential association theory is today less prominent than before, despite attempts to broaden (Glaser, 1956) and reformulate (Akers, 1985) the central argument. Because of the difficulty of testing the theory and its omission of what causes the culture that transmits crime, it is used either in conjunction with other theories or as a general orientation, rather than as a specific explanation of crime.

Differential association theory in many respects resembles Thorsten Sellin's (1938) theory of culture conflict. For Sellin, crime in heterogeneous societies results from the clash between the traditional cultures of ethnic groups and the culture of the dominant society, which is codified in law. For example, because Canada is a multi-ethnic society, there are groups of people with allegiance to two sets of cultural values — the culture of the "larger Canadian society" and the culture of a specific ethnic group. Sellin argued that culture conflict involves those situations in which ethnic norms conflict with the norms embodied in legal codes. Thus some immigrants to Canada may bring with them the belief that it is appropriate to use physical violence in the defence of personal honour. The law, and the wider society from which the law might be seen to derive, may define the violent defence of personal honour as criminal assault.

Sellin's theory of culture conflict became very popular in a historical period during which much of the crime in North America was attributed to rapid and large-scale immigration. The argument has also been applied to other societies that have experienced rapid immigration (Rahav, 1981). Although the value of the culture conflict model has been disputed by some empirical researchers, it may still have some limited utility. For instance, Ribordy (1980) discussed how the culture conflict experienced by Italian immigrants in Montreal was related to levels of criminal offending. Still, since most crime in Canada is committed by people born in Canada, culture conflict cannot be used as a major explanation of criminal activity.

As a final example of cultural theory, Claude Fischer (1975, 1976) attempted to wed ecological and subcultural accounts in order to explain why cities generally have higher rates of crime than less urban places. With respect to crime, or any type of cultural activity, he argued that the sheer size of cities allows for the development of a "critical mass" of individuals that permits and sustains distinctive lifestyles. Thus the concentration of people in one place who share an interest, talent, or preference allows for the development of subcultural worlds that are frequently organized around unconventional values. In towns or villages, on the other hand, the absolute number of deviant or criminal individuals will be smaller, and when crime does occur in such settings, it is less likely to take a subcultural form. Because big cities facilitate subcultural growth and diversity, urbanism is inevitably associated with crime and other forms of deviance:

> Large population size provides a "critical mass" of criminals and customers for crime in the same way it provides a critical mass of customers for other services. The aggregation of population promotes "markets" of clients — people interested in purchasing drugs or the services of prostitutes, for example; and it provides a sufficient concentration of potential victims — for example, affluent persons and their property. Size also provides a critical mass of criminals sufficient to generate organization, supportive services (such as fences, "bought" policemen and a criminal underground) and full-time specialization (Fischer, 1976, p. 93).

While Fischer marshalled considerable evidence in support of his subcultural theory of urbanism, a comprehensive test of the hypothesis by Tittle (1989) produced mixed findings.

In general terms, the utility of cultural and subcultural theories for Canadian criminologists resides in the fact that they can be applied to any setting in which a group of people have norms and values that are different from the majority norms and values. As mentioned above, this is descriptive of the Canadian case as well as of all large, heterogeneous societies. Of particular interest to Canadian criminologists, however, has been the cultural character of crime rate differences between Canada and the United States. To what extent, analysts have asked, are higher rates of violence in the United States a product of differences in values rather than differences in the structural nature of the two societies (Grandin & Lupri, 1997; Hagan, 1989; Sacco, 1993)?

On the other hand, cultural theories are judged by many to be deficient in several respects. Some critics (e.g., Goode, 1994) suggest that their reasoning is circular. Such theories explain illegal or delinquent behaviour by arguing that the individuals so engaged possess values that are supportive of such activities. Thus, in a sense, they merely describe what we already know and do not tell us which conditions are conducive to holding the values that are favourable to illegal or delinquent conduct. Also, the proportion of criminality or delinquency accounted for by cultural rather than by individual factors is not known. It is possible that much of what has been labelled "subcultural" crime is in fact "situational" crime, in that it occurs in response to opportunities available in particular areas at particular times, or that it results from pressures placed on individuals in groups, even when they do not share a common culture (Matza, 1964).

Social Control Theory

Whereas other theories assume conformity and attempt to explain deviance, social control theories argue that it is safer to assume that people will deviate and that it is therefore necessary to explain why so many conform. Control theorists maintain that if individuals are to conform to normative expectations, they must be taught the lessons of conformity. From a sociological point of view, the training of individuals to conform is known as *socialization*. The essence of socialization involves reward and punishment. While psychological principles indicate that reward techniques are more effective than punishment techniques in producing desired outcomes, most of those involved in the socialization of children (parents and teachers) combine punishment and reward.

Not everyone, however, responds to this training in the same way. Some respond quickly, some slowly; and some trainers are more effective than others. Thus in the long run, some individuals are more likely than others to conform. Individuals who do not conform might be thought of as products of poor or inadequate socialization. In speaking of adult criminals, we may indicate that "something went wrong with their childhood or upbringing." Perhaps their antisocial impulses were not punished enough or their pro-social activities not rewarded sufficiently. When we make such comments, we are tacitly accepting the tenets of control theory.

Research concerning social control and crime generally examines how socialization leads to conformity or how punishment decreases nonconformity. Probably the greatest amount of research and theory involves this latter, negative, aspect of social control, that is, the potential of punishment for deterring criminal activities. As stated above, Beccaria (1764) and Bentham (1843), early social control theorists, saw people as hedonists or pleasure seekers, and argued that in order to deter crime the state must make the potential punishment and pain for crime greater than its potential pleasures and rewards. Rational individuals would then conform in order to avoid the pain and punishment that would follow criminal activity. More specifically, they argued, the more certain, the more severe, the more public, and the quicker the punishment, the less crime there would be.

Over the last several decades, considerable research attention has been directed toward the study of deterring crime (Cusson, 1993; Krohn, 1991). While theoretical and methodological approaches to the problem do not allow this literature to be easily summarized, it appears that "severity of punishment is probably less important in deterring crime than certainty of punishment" (Conklin, 1986, p. 409). In addition, in a review of relevant experimental studies, Clark (1988) concluded that although the swiftness (or celerity) of punishment appears to be an important aspect of the deterrence process, its importance is diminished when other factors are taken into account. Even more generally, some researchers have called into question the broad assumption that the law is an important deterrent to criminal conduct (Paternoster, Saltzman, Waldo, & Chiricos, 1983).

Finally, some writers contend that, in the main, deterrence theorists have taken a position on the deterrence effects of law that is too narrow in scope (Baron & Kennedy, 1998). Instead, they argue that whatever effect the threat of legal sanction has on potential offenders is mediated by the informal networks to which those potential offenders belong. For example, a potential offender may not fear being arrested so much as the "attachment costs" associated with being arrested, meaning the fallout arrest might have for the offender's relationships with family, friends, neighbours, and co-workers. While an offender might not be afraid of jail or a fine per se, he or she may be afraid of losing the respect and support of friends or family. This awareness complicates our understanding of how deterrence might work, since the effects of legal threats might vary considerably depending on the strength of an individual's informal networks and according to the importance of those networks for the individual.

As stated, a second variant of control theory is less concerned with punishment and emphasizes instead the "positive" role that socialization plays in the promotion of conformity. Thus, from this perspective, socialization is seen as the process that results in the establishment of strong social bonds between the individual and others in society who are carriers of conformist values. When such bonds are effective, they discourage delinquent or criminal conduct.

The best known version of this argument has been provided by Travis Hirschi (1969). According to him, when our connections to conformist others are meaningful, we are forced to take their opinions into account when we act. If, however, we are detached from those who hold values of conformity, we are free to do as we please — and frequently this may mean that we are free to behave in a criminal fashion. For Hirschi, the "bond to society" can be conceptualized as being made up of four distinct but related strands. The first element, *attachment,* refers to the degree to which individuals are sensitive to the expectations of others who represent the world of conformity. The second element, *commitment,* refers to investments of time and energy made to conventional lines of activity; the greater these investments, the more likely they are to discourage criminal behaviour that might place them in jeopardy. *Involvement* refers to the extent to which time and energy are used up by non-criminal pursuits and thus made unavailable for the exploration of criminal opportunity. Finally, what Hirschi terms *belief* refers to perceptions that conformist values are deserving of respect. Hirschi's version of control theory suggests that one should attempt to induce conformity by attaching individuals to society with positive bonds, that is, by making them want to conform.

A somewhat more complicated version of the control argument is found in the work of Matza (1964; Sykes & Matza, 1957), who suggested that the relationship between the bond to society and delinquent behaviour must be understood in situational terms. Matza maintained that in order to commit delinquent acts, youths must be able to rationalize their behaviour and thus be released from the moral constraints that would normally prohibit the performance of these acts. The rationalization process that allows youth to "drift" in and out of delinquency is known as *neutralization.* Through this process the law may be temporarily and sporadically deprived of moral constraint to the point where the offender is able to transgress it. Matza described a "negation of events," a feeling on the part of the delinquents that the deviant acts are not really important, that people act that way all the time, or that adults are allowed to get away with similar acts and thus there is no reason why they should not also get away with them. For example, alcohol regulations may be considered irrational by juveniles, auto theft may be redefined as "joyriding," and vandalism may come to be viewed as a harmless prank. Hence the juveniles question the moral validity of such rules, find them wanting, and feel free to violate them. By neutralizing the law, they create a situation in which they are free to choose whether to violate it.

The concept of neutralization is viewed by many as offering a useful insight into the problems of crime and victimization. Recent work suggests that neutralization processes are important in the facilitation of crime when individuals believe in the sentiment expressed in the neutralization technique, when they find themselves in situations to which the technique of neutralization applies, and when they morally disapprove of the behaviour in question (Agnew & Peters, 1986). Some of this research also supports the view that neutralization may be part of a "hardening process" such that over time the prohibited behaviour and the neutralization that allows it reinforce each other. As a result, the commitment to both the behaviour and the neutralization intensifies (Minor, 1984).

More recently, Gottfredson and Hirschi (1990) have proposed a "general theory of crime" that to some extent builds upon Hirschi's earlier contributions to social control theory. Gottfredson and Hirschi define crime as the use of "force or fraud undertaken in pursuit of self-interest" (1990, p. 15). They maintained that because crimes of various types share these definitional properties in common, it is possible to have a "general theory," and as a result it is unnecessary to have specific theories of, for instance, robbery, homicide, organized crime, or white-collar crime. Gottfredson and Hirschi said that the key to criminal involvement is the concept of low self-control. Individuals who are lacking in self-control will be attracted to crime because such behaviours require little skill or planning, promise immediate gratification, and are risky and thrilling. These same individuals are also likely to have higher than average levels of involvement in other behaviours (for example, drug use, skipping school) that have similar characteristics. According to Gottfredson and Hirschi, low self-control is rooted in childhood and reflects the influence of family contexts in which parents do not monitor their children's behaviour effectively, do not recognize delinquency when it occurs, and do not punish it when it is recognized. To date, a limited (and somewhat mixed) body of empirical research has begun to accumulate in support of this general theory of crime (Brownfield & Sorenson, 1993; Grasmick, Tittle, Bursik, & Arneklev, 1993; Keane, Maxim, & Teevan, 1993; Sorenson & Brownfield, 1995).

Finally, "life course theory" attempts to develop an empirically based developmental version of the social control argument. The architects of this theory, Robert Sampson and John Laub (1993) were interested in understanding the ways in which controls over the propensity to behave criminally change or remain stable over the life course. In this respect, they made an important distinction between *trajectories* and *transitions*. The former term refers to the pathways on which people are located or the general directions in which their lives seem to be heading. Transitions, on the other hand, are specific life events (a first job, a divorce, the birth of a child) that may alter personal trajectories. Thus, an individual's early childhood experiences of abuse and poverty might set him or her on a criminal trajectory. However, a specific life event (meeting and settling down with a "nurturing mate") might alter the trajectory. Thus, trajectories change when transitions alter the number and the nature of social connections that help to ensure conformity.

Recently, Macmillan (Chapter 16, this volume) has drawn on life course theory in an attempt to explain the increase in rates of property crime in Canada over the last several decades. Macmillan notes that during this period, young males (who commit the majority of such crimes) were more likely to have left their parents' homes earlier, and to have waited longer to marry or become parents. The net effect of such changes was to delay (or even prevent) young males from connecting with those social networks that would have controlled criminal behaviour. One implication of this analysis is that there are structural as well as individual dimensions to the relationship between life course and crime.

As several writers have noted, the body of evidence that has accumulated in support of the general logic of social control theory is quite impressive (Vold et al., 1998). Still, some critics question the assumptions from which such arguments proceed. Thio (1988), for instance, argued that the distinction that is frequently made in control theory between individual deviants and the world of "conformist others" is too simplistic to capture the cultural pluralism of complex societies. Others doubt the generalizability of control arguments, given that most of the supporting research has involved the study of adolescent populations only. Perhaps the most frequently voiced criticism of control theory, however, concerns the charge that it is inattentive to the possible ways in which the application of social control might increase — rather than reduce — the propensity to criminality. This is a theme that has been pursued in the context of societal reaction theories.

Societal Reaction Theories

Societal reaction theories attempt to understand crime or delinquency as outcomes that result from interactions involving offenders and agents of social control such as police or judges. Thus crime is seen not as something that emerges full-blown from the motivations or values of the criminal, but rather as rooted in the social exchange between those who are judged to be lawbreakers and those who make those judgements. Societal reaction theories attempt to demonstrate that the behaviour of those who are supposedly involved in the control of crime may actually have consequences that produce the opposite effect.

Most of the research and theorizing on the role of societal reaction in generating crime has been organized in terms of a set of arguments known as the labelling perspective. This approach to the study of crime and control gained considerable popularity in the 1960s and 1970s and exerted considerable influence on an entire generation of sociologists.

In simple terms, labelling theorists argue that the response of control agents to a presumed lawbreaker may create conditions that increase the probability of further (and perhaps more serious) rule breaking. Thus the application of labels such as "criminal" or "delinquent" may create a self-fulfilling prophecy such that the individual so labelled comes to behave in ways that are consistent with the behavioural expectations that such labels embody. Labelling theorists encourage us to ask two important questions about the relationship between crime and the labelling process: (1) What factors determine who does and who does not end up being labelled? and (2) What consequences do the application of these labels have for the labelled individuals?

With respect to the first question, labelling theory suggests that criminality is more evenly distributed throughout the social system than police or other types of official statistics would lead us to believe. Thus the overrepresentation of crime in the lower social classes or among some ethnic minorities may be thought to reflect the uneven application of legal control rather than the greater tendency on the part of some groups in society to engage in criminal conduct. Several factors, such as race or economic status, may be thought to affect the likelihood that an individual will be arrested by the police or sentenced by the court. It has also been argued that offence characteristics (such as the visibility of the act or the relationship between the victim and the offender) as well as characteristics of the social control agencies themselves (the size of the agency, organizational priorities, resources available) may also affect the directional flow of social control activity.

The second set of issues raised by labelling theorists concerns the effects of labelling processes. One of the first sociologists to focus attention on this problem was Tannenbaum (1938). He argued that if children are labelled as "bad" and then segregated from "good" children, they are more likely to continue their deviance than if they are simply ignored. A change in self-concept occurs because of the labelling, and the situation worsens with each subsequent labelling. These children come to think of themselves as bad and isolate themselves or are isolated from conforming others. Eventually they move closer to deviant groups that have antisocial values, they spend much of their time attacking the labellers, and ultimately they engage in deviance because they are cut off from legitimate alternatives. This cycle is repeated with each new "delinquent" act.

Lemert (1951) attempted to understand this process in a somewhat more systematic manner, introducing a distinction between what he called "primary" and "secondary" deviance. According to Lemert, primary deviance refers to those types of rule-breaking behaviour that are engaged in by many members of society, but do not attract the attention of control agents and have no serious implications for the self-concept of the rule-breaker. Although most of us have at one time or another broken the law (e.g., fighting, shoplifting), we do not see ourselves as criminal for having done so. Lemert would suggest that this is largely because our actions are transitory and episodic and, in most cases, do not attract the attention of social control agents. Lemert argued that there is an important difference between such acts of primary deviance and what he defined as secondary deviance. The latter term refers to the behaviour of the person who is immersed in a deviant role and whose self-concept is organized around a deviant lifestyle. For Lemert, the central task of the sociologist is to explain how the processes of societal reaction transform primary deviance into secondary deviance. In a similar manner, Becker (1963) maintained that an understanding of nonconformity requires an appreciation of the role of societal reaction in the development of deviant careers.

For Lemert, Becker, and many other labelling theorists, the societal reaction process is a complex one. If an individual, on the basis of an isolated criminal act, attracts the attention of control agents, this may have important implications for the ways in which others see that individual and ultimately for the ways in which that individual sees himself or herself. The application of an emotionally laden label such as "criminal" or "delinquent" will influence the quality and quantity of subsequent interaction in which that individual is involved. The individual may be stigmatized and isolated from conformist others. As opportunities for association with conventional others become blocked, opportunities for association with criminal others may open up. When conventional people do interact with the stigmatized individual, they may do so largely in terms of the negative stereotypes that they have come to associate with people who bear these labels. These stereotypes may encourage the individual to adopt a self-image consistent with the expectations contained in these stereotypes. The overall effect of the societal reaction, according to this logic, is to increase the likelihood that sporadic acts of nonconformity will coalesce into stable patterns.

Analyses provided by labelling theorists have been useful in forging a reconceptualization of the relationship between crime and social control. However, in recent years, the influence of labelling theory has diminished considerably, in part due to the growth of a large body of critical literature and empirical data that has questioned the validity of the perspective (Rosenberg & Lewis, 1993). In the absence of a compelling empirical case, critics have concluded that, while labelling processes may play a role in the development of criminal careers, they

are probably not as important as proponents of the perspective make them out to be — especially in the case of serious, repetitive, criminal offending.

The general value of societal reaction approaches derives from the fact that they encourage us to conceptualize the activities of control agents such as the police as something other than mere reactions to the behaviour of criminal offenders. On the other hand, while societal reaction theorists focus our attention upon the role of power and conflict in the creation of crime, they do not draw explicit linkages between the activities of control agents and the larger social structure. This question was taken up by conflict theorists who, while building upon the work of societal reaction writers, took the study of crime and social control in new directions.

Conflict Theories

Conflict theories see social conflict as central to any theoretical explanation of crime and delinquency. These theories reject the assumption that societies are based upon a shared consensus about important norms and values. Instead, they assume that the most noteworthy feature of any complex society is the presence of conflict between segments of that society that differ from each other in terms of the social power and other resources to which they have access. The important task for criminological theory, conflict theorists argue, is to understand processes of lawmaking and lawbreaking in a manner that takes the conflict-oriented nature of society into account.

At the risk of oversimplification, it is possible to recognize two broad categories of conflict theory (Williams & McShane, 1994; see also Turk, 1986). Conservative conflict theorists tend to view social conflict as involving a wide variety of groups in society. They conceptualize conflicts as emerging in response to particular situations or particular events that bring into sharp relief their competition for social or economic advantage. In contrast, radical theories of social conflict, which derive primarily from the writings of Marx, conceptualize social conflict primarily in terms of a struggle between social classes in the context of the structured inequalities of capitalist societies.

George Vold (1958; Vold et al., 1998) provided an early example of conservative conflict theory in criminology. Vold's argument begins with the assumption that people are fundamentally "group-involved" in that their lives are both a part of, and a product of, group belonging. Groups are formed because individuals have common interests and common needs that are best met through collective action. Moreover, Vold maintained, groups come into conflict with each other as "the interest and purposes they serve tend to overlap, encroach on one another and become competitive" (Vold et al., 1998, p. 236).

Vold suggested that legislation is one arena in which the processes of group conflict are especially apparent. Groups with the power to do so will attempt to influence the content of law so that it reflects their interests and preference. As a consequence, those in society who promote the passage of a given law will likely abide by it, while those against whom the law is directed will be more likely to violate the law, since it defends interests and values that are in conflict with their own. Seen in this way, crime may be the behaviour of a group in society that lacks the power to exert its will through the legal machinery of the state. Vold maintained, for instance, that much juvenile misbehaviour could be understood in precisely this way. The law (and the behaviour of police, judges, and others who enforce law) may be said to reflect the interests, values, and preferences of the adult world. Thus juvenile crime and delinquency are very much reactions against the rules and regulations that the adult world attempts to impose upon the behaviour of youth. Juvenile crime, which is very often a group phenomenon, according to Vold, represents a minority response to the domination exerted by the more powerful adult majority.

As Vold's work makes clear, an important theme in conflict theory is "criminalization," the process by which behaviour comes to be designated as criminal. Criminalization is not seen to emerge, conflict theorists argue, from the common will of the members of society, but rather from the ability of more powerful members of society to impose their definition of behaviour upon those who are less powerful. Thus Austin Turk (1976) argued that it is useful to think of the law as a "weapon in social conflict." Turk rejected older consensus views of law as a reflection of the compromise between conflicting segments of society. Instead, he maintained, law should be viewed as a resource that more powerful groups may be able to secure in order to resolve conflicts in their favour. The law does not express a common morality, but rather the morality of the group that is able to influence the content of the law.

Some critics have questioned, however, whether the conflict between interest groups characterizes the emergence of all laws or merely those that are directed toward the regulation of "vices" such as drug or alcohol use. Other critics have maintained that while the movement away from the study of crime and toward the study of criminalization was an important step, conservative conflict theorists offered only limited insight into these processes. In particular, Marxian criminologists maintain that the emphasis that conservative conflict theory places upon interest groups diverts attention from the study of how social conflict is rooted in the structure of society.

These more radical theories of social conflict proceed from general Marxian assumptions about history and social change, and are not easily summarized. Pfohl (1985, p. 347), however, characterized these assumptions as follows:

> The Marxist image of deviance suggests that the social organization of material existence is a primary factor in determining the style and content of social control. . . . Material resources, human population, and technological know-how must be socially organized if they are to provide for a stable economic environment. Economic production is a social art. It is structured by organized social relations. The way this structuring occurs is what Marx referred to as the "mode of production." Central as it is to the very survival of the social

group, the mode of production is said to influence all other social relations, be they legal, religious, formal, or whatever. How the mode of production influences the relations of social control is central to the critical understanding of social deviance. . . . The Marxist interpretation of history stresses the impact of unequal economic resources on the entirety of social life.

Building upon these assumptions (and upon the insights provided by the writings of more conservative conflict theorists), Marxian criminologists have attempted to understand the relationship between crime and social control, and the structured inequalities of capitalist societies. Consistent with much Marxist scholarship, they have argued that capitalist forms of economic production contain within them the elements of a conflict between a capitalist class, which controls the mode of production, and a labouring class, which must sell its labour in order to survive.

During the 1970s, many Marxian scholars argued that processes of criminalization could be understood as the means by which the capitalist ruling class attempts to control the labour class and thereby maintain its advantage (Chambliss, 1975; Quinney, 1974). Criminal law, as a social institution, was thus viewed as an instrument of class oppression, and behaviour that threatened the interests and privileges of the ruling class was seen as subject to criminalization. Moreover, it was argued that, while "capitalist crimes" such as price-fixing, union busting, the pollution of the environment, or the endangerment of worker safety may result in greater harm than the garden-variety offences of robbery or assault, they are either ignored by the state or defined as less serious regulatory offences.

Proponents of more mainstream criminological approaches maintained that these attempts to develop a Marxian theory of crime were too simplistic. A similar criticism was made by a subsequent generation of Marxian scholars who attempted to refine the approach and to offer a view of the relationship between capitalism and

crime that is considerably more sophisticated. For example, a recent trend in Marxian criminology, "left realism," has faulted earlier approaches for their insensitivity to the kinds of crimes about which most members of society show the greatest concern (Matthews & Young, 1986; MacLean, 1989). Left realists argue that while Marxian criminology must increase awareness of the crimes of capitalists, it must also attempt to understand the origins and consequences of street crimes, since such offences disproportionately victimize women, the poor, and others who are made vulnerable by capitalist economic relations.

The range of theoretical approaches that may be labelled Marxian is extremely broad, and as a result, it is difficult to describe the limitations that they share in common. Two points, however, require comment. First, as many critics have pointed out, Marxian theories have frequently evaded empirical test. This was especially true of the first wave of Marxian theory, which was frequently distrustful of traditional criminological methodology and thus resisted attempts at empirical verification. In general, however, the empirical evidence supportive of Marxian models of crime and social control is safely characterized as piecemeal and frequently inconsistent. Second, the value of a Marxian theory of crime ultimately rests upon the more general assumptions that such a theory makes about the nature of social organization and social change, and such assumptions have not gone unchallenged (Turk, 1986).

Victim-Centred Theories

As the above review makes quite evident, criminological theory has, for the most part, been focussed on the study of offenders. More recent years, however, have witnessed the emergence of a large body of criminological theory intended to place the victim rather than the offender at centre stage. Whereas previous theories assume a steady supply of victims and attempt to explain the behaviour of offenders, these victim-centred theories are more likely to assume a steady supply of offenders and attempt to understand, instead, the behaviour of victims. The growth of victim-centred theories may be traced to three important developments. The first was the emergence of the "crime victim" as a social and political issue in the 1970s and 1980s (Elias, 1986). The second development concerned a disenchantment on the part of many criminologists with the explanations offered by the offender-based theories that have dominated criminology since its inception. Finally, the emergence of victim-centred theories may be linked to the proliferation of victim surveys, which have yielded a wealth of information relating to the social characteristics of victims and victimization.

One important line of theoretical inquiry into victim processes emphasizes the *situational* nature of victim-offender interactions. In an early empirical study, Wolfgang (1958) discovered that in about one in four of the homicides in the city of Philadelphia between 1948 and 1952, the victim, rather than the offender, was the first party in the exchange to engage in some sort of aggressive action. Wolfgang conceptualized such murders as "victim-precipitated." He intended the term to describe such homicides in terms of the situational dynamic that led to the lethal outcome. Typical of the victim-precipitated homicide would be the situation in which the following occurred:

> The person who ended up the victim was the one who had started a barroom brawl. His friends tried to break up the fight, but he persisted. Finally, the tide turned, and the aggressor was knocked down; he hit his head on the floor and died from the injuries (Karmen, 1984, p. 79).

Wolfgang's general point was that in a relatively large proportion of the homicides that he studied, the stereotypical image of an exchange between a completely innocent victim and a completely guilty offender was not applicable.

Although the concept of victim-precipitation has been very influential in forcing a rethinking of the situational determinants of criminal incidents, it has also been widely criticized. Much of this criticism has centred on the tendency toward "victim blaming." Thus, in recent years, attention has moved beyond victim-precipitation, looking more fully at the interaction between the offender and the victim (Luckenbill, 1984). In a study of 70 California homicides, Luckenbill (1977) analyzed murder as a "situated transaction." His analysis revealed that homicide is generally the result of a "character contest." Such contests take the form of a gamelike confrontation in which offender and victim each attempt to save face at the expense of the other. In a similar way, Felson and Steadman (1983) analyzed the ways in which the escalation of offender and victim aggression eventuates in criminal violence. While such analyses may be said to find their theoretical origins in the concept of victim-precipitation, they provide important elaborations and in doing so provide a more balanced assessment of the role played by victim-offender exchanges in the generation of crime.

A somewhat different approach to the study of crime victims is provided by lifestyle-exposure theory. This theoretical position, originally formulated by Hindelang, Gottfredson, and Garofalo (1978), tries to explain why some groups in society (males, the young, racial and economic minorities) face much higher risks of victimization than do other groups. For Hindelang and his colleagues, the principal link between the social and demographic characteristics of people and the victimization risks that they face is the concept of "lifestyle." This concept is defined by the authors in terms of daily activities of both a vocational and leisure nature. Stated differently, lifestyles may be defined as the patterned ways in which people distribute their time and energies across a range of activities. We can recognize without much difficulty that a retired middle-class female typically has a different lifestyle than a young male working-class high school student. The retiree and the student would differ with respect to how they put in an average day, how they spend their leisure time, how often they go out in the evening, where they go when they do go out in the evening, and with whom they routinely associate.

Hindelang and his colleagues argued that some lifestyles are more likely than others to put people at risk of criminal victimization. For example, to the extent that the style of life regularly puts a person on the street or in bars late at night, or brings the person into regular contact with people who have the social and demographic characteristics of typical offenders, the risk of criminal victimization increases. Young members of minority groups, therefore, have a higher level of victimization than middle-class retirees because the lifestyle of the former group entails much more exposure to victimization risk than does the lifestyle of the latter group.

An allied approach to the study of victimization is known as "routine activity theory." As originally developed by Cohen and Felson (1979), routine activity theory attempts to explain variations in victimization rates independently of changes in the size of the offender population. They argued that in order for a direct-contact predatory victimization (such as assault, personal theft, or break and enter) to occur, three elements must come together in time and space. A *motivated offender* must come into contact with a *suitable target* in the absence of *capable guardianship* (that might otherwise prevent the occurrence of the victimization).

While most criminological theorists have emphasized the study of the factors that motivate offenders, Cohen and Felson wanted to concentrate on the other two factors as well as upon the changes in society that affect the rates at which offenders, targets, and the lack of guardianship converge. Beginning with these assumptions, Cohen and Felson argued that since the end of the Second World War, several changes have occurred in North American society to increase the likelihood of victimization. In general, they argued, the world beyond the household, rather than the household, has increasingly become the locus of routine activities. People are, for instance, more likely to eat out at restaurants or to take longer vacations than in earlier periods. In a related way, many women who in previous times would have been homemakers are now in school or in the paid labour force. Moreover, the growth in the number of single-person households brought about by rising divorce rates and the tendency on the part of

many people to marry at a later stage in the life cycle has accelerated the shift in routine activities away from the home.

According to Cohen and Felson, such changes have important implications for the levels of victimization. First, the dispersion of activities away from the home increases the probability that people will come into contact with strangers who might threaten them with criminal harm. Second, these changes mean that homes are occupied at a much lower rate than in previous decades and, as a result, households and their contents are subject to generally lower levels of guardianship. Finally, these changes have increased consumer demand for lightweight durable consumer goods (such as portable radios, television sets, computers, and VCRs) that are defined by offenders as suitable targets.

Overall, Cohen and Felson maintained, these broad social changes have increased the likelihood that motivated offenders and suitable targets will converge in time and space in the absence of capable guardians and, as a result, rates of direct contact victimization will be expected to climb. Importantly, however, their analysis implies that these changes will increase victimization levels even if the number of motivated offenders does not increase. Crime is not simply the product of an offender's intention, but of the spatial and temporal combination of this intention with other elements.

It is apparent that lifestyle-exposure and routine activity theorists share many common themes. In fact, some writers suggest that the differences between the approaches are more apparent than real (Sampson, 1987) and that both positions should be viewed as aspects of a more general theory of victimization opportunity. To be sure, empirical tests of these theories blur whatever distinctions may exist, and many researchers use the terms *lifestyle-exposure* and *routine activity* interchangeably.

But how are we to understand the offender's role in the context of theories of opportunity? This role is usually understood in terms of theories of rational choice (Birckbeck & LaFree, 1993; Clarke & Felson, 1993; Cornish & Clarke, 1986; Tunnell, 1992). Rather than begin with questions about what motivates offenders, rational choice theory assumes that offenders seek to benefit from their crimes. Moreover, it is argued that in order to benefit from crime the offender must make decisions and choices about when and where the crime will occur or who will be victimized. It is recognized that offenders' rationality in this respect is compromised by time, available information, and cognitive ability. Thus the offender operates on the basis of a "limited" rather than a "pure" rationality. Rational choice theory encourages us to try to understand how offenders create or exploit criminal opportunities. In theorizing about break and enter, for instance, we might ask how the offender assesses the ease with which the crime can be committed, the risks associated with the offence, or the relative gains that the crime can potentially provide (Clarke, 1992). In contrast to Gottfredson and Hirschi's general theory of crime, rational choice theories suggest that different types of offending situations involve quite distinct choice criteria, and so there is little to be gained from efforts to theorize about crime as a generic category.

In any case, these approaches have generated a large body of empirical literature in recent years, and analysts have attempted to apply the logic of these arguments to a broad range of victimization problems (Fattah, 1991; Felson, 1998). Although victimization research in Canada has lagged behind that of other countries, researchers in this country have also begun in recent years to apply lifestyle and routine activity models to the study of crime (Baron, Chapter 13, this volume; Kennedy & Forde, 1990; Silverman & Kennedy, 1993; Sacco & Kennedy, 1994; Sacco, Johnson, & Arnold, 1993).

Victimization opportunity theories have significantly reoriented the study of direct contact predatory offences. In so doing, they have overcome some of the obstacles that beset traditional offender-based explanations of such behaviour (Miethe & Meier, 1994). Moreover, such accounts are well supported by the existing body of empirical evidence (Garofalo, 1986; Maxfield, 1987b). Critics suggest, however, that the utility of such theories ultimately will depend upon the ability of investigators to over-

come the limitations of current formulations. For instance, victimization opportunity theories have, to date, utilized rather crude conceptual and operational definitions of "lifestyle" and "routine activities" (Miethe, Stafford, & Long, 1987) and have failed to devote sufficient attention to the relationship between lifestyle activities and wider community settings (Sampson & Wooldredge, 1987; Kennedy & Forde, 1990). Other critics have argued that there is a need to shift attention away from the general relationship between routine activities and victimization and toward the study of such relationships in the context of specific domains such as the workplace (Lynch, 1987), the school (Garofalo, Siegel, & Laub, 1987), or the household (Maxfield, 1987a). It should also be re-emphasized that thus far the applicability of lifestyle and routine activity theories has been limited to the study of direct contact offences, with little investigation of victimless, corporate, or white-collar crimes.

Feminist Theories

A new group of theories, termed feminist theories, has begun to influence criminological thinking with respect to a diverse range of issues (Boritch, 1997; Comack, 1992; Daly & Chesney-Lind, 1988). In general, these theories emerged as a response to the tendency of mainstream criminology to ignore the study of women as victims and offenders and the role of gender in organizing social relations. It is argued that criminological theories have focussed, implicitly and explicitly, on the study of men, and that crime and criminal justice issues that uniquely affect women — such as sexual assault or wife assault — have been neglected (Boritch, 1997). Feminist theories intend to correct this imbalance. However, contemporary feminist theories are not simply theories of women's crime and victimization. They more generally attempt to move beyond the study of women to a "gendered understanding" of crime and crime control (Simpson, 1989). In other words, these theories ask how gender inequality is implicated in the crime and victimization of both females and males (Gibbons, 1994).

While they share many assumptions in common, feminist theories are not of one type. Hinch (1994) identified three broad categories. "Liberal feminism" seeks to explain male-female differences in crime and victimization in terms of variations in sex-role socialization. As a critique of law and the criminal justice system, liberal feminism seeks equality of protection and of treatment. "Radical feminism" is organized around the theme of "patriarchy." This term describes the many and varied ways in which the male domination of women is built into the structure of society. Radical feminism argues that problems such as male violence against women (or the inability or unwillingness of the justice system to address such violence) is rooted in and underwritten by social institutions such as the family or the police. Finally, "socialist feminism" seeks to explore the problem of crime and social control in terms of the intersection of gender relations and class relations. Socialist feminism, therefore, combines elements of feminist thought with elements of Marxian analysis.

Some of these ideas are reflected in the writings of John Hagan, A. R. Gillis, and John Simpson, (1979, 1985, 1987, 1988), whose work offers an analysis of why male rather than female adolescents are more frequently involved in delinquent activity. In constructing a theoretical account of this pattern, they attempted to integrate the logic of control theory with insights offered by Marxian and feminist criminologists. In their theoretical approach, called "power-control theory," Hagan and his colleagues maintained that gender differences in delinquency are rooted in historical changes that have assigned men and women to different social realms and have created differences in the kinds of social control to which each gender group is subjected. Specifically, as modern industrial economies developed, there emerged a sphere of consumption and a sphere of production. The former is best typified by the home environment (to which women were largely segregated), while the latter is best typified by the workplace (in which men have largely been dominant). The growth of the criminal justice system, which coincided with these economic changes, was largely concerned with the regulation of behaviour in the public sphere. As a result, criminal justice has had to do with controlling the behaviour of men more than the behaviour of women. By contrast, the household has come to be characterized by informal rather than formal control processes in which women are more actively involved than men. Hagan and his colleagues argued that these changes stratified social control in such a way that men more than women have become both the "instruments" and "objects" of formal control, while women more than men have become the "instruments" and "objects" of informal control.

They also argued that the family, because it is the social agency primarily responsible for early socialization, provides the means by which these differences are maintained from one generation to the next. Mothers more than fathers are assigned the responsibility for the control of children, and daughters more than sons are subjected to these control processes, especially in the area of attitudes toward risk taking. The socialization of daughters may encourage passivity and in so doing may prepare females for "the cult of domesticity." The socialization of sons, however, frees males from many forms of control, including those that might discourage risk taking, thus preparing them for activities associated with the production sphere. Since much delinquency may be understood as risk-taking activity, gender differences in delinquent conduct follow logically from these more general differences in socialization processes.

Integrated Theories

As the foregoing makes obvious, there has been no shortage of attempts to theorize about the nature and the causes of crime. For many criminologists, however, the existence of such a large number of theories is dismaying. Thomas Bernard (1990) noted that many of these theories have been around at least 25 years while new theories are always being developed. As more and more theories proliferate, Bernard warned, scientific progress is impeded rather than advanced.

How then do we resolve the problem of too many theories? Two kinds of solutions are advanced in the contemporary criminological literature. One solution stresses the falsification of theories, and the other stresses theoretical integration. By falsification is meant the use of research to reject those explanations that are inconsistent with our empirical observations of the world. In other words, we should be able to use the results of our research to tell us which arguments are false and can therefore be discarded. However, as Bernard observed, despite very high levels of research activity, no theory of crime has truly been falsified in the entire history of criminology, largely because theories are rarely stated in terms that allow them to be falsified. We are rarely told, in explicit terms, by those who construct theories, what empirical evidence would allow us to say that the theory is *wrong*. Instead, we tend to accumulate large numbers of explanations, all of which seem to derive at least partial support from the available research.

Theoretical integration provides an alternative solution to the problem. It may be defined as "the combination of 2 or more pre-existing theories, selected on the basis of their perceived commonalities, into a single reformulated theoretical model with greater comprehensiveness and explanatory value than any one of its components" (Farnworth, 1989, p. 95). Of course, all theories are to some extent integrative in that they tend to be influenced by and thus reflect ideas that have gone before them. When we talk about integrated theories, however, we are talking about a more deliberate process by which ideas can be combined so as to increase their explanatory power.

In recent years, theoretical integration has been given a variety of expressions, some of which take an interdisciplinary approach, attempting to combine the theoretical insights derived from one discipline (e.g., biology or psychology) with those derived from another discipline (e.g., sociology). For example, Booth and Osgood (1993) reported evidence of a causal relationship between testosterone levels and adult crime. However, they suggested that this effect is influenced by social factors such as social integration and prior involvement in juvenile crime. Most social scientists would probably agree that both biological and environmental factors play a role in antisocial behaviours (Lilly et al., 1989). What they probably would not be able to agree on is the relative contribution of each to particular cases. For example, after a rather exhaustive review of the literature in these areas, Fishbein (1990, p. 55) concluded:

> How biological variables interact with social and psychological factors to produce human behaviour generally and antisocial behaviour specifically is unknown. . . . The bulk of biological studies . . . have examined only a few isolated variables and have generally failed to evaluate dynamic interrelationships among biological and socioenvironmental conditions.

A causal link is similarly found in learning disability research (Carrier, 1986; Crealock, 1987), which attempts to tie neurologically based learning disability (e.g., dyslexia, aphasia, hyperkinesis) to juvenile delinquency through a chain of events including learning problems, poor school performance, labelling by adults and peers, association with similar peers, dropping out of school, and finally, increased susceptibility to delinquent behaviour. The causal chain suggested here is consistent with most of the sociological theories discussed in this chapter and with sociological findings concerning the link between poor school performance and delinquency. However, learning disability research emphasizes a different major cause — neurological malfunction. Unfortunately, this research is fraught with problems, not the least of which is the difficulty involved in measuring the independent variable (learning disabilities).

In a distinct way, Terence Thornberry (1987) attempted to integrate ideas derived from social control and cultural theories. For Thornberry, a major problem of most contemporary theories of delinquency is that they present a static understanding of the process of crime causation. In contrast, Thornberry developed an "interactional theory of delinquency" that regards the relationship between delinquency and social bonds as dynamic. He argues that while low levels of attachment to parents, of commitment to school, or of belief in conventional values may allow delinquency to happen, they do not make it happen. Rather than resulting in delinquency, weak social bonds may instead result in mental illness, alcoholism, or even continued conventional behaviour. The likelihood of delinquency increases when adolescents with weak bonds have delinquent values or associate with delinquent peers. Thus for Thornberry, it is not only the weakness or the strength of the parent-child bond but also the cultural values of delinquency that have causal significance. In addition, Thornberry maintained, while weak social bonds may affect the occurrence of delinquency, the delinquency may in turn affect the strength of the bond. When parents grow more distant from a child who behaves badly, acts of delinquency may contribute to the erosion of social bonds. In general, Thornberry's position is that social control and delinquency interact over time in a process that involves mutual influence.

A final example of theoretical integration illustrates the ways in which theories of offending and theories of victimization may be combined in the context of a single explanatory framework. Terance Miethe and Robert Meier (1994) have argued that a major problem with contemporary explanations of crime is that theories that have focussed on explaining crime in terms of what offenders do (e.g., social disorganization or social control) and theories that have attempted to explain crime in terms of what potential victims do (e.g., routine activities theory) have not paid attention to each other. However, both elements are essential to any comprehensive account of why crime occurs. Moreover, they argue, it is important to be attentive to the specific character of the social context under which "offender and victim characteristics combine" (1994, p. 59). In other words, the linchpin of any attempt to integrate our understanding of the causes of offending with our understanding of the causes of victimization are those situational factors that enhance offender motivation and victim risk. Most notably, for Miethe and Meier, these include the physical location of crimes, the interpersonal relationship between victim and offender, and the behavioural setting (e.g., home versus work) in which the crime occurs.

There are objections to be raised with respect to the trend toward theoretical integration. First, it might be argued that integration that mixes and matches theoretical viewpoints does little to reduce the clutter and thus represents little more than a second-order form of theoretical diffusion. Additionally, some writers charge that the major theories in criminology — such as cultural theory and social control theory — are not really compatible with each other. In this respect, Hirschi (1979) has argued that these explanations reflect quite different assumptions about social life, and thus any attempt to make them compatible with each other must distort their original meaning to such a degree that they cease to resemble their original formulations. Such criticisms aside, it is likely that the trend toward theoretical economy through integration will continue (Brannigan, 1997; Sorenson & Brownfield, 1995).

CONCLUSIONS

This section has provided a brief overview of the major sociological perspectives that have dominated the study of crime. However, given their vast array, it is important to ask how we go about assessing the relative merits of these explanations. Most criminologists answer this question by arguing that if theories are to be valid and reliable guides to understanding behaviour, they must be supported by research evidence and be consistent with empirical observations.

THE READINGS

Not surprisingly, given the statement above, all of the articles in this part demonstrate an awareness of the intricate relationship between theoretical explanation and empirical research. In the first selection,

"Power-Control Theory," John Hagan details the criminological foundations of power-control theory and the types of questions the theory encourages us to ask. The discussion emphasizes how the long-standing sociological interest in class and crime may be combined with the emerging body of theory and research on crime and gender.

In "Crime among the Provinces," Timothy F. Hartnagel examines regional trends in Canadian crime rates. Why is it, he asks, that rates of many kinds of crime increase from east to west? Hartnagel argues that at least in part, the answer to this question is to be found in the effects created by geographic mobility. Mobile populations imply disintegrative forces that weaken informal social control. His analysis suggests strong links to the earlier versions of social disorganization theory discussed above.

Marginalized, homeless youth are the subject of the empirical test described in "Risky Lifestyles and the Link between Offending and Victimization." Drawing on the general theoretical insights of lifestyle and routine activities theory, Stephen W. Baron investigates the link between being a victim and victimizing others. Among his sample of street youth, Baron reports, the relationship is a strong one. The capricious nature of violence, the commitment to subcultural norms supportive of violence, and the behaviour typical of offenders leaves these youth vulnerable to victimization. His evidence also suggests that the childhood victimization experienced by many of these youths increases their victimization risks because it encourages them to adopt styles of interaction that increase the likelihood of criminal conflict.

In "Inattention to Sanctions in Criminal Conduct," Lucia Benaquisto addresses questions derived from rational choice and deterrence theories of crime. Benaquisto's research involves the analysis of interviews conducted with 152 prison inmates who were asked about the decision-making processes that led to the commission of the offences for which they were incarcerated. Her conclusion, that only a minority of the inmates claim to have considered the risks of punishment, casts doubt on the popular assumption that lengthier sentences would be an effective means of crime control.

A test of the general theory of crime is described in the selection by Teresa C. LaGrange and Robert A. Silverman, entitled "Low Self-Control and Opportunity." Employing data gathered from 2000 secondary school students, LaGrange and Silverman attempt to determine whether low self-control is related to offending patterns. Their results provide only partial support for the general theory and reveal that the relationship between self-control and delinquency varies across gender groups and for different offence types.

Finally, in "Changes in the Structure of Life Courses and the Decline of Social Capital," Ross Macmillan uses life course theory to explain increases in rates of crime over the last few decades. As discussed above, Macmillan argues that changes in the character of major life transitions (especially for young males) over the period in question may have increased the size of the pool of motivated offenders. His results provide strong support for the argument.

REFERENCES

Adler, F. (1975). *Sisters in crime.* New York: McGraw-Hill.

Agnew, R. (1984). Goal achievement and delinquency. *Sociology and Social Research, 68*, 435–451.

Agnew, R. (1992). Foundation for a general strain theory of crime and delinquency. *Criminology, 30*(1), 47–83.

Agnew, R., & Peters, A. R. (1986). The techniques of neutralization: An analysis of predisposing and situational factors. *Criminal Justice and Behavior, 13*(1), 81–97.

Agnew, R., & White, H. R. (1992). An empirical test of general strain theory. *Criminology, 30*(4), 475–499.

Akers, R. L. (1985). *Deviant behavior: A social learning approach* (3rd ed.). Belmont, CA: Wadsworth Publishing Co.

Baron, S. W., & Hartnagel, T. F. (1997). Street youth and strain: Testing Agnew's revised theory. Paper presented to the Annual Meetings of the American Society of Criminology, San Diego.

Baron, S. W., & Kennedy, L. W. (1998). Deterrence and homeless male street youth. *Canadian Journal of Criminology* (January), 27–60.

Beccaria, C. (1764). *Essays on crime and punishment.* H. Paolucci (Trans. 1963). Indianapolis, IN: Bobbs-Merrill Co.

Becker, H. S. (1963). *Outsiders: Studies in the sociology of deviance.* New York: Free Press.

Bentham, J. (1843). Principles of penal law. In J. Bowing (Ed.), *The works of Jeremy Bentham.* Edinburgh: W. Tait.

Bernard, T. J. (1981). The distinction between conflict and radical criminology. *Journal of Criminal Law and Criminology, 72,* 362–379.

Bernard, T. J. (1990). Twenty years of testing theories: What have we learned and why? *Journal of Research in Crime and Delinquency, 27*(4), 325–347.

Birckbeck, C., & LaFree, G. (1993). The situational analysis of crime and deviance. *Annual Review of Sociology, 19,* 113–137.

Booth, A., & Osgood, D. W. (1993). The influence of testosterone on deviance in adulthood: Assessing and explaining the relationship. *Criminology, 31*(l), 93–117.

Boritch, H. (1997). *Fallen women: Female crime and criminal justice in Canada.* Scarborough, ON: Nelson Canada.

Brannigan, A. (1997). Self-control, social control and evolutionary psychology: Towards an integrated perspective on crime. *Canadian Journal of Criminology* (October), 403–431.

Brownfield, D., & Sorenson, A. M. (1993). Self-control and juvenile delinquency: Theoretical issues and an empirical assessment of selected elements of a general theory of crime. *Deviant Behavior, 14,* 243–264.

Burgess, E. W. (1923). The growth of the city. Paper prepared for the meetings of the American Sociological Society. Reprinted in R. Park, *The city.* Chicago: University of Chicago Press.

Bursik, R. J., & Grasmick, H. G. (1993). *Neighborhoods and crime.* New York: Lexington Books.

Carrier, J. G. (1986). *Learning disability: Social class and the construction of inequality in American education.* New York: Greenwood Press.

Chambliss, W. J. (1975). Toward a political economy of crime. *Theory and Society, 2*(Summer), 152–153.

Clark, R. O. (1988). Celerity and specific deterrence: A look at the evidence. *Canadian Journal of Criminology, 30,* 109–120.

Clarke, R. V. (1992). Introduction. In R. V. Clarke (Ed.), *Situational crime prevention.* Albany, NY: Harrow and Heston.

Clarke, R. V., & Felson, M. (1993). Introduction: Criminology, routine activity and rational choice. In R. V. Clarke & M. Felson (Eds.), *Routine activity and rational choice.* New Brunswick: Transaction Publishers.

Cloward, R. A., & Ohlin, L. E. (1960). *Delinquency and opportunity: A theory of delinquent gangs.* New York: Free Press.

Cohen, A. K. (1955). *Delinquent boys: The culture of the gang.* Glencoe, IL: Free Press.

Cohen, L. E., & Felson, M. (1979). Social change and crime rate trends: A routine activity approach. *American Sociological Review, 44,* 588–608.

Coleman, J. (1990). *Foundations of social theory.* Cambridge, MA: Harvard University Press.

Comack, E. (1992). Women and crime. In R. Linden (Ed.), *Criminology: A Canadian perspective.* Toronto: Harcourt Brace Jovanovich.

Conklin, J. E. (1986). *Criminology.* New York: Macmillan Publishing Co.

Cornish, D. B., & Clarke, R. V. (1986). *The reasoning criminal.* New York: Springer-Verlag.

Crealock, C. M. (1987). The *LD/JD Link: Causation or correlation.* Ottawa: Solicitor General of Canada.

Cusson, M. (1993). Situational deterrence: Fear during the criminal event. In R. V. Clarke (Ed.), *Crime prevention studies, Vol. 1.* Monsey, NY: Criminal Justice Press.

Daly, K., & Chesney-Lind, M. (1988). Feminism and criminology. *Justice Quarterly, 5,* 497–583.

Doob, A. N., Grossman, M. G., & Auger, R. P. (1994). Aboriginal homicides in Ontario. *Canadian Journal of Criminology, 36*(1), 29–62.

Downes, D., & Rock, P. (1988). *Understanding deviance* (2nd ed.). Oxford: Clarendon Press.

Elias, R. (1986). *The politics of victimization.* New York: Oxford University Press.

Farnworth, M. (1989). Theory integration versus model building. In S. F. Messner, M. D. Krohn, & A. E. Liska (Eds.), *Theoretical integration in the study of deviance and crime.* Albany: State University of New York Press.

Fattah, E. A. (1991). *Understanding criminal victimization.* Scarborough: Prentice-Hall Canada.

Felson, M. (1998). *Crime and everyday life* (2nd ed.). Thousand Oaks, CA: Pine Forge Press.

Felson, R. B., & Steadman, H. J. (1983). Situational factors in disputes leading to criminal violence. *Criminology, 21* (l), 59–74.

Fischer, C. S. (1975). Toward a subcultural theory of urbanism, race, and gender: The Canadian case. *Crime and Delinquency, 31* (l), 129–146.

Fischer, C. S. (1976). *The urban experience.* New York: Pine Forge Press.

Fishbein, D. H. (1990). Biological perspectives in criminology. *Criminology, 28* (l), 27–72.

Garofalo, J. (1986). Lifestyles and victimization: An update. In E. A. Fattah (Ed.), *From crime policy to victim policy: Reorienting the justice system.* London: Macmillan.

Garofalo, J., Siegel, L., & Laub, J. (1987). School related victimizations among adolescents: An analysis of National Crime Survey (NCS) narratives. *Journal of Quantitative Criminology, 3* (4), 321–338.

Gibbons, D.C. (1994). *Talking about crime and criminals.* Englewood Cliffs, NJ: Prentice-Hall.

Glaser, D. (1956). Criminality theories and behavioral images. *American Journal of Sociology, 61* (March), 433–444.

Goode, E. (1994). *Deviant behaviour* (4th ed.). Englewood Cliffs, NJ: Prentice-Hall Inc.

Goring, C. (1913). *The English convict.* London: His Majesty's Stationery Office.

Gottfredson, M. R., & Hirschi, T. (1990). *A general theory of crime.* Stanford, CA: Stanford University Press.

Grandin, E., & Lupri, E. (1997). Intimate violence in Canada and the United States: A cross-national comparison. *Journal of Family Violence, 12* (4), 417–443.

Grasmick, H. G., Tittle, C. R., Bursik, R. J., Jr., & Arneklev, B. J. (1993). Testing the core empirical implications of Gottfredson and Hirschi's general theory of crime. *Journal of Research in Crime and Delinquency, 30* (1), 5–29.

Guest, A. (1969). *The applicability of the Burgess zonal United States 1800–1915.* Philadelphia: University of Pennsylvania Press.

Hagan, J. (1989). Comparing crime and criminalization in Canada and the U.S.A. *Canadian Journal of Sociology, 14,* 361–371.

Hagan, J. (1994). *Crime and disrepute.* Thousand Oaks, CA: Harcourt Brace Jovanovich.

Hagan, J., Gillis, A. R., & Simpson, J. (1985). The class structure of gender and delinquency: Toward a power-control theory of common delinquent behavior. *American Journal of Sociology, 90* (6), 1151–1178.

Hagan, J., Simpson, J. H., & Gillis, A. R. (1979). The sexual stratification of social control: A gender-based perspective. *British Journal of Sociology, 30,* 25–38.

Hagan, J., Simpson, J. H., & Gillis, A. R. (1987). Class in the household: Deprivation, liberation and a power-control theory of gender and delinquency. *American Journal of Sociology, 92* (4), 788–816.

Hagan, J., Simpson, J. H., & Gillis, A. R. (1988). Feminist scholarship, relational and instrumental control, and a power-control theory of gender and delinquency. *British Journal of Sociology, 39* (3), 301–336.

Hinch, R. (1994). *Readings in critical criminology.* Scarborough: Prentice-Hall Canada Inc.

Hindelang, M. J., Gottfredson, M. R., & Garofalo, J. (1978). *Victims of personal crime: An empirical foundation for a theory of personal victimization.* Cambridge, MA: Ballinger Publishing Co.

Hirschi, T. (1969). *Causes of delinquency.* Berkeley: University of California Press.

Hirschi, T. (1979). Separate and unequal is better. *Journal of Research in Crime and Delinquency, 16,* 34–38.

Jackson, P. I. (1984). Opportunity and crime: A function of city size. *Sociology and Social Research, 68,* 172–193.

Karmen, A. (1984). *Crime victims: An introduction to criminology.* Monterey, CA: Brooks/Cole Publishing Co.

Katz, J., & Chambliss, W. J. (1995). Biology and crime. in J. F. Sheley (Ed.), *Criminology: A contemporary handbook.* Belmont, CA: Wadsworth Publishing Co.

Keane, C., Maxim, P. S., & Teevan, J. J. (1993). Drinking and driving, self-control and gender: Testing a general theory of crime. *Journal of Research in Crime and Delinquency, 30* (l), 30–46.

Kennedy, L. W., & Forde, D. (1990). Routine activities and crime: An analysis of victimization in Canada. *Criminology, 28,* 137–152.

Krohn, M. (1991). Control and deterrence theories. In J. F. Sheley (Ed.), *Criminology: A contemporary handbook.* Belmont, CA: Wadsworth Publishing Co.

Lander, B. (1954). *Toward an understanding of juvenile delinquency.* New York: Columbia University Press.

Lemert, E. M. (1951). *Social pathology.* New York: McGraw-Hill.

Lilly, J. R., Cullen, F. T., & Ball, R. A. (1989). *Criminological theory: Context and consequences.* Newbury Park, CA: Sage.

Lombroso, C. (1876). *L'uomo delinquente [The criminal man].* Milano: Hoepli.

Luckenbill, D. F. (1977). Criminal homicide as a situated transaction. *Social Problems, 25*, 176–186.

Luckenbill, D. F. (1984). Murder and assault. In R. F. Meier (Ed.), *Major forms of crime.* Beverly Hills, CA: Sage Publications.

Lynch, J. P. (1987). Routine activity and victimization at work. *Journal of Quantitative Criminology, 3*(4), 283–300.

MacLean, B. (1989). Framing the law and order debate: Left realism, local crime surveys and police accountability. Paper presented at the annual meetings of the American Society of Criminology, Reno, Nevada.

Matthews, R., & Young, J. (1986). *Confronting crime.* London: Sage Publications.

Matza, D. (1964). *Delinquency and drift.* New York: John Wiley and Sons.

Maxfield, M. G. (1987a). Household composition, routine activity and victimization: A comparative analysis. *Journal of Quantitative Criminology, 3*(4), 301–320.

Maxfield, M. G. (1987b). Lifestyle and routine activity theories of crime: Empirical studies of victimization, delinquency and offender decision-making. *Journal of Quantitative Criminology, 3*(4), 275–282.

Merton, R. K. (1938). Social structure and anomie. *American Sociological Review, 3*, 672–682.

Merton, R. K. (1957). *Social theory and social structure.* New York: Free Press.

Miethe, T. D., & Meier, R. F. (1994). *Crime and its social context.* Albany: State University of New York Press.

Miethe, T. D., Stafford, M. C., & Long, J. S. (1987). Social differentiation in criminal victimization: A test of routine activities/lifestyle theories. *American Sociological Review, 52*(April), 184–194.

Mills, C. W. (1943). The professional ideology of social pathologists. *American Journal of Sociology, 49*, 165–180.

Minor, W. W. (1984). Neutralization as a hardening process: Considerations in the modelling of change. *Social Forces, 62*(4), 995–1019.

Nettler, G. (1984). *Explaining crime* (3rd ed.). New York: McGraw-Hill.

Nisbett, R. E., & Cohen, D. (1996). *Culture of honor: The psychology of violence in the south.* Boulder, CO: Westview Press.

O'Brien, R.M. (1985). *Crime and victimization data.* Beverly Hills, CA: Sage Publications.

Paternoster, R., Saltzman, L. E., Waldo, G. P., & Chiricos, T. G. (1983). Perceived risk and social control: Do sanctions really deter? *Law and Society Review, 17*, 457–480.

Pfohl, S. J. (1985). *Images of deviance and social control.* New York: McGraw-Hill.

Quinney, R. (1974). *Critique of legal order.* Boston: Little, Brown & Co.

Rahav, G. (1981). Culture conflict, urbanism, and delinquency. *Criminology, 18*(4), 523–530.

Ribordy, F. (1980). Culture conflict and crime among Italian immigrants. In R. A. Silverman & J. Teevan (Eds.), *Crime in Canadian society* (2nd ed.). Toronto: Butterworths.

Rosenberg, M., & Lewis, A. (1993). *Social deviance: An integrated approach.* Scarborough: Prentice-Hall Canada Inc.

Rosenfeld, R. (1986). Urban crime rates: Effects of inequality, welfare dependency, region, and race. In J. M. Byrne & R. J. Sampson (Eds.), *The social ecology of crime.* New York: Springer-Verlag.

Sacco, V. F. (1993). Violent crime in Canada and the United States: A theoretical assessment. *Canadian Review of American Studies, 23*(4), 89–112.

Sacco, V. F., & Kennedy, L. W. (1994). *The criminal event.* Toronto: Nelson Canada.

Sacco, V. F., Johnson, H., & Arnold, R. (1993). Urban-rural residence and criminal victimization. *Canadian Journal of Sociology, 18*(4), 431–451.

Sampson, R. J. (1987). Personal violence by strangers: An extension and test of the opportunity model of predatory victimization. *Journal of Criminal Law and Criminology, 78*(2), 327–356

Sampson, R. J. (1995). The community. In J. Q. Wilson & J. Petersilia (Eds.), *Crime.* San Francisco, CA: ICS Press.

Sampson, R. J., & Laub, J. H. (1993). *Crime in the making: Pathways and turning points through life.* Cambridge MA: Harvard University Press.

Sampson, R. J., & Wooldredge, J. D. (1987). Linking the micro- and macro-level dimensions of lifestyle/routine activity and opportunity models of predatory victimization. *Journal of Quantitative Criminology, 3*(4), 371–393.

Sellin, T. (1938). *Culture conflict and crime*. New York: Social Science Research Council.

Shaw, C., & McKay, H. (1942). *Juvenile delinquency and urban areas*. Chicago: University of Chicago Press.

Sherman, L. W., Gartin, P., & Buerger, M. E. (1989). Hot spots of predatory crime: Routine activities and the sociology of place. *Criminology, 27*(l), 27–55.

Silverman, R. A., & Kennedy, L. W. (1993). *Deadly deeds*. Toronto: Nelson Canada.

Simpson, S. S. (1989). Feminist theory, crime and justice. *Criminology, 27*(4), 605–631.

Sorenson, A. M., & Brownfield, D. (1995). Adolescent drug use and a general theory of crime. *Canadian Journal of Criminology, 37*(1), 19–37.

Steffensmeier, D. (1983). Organizational properties and sex-segregation in the underworld: Building a sociological theory of sex differences in crime. *Social Forces, 61*, 1010–1032.

Sutherland, E. (1939). *Criminology*. Philadelphia: J. B. Lippincott.

Sutherland, E. H., & Cressey, D. R. (1978). *Criminology* (10th ed.). Philadelphia: J. B. Lippincott.

Sykes, G., & Matza, D. (1957). Techniques of neutralization: A theory of delinquency. *American Sociological Review, 22*, 664–670.

Tannenbaum, F. (1938). *Crime and the community*. Boston: Ginn.

Thio, A. (1988). *Deviant behavior* (3rd ed.). Cambridge: Harper and Row.

Thornberry, T. P. (1987). Toward an interactional theory of delinquency. *Criminology, 25*(4), 863–891.

Tittle, C. R. (1983). Social class and criminal behavior: A critique of the theoretical foundation. *Social Forces, 62*, 334–358.

Tittle, C. R. (1989). Urbanness and unconventional behavior: A partial test of Claude Fischer's subcultural theory. *Criminology, 27*(2), 273–306.

Tunnell, K. D. (1992). *Choosing crime*. Chicago: Nelson-Hall Publishers.

Turk, A. (1976). Law as a weapon in social conflict. *Social Problems, 23*, 276–292.

Turk, A. (1986). Class, conflict and criminalization. In R. A. Silverman & J. Teevan (Eds.), *Crime in Canadian society* (3rd ed.). Toronto: Butterworths.

Vold, G. B. (1958). *Theoretical criminology*. New York: Oxford University Press.

Vold, G. B., & Bernard, T. J. (1986). *Theoretical criminology* (3rd ed.). New York: Oxford University Press.

Vold, G. B., Bernard, T. J., & Snipes, J. B. (1998). *Theoretical criminology*, (4th ed.). New York: Oxford University Press.

Walters, G. D., & White, T. W. (1989). Heredity and crime: Bad genes or bad research. *Criminology, 27*(3), 455–485.

Whyte, W. E. (1955). *Street corner society: The social structure of an Italian slum*. Chicago: University of Chicago Press.

Williams, F. P., & McShane, M. D. (1994). *Criminological theory* (2nd ed.). Englewood Cliffs, NJ: Prentice-Hall.

Wolfgang, M. E. (1958). *Patterns in criminal homicide*. New York: John Wiley & Sons.

Power-Control Theory

JOHN HAGAN

INTRODUCTION

In its most general form, power-control theory asserts that the class structure of the family plays a significant role in explaining the social distribution of delinquent behaviour through the social reproduction of gender relations. "Family class structure" and "the social reproduction of gender relations" are not commonly used concepts in sociological criminology, and so we begin with some definitions.

Family class structure consists of the configurations of power between spouses that derive from the positions these spouses occupy in their work inside and outside the home. Spouses often gain power in the family through their work outside the home. So the occupational advances of women in recent decades are of particular interest to our understanding of family class structure.

The social reproduction of gender relations refers to the activities, institutions, and relationships that are involved in the maintenance and renewal of gender roles, in the family and elsewhere. These activities include the parenting involved in caring for, protecting, and socializing children for the roles they will occupy as adults. According to power-control theory, family class structure shapes the social reproduction of gender relations, and in turn the social distribution of delinquency.

POWER, PATRIARCHY, AND DELINQUENCY

The concepts of power and control typically are treated as being, respectively, macro- and micro-structural in content. The macro-micro distinction may or may not be one of simple aggregation, as for example when classes are thought of as all persons found in common social relations of production, or as in addition sharing views of these conditions that result in group-based actions organized and carried out in ways that go beyond any simple summation of individual preferences (see Coleman, 1986). In either event, conceptual and empirical considerations of power typically occur at higher levels of aggregation and abstraction than do discussions of control, and they therefore are characteristically kept separate.

Considerations of power and control nonetheless have important features in common: for example, they are both relational in content. Power theories often focus on relations of domination in the workplace, while control theories frequently focus on relations of domination in the family. We do both here. Essential to the conceptualization and measurement in both areas of theory construction is the effort to capture a relational component of social structure. In power theories of the workplace, the relational structure may be that between owner and worker, or between supervisor and supervisee. In control theories of the family, the relational structure may be that between parent and child, or between parents themselves. In both cases, however, it is a sociological concern with relational and hierarchical structure that drives the conceptualization and measurement.

Power-control theory brings together these relational concerns in a multilevel framework. In doing so, this theory highlights another concern that the power and control traditions share. This common concern is with the conditions under which actors are free to deviate from social norms. Both the presence of power and the absence of control contribute to these conditions. A particular concern of power-control theory, for example, is to identify intersections of class and family relations that provide the greatest freedom for adolescent deviation. Power-control theory assumes that the concept of patriarchy is of fundamental importance in identifying such intersections.

Curtis (1986: 171) persuasively argues that patriarchy should not be seen as a theoretical concept with a standard definition, but as a generalization about social relations that calls for sociological investigation and explication. This generalization involves the propensity of males to create hierarchical structures through which they dominate others.

It is important to emphasize here that these others may be male as well as female. So the study of patriarchy includes within it the analysis of structures through which men exercise hierarchical domination over both males and females, for example, including children of both genders in the family. Curtis goes on to point out that patriarchy is extremely widespread, including structures of the state (such as police, courts, and correctional agencies) as well as the workplace and the family. But the source of patriarchy nonetheless is assumed to be the family. Millett (1970: 33) calls the family patriarchy's "chief institution," suggesting that the family is the fundamental instrument and the foundation unit of patriarchal society, and that the family and its roles are prototypical.

We are now in a position to begin sketching the outlines of a power-control theory of delinquency. We begin with the three levels of the theory, as illustrated in Figure 11.1. These include, in order of level of abstraction, *social-psychological process* involving the adolescents whose behaviours we wish to explain, *social positions* consisting of the gender and delinquency roles in which these adolescents are located, and the *class structures* by which families are socially organized. Five kinds of links, described further below, bring together the

Figure 11.1
A Power-Control Theory of Gender and Delinquency

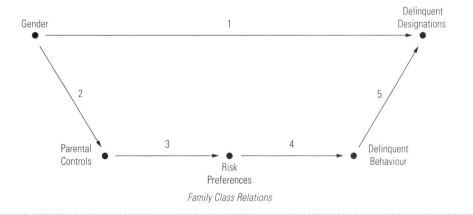

social positions and social-psychological processes that are the core of power-control theory.

We begin with the connections between the social positions and social-psychological processes identified in Figure 11.1. Link 1 is the correlation between gender and state-defined delinquency that criminologists long have observed. We need only note here that gender and delinquency both constitute ascribed positions that are socially designated and legally identified. Our interest is in establishing the family class structures and social-psychological processes that account for these social positions being joined in the correlations so consistently recorded by criminologists. Note that the interest of power-control theory is in individuals only insofar as they are located as occupants of these positions, and not, therefore, in the individuals per se. By virtue of the premises noted above, the question power-control theory inevitably asks is: how and why are individuals located in male adolescent positions freer to deviate in ways defined by the state as delinquent than are individuals located in female adolescent positions?

The reference to state definition above indicates that the connection between officially defined delinquency and delinquent behaviour is not assumed. Nor is a consensus assumed about what is to be called delinquent behaviour. Indeed, it is assumed that police and court practices sometimes operate to inflate the gender-delinquency correlation. As we will discuss further below, the effect of this inflation is to reinforce a sexual stratification of family and work activities, with females ascripted disproportionately for the former, and males appropriated disproportionately for the latter. Nonetheless, a sufficient consistency is hypothesized between police processing and delinquent behaviour to make the above kind of question relevant in behavioural terms.

Note also that while the above question makes no value judgements as to the "goodness" or "badness" of delinquency, it does nonetheless imply that there is a pleasurable or enjoyable aspect of delinquency. Indeed, power-control theory assumes that delinquency can be fun, if not liberating, as well as

rewarding in other ways. Bordua (1961) notes that theories of delinquency too often, at least implicitly, assume that delinquency is a grim and somewhat desperate pursuit. In contrast, our assumption is that delinquency frequently is fun — and even more importantly, a kind of fun infrequently allowed to females. Said differently, delinquency may involve a spirit of liberation, the opportunity to take risks, and a chance to pursue publicly some of the pleasures that are symbolic of adult male status outside the family. One reason why delinquency is fun, then, is because it anticipates a range of activities, some criminal and some more conventional, that are more open to men than women. The interests of power-control theory are in how a sense of this sexually stratified world of licit and illicit adult pleasures, and restrictions of access to them, are communicated and reproduced across generations through gender relations.

Link 2 takes the first step in addressing such issues by explicating a connection between gender positions and the parental control of children. This link first calls attention to the proposition that parental controls are imposed selectively: that is, daughters are controlled more extensively than sons. Conceptually we represent this by noting that parents are characteristically the instruments of familial controls, while children are the objects; but most significantly, *daughters* are disproportionately the objects of this socially structured domination. So the instrument-object relationship established between parents and children is applied more selectively and extensively to daughters than sons. Beyond this, within patriarchal family structures mothers are particularly likely to be placed in the primary position of implementing this instrument-object relationship: that is, mothers more than fathers are assigned responsibility for perpetuating this instrument-object relationship.

Of course, control can be established through ties of affiliation as well as through subordination. Indeed, it might well be argued that a lot of affiliation and a little subordination is the most effective basis of social domination. Again, however, power-control theory predicts that ties of affiliation selectively and more extensively will be applied to daughters than sons. We will refer to these affiliative ties as relational controls, as contrasted with more instrumental kinds of controls involving supervision and surveillance. However, it is again the sexual asymmetry that is of greatest importance here, with power-control theory predicting that the larger burden of these controls is imposed on daughters rather than sons. Furthermore, it is mothers more than fathers that the patriarchal family holds responsible for the everyday imposition of these controls, again, on daughters more than sons.

Links 3, 4, and 5 in our theoretical framework lead us to a consideration of the consequences of this sexual stratification of social control. In link 3 the focus is on the risk preferences of adolescents. Risk-taking can be regarded as an expression of freedom, an expression that power-control theory predicts will be allowed selectively and more extensively to males than females. Delinquency can be regarded as an adolescent form of risk-taking (hence links 4 and 5) that we have argued can carry with it an element of pleasure, excitement, and therefore fun. The interest of power-control theory is in how a taste for such risk-taking is channelled along sexually stratified lines.

Link 3 in our theoretical framework predicts that gender differences in risk preferences will be observed and that they are mediated by the structures of parental control introduced above. That is, parents control their daughters more than their sons, and in so doing they diminish the preferences of daughters to take risks. The logical links in this theory therefore predict that daughters will be more risk-averse than sons, and that therefore daughters will be less delinquent in their behaviour than sons. In an important sense, then, what a power-control theory of delinquency is saying is that the higher likelihood of delinquency among boys than girls, and ultimately the higher likelihood of crime among men than women, is an expression of gender differences in risk preferences, which in turn are a product of the different patterns of parental control imposed on daughters compared to sons. In a still more ultimate sense,

however, power-control theory goes beyond this to locate the source of such gender differences in a patriarchal connection between the family and the world of work outside it. We turn next to an explication of this connection between work and family.

CLASS, STATE, AND HOUSEHOLD

We have made recurring references to the role of the patriarchal family in reproducing the five links presented in Figure 11.1 as the core of power-control theory. In this section we will argue that the patriarchal family is one distinct type of family class structure. Power-control theory predicts that the links identified in Figure 11.1 are strongest within this family class relation, and therefore that this type of family structure plays a central role in accounting for a strong connection between gender and crime. Because patriarchal family structures historically have played such a prominent role in the development of industrial capitalist societies, the effects of this family structure may be seen throughout our society, even within families that seek to reduce or eliminate patriarchy. We live, in short, in a patriarchal society. Nonetheless, if power-control theory is correct, it should be possible to identify variations in the effects of patriarchy across family class structures. First, however, we consider the historical roots of the patriarchal family structure to which we attach so much importance, and the place of this family structure in the theory we propose.

Power-control theory focuses on the social organization of gender relations. It is concerned with the way in which gender relations are established, maintained, perpetuated, or in other words, reproduced. The social reproduction of gender relations occurs across generations, and so adolescence provides a crucial context in which to address such issues. Meanwhile, societies vary in the social organization and reproduction of their gender relations, and so it is highly significant that our development of power-control theory occurs within an industrial capitalist society. Indeed, the question we must initially confront is: what is it about the macrolevel development of industrial capitalist societies that accounts for the way in which they reproduce gender relations?

Weber (1947) answers this question by noting that an important juncture in the development of modern capitalism involved the separation of the workplace from the home. Two distinct spheres, which Weber regarded as crucial to the rationalization of an industrial capitalist economy, resulted from this separation: the first was populated by women and focused on domestic labour and consumption, and the second was populated by men and centred around labour power and direct production. Weber referred to these respectively as the consumption and production spheres.

The differentiation of the production and consumption spheres is significant for the social reproduction of gender relations. The reproduction of gender relations occurs in both spheres. The state (through police, courts, and correctional agencies) assumes responsibility for reproductive functions in the production sphere, while the family assumes responsibility for such functions in the consumption sphere. These reproductive functions are inversely related and sexually stratified.

The inverse relationship derives from the fact that as the reproductive activities of the family and kinship groups decline, the reproductive activities of state agencies increase. So, for example, we have elsewhere (Hagan et al., 1979) tested the thesis that as informal social controls of family and kinship groups decrease, contact with state agencies such as the police increases. This inverse relationship between state and family based systems of social control is discussed by Donald Black (1970) and Andrew Scull (1977), among recent sociologists interested in issues of social control. The important point here is that this differentiation of state and family reproductive functions, and the inverse relationship between them, also has its source in the separation of the workplace from the home that accompanied the emergence of Western capitalist societies. So the separation of the workplace from the home brought a change in production relations that in turn resulted in changes in reproductive relations, both of which had profound implications

for gender relations. Among the most significant of the new gender relations was an intensification of the sexual stratification of reproductive functions.

The sexual stratification of reproductive functions in the production and consumption spheres inheres in the fact that while females disproportionately are the instruments and objects of the informal social control activities of the family, males disproportionately are the instruments and objects of formal social control agencies of the state, such as the police. The overall effect of the sexual stratification of these functions is to perpetuate a gender division in the production and consumption spheres, with females restricted to the home-based consumption sphere, and males appropriated to the production sphere; where, among other things, males are more liable to police contact.

The new family that emerged from the separation of work and home assumed responsibility for reproducing the gender division of the production and consumption spheres (Vogel, 1983). This family was patriarchal in form and created a "cult of domesticity" around women (Welter, 1966). Today, however, Coser (1985) notes that there is a declining division of the consumption and production spheres, which is reflected in the increased participation of women in the labour force. Coser goes on to note that as women have joined the labour force, they have gained new power in the family, particularly in the upper classes. We consider a highly abridged version of a model of family class structure, noting that these structures vary between two extreme family class relations that form real-life counterparts of two ideal-type families.

The first of these ideal types is largely a residue from an earlier period in which the consumption and production spheres were more strictly divided by gender. To reflect this legacy, we will call this the patriarchal family. Of the family class relations we identify, the one that should most closely correspond to the ideal-type patriarchal family consists of a husband who is employed outside the home in a position of authority over others, and a wife who is not employed outside the home. Power-control theory predicts that patriarchal families will tend to reproduce daughters who focus their futures around domestic labour and consumption, as contrasted with sons who are prepared for participation in direct production. We say more about how this happens below. Here we simply repeat that Weber regarded this process of social reproduction, and implicitly the social reproduction of gender relations, as crucial to the rationalization of industrial capitalism.

At the other extreme is an ideal type we call the egalitarian family, in which the consumption and production spheres are undivided by gender. Of the family class relations we identify, the one that should most closely correspond to the ideal-type egalitarian family includes a mother and father who both are employed in positions with authority over others outside the home. Power-control theory predicts that egalitarian families tend to socially reproduce daughters who are prepared along with sons to join the production sphere. Such families are therefore a part of an overlapping of the consumption and production spheres, which a post-industrial society no longer so clearly keeps apart; such families are a part as well as a product of changing economic relations.

So the patriarchal family perpetuates a gender division in the consumption and production spheres, whereas the egalitarian family facilitates an overlapping of these spheres. The question is how this occurs. How does this happen and what are its consequences? Power-control theory answers these questions by joining a class analysis of the family with an analysis of the division of parental social control labour discussed above. The link is that parents socially reproduce their own power relationships through the control of their children. The key process involves the instrument-object relationship described under link 2 of Figure 11.1 above, which is assumed to be at its extreme in the patriarchal family. Here fathers and especially mothers (i.e., as instruments of social control) are expected to control their daughters more than their sons (i.e., as objects of social control). In regard to mothers, we should emphasize that our point is not that they are, in any ultimate causal sense, more

important than fathers in the control of daughters, but rather that mothers in patriarchal families are assigned a key instrumental role that involves them more in the day-to-day control of their children, especially their daughters. This imbalanced instrument-object relationship is a product of a division in domestic social control labour and it is a distinguishing feature of the control of daughters in patriarchal families. This instrument-object relationship is a key part of the way in which patriarchal families socially reproduce a gender division in the spheres of consumption and production.

Alternatively, a reduction of this relationship enables egalitarian families to reproduce an overlap of the production and consumption spheres. This does not mean that in these families fathers are as involved as mothers in the parental control of children; indeed, evidence mounts that this is not the case. What it does mean is that parents in egalitarian families will redistribute their control efforts so that daughters are subjected to controls more like those imposed on sons. In other words, in egalitarian families, as mothers gain power relative to husbands, daughters gain freedom relative to sons. In terms of the social reproduction of gender relations, the presence of the imbalanced instrument-object relationship helps perpetuate patriarchy, and its absence facilitates equality.

Our final task at this stage is to link this discussion of ideal-type families and the instrument-object relationship with predicted gender differences in common delinquent behaviour. This final intervening connection involves the attitudes toward risk-taking involved in the discussion of links 3 and 4 in Figure 11.1. At one extreme, the patriarchal family and its acute instrument-object relationship between parents and daughters engenders a lower preference for risk-taking among daughters. Risk-taking is the antithesis of the passivity that distinguishes the "cult of domesticity." So, in patriarchal families, daughters are taught by their parents to be risk-averse. Alternatively, in egalitarian families, daughters and sons alike are encouraged to be more open to risk-taking. In part, this accommodation of risk is an anticipation of role in the entrepreneurial and other activities associated with the production sphere, for which daughters and sons are similarly prepared in egalitarian families.

CONCLUSIONS

Control theories often regard delinquency as a form of risk-taking (Thrasher, 1927; Hirschi, 1969), sometimes as an unanticipated consequence of a rewarded willingness to take risks. The result is a correspondence in delinquent and entrepreneurial orientations that is reflected in Veblen's frequently quoted observation that "the ideal pecuniary man is like the ideal delinquent in his unscrupulous conversion of goods and persons to his own ends, and in a callous disregard of (i.e., freedom from) the feelings and wishes of others or the remoter effects of his actions" (1967: 237). Power-control theory does not regard this parallel as simple irony, but as an unintended consequence of a patriarchal social structure that is valued for its capacity to foster entrepreneurial, risk-taking orientations. With this in mind, power-control theory predicts that patriarchal families will be characterized by large gender differences in common delinquent behaviour, while egalitarian families will be characterized by smaller gender differences in delinquency. In egalitarian families, daughters become more like sons in their involvement in such forms of risk-taking as delinquency.

DISCUSSION QUESTIONS

1. In what way does power-control derive from theories of power and from theories of control?
2. What is "patriarchy" and what role does this concept play in the overall power-control framework?
3. In general terms, what are the three levels at which power-control theory operates?
4. Distinguish between "patriarchal" and "egalitarian" families and describe the relevance of this distinction to the study of delinquency.
5. According to Hagan, what are the major gender differences that exist with respect to processes of social control within the family?

REFERENCES

Black, D. J. (1970). Production of crime rates. *American Sociological Review, 35,* 733–747.

Bordua, D. (1961). Delinquent subcultures: Sociological interpretations of gang delinquency. *Annals of the American Academy of Political and Social Science, 338,* 119–138.

Coleman, J. (1986). Social theory, social research and a theory of action. *American Journal of Sociology, 91,* 1309–1335.

Coser, R. (1985). Power lost and status gained: The American middle class husband. Paper presented at the American Sociological Association Meetings, Washington, DC.

Curtis, R. (1986). Household and family in theory on equality. *American Sociological Review, 51,* 168–183.

Hagan, J., Simpson, J. H., & Gillis, A. R. (1979). The sexual stratification of social control: A gender-based perspective. *British Journal of Sociology, 30,* 25–38.

Hirschi, T. (1969). *Causes of delinquency.* Berkeley: University of California Press.

Millett, K. (1970). *Sexual politics.* Garden City, NY: Doubleday.

Scull, A. (1977). Madness and segregative controls: The rise of the insane asylum. *Social Problems, 24,* 346.

Thrasher, F. M. (1963) [1927]. *The gang.* Chicago: University of Chicago Press.

Veblen, T. (1967) [1899]. *The theory of the leisure class.* New York: Viking Press.

Vogel, L. (1983). *Marxism and the oppression of women: Toward a unifying theory.* New Brunswick, NJ: Rutgers University Press.

Weber, M. (1947). *The theory of social and economic organization.* Glencoe, IL: Free Press.

Welter, B. (1966). The cult of womanhood, 1820–1860. *American Quarterly, 18,* 151–174.

CHAPTER

12

Crime among the Provinces[1]

TIMOTHY F. HARTNAGEL

INTRODUCTION

Canadian provincial crime rates have exhibited an east-west trend for a number of years, with the Maritime provinces having relatively low rates while the Western provinces record higher rates. Ontario and Quebec have rates that are intermediate between those of the Maritimes and the West, with Quebec's rates usually somewhat lower than Ontario's (Hackler and Don 1987; Brantingham and Brantingham 1984). These patterns persist for both violent and property crimes, with only occasional exceptions. Table 12.1 displays the provincial

rates of violent and property crime known to the police (per 100 000 population age 15 and above) for 1962, 1972, and 1982.[2] The usual east-west trend is readily observable for all three years and the two types of crime.

The present research also uses multiple regression methods in an attempt to explain provincial differences in violent and property crime rates. The impact of geographic mobility on these crime rates is examined in the context of several other potential predictors of regional crime rates. Violent and property crime rates for the years 1962, 1972, and 1982 are regressed on a set of predictors drawn

Table 12.1

Canadian Provincial Crime Rates (per 100 000 population age 15 and above), 1962, 1972, 1982

	1962		1972		1982	
	Violent	**Property**	**Violent**	**Property**	**Violent**	**Property**
Newfoundland	249	2 266	672	4 156	854	5 400
Prince Edward Island	210	1 126	482	2 612	554	4 852
Nova Scotia	389	1 868	620	3 269	776	5 741
New Brunswick	208	1 402	539	3 246	714	5 454
Quebec	245	2 508	451	3 924	640	6 853
Ontario	357	3 044	814	5 720	866	7 607
Manitoba	312	3 611	666	6 235	938	9 797
Saskatchewan	395	2 835	882	5 666	883	8 776
Alberta	497	4 096	1 170	7 459	1 204	9 396
British Columbia	550	4 461	1 027	8 596	1 507	11 239

SOURCE: Dominion Bureau of Statistics 1966; Statistics Canada 1974; 1984.

Adapted from Crime among the Provinces: The Effect of Geographic Mobility, by Timothy F. Hartnagel (1997). *Canadian Journal of Criminology, 39*(4), p. 387–402. Copyright by the Canadian Criminal Justice Association. Reproduced by permission of the *Canadian Journal of Criminology*.

from related research and lagged by one year (1961, 1971, and 1981), since it is unlikely that these predictors would have instantaneous effects on crime.

Criminologists have long been interested in regional variation in crime rates. Brantingham and Brantingham (1984) have pointed out that the analysis of the spatial distribution of crime within particular nations was the first scientific research by criminologists. These early studies suggested that crime was distributed unevenly by region, that different mechanisms might be important for explaining violent and property crime, and that these regional patterns appeared to be related to demographic trends and opportunity variables (Brantingham and Brantingham 1984).

One demographic trend which has not received much criminological research attention is geographic mobility. While the criminality of migrants has been of some interest (Savitz 1960; Kinman and Lee 1966; Green 1970; Tilly 1970; Tittle and Paternoster 1988), the potential impact of population mobility on regional crime rates has received little attention. Tittle and Paternoster (1988: 325) have reiterated the distinction between these micro and macro aspects of the connection between geographic mobility and crime. They concluded that much remains to be learned about the effects of mobility rates on the overall amount or rates of crime in social units, and considered quite plausible the hypothesis "that high rates of geographic mobility in a community or social unit could lead to poor community integration and weak social control that might, in turn, generate high rates of crime or deviance independent of whether individual movers were more or less likely to engage in crime or deviance than nonmovers."

Crutchfield, Geerken, and Gove (1982) investigated the effects of geographic mobility on the crime rates of the 65 largest U.S. Standard Metropolitan Statistical Areas. They hypothesized that environments with higher rates of geographic mobility would manifest weaker social integration with resulting higher crime rates. Communities with very mobile populations would be subject to breakdowns in their relational structures, since the costs of maintaining special contacts over long distances mean that the greater the degree of population mobility, the less permanence, depth of feeling, and stability there will be in social relationships. A weakened relational structure would decrease the effectiveness of community informal social control mechanisms, resulting in higher crime rates. Crutchfield et al.'s (1982) results were consistent with this contextual interpretation of the mobility-crime rate relationship, net of controls for population size and measures thought to reflect restricted legitimate opportunities, but primarily for property rather than other crime types. In addition, Clinard and Abbott's (1973) African research suggested that migration from rural areas to cities was associated with a breakdown of traditional tribal relations and increased crime. Furthermore, they reported that in an urban slum area with less mobility there was also less crime.

HYPOTHESES

The present research is designed to test the hypothesis that the observed variation in provincial crime rates will be positively related to the amount of provincial geographic mobility. Following the argument of Crutchfield et al. (1982), provinces exhibiting more geographic mobility should experience a lower degree of integration in their relational structures, and hence, a weakening of their informal mechanisms of social control, resulting in higher crime rates. This positive relationship between geographic mobility and crime should be maintained even with controls for other variables known to be predictors of aggregate crime rates.

Urban crime rates are generally higher than rural/small town rates (Harries 1974; Nettler 1984) and indeed much of the literature on social integration and crime has been focused upon urban communities. So we will control for differences in provincial urbanization and expect a positive zero-order relationship between provincial urbanization and their crime rates.

Studies of regional variation in crime rates have usually demonstrated effects of economic deprivation variables (Ehrlich 1973; Loftin and Hill 1974; Braithwaite 1979; Smith and Parker 1980; Kennedy et al. 1988; 1991). Therefore, we expect a positive zero-order relationship between the economic deprivation of a province and its crime rates. Provinces experiencing greater economic deprivation should exhibit higher crime rates.

Labelling and critical theory both emphasize the role of the criminal justice system itself in affecting the level of officially recorded crime and various researchers have demonstrated such effects (Kitsuse and Cicourel 1963; Wheeler 1967; Swimmer 1974; Jones 1974; Land and Felson 1976; Jacobs 1979; Quinney 1979). In Canada, McDonald (1969) reported that increases in the number of police per capita were positively related to particular measures of crime rates, generally for the less serious types. So provinces that have a larger number of police per capita should also have higher crime rates.

Finally, relative to their proportion in the population, young people are arrested far more frequently than other age groups (Nettler 1984; Hartnagel 1996). A number of studies have demonstrated the effect of age composition of the population on crime rates (Sagi and Wellford 1968; Wellford 1973; Flango and Sherbenou 1976; Lee 1984). Research by Marlin (1973), McCarthy, Gaile, and Zimmern (1975), Loftin and Hill (1974), and Cohen and Felson (1979) reported a positive relation between crime rates and the young adult proportion of the population. Therefore, we expect that provinces with a higher proportion of youth and young adults in their population will have higher crime rates.

METHODOLOGY

Crimes known to the police recorded in *Crime Statistics* (Dominion Bureau of Statistics, 1966; title later changed to *Crime and Traffic Enforcement Statistics*, Statistics Canada, 1974; 1984) for the years 1962, 1972, and 1982 were obtained to measure the dependent variables. These crimes were categorized into two types: violent crime and property crime. The rate per 100 000 population age 15 and above was calculated for each type.

DATA ANALYSIS

The results from regressing the two crime rates on the five predictors are displayed in Table 12.2. A substantial amount of the observed variation in these provincial crime rates can be accounted for by the five predictors. Further, the pattern of net effects of these predictors is similar for the two crime rates. The hypothesis of a positive net effect of the migration rate is confirmed for both violent and property crime. In fact, the migration rate is by far the strongest net predictor of both crime rates. The only other predictor variable to have much of a net effect on either crime rate is the percent low income in a province; as this percentage increases so do the violent and property crime rates. Police per capita has a small positive net effect on the property crime rate, but its effect on violent crime is negligible. Neither the percent urban nor age composition of provinces makes a net contribution to the explanation of provincial crime rates.

DISCUSSION

These results support the hypothesis that provincial differences in crime rates are at least partly a function of differences in the amount of geographic mobility experienced in different provinces. Those provinces that have more migration from other provinces also have higher rates of both violent and property crime. This impact of geographic mobility is fairly strong net of the effects of four other potential predictors. In line with previous interpretations of the effect of geographic mobility (Crutchfield et al. 1982; Tittle and Paternoster 1988), this result suggests that higher provincial rates of geographic mobility produce a weakening of the structure of social relations, with a consequent decline in the power of informal social controls, resulting in higher crime rates. In common

Table 12.2

Multiple Regression of Violent and Property Crime Rates on Five Predictors

Predictor	B	Beta
VIOLENT		
Urban	.812	.0583
Age 15–24	4.81	.0355
Police	58.21	.0797
Migration	2 527.80	.7253
Low income	15.50	.4851

R^2_{ADJ} = .747 SE = 160.38
Durbin-Watson = 1.70

Predictor	B	Beta
PROPERTY		
Urban	17.76	.1532
Age 15–24	–43.73	–.0388
Police	1 558.05	.2562
Migration	17 087.33	.5892
Low income	106.22	.3996

R^2_{ADJ} = .767 SE = 1281.91
Durbin-Watson = 1.95

with previous aggregate level research on geographic mobility and crime, we can only infer the presence of these intervening mechanisms; more direct evidence for their presence and operation must come from local community and individual level research. But our results certainly add to the previous evidence of Crutchfield et al. (1982) for this type of argument. It is also worth noting that, as expected, the positive effect of migration applies to both property and violent crime as this social control perspective predicts. A weakening of the structure of informal social control will permit either type of crime to occur rather than being limited to a more specific form of criminal response.

As Table 12.1 indicated, the Western provinces, particularly British Columbia and Alberta, have consistently higher violent and property crime rates over this time period. Not surprisingly, in view of the above results, they are also the provinces that experienced the greatest migration from other provinces during these years. This migration is probably related to regional changes in the economy. These Western provinces have experienced cycles of rapid change in their economies. Employment-driven migrations spurred by economic booms and busts in the Western provinces seem, then, to play an important role in explaining the regional patterning of crime rates in Canada (Kennedy et al. 1988; 1991). These findings suggest that economic change that results in relatively rapid population increase through geographic mobility is destabilizing and weakens the structure of informal social control. Alternatively, the relationship between migration and crime may result from their joint dependence upon economic change.[3] Periods of rapid economic change may affect the level of both migration and crime. Economic booms and busts may lead to corresponding changes in migration, as well as directly to increases in crime through such mechanisms as changes in social controls, opportunities, and/or deprivation. Caution, then, is required in interpreting these results, since they may be subject to the influence of other variables not included in the regression equation. Furthermore, it would be fallacious to conclude from these aggregate results that the individuals migrating from east to west are the persons committing crimes at a higher rate in the Western provinces. Such a conclusion would require data from individuals.

So economic factors may be an important underlying source for some of the impact of geographic mobility on provincial crime rates. The significance of economic variables in contributing to the explanation of provincial variation in crime rates is further indicated by the net effect of percent low income in a province on property and, particularly, violent crime rates. Although not as strong as the effect of migration, percent low income does appear to affect provincial crime rates when the effects of the other predictors are controlled.

While the other three independent variables exhibited the hypothesized zero-order relationships with provincial crime rates, only police per capita was a net predictor of property crime. This may, for example, reflect the impact of police resources on the recording of less serious theft and fraud, or of intensified police surveillance directed toward certain offences/offenders. Alternatively, migration and its resultant disorganization might lead to both increased crime and an increase in police personnel per capita as the state employs measures to control disorganized, "problem populations" (Spitzer 1975). Other specifications involving additional variables are also possible but would require a larger number of observations to test.

Little research attention has been directed toward explaining the regional patterns of Canadian crime rates. Additional research could be pursued in a number of areas. For example, more specific types of violent and property crime could be examined in an effort to determine the generality of the effect of geographic mobility, since the categories of violent and property crime may mask important internal variation. Measures of change in the predictor variables could be calculated and used in a regression equation to capture more adequately how the process of demographic and economic change leads to increased crime. This could be accompanied by a more detailed time-series analysis examining year-to-year fluctuations with a few additional predictor variables. The analysis could also be extended historically by changing to court-based measures of crime (e.g., convictions). This aggregate level research could be supplemented with community surveys to measure more directly the intervening processes hypothesized to link geographic mobility and crime. Clearly, more work is required to gain a better understanding of the structural sources of regional crime patterns.

NOTES

1. This paper was completed while the author was a Visiting Fellow at the Institute of Criminology, Cambridge University. Partial financial support was provided by Solicitor General Canada through the contributions grant to the Centre for Criminological Research, University of Alberta. Ed Ng and Terri Bose provided research assistance. The comments of Leslie Kennedy, Robert Silverman, and an anonymous reviewer on earlier drafts are gratefully acknowledged.

2. The specific crimes included within each type are, respectively: murder, manslaughter (both combined into homicide by 1982), attempted murder, rape and other sexual offences (combined into sexual offences by 1982), and robbery; break and enter, car theft, theft over and under $50 (later increased to $200 by 1982), possession of stolen goods, and fraud. The year 1962 is the first for which national data for crimes known to the police are available.

3. This possibility was suggested by an anonymous reviewer.

DISCUSSION QUESTIONS

1. Aside from the factors discussed in this analysis, can you suggest any other reasons for the observed geographic variation in Canadian crime rates?

2. According to Hartnagel, what is the hypothesized relationship between geographic mobility and social control?

3. How would you attempt to explain the observed effects of police per capita on property and violent crime rates?

4. If the research shows that *rates of crime* are correlated with *rates of migration*, why would it be an error to assume that it is the migrants themselves who are more likely to be committing crime?

REFERENCES

Braithwaite, J. B. (1979). *Inequality, crime and public policy*. London: Routledge and Kegan Paul.

Brantingham, P., & Brantingham, P. (1984). *Patterns in crime*. New York: Macmillan.

Clinard, M. B., & Abbott, D. J. (1973). *Crime in developing countries*. New York: Wiley.

Cohen, L. E., & Felson, M. (1979). Social change and crime rate trends. *American Sociological Review, 44*, 588–608.

Crutchfield, R. D., Geerken, M. R., & Gove, W. R. (1982). Crime rate and social integration. *Criminology, 20*, 467–478.

Dominion Bureau of Statistics. (1966). *Crime Statistics, 1962*. Cat. no. 85-205. Ottawa: Trade and Commerce.

Ehrlich, I. (1973). Participation in illegitimate activities. *Journal of Political Economy, 81*, 521–565.

Flango, V. E., & Sherbenou, E. L. (1976). Poverty, urbanization and crime. *Criminology, 14*, 331–346.

Green, E. (1970). Race, social status and criminal arrest. *American Sociological Review, 35*, 476–490.

Hackler, J. C., & Don, K. (1987). Estimating system biases. Discussion Paper 12, Centre for Criminological Research, University of Alberta.

Harries, K. D. (1974). *The geography of crime and justice*. New York: McGraw-Hill.

Hartnagel, T. (1996). Correlates of criminal behaviour. In R. Linden (Ed.), *Criminology: A Canadian perspective* (3rd ed.). Toronto: Harcourt, Brace & Company.

Jacobs, D. (1979). Inequality and police strength. *American Sociological Review, 44*, 913–925.

Jones, E. T. (1974). The impact of crime rate changes on police expenditures in American cities. *Criminology, 11*, 516–524.

Kennedy, L. W., Silverman, R. A., & Forde, D. R. (1988). Homicide from east to west. Discussion

Paper 17, Centre for Criminological Research, University of Alberta.

Kennedy, L. W., Silverman, R. A., & Forde, D. R. (1991). Homicide in urban Canada. *Canadian Journal of Sociology, 16*, 397–410.

Kinman, J. E., & Lee, S. (1966). Migration and crime. *International Migration Digest, 3*, 7–14.

Kitsuse, J. I., & Cicourel, A. V. (1963). A note on the use of official statistics. *Social Problems, 11*, 131–139.

Land, K. C., & Felson, M. (1976). A general framework for building dynamic macro social indicator models. *American Journal of Sociology, 82*, 565–604.

Lee, G. W. (1984). Are crime rates increasing? *Canadian Journal of Criminology, 26*, 29–41.

Loftin, C., & Hill, R. H. (1974). Regional subculture and homicide. *American Sociological Review, 39*, 714–724.

Marlin, J. T. (1973). City crime: Report of council on municipal performance. *Criminal Law Bulletin, 9*, 557–604.

McCarthy, J. D., Galle, O. R., & Zimmern, W. (1975). Population density, social structure, and interpersonal violence. *American Behavioral Scientist, 18*, 771–789.

McDonald, L. (1969). Crime and punishment in Canada. *Canadian Review of Sociology and Anthropology, 6*, 212–236.

Nettler, G. (1984). *Explaining crime*. New York: McGraw-Hill.

Quinney, R. (1979). *Criminology*. Boston: Little, Brown.

Sagi, P. C., & Wellford, C. F. (1968). Age composition and patterns of change in criminal statistics. *Journal of Criminal Law, Criminology and Police Science, 59*, 29–36.

Savitz, L. (1960). *Delinquency and migration, human relations*. Philadelphia: Commission on Human Relations.

Smith, M. D., & Parker, R. N. (1980). Type of homicide and variation in regional rates. *Social Forces, 59*, 136–147.

Spitzer, S. (1975). Towards a Marxian theory of deviance. *Social Problems, 22*, 638–651.

Statistics Canada. (1974). *Crime and Traffic Enforcement Statistics, 1972–73*. Ottawa: Supply and Services Canada.

Statistics Canada. (1984). *Crime and traffic enforcement statistics*, Cat. no. 85-205. Ottawa: Supply and Services Canada.

Swimmer, G. (1974). The relationship of police and crime. *Criminology, 12*, 293–314.

Tilly, C. (1970). Race and migration to the American city. In J. Q. Wilson (Ed.), *The metropolitan enigma*. Garden City, NY: Doubleday.

Tittle, C. R., & Paternoster, R. (1988). Geographic mobility and criminal behavior. *Journal of Research in Crime and Delinquency, 25*, 301–343.

Wellford, C. F. (1973). Age composition and the increase in recorded crime. *Criminology, 11*, 61–70.

Wheeler, S. (1967). Criminal statistics: A reformulation of the problem. *Journal of Criminal Law, Criminology and Police Science, 58*, 317–324.

13

Risky Lifestyles and the Link between Offending and Victimization[1]

STEPHEN W. BARON

INTRODUCTION

Research focusing on risk factors for criminal victimization suggests that the probability of becoming a victim of crime varies across persons or groups (Jensen & Brownfield, 1986; Kennedy & Forde, 1990a; 1990b). Findings reveal that actors with certain attributes are particularly vulnerable to crime because they are more likely to follow lifestyles that expose them to victimogenic situations. Young, unemployed, single males who pursue activities outside the home are at greater risk for victimization because their public lifestyles increase their proximity and availability to potential offenders (Kennedy & Forde, 1990a; 1990b).

A comparison of victim attributes with those of offenders reveals a surprising similarity. Offenders like victims tend to be young, unemployed, single, and male (Hindelang et al., 1978; Sampson & Lauritsen, 1990). These similarities imply that there may be a link between offending behaviour and victimization in that participation in a deviant risky lifestyle may contribute to both crime and victimization (Fagan et al., 1987; Kennedy & Baron, 1993; Sampson & Lauritsen, 1990; Lauritsen et al., 1991; Singer, 1986).

THEORETICAL EXPLANATIONS

A general explanation for the connection between victimization and offending has been derived from the routine activities and lifestyle exposure perspectives. Central to the arguments of these approaches is the convergence in time and space of motivated offenders and suitable targets in the absence of capable guardians. Together these factors are said to increase criminal victimization. Derived from this general proposition is the suggestion that the risks of victimization increase the more frequently actors associate, or come into contact, with members of demographic groups which contain a disproportionate share of offenders. In other words, the amount of exposure an individual has to offenders is the key in helping to explain criminal victimization (Cohen & Felson, 1979; Felson & Cohen, 1980; Hindelang et al., 1978).

Sampson and Lauritsen (1990) note that, although rarely studied, the logic of the routine activities/lifestyle exposure perspectives implies that criminal and deviant lifestyles may directly increase victimization owing to the element of offending. Crime and deviance are characteristics of a risky lifestyle or type of routine activity which increases the actors' risks for victimization because it augments their exposure and contact to other offenders who are themselves disproportionately involved in criminal activity.

For example, the frequency with which actors involve themselves in situations prone to violence not only affects their chances of using violence and injuring others but also of being on the receiving

Adapted from Risky Lifestyles and the Link between Offending and Victimization, by Stephen W. Baron (1997). *Studies on Crime and Crime Prevention*, 6, p. 53–71. Reprinted with permission.

end of violence and being injured (Fattah, 1991). Furthermore, the victimogenic potential of fighting is at a maximum because outcomes, in which the participant ends up the victim, often depend on factors other than intent or deliberate action. Thus, the risk of becoming a victim, given that one is the initial offender, can be at its most extreme (Lauritsen et al., 1991, Kennedy & Baron, 1993). This can involve either one-on-one altercations or group or gang contests which involve close proximity to other offenders and criminal events (the group battle) where rival offenders are present (Lauritsen et al., 1991; Kennedy & Baron, 1993; Sampson & Lauritsen, 1990). It is also the case that violence, or offending behaviour, can increase the chances of becoming a victim of retaliatory violence or property victimization. In other words, previous offending can often lead to later victimization since it increases the motivation of others (victims) for offending (Fattah, 1991). In sum, persons whose lifestyles include violence face a heightened risk of victimization as a direct result of their predatory offending and their association with other offenders.

Other forms of deviance might also be expected to be related to a high degree of victim proneness. For example, deviant transactions can generally be considered high risk activities where the potential for victimization is high (Fattah, 1991). Transactions involving drugs or other illicit goods or services are often characterized by distrust, mistrust, antagonism or outright conflict. Being "ripped off" in drug transactions, arguments over the control of trafficking fields of influence and other conflicts related to the supply and securing of drugs can lead to the victimization of an offender. This is exacerbated by the reality that the buying, selling and distributing of illegal goods are clandestine operations that are undertaken in "out of the way" locations, making participants vulnerable to robberies and extortions by those who also populate these environments (Fattah, 1991; Zahn & Bencivengo, 1974; 1975).

In addition, Sparks (1982) has suggested that offenders are ideal targets for other offenders because they can be victimized with relative im-

punity. Offender/victims are less likely to go to the police to report transgressions for fear of implicating themselves in other offenses. Sparks also implies that offenders believe that enforcement officials will discount their victimization experiences, making efforts to report victimizations futile.

Aspects of deviant lifestyles not directly tied to offending can also place persons at risk for victimization. Included here is the use of drugs and/or alcohol. These various substances can lead to a reduction of vigilance or an increase in negligence on the part of the user, leading to property losses and violent attacks. The use of these intoxicants can diminish users' critical judgements and increase their recklessness and imprudence, factors that often foster provocation. Drinking and/or drug use might also lower actor inhibitions and release provocative, aggressive tendencies and at the same time serve to slow important defensive reflexes (Fattah, 1991). Apart from these bodily effects, it is also the case that the environments where these substances are consumed can be considered high risk areas that create conflict situations and inflame violent actions (Jensen & Brownfield, 1986; Lauritsen et al., 1991; Sampson & Lauritsen, 1990).

There may also be a number of structural explanations for victimization. First there is the idea that proximity to criminal activity has an effect on victimization. Living in certain areas, for example, low-income urban areas where the offender pool is large, can increase the victimization risk for all types of crime regardless of individual propensities to engage in crime (Garofalo, 1987; Kennedy & Baron, 1993; Lauritsen et al., 1991). However, it is also true that the chronic stresses of poverty and lower class life in these areas generate resentment and hostility which can ultimately be expressed in angry aggression (Bernard, 1990). If those experiencing this stress are socially segregated from others, then an aggressive environment can be created where there is a constant threat of physical injury.

There are also subcultural explanations for the link between victims and offenders. Wolfgang and Ferracuti (1967) suggest that within certain subgroups of the population, and in certain geographical areas, there are value systems that support the use of violence.

Linked to this subcultural factor are peers. Felson and Steadman (1983) suggest that "third parties" are influential in the outcome of violent incidents in at least two ways. First, they can engage in physical and verbal attacks themselves, acting as allies for one of the antagonists. Second, they may instigate conflict by defining a situation as one in which violence is an appropriate response. Again, participation leaves the actors at risk for injury. These types of groups may also designate certain other groups or individuals as appropriate targets for victimization. In this scenario the violence of delinquent groups directed against members of outgroups is tolerated and sometimes encouraged. This, however, leaves group members vulnerable to attacks from others because of their group membership and past violations.

There is also the recognition that prior childhood victimization at the hands of parents or guardians is linked to later antisocial behaviour (Elliott, 1994; Hartstone & Hansen, 1984; Hotaling et al., 1989; McCord 1979; Sedgely & Lund, 1979; Smith & Thornberry, 1995; Straus, 1985; Widom, 1989; Whitbeck & Simons, 1990). It is argued that children in these circumstances come to model their behaviour on that of their parents (Fagan & Jones, 1984; Fagan & Wexler, 1987; Farrington, 1978; Sorrels, 1977), and adopt aggression as an interpersonal strategy and/or tactic. The violent experience encourages the youths to utilize aggression as a means of problem solving and/or of gaining compliance from others (Fagan & Wexler, 1987; Siegal & Senna, 1994).

This review suggests that the risk of victimization may be increased by a number of different factors including various demographic, behaviorial, attitudinal and lifestyle characteristics. Despite this recognition most research has failed to take account of these factors and has almost ignored those theoretically most at risk for victimization — juveniles and young adults on the margins of society leading risky lifestyles. Much of the recent work that does focus on youth utilizes conventional samples and neglects many of the variables identified as being linked to victimization including subculture, criminal peers, child abuse, and structural location (Garofalo 1987; Jensen & Brownfield, 1986; Sampson & Lauritsen, 1990). Therefore, despite theoretical speculation, it can be argued that it has yet to be empirically demonstrated that the various factors reviewed above are linked to the victimization of marginal youths. In the analysis that follows we attempt to utilize the variables identified in our review and explore their effects on homeless street youths. It is hoped that by applying a more complete set of variables to an extremely economically marginal target group we shall be able to address some of the weaknesses of past work.

HYPOTHESES

Drawing from the extensive literature reviewed above we can hypothesize how structural, subcultural and lifestyle factors might contribute to the victimization of homeless street youths. First, the literature stresses the importance of exposure to offenders. It can be argued that homeless people who inhabit high risk ecological locations are at an extreme risk because they are more likely to come into contact with offenders and lack the resources to isolate themselves and their possessions from these offenders. This suggests that 1) the longer the period of homelessness, the greater the risks of personal and property victimization due to maximal exposure to potential offenders. The literature also outlines how participation in various illegal activities can increase one's risk for victimization. First, in terms of violence, the evidence suggests that outcomes in violent altercations are unpredictable, thus making participation risky. Further, violence can lead to property or violent victimization if past victims seek retribution for their previous victimizations. Therefore, we hypothesize that 2A) the more violent events that offenders are involved in, the greater the likelihood that they will suffer personal and property victimization. Turning to property crime, the literature implies that property offenders may be subjected to violent retaliation for their thefts, and might themselves be subjected to property loss in retribution for their earlier behaviours. Thus we would expect that 2B) the greater the number of property offenses committed by the subjects, the greater the likelihood that they will be the victims of property and violent offenses. Finally, drug distribution can also lead to both violent and property victimization (ripoffs) because of the offender status of the purchasers and the clandestine nature of these operations. Further, battles over territory, drug quality and disputed transactions can all increase an offender's risk for victimization. Therefore, we suggest that 2C) the greater the involvement in drug trafficking the greater the risk of violent and property victimization. In terms of other aspects of the risky lifestyle, the literature indicates that drug and/or alcohol consumption might lead to both property and violent victimization because of the potential increases in provocative and negligent behaviours on the part of users. In light of this we argue that 3) the greater the substance use, the greater the likelihood of violent and property victimization. Some research has suggested that subcultural understandings between offenders to use violence to settle disputes increases not only the number of violent incidents but also victimization, as the roles of victim and offender in these unpredictable incidents alternate over time. It may also be the case that violent subcultures require retaliation, making a prior victory reason for subsequent attacks. We therefore predict that 4) offenders who adhere to violent subcultural values are at greater risk for violent victimization. Finally, the literature indicates that actors who are physically abused in childhood develop a coercive interaction style that utilizes aggression and can provoke violent altercations which might ultimately result in victimization. Therefore, we would expect that 5) offenders who have experienced physical abuse as children are more likely to become victims of violence.

METHODS

The term "street youths" usually refers to youths who have been forced, or have run, from their homes and/or who spend some or all of their time in various public locations. The street population is made up of both sporadic, irregular participants and youths who "hang out" on the street on a regular and permanent basis. The street contains students, school drop-outs, part-time and full-time employees and the unemployed. Some rely on state assistance or the good will of social agencies to support themselves, while others rely on illegal subsistence strategies. These youth range in age from pre-teens to those in their mid-twenties. Thus, street involvement can be characterized as a continuum rather than a categorical entity.

DATA COLLECTION

Sample selection began with the researcher situating himself in geographical areas known to be frequented by the population under study. The researcher approached potential respondents, and screened them for study eligibility while informing them of the project.

Additional contacts were initiated by street youths who were made aware of the researcher's presence and solicited interviews, or through introductions from previously interviewed subjects. These procedures provided a sample of 200 youths of an average age of almost nineteen (X = 18.86). All but fifteen of these youths had spent some time during the year living away from their parents, and a full three-quarters of the sample had been without a fixed address during the last year (N = 153). Those who had been homeless had spent on average almost five months (4.93) in total living time on the street in the previous year.

MEASURING VICTIMIZATION

Information on a number of measures of victimization were obtained via self-report.[2] The respondents were asked "How many times in the past year did you have physical force used against you to get your money or things; been attacked with a weapon or fists/feet, injuring you so badly you needed a doctor; been physically attacked for no apparent reason; had something taken from you?" The first three measures were summed to create a violent victimization measure, while the fourth represents a measure of property victimization. A measure of total victimization was created by adding all four of the measures together.

After recording the amount of victimization in each of these categories, respondents were requested to recall the most recent incident in each of the victimization categories and indicate where the incident took place (open ended), the number of offenders involved and their relationship to these offenders (five offered categories: friend, relative, acquaintance, stranger, unknown).

INDEPENDENT VARIABLES

Demographic and Structural Measures

Information was obtained in the interviews on a range of demographic, structural, lifestyle, and subcultural variables hypothesized to be important in explaining the victimization of street youth. To control for the demographic and structural factors outlined in other research, the respondent's age, employment history, financial well being, and living status were determined.

Deviant Lifestyle Measures

A number of measures were created to represent the deviant or risky lifestyles alluded to in the literature review. First, respondents were queried about the number of times they drank alcohol during a month, and the number of times they smoked marijuana or hash during a month (1 = never, 2 = once per month, 3 = 2–3 times per month, 4 = once per week, 5 = 2–3 times per week, 6 = 4–6 times per week, 7 = daily).

After completing the self-report delinquency items the youths were asked "Do you ever do any of these illegal activities to impress your friends?" This measure was used to determine the role of third parties and subcultural influences on the youths' behaviour. To provide us with some indication of

the sample's interaction with other offenders (Fagan et al. 1987; Whitbeck & Simons, 1990) respondents were asked how many of their current friends had been picked up by the police. Finally, to explore for the effects of childhood victimization on conflict styles that might contribute to current victimization, the questions "Did your parents or guardians ever use physical forms of discipline?" and "Have you ever been intentionally struck so hard by a parent or guardian that it caused a bruise or bleeding?" were coupled to produce a measure reflecting physical abuse in childhood.

Criminal Involvement

Information on a number of measures of criminal involvement was also obtained via a self-report. The respondents were asked how many times in the past year they had used physical force to get money or things from another person; attacked someone with a weapon or fists, injuring them so badly they probably needed a doctor; got into a fight for the fun of it; taken part in a fight where a group of their friends was against another group; sold marijuana or other non-prescription drugs; broken into a car; broken into a building; taken something worth less than $50; taken something worth more than $50; stolen food; or taken a car without permission of the owner. The first four measures, representing robbery, aggravated assault, assault, gang fights and drug dealing, were used as individual variables to explore for their effects on various forms of victimization. The various property offenses were aggregated to form a property crime index.

FINDINGS

Descriptive Results

Table 13.1 shows the distributions of the various types of victimization experienced by our sample of street youths. Beginning with our violent crime measures we note that 30% of the respondents had been robbed, 20% had been the victims of aggravated assault, and 44% had suffered a common

Table 13.1

Percentage of Respondents Victimized

	Number of victimizations			
Type of victimization	0	1	2	>3
Robbery	70.0	17.0	7.0	6.0
Aggravated assault	80.5	10.5	3.0	6.0
Assault	54.0	21.5	13.5	11.0
Total violent victimization	39.0	18.0	15.5	27.5
Property victimization	30.0	24.0	11.0	35.0
Total victimization	16.0	17.5	14.0	57.5

assault. The table also reveals that within each offense category a number of street youths can be characterized as chronic victims. For example, Table 13.1 shows that 13% of the sample had been forced to give up their personal material goods two or more times in the twelve month period surveyed. In fact, 7% of the youths had been robbed three or more times. Thus, those who are robbed once seem to be at risk to be robbed again. This type of pattern is replicated across each disaggregated category of violent victimization: a minority of youths are recidivist victims.

When we add up the three types of violence we discover that the majority (61%) of the sample had experienced some sort of negative violent happening during the previous year. In addition, a large minority (43%) of the sample had suffered more than one violent victimization during the survey period and over one-quarter had suffered three or more. Thus, we see that this population is at risk for violent victimization and prone to multiple violent victimization.

An examination of personal property victimization echoes the above findings.

Number of Offenders

Table 13.2 begins to provide us with some insights into the situations that street youths encounter in their lifestyle. This summary of the number of offenders the respondents encountered in their most recent violent victimization reveals that our street youth victims tend to be faced with multiple offenders. Over 60% of the robbery victims in our sample encountered two or more offenders the last time they were robbed. These findings suggest that street youths find themselves in situations and locations that expose them to large populations of networked offenders. In the case of robbery it is likely that these networked offenders choose to prey on those lacking guardianship so as to decrease the potential for victim resistance and increase the overall odds of success (Kennedy & Baron, 1993). In terms of the other types of victimizations it seems probable that street youths often find themselves in confrontations where their protagonists are verbally and physically assisted by third party allies (Felson & Steadman, 1983).

Table 13.2

Number of Offenders

	Number of offenders		
Type of victimization	1	2	>3
Robbery	38.3	21.7	40.0
Aggravated assault	56.4	15.4	28.2
Assault	65.2	14.1	20.6

Location of Victimization

Table 13.3 illustrates the location of our subjects' most recent victimization within each type. The majority of the violent victimization took place on the street. Since the street is where these youths live and spend most of their time, this is not surprising. However, we also see that a smaller number of offenses take place in dangerous commercial locations, like bars, and in private dwellings, where parties create risky conditions. In both cases it might be argued that risk is increased because these locations attract members of the offender population and the substances consumed in these locations increase the likelihood of victimization.

Victim/Offender Relationship

As mentioned above, many of the thefts experienced by our sample took place in private dwellings under conditions where pools of potential offenders were present. Normally, victims of theft cannot provide much information about the offender because it is usually sometime after the theft that they realize their property is missing, by which time the offender has escaped undetected (Koenig, 1996). However, the majority of youths in our sample could identify, if not name, the person who had taken their property. Only 35% of the respondents indicated that they did not know who had stolen their property (see Table 13.4). In contrast, 42% indicated that it was a friend who had stolen from them. Another 18% reported being victimized by an acquaintance. Thus, because of a lifestyle that maximally exposes them

to offenders, street youths tend to know their thieves.

In contrast, strangers were identified as the offender in 70% of the robberies, 65% of the common assaults, and 50% of the aggravated assaults. With our descriptive analysis complete we now move to a multivariate examination of our measures.

REGRESSION ANALYSIS

Violent Victimization

Our multivariate analysis begins with an examination of violent victimization. Table 13.5 reveals that serious violent offenders are more likely to suffer violent victimization. The more aggravated assaults respondents reported, the greater the risk of being a violent victim. The fact that these youths are involved in large numbers of violent altercations leaves them at risk of injury because the outcomes of these disputes are obviously extremely unpredictable. Each time a youth participates in a conflict he risks serious injury. It is also likely that these youths are subjected to extreme violence in retribution for their own past offensive behaviours. Thus, each victory increases their chances of violent retribution. Further, we must also admit that their own serious violent offenses may be retribution for the serious victimizations that they themselves have suffered in the past.

We also discover that a history of child abuse increases one's risk of violent victimization. Our literature review suggests that these abusive experiences leave youths more likely to adopt an

Table 13.3
Location of Victimization

| Type of victimization | Street | Commercial | Location of victimization | | |
			Public transit	Private dwelling	Other dwelling
Robbery	75.0	11.7	6.7	5.0	1.6
Aggravated assault	58.0	15.8	0.0	26.2	0.0
Assault	66.2	15.7	1.1	14.6	2.2
Theft	8.2	6.7	0.0	81.3	3.7

Table 13.4

Victim/Offender Relationship

Type of victimization	Victim/Offender relationship				
	Relative	Friend	Acquaintance	Stranger	Not known
Robbery	0.0	6.7	23.3	68.3	1.7
Aggravated assault	5.3	18.4	26.3	50.0	0.0
Assault	2.2	12.2	20.0	65.6	0.0
Theft	2.2	41.6	17.5	3.6	35.0

aggressive, often provocative interaction style. This type of manner may stimulate conflict, particularly when the parties towards whom this bearing is directed are offenders. Thus, abused youths may risk serious victimization because they are more likely to behave in a fashion that rouses conflict in environments where other offenders are present.

Peer support also helps predict violent victimization. Those youths who indicated that they often engaged in criminal activities to impress their friends also reported higher violent victimization totals. Our literature review suggested that subcultural and peer expectations help to define those situations where violence is an appropriate response. These expectations and attempts to placate and impress peers may lead respondents into violent altercations where outcomes are unpredictable, leaving the respondent as the victim. Further, peers may contribute to the need to retaliate for past indiscretions. It is also likely that these peer expectations

Table 13.5

OLS Regression Standardized Beta Coefficients Violent, Property and Total Victimization

Variable name	Violent victimization	Property victimization	Total victimization
Age	.0591	.0210	.0550
Length no fixed abode	.0072	.0029	.0069
Length unemployed	.0008	.0281	.0187
Income	.0250	.0082	.0229
Child abuse	.1576**	.1463*	.2071**
Offender friends	−.1367*	.1152	−.0182
Subculture	.1796**	−.0122	.1167
Alcohol use	.0925	.0817	.1187
Drug use	.0295	.1187	.0538
Log robberies	.0840	.2478**	.2234**
Log aggravated assaults	.2564***	−.2374**	.0200
Log assaults	−.0311	−.1044	−.0912
Log group fights	.0264	.2417**	.1426
Log property crime	−.0572	−.1523	−.1412
Log drug sales	.0072	.1662*	.1107
R2	.1596	.1791	.2064
Ad R2	.0837	.1049	.1347

Sig. 10 *

Sig .05 **

Sig .01 ***

and subcultural values can help to explain why offenders attack people who demonstrate coercive interaction styles. These behavioural styles are probably defined as challenges that must be responded to with violence.

Finally, our findings suggest that youths without criminal peers are more likely to suffer violent victimization. This suggests that conventional peers are poorly equipped as guardians. They may lack the skills and tendencies to become involved in violent altercations, leaving associates to fend for themselves. It may also simply be that these youths lack peer networks on the street, meaning there is no human guardianship available. In sum, violent victimization can be limited by choosing criminal peers who are better suited to tackle the guardian role.

Personal Property Victimization

An examination of the property victimization model reveals that four of the five significant predictors are measures of the respondents' criminal activities. Respondents who admitted to robbery, participation in group fights and drug distribution were at increased risk to become victims of theft. This suggests that offenders may make attractive targets because of the relative legal impunity with which they can be victimized. We also know from our descriptive results that the lifestyles of these street youths, including sharing shelter with other offenders, leaves them maximally exposed for victimization. Through these relationships, it is likely that offenders are well aware that their victims are also offenders. In other cases, drug dealing, robbery and gang fights are activities that communicate to others on the street when given youth are offenders, making more likely that they will lose their property on the street or in the bar.

It is also possible that the respondents' property victimizations are retribution for their past offenses. Thus, they may have "shorted" someone in a drug deal, they may have robbed someone for their coat, or they may have been involved in a group fight where they were victorious and/or injured the party. A past victim may seek "pay

back" by later taking the victors' property. We must also note that the robbery and group fights related with thefts may have been the respondents' aggressive retaliation for their property victimizations.

What is perhaps most interesting in this model is the fact that those youths with higher aggravated assault totals were less likely to lose their property. Perhaps their reputations as extreme violent offenders deterred other offenders from taking their property. A minicassette player was not worth stealing if it was common knowledge that the potential retribution would result in the need for medical attention.

DISCUSSION

Our exploration of the victimization experiences of homeless street youths reveals that this marginal population is at extreme risk. Almost all of these youths have suffered some sort of criminal victimization and the majority have been victimized repeatedly. Contrary to expectation, homelessness does not have a direct effect on their victimization. Instead it is likely that the effects of homelessness are felt indirectly through its influence on offending and criminal peers. Homelessness may lead to greater participation in criminal activities and place youths in environments where they come into contact with other offenders. As we have shown, the pressure of peers and offending are important predictors of victimization.

In fact a key component of these youths' risky lifestyle is their own criminal behaviour. Our results suggest that there is a strong link between offending behaviour and chronic victimization. In support of hypothesis 2A we find that the more violent altercations that street youths participate in, the greater their risk for violent victimization. It is likely that the capricious nature of these confrontations leaves participants vulnerable to serious injury. Therefore, each and every physical conflict an offender enters into puts him at risk for physical injury. It also appears that youths who are violent offenders are at risk for retributive victimization. On the street, past violations are subject to "even up" tactics that often leave victims needing medical attention. Also supporting hypothesis 2A are the results that indicate that participating in robberies and group conflicts increases the risk for property victimization. The profile of these offenses communicates to others that they are offenders who can be victimized with relative impunity and provides an avenue of retaliation for past offenses.

What we did not predict in our hypotheses is that violent offending can also inhibit victimization under certain conditions. Involvement in serious assaults can stunt the risk of certain types of victimization. While these types of assaults often lead to violent retribution, they appear to deter those less inclined towards violence from taking property. It is likely that certain offenders fear discovery and the potential injury associated with this revelation. Thus, risky lifestyles can promote and deter victimization depending on the situations and offenses.

There is little support for our prediction that property offending increases victimization. This is surprising in light of our finding that most youths can identify their victimizers. If we reverse this, it suggests that property offenders should be vulnerable to victimization because they lack the safety of anonymity. Yet they appear able to offend with impunity. It may be the case that the bulk of street youth property offending is directed towards the wider community in the form of shoplifting and breaking into cars and houses. This suggests that anonymity does in fact exist and shelters these property offenders from victimization.

As predicted in hypothesis 2C, drug distribution increases the risk of property victimization. The constant suspicion and distrust about the quality and quantity of the product, and the status of offender, leave dealers at risk to have their property stolen. What we did not find was the expected relationship between violent victimization and drug distribution. This is somewhat surprising and is certainly an avenue for exploration in future research.

The fact that both violent and drug offending increases risk suggests that there is something about the status of being an "offender" that might help to explain victimization. It can be argued that youths with offender status make attractive targets because they are less likely to report their victimizations to the police for fear of implicating themselves. Their status also increases the likelihood that legal authorities will dismiss their claims. This essentially eliminates all potential legal repercussions for those who might victimize an offender. In sum, offenders make attractive targets because they can be preyed upon with legal impunity.

Victimization may also contribute to an increase in offending on the part of street youths (Agnew, 1992; Fagan et al., 1987; Singer, 1981; 1986). It is likely that just as street youths are subjected to violent retaliations because of their offensive behaviour, they themselves seek retribution for their own victimizations. Thus, we see that offending and victimization contribute to each other. Offending can increase victimization, but victimization can also increase offending.

Moving to other aspects of deviant lifestyles, we find little support for hypothesis 3. There is little evidence that regular drug or alcohol use increases the risk of victimization among homeless street youths. In contrast, in support of hypothesis 4 we find that those youths who are influenced by their peers and a violent subculture are at increased risk for victimization. The idea that certain cues and situations are to be aggressively acted upon, in addition to the expectations and pressures of peers, all serve to increase the likelihood that youths will enter into volatile situations with unpredictable outcomes. It also seems likely that these same expectations and pressures promote retribution, thus strengthening the link between victimization and increased offending.

Finally, we found, as predicted in hypothesis 5 that those youths from abusive family backgrounds were more likely to be victimized. Their histories create styles of intercommunication that can be provocative, belligerent, hostile and conflictual, all of which can serve to instigate violence and make them targets for victimization. This is particularly true if they display these characteristics in the presence of other offenders. In the context of the third party expectations and situational definitions just described, these behaviours can serve as cues that stimulate violent reactions. What this suggests is that childhood victimization increases the odds of later victimization on the street because it can create characteristics that are victimogenic within the street environment. Thus, victimization can lead to youths being on the street (Hagan & McCarthy, 1992; McCarthy & Hagan, 1992; Whitbeck & Simons, 1990), which in turn because of the lack of shelter, deviant subsistence strategies and their aggressive socialization can lead to even further victimization (Whitbeck & Simons, 1990).

Together, the poverty, exposure to offenders, offending, deviant leisure activities, peer expectations and childhood socialization histories create a complex lifestyle that leaves many street youths as chronic victims. The idea that victims are offenders runs counter to public perceptions and stereotypes of victims. Future research should continue to focus on those "at risk" populations often overlooked in traditional victimization surveys and further explore the links between poverty, offending, deviant lifestyles, subculture and socialization. Research must go beyond the traditional demographic factors to include behaviour patterns and attitudes that can produce both offending and victimization. It is only through broadening our approach that we will be able to obtain greater understanding of the link between lifestyle and victimization.

NOTES

1. The author would like to thank David Forde for his comments. Financial support for this research came in part from a Social Science and Humanities Research Council doctoral fellowship, a contributions grant from the Solicitor General of Canada through the Centre for Criminological Research at the University of Alberta, and the financial assistance of the Department of Sociology at the University of Alberta.
2. An extensive literature has developed on the self-report methodology, indicating that its use with normal youth populations gives results that are both sufficiently accurate and fairly compatible with the conclusions drawn from analyses of arrest data (for summaries see Elliott et al., 1989: 4–9; Hindelang et al., 1981: 13–25; Johnson, 1979: 89–93. Studies of more serious drug/crime participants consistently find that the respondents' self-reports are "surprisingly truthful and accurate" (Inciardi et al., 1993). Further, research has determined that the most accurate self-reported delinquency measures are those that ask questions about serious as opposed to trivial offenses, do not restrict response categories, do not request information beyond a one year period, and utilize face to face interviews as opposed to paper and pencil written questionnaires (see Huizinga & Elliott, 1986). The present research contained all of these characteristics.

DISCUSSION QUESTIONS

1. Why do the results of this study suggest that the tendency of the mass media and politicians to talk about "offenders" and "victims" as separate classes in society may be far too simplistic?
2. Can you think of any reasons why some interest groups might oppose research efforts to investigate the link between offending and victimization?
3. According to the author, how and under what kind of conditions does violent offending inhibit victimization?
4. How do the results of this study make sense in terms of routine activity and lifestyle theories of criminal victimization?
5. What does this research have to say about the relationship between abusive family background and subsequent victimization?

REFERENCES

Agnew, R. (1992). Foundations for a general strain theory of crime and delinquency. *Criminology, 30*, 47–87.
Bernard, T. J. (1990). Angry aggression among the truly disadvantaged. *Criminology, 28*, 73–95.

Cohen, L. E., & Felson, M. (1979). Social change and crime rate trends: A routine activity approach. *American Sociological Review, 44*, 588–608.

Elliott, D. S. (1994). Serious violent offenders: Onset, developmental course and termination. *Criminology, 32*, 1–22.

Elliott, D. S., Huizinga, D., & Menard, S. (1989). *Multiple problem youth: Delinquency, substance abuse and mental health problems.* New York: Springer Verlag.

Fagan, J. A., & Jones, S. J. (1984). Towards an integrated model of violent delinquency. In R. Mathias, P. DeMuro, & R. S. Allinson (Eds.), *An anthology on violent juvenile offenders.* Newark: National Council on Crime and Delinquency.

Fagan, J. A., & Wexler, S. (1987). Family origins of violent delinquents. *Criminology, 25*, 643–669.

Fagan, J. A., Piper, E. S., & Cheng, Y. T. (1987). Contributions of victimization to delinquency in inner cities. *Journal of Criminal Law and Criminology, 78*, 586–609.

Farrington, D. P. (1978). Family backgrounds and aggressive youths. In L. Hersov et al. (Eds.), *Aggressive and anti-social behavior in childhood and adolescence.* Oxford: Pergamon Press.

Fattah, E. A. (1991). *Understanding criminal victimization.* Scarborough: Prentice-Hall.

Felson, M., & Cohen, L. E. (1980). Human ecology and crime: A routine activities approach. *Human Ecology, 4*, 389–406.

Felson, R. B., & Steadman, H. J. (1983). Situational factors in disputes leading to criminal violence. *Criminology, 21*, 59–74.

Garofalo, J. (1987). Reassessing the life-style model of criminal victimization. In M. R. Gottfredson & T. Hirschi (Eds.), *Positive criminology.* Newbury Park: Sage.

Hagan, J., & McCarthy, B. (1992). Streetlife and delinquency. *British Journal of Sociology, 42*, 533–561.

Hartstone, E., & Hansen, V. (1984). The violent juvenile offender: An empirical portrait. In R. Mathias, P. DeMuro, & R. S. Allinson (Eds.), *An anthology on violent juvenile offenders.* Newark: National Council on Crime and Delinquency.

Hindelang, M. J., Gottfredson, M. R., & Garofalo, J. (1978). *Victims of personal crime: An empirical foundation for a theory of personal victimization.* Cambridge: Ballinger.

Hindelang, M. J., Hirschi, T., & Weiss, J. G. (1981). *Measuring delinquency.* Beverly Hills, CA: Sage.

Hotaling, G. T., Straus, M. A., & Lincoln, A. J. (1989). Intrafamily violence, and crime and violence outside the family. In M. Tonry (Ed.), *Crime and justice: A review of research.* Chicago: University of Chicago Press.

Huizinga, D., & Elliott, D. S. (1986). Reassessing the reliability and validity of self-report delinquency measures. *Journal of Quantitative Criminology, 2*, 293–327.

Inciardi, J. A., Horowitz, R., & Pottieger, A. E. (1993). *Street kids, street drugs, street crime.* Belmont: Wadsworth Pub. Co.

Jensen, G. F., & Brownfield, D. (1986). Gender, lifestyles and victimization: Beyond routine activity. *Violence and Victims, 1*, 85–99.

Johnson, R. E. (1979). *Juvenile delinquency and its origins: An integrated theoretical approach.* New York: Cambridge University Press.

Kennedy, L. W., & Baron, S. W. (1993). Routine activities and a subculture of violence: A study of violence on the street. *Journal of Research in Crime and Delinquency, 30*, 88–113.

Kennedy, L. W., & Forde, D. R. (1990a). Routine activities and crime: An analysis of victimization in Canada. *Criminology, 28*, 137–152.

Kennedy, L. W., & Forde, D. R. (1990b). Risky lifestyles and dangerous results: Routine activities and exposure to crime. *Sociology and Social Research, 74*, 208–211.

Koenig, D. (1996). Conventional crime. In R. Linden (Ed.), *Criminology: A Canadian perspective.* Toronto: Harcourt Brace & Company.

Lauritsen, J. L., Sampson, R. J., & Laub, J. (1991). The link between offending and victimization among adolescents. *Criminology, 29*, 265–291.

McCarthy, B., & Hagan, J. (1992). Mean streets: The theoretical significance of desperation and delinquency among homeless youth. *American Sociological Review, 98*, 597–627.

McCord, J. (1979). Some child-rearing antecedents of criminal behavior in adult men. *Journal of Personality and Social Psychology, 37*, 1477–1486.

Sampson, R. J., & Lauritsen, J. L. (1990). Deviant lifestyles, proximity to crime, and the offender-victim link in personal violence. *Journal of Research in Crime and Delinquency, 27*(2), 110–139.

Sedgely, J., & Lund, D. (1979). Self-reported beatings and subsequent tolerance for violence. *Review of Public Data Use, 7*, 30–38.

Siegal, L. J., & Senna, J. J. (1994). *Juvenile delinquency: Theory practice and law* (5th ed.). New York: West Pub. Co.

Singer, S. (1981). Homogeneous victim-offender populations: A review of some research implications. *Journal of Criminal Law and Criminology, 72,* 779–788.

Singer, S. (1986). Victims of serious violence and their criminal behavior: Sub-cultural theory and beyond. *Victims and Violence, 1* (1), 61–69.

Smith, C., & Thornberry, T. P. (1995). The relationship between childhood maltreatment and adolescent involvement in delinquency. *Criminology, 33,* 451–482.

Sorrells, J. M. (1977). Kids who kill. *Crime and Delinquency, 23,* 312–320.

Sparks, R. (1982). *Research on victims of crime.* Washington, DC: U.S. Government Printing Office.

Straus, M. A. (1985). Family training in crime and violence. In A. J. Lincoln & M. A. Straus (Eds.), *Crime in the family.* Springfield: Thomas.

Whitbeck, L. B., & Simons, R. L. (1990). Life on the streets: The victimization of runaway and homeless adolescents. *Youth and Society, 22,* 108–125.

Widom, C. S. (1989). Child abuse, neglect, and violent criminal behavior. *Criminology, 27,* 251–271.

Wolfgang, M. E., & Ferracuti, F. (1967). *The subculture of violence.* London: Tavistock.

Zahn, M. A., & Bencivengo, M. (1974). Violent death: A comparison between drug users and non-drug users. *Addictive Diseases: An International Journal, 1* (3).

Zahn, M. A., & Bencivengo, M. (1975). Murder in a drug using population. In M. Reidl & T. Thornberry (Eds.), *Crime and delinquency: Dimensions of deviance.* New York: Praeger.

Inattention to Sanctions in Criminal Conduct[1]

LUCIA BENAQUISTO

INTRODUCTION

An important, even dominant, ideology underpinning the North American system of criminal justice is that people will respond rationally to punishment. There is an underlying belief that there is a moral calculus that guides, and hence determines, whether or not a person will commit an offense. As an example of ideological discourse, opponents of gun control commonly argue that more severe sanctions for the use of guns for criminal purposes will deter their use in illegal activities. Such models of crime control require empirical investigation.

This paper reports on criminal reasoning. This, it will become apparent, is largely a misnomer. The analysis employs data gathered from a sample of inmates in three Canadian prisons. In the process of a lengthy interview schedule, each man was asked to tell us the crime(s) he had been charged with and the crime(s) for which he had been convicted. He was then asked to tell us what happened at the time of the event for which he was convicted. So what I speak of as criminal reasoning is the mental processing, the decision making, that is revealed by these crime stories.

RATIONALITY AND THE DECISION TO COMMIT CRIME

The idea that criminal decision making is "rational" has taken on new meaning in criminological research (Felson, 1993; Tunnell, 1992; see also Akers, 1997, p. 23–26). The idea that "punishment is the key to crime prevention is not embraced by new rational choice criminologists . . ." and investigating "[h]ow people make decisions to commit criminal acts is a growing area of research and theory" (Felson, 1993, p. 1497).

As is well known, general deterrence refers to punishment of offenders in an attempt to prevent others from committing illegal acts. On the other hand, specific deterrence is the punishment of individual offenders in an attempt to change their behavior, that is, to prevent them from committing any further offenses. The debate at issue in this paper is whether enhancing sanctions, everything else held constant about society, would enhance crime control. The referent population is therefore not the great majority of the population who do not presently engage in the kinds of major crimes addressed below. It would be moot to employ harsher sanctions to stop people who already do not engage in crime.

Enhanced general deterrence can work, if at all, only against persons who under present conditions commit crimes. Enhanced general deterrence corresponds to what economists call a marginal effect. The implicit referent is a change in the penalty schedule that applies to all adults. It is only in a manner of speaking that the analytic "marginal individual" is subject to something reminiscent of specific deterrence.

Written for this volume.

Thus a relevant population for the empirical investigation of the issue is offenders who have been caught and punished. (One could, of course, argue that there are people who commit crimes but somehow systematically avoid getting caught or punished, but enhancing sanctions would have little effect on their rational choices.) Assuming conditions do not change, those who have been caught and punished are reasonably representative of those who will commit crimes in the future and would be at risk of any greater (or lesser) penalty schedules that might be enacted.

The particular contribution of the present study is to examine the reasoning (or lack thereof) that accompanied the criminal deeds that have in fact been sanctioned. It therefore addresses a general presumption of advocates of enhanced general deterrence; whether, how, or in what degree possible sanctions influence actual offenders when they commit violations. The presumption is one of a modicum or more of rational attention to consequences like sanctions. As shall be seen, even in the weaker form known as common sense, rationality is not strikingly evident in many of the decisions to commit crime.

The current study was in part motivated by previous research concerning inmates' views toward crime and punishment. A random sample of inmates in Massachusetts were interviewed (Benaquisto and Freed, 1996). A key finding, which is replicated in the present study, is that most inmates acknowledge their crimes and are willing to discuss them. A further minority acknowledge a criminal pattern of conduct, although they dispute some of the specifics of the official charges and convictions. Relatively few assert their innocence.

In a more elaborate analysis of their perceptions of legal sanctioning, we found that very few indicate dissent at a personal level. In fact, most are willing to inflict punishment on offenders and offenses in a manner quite similar to the sentences they attribute as the most likely response of actual judges. They are also quite willing to accept such punishment for their own crimes. They do, however, perceive the other inmates as a group as dissenters from sanctioning norms, despite the fact that the generally conformist responses of their fellow inmates negate the perceptions that each (strictly, "most") holds of the others. Nonetheless, if they perceive their actions as worthy of punishment, it raised the issue of why they nevertheless engaged in criminal activity. Further investigation of this issue was thus pursued in this study.

SAMPLE AND METHOD

The samples were drawn from three federal correctional facilities in Canada (one each of minimum, medium, and maximum level security prisons). Interviews with a random sample of approximately 50 men from each prison were conducted. The interviews within the facilities discussed in this paper were begun in 1993 and completed in 1994. They were conducted in private with the inmate and lasted from one to slightly over three hours, with most running about one hour and forty-five minutes. The total sample consists of 152 men.[2] The overall response rate was 76%. Access to men in both administrative and punitive detention was allowed.

Background factors were obtained in two ways. We asked the inmates a number of questions about their prior criminal histories, their prior experience with incarceration, their work history, educational background and other demographic questions. We also obtained answers to a large majority of these same questions from the inmates' files, from which we gained, in addition, a summary of both the inmate's and the police's report on the offense that resulted in the most recent conviction. Information from the files was also obtained about the inmate's psychological assessment.

The crimes for which they were convicted ranged from first degree murder to forgery and fraud. Looking at the primary crime for which they were convicted, 37% of the sample were convicted of murder, homicide and attempted homicide (first degree murder [6.6%], second degree murder [17%], and manslaughter [7%]). Approximately 5% were in for assault, 27% for robberies, 14% for burglaries, 9% for drug offenses, and 3% for sexual assault. The remainder were a tiny minority of forgers, extortionists, and those who committed serious motor vehicle violations (5% in total).

Thirty percent of these men never completed the eighth grade and 65% (in total) never graduated from high school prior to being incarcerated. Only 2% had university degrees and one person had some postgraduate schooling. There were 81.6% caucasians, 8.6% blacks, 6.6% aboriginals, and 3.3% categorized as other. The average age of the men was about 33 years (with the vast majority less than 45 years old (82%), and most had previously been incarcerated (71%), 54% more than once. Thus there were relatively few who had never previously experienced legal punishment, or in fact been in prison before, and relatively fewer who had never had a prior conviction (only 18%), with the average number of prior convictions just over six. The average inmate has spent eight years (in total) of his life behind bars, ranging from 4.5 months to 31 years.

The questions we pursued in the interview that were most relevant to this paper are as follows. "Describe for me briefly the circumstances that led up to your arrest?" and "What if anything were you doing at the time and with whom?" The hope was to elicit information on motivation and reasoning. The larger question — lurking in the background — was whether they had anything in mind about whether they would be punished.

The main goal from the outset was to provide the inmate the freedom to tell his story. Only after he concluded would he be asked specific, follow-up questions, for example, about his thoughts, if any, concerning risks and consequences prior to and during the commission of the criminal act(s) and after being caught. By and large, however, what became strikingly evident was that in the telling of their stories, an explanation of self in light of the circumstances incorporated responses to these questions.

The unspecific invitation to provide narrative quite generally brought forth responses that spoke to the kind of mental state that went into the commission of the deed. It is uncommon for humans,

or at least my respondents, to construct a narrative without referring to the consequences (even the lack of consideration of them). They take for granted, as most of us do, that people act with an eye on what that will bring about for them. Failure to do so "calls for explanation" and thus such explanation tends to be volunteered. This is especially true here given the social setting of the interview. The interviewee is trying to give an account of/for self. The narratives then refer to motive in light of consequences that are self-evident. Thus without being directly prompted, most volunteered an account of the consequences that they had or did not have in mind before they committed the act. This rather often came down to whether or not they could be perceived as considering outcomes when they committed the act.

An initial coding of rationale or "criminal reasoning" with respect to deterrence thus emerged from common central motifs in "crime stories" offered by inmates. This coding scheme evolved from themes that became evident throughout the interviewing process and upon the first reading of the assembled responses to the question of what happened regarding the crime for which they were convicted.

In addition to the personal stories told to us by the inmates, we also gathered information from their files concerning the official accounts of what had taken place, as noted above. I, therefore, conducted an additional coding that consisted of examining the official summary reports in light of the accounts provided us by the inmates for degree of discrepancy. The degree of discrepancy was quite low.

The crime stories provided by the inmates, therefore, were first roughly coded by recording elements that were common across stories. In many stories, more than one element occurred. The next step was to attribute a dominant motif, relegating others to secondary status. From an observer's point of view, the dominant motif summarizes the motivation or inner mental states that lead to the crime. From the subject's point of view, it summarizes the "reasons" offered to explain the deed, although, of course, "reasons" need not include much recognizable as "reasoned thinking."

A small percentage of crime stories, labelled Baroque, defied any standard categorization (2.6%), and another 10% had essentially unique motifs and were thus placed together in a category of Other. Yet, despite the usual complexities of most "real" situations, in the remaining cases, making up the vast majority, the dominant motifs emerged quite clearly and were readily recognizable as substantially parallel across cases.

Since the goal was to code the dominant motif of action from the standpoint of the respondents' mental state, implicitly, focus was directed to code the "prime" criminal act that was being attempted by the offender at the time of the offense. The crime at issue is, accordingly, what the individual defines himself as having done and is thus not always equivalent to the offense for which he was ultimately convicted (or even the most serious thing for which he was convicted), since, for example, there are many instances of plea bargaining. There are also the rarer cases when an intended lesser crime like robbery evolves into a conviction for a murder that the individual himself did not actually commit. He, nonetheless, may have borne legal responsibility due to his involvement in the robbery. Under such circumstances, the individual's motivations and thoughts concern the robbery, because that is what he thinks of as his offense and hence what he talks about in the context of the question concerning the criminal behavior in which he engaged. In essence, without intent there is no motive, or more precisely no direct thoughts concerning the act. Also, it would be highly misleading to code an intended robbery, with clear motivations, as an act without thought based on a conviction for an unintended murder committed during a robbery (particularly if the individual in question did not commit the murder). This would not be reflective of the dominant motif in terms of motivation for the criminal event in question. So, the dominant motif is evaluated in terms of the principal offense in which the person engaged, and what he talks about as "his crime." As noted, this corresponds reasonably well to the acts for which they were arrested and/or convicted (taking into account plea bargains).

There were ultimately 11 categories of motivation in light of consequences, making up the 15 dominant motifs that emerged. These 11 categories were further aggregated, for purposes of summary, into four overarching categories. The distinguishing labels for these summary categories are Noncalculators (65%) (made up of Reduced Mental Capacity, the Negligent, Drug/Alcohol Addiction, and Thoughtless Greedy), Miscalculators (16.5%) (composed of Prideful Neutralizers and Thrill Seekers), Calculators (13%), and Fatalists (6%).[3] The following accounts taken from interviews will illustrate what went into these four categories, and in the process describe the key dominant motifs that they comprise.

CATEGORIES OF CRIMINAL MOTIVATION IN LIGHT OF CONSEQUENCES

The smallest of the overarching categories I term Fatalists (6%). Members of this category emphasized in their "crime stories" that they really did not care whether or not they went to prison. Many explicitly said they might just as well be in prison. Some explicitly stated that they were better off in prison because they were destroying themselves on the outside by overeating, overdrinking and taking too many drugs. It seems quite clear that for members of this category, the likelihood of incarceration is anything but a deterrent.

The typical Fatalist had limited education and faced various serious problems with life. Most, at the time of the crime, were unemployed or on welfare and many have drug problems. They are people who report feeling that they have no good choices in life, and some indicate that they feel as if their life is out of control. When they engage in criminal acts they often think about the outcome in terms of a high expectation of getting caught and not caring one way or the other. Their life outside, in their view, is no better or worse than inside. And, as noted above, there are some who actively desire to be caught, believing life inside would be better for them.

The second smallest of the four categories, 13% of the sample, is the Calculators. Those categorized as Calculators explicitly spoke of their actions in terms of costs and benefits. They report having determined (rightly or wrongly) that in their situation the potential benefits of or gains from committing the act outweighed costs or perceived risks. For example there was a document forger who said the lifestyle was really hard but the money was very good. He said, given the money, "I can always hire a good lawyer and with a good lawyer you can get smaller sentences and time in a minimum [security institution]." He went on to say that he made so much more money doing this than anything else he knew of that he could do that it was worth serving a sentence in a minimum security prison.

The third smallest category, 16.5% of the sample, is the Miscalculators. These are individuals who overestimate their capacity to escape detection or underestimate the abilities of the criminal justice actors. This overarching category consists primarily of two types of dominant motifs. One I call Prideful Neutralizers; the second type I refer to as Thrill Seekers. There is a third type that is quite rare but also fits within this category, the Politically Motivated offender.

The Prideful Neutralizers (9%) expressed the belief that the odds, likelihood or probability that they themselves would get caught was minimal or zero. Given the context of the interview, they were obviously in error. They understood that too, because they would go on to explain in various ways how this was another one of the flukes (since many have rather extensive prior records). One example is a man who said in the course of his crime story, "I'm a great burglar. I'm really good at this." When asked how many years he has spent behind bars, he responded, "Well, I was out for 6 months between the age of 16 and 18. And I was out again for 3 months between [the ages of] 18 and 21." I then asked, "So why do you think you are good at it?" He replied, "Because I've done a lot of them where I haven't gotten caught."

The second type of Miscalculator, I refer to as the Thrill Seekers (6%), those who like the sense of risk involved in the act, and the rush of getting away with it. They are Miscalculators because, while the dominant motif in their explanations of their actions is the sense of thrift, this is combined with the idea that their competence is more than sufficient to insure getting away with their plan. One might compare them to people who go sky diving or rock climbing. They like the thrill involved and the risk of death, but clearly they have no intention of dying.

A final type of Miscalculator is the Politically Motivated offender. While not common in the sample (1.6%), some individuals are undeterred because, in their minds, their goal is pure. The commission of the act is not furtive and the purpose, in essence, is to be apprehended in order to bring attention to their cause — to make a political statement.

There are but two Politically Motivated offenders and for reasons of confidentiality it is not appropriate to supply detail. Such men, however, see themselves as extremely moral and upright in their actions. There is a high degree of expectation that others will recognize this moral behavior and, as a result, see their acts as distinct from those of "common criminals" (as they themselves do). This, of course, neutralizes any "reasonable" consideration of consequences. The consequences upon which these men focus are the positive outcomes for their "cause" and not what they perceive as unlikely harsh punishments in response to their noble acts. In this respect, they insist that their acts are not crimes at all. They note that they do it to be caught but expect that once people hear the reasons for their acts, the consequences of punishment that are normally meted out for actions such as theirs will be set aside.

Finally, the fourth overarching category, and largest by far, is the Noncalculators. They make up about 65% of the sample. Noncalculators are defined as those who did not think about the consequences. I distinguish two main subcategories within the Noncalculators, those with Mental

Capacity (31%) and the Nonthinkers (34.1%, who could be unflatteringly characterized as the thoughtless criminals). Each of these subcategories comprise several distinct dominant motifs.

The narratives of all of the Noncalculators have a common theme. There is explicit reference to how they were unable to think about the consequences or how they did not think about the consequences. The category gathers together those who could not think and those who did not think. Their self-accounts directly emphasized their disconnection from consequence.

Turning first to Extreme Intoxication (13%), this motif comprises those who are so completely intoxicated due to heavy use of drugs and/or alcohol that they can barely recall their actions, let alone consider the consequences of their acts.

One man described for us the events surrounding his criminal act, but was only able to describe the act itself through the eyes of others — what he was told had to have happened. This man was so high from a combination of drugs and alcohol that after he had stabbed his wife in their own home, at some point during the course of an evening, he fell asleep in a chair in the living room. The next morning neighbors noticed the door to his house was left wide open. When they went in to see if everything was all right, they found him solidly asleep in the chair and his wife dead in the bedroom. They called the police. When the police arrived, they woke him up. He was still quite intoxicated. He does not really recall committing the act, but he said he knew he must have done it, and he clearly stated that he accepts responsibility for it.

There is also a fairly large number of these men who committed criminal acts out of passion or in a state of situational Rage (13%). And, for some of these people it is somewhat out of character. For example, we interviewed a 44-year-old high school graduate who was convicted of killing his wife. The man had a record of stable employment, and his file indicates that he had had a good work record. He had a nearly clean criminal record, the exception being an experience with the law over a minor theft 21 years prior to the murder. He killed his wife during a heated argument with her about his belief that she was sleeping with his brother. While he clearly reported that he was not thinking of the consequences at all when he committed the act, that he was "out of his head," he also offered no excuses for what he did. "I accept responsibility for what I've done. I'm not saying that on my behalf I was in another state of mind. The judge was fair." He tried to make it clear to us on several occasions that just because he was telling us about his state of mind when he committed the act, that did not mean he wanted us to think he was using it as an excuse to lessen his responsibility. For him, the fact that he "lost his head" was merely a "fact" that he was reporting to us about the event, along with his belief that he bore responsibility for his actions and deserved to be punished. He did report to us, however, that he contemplated killing himself after he had killed his wife.

Finally there is a dominant motif of Permanent Mental Incapacity (5%) that also falls within the subcategory of Reduced Mental Capacity. These are primarily cases where the offenders have serious mental problems, e.g., mental retardation or psychosis. To briefly illustrate, one man told us that when he was drunk and in the process of committing a theft, he completely lost control and assaulted someone. (This man was from an exceptionally poor background, had an extremely low level of education and was an alcoholic with bipolar disorder who also suffered from psychotic episodes. Despite repeated system contact, one finds in his file a statement indicating that his mental disorders were not diagnosed until late in his criminal career.) In the process of telling us his crime story, he said that he had stopped drinking, adjusted to his medication and got a job. When he was laid off from his job he started drinking again, stopped taking his lithium and ended up committing another crime.

Those with Reduced Mental Capacity may be distinguished from another type of Noncalculator, the Nonthinkers (34%), those who for the most part had the ability to think about the consequences but simply did not. Their self claim is that they were thoughtless when it came to consequences. They did not weigh potential risks of their actions. There are two principal dominant motifs within this subcategory.

The first type of Nonthinker to be discussed is the Severe Drug Addict (20%). He often reports being compelled to steal as a way of life, for money to support himself in his habit. The addicts often report being induced to their criminal acts while high, but this is not always the case. The following is an illustrative example of a repeat offender who is an addict. At 39 years of age he was convicted and sentenced for possession of weapons and drugs and for armed robbery. He, like most, admits to committing these offenses. While describing the events, he states that he was stealing to get money to buy drugs. He said:

> I was doing armed robberies for money for drugs. It was never planned, always on the spot or at the moment, never even planned an hour before or anything . . . I've done at least 20 armed robberies, sometimes with other people, sometimes alone . . . It was madness, always stealing for the drugs.

He was high when doing it. He said, "It would bother me when I got straight, but when I was on a trip, I couldn't think."

The dominant motif for the second type of Nonthinker was a claim that the desire or need for money was his motivation, and that he gave no thought at all to potential consequences of acting criminally to get it (the Thoughtless Greedy, 10%). To illustrate this type, there was an Iranian immigrant who claimed money had always been important to him. He said he grew up without it, and that he also grew up believing "you can't have a wife or family without money." One day he was given an opportunity by his employer to run some drugs. He said that he told himself, "This is your chance for the money." He said, it wasn't until he got caught that he realized how "stupid" he was. He said, "I just never really thought about what could happen to me." He also said, "When I got 12 years, I can't believe I never really thought about it." In

this sort of story, greed, or the quest for money, overrode any attention to the consequences.

A final dominant motif found within the category of Noncalculator (unrelated to the two principal variants discussed above) is commission of crime through acts of Negligence (4%). There is no calculation because there was no intended criminal behavior. A brief illustration is a man who, after having had a few beers, improperly hooked a trailer to the back of his truck. As a result, he accidentally caused severe injury to another when the trailer detached from the truck.

This survey, and coding, of criminal reasoning is sufficient to reveal a preliminary conclusion. Consequences in terms of possible punishment are not a very prominent consideration in the accounts of how crime was chosen. Indeed, the very term "choice" is an unrealistically flattering description for the frequently reported absence of any very creditable mental processing. Further elaboration of this can be obtained from inspection of Table 14.1, which reports on the kinds of crime stories that are associated with the several types of offense.

While 65% of the random sample of incarcerated criminals are what I call Noncalculators, one can see from examining Table 14.1 that the property offenders (e.g., robbers and burglars) are more likely, even if still not very likely, to include among their ranks persons whose reasoning (such as it is) does include some attention to the consequences of likely punishment. In contrast, the violent criminals (e.g., those convicted of murders and assaults) are overwhelmingly Noncalculators. The notion that murder is carried out as a calculated deed is essentially a myth of television dramas.

Thus, in contrast to deterrence theory, such acts are immune to much in the way of rational considerations. There is, however, one category of crime in which a relatively large percentage of calculators can be found (such criminals are a rather small percentage of the prison population, however, which may be significant), drug dealers. And at least one of these individuals is probably right in his calculations. He told us (and several officials at the prison later confirmed his story), that he had millions of

Table 14.1

Overarching Categories of Criminal Motivation by Major Categories of Criminal Offense

	Overarching Categories — Motivation				
	Noncalculators	**Miscalculators**	**Calculators**	**Fatalists**	**Total**
Offenses					
Violent Crimes — Count	40	3	5	1	49
% within Offenses	81.6%	6.1%	10.2%	2.0%	100.0%
Property Crimes — Count	33	13	6	4	56
% within Offenses	58.9%	23.2%	10.7%	7.1%	100.0%
Drug Offenses — Count	4	1	4	1	10
% within Offenses	40.0%	10.0%	40.0%	10.0%	100.0%
Other — Count	2	3	1	1	7
% within Offenses	28.6%	42.9%	14.3%	14.3%	100.0%
Total — Count	79	20	16	7	122
% within Offenses	64.8%	16.4%	13.1%	5.7%	100.0%

dollars waiting for him upon his release after serving his five year sentence in a minimum security facility. He insisted that this was "worth it." One could argue that this is not much worse than attending graduate school. Nonetheless, this is one of the very few instances I encountered in which crime, in any sense, was a reasonable or thoughtful choice. The inmate did provide us with an elaborate account of his thought processes when considering the risks of engaging in high level drug dealing. He considered his risks of being caught, the probability of his length of sentence should this occur, and the likelihood that he would be sent to a minimum security facility if convicted. He weighed the impact of his ability to accumulate wealth, facilitating a good

defense, against the lack of such wealth and decided that the odds were in his favor. He determined the probable costs or risks would likely be more than offset by the potential gains. He therefore proceeded with and continued in his drug dealing activities.

Yet another issue one can explore with these data is the impact of criminal histories, if any, on the types of mental images and concerns (mind sets) that figured in the decision to commit crime. Does past experience with the criminal justice system have any systematic impact on how these men "reason" about crime in terms of consequences? There are several summary variables that can be used to indicate the criminal histories of these inmates. One is their experience with juvenile institutions,

Table 14.2

Overarching Categories of Criminal Motivation by Record of Juvenile Institutionalization

	Overarching Categories — Motivation				
	Noncalculators	**Miscalculators**	**Calculators**	**Fatalists**	**Total**
Juvenile Institution					
yes — Count	29	10	5	1	45
% within Juvenile Insitution	64.4%	22.2%	11.1%	2.2%	100.0%
no — Count	50	10	11	6	77
% within Juvenile Institution	64.9%	13.0%	14.3%	7.8%	100.0%
Total — Count	79	20	16	7	122
% within Juvenile Institution	64.8%	16.4%	13.1%	5.7%	100.0%

Table 14.3

Overarching Categories of Criminal Motivation by Prior Conviction Record

	Noncalculators	Overarching Categories — Motivation			
	Noncalculators	Miscalculators	Calculators	Fatalists	Total
Total Convictions					
Four or less — Count	34	4	5	1	44
% within Total Convictions	77.3%	9.1%	11.4%	2.3%	100.0%
Five or more — Count	43	13	11	5	72
% within Total Convictions	59.7%	18.1%	15.3%	6.9%	100.0%
Total — Count	77	17	16	6	116
% within Total Convictions	66.4%	14.7%	13.8%	5.2%	100.0%

another is the number of times they were previously incarcerated, and a third is the number of previous convictions they have had. Of particular interest is whether there is any evidence of any kind of learning from experience.[4]

The story of the effect of juvenile incarceration can be briefly told from a look at Table 14.2. It appears that sending people to juvenile institutions has little impact on making them more calculating about committing crime. Nor, for that matter, does it make them less. In fact, this factor appears to be irrelevant to the types of reasoning they deploy.

It appears, however, that one's prior criminal experience as measured by number of previous convictions does have some impact on the type of reasoning employed (or not, as the case may be) by the criminal actors. As Table 14.3 shows, the Noncalculators are somewhat more concentrated among those with no previous convictions or four

or fewer previous convictions and are somewhat rarer among those with five or more previous convictions. The difference in frequency is 17.6%. Table 14.4 shows that what becomes more common as one increases his number of prison experiences is miscalculation.[5] Calculators actually become slightly more frequent also.

DISCUSSION

The "crime stories" offered by inmates summarize the range and qualities of motivations and decisions that lead to crime and punishment. Because the sample is random, it more or less accurately recapitulates how the crimes that lead to detection and incarceration, under present social conditions, arise in individuals "reasoning" to decisions. This offers a potentially important corrective to any notion that crime is somehow a decision like any other, and

Table 14.4

Overarching Categories of Criminal Motivation by Prior Prison Term

	Noncalculators	Overarching Categories — Motivation			
	Noncalculators	Miscalculators	Calculators	Fatalists	Total
Prior Prison Terms					
None — Count	25	2	4	1	32
% within Prior Prison Terms	78.1%	6.3%	12.5%	3.1%	100.0%
One or more — Count	53	18	12	6	89
% within Prior Prison Terms	59.6%	20.2%	13.5%	6.7%	100.0%
Total — Count	78	20	16	7	121
% within Prior Prison Terms	64.5%	16.5%	13.2%	5.8%	100.0%

that the decision to undertake crime may be understood through models of rationality or reasoned choice, especially if one expects the reasoning to reflect middle-class lifestyles and standards. Deterrence models, in essence, do that. They do not take into consideration the circumstances and life conditions of the majority of these men. This especially affects any claims that crime might be controlled by altering the conditions that a rational decision-maker would take into account. The case for enhanced general deterrence rests on such a claim. Evaluation of that claim involves inference over a counter-factual: what impact would one expect from a harsher schedule of penalties, if any at all?

In pursuing the criminal motivations in light of consequences through analysis of the inmates' crime stories, it very quickly became apparent that the vast majority of those already engaging in criminal activities, activities of the most serious nature (and who have, for the most part, experienced punishments prior to the one they are currently experiencing), are very bad candidates for an enhanced deterrence model. And as noted in the introduction, a model of enhanced deterrence does not make much sense unless the target population of the model is any other than those already engaging in the most serious crimes, for one need not increase deterrence to stop people who do not commit criminal acts.

This analysis shows that most offenders who repeatedly engage in criminal activities do not calculate their actions in terms of the potential risks they may face if they engage in a given illegal act. Many simply do not think about the potential consequences at all. Some even report not thinking at all about the illegal act itself prior to its commission. It is even difficult to use the term decision when talking about the majority of these men. Clearly, rational calculation — the weighing of potential gains or benefits against potential costs or risk — is hardly evidenced. As the dominant motifs identified above clearly display, crime that results in incarceration is, much more often than not, action taken without any attention, much less reasoned attention, to possible incarceration as a consequence.

It appears also that past experience with legal punishments, if anything, merely acts to alter slightly one's rationales — creating more Miscalculators and a few more who claim calculation. This small number of Calculators are the clearest case in support of an enhanced deterrence model (but they represent only 13%). And an analysis of the relationship between categories of criminal motivation and types of crimes engaged in show that these types are found largely among high level drug dealers and not among violent criminals. Enhancing the punishments for crime generally, in an attempt to address violent crime, would thus serve little purpose.

Perhaps the least likely candidates for response to enhanced deterrence are those contained within the category of Noncalculator (65%). This is especially true for those with reduced mental capacity. Harsher penalties would prove quite ineffective against acts engaged in by those who at the time were without the capacity to think, either due to rage, severe intoxication (especially if addicted) or mental incapacities of a permanent nature. If one is not in one's right mind (so to speak, without a mind), no amount of deterrence — a concept which demands the capacity for rational thought — can have an impact.

There is one category of Noncalculator that might be receptive to deterrence, the Thoughtless Greedy, had the men thought at all about the consequences at the time of their act, but they did not. Therefore, if many of these men (two-thirds of whom had no prior records) had thought about their acts in terms of consequences they might have been deterred by the current level of punishment, as some of them reported after the fact. A higher level of punishment, an enhanced general deterrence model, however, is not a very plausible solution to this problem. Many report substantial dismay at what they have brought upon themselves. There is no reason to believe that higher levels of punishment would have any greater effect than the current level of punishment in making them consider the potential consequences in the first place. As noted above, this group includes many reasonable candidates for responding to their current sentence as a specific deterrent. This in no way, however, indicates the need for harsher punishments.

The Fatalists, while only a small percentage (6%), clearly are not good candidates for a model of enhanced deterrence. They report a condition of life that is so desperate that, at best, they are indifferent to the punishment; some actively seek out prison. These men told their own stories, and, in the cases they reported to us, it was all too easy to imagine why, given the life circumstances they revealed, they saw life on the street as no better, and sometimes worse, than being locked away in prison. While it is not always easy to communicate in a paragraph or two a state of mind, the illustrative case of the unemployed male with barely a fifth grade education who was raised by an alcoholic mother and who is himself an alcoholic suffering from severe asthma may provide some insights.

There remain the Miscalculators (16.5%). The label describes well enough their dominant motifs, yet a closer look serves to underscore the essentially conservative nature of the above codes. In academic language, Miscalculators report reasoning that features a misestimation of the probabilities of apprehension. But such language falls short of evoking the distinctive quality of their self-attributions. Most of these individuals had been arrested and imprisoned more than once, or even many times, for spells amounting to the greater part of their adult life. And, of course, they made their claims while in prison. Yet they would insist, sometimes quite vehemently, that their skills or qualities rendered apprehension and incarceration somehow unlikely and/or irrelevant. The reasoning involved is, on its face, not what is ordinarily deemed "rational." The statements reflected a willful incomprehension (often grounded in pride) that fell very far short of incorporating key aspects of reality that had the most direct bearing on key circumstances of life. They expressed an adherence to fixed views about potential outcomes — views that are unalterable in the face of evidence to the contrary. And these misunderstandings or incomprehensions were not casual or tangential. They were raised, even emphatically and repeatedly raised, as central elements in accounting for self.

One can always imagine that such persons "might think a little more carefully" about harsher penalties. But, this is wishful thinking. Precisely what they have refused to do, with altogether serious results, is to pay any mind to consequences.

In the everyday life of middle-class adults, to tell many of the tales offered as "crime stories" would be to mark oneself as woefully lacking in fundamental judgment and/or reasoning capacity. (Of course, many of the inmates would agree to precisely such a characterization of their mental state at the time of their crimes.) What the bare codes only summarily communicate is the depth or degree to which this is apparent in the variety of motifs summarized above. It was very rare to encounter an inmate who conveyed anything remotely suggesting someone "who knew the odds and consciously took his chances." What comes through was an inability (often situational, sometimes persistent) to comprehend or grasp consequences. The common denominator that unites the vast majority is that the deeds that landed them in prison were undertaken precisely because they did not think clearly (or were quite unable to think clearly) about the consequences.

Most of the crimes that were described were anything but romantic. Real people were often hurt, and often for "reasons" that hardly inspired sympathy. This is not to gainsay the appalling conditions of alcoholism, abuse or poverty that figure prominently in the childhoods of many such men. Nor is it at all rare that they regret their deeds. It is not that hard to envision remedies that might divert some of those who end up as adults making bad decisions that hurt others. But there is little reason to suspect that decisions that are already bad, but nevertheless occur, would become less frequent if only harsher penalties made them even worse decisions.

Enhanced general deterrence is not, of course, the only rationale for urging longer sentences. Vengeance, for example, is attainable quite independently of the mental capacities or reasoning process that led to offensive acts. And one can hardly say from the above that enhanced general deterrence would affect *no* one; a few did calculate that for them "crime paid," and one cannot rule out that some who suffered from disattention might be jolted into sharper focus. But, as a strategy of altering the behavior of those who under current conditions engage in crime, enhanced general deterrence is not at all promising. What "crime stories" show is quite otherwise. Enhanced general deterrence comes down to disincentive that would discourage a rational actor or person thinking clearly. A less promising target than the mental states of those who currently manage to end up imprisoned is not easy to imagine.

NOTES

1. I would like to thank FCAR for the grant (#95-NC-0986) that made this research possible. I would also like to thank Correctional Service of Canada for the high level of assistance and support they provided. Thanks also to the many individuals within the various institutions and organizations of Correctional Service of Canada who opened their doors to me and provided me with invaluable aid. I am grateful to Sharon Nixon, André Smith, Marie Anik Gangé, and Ronit Dinovitzer for the excellent research assistance they provided. I would also like to thank Carolyn Boyes-Watson and Steve Rytina for their extensive comments on this or earlier versions of this paper. Most of all, I would like to thank the men in the prison for agreeing to be interviewed and responding so extensively to our queries. I am truly grateful. Earlier versions of parts of this paper were presented at the American Sociological Association Meetings, Los Angeles, 1994, and the Social Science History Association Meetings, New Orleans, 1996. Please direct any correspondence to Lucia Benaquisto, Department of Sociology, McGill University, Stephen Leacock Bldg., 855 Sherbrooke St. W., Montreal, P.Q. H3A-2T7.

2. I gained permission and support from Correctional Service of Canada to conduct this study.

The study, however, was independently funded by FCAR. Therefore, the men were guaranteed the confidentiality of their responses and assured that the individual level information would not be shared with the institution or any government agency. All interviews were voluntary. The men were informed of the study prior to the first interviews by notices that we distributed within each institution. They were told that men would be chosen by chance to participate, if they were willing, in an interview concerning their views on issues of punishment and sentencing, and that if their name had been selected they would be called for an interview. They were also assured that the interview was unaffiliated with the institution and would be kept strictly confidential. When the men arrived for an interview, we informed them about the study, read them a form assuring them of the confidentiality of their responses and of the voluntariness of their participation. If they chose to participate, they would sign the form. We also requested from each inmate written permission to review their individual files.

3. The percents add to 100.5 due to rounding error. These summaries, of course, omit the motif categories of Denial (7.2%) and Baroque (2.6%). An additional motif category that was not incorporated in this summarizing scheme was that of Other (9.9%). Therefore, the overarching categories consist of 122 cases. The percentages reported here and in the remainder of this paper correspond to this reduced number.

4. This is at least partially relevant to concerns about specific deterrence. However, an obvious caveat is that the sample does not include those who learned enough from earlier run-ins with the law so as not to show up here among the (many) repeat offenders.

5. When Table 14.3 is collapsed to contrast Non-calculators with the other categories, a chi-squared test yields p = .052, or borderline support for rejecting the hypothesis of no difference. When Table 14.4 is collapsed to

contrast Miscalculators with the other modes, a chi-squared test yields p = .068. Both tables hint of pattern, but the evidence for differences is, at best, modest.

DISCUSSION QUESTIONS

1. What do you see as some of the more significant lessons of this study for those who believe that the solution to the problem of crime is the imposition of harsher sentences?
2. What do you think might be some of the more formidable problems involved in research with prison inmates?
3. Distinguish between "general" and "specific" deterrence.
4. According to Benaquisto, among the various groups of offenders that she identifies, which is probably least likely to respond to enhanced deterrence?

5. Why does Benaquisto's analysis lead her to conclude that the term "criminal reasoning" is somewhat of a misnomer?

REFERENCES

Akers, R. L. (1997). *Criminological theories.* (2nd ed.). Los Angeles: Roxbury Publishing Company.

Benaquisto, L., & Freed, P. J. (1996). The myth of inmate lawlessness: The perceived contradiction between self and other in inmates' support for criminal justice sanctioning norms. *Law and Society Review, 30,* 481–511.

Felson, M. (1993). Review of choosing crime: The criminal calculus of property offenders. *American Journal of Sociology, 98,* 1497–1499.

Tunnell, K. D. (1992). *Choosing crime: The criminal calculus of property offenders.* Chicago: Nelson-Hall.

CHAPTER

15

Low Self-Control and Opportunity[1]

TERESA C. LAGRANGE
ROBERT A. SILVERMAN

INTRODUCTION

General Theory of Crime (1990) claims to be *general*, in part, due to its assertion that the operation of a single mechanism, low self-control, accounts for "all crime, at all times": acts ranging from vandalism to homicide, from rape to white-collar crime (Gottfredson and Hirschi 1990:117). Whether or to what extent an individual engages in any one or more of these crimes or analogous actions such as smoking, drinking, gambling, or prostitution, may depend on individual circumstances and opportunities; but it is low self-control which provides the impetus to commit them (Hirschi and Gottfredson 1994). Beyond this, however, General Theory claims to be a *general* theory by offering an explanation for all of the persistent, well-documented correlates of crime. Gender, age, race, social class, peer relationships, family structure and relations, school performance or employment — all are assumed to be significant not as proximate causes, but only in whether they discourage or encourage the internalization of self-control, or reflect its expression (Gottfredson and Hirschi 1990).

A growing body of empirical research has demonstrated at least moderate support for the first of the theory's contentions: that low self-control predicts a variety of criminal and non-criminal deviant behaviors (Arneklev et al. 1993; Brownfield and Sorenson 1993; Creechan 1995; Grasmick et al. 1993; Keane et al. 1993; Kennedy and Forde 1995; Polakowski 1994). What remains unclear, however, is the degree to which the theory can appropriately claim to be a general one by explaining common correlates of crime such as gender. It is this issue that the current research examines, using data from a recent cross-sectional survey of Canadian secondary-school students. Consistent with previous research, we assess low self-control by self-reported psychological traits (Arneklev et al. 1993; Grasmick et al. 1993). Additional indicators of low self-control are obtained from self-reported frequency of equivalent but non-criminal behaviors (smoking and drinking). We use these measures of low self-control, opportunity and their interactions to predict self-reported *general delinquency* as measured by a summed 20-item scale, and *property*, *violent*, and *drug offenses*, among males and females.

THEORY AND PREVIOUS RESEARCH

Gender, traditionally one of the most significant correlates of crime, has over the last few decades become the subject of considerable debate. The debate centers on two related questions: *why*

Adapted from Low Self-Control and Opportunity: Testing General Theory of Crime as an Explanation for Gender Differences in Delinquency, by Teresa C. LaGrange and Robert A. Silverman (February 1999). *Criminology, 37*(1), p. 41–72. Reprinted with permission.

females are substantially less delinquent/criminal than males; and whether females, when they *are* delinquent/criminal, act for the same reasons as males (Broidy and Agnew 1997; Chesney-Lind and Shelden 1998; Ensminger et al. 1983). Several prominent and influential theorists, beginning in the mid-70s, attributed persistent gender differences in crime and delinquency to differences in opportunity (Adler 1975, 1977, 1981; Simon 1975, 1979). Females, traditionally delegated to uniquely "feminine" roles that kept them at home, or more closely supervised at school and at work, were less likely to engage in "drinking, stealing, gang activity, and fighting" (Adler 1975:95) because they had fewer opportunities to do so.

The corollary of this explanation for lesser female participation in crime/delinquency is that, given similar opportunities to those already enjoyed by males, females will behave similarly; in other words, that female crime arises from the same mechanisms, and in a parallel way, to male crime. Underscoring this, theorists writing from this perspective predicted that as females gained greater freedom and wider social participation, their involvement in crime would also increase and converge with males (Adler 1975; Simon 1975). Early studies based on female arrests for serious (index) crimes, seemed initially to support this prediction, reporting dramatic increases for females in such non-traditional, "masculine" categories as robbery and even homicide. Subsequent and more systematic research, however, has failed to demonstrate that such a trend towards equality in crime is occurring (Steffensmeier 1978, 1980, 1981, 1989). Overall, the actual differences between male and female crime participation remain substantial, and in fact appear to have stabilized in recent years.

In spite of the debates and controversies surrounding the issue of gender, General Theory devotes a relatively brief discussion to the topic, arguing that "gender differences appear to be invariant over time and space" (1990:145). Gottfredson and Hirschi note that males are not only more likely to commit delinquent or criminal acts; they are also more likely to engage in analogous behaviors such as drinking, smoking, and drug use — behaviors so easily committed that opportunity is not an issue, even for juveniles (1990:147). Furthermore, even where female opportunities have increased, female involvement in crime has not increased in proportion. And for personal offenses, females are portrayed as having at least potentially the same opportunities as males — they spend equal or even greater amounts of time in the close, intimate contact that usually generates these offenses. Yet in spite of the possibility for relatively high rates of female violence, female participation in this sort of offending remains significantly lower than that reported for males.

These observations, Gottfredson and Hirschi argue, provide evidence of "a substantial self-control difference between the sexes" (1990:147). Given that the development of self-control is linked directly to early childhood socialization, this suggests differential socialization of females (as argued by feminist theorists); but these differences are not implicated in the development of a distinctively different feminine pattern. Their significance lies in the mechanism of low self-control: effective socialization results in its development, while ineffective socialization does not. Hence, more intensive socialization of girls results in their having, in general, more self-control than boys. These differences in propensity, moreover, are compounded by differences in opportunity: females tend to be more closely monitored than males throughout childhood (and into adulthood). They therefore have fewer opportunities to express their propensities in antisocial actions, even if such propensities exist. Gottfredson and Hirschi conclude that gender-based differences in crime participation are due to the combination of differential socialization of males and females, resulting in the gender stratification of self-control, and the element of opportunity. General Theory thus provides an answer to both of the previously noted issues about gender differences in offending. On the one hand, lesser female crime and delinquency is attributed to the combination of greater self-control and lesser opportunity; but when female offending occurs, it can be expected to parallel male offending, since it is seen as arising from the same sources.

Controlling for Opportunity

Opportunity is a key factor in many causal models of gender-stratified offending; in addition, it is central to General Theory. According to Gottfredson and Hirschi, *crimes* are specific acts of "force or fraud" committed in the pursuit of self-interest; *criminality*, by contrast, is the propensity to commit such acts (Gottfredson and Hirschi 1990:91–94). It is this distinction that allows them to conclude that the actual occurrence of crimes is shaped by a number of "necessary conditions" including "activity, opportunity, adversaries, victims, [and] goods" (Gottfredson and Hirschi 1990:137). Opportunity in this context, and as it has been addressed by previous tests of General Theory, refers primarily to the structural conditions of access and target availability (Grasmick et al. 1993; Kennedy and Forde 1995).[2] Drug abuse presupposes access to drugs; driving under the influence of alcohol entails access to both a vehicle and alcohol; theft from an employer requires having a job; getting into brawls may be related to frequenting bars.

For adolescents, however, opportunity is further constrained by adult supervision. The degree to which parents monitor where teens are and who they are with can be expected to have a direct impact on their opportunities to offend. In support of this, a substantial body of research has demonstrated that weak parental supervision predicts increased delinquency (Canter 1982; Gove and Crutchfield 1982; Hagan et al. 1985, 1988; Krohn and Massey 1980; LaGrange and White 1985; Rankin and Kern 1994). More importantly, from the perspective of the current discussion of gender differences, differential supervision of male and female children has been identified as a significant factor in the gender stratification of delinquency. Since females of all ages are assumed to be monitored more closely than their male counterparts, they could be expected to have fewer delinquent opportunities. Some evidence suggests, however, that the differences in opportunity accorded to males and females vary according to age. While both sexes are more closely monitored in the early teen years, mid- to late-adolescence often results in a substantial relaxation of supervision for boys, but not for girls (Chesney-Lind and Shelden 1992).

The differential supervision of girls in later adolescence and the implication for opportunity is consistent with General Theory's explanation of gender differences. The claim that the expression of low self-control in delinquency and crime is dependent on situational opportunities suggests that closer supervision of girls in the later teens would tend to limit their delinquent involvement. Nevertheless, to the extent that they are lacking in self-control, females of any age should be just as likely as males to act on their propensities when they have the chance. When differences in levels of self-control and opportunity are controlled, therefore, General Theory predicts that low self-control will manifest itself in similar patterns of delinquent behavior for both sexes.

Measures of Low Self-Control

The issue of what, precisely, is embraced by the concept of low self-control, and how it might best be measured, has been raised in several critiques of the theory (Akers 1991; Barlow 1991), and recently has become the subject of some empirical debate (Longshore et al. 1998; Piquero and Rosay 1998). Gottfredson and Hirschi contend that the low self-control individual is "impulsive, insensitive, physical (as opposed to mental), risk-taking, short-sighted, and nonverbal," although they offer little evidence to support this description, nor for their subsequent contention that "there is considerable tendency for these traits to come together in the same people" (1990:90).

Gottfredson and Hirschi claim that low self-control should not be thought of as a coherent "criminal personality." In their commentary on Grasmick et al.'s 1993 study, for example, they note that while low self-control is a single underlying propensity, it may be expressed in multidimensional ways, ways shaped largely by situational and opportunity differences (1993:53). Just as low self-control persons will be likely to commit crimes, they will be similarly likely to display characteristics such as temper, impulsivity, a preference for risk-taking, and so forth. These traits can therefore be seen as by-products of low self-control, and the extent to which they occur does provide some indication of the construct. Nevertheless, the implication is that *low self-control* refers to some distinctive, underlying characteristic (or propensity, as Gottfredson and Hirschi identify it) that encompasses these various traits. The question remains, then, whether all of these assumed by-products of low self-control are equally predictive of delinquency and crime, or whether only some more specific traits are associated with offending. Is low self-control simply another name for impulsivity or risk-seeking? If so, it would seem preferable to use the more concise and specific concept, one which more clearly identifies the characteristics leading to crime/delinquency, than the broader, vaguer term of low self-control.

To address this issue, and in view of the role assigned to traits such as impulsivity and risk-taking in other models of gender differences in offending, we have chosen not to combine all personality traits into a single unweighted scale for the present analysis. Instead, we have retained each of the personality traits as separate measures. In addition, we have included two behavioral measures of the concept, self-reported smoking and drinking, as advocated by Akers (1991:204), and by Hirschi and Gottfredson (1993:53).

We use these measures of low self-control to predict self-reported delinquency, measured as general delinquency, and as specific offense types (property, violence, and drugs), controlling for opportunity and its interactions with low self-control, age, social class, and race. Consistent with Gottfredson and Hirschi's explanation of gender differences in offending, we expect that when differences in inclination and situational opportunities are controlled, both genders will offend in similar ways.

METHOD

Study and Data

Data for this research were taken from the *University of Alberta Study of Juvenile and Adolescent Behavior*, a cross-sectional survey of secondary-school students completed in Edmonton, Alberta in 1994. Edmonton is a medium-sized western Canadian city, with a population of approximately one-half million. Secondary schools in the city's public school district include thirteen senior high schools serving grades ten to twelve and thirty junior high schools for grades seven to nine. In addition, a separate Catholic school district includes six high schools and ten junior high schools. A multistage cluster sampling design was used to select fifteen schools for this study: five public senior high schools, six public junior highs, two Catholic high schools, and two Catholic junior highs. School selection was initially based on school and neighborhood vandalism rates, obtained from a previous city-wide study of vandalism (LaGrange 1994). Schools were selected to represent all sections of the city, with oversampling of schools in high-vandalism areas. Within each school, cluster sampling was used across grades. Individual classes were selected from the language arts and social studies programs (required courses for all enrolled students), to ensure full coverage of each school's population and to eliminate overlap.

Questionnaires were administered to students in each school during October and November of 1994 by a team of trained graduate students. Participating students completed the questionnaire during one of their regularly scheduled class periods of approximately 50 minutes. Of the 2425 questionnaires completed, a total usable sample of 2095 was obtained, consisting of 961 males (45.9%) and 1134 females (54.1%) between the ages of 11 and 18.

For purposes of this analysis, sixty-five variables were extracted to measure low self-control, opportunity, and delinquency. Opportunity measures, taken from items about family and/or adult supervision, were combined into summed indices, as were the delinquency items; factor analysis was used to construct measures of the psychological expressions of self-control; and questions about smoking and drinking behavior were retained as separate measures. Age, race, and a family income measure were included as variables. To examine General Theory's predictions regarding gender, we first analyze general delinquency and specific offense types for the total sample of 2095. To further examine differences between males and females, we then analyze the two groups separately.

MEASURES

Personality Expressions of Low Self-Control

The study contained an inventory of twenty-six items that correspond to the traits identified in previous research as reflective of low self-control (impulsivity, a preference for simple tasks and physical activities, a taste for risk-seeking, self-centeredness, and temper [Arneklev et al. 1993; Grasmick et al. 1993:13–16; Kennedy and Forde 1995]).

Smoking and Drinking

In addition to personality traits, low self-control was measured by two items about frequency of smoking and drinking. The survey had asked "How often do you smoke cigarettes?" and "How often do you drink alcoholic beverages?" Each question provided five response categories, ranging from "never" to "every day" ("a pack a day," for smoking). The majority of respondents (80%) had answered "never" on each of these questions.

Opportunity

Eight questions regarding parental and adult supervision were used to measure opportunity. Four of these asked about parents' knowledge of where

youths were during the course of a day, and who they were with; two others asked respondents about whether or not they had a curfew. Two further questions dealt with adult supervision more generally, asking respondents about time spent with companions in the absence of adults.

Dependent Variable

The dependent variable, delinquency, was measured by a summed 20-item scale. Respondents had been asked how many times during the last year they had committed actions that corresponded to crimes ranging from shoplifting to armed robbery. For each question, response categories ranged from "never" to "more than three times." The most frequently reported of the delinquency items, "hitting someone to hurt them," was reported by 35% of respondents; the least frequent, "physically hurt someone to force them to have sex," was reported by less than 1%. An additional six questions asked how many times (actual count) respondents had committed six different types of vandalism.

In addition to measures of low self-control, opportunity, and delinquency, four other variables were included: age, two dummy variables representing categories of racial minority (Asian and Aboriginal),[3] and mean neighborhood income as a measure of socioeconomic status. Three hundred and thirty-nine of the respondents (16.2%) were of Asian background; an additional 136 (6.5%) were Aboriginal,[4] and the remaining 1620 (77.3%) were non-Asian, non-Aboriginal. A measure of family socioeconomic status was taken from Canadian National Census data regarding the mean annual income for similar households in the respondent's neighborhood. For the present analysis, raw income estimates were recoded into eight categories, ranging from less than $19 900/year to $80 000+/year.

To evaluate the prediction that delinquency will be most likely when persons with low self-control have greater opportunity, the interaction between the two constructs was assessed by multiplying measures of the two together (Friedrich 1982;

Jaccard et al. 1990). Relationships between independent and dependent variables were then analyzed using Ordinary Least Squares regression.

RESULTS

Regression Analysis for Total Sample

The results of regressing general delinquency and specific offense types on predictors for the total sample, with gender as a dummy variable and age continuous, are reported in Table 15.1. For general delinquency, all measures of low self-control are statistically significant predictors of increased delinquency. The strongest predictor for this group of teens as a whole, based on a comparison of the standardized coefficients, is risk-seeking (b = 1.44, Beta = .26), followed by the behavioral indicators of smoking (b = .71, Beta = .21) and drinking (b = .86, Beta = .19). When the dependent variable is restricted to property offenses, which composed approximately half of the delinquency items and were the most frequently reported delinquent acts for these teens, results are very similar: almost all measures of low self-control are strong and statistically significant predictors, with risk-seeking again having the largest effect (b = 1.00, Beta = .25). For violent offenses, however, it is the interactions between low self-control and opportunity that are the strongest predictors of increased offending, with the largest effects reported for the interaction between risk-seeking and getting together with friends in the absence of adults (b = 12, Beta = .27). While the other measures of low self-control predict modest increases in this type of delinquency, the effects are substantially less than those reported for interactions. This pattern is even more apparent for drug offenses: almost all statistically significant effects are associated with the interactions between low self-control and opportunity, rather than low self-control alone.

Based on the previous discussion of male and female differences, females are assumed to be less likely to exhibit traits reflecting low self-control than males. In addition, previous research has suggested that males and females have differential access to opportunity. When these differences are controlled, however, predictions based on General Theory were that male and female effects would be similar: low self-control and opportunity should translate into delinquency in the same way for all teens, regardless of their gender. This expectation, in turn, suggests that when the causal factors identified by the theory are controlled, gender will no longer be a significant predictor of delinquency. In the present analysis, however, that assumption is not supported. For general delinquency, property offenses, and violent offenses, gender retains a statistically significant effect (b = 1.01, b = .70, and b = .50, respectively, p < .01 for all), indicating that the variables in the regression analyses do not fully explain gender differences in offending. For drug offenses, however, a non-significant effect is reported for gender; any gender differences among teens in this sample are explained by differences in the measures of low self-control and opportunity.

Regression Results for Sample Split on Gender

Splitting the sample into two groups consisting of females (N = 1134) and males (N = 961) of all ages (reported in Table 15.2) gives some indication of the patterns of gender differences. For both genders, the strongest predictors of general delinquency are measures of low self-control; for females, however, the largest effects are reported for risk-seeking (b = 1.58, p < .01), while impulsivity has the largest effect for males (b = 1.49). Smoking and drinking are significant predictors for both sexes, and their effect is similar (for smoking, b = .65 for females and b = .75 for males; for drinking, b = .86 and b = .80 for females and males, respectively).

Property offences follow a similar pattern, with largest effects for females associated with risk-seeking (b = .93). As with general delinquency, smoking and drinking are significant predictors of increased offending, for both genders. For females, however, the interaction between low self-control and opportunity predicts increased offending,

Table 15.1

Regression Coefficients for General Delinquency and Specific Offenses on Measures of Low Self-Control, Opportunity, and Interaction for Total Sample (Standardized Coefficients in Parentheses)

	General Delinquency	Property Offenses	Violent Offenses	Drug Offenses
Gender	1.01 (.09)**	.70 (.09)**	.50 (.13)**	.01 (.00)
Age	−.09 (−.03)	−.05 (−.03)	−.11 (−.10)**	.06 (.08)**
Race/Asian	−.37 (−.02)	−.13 (−.01)	−.01 (.00)	−.17 (−.05)**
Race/Aboriginal	.43 (.02)	.26 (.02)	.45 (.06)**	−.03 (−.00)
Neighborhood income	.02 (.00)	.05 (.02)	−.03 (−.02)	.00 (.00)
Measures of Low Self-Control				
Impulsivity	.46 (.08)*	.08 (.02)	.10 (.05)	−.03 (−.02)
Risk-seeking	1.44 (.26)**	1.00 (.25)**	−.05 (−.02)	.02 (.01)
Temper	.60 (.11)**	.41 (.10)**	.11 (.06)	.09 (.06)
Carelessness	.72 (.13)**	.51 (.13)**	.13 (.07)**	.04 (.03)
Present-oriented	.39 (.07)**	.21 (.05)**	.17 (.09)**	.10 (.07)*
Smoking	.71 (.21)**	.32 (.13)**	−.01 (−.01)	.06 (.07)
Drinking	.86 (.19)**	.55 (.17)**	.18 (.11)**	−.15 (−.14)
Measures of Opportunity				
Mother's supervision	.39 (.11)**	.23 (.09)**	.06 (.05)	.00 (.00)
Father's supervision	.15 (.06)**	.09 (.05)*	.05 (.05)**	.00 (.00)
Curfew	.01 (.00)	.01 (.00)	.01 (.01)	−.01 (−.01)
Together w/friends	.19 (.04)*	.07 (.02)	.10 (.05)**	.00 (.00)
Drive around	.15 (.03)*	.17 (.06)**	−.01 (−.01)	.00 (.00)
Interactions between Low Self-Control & Opportunity[a]				
Impuls x Mother super	.27 (.16)**	.18 (.15)**	.07 (.12)**	—
Impuls x Drive around	—	.13 (.08)	—	.05 (.09)**
Risk x Together friends	—	—	.12 (.27)**	—
Risk x Drive around	—	—	—	.06 (.12)**
Temper x Mother super	—	—	.05 (.09)*	—
Temper x Father super	—	—	—	−.02 (−.09)*
Careless x Curfew	—	—	—	−.04 (−.06)*
Careless x Drive around	—	—	—	.04 (.07)*
Present x Mother super	—	—	.03 (.12)	—
Present x Father super	—	—	—	−.03 (−.11)**
Smoke x Mother super	—	—	—	.03 (.15)**
Smoke x Curfew	—	—	—	.04 (.12)**
Smoke x Drive around	—	—	—	.04 (.14)**
Drink x Father super	—	—	—	.04 (.19)**
Drink x Curfew	—	—	—	−.03 (−.07)*
Drink x Together friends	—	—	—	.10 (.42)**
Drink x Drive around	—	—	—	−.07 (−.19)**
Rsq.	.55	.45	.31	.50

[a] Only interaction effects retained in final regression equations shown.

* Statistically significant, $p < .05$

** Statistically significant, $p < .01$

Table 15.2

Regression Coefficients for Delinquency and Offense Types on Measures of Low Self-Control, Opportunity, and Interactions for Females and Males (Standardized Coefficients in Parentheses)

	Total Females (N = 1134)				Total Males (N = 961)			
	Delinq.	**Property**	**Violent**	**Drugs**	**Delinq.**	**Property**	**Violent**	**Drugs**
Age	-.16(-.06)**	-.10(-.06)**	-.13(-.15)**	.05(.09)**	-.01(-.00)	.01(.01)	-.09(-.08)*	.07(.08)**
Race/Asian	-.21(-.02)	-.06(-.01)	.05(.11)	-.13(-.04)	-.56(-.04)	-.16(-.00)	-.09(-.02)	-.21(-.06)*
Race/Aboriginal	.97(.04)*	.68(.05)*	.53(.07)**	.10(.02)	.03(.00)	-.10(-.01)	.32(.04)	-.17(-.03)
Neighborhood income	-.08(-.03)	.01(.00)	-.05(-.05)	-.01(-.01)	.09(.03)	.07(.03)	-.02(-.01)	.01(.01)
Measures of Low Self-Control								
Impulsivity	.14(.03)	-.02(-.01)	-.05(-.03)	.08(.07)**	1.49(.25)**	1.05(.24)**	.38(.17)**	.06(.04)
Risk-seeking	1.58(.27)**	.93(.24)**	.41(.21)**	.08(.05)	.18(.03)	.89(.23)**	.49(.24)**	-.39(-.29)**
Temper	.70(.14)**	.45(.13)**	.32(.19)**	.15(.11)*	.44(.08)**	.34(.08)**	.08(.04)	-.01(-.01)
Carelessness	.14(.03)	.44(.13)**	-.05(-.03)	-.04(-.03)	.72(.12)**	.57(.13)**	.10(.05)	.07(.05)*
Present-oriented	.43(.09)**	.25(.07)**	.16(.09)**	.14(.11)*	.80(.13)**	.17(.04)*	.20(.09)**	.08(.06)
Smoking	.65(.21)**	.26(.13)**	.18(.18)**	.06(.08)	.75(.20)**	.38(.14)**	-.31(-.23)	.19(.22)**
Drinking	.86(.20)**	.80(.27)**	.13(.09)**	-.20(-.18)	.80(.17)**	.51(.16)**	.19(.11)**	-.16(-.15)
Measures of Opportunity								
Mother's supervision	.31(.09)**	.16(.07)*	.11(.09)**	-.02(-.02)	.49(.13)**	.29(.10)**	.11(.08)*	.03(.03)
Father's supervision	.09(.03)	.03(.02)	.02(.03)	-.01(-.02)	.24(.08)**	.14(.07)*	.06(.06)	.00(.00)
Curfew	.02(.01)	.19(.09)**	.01(.01)	.04(.05)	-.03(-.01)	-.01(-.00)	.00(.00)	-.02(-.02)
Together w/friends	.08(.02)	-.02(-.01)	.03(.02)	.00(.00)	.37(.06)**	.21(.05)	.15(.07)*	.00(.00)
Drive around	.10(.02)	.15(.05)*	-.02(-.01)	-.02(-.02)	.16(.04)	.20(.06)*	.04(.03)	-.01(-.01)

(continued)

Table 15.2 (continued)

Interactions between Low Self-Control & Opportunity[a]

	Total Females (N = 1134)				Total Males (N = 961)			
	Delinq.	Property	Violent	Drugs	Deling.	Property	Violent	Drugs
Impuls x Mother super	.36(.23)**	.19(.18)**	.12(.22)**	—	—	—	—	—
Impuls x Curfew	—	.17(.10)**	—	—	—	—	—	—
Risk x Curfew	—	.13(.07)**	—	.07(.09)**	−.22(−.09)*	—	—	.10(.33)*
Risk x Together	—	—	—	—	—	—	—	—
Risk x Drive around	—	—	—	—	—	—	—	.05(.11)*
Temper x Father super	—	—	—	−.05(−.18)**	—	—	—	—
Temper x Curfew	—	—	—	—	—	—	.10(.11)*	—
Careless x Father super	.13(.13)*	—	.05(.14)*	.05(.09)*	—	—	—	—
Careless x Drive around	—	—	—	−.04(−.15)**	—	—	—	—
Present x Father super	—	—	—	—	—	—	—	—
Present x Curfew	—	—	—	—	.27(.22)*	—	—	—
Present x Drive around	—	—	—	—	—	—	—	−.06(−.10)*
Smoke x Mother super	—	—	—	.04(.19)**	—	—	—	.03(.08)**
Smoke x Curfew	—	—	—	.06(.17)**	—	—	—	.05(.19)**
Smoke x Drive around	—	—	−.04(−.13)**	—	—	—	—	—
Drink x Father super	—	—	—	.04(.22)**	—	—	—	.03(.17)*
Drink x Drive around	—	—	—	—	—	—	—	−.05(−.17)*
Drink x Together friends	—	—	—	.10(.40)**	—	—	.11(.37)*	—
Drink x Curfew	—	−.13(−.12)*	—	−.09(−.22)**	—	—	—	.08(.34)*
Rsq	.54	.44	.27	.47	.53	.42	.30	.53.

[a] Only interaction effects retained in final regression equations shown.

* Statistically significant, p < .05

** Statistically significant, p < .01

beyond the effects identified for low self-control alone, as is apparent by the significant effects identified for three of the interaction terms. For males, by contrast, property offending is predicted almost entirely by measures of low self-control alone, with all indicators of the concept statistically significant. Violent offenses are linked to the factor of risk-seeking (b = .41 for females, b = .49 for males), and to the interaction between low self-control and opportunity — for both genders, the coefficients for interaction terms exceed in magnitude those for measures of low self-control by itself. The interactions between low self-control and opportunity are also the most important predictors for drug offenses; they account for almost all of the explained variance in this form of offending for females, while for males additional increases in drug offences are predicted by smoking (b = .19).

DISCUSSION AND CONCLUSION

According to General Theory, females commit fewer crimes than males due in part to lesser inclination (self-control), as a product of differential socialization, and also to fewer opportunities. Nevertheless, low self-control persons are predicted to commit a variety of criminal and non-criminal deviant acts when they have the chance to do so, regardless of their gender. When differences in opportunity are controlled, we expect to find that low self-control translates into behavior similarly for both genders.

When measures of delinquency are regressed on these predictors, results for both males and females identify consistent relationships between *some* measures of low self-control and reported delinquency. A preference for risk-seeking and impulsivity, in particular, were found to be robust predictors of increased delinquency, of various types and to varying degrees. It should be noted, too, that consistent with the theory, those teens in our sample who reported smoking and drinking were also significantly more likely to engage in delinquency; and these effects were most consistent and pronounced for girls. Given that General Theory identifies all of these specific measures — risk-seeking, impulsivity, smoking and drinking — as indicators of low self-control, these observations seem to offer support for the theory.

Yet the specific *component* of low self-control leading to increased delinquency differs between the two genders; and the nature and magnitude of differences varies for different types of offenses. Girls reported a significantly lower propensity for risk-taking behaviors than boys; but this specific trait is associated with a very substantial increase in delinquency. For boys, on the other hand, impulsivity is an additional consistent and robust predictor of increased delinquency. Differences between males and females are large enough in magnitude to be statistically significant; they also vary, depending on how delinquency is measured. The contrast in effects is much more marked for general delinquency and for property offenses than for violent offenses or drugs. Property offenses, as previously noted, made up half of the offenses included in our delinquency items, and they were also the most frequently reported. These results suggest, then, that the factor structure of low self-control, to the extent that it can be viewed as a unitary construct, differs between males and females. This, in turn, implies that there may be different patterns of causality leading to male and female offending — a conclusion that does not support General Theory's explanation of the relationship between gender and crime/delinquency. Beyond that, the results of this study provide little support for the contention that low self-control is a unitary construct. The traits used here to assess the psychological dimensions of low self-control — risk-seeking, impulsivity, temper, present-orientedness, and carelessness — are all associated with some increases in delinquency of different types, as argued by the theory. Yet they function very distinctively in terms of consistency and magnitude, and in relationship to different categories of offenders (male vs. female) and offenses (general delinquency, property, violence, and drugs). By far the most consistent and robust predictors throughout this analysis are the factors of risk-seeking and impulsivity, and the behavioral measures of smoking and drinking — although, as noted above, effects differ for offenders and offense types. Carelessness and being present-oriented, by contrast, were found to be weak or inconsistent predictors.

It remains unclear whether the broader, more general construct of low self-control adds anything to the understanding of crime and delinquency, when greater precision might be obtained by restricting the causal mechanisms to narrower concepts like risk-seeking and impulsivity — concepts that have been well established in previous literature (Longshore et al. 1998). Hagan and his associates (1985, 1988), for example, attribute lower female delinquency to differences in the preference for risk-seeking, and the closer supervision of females — two factors consistently identified as significantly associated with delinquency in this analysis. And research going back several decades has identified impulsivity as an important predictor of gender-stratified delinquency (Eysenck and Eysenck 1985; Wilson and Herrnstein 1985).

Our results suggest that further research into the theory's explanations of gender differences is warranted. Aside from gender, however, other variables such as race and social class are also, in General Theory's causal model, attributable to differences in low self-control; and these issues have not been addressed in any depth in the empirical literature. General Theory attributes racial differences in rates of offending, in large part, to differential child-rearing practices among ethnic/racial categories (1990:153). Class, by contrast, along with other structural factors, is generally irrelevant to the theory's micro-social focus, receiving only a peripheral discussion in relation to white collar crime (Gottfredson and Hirschi 1990:181–183) and in a brief review of Social Disorganization (Shaw and McKay 1942) and Strain (Merton 1938) theories as earlier representatives of "positivist social science" (1990:79–80).

In the present analysis, we controlled for two categories of racial minority, and a measure of neighborhood level of social class. A consideration of the results, based on the coefficients for these measures in each of the regression analyses, suggests

that for these teens, being of Aboriginal background is associated with an increase in violent behavior (especially among girls), while being of Asian background is associated with a decrease in drug offending, especially among boys; and that these effects persist even while controlling for differences in self-control and opportunity. The measure for social class, by contrast, has little impact. While an exploration of these relationships is beyond the scope of this paper, they nevertheless suggest that an evaluation of the significance of such factors would be an important direction for future discussions of the theory.

In addition to its relative neglect of structural factors, General Theory also dismisses the relevance of more temporally proximate individual factors such as peers. Teens who are delinquent tend to have friends who are delinquent; and some types of delinquency, particularly drug abuse, seem to be closely related to group activity (Elliott et al. 1979, 1985; Erickson and Jensen 1977). Consistent with this literature, drug offences and violence in our results were both found to be dependent to some degree on the opportunities provided by spending a great deal of unsupervised time with peers. General Theory does not dispute the existence of these relationships, however; instead, its disagreement with other perspectives centers on the direction and time-order of the apparent relationship. Gottfredson and Hirschi contend that peer relationships are a reflection of low self-control: youths who lack self-control, who are risk-seeking and prone to delinquency, are inclined to associate with like-minded others, and these circumstances may provide the situational opportunities for some types of deviance. Alternative interpretations, however, are that youths learn to engage in such behaviors as smoking and risk-seeking from their association with others (Akers et al. 1979; Krohn et al. 1985; Sutherland and Cressey 1978); or that there is actually an interaction between individual propensities and peer influences (Agnew 1991; Thornberry et al. 1994). These issues, too, are in need of further exploration.

Our analysis of the *University of Alberta Study of Juvenile and Adolescent Behavior* suggests that

General Theory's concept of low self-control provides an inadequate explanation of marked gender differences in offending among these teens. The validity of the theory's claim to explain "all crime, at all times" (1990:117), among all offenders, thereby proving itself to be a "general theory of crime," thus remains to be demonstrated in further research.

NOTES

1. Funding for this research was received from the Social Sciences and Humanities Research Council of Canada.

2. This argument on the role of opportunity in specific actions closely parallels routine activities and opportunity perspectives (Cohen and Felson 1979; Felson and Cohen 1980; Sherman, Gartin, and Buerger 1989). And, in fact, Gottfredson and Hirschi acknowledge the affinity, observing that the two viewpoints "are not necessarily inconsistent" (Gottfredson and Hirschi 1990:23; Hirschi 1986).

3. Canadian research has identified these two ethnic categories as overrepresented in crime statistics; they also represent the two largest minorities for the city where the questionnaire was administered (see Gordon and Nelson 1996; Wood and Griffiths 1996).

4. This figure differs from the officially recorded proportion of Aboriginals in the population of Edmonton, reported variously as between 3 and 4%. Our higher figure may be due to the fact that subjects categorized as Aboriginal in this research include all three groups of Natives, Inuit, and Métis. Official figures, on the other hand, are based on legal status criteria that do not include "non-status" Aboriginals or the much larger group of Métis (Morrison and Wilson 1986:524).

DISCUSSION QUESTIONS

1. What is "general" about the General Theory of Crime?

2. If you were to undertake research of the sort described in this article, would you operationalize "low self-control" in the same way as or differently than LaGrange and Silverman?

3. According to the authors of this study, what role does criminal opportunity play in the promotion of crime?

4. Gender differences in crime are among the most consistently reported in the research literature. What does the General Theory of Crime have to say about these differences.

REFERENCES

Adler, F. (1975). *Sisters in crime.* New York: McGraw-Hill.

Adler, F. (1977). The interaction between women's emancipation and female criminality. *International Journal of Criminology and Penology, 5*, 102–112.

Adler, F. (1981). *The incidence of female criminality in the contemporary world.* New York: New York University Press.

Agnew, R. (1991). The interactive effect of peer variables on delinquency. *Criminology, 29*(1), 47–72.

Akers, R. L. (1991). Self-control as a general theory of crime. *Journal of Quantitative Criminology, 7*(20), 201–211.

Akers, R., Krohn, M., Lonza-Kaduce, L., & Radosevich, M. (1979). Social learning and deviant behavior: A specific test of a general theory. *American Sociological Review, 44*, 636–655.

Arneklev, B. J., Grasmick, H. G., & Tittle, C. R. (1993). Low self-control and imprudent behavior. *Journal of Quantitative Criminology, 9*(3), 225–247.

Barlow, H. D. (1991). Explaining crime and analogous acts, or the unrestrained will grab at pleasure whenever they can. *Journal of Criminal Law and Criminology, 82*, 229–242.

Broidy, L., & Agnew, R. (1997). Gender and crime: A general strain theory perspective. *Journal of Research in Crime and Delinquency, 34*(3), 275–306.

Brownfield, D., & Sorenson, A. (1993). Self-control and juvenile delinquency: Theoretical issues and an empirical assessment of selected elements of a general theory of crime. *Deviant Behavior, 14*(3), 242–264.

Canter, R. J. (1982). Family correlates of male and female delinquency. *Criminology, 20*(2), 149–167.

Chesney-Lind, M., & Shelden, R. G. (1992). *Girls, delinquency and juvenile justice.* Pacific Grove, CA: Brooks/Cole Publishing Company.

Chesney-Lind, M., & Shelden, R. G. (1998). *Girls, delinquency, and juvenile justice* (2nd ed.). Belmont, CA: Wadsworth Publishing Company.

Cohen, L., & Felson, M. (1979). Social change and crime rate trends: A routine activity approach. *American Sociological Review, 44*, 588–608.

Creechan, J. H. (1995). A test of the general theory of crime: Delinquency and school dropouts. In J. H. Creechan & R. A. Silverman (Eds.), *Canadian delinquency.* Scarborough, ON: Prentice-Hall Canada Inc.

Elliott, D. S., Ageton, S. S., & Canter, R. J. (1979). An integrated theoretical perspective on delinquent behavior. *Journal of Research in Crime and Delinquency, 16*, 3–27.

Elliott, D. S., Huizinga, D., & Ageton, S. S. (1985). *Explaining delinquency and drug use.* Beverly Hills: Sage.

Ensminger, M. E., Kellam, S. G., & Rubin, B. R. (1983). School and family origins of delinquency: Comparisons by sex. In K. Teilman Van Dusen & S. A. Mednick (Eds.), *Prospective studies of crime and delinquency.* Boston: Kluwer-Nijhoff Publishing.

Erickson, M. L., & Jensen, G. F. (1977). Delinquency is still group behavior! Toward revitalizing the group premise in the sociology of deviance. *Journal of Criminal Law and Criminology, 68*(2), 262–273.

Eysenck, H., & Eysenck, M. W. (1985). *Personality and individual differences.* New York: Plenum.

Felson, M., & Cohen, L. (1980). Human ecology and crime: A routine activity approach. *Human Ecology, 8*, 389–406.

Friedrich, R. J. (1982). In defense of multiplicative terms in multiple regression equations. *American Journal of Political Science, 16*, 797–833.

Gordon, R. M., & Nelson, J. (1996). Crime, ethnicity, and immigration. In R. A. Silverman, J. J. Teevan, & V. F. Sacco (Eds.), *Crime in Canadian society* (5th ed.). Toronto: Harcourt Brace & Co., Canada.

Gottfredson, M. R., & Hirschi, T. (1990). *A general theory of crime.* Stanford, CA: Stanford University Press.

Gove, W. R., & Crutchfield, R. D. (1982). The family and juvenile delinquency. *The Sociological Quarterly, 23*, 301–319.

Grasmick, H. G., Tittle, C. R., Bursik, R. J., Jr., & Arneklev, B. J. (1993). Testing the core empirical

implications of Gottfredson and Hirschi's general theory of crime. *Journal of Research in Crime and Delinquency, 30*(1), 5–29.

Hagan, J., Gillis, A. R., & Simpson, J. (1985). The class structure of gender and delinquency: Toward a power-control theory of common delinquent behavior. *American Journal of Sociology, 90*, 1151–1178.

Hagan, J., Gillis, A. R., & Simpson, J. (1988). Feminist scholarship, relational and instrumental control and a power-control theory of gender and delinquency. *British Journal of Sociology, 30*, 301–336.

Hagan, J., Simpson, J., & Gillis, A. R. (1989). The sexual stratification of social control: A gender-based perspective on crime and delinquency. *British Journal of Sociology, 30*, 25–38.

Hirschi, T. (1986). On the compatibility of rational choice and social control theories of crime. In D. Cornish & R. Clarke (Eds.), *The reasoning criminal: Rational choice perspectives in offending.* New York: Springer-Verlag Press.

Hirschi, T., & Gottfredson, M. (1993). Commentary: Testing the general theory of crime. *Journal of Research in Crime and Delinquency, 30*(1), 47–54.

Hirschi, T., & Gottfredson, M. (1994). *The generality of deviance.* New Brunswick, NJ: Transaction.

Jaccard, J., Turrisi, R., & Wan, C. K. (1990). *Interaction effects in multiple regression.* Newbury Park, CA: Sage.

Jackson, D. N. (1986). *Basic personality inventory.* London, ON: Sigma Assessment Systems, Research Psychology Press Division.

Keane, C., Maxim, P. S., & Teevan, J. J. (1993). Drinking and driving, self-control, and gender: Testing a general theory of crime. *Journal of Research in Crime and Delinquency, 30*(1), 30–46.

Kennedy, L. W., & Forde, D. R. (1995). Self-control, risky lifestyles, routine conflict and crime: A respecification of the general theory of crime. Edmonton: University of Alberta, Centre for Criminological Research.

Krohn, M., & Massey, J. (1980). Social control and delinquent behavior: An examination of the elements of the social bond. *Sociological Quarterly, 21*, 529–543.

Krohn, M., Skinner, W., Massey, J., & Akers, R. (1985). Social learning theory and adolescent cigarette smoking: A longitudinal study. *Social Problems, 32*, 455–471.

LaGrange, R. L., & White, H. R. (1985). Age differences in delinquency: A test of theory. *Criminology, 23,* 19–45.

LaGrange, T. C., (1994). Routine activities and vandalism. Unpublished MA Thesis, Edmonton, AB: University of Alberta.

Longshore, D., Stein, J. A., & Turner, S. (1998). Reliability and validity of a self-control measures: A rejoinder. *Criminology, 35*(1), 175–182.

Longshore, D., Turner, S., & Stein, J. A. (1996). Self-control in a criminal sample: An examination of construct validity. *Criminology, 34*(1), 209–228.

Merton, R. K. (1938). Social structure and "anomie." *American Sociological Review, 3,* 672–682.

Morrison, R. B., & Wilson, C. R. (1986). *Native peoples: The Canadian experience.* Toronto: McClelland & Stewart Inc.

Piquero, A. R., & Rosay, A. B. (1998). The reliability and validity of Grasmick, et al.'s self-control scale: A comment on Longshore, et al. *Criminology, 35*(1), 157–174.

Polakowski, M. (1994). Linking self- and social control with deviance: Illuminating the structure underlying a general theory of crime and its relation to deviant activity. *Journal of Quantitative Criminology, 10*(1), 41–78.

Rankin, J., & Kern, R. (1994). Parental attachments and delinquency. *Criminology, 32*(4), 495–516.

Shaw, C., & McKay, H. (1942). *Juvenile delinquency and urban areas.* Chicago: University of Chicago Press.

Sherman, L. W., Gartin, P. R., & Buerger, M. E. (1989). Hot spots of predatory crime: Routine activities and the criminology of place. *Criminology, 14*(1), 17–49.

Simon, R. J. (1975). *Women and crime.* Lexington, MA: Lexington Books.

Simon, R. J. (1979). Arrest statistics. In F. Adler & R. J. Simon (Eds.), *The criminology of deviant women.* Boston: Houghton Mifflin Co.

Steffensmeier, D. (1978). Crime and the contemporary woman, 1960–1975. *Social Forces, 57,* 566–584.

Steffensmeier, D. (1980). Sex differences in patterns of adult crime, 1965–1977. *Social Forces, 58,* 1080–1109.

Steffensmeier, D. (1981). Patterns of female property crime, 1960–1978: A postscript. In L. Bowker (Ed.), *Women and crime in America.* New York: Macmillan.

Steffensmeier, D. (1989). Trends in female crime: It's still a man's world. In R. C. Monk (Ed.), *Taking sides: Clashing views on controversial issues in crime and criminology.* Guilford, CT: The Dushkin Publishing Group, Inc.

Sutherland, E., & Cressey, D. (1978). *Principles of criminology* (10th ed.). Philadelphia, PA: Lippincott.

Thornberry, T. P., Lizotte, A. J., Krohn, M. D., Farnworth, M., & Sang, S. J. (1994). Delinquent peers, beliefs, and delinquent behavior: A longitudinal test of interactional theory. *Criminology, 32*(1) 47–84.

University of Alberta study of juvenile and adolescent behavior. (1994). Computer data file. Edmonton: University of Alberta.

University of Alberta study of juvenile and adolescent behavior. (1994). Study codebook. Edmonton: University of Alberta.

Wilson, J. Q., & Herrnstein, R. (1985). *Crime and human nature.* New York: Simon & Schuster.

Wood, D. S., & Griffiths, C. T. (1996). Patterns of Aboriginal crime. In R. A. Silverman, J. J. Teevan, & V. F. Sacco (Eds.), *Crime in Canadian society* (5th ed.). Toronto: Harcourt Brace & Co., Canada.

16

Changes in the Structure of Life Courses and the Decline of Social Capital[1]

ROSS MACMILLAN

INTRODUCTION

Arguably one of the more interesting empirical phenomena in contemporary society is the temporal trend in aggregate crime rates, a trend that, for all intents and purposes, has been largely upward for several decades. This empirical phenomenon appears to characterize most developed and developing countries during the post-World War II period (Braithwaite, 1989: 49; Wilson and Hermstein, 1985: 409–10; Hagan, 1994: 19). In Canada, aggregate crime rates increased steadily from the 1940s through to the 1970s, levelled off for the decade of the 1980s, and then continued to rise in the late 1980s and early 1990s.

In many respects this trend is either a blatant embarrassment or, more generously, an enduring puzzle for criminologists, because the increase was neither anticipated nor adequately explained by the dominant theoretical perspectives of the 1950s, 1960s, and 1970s (Cohen and Felson, 1979). In an effort to extend theory and research in this area, this paper integrates insights from life course research (Elder, 1985) with a conception of the *age stratification of informal social control* (Sampson and Laub, 1993) to provide an account of changes in the size of the pool of motivated or potential offenders over time. In examining changes in the order and timing of life course transitions for successive cohorts, the proposed model suggests that changing degrees of institutional bonds and social capital for late teens and young adults have direct associations with secular trends in aggregate crime rates. Life course transitions have been identified as an important element of informal social control (Sampson and Laub, 1993), and changes in the timing of these events may result in an increased and increasing pool of potential offenders who are less constrained by institutional controls. Using a life course approach to the study of crime (Hagan and Palloni, 1988), this argument highlights changes in the availability and application of informal social control mechanisms for recent periods and will be tested in a time series analysis of temporal trends in property crime rates in Canada, from 1963 to 1992.

INFORMAL SOCIAL CONTROL AND CHANGES IN THE NORMATIVE STRUCTURE OF THE LIFE COURSE

As an emerging paradigm in sociology, a life course perspective generally involves four central themes: the interplay of human lives and historical times; the timing of lives; linked or interdependent lives; and human agency in making choices (Elder, 1994). Elder defines life courses as "pathways

Adapted from Changes in the Structure of Life Courses and the Decline of Social Capital in Canadian Society: A Time Series Analysis of Property Crime Rates, by Ross Macmillan (1995). *Canadian Journal of Sociology, 20*(1), p. 51–78. Reprinted with permission.

through the age differentiated life span" where differences in age influence the various "expectations and options that impinge on decision processes and the course of events that give shape to life stages, transitions, and turning points" (1985: 17). It has long been recognized that age and aging are fundamental elements in social relations and that many of the qualitative aspects of social life are contingent on one's progress through the life course. In age differentiated societies, specific ages are bound up with differential role expectations and role transitions that are embedded in social institutions (Caspi, Elder, and Herbener, 1990: 15).

The central notion of the life course generally revolves around two central concepts: trajectories and transitions, both of which are contingent on socio-historical context, social interdependency, and particular stage of the life course. Life course trajectories refer to long-term patterns and sequences of behaviour that constitute pathways or lines of social development, while transitions are identified as specific, consequential life events that are embedded in trajectories and constitute "changes in state that are more or less abrupt" (Elder, 1985: 31–2). Specific types of transitions characteristic of life course progression in Western societies include high school graduation, leaving home, the first marriage, the first full-time job, entry into parenthood, and divorce. Because transitions constitute significant life events, their interlocking with specific trajectories can result in turning points or changes in the life course. These trajectories, characteristic of particular life courses, are contingent on the specific transitions undergone or not undergone. In the example of high school completion (i.e., the presence or absence of a particular life course transition), there are significant social consequences associated with either outcome (Elder, 1985: 32). Although one type of life course transition can trigger specific long-term trajectories, the specific nature of later life course transitions can also serve to redirect life course trajectories (Sampson and Laub, 1993; Rutter, Quinton, and Hill, 1990).

CRIME AND THE LIFE COURSE

Sampson and Laub (1993) apply insights derived from the life course perspective to the study of crime and deviance in their age-graded theory of informal social control. While previous studies of social control have tended to focus on either adolescents or formal mechanisms of social control (see the review in Gottfredson and Hirschi, 1990), Sampson and Laub propose a theory that encompasses the nature, diversity, and changes in social bonds and informal social controls over the life course.

As the experience of individuals with social institutions and specific significant others is age-stratified (Elder, 1975), aging is characterized by an embedding or disembedding in different social relations. For example, the transition to adulthood is characterized by a disembedding of the relations between parents and children in order to accommodate new sets of social relations that are characteristic of adulthood. The age-graded movements from one set of these social relations to another constitute the various life course transitions that have a significant influence on an individual's engagement, continuity, and discontinuity in criminal activity (Sampson and Laub, 1993). In examining contexts of social control across the life cycle, Sampson and Laub emphasize both the character of and changes in social relationships. Because these relations are resources that individuals can draw upon in their everyday lives, they constitute distinct forms of social capital.

While Coleman (1988) defines social capital primarily in relation to the achievement of capabilities for action, the source of social capital is the socially structured relations between individuals in groups. In the context of the life course, social capital can provide resources that allow individuals to enact life course transitions. Yet because social structures are both enabling and constraining (Giddens, 1984), the social capital and institutional bonds inherent in these relations also constitute an important dimension of informal social control. By emphasizing the control aspect of intimate social relations, Sampson and Laub demonstrate the importance of life course transitions for understanding criminal activity.

While Sampson and Laub (1993) focus explicitly on intra-individual change in criminal and deviant activity over the life span, contemporary life course perspectives emphasize the importance of historical and structural conditions (Elder, 1994). As is consistent with this approach, insights derived from life course research can further the understanding of secular trends in crime rates over time by acknowledging how temporal changes in the timing, duration, and sequencing of life course transitions (Elder, 1985) result in changes in the patterning of social control.

THE STRUCTURE OF LIFE COURSES, SOCIAL CHANGE, AND CRIME

In examining historical changes in the order and timing of life course transitions, one of the more significant transitions is that from adolescence to adulthood. Although a normative life course conception suggests an inter-related process of leaving home and starting one's own family and/or one's first full-time job (Modell, 1989; Rindfuss et al., 1987), research indicates that recent cohorts have been increasingly less likely to follow such a pattern. In North America, there is a general trend of declining proportions of persons 15 to 24 who live with their parents (Goldscheider and Goldscheider, 1993; Goldscheider and LeBourdais, 1986; Boyd and Pryor, 1990). Additionally, recent research also indicates that adolescents now spend less time in household and family settings, particularly with parents nearby (Felson and Gottfredson, 1984).

While leaving home represents an important life course transition in itself, traditional conceptions of a normative life course have generally examined its interconnection with other life course transitions, particularly marriage, parenthood, and the first full-time job. As was the case with leaving home, recent research indicates that people, particularly males, are waiting longer to get married (Adams and Nagnur, 1990; Glick, 1990; Modell,

1989: figure 20). Equally interesting, some research has reported that people have expressed less interest in the qualitative dimensions of marriage in recent years (Modell, 1989: Table 37). Comparing survey responses in 1957 and 1976, Modell found that more than twice as many men in the earlier period reported that one positive aspect of marriage was in helping men to "settle down."

With similar effects, more widespread availability of contraceptives have allowed recent cohorts to exercise greater control over the timing of parenthood, resulting in a tendency for couples to wait longer for parenthood and to have fewer children (Modell, 1989: 280; Rindfuss, Morgan, and Swicegood, 1988). In this regard, Rindfuss et al. (1988: figure 14) indicate that the proportion of persons ages 20 and 25 who were childless increased dramatically in the post-war era. Similarly, Devereaux (1994) reports Canadian data showing an increase in childlessness of 15 percent (from 21 to 36 percent) for families with husbands under the age of 35 between the years 1966 and 1986.

In addition to changes in institutional bonds characteristic of familiar relationships, there is also evidence of changes in the order and timing of occupational bonds. Gower (1990) reports lower proportions of males 16 to 24 in the labour force in recent years, a trend that is apparent in both the United States and Canada. Furthermore, decreases in the average real wage for workers aged 16 to 24 (Wannell, 1990) suggest decreases in the qualitative dimensions of work for young Canadians.

While the previous review has sketched out just a few significant temporal trends in the timing of early life course transitions; there are two aspects which are of particular note for understanding criminal activity. First, there is a general decline in the age of first leaving home and consequently an increase in the proportion of adolescents and early adults who are not living with their parents. Second, there is also evidence of delays in the formation of adult social bonds connected with marriage, parenting, and full-time employment (see also Stevens, 1990: figure 1). In terms of a life course conceptualization, these trends suggest a process by which recent periods are characterized by a disembedding from the familial relations of adolescence and lessened or delayed embedding in the familial and economic relationships characteristic of adulthood. Research on age and crime shows that (1) crime is predominantly engaged in by teenagers and young adults and (2) there is tremendous variation within this subpopulation due to the presence and salience of social bonds (Gottfredson and Hirschi, 1990; Hagan, 1989). These findings indicate that the recent changes in the timing of life course events that constitute institutional bonds and social capital have weakened mechanisms of informal social control for the high-crime age group.

While the majority of sociological criminology, particularly macro-level research, has focused on the question of why people commit crimes and has sought to identify forces that impel or influence criminal activity, the present research utilizes a control perspective such that motivation is assumed and theoretical interest rests on that which restrains offending. In seeking such an explanation, control theorists assert that conformity arises from strong social bonds, such as attachment, commitment, involvement, and belief (Hirschi, 1969). Consequently, the possibility of criminal activity increases when the social bonds of individuals are attenuated (Hagan, 1989; Hirschi, 1969; Matza, 1964). Rather than develop an overly deterministic account of human activity in which persons are impelled to criminal activity, control perspectives assert that offending simply becomes a greater possibility when bonds are weak or weakened (Matza, 1964).

While control approaches have generated a large volume of empirical support, virtually all of the research has focused on individual differences (see review in Hagan, 1991a; Gottfredson and Hirschi, 1990). In extending this approach to macro-level research, the primary interest of this paper is how changes in age-stratified social controls and social bonds over time can be seen to influence the size of the pool of potential offenders in any given period. Because of the significant role of intimate relations and institutional commitments in networks of social control, the general decline of adolescent and young adult familial and economic activity should have significant consequences for the criminal or delinquent activity of adolescents and young adults. This issue is explored in an analysis of aggregate crime rates that are primarily influenced by the activities of adolescents and young adults (Wilson and Hermstein, 1985; Cohen and Land, 1987; Steffensmeier and Harer, 1991).

DATA AND METHODOLOGY

The data used in this analysis consist of time series data for Canada for the years 1963 to 1992.[2] In order to assess generalizability, the analysis estimates models for three different types of property crime: robbery, break and enter, and motor vehicle theft. All crime data were taken from Statistics Canada's *Criminal Statistics Reports*.[3]

INDEPENDENT VARIABLES

Because the current research is focused primarily towards developing a theoretically and empirically tenable account of the motivational dimension of criminal activity, the relevant independent variables consist of measures of the size of the pool of motivated or potential offenders in relation to changing patterns of social capital and informal social control. These measures tap changes in the character and content of the institutional bonds and social relations experienced by young persons in Canadian society. In addition, other independent variables intended to control for further influences include an age-sex structure measure, criminal opportunity measures, measures of economic conditions, and a criminal deterrence measure. As the latter measures have been extensively described elsewhere (Cohen, Felson, and Land, 1980; Cantor and Land, 1985; Cohen and Land, 1987), they will be described only briefly here. Whenever possible, measures were constructed to be consistent with previous research.

Informal Social Control and Potential Offenders

Consistent with the structural changes in the order and timing of life course transitions identified in the previous section, the present research focuses on the three measures of "leaving home," "marriage," and "employment" to operationalize period differences in informal social control and social capital during late adolescence and early adulthood. The first measure, the proportion of males 15 to 24 who are married, is intended to tap both social capital and social bonds for those most at risk of criminal behaviour. The second measure is the percentage of persons between the ages of 15 and 24 living with their parents. The third measure is the proportion of males 15 to 24 who are active members of the labour force. All measures are intended to capture the degree to which specific cohorts differ in terms of institutional relations and institutional bonds and thus how the size of the pool of potential offenders fluctuates over time. Each measure is expected to be associated negatively with crime rates.

Age-Sex Structure of the Population

In addition to the social control measures, the present research also includes a measure of the age-sex structure of the population. In micro-level research, the relationship between age and crime can best be characterized as an empirical regularity with offending activity increasing through the teenage years, peaking during mid to late adolescence or early adulthood, and then declining continually through the life course. Because this pattern has been consistently demonstrated across time and space, and regardless of data source, offense type, or methodology (Gottfredson and Hirschi, 1990; Braithwaite, 1989), it follows logically that periods characterized by increased proportions of young adults, particularly young males, will tend to have higher crime rates (Cohen and Land, 1987).

In order to control for gross changes in demographic composition that may affect crime rates,

the proportion of the population that is male and between the ages of 15 and 24 is included in the analysis.

Deterrence/Incapacitation

While the previous measures have all focused on structural features of society, a fifth measure captures the effects of activities of criminal justice agencies on crime. In order to capture these effects, the present research incorporates a measure of the imprisonment rate.

Unemployment

In conceptualizing the social ecology of criminal activity, Cohen and Felson (1979) identify the logical requirements of any predatory criminal event as a motivated offender, a suitable target, and an absence of capable guardianship. From this perspective, motivation, by itself, is an insufficient cause of crime because it does not account for the patterns and activities of social life that facilitate or inhibit the convergence of these three elements. Without a convergence of these three elements, there is no *opportunity* for crime.

Incorporating this perspective, unemployment can be seen to produce two separate effects on aggregate crime rates: a positive motivational association that is theoretically consistent with traditional, deprivation-based theories of crime; and a negative opportunity association through increased home activity (i.e., greater guardianship) and a slower circulation of goods (i.e., fewer suitable targets). While unemployment can be expected to display both effects, Cantor and Land (1985) suggest that the timing of these effects is not simultaneous, because motivational effects occur more slowly due to institutional social supports that cushion the economic impact of unemployment (Devine, Sheley, and Smith, 1988; Cantor and Land, 1985; DeFronzo, 1983).

To capture this process, the present analysis includes both the aggregate unemployment rate derived from the *Historical Labour Force Statistics* for the years 1962 through 1992 and its first-difference, computed directly from the series (see Cantor and Land, 1985, for a more elaborate discussion of these measures). The former measure is expected to be negatively associated with crime rates, while the latter is expected to be positively associated.

Residential Population Density Ratio and Automobile Registration

In addition to the opportunity effects of economic slow-downs, the present analysis also includes direct indicators of criminal opportunities.

To operationalize opportunities for crime, Cohen et al. (1980; Cohen and Felson, 1979) propose two measures. First, a residential population density ratio measures the proportion of households that are either non-family or family households in which both the husband and the wife are in the labour force. This variable measures both households that are less likely to have persons in them at all times of the day, and persons in public spaces. Second, in the specific models for motor vehicle theft, Cohen et al. (1980; Cohen and Land, 1987) include a measure of registered motor vehicles per capita to indicate the number of available targets.

Using the same formula as Cohen et al. (1980), a residential population density ratio for Canada was constructed from data derived from Statistics Canada's *Census Reports on Families and Households* for the census years 1962 through 1991. Additionally, the number of registered passenger vehicles per capita was derived from Statistics Canada's *Canada Year Book*, as well as the *Road Motor Vehicles, Registrations* for the same time period. Both measures are expected to display positive associations with the aggregate crime rates.

SUMMARY OF RESULTS AND DISCUSSION

The current research began with the empirical observation of increasing crime rates in Canada and the recognition that dominant theoretical approaches were either unable to account for these increases or offered only partial explanations. In particular, efforts to explain crime rate trends were relatively weak in explaining the motivational component of crimes. The argument presented in this paper drew on two empirical regularities from criminological research to formulate a theoretically tenable account of this component. First is the consistent finding that crime is an activity predominantly engaged in by young persons, particularly males (Gottfredson and Hirschi, 1990); and second is the evidence of substantial variation in offending within this population, due, at least in part, to variations in informal social control and social capital (Sampson and Laub, 1993; Hirschi, 1969). With these patterns as a starting point, this research drew on recent formulations in both criminology and life course research to propose a model that incorporates changing degrees of informal social control, indicated by changes in institutional bonds and social capital over time. The goal of this analysis was to identify changes in the proportions of subpopulations that are substantively less bonded and have less interdependency, and to relate fluctuations in the size of these populations to secular trends in aggregate property crime rates.

This model was tested on three distinct measures of property crime. The effects of the theoretically derived measures of social control and social capital were consistent with expectations and were generalized across crime types (Table 16.1). For robbery rates, all three measures of social bonds displayed significant and theoretically expected associations. For break and enter rates, both familial social capital measures were significant, while the labour force measure was not. Finally, for rates of motor vehicle theft, two of the three social capital measures were significant. Altogether, seven of nine possible effects were statistically significant and theoretically consistent, suggesting good preliminary support for the model. Of the three social control and social capital measures, the most consistent effects were found for the proportion of persons living at home.

The analysis also revealed general support for the utility of the various control variables in explaining crime rate trends. Interestingly, the age-sex structure

Table 16.1
Summary of Results

Variable	Expected effect	Robbery effect	Break and enter effect	Motor Vehicle theft effect	Summary
Proportion married					
Males 15–24	Neg	Neg	Neg	None	2 of 3
Proportion 15–24					
living at home	Neg	Neg	Neg	Neg	3 of 3
Proportion males 15–24					
in labour force	Neg	Neg	None	Neg	2 of 3
CONTROL VARIABLES					
Age structure	Pos	None	Pos	Neg	1 of 3
Residential population density	Pos	Pos	Pos	Pos	3 of 3
Registered motor vehicles per capita	Pos	—	—	Pos	1 of 1
Unemployment	Neg	Neg	Pos	Neg	2 of 3
First-difference unemployment	Pos	Pos	None	Pos	2 of 3
Incarceration rate	Neg	None	Neg	Neg	2 of 3

measure was significant and theoretically consistent in only one of the three models. More theoretically consistent findings were indicated for the unemployment effects, which were consistent in two of three equations. Although Cantor and Land have been criticized for their argument (Hale and Sabbagh, 1991), these findings provide further evidence of the viability and generalizability of their argument. While the contemporaneous effects of unemployment were statistically significant in all models, it yielded a positive effect in the break and enter equations, which was opposite from expectations.

There is currently considerable debate over the effectiveness of criminal justice sanctions on deterring crime. While public discourse suggests considerable faith in the effectiveness of sanctions, at least in an incapacitative sense, sociological research has been far from conclusive (Sherman, 1993; Braithwaite, 1989). In this regard, the present findings suggest some support for a deterrence or incapacitative argument, at least at a macro level. The deterrence measure was moderately consistent, being statistically significant in two of three equations. In concert with previous Canadian research findings (Schissel, 1992), it appears that criminal justice activity does have a significant deterrent effect on some types of property crime.

Finally, the control measure with the strongest effects was the opportunity measure of residential population density ratio. It was significant in all models at a probability level of less than 0.001. These findings further indicate the importance of including dimensions of criminal opportunities in both criminological theory and criminological research, as well as the generalizability of the opportunity perspective to countries other than the United States. These findings also have implications for both criminological and sociological theory. Recent sociological formulations have posited social capital as a central feature of modem social organization and a fundamental indicator of social change (Coleman, 1993). Foremost in this perspective is an analysis of changes or declines in *primordial social organization*, the intimate networks that generate social capital. While much research has focused on differences in social capital at an individual level (Coleman, 1988), much less has sought to examine the macro, structural consequences of these changes. Recent years have witnessed a diverging trend in the sequential order and timing of major life course transitions, and we are also witnessing a concomitant decline in primordial social organization. In this regard, late teens and young adults are increasingly less likely to live at home, yet are also less likely to be embedded in other closed networks. Consistent with Coleman's (1993: 9) argument that the effectiveness of social norms depends heavily on the viability of these networks, the present research clearly indicates the social costs attached to this process of social change. In the current research, fundamental changes in the organization of social activity within the life cycle are clearly related to changes in crime rates over time.

The current research also indicates further benefits of a social indicators approach to criminological theorizing (Felson, 1993). Over three decades ago, Donald Cressey, one of the more influential criminologists of the last century, argued that effective theory

> . . . explaining social behaviour in general, or any specific kind of social behaviour, should have two distinct but consistent aspects. First, there must be a statement that explains the statistical distribution of the behaviour in time and space . . . and from which predictive statements about unknown statistical distributions can be derived. Second, there must be a statement that identifies, at least by implication, the process by which individuals come to exhibit the behaviour in question, and from which can be derived predictive statements about the behaviours of individuals. (Cressey, 1960: 47)

While many micro-level approaches to understanding crime and deviance emphasize complex causal sequences with crime resulting from drug use (Elliott, Huizinga, and Ageton, 1985; Reiss and Roth, 1993), violence and abuse (Widom, 1989), gangs (Esbensen and Huizinga, 1993), or strain (Agnew, 1992), the majority of macro-level research on criminal offending has tended to seek ecological correlates such as racial composition that often bear only limited connection to contemporary theory. In contrast to these perspectives, the current research suggests a simpler explanation that is consistent across levels of aggregation. Criminal activity is

made possible by an absence of social bonds. This is compatible with both general control perspectives (Hirschi, 1969) and Sampson and Laub's (1993) recent formulation. While research at a micro level is consistently supportive of this position (Gottfredson and Hirschi, 1990), the present findings suggest that the same process is applicable at a structural level.

Although the present research was modelled in a uni-directional causal manner, it also seems reasonable to envision reflexive or reciprocal effects that are further consistent with Coleman (1993) and Sampson and Laub (1993). In the latter research, Sampson and Laub found that problem behaviour in children had direct effects on the nature of social bonds that formed in both the home and the school. Similarly, recent work by Hagan (1993; 1991b) suggests that criminal activity, beyond the consequences of official labelling (Braithwaite, 1989), plays a significant role in the erosion of social capital by embedding individuals in crime networks and distancing them from educational and occupational ones. This results in increased bouts of unemployment and lower occupational status (see also Sampson and Laub, 1993). It seems reasonable and consistent with this research to suggest a reflexive model that explores the bi-directional effects of crime and social capital in terms of the possibility that greater involvement in criminal activity for recent cohorts has the potential to erode social capital by further disrupting intimate, educational, and occupational relationships. The potential outcome of this process is the emergence of a "criminal class" with only limited life prospects.

While the present research indicates the importance of incorporating indicators of social bonds or social capital in modelling crime rate trends, the results are far from definitive. Future research could expand on these conceptions by including more measures that reflect a wider range of social bonds. As research by Sampson and Laub (1993) has identified the school as an important area for the generation of social bonds, future research could benefit from an exploration of the effects of educational investments on crime. Additionally, future research could be enriched by applying the analysis to a longer time frame. This would allow for an examination of longer trends in both informal social control and crime rates, allow for the inclusion of a wider variety of measures, and also allow for an exploration of whether the effects of social capital and social bonds are time or cultural dependent (see Gartner and Parker, 1990). The argument can also be extended to examine whether differences in criminal activity between social groups is influenced by sub-group differences in life course progress.[4] Finally, future research could explore the more qualitative dimensions of social bonds. Recent criminological research (Hagan, 1989; Sampson and Laub, 1993; Braithwaite, 1989) has recognized the significance of the quality of social relations on life outcomes, and this area seems a promising route of enquiry.

NOTES

1. I would like to thank Rosemary Gartner, Ron Gillis, John Hagan, Annette Nierobisz, and three reviewers from the *Canadian Journal of Sociology* for their helpful advice and/or comments throughout the research.

2. This time period was chosen because 1962 was the first year that Statistics Canada initiated the Uniform Crime Reporting system, and thus standardizes the various crime indicators. The actual analysis begins with the year 1963 in order to account for the first differencing of one of the independent variables.

3. The inclusion of theft was also considered because it represents a distinct form of property crime and has been included in previous Canadian research on crime rate trends (Schissel, 1992). However, over the time period under study, the definition of theft changed three times and thus does not provide a reliable measure of criminal activity.

4. I would like to thank two of my reviewers for alerting me to the possible extensions of the argument to explain differences in offending between social groups.

DISCUSSION QUESTIONS

1. With respect to the life course perspective, distinguish between trajectories and transitions.
2. What is "social capital" and how does this concept help us understand patterns of crime?
3. What are some of the more significant changes, in recent years, in the transition from adolescence to adulthood?
4. How does Macmillan's argument reflect the assumptions of social control theory?
5. In what way is Macmillan's argument a "structural" explanation of crime?

REFERENCES

Adams, O., & Nagnur, D. (1990). Marrying and divorcing: A status report for Canada. In C. McKie & K. Thompson (Eds.), *Canadian social trends*. Toronto: Thompson Educational Publishing.

Agnew, R. (1992). Foundation for a general strain theory of crime and delinquency. *Criminology, 30*, 47–88.

Boyd, M., & Pryor, E. (1990). Young adults living in their parents' homes. In C. McKie & K. Thompson (Eds.), *Canadian social trends*. Toronto: Thompson Educational Publishing.

Braithwaite, J. (1989). *Crime, shame and reintegration*. New York: Cambridge University Press.

Cantor, D., & Land, K. (1985). Unemployment and crime rates in the post-World War II United States: A theoretical and empirical analysis. *American Sociological Review, 50*, 317–332.

Caspi, A., Elder, G., & Herbener, E. (1990). Childhood personality and the prediction of life course patterns. In L. Robins & M. Rutter (Eds.), *Straight and devious pathways from childhood to adulthood*. Cambridge: Cambridge University Press.

Cohen, L., & Felson, M. (1979). Social change and crime rate trends: A routine activity approach. *American Sociological Review, 44*, 588–608.

Cohen, L., & Land, K. (1987). Age structure and crime: Symmetry versus asymmetry and the projection of crime rates through the 1990s. *American Sociological Review, 52*, 170–183.

Cohen, L., Felson, M., & Land, K. (1980). Property crime rates in the United States: A macrodynamic analysis, 1947–1977; with ex ante forecasts for the mid-1980s. *American Journal of Sociology, 86,* 90–118.

Coleman, J. (1988). Social capital in the creation of human capital. *American Journal of Sociology, 94,* 95–120.

Coleman, J. (1993). The rational reconstruction of society. *American Sociological Review, 58,* 1–15.

Cressey, D. (1960). Epidemiology and individual conduct: A case from criminology. *Pacific Sociological Review, 1,* 47–58.

DeFronzo, J. (1983). Economic assistance to impoverished Americans: Relationship to incidence of crime. *Criminology, 21,* 119–136.

Devereaux, M. (1994). Decline in the number of children. In C. McKie & K. Thompson (Eds.), *Canadian social trends, vol, 2,* (pp. 201–203). Toronto: Thompson Educational Publishing.

Devine, J., Sheley, J., & Smith, M. D. (1988). Macroeconomic and social-control policy influences on crime rate changes, 1948–1985. *American Sociological Review, 53,* 407–420.

Elder, G. (1975). Age differentiation and the life course. *Annual Review of Sociology, 1,* 165–190.

Elder, G. (1985). Perspectives on the life course. In G. Elder (Ed.), *Life course dynamics: Trajectories and transitions, 1968–1980.* Ithaca: Cornell University Press.

Elder, G. (1994). Time, human agency, and social change: Perspectives on the life course. *Social Psychology Quarterly, 57,* 4–15.

Elliott, D., Huizinga, D., & Ageton, S. (1985). *Explaining delinquency and drug use.* Beverly Hills, CA: Sage.

Esbensen, F., & Huizinga, D. (1993). Gangs, drugs and delinquency in a survey of urban youth. *Criminology, 31,* 565–587.

Felson, M. (1993). Social indicators for criminology. *Journal of Research in Crime and Delinquency, 30,* 400–411.

Felson, M., & Gottfredson, M. (1984). Social indicators of adolescent activities near peers and parents. *Journal of Marriage and the Family, 45,* 709–714.

Gartner, R., & Parker, R. (1990). Cross-national evidence on homicide and the age structure of the population. *Social Forces, 69*(2), 351–371.

Giddens, A. (1984). *The constitution of society.* London: Polity Press.

Glick, P. (1990). American families: As they are and were. *Sociology and Social Research, 74,* 139–145.

Goldscheider, F., & Goldscheider, C. (1993). *Leaving home before marriage: Ethnicity, familism, and generational relationships.* Madison: University of Wisconsin Press.

Goldscheider, F., & LeBourdais, C. (1986). The decline in age at leaving home, 1920–1979. *Sociology and Social Research, 70*(2), 143–145.

Gottfredson, M., & Hirschi, T. (1990). *A general theory of crime.* Stanford: Stanford University Press.

Gower, D. (1990). Labour force trends: Canada and the United States. In C. McKie & K. Thompson (Eds.), *Canadian social trends.* Toronto: Thompson Educational Publishing.

Hagan, J. (1989). *Structural criminology.* New Brunswick: Rutgers University Press.

Hagan, J. (1991a). *The disreputable pleasures: Crime and deviance in Canada.* (3rd ed.). Toronto: McGraw-Hill Ryerson Ltd.

Hagan, J. (1991b). Destiny and drift: Subcultural preferences, status attainments, and the risks and rewards of youth. *American Sociological Review, 56,* 567–582.

Hagan, J. (1993). The social embeddedness of crime and unemployment. *Criminology, 31,* 465–492.

Hagan, J. (1994). *Crime and disrepute.* Thousand Oaks: Pine Forge Press.

Hagan, J., & Palloni, A. (1988). Crimes as social events in the life course: Reconceiving a criminological controversy. *Criminology, 26,* 87–100.

Hale, C., & Sabbagh, D. (1991). Testing the relationship between unemployment and crime: A methodological comment and empirical analysis using time series data from England and Wales. *Journal of Research in Crime and Delinquency, 28,* 400–417.

Hirschi, T. (1969). *Causes of delinquency.* Berkeley, CA: University of California Press.

Land, K., McCall, P., & Cohen, L. (1990). Structural covariates of homicide rates: Are there any invariances across time and space? *American Journal of Sociology, 95,* 922–963.

Matza, D. (1964). *Delinquency and drift.* New York: Wiley.

Modell, J. (1989). *Into one's own: From youth to adulthood in the United States, 1920–1975.* Berkeley: University of California Press.

Reiss, A., & Roth, J. (Eds.). (1993). *Understanding and preventing violence.* Washington, DC: National Academy Press.

Rindfuss, R., Morgan, P., & Swicegood, G. (1988). *First births in America.* Berkeley, CA: University of California Press.

Rindfuss, R., Swicegood, G., & Rosenfeld, R. (1987). Disorder in the life course: How common and does it matter? *American Sociological Review, 52,* 785–801.

Rutter, M., Quinton, D., & Hill, J. (1990). Adult outcomes of institution-reared children: Males and females compared. In R. Lee & M. Rutter (Eds.), *Straight and devious pathways from childhood to adulthood.* Cambridge: Cambridge University Press.

Sampson, R., & Laub, J. (1993). *Crime in the making: Pathways and turning points through life.* Cambridge: Harvard University Press.

Schissel, B. (1992). The influence of economic factors and social control policy on crime rate changes in Canada, 1962–1988. *Canadian Journal of Sociology, 17,* 405–428.

Sherman, L. (1993). Defiance, deterrence, and irrelevance: A theory of the criminal sanction. *Journal of Research in Crime and Delinquency, 30,* 445–473.

Steffensmeier, D., & Harer, M. (1991). Did crime rise or fall during the Reagan presidency? The effects of an "aging" U.S. population on the nation's crime rate. *Journal of Research in Crime and Delinquency, 28,* 330–359.

Stevens, D. (1990). New evidence of the timing of early life course transitions: The United States 1900 to 1980. *Journal of Family History, 15,* 163–178.

Wannell, T. (1990). Losing ground: Wages of young people, 1981–1986. In C. McKie & K. Thompson (Eds.), *Canadian social trends.* Toronto: Thompson Educational Publishing.

Widom, C. (1989). The cycle of violence. *Science, 244,* 160–166.

Wilson, J., & Herrnstein, R. (1985). *Crime and human nature: The definitive study of the causes of crime.* New York: Simon and Schuster.

PART

4

Crime and Criminals: Selected Research

Introduction

This section is designed to introduce students to Canadian research on a variety of topics. Themes that were introduced in the first three parts of the book are revisited in some of these articles. For instance, theoretical issues are raised in several of the pieces, as are measurement issues. Some of these pieces are designed to give students an overview of a particular situation with regard to crime in Canada (e.g., aboriginal crime). Most of these articles appeared in our last edition, but those have all been revised and updated.

The first article deals with juvenile females as offenders. Issues involving gender and crime have been around since the early days of criminology. It is an accepted fact that boys commit more crimes than girls. Linda Simourd and Donald A. Andrews explore issues regarding the identification of risk factors for female youth. Their article reviews the findings of many other studies, and they conclude that some factors associated with male delinquency are also important for females, including associating with anti-social peers, misconduct problems, and poor parent-child relations, to name only a few.

The next two articles deal with some group differences in behaviour. In the first, Darryl S. Wood and Curt T. Griffiths explore patterns of aboriginal crime in Canada. They show that, while patterns of crime are often similar for aboriginal and non-aboriginal peoples, the rates among aboriginals are much higher, for both violent and property crime.

This piece surveys the literature on aboriginal crimes and suggests directions for future research.

The relationship between immigration, ethnicity, and criminality is examined by Robert M. Gordon and Jacquelyn Nelson. After reviewing the literature, they report on their research conducted in British Columbia. They find that, overall, immigrants and non-aboriginal ethnic minorities are significantly underrepresented in the federal corrections system as well as in British Columbia youth and adult correctional centres.

Gartner, Dawson, and Crawford report on their original research on women as the victims of intimate homicide (femicide). They document trends in intimate femicide, characteristics of victims and offenders, circumstances of the killings, and criminal justice responses to offenders. They also discuss the gender-specific nature of intimate femicides and identify ways in which intimate partner killings by males and females are distinctly different.

"Organized Crime and Money Laundering" provides an extensive review of information available about organized crime in Canada. As the reader will see, organized crime takes many more forms than are presented in the media. Margaret Beare shows that organized crime activity is market-driven and is defined by political, social, and economic elements. No one ethnic group has a monopoly on these illegal endeavours. After a thorough discussion of the problem, the author examines some possible solutions.

The concluding article deals with white collar crime — in this case, crime in and by corporations. These crimes, by middle- and upper-class individuals holding positions of responsibility, have not been well studied in Canada. Carl Keane shows how corporate criminals are spared the stigma of criminalization despite the fact that millions of dollars are involved in their crimes. His findings also show that the current sanctions have little deterrent effect. He concludes by discussing remedies for the current situation.

CHAPTER

17

Correlates of Delinquency:
A Look at Gender Differences

LINDA SIMOURD
DONALD A. ANDREWS

INTRODUCTION

Contemporary research on delinquency is challenging fundamental assumptions regarding female delinquency made by early theorists and researchers.

One important issue is the identification of risk factors for female youth. The apparent social bias of early female-delinquency theories suggests that exclusive reliance on personal and familial problems in the assessment of female risk may be inadequate. Yet, the relevance of male-based risk factors has not been fully evaluated.

Our study attempted to fill this gap through a systematic review of research that has examined the same risk factors for male and female youths separately. It should be noted here that our research and its findings focused on youth criminality (delinquency) rather than on adult criminality.

Female delinquency has historically been perceived as relatively rare and less serious than male delinquency (Canter, 1982a; Richards, 1981). Early research using police and court records showed that for each female delinquent, there were three to seven male delinquents (Canter, 1982a). In terms of offence type, female youths were perceived as committing relatively minor offences, such as running away, truancy, and sexual acting out, while male youths were perceived as committing a much wider and more serious range of offences (Canter, 1982a).

Early female-delinquency theories were also dramatically different from those developed for male youths. Personal maladjustment was viewed as a fundamental cause of problem behaviour in female youths. Psychological problems, inadequate performance of the proper sex role, and a problematic home life were some of the proposed explanations for female deviance (Giordano, 1978). In contrast, early male-delinquency theories focused on more external risk factors, such as peer group, lower social class, and lack of educational or occupational resources (Giordano, 1978).

Within the past 20 years, research has challenged some of these traditional views. Contemporary self-report studies, for example, have suggested a more accurate gender ratio of no more than three male delinquents to each female delinquent.[1] Recent studies have also found that female youth are involved in a broad range of criminal behaviours, not just minor offences. One exception to the similarity of offences is the use of physical aggression; here, female involvement remains lower than that of male youths (Gomme, 1985).

To explain and predict delinquency, contemporary research has expanded its scope to consider personal factors (such as behaviour, personality, and cognition), interpersonal factors (such as family and peers), and structural factors (such as school and church). Although the tendency to omit female

Adapted from Correlates of Delinquency: A Look at Gender Differences, by Linda Simourd and D. A. Andrews (1994). *Forum on Corrections Research*, 6(1), p. 26–31. Reprinted with the permission of The Research and Statistics Branch of the Correctional Service of Canada.

youths continues, there has been an emerging interest in female involvement in delinquency. Increasingly, studies on risk are including male and female youths in their research samples. Until now, these studies were never examined as a group.

OUR STUDY

The primary goal of our research was to review this portion of the delinquency literature. Specifically, we looked at published and unpublished studies conducted over the past 30 years. This review gave us an opportunity to comprehensively examine female youths on a wide range of risk factors. It also allowed us to examine risk factors not typically investigated among male samples. We sought answers to two basic questions:

◆ What are the important risk factors for *each* gender? For example, does associating with criminal peers place male youths at risk for delinquency, and does this factor also place female youths at risk?

◆ Are specific risk factors *more important* for a particular gender? For example, are family problems more strongly related to female delinquency than to male delinquency, and are school difficulties more strongly associated with male delinquency than with female delinquency?

We used a technique called "meta-analysis" to conduct this review (Rosenthal, 1991). One of the main advantages of meta-analysis over the traditional (narrative) form of literature review is that meta-analysis summarizes large bodies of literature and reaches more definitive conclusions. This quantitative approach combines numerical information (actual data) from selected studies and computes an average result for each risk factor for males and females separately. This information then indicates the degree of association between delinquency and a particular risk factor.[2]

Each study included in this review met three criteria:

◆ Male and female youths were sampled.
◆ Each gender was examined on the same risk factor.
◆ The data for each gender were reported separately.

These criteria ensured that male-female comparisons were based on the same delinquency and risk measures, thus eliminating biases that could result from using different measures for each gender.

Sixty studies met these requirements and provided 464 correlations between delinquency and risk factors. We then grouped the risk factors examined within these correlations into eight general risk categories based on previous reviews and common themes in the delinquency literature. Table 17.1 lists the eight risk factors and provides a brief indication of their content.

What risk factors are most important for delinquency in each gender? For female youths, the most important risk factors in descending order were antisocial peers or attitudes, temperament or misconduct problems, educational difficulties, poor parent-child relations, and minor personality

Table 17.1
Risk Factors

◆ Antisocial peers or attitudes
◆ Temperament or misconduct problems (psychopathy, impulsivity, substance use)
◆ Educational difficulties (poor grades, dropout)
◆ Poor parent-child relations (attachment, supervision)
◆ Minor personality variables (empathy, moral reasoning)
◆ Personal distress (anxiety, low self-esteem, apathy)
◆ Family structure or parental problems (broken home, marital problems)
◆ Lower social class

variables. Personal distress, family structure or parental problems, and lower social class did not appear to be strongly related to delinquency. A similar pattern emerged for the male youths.[3]

ARE SPECIFIC RISK FACTORS MORE IMPORTANT FOR A PARTICULAR GENDER?

There were no statistical or substantive differences in the risk factors across gender. In other words, the general risk factors that were important for male delinquency were also important for female delinquency.

PRACTICAL IMPORTANCE

In practical terms, these data suggest that knowing a youth's socioeconomic status or family structure would provide little information about his or her risk of delinquency. However, information indicating difficulties in the area of family relations, conduct, or peers would provide valuable information about that individual's risk of delinquency. These findings are consistent with social psychological models of criminal conduct that suggest that a variety of factors are associated with delinquency (Andrews and Bonta, in press; LeBlanc et al., 1988).

CONTROL VARIABLES

The next step in our research process was to assess whether particular aspects of these 60 studies contained systematic bias. For example, would the results change dramatically if we took into account the source of the information — that is, whether delinquency was measured by self-reports from the delinquents or by officials from the justice system? Would it matter if the sample consisted of high-school students or a group of offenders?

We considered 15 aspects related to the studies and their samples.[4] While certain aspects did influence the size of the correlations, the overall ranking of factors did not change. That is, despite taking into account various study characteristics, the data on social class, family structure or parent problems, and personal distress still provided little information about an individual's risk for delinquency. Parent-child difficulties and school problems remained important. Finally, temperament or misconduct problems and antisocial peers or attitudes remained the factors most significantly related to delinquency, regardless of study characteristics.

To summarize, this meta-analytical review yielded three conclusions with respect to eight general risk factors:

♦ The general risk factors that were important for female youths were also important for male youths. Further, no risk factor was more important for a particular gender.

♦ The most important risk factors for both genders, in descending order, were antisocial attitudes and peers, temperament or misconduct problems, educational difficulties, poor parent-child relations, and minor personality variables. In contrast, lower social class, family structure or parental problems, and personal distress were not strongly related to delinquency.

♦ When various sample and study characteristics were taken into account, the general pattern of results remained the same.

OTHER RISK FACTORS

Although this review suggests that the same risk factors are important for male and female youths, some might argue that gender differences may exist for other factors not captured by the eight areas we examined.

To explore this possibility, we grouped 96 correlations not captured by the eight general risk factors into 10 additional risk areas and assessed them for possible gender differences. Table 17.2 lists these factors and the number of times each factor was found in the studies examined. Undoubtedly more research has been conducted within each area; however, recall that we selected the studies based on three criteria listed earlier.

Table 17.2

Other Risk Factors

- Victimization (1)
- Illegitimate opportunity (2)
- Lack of legitimate opportunity (3)
- Sexual behaviour (3)
- Lack of hobbies or involvement (4)
- Accommodation problems (4)
- Self-concept issues (6)
- Race (7)
- Sex-role orientation (8)
- Lack of attachment to convention (10)

Since only a total of 96 correlations pertained to these 10 categories, we treated this set of findings as exploratory. A few highlights will be mentioned.

Two very promising categories of risk were lack of attachment to convention and sexual behaviour. Lack of attachment to convention pertained to an individual's lack of affiliation with prosocial people (such as parents and teachers) or institutions (such as family, school, and church). Because these measures assessed attachment to multiple individuals or institutions, they could not be incorporated in any of the earlier categories, such as education or parent-child relations.

The data indicated that lack of attachment to convention was associated with delinquency for each gender. This was to be expected given that our earlier analysis found that lack of attachment to specific institutions (such as educational difficulties) and people (poor parent-child relations) were important risk factors.

Although the data for sexual behaviour were obtained from only three studies, there was consensus about the importance of this factor. What remains unclear is whether gender differences exist — one study found large gender differences, another found minor differences, and the third found none.

The significance of sexual behaviour as a correlate of delinquency may be somewhat surprising, given current rates of sexual activity among teenagers. However, these three studies were conducted

between 1966 and 1971. Sexual behaviour in those days may have served as an indicator of an individual's tolerance of rule/norm violations. An interesting question is whether the same degree of association would be noted for high-school students in the 1990s.

Sex-role orientation (masculinity or femininity) was found to be unrelated to delinquency. There may be a minor association of delinquency with sex-role orientation when lack of feminine traits (communal traits, such as sharing and caring) are examined. A narrative literature review of research in this area found similar results and concluded this line of research should be abandoned (Naffin, 1985).

The jury is still out for the six remaining risk categories. For these factors (victimization, illegitimate opportunity, lack of legitimate opportunity, lack of hobbies or involvement, accommodation problems, and self-concept issues), either too few studies were obtained or various study characteristics made interpretation of the findings difficult. Victimization, for example, was only measured by one study, which asked students between the ages of 12 and 16 whether they personally were a victim of five types of crimes ranging from theft of unguarded possessions to attack and assault (Mawby, 1980). The correlations, based on overall victimization, not on victimization specific to violence, yielded no gender differences. Given the growing clinical interest in sexual abuse and victimization, particularly for females (Darke and McLean, 1990; Einbender and Friedrich, 1989), future gender research should examine this issue empirically.

Another category, accommodation problems (e.g., crowding, high-crime neighbourhood), was assessed by four studies, whose results varied across sample and design, thus making interpretation difficult. The two cross-sectional studies indicated no association between accommodation problems and delinquency in male youths, but a minor association between them for female youths. The longitudinal study reported a significant association for men, but not for women. Finally, the offender versus non-offender sample found accommodation problems to be a significant risk factor for both genders, although more important for women.

More questions are raised than answered when variation occurs to this extent in the data. Clearly, for these six categories, more research must be gathered before any conclusions can be drawn.

In summary, our conclusions about the 10 categories described in this section are limited by the small number of correlations and the sometimes varying results. Future research could examine some of these factors for their use as risk factors and for possible gender differences.

CONCLUSIONS

The results of this literature review are clear. The risk factors that are important for male delinquency are also important for female delinquency. Of the risk factors examined, the most important are anti-social peers or attitudes, temperament or misconduct problems, educational difficulties, poor parent-child relations, and minor personality variables. In contrast, lower social class, family structure or parental problems, and personal distress are not strongly related to delinquency for either gender. These results support recent social psychological models of criminal conduct that suggest a variety of personal, interpersonal, and structural factors are related to delinquent behaviour in males and females.

However, our results seriously challenge the value of early delinquency theories. Most impor-

tantly, notions of female delinquency as exclusively symptomatic of personal distress or familial difficulties have been shown to be inadequate. Early male theories, which focused on lower social class as a major route to criminal behaviour, can also be questioned. Others previously challenged this social-location perspective, and a contemporary understanding of male delinquency has moved beyond this limited view.[5]

Several challenges remain for researchers and scientist-practitioners. First, these results do not eliminate the possibility that other factors are associated with delinquency in one or both genders. Future research could investigate, for example, the role of some of the less frequently measured factors explored in this study. Weaker personality variables, sexual behaviour, and sexual abuse and victimization are a few areas worthy of further consideration.

Second, these findings should lead to reformulated ideas and directions about theory and research on female delinquency. Those interested in female delinquency should learn from male-delinquency literature that has progressed beyond the early reliance on social class as the major explanation of male deviance. It is time to set aside antiquated ideas and to consider a larger group of factors as causes of delinquency. Our review examined gender differences and similarities in the correlates of delinquency, so the next step is to examine causal factors for individual female and male youths in the context of their experiences. That research would inform us of the need for gender-specific or gender-neutral theories of delinquency.

In conclusion, for some, the results of this review may simply state the obvious. For years, a small portion of the literature on delinquency has examined the same risk factors for male and female youths and independently, yet repeatedly, found the same results across gender. This review of the literature has pulled those results together in a quantitative fashion, and the similarity across gender can no longer be ignored. The factors examined to date suggest a unique set of correlates may not be required for female delinquency.

Future research will inform us about the role gender plays with respect to predictors and theories of criminal conduct. Consistent with this approach is the need to incorporate gender into the research design and to present the male and female data separately. Only then can a clearer understanding of the similarities and differences across gender be obtained.

NOTES

1. The precise ratios are 1.2:1 to 2.5:1 as reported in Canter, "Sex Differences in Self-Report Delinquency."
2. Measures of variability are available from Linda Simourd; they are not discussed in this paper.
3. The findings for minor personality variables should be viewed with caution, given the small number of correlations representing this factor and fluctuations noted within this category.
4. These were (1) sample, (2) design, (3) sample size, (4) period of data collection, (5) gender focus of study, (6) predominant ethnicity, (7) source of delinquency information, (8) source of risk information, (9) retrieval source, (10) gender of author, (11) psychometrics of risk measure, (13) social class, (14) type of delinquency, and (15) nature of delinquency. [Editor's note: Number 12 was omitted in the original paper.]
5. This conclusion is consistent with that of a study conducted by Tittle and Meir (1990).

DISCUSSION QUESTIONS

1. Discuss the major risk factors involved in delinquency. How do males and females differ?
2. What implications does this research have for early theories about delinquency?
3. Discuss the value of meta-analysis. What other kinds of research might be done to explore the differences between male and female delinquency?

REFERENCES

Andrews, D. A., & Bonta, J. (1998). *The psychology of criminal conduct.* Cincinnati: Anderson.

Canter, R. (1982a). Family correlates of male and female delinquency. *Criminology. An Interdisciplinary Journal, 20,* 149–167.

Canter, R. (1982b). Sex differences in self-report delinquency. *Criminology. An Interdisciplinary Journal, 20,* 373–393.

Darke, J., & McLean, H. (1990). Invisible women: The treatment and research needs of female offenders. In A. Loucks (Ed.), *The treatment of female offenders,* symposium conducted at the annual meeting of the Canadian Psychological Association, Ottawa, May 1990.

Einbender, A., & Friedrich, W. (1989). Psychological functioning and behaviour of sexually abused girls. *Journal of Consulting and Clinical Psychology, 57,* 155–157.

Giordano, P. (1978). Girls, guys and gangs: The changing social context of female delinquency. *The Journal of Criminal Law and Criminology, 69,* 126–132.

Gomme, I. (1985). Predictors of status and criminal offences among male and female adolescents in an Ontario community. *Canadian Journal of Criminology, 27,* 147–159.

LeBlanc, M., Ouimet, M., & Tremblay, R. E. (1988). An integrative control theory of delinquent behaviour: A validation, 1976–1985. *Psychiatry, 51,* 164–176.

Mawby, R. (1980). Sex and crime: The results of a self-report study. *British Journal of Sociology, 31,* 525–543.

Naffin, N. (1985). The masculinity-femininity hypothesis: A consideration of gender-based personality theories of female crime. *British Journal of Criminology, 25,* 365–381.

Richards, P. (1981). Quantitative and qualitative sex differences in middle-class delinquency. *Criminology: An Interdisciplinary Journal, 18,* 453–470.

Rosenthal, R. (1991). Meta-analysis: A review. *Psychosomatic Medicine, 53,* 247–271.

Tittle, C., & Meir, R. (1990). Specifying the SES/delinquency relationship. *Criminology: An Interdisciplinary Journal, 28,* 271–296.

Patterns of Aboriginal Crime

DARRYL S. WOOD
CURT T. GRIFFITHS

INTRODUCTION

Canada has one of the world's most diverse Aboriginal populations. From the small Inuit settlements of the Eastern Arctic, to the woodlands of western Ontario, to the West Coast, the 800 000 persons (about 3 percent of the Canadian population) who identify themselves as Aboriginal are distinguished by their culture and language, their legal status and the diversity of geographic settings in which they live (Statistics Canada, 1998). Aboriginal people live in isolated settlements accessible only by air and/or sea; on reserves; and in cities and towns from sea to sea to sea.

Despite this diversity, there is one attribute that many Aboriginal bands and communities share — a high rate of violent crime and victimization. In recent years, numerous task forces and commissions of inquiry have documented the conflict which Aboriginal people experience with the criminal law and their overrepresentation in the criminal justice system (see Griffiths & Verdun-Jones, 1993; Silverman & Nielsen, 1992). And Aboriginal bands and communities have become increasingly involved in developing alternative, community-based programs and services which are designed to address the needs of Aboriginal victims and offenders. This has included Aboriginal police forces, community courts, and localized corrections programs. Considerably less attention, however, has been given to the patterns of Aboriginal crime. Understanding Aboriginal crime is a prerequisite for the design of effective prevention programs and criminal justice services.

In the following discussion, we explore the patterns of Aboriginal crime in Canada. We will first consider the findings of research conducted in rural and remote areas of the country as well as in urban centres. From this, a general picture of Aboriginal crime can be constructed. The discussion will then shift to a consideration of the various explanations that have been offered for Aboriginal criminality and for the differences which exist between Aboriginal and non-Aboriginal patterns of crime and victimization.

One way Aboriginal and non-Aboriginal crime patterns can be compared is by examining the proportion of the population in a given jurisdiction that is Aboriginal with the proportion of individuals who are accused of criminal offences that are Aboriginal. Where this proportion is high (i.e., Aboriginal peoples commit more offences than one would expect given the relative size of the Aboriginal population), it can be said that Aboriginal peoples are more likely to be represented in measures of criminal behaviour than are non-Aboriginal peoples. Three recent studies (Griffiths, Wood, Zellerer, & Simon, 1994a; Trevethan, 1993; Wolff, 1991) included such comparisons.

It is, of course, not possible to explore all facets of what is a very complex issue, and we must keep in mind that it is often difficult to compare the findings from different research studies. Neverthe-

Written for this volume. Adapted from the article that appeared in the fifth edition of *Crime in Canadian Society*.

less, it is possible to piece together a general picture of Aboriginal crime in Canada which can be utilized in attempts to explain the causes of Aboriginal criminality.

PATTERNS OF ABORIGINAL CRIME: A PROFILE

There are several identifiable patterns of crime in Aboriginal communities and among Aboriginal populations in Canada:

* the rates of violent crime and property crime in Aboriginal communities and in Aboriginal populations are very high, particularly in comparison with the rates for non-Aboriginal peoples;
* there is considerable variation in official crime rates between Aboriginal communities and among Aboriginal populations across Canada; and
* the types of offences committed by Aboriginal persons vary by age: younger individuals tend to be more involved in committing property offences, while violent offences are generally committed by individuals who are somewhat older.

Aboriginal and Non-Aboriginal Crime Patterns

Aboriginal peoples are overrepresented in crime statistics and in the criminal justice system in many areas of the country. This pattern extends to reserves, urban areas, and remote settlements. Generally, Aboriginal communities and populations experience much more violence than their non-Aboriginal counterparts. There are, however, fewer differences in the rates of property crimes between Aboriginal and non-Aboriginal persons and communities; in fact, in many areas of the country, Aboriginal communities have lower property crime rates than non-Aboriginal communities.

RESERVE VS. OFF-RESERVE, SASKATCHEWAN
Wolff (1991) compared the crime rates of on-reserve and off-reserve populations in Saskatchewan. He found that, although only 3 percent of the population resided on Indian reserves, 15 percent of all violent crimes in Saskatchewan were committed on reserves (Wolff, 1991:30). This means that, on reserves in Saskatchewan, where 98 percent of the population is Aboriginal, the violent crime rate is five times higher than one would expect. For property crimes in Saskatchewan, however, the proportion of the population that are reserve residents is equal to the proportion of property crimes that were committed on reserves (Wolff, 1991:33); this means that reserves in Saskatchewan have rates of property crime that are roughly equal to those of the rest of the province.

URBAN ABORIGINAL CRIME:
FOUR WESTERN CITIES
Table 18.1 includes findings from studies of urban Aboriginal crime conducted by Trevethan (1993) and Griffiths et al. (1994a). These studies allow a comparison of the percentage of the population that is Aboriginal with (1) the percentage of Aboriginal persons accused of property and violent offences, and (2) the percentage of Aboriginal individuals who were the victim of a violent offence. The figures in Table 18.1 indicate that, in Saskatoon, Regina, Calgary, and Vancouver, Aboriginal persons are more likely than non-Aboriginal persons to be accused of committing a property or a violent offence and are more likely than non-Aboriginals to have been the victim of a violent crime. More specifically, Aboriginal people are four to eight times more likely than non-Aboriginal people to be accused of a property offence, five to nine times more likely to be accused of having committed a violent crime, and three to six times more likely to be the victim of a violent offence.

THE BAFFIN REGION, EASTERN ARCTIC,
NORTHWEST TERRITORIES
The Baffin Region is situated in the Eastern Arctic of the Northwest Territories and comprises thirteen communities, ranging in size from Grise Fiord with a population of 150, to Iqaluit, which has approximately 4200 residents. The average size of the

Table 18.1

Patterns of Crime and Victimization in Four Western Cities, 1990 and 1992

City	% Population That is Aboriginal	% Aboriginal of Accused of Violent Offences	% Aboriginal of Accused of Property Offences	% Aboriginal of Victims of Violent Offences
Saskatoon	6	36	29	(Not Reported)
Regina	5	47	42	31
Calgary	2	10	8	6
Vancouver	3	17	15	10

SOURCE: Adapted from material from S. Trevethan, *Police-Reported Aboriginal Crime in Calgary, Regina and Saskatoon* (Ottawa: Canadian Centre for Justice Statistics, 1993) and C.T. Griffiths, D.S. Wood, E. Zellerer, and J. Simon, *Aboriginal Policing in British Columbia*, report prepared for Commission of Inquiry, Policing in British Columbia, (Victoria, BC, Ministry of Attorney General, 1994a).

communities is slightly less than 1000, although most have under 700 residents. These communities are accessible only by air, or, for a few months during the late summer, by sea. The levels of crime for these communities generally are much higher than the national rates for all Canadians. The figures in Table 18.2 indicate that all of the Baffin Region communities had rates of violent crime which were higher than the national rate in Canada. In 1996, the Baffin Region property crime rate was nearly double the Canadian property crime rate, and the violent crime rate was more than six times the national rate. In six of the communities, however, the property crime rate was lower than the national rate (see also Griffiths, Saville, Wood, & Zellerer, 1994b).

Table 18.2

Violent and Property Crime Rates per 1000 Total Population, Baffin Region, N.W.T. Communities, and Canada, 1996

Community	Violent Crime Rate	Property Crime Rate
Broughton Island	36.9	90.2
Cape Dorset	75.1	81.4
Clyde River	42.4	48.0
Grise Fiord	13.5	6.8
Hall Beach	42.4	58.9
Igloolik	80.9	66.4
Iqaluit	118.2	147.2
Lake Harbour	35.3	45.3
Nanasivik	29.2	47.5
Pangnirtung	20.9	69.2
Pond Inlet	20.8	25.1
Resolute Bay	111.1	40.4
Sanikiluaq	26.9	74.5
Baffin Region	66.7	85.7
Canada	9.7	52.0

SOURCE: Adapted from Canadian Centre for Justice Statistics, *Uniform Crime Reports, 1996* (Ottawa: Statistics Canada, 1997).

AUTONOMOUS "STAND ALONE" ABORIGINAL POLICE JURISDICTIONS

As Aboriginal peoples have become increasingly involved in the creation and control of justice programs in recent years, a number of Aboriginal controlled autonomous police departments have been established. These "stand alone" departments, as they are sometimes called, have jurisdiction over the enforcement of the *Criminal Code* in the reserve communities they serve. Violent and property crime statistics compiled by these autonomous departments for the reserves they police are shown in Table 18.3. A comparison of these crime rates with those found nationally provides results similar to the comparisons made above. The Aboriginal police jurisdictions report violent crime rates that are much higher than average, while property crime is reported at levels similar to the national rate. As seen in Table 18.3, six of the eight "stand alone" jurisdictions had reported violent crime rates that were at least double those found nationally. The property crime rates, on the other hand, are much like those found in non-Aboriginal jurisdictions; three of the eight autonomous police jurisdictions had property crime rates less than the national rate.

HOMICIDE RATES

Of all of the indicators of criminal behaviour, homicide statistics tend to be the most reliable and valid (Brantingham & Brantingham, 1984). Homicide statistics, therefore, can be utilized to determine the extent to which Aboriginal peoples are overrepresented in terms of criminal behaviour and as another basis of comparison with non-Aboriginal populations. Table 18.4 compares the rates (per 100 000 population) at which Aboriginal and non-Aboriginal persons were suspected of committing homicides and were the victims of homicide in the major cities of Canada over the 10 year period 1980–1989.

The figures in Table 18.4 indicate that as one moves east from Ottawa, Aboriginal peoples are much more likely to be suspected of committing homicides than are non-Aboriginals and, except in Ottawa, Montreal, and Halifax, they were also more likely than non-Aboriginal persons to be the victim of a homicide.

ABORIGINAL AND NON-ABORIGINAL PERCEPTIONS OF SAFETY

In addition to official statistics, the findings of general social surveys and victimization surveys provide insights into crime in Aboriginal communities and

Table 18.3

Violent and Property Crime Rates per 1000 Total Population, "Stand Alone" Aboriginal Police Jurisdictions, 1995 and 1996

Police Jurisdiction	Violent Crime Rate		Property Crime Rate	
	1995	1996	1995	1996
Unama'ki Tribal Police	57.4	47.2	41.1	46.5
Akwesasne Mohawk Police	8.4	10.0	22.6	25.4
UCCM Police Service	47.0	50.9	70.4	108.1
Lac Seul Police Service	133.3	161.7	83.3	108.3
Six Nations Police	15.0	17.7	33.6	28.8
Dakota Ojibway Police Service	65.8	80.5	69.5	64.6
Louis Bull Police Service	42.7	34.5	92.7	70.0
Siksika Nation Police		75.3		61.0
CANADA	9.9	9.7	52.3	52.0

SOURCE: Adapted from Canadian Centre for Justice Statistics, *Uniform Crime Reports, 1995* (Ottawa: Statistics Canada, 1996); Canadian Centre for Justice Statistics, *Uniform Crime Reports, 1996* (Ottawa: Statistics Canada, 1997).

Table 18.4

Non-Aboriginal and Aboriginal Homicide, Suspect and Victim Rates (per 100 000 Population), by Selected Cities, 1980–1989.

City	Non-Aboriginal Suspects	Aboriginal Suspects	Non-Aboriginal Victims	Aboriginal Victims
Halifax	3.4	0.0	2.9	0.0
Montreal	2.5	0.4	4.3	0.8
Ottawa	1.7	3.8	1.8	0.0
Toronto	2.1	7.5	2.3	4.8
Thunder Bay	1.3	17.4	1.5	15.3
Winnipeg	2.1	25.7	1.6	19.1
Saskatoon	1.1	19.9	1.0	12.9
Regina	0.9	76.6	1.2	45.3
Edmonton	2.6	27.9	2.7	21.1
Calgary	1.7	19.7	1.8	12.5
Vancouver	3.9	15.3	5.5	14.4

SOURCE: Based on material from C. LaPrairie, *Dimensions of Aboriginal Over-Representation in Correctional Institutions and Implications for Crime Prevention* (Ottawa: Ministry of Solicitor General Canada, 1992), p. 6. Reproduced with the permission of the Minister of Public Works and Government Services Canada, 1999.

populations. A survey by Sacco and Johnson (1990) asked a sample of all Canadians (including Aboriginal peoples) whether they felt safe walking alone in their community at night. The same question was asked by Statistics Canada (1994) in the Aboriginal Peoples Survey, which surveyed Aboriginal persons in communities across Canada. In comparing the findings of these two surveys, it appears that Aboriginal people feel just as safe in their communities as non-Aboriginal people, a very interesting finding considering the high rates of violent crime and victimization that afflict many Aboriginal communities. More specifically, the figures presented in Table 18.5 show that 73 percent of Canadians in 1987 and 73 percent of Aboriginal peoples in 1991 said that they felt safe walking alone in their community at night. In only three of the twelve provinces and territories (Alberta, British Columbia, and Ontario) was the percentage of Aboriginal peoples who said they felt safe less than the national average for Aboriginal peoples and non-Aboriginal peoples.

Perceptions of personal safety, however, are much lower among Aboriginal peoples residing in metropolitan areas. Table 18.5 indicates that Aboriginal peoples surveyed by the Aboriginal Peoples

Survey in 1991 were 10 percent less likely to report feeling safe when walking alone in their community at night than their non-Aboriginal urban counterparts surveyed by Sacco and Johnson in 1987. In three metropolitan areas (Toronto, Vancouver, and Victoria), almost half of Aboriginal peoples reported feeling unsafe walking alone at night in their community (Statistics Canada, 1994).[1]

Variation in Aboriginal Communities and Aboriginal Populations

In our discussion thus far, we have identified some of the general patterns of Aboriginal crime and victimization and noted the similarities and differences between Aboriginal and non-Aboriginal communities and populations. These findings might lead us to expect that all Aboriginal communities are afflicted by high rates of crime and victimization. The findings of field research projects conducted in a number of provinces and in a number of different geographic settings, however, indicate that this is not the case. Table 18.6 presents the results of several research studies of Aboriginal crime, including (1) a study on several

Table 18.5

Perceptions of Safety among Aboriginal Peoples, by Province and by Metropolitan Area, 1991, and Perceptions of Safety of Non-Aboriginal Peoples, Canada, 1987

Province	Percentage That Feel Safe Walking Alone at Night in Their Community	Metropolitan Area	Percentage That Feel Safe Walking Alone at Night in Their Community
Newfoundland	86	Halifax	61
P.E.I.	73	Montreal	64
Nova Scotia	81	Ottawa	60
New Brunswick	76	Toronto	48
Quebec	73	Winnipeg	65
Ontario	71	Regina	76
Manitoba	75	Saskatoon	70
Saskatchewan	75	Calgary	68
Alberta	69	Edmonton	62
B.C.	69	Vancouver	56
Yukon	81	Victoria	56
N.W.T.	80		
Aboriginal, Canada	73	Urban Aboriginal, Canada	61
Non-Aboriginal, Canada	73	Urban Non-Aboriginal, Canada	71

SOURCE: Adapted from Statistics Canada, *Aboriginal Peoples Survey: Language, Tradition, Health, and Social Issues* (Ottawa: Minister of Supply and Services Canada, 1993); and V. F. Sacco and H. Johnson, *Patterns of Criminal Victimization in Canada* (Ottawa: Minister of Supply and Services Canada, 1990). Reproduced with the permission of the Minister of Public Works and Government Services Canada, 1999.

Amerindian reserves in the province of Quebec; (2) two studies of crime patterns among Aboriginal peoples in urban areas; (3) an inquiry into crime in Nishnawbe-Aski Nation communities in northwest Ontario; and (4) Wolff's study of crime on Aboriginal reserves in Saskatchewan. The findings of these studies indicate that there is a great deal of variation in both property and violent crime rates among the jurisdictions in which Aboriginal people reside as well as among Aboriginal communities.

A comparison of the jurisdictions covered by the research studies indicates that the mean of the rates for violent crimes varied between 19 per 1000 population on Amerindian reserves in Quebec to 50 per 1000 population in the Baffin Region, N.W.T. For property crimes, the rates ranged from 22 per 1000 population on Amerindian reserves to 106 per 1000 population in the Nishnawbe-Aski Nation commu-

nities. Even within jurisdictions, there is a great amount of variation in crime rates. Several of the Amerindian reserve communities in Quebec experienced no violent or property crime between 1978 and 1983, while other Amerindian communities had rates that were many times the national average.

The studies of crime rates in four western cities found that Aboriginal peoples in Regina (at a rate of 246 per 1000) were 6 times more likely to be accused of a property crime than Aboriginal peoples in Calgary (at a rate of 36 per 1000). Similar ranges in the rates of crime exist among communities of the Nishnawbe-Aski Nation, on Saskatchewan reserves, and Baffin Region communities.

Offence Type and Age of Offender

A final pattern in Aboriginal crime that will be examined is the age structure for property and

Table 18.6

Violent and Property Crime Rates per 1000 Population for Aboriginal Communities and Populations

Jurisdiction, Year, and Offence Type	Mean Rate of Offences	Range of Offence Rates	Study Sources
Amerindian Reserves, Quebec, 1978 to 1983			Hyde & LaPrairie, 1987
Violent	19	0 to 57	
Property	22	0 to 58	
Aboriginal Residents, 4 Western Cities, 1990* & 1992**			Trevethan, 1993; Griffiths et al., 1994a
Violent	32	17 to 58	
Property	96	36 to 246	
Nishnawbe-Aski Nation Communities, Ontario, 1990			Auger et al., 1992
Violent	36	18 to 63	
Property***	106	50 to 161	
Saskatchewan Reserves, 1989			Wolff, 1991
Violent	51	32 to 93****	
Property	73	39 to 167****	
Baffin Region Communities N.W.T., 1996			CCJS, 1997
Violent	50	14 to 118	
Property	62	7 to 147	

* Calgary, Regina, and Saskatoon

** Vancouver

*** Property crime rates for these communities include property damage.

**** Range for Saskatchewan reserves is across the 13 Justice Administration Areas in the province rather than across all Indian reserves.

violent offences. Research studies indicate that there is an indirect relationship between age and the likelihood that an offender will commit a property offence. More often than not, property offences are committed by youth or young adults in their early 20s. Violent crimes, on the other hand, tend to be committed by older persons. Up until age 40, there is a direct relationship between age and the propensity to commit violent crimes.

In their study of crime on 25 Amerindian reserves in the province of Quebec, Hyde and LaPrairie (1987:29–30) found that young offenders were more likely to have committed property offences, while adults were more likely to have committed violent offences. This pattern holds

true in other Aboriginal jurisdictions. On Indian reserves in Saskatchewan, where 98 percent of residents are Aboriginal, Wolff (1991) found that the rates of being charged for violent offences were highest among adults. On average, 51 out of 1000 adults age 18 and over were charged with violent offences, while only 16 out of every 1000 youths age 12 to 17 were charged with violent offences (Wolff, 1991:31–32). This relationship is reversed for property offences. Twenty-nine out of every 1000 adults were charged with property offences, while 88 out of 1000 youths age 12 to 17 were charged with a property offence (Wolff, 1991:35).

The relationship between age and type of crime also holds true for Aboriginal peoples in urban areas. Aboriginal individuals accused of violent offences were older than those individuals accused of property offences in the four western Canadian cities studied by Trevethan in 1990. In Saskatoon, 58 percent of offenders accused of property crimes were under the age of 25, while 61 percent of offenders accused of violent crimes were age 25 and over (Trevethan, 1993:50). Likewise, in Calgary in 1990, 56 percent of offenders accused of property crimes were under the age of 25, while 59 percent of offenders accused of violent crimes were 25 years old and over (Trevethan, 1993:42). An exception to this rule is in Regina, where the majority of individuals charged with violent crimes (56 percent) were under the age of 25, although 73 percent of Aboriginal individuals charged with property crimes were under the age of 25 (Trevethan, 1993:46).

Among the Inuit of the Baffin Region, Northwest Territories, individuals accused of violent offences tend to be older than individuals accused of property offences (Griffiths et al., 1994b). Information recorded from RCMP operational files in each of the communities for the year 1991 shows

that in the Baffin Region, the median age of Inuit accused of violent offences was 28 years, whereas the median age of Inuit accused of property offences was 20 years. Table 18.7 shows the median age of accused of property and violent offences in the 13 different Baffin Region communities. In 11 of the 12 communities in which Inuit were accused of violent offences, the median age of those who were accused of violent offences was higher than that of those who were accused of property offences.

UNDERSTANDING ABORIGINAL CRIME PATTERNS

Any explanation that is offered for Aboriginal crime must consider the findings of the research studies discussed above. More specifically, the following questions must be addressed:

* Why are Aboriginal people, whether considered as a population or as communities, more likely than non-Aboriginals to be accused of committing offences and to be the victims of crime?

Table 18.7

Median Age of Individuals Accused of Property and Violent Offences, Baffin Region Communities, 1991

Community	Median Age, Property Offences	Median Age, Violent Offences
Pangnirtung	21	28
Lake Harbour	24	22
Cape Dorset	21	28
Broughton Island	23	24
Clyde River	19	26
Hall Beach	18	27
Igloolik	18	27
Pond Inlet	17	26
Sanikiluaq	21	27
Resolute	30	32
Grise Fiord	(Not Applicable)	29
Nanasivik	19	28
Iqaluit	21	30
Baffin Region	20	28

SOURCE: Based on material from RCMP Operational Files.

- Why is there often considerable variation in the rates of crime between Aboriginal communities and populations in different regions of the country and within the same region?
- Why are property offences more likely to be committed by Aboriginal youth and young adults, while violent crimes are committed by older Aboriginal persons?

The High Rates of Crime, Particularly Violence, in Aboriginal Communities

There are a number of approaches which have been taken in an attempt to explain the high rates of crime among Aboriginal peoples. One of the most common focuses on the colonization and conquest of Aboriginal peoples by the European settlers and the resulting destruction of Aboriginal culture, communities, and lifeways. A long-term consequence of colonization, it has been argued, is the marginalization of Aboriginal peoples in Canadian society, which is reflected in high rates of unemployment, low levels of formal education, poverty, and substandard living conditions. Taken together, the condition of Aboriginal peoples is seen to contribute to high rates of criminal behaviour. Fleras and Elliott (1992:16–18), for example, have argued that Aboriginal overrepresentation in crime statistics is but one outcome of "colonialist domination" (see also Berger, 1991:36).

Colonization and its consequences for Aboriginal peoples has also been offered as an explanation for why the crime rates for Aboriginal peoples are higher than for non-Aboriginals. In explaining the patterns of Aboriginal crime in the urban centres of Calgary, Regina, and Saskatoon, Trevethan (1993:34) argues that "the differences in crime patterns between Aboriginal and non-Aboriginal persons may be attributed to several socio-demographic variables" including lower levels of educational attainment, labour force participation, average income, and higher levels of unemployment.[2]

Another explanation that has been offered for why Aboriginal peoples have higher crime rates when compared with non-Aboriginal peoples is

that the Aboriginal population is, on average, younger than the non-Aboriginal population in Canada. Trevethan (1993) has argued that Aboriginal/non-Aboriginal differences in crime rates are due, at least in part, to the larger percentage of Aboriginal people in the 15–34 year old age group. Wolff (1991), however, considered the role of age in comparing on-reserve and off-reserve crime rates in Saskatchewan and found only modest support for this explanation. By adjusting the rates of on-reserve violent and property crime so that the on-reserve population age structure matched the off-reserve population age structure, the on-reserve charged rates for property crime dropped from 44 per 1000 to 36 per 1000, while the on-reserve charged rates for violent crime actually rose from 42 per 1000 to 47 per 1000 (Wolff, 1991:40). In other words, in Saskatchewan, the on-reserve age structure had a modest impact on the rate of property crime but not on the rate of violent crime.

Another explanation that has been offered for the overrepresentation of Aboriginal people in official crime statistics is discriminatory treatment of Aboriginal people by the criminal justice system. Several task forces and commissions of inquiry have suggested that Aboriginal people are much more likely to be arrested, found guilty, and sent to a correctional institution than non-Aboriginal people (see Cawsey, 1991; Hamilton & Sinclair, 1991a). In particular, concerns have been raised about the discriminatory treatment of Aboriginal peoples by the police (see Hamilton & Sinclair, 1991b). Caution, however, must be exercised in assessing the extent to which such discriminatory treatment, where it exists, has an effect on Aboriginal crime rates. Research studies indicate that most criminal offences are discovered not by the police, but by community residents who report to the police. In the Baffin Region, for example, Griffiths et al. (1994b) found that only 6 percent of officially recorded offences were originally discovered by the RCMP.[3] And LaPrairie (1992:7) has argued that "some data allude to differential treatment by police but it is neither empirical nor recent." Suffice it to say that there is still a great deal of field study which is required before the connections between high crime rates among Aboriginal peoples and the response to Aboriginal peoples by the criminal justice system can be firmly established.

The Variations in Aboriginal Crime Patterns

Complicating our attempt to explain Aboriginal crime are the variations in crime patterns which exist between different regions of the country and between communities in the same jurisdiction. Why is it, for example, that there are differences in the patterns of crime among the thirteen isolated Inuit communities of the Baffin Region, Eastern Arctic? The colonization perspective would lead us to predict that the consequences of colonization were equally as disastrous for all Aboriginal cultures and communities, yet the findings of field studies suggest otherwise. Variations in crime patterns exist between communities that share many of the same difficulties — low levels of education, employment, and income, and loss of traditional cultural practices. This suggests that these types of variables are unable to tell us why some Aboriginal communities have higher rates of crime than others (Marenin, 1992; Wood, 1991).

Two different studies have shown the inability of the colonization perspective to explain variations in Aboriginal community crime patterns. Wolff (1991:28), in a rank order analysis of the crime patterns on Saskatchewan reserves, found no relationship between these manifestations of colonization (including single parent families, persons per dwelling, unemployment, labour force participation, education, average income, and income from government transfer payments) and violent and property crime rates. The only relationship that Wolff (1991:28) did discover was one between property and violent crime, meaning that communities that have high violent crime rates are also more likely to have high property crime rates. A similar study by Wood (1997), looking at the Inuit communities of the Baffin Region, found no relationship between the rates of violent crime and

community relocation or the impact of the seal fur market decline. Wood (1997) also found, contrary to the colonization perspective, that high violent crime rates were associated with high, rather than low, levels of income, employment, and education.

Other approaches have been more successful in explaining why some Aboriginal communities have higher crime rates than others. In an attempt to explain crime patterns between Aboriginal communities, LaPrairie (1988) compared the ways in which Aboriginal communities had responded to the pressures to modernize. By classifying reserves according to the extent to which they had adapted to modern conditions, and the methods that communities had used to adapt, LaPrairie (1988) was able to explain some of this inter-community variation. Bands which had responded to the forces of modernization by developing educational programs, administrative services, and an economic base on the reserve had higher levels of violent crime than those bands that had dealt with the pressures of modernization by developing the personal, educational, and job skills of individual band members in settings outside the reserve. These bands, in contrast, had higher rates of property offences.

LaPrairie (1988) argues that part of the reason why these two different approaches to modernization have produced a differential influence on the rates of property and violent crime is the impact of each of the approaches on the daily patterns of interaction between community residents. In other words, the ways in which the bands have modernized have affected their "routine activities." Aboriginal bands that have focused their energies on developing programs and services on the reserve have tended to keep more people on the reserve, which, in turn, leads to increased opportunities for interpersonal conflicts, including violent offences, to occur. On the other hand, bands which have reacted to modernization by becoming involved in off-reserve school systems and employment opportunities have, at the same time, become more vulnerable to property offences because of the absence of property owners.

The Role of Age in Aboriginal Crime Patterns

Few attempts have been made to explain the role that age plays in the types of offences committed by Aboriginal persons (younger persons tend to commit property offences, while older Aboriginal persons tend to become involved in crimes of violence). However, it is important to note that a similar pattern exists among non-Aboriginal people as well. Gottfredson and Hirschi (1990:127) point out that in official crime statistics, there is "a consistent difference in the age distributions for person [i.e., violent] and property offences [which] appears to be well established." These researchers (Gottfredson & Hirschi 1990:127) have also found that "person crimes peak later than property crimes, and the rate declines more slowly with age."

One possible explanation for the higher rates of violent crime, particularly spousal and sexual assault, among older Aboriginal peoples is that older individuals are more likely to be in a relationship than are younger persons. This would provide more opportunities for such behaviour to occur. An examination of the relationships between victims and offenders in the Baffin Region (Griffiths et al., 1994b) shows that most violent offences occur in immediate family relationships. While it was impossible to determine the victim/offender relationship in 30 percent of the police files sampled, of the violent offence files where it was possible to determine the victim/offender relationship, 66 percent involved violence between two people who were in an immediate family relationship. Of the remaining cases involving violent offences, 30 percent involved violence between acquaintances, while only 4 percent involved an offender who was a stranger to the victim.

CONCLUSIONS

In the preceding discussion, we have identified several major attributes of Aboriginal crime that future researchers and those involved in the formulation of policy and programs must address. To date, there has been very little research on the causes of Aboriginal criminality or on ways in which crime among Aboriginal people can be prevented. It is important to point out that, although the rates of crime among Aboriginal peoples are much higher than those for non-Aboriginals, many of the *patterns* of crime committed by Aboriginals and non-Aboriginals are the same. From research on crime patterns in Alaska Native villages, Marenin (1992:356) has argued: ". . . native American crime is not a *sui generis* category. It is crime done by people who happen to be native Americans. Their status is one, but not the only determining factor in behavior." And McCaskill (1985:62), who has conducted several studies of Aboriginal crime in Canada, has cautioned us that Aboriginal criminality is quite complex and that it must be considered to be, in many instances, the result of an individual pathology: "For some Native offenders being Native may be almost irrelevant to their criminal activity."

This suggests that the root causes of crime among Aboriginal and non-Aboriginal peoples may be similar and that researchers exploring Aboriginal criminality may want to utilize theoretical approaches which consider criminal behaviour across all races and ethnicities. Such lines of inquiry may be more productive than those adopted to date. As Aboriginal Bands and communities and the federal, provincial, and territorial governments in Canada increase their efforts to reduce the overrepresentation of Aboriginal peoples in the criminal justice system, more attention will be focused on the causes of patterns of Aboriginal crime. The extent to which criminologists can develop theories of crime which explain the patterns of Aboriginal criminality will contribute to the success of initiatives designed to prevent and respond to Aboriginal crime.

NOTES

1. Given the four year time difference between the two surveys, it is difficult to determine the exact nature and extent of the differences in feelings of safety among Aboriginal and non-

Aboriginal people. The General Social Survey of all Canadians was conducted in 1987, and since that time it is possible that non-Aboriginal perceptions of safety have decreased to the point that they may be similar to those of Aboriginal peoples.

2. While many observers have argued that there is an association between the use (and abuse) of alcoholic beverages and Aboriginal crime, it is important to point out that alcohol is also closely associated with criminal behaviour among non-Aboriginals. To date, there have been no published research studies which have compared Aboriginal and non-Aboriginal alcohol use or consumption patterns with crime patterns. Studies of Aboriginal drinking in the United States (see May, 1989) which indicate that, per capita, fewer Aboriginal people drink than non-Aboriginals, suggest that the role of alcohol as a causal factor in Aboriginal crime should be closely examined.

3. Of the criminal offences discovered by the RCMP, more than half involved violations against the *Narcotic Control Act*, the N.W.T. *Liquor Act*, or were offences in which the RCMP or one of its members was a victim (e.g., assault on a police officer or property damage to a police vehicle).

DISCUSSION QUESTIONS

1. What factors distinguish Aboriginal crime from non-Aboriginal crime? Discuss "patterns" as well as "substance" (types).
2. What can be said about the underlying causes of Aboriginal versus non-Aboriginal crime?
3. How do Wood and Griffiths explain the high rates of crime among Aboriginal people?

REFERENCES

Auger, D. J., Doob, A. N., Auger, R. P., & Driben. P. (1992). Crime and control in three Nishnawbe-Aski nation communities: An exploratory investigation. *Canadian Journal of Criminology, 34*, 317–338.

Berger, T. R. (1991). *A long and terrible shadow*. Vancouver: Douglas and McIntyre.

Brantingham, P., & Brantingham. P. (1984). *Patterns in crime*. New York: Macmillan.

Canadian Centre for Justice Statistics. (1996). *Uniform crime reports, 1995*. Ottawa: Statistics Canada.

Canadian Centre for Justice Statistics. (1997). *Uniform crime Reports, 1996*. Ottawa: Statistics Canada.

Cawsey, Mr. Justice R. A. (Chair). (1991). *Justice on trial: Report of the task force on the criminal justice system and its impact on the Indian and Metis people of Alberta, Vol. 1. Main report*. Edmonton: Attorney General and Solicitor General of Alberta.

Fleras, A., & Elliott, J. L. (1992). *The nations within*. Toronto: Oxford University Press.

Gottfredson, M. R., & Hirschi, T. (1990). *A general theory of crime*. Stanford: Stanford University Press.

Griffiths, C. T., & Verdun-Jones, S. N. (1993). *Canadian criminal justice* (2nd ed.). Toronto: Harcourt Brace.

Griffiths, C. T., Wood, D. S., Zellerer, E., & Simon, J. (1994a). *Aboriginal policing in British Columbia*. Report prepared for Commission of Inquiry, Policing in British Columbia. Victoria, BC: Ministry of Attorney General.

Griffiths, C. T., Saville, G., Wood, D. S., & Zellerer, E. (1994b). *Crime and justice in the Baffin region, N.W.T.* Unpublished report. Burnaby: School of Criminology, Simon Fraser University.

Hamilton, Associate Chief Justice A. C., & Sinclair, Associate Chief Judge C. M. (1991a). *Report of the Aboriginal justice inquiry of Manitoba. The justice system and Aboriginal people, vol. 1*. Winnipeg: Queen's Printer.

Hamilton, Associate Chief Justice A. C., & Sinclair, Associate Chief Judge C. M. (1991b). *Report of the Aboriginal justice inquiry of Manitoba: The deaths of Helen Betty Osborne and John Joseph Harper, vol. 2*. Winnipeg: Queen's Printer.

Hyde, M., & LaPrairie, C. (1987). *Amerindian police crime prevention*. Ottawa: Ministry of the Solicitor General.

LaPrairie, C. (1988). Community types, crime, and police services on Canadian Indian reserves. *Journal of Research in Crime and Delinquency, 25*, 375–391.

LaPrairie, C. (1992). *Dimensions of Aboriginal over-representation in correctional institutions and implications for crime prevention*. Ottawa: Ministry of Solicitor General Canada.

Marenin, O. (1992). Explaining patterns of crime in the Native villages of Alaska. *Canadian Journal of Criminology, 34*, 339–368.

May, P. A. (1989). Alcohol abuse and alcoholism among Native American Indians: An overview. In T. D. Watts & R. Wright, Jr. (Eds.), *Alcoholism in minority populations*. Springfield: Charles C. Thomas Publisher.

McCaskill, D. (1985). *Patterns of criminality and correction among Native offenders in Manitoba: A longitudinal analysis*. Saskatoon: Prairie Region, Correctional Service of Canada.

Sacco, V. F., & Johnson, H. (1990). *Patterns of criminal victimization in Canada*. Ottawa: Minister of Supply and Services Canada.

Silverman, R. A., & Nielsen, M. O. (1992). *Aboriginal peoples and Canadian criminal justice*. Toronto: Butterworths.

Statistics Canada. (1993). *Aboriginal peoples survey: Language, tradition, health, and social issues*. Ottawa: Minister of Supply and Services Canada.

Statistics Canada. (1994). *Aboriginal peoples survey: Aboriginal community profiles*. Ottawa: Minister of Supply and Services Canada.

Statistics Canada. (1998). *The nation: 1996 census of population*. Ottawa: Minister of Supply and Services Canada.

Trevethan, S. (1993). *Police-reported Aboriginal crime in Calgary, Regina and Saskatoon*. Ottawa: Canadian Centre for Justice Statistics.

Wolff, L. (1991). *Crime in Aboriginal communities, Saskatchewan 1989*. Ottawa: Canadian Centre for Justice Statistics.

Wood, D. S. (1991). Demographic change, relocation, and patterns of crime in the Baffin Region, Northwest Territories, Canada. Unpublished paper, presented at the annual meeting of the Academy of Criminal Justice Sciences, Pittsburgh.

Wood, D. S. (1997). *Violent crime and characteristics of twelve Inuit communities in the Baffin Region, NWT*. Doctoral dissertation, School of Criminology, Simon Fraser University, Burnaby, B.C.

Crime, Ethnicity, and Immigration

ROBERT M. GORDON
JACQUELYN NELSON

INTRODUCTION

The relationships among factors such as crime, ethnicity, and immigration have been of sporadic interest to policy-makers and academics in North America for at least 60 years, beginning with the work of the Chicago School of sociology. Canadian contributions have been limited, but include the early work of Dandurand (1974) and Giffen (1976), and more contemporary contributions made by Cheung (1980), Ribordy (1980), and Samuel and Faustino-Santos (1991). Of late, the connections between the variables have received renewed attention in Canada (see, e.g., Yeager, 1997). This is due, in part, to a vigorous politicization of crime and punishment by conservative politicians and media reports that immigrants and particular ethnic groups are responsible for a disproportionate amount of crime (especially "gang-related" crime, welfare fraud, and drug trafficking). There have also been commissions and committees of inquiry into systemic racism in the criminal justice systems of several provinces (and especially in police departments), and a heated debate among policy-makers, practitioners, and academics over the ethics of recording and using crime, ethnicity (or race), and immigration statistics.[1]

Discussions of crime, ethnicity, and immigration tend to centre around two main issues: criminal justice system bias; and the causal connections

(if any) among the variables. In Canada, the United States, and Britain, allegations of ethno-cultural bias in the criminal justice system are not uncommon. These allegations may be directed toward any point in the criminal justice process: police arrests or practices (Jefferson and Walker, 1992); bail and remand hearings (Brown and Hullin, 1993); jury selection (O'Connell, 1991); the activities of court personnel, prosecutors, and judges (Frazier, Bishop, and Hennelly, 1992; Johnson, 1988); sentencing including, in the United States, the differential use of the death penalty (Gross and Mauro, 1984; Johnson, 1988); and parole and other alternatives to incarceration (LaPrairie, 1992). Some commissions of inquiry have taken a more comprehensive view, examining systemic bias at all points in the criminal justice system. An important Canadian example is the recent work of the Commission on Systemic Racism in the Ontario Criminal Justice System (1995), the final report of which is commonly known as the "Cole-Gittens Report."

Charges of justice system bias range from allegations of overt racism to more subtle evidence of so-called "adverse effects" discrimination: policies that are appropriate for one group (usually white, non-immigrant males) but that have adverse effects on others. Archibald (1989) has explored the rise in the importance of "adverse impacts" or systemic discrimination in the Canadian courts, noting that there is an increasing demand to determine whether

---

Written for this volume. Adapted from the article that appeared in the fifth edition of *Crime in Canadian Society*.

discrimination exists based on evidence of social patterns or legal practices, rather than simply stereotypes and attitudes.

Suggestions of bias may be countered by claims that certain ethno-cultural groups, or immigrant groups, are simply more disposed to commit crimes than others. This may be supported by evidence of the overrepresentation of ethnic minorities or immigrant groups in prisons (see, for example, Walmsley, Howard, and White, 1993) coupled with media reports of the crimes of ethnic minorities such as "Asian gangs," Hispanic drug traffickers, and the involvement of blacks in prostitution. Criminologists and sociologists tend either to debunk such claims by pointing to the effects of justice system bias on the police exercise of discretion and court sentencing practices, or to point the finger of blame at social structural variables such as systemic racism, class, and gender (Etherington et al., 1991). Some search for causality in the oppression of particular groups, in the barriers blocking access to society's material rewards and other symbols of success, and in the way the criminal law maintains differential power relations and maintains the traditional hierarchies of race, class, and gender (Reiman, 1989; Burtch, 1992). Other criminologists have invoked concepts such as culture conflict, friction between old and new world moralities (especially in the case of immigrants); social environmental factors such as the ecology of cities; and the strains of integration (see, for example, Thomas, 1992). More recently, the Cole-Gittens Report provided a "process definition" to explain the manifestation of systemic racism in the Ontario criminal justice system. Systemic racism, according to this explanation, is based in two social processes: racialization; and the social system. "Racialization" is the term used to refer to the process of classifying people, referring to signs of origin and making judgments regarding the capacities of people of certain origins to belong in Canadian society.

Unfortunately, as Etherington et al. (1991) note, there has been little empirical research in Canada on systemic ethno-cultural bias at discretion points in the criminal justice system. The exceptions are in two areas, both related to crime and ethnicity, but neither of which include an examination of the significance of immigration.

The first area is the body of work on aboriginal offenders, which tends to point to the overrepresentation of such peoples in prisons, and the various systemic and social structural biases that may account for this phenomenon (see, e.g., Jackson, 1989; Archibald, 1989; and LaPrairie, 1990). The second, and more recent, area of research on crime and ethnicity in Canada is the study of the impact of the criminal justice system on black people in urban Ontario. This body of work largely resides in the Cole-Gittens Report (Report of the Commission on Systemic Racism, 1995); however, other studies such as the work of Henry (1994) and Kallen (1995) are worthy of note. Cole-Gittens uncovered a significant body of evidence on the differential treatment of black people, compared with those of European ethnic origin (i.e., "Caucasians"), in Ontario's criminal justice system. The Commission's report provides data on, and an analysis of, systemic racism in policing, imprisonment before trial, charge management, court dynamics, imprisonment following conviction, prison administration, and prison discipline and control.

The relationship between crime and *immigration* in Canada remains largely unexplored, although it should be noted that the Cole-Gittens Report includes some discussion of the impact of immigration status as a person moves through the criminal justice process. However, since the focus of the Commission's work was on the impact of racialization, immigration as a separate factor was not addressed specifically. For example, in a compelling analysis of the references to "foreignness" in Ontario criminal courts, the Commission documented a higher number of references to a person's non-Canadian origins when the accused belonged to a racialized minority. The discussion of the use of references to foreignness by judges and lawyers in court is done within the context of compound racial biases. Similarly, the Commission documents cases of inappropriate judicial recommendations for deportations of convicted persons who were not citizens. The Commission noted that this is an area over which the court had no authority, and refers to the racism inherent in such remarks. There is, however, no discussion of the occurrence or impact of such comments when the convicted person is not a member of a racialized minority.

The more complex dynamics of crime, the criminal justice processes, ethnicity, and immigration remain largely unexplored. This may, in part, be due to a lack of availability of such data coupled with concerns about the potential misuse of the results of such an analysis, such as the entrenchment of cultural stereotypes or the undermining of multicultural policies (see, for example, Roberts, 1994). An analysis of two studies of corrections populations in Canada (Thomas, 1992; and Gordon and Nelson, 1993) may assist in developing an approach to understanding the relationships among crime, ethnicity, and immigration, and demonstrate how such analyses need not undermine multiculturalism or entrench damaging stereotypes.

STUDIES OF CORRECTIONS POPULATIONS IN CANADA

Prior to examining these studies of corrections populations, it is necessary both to define some key terms and to provide an important caveat with respect to the limitations of the data. The authors of both studies (Thomas, 1992; Gordon and Nelson, 1993) focused upon three overlapping groups: offenders who were members of visible ethnic minorities; offenders who, regardless of ethnicity, were not born in Canada (i.e., "immigrants" or "foreign-born"); and offenders who fell into both groups — those from visible ethnic minorities who were immigrants. In both studies, an offender was considered to be a member of a visible ethnic minority if he or she differed in physical appearance from the dominant ethnic (or racial) group in Canada, namely, fair skinned, Euro-Canadians commonly referred to as "Caucasians."

Gordon and Nelson (1993) divided their prisoner population into six major ethnic groups: aboriginal, Caucasian, Indo-Canadian, Hispanic, black,

and Asian. Each group was further divided into subgroups according to the prisoner's region or country of origin. Thus, for example, the Hispanic group included those of Spanish-American ethnic origin from regions such as the Caribbean and Central America. The Asian group included inmates of Chinese ethnic origin from Hong Kong and from China and those from Vietnam and the Philippines. The ethnic categorization of prisoners was an open-ended process, the outcome of which was ultimately determined by the data rather than by predetermined and rigid categories, and the authors ended up with 32 different subgroups.

An inmate was considered to be an "immigrant" if he or she was not born in Canada, a definition that is not free of problems. The two corrections studies, and other work conducted earlier, indicate that the majority of immigrants who are convicted of crimes have lived in Canada for a long period of time; very few are recent arrivals (in the Gordon and Nelson study, less than 1.0 percent of the inmate population). Some have lived in Canada longer than Canadian-born offenders and for such a long period that their status as immigrants hardly seems relevant to an understanding of their behaviour. Further, no distinction is made between those who are refugees or refugee claimants, and those who migrated to Canada in other ways. This distinction may well be important and should be carefully considered in any future research in this area.

The caveat with respect to the two corrections studies concerns the representativeness of such populations: Is it valid to generalize on the basis of research conducted with the inmates of provincial and federal correctional facilities? This is an important question because prison populations can be either over- or underrepresentative of the population at large, and of subgroups within that population such as all immigrants or all offenders. Overrepresentation could occur as a result of the kinds of systemic biases outlined at the beginning of this chapter (e.g., the police may pursue and prosecute individuals from particular ethnic groups with greater enthusiasm because of entrenched racist attitudes). Underrepresentation could occur as a result of reverse discrimination or, where discrimination is not a factor, as a result of routine practices within the criminal justice system. Even if an offender is caught, and then prosecuted, and then convicted — each step containing a filter that excludes subjects — terms of imprisonment are not the first choice for most courts in most cases. And even fewer offenders are sentenced to terms of imprisonment for two years or more that must be served in a federal facility. All of this means that prison populations are a select sample of the offenders found in, for example, a particular ethnic group, and may not represent the total offender "population" of such groups in society as a whole. At the same time, the inmates of provincial and federal facilities can be considered to be the more serious and persistent of offenders and, arguably, are interesting and important individuals for the purposes of both general criminological inquiry and government policy-making.

The two corrections studies proceeded with similar research questions and assumptions. If the rate of incarceration of visible ethnic minorities or of immigrants reflects the proportion of such groups in the population as a whole, it is probably safe to argue that ethnicity and immigration either are not significant factors in explaining crime among these groups or that any negative experiences associated with ethnicity or immigrant status (e.g., persistent and blatant discrimination) are counterbalanced by powerful contrary influences. These influences can include the resources of a particular community, the presence of strong supportive networks within it (Goldenberg and Haines, 1992), or its "institutional completeness" (Breton, 1964). These kinds of assets can protect the group from the damaging effects of racist stereotypes and non-inclusive practices.

Thomas's study (1992) of the population of the federal correctional system in Canada is especially helpful in determining the extent to which the members of visible ethnic minorities and immigrants — two separable although not always separate groups — are over- or underrepresented. Thomas's work began with the assumption that if

there is no systemic bias and if the members of ethnic minorities and immigrants are equally predisposed to commit crimes, then the percentage of these individuals who are charged, convicted, or incarcerated would equal the proportions of those from ethnic minorities and those who are immigrants in the population as a whole. An overrepresentation in the correctional system could suggest either systemic bias or a higher disposition to commit crimes, phenomena that would then need to be explored further. In fact, his study found an underrepresentation.

Using data from the Correctional Services of Canada and from the 1986 national census, Thomas found that offenders from non-aboriginal, visible ethnic minorities, regardless of whether they were foreign-born or not, were underrepresented in the population of the federal correctional system. In 1989, only 5.2 percent of the federal corrections population were from an ethnic minority, compared with approximately 6.3 percent in the national population (1986 census). By 1991, these proportions had increased to 6.3 percent and a projected 8.5 percent respectively. According to Thomas, the most common region of birth among those from visible ethnic minorities was the West Indies (especially Jamaica) followed by South and Central America. These particular ethnic groups were both overrepresented[2] and the fastest growing visible minorities in the federal system. The numbers of those of West Indian ethnic origin had increased from 265 in 1989 to 420 in 1991, while the numbers of those from South and Central America had increased from 157 to 238 in the same time period.

Thomas (1992) also explored the representation of immigrants in the federal correctional system, regardless of their ethnic origin. He found that immigrants were very significantly underrepresented in the population of those incarcerated for serious crimes in 1989 and 1991. The underrepresentation appeared to be most pronounced in British Columbia and the Prairies. In British Columbia, 13.5 percent of the federal corrections population in 1989 were foreign-born, and by

1991, this had remained reasonably stable at 13.2 percent. The 1986 national census data showed that 26.6 percent of the general population of the province were foreign-born. Of particular interest, given the high level of immigration to the area, is the fact that between 1989 and 1991, the representation of foreign-born people in the Pacific region actually declined slightly whereas in all other regions there was a noticeable increase.

These data represent the more than 20 000 offenders in the federal correctional system and include both those in facilities serving sentences of two years or more and those on conditional release. These offenders are usually individuals who have either committed the most serious of crimes (e.g., murder) or who have been persistent in the commission of crime, such as those who have chosen a "career" in the field of armed robbery. An obvious question then emerges of whether similar patterns would be found among people incarcerated in provincial correctional systems — young offenders or adult offenders serving sentences of up to two years less one day — and especially in those provinces where there was a significant underrepresentation of visible ethnic minorities and immigrants in the federal correctional system.

A study by Gordon and Nelson (1993) of the entire population of provincial youth and adult correctional centres in British Columbia mirrored Thomas's findings in the federal system. Only 8.2 percent of the prison population were members of non-aboriginal, visible ethnic minorities compared with an estimated 13.5 percent in the general population of the province. More important, only 11 percent of inmates — 215 of the 1952 prisoners contained in correctional centres on the day of the census — were not born in Canada compared with 22.3 percent in the general population of the province, a significant underrepresentation.

Immigrant inmates came from three main regions: Europe, including Britain (22 percent), South East Asia (15 percent), and Central America (12.1 percent). Other much smaller groups hailed from a variety of regions and countries including India, Fiji, Iran, Hong Kong, and Jamaica, but in each case these individuals accounted for less than 0.5 percent of the prisoner population. Approximately one-half of the immigrant inmates had been in Canada for a considerable period (ten years or more), and more than two-thirds had been residents for more than five years. Only 59 inmates (3.0 percent of the inmate population) had been living in Canada for five years or less, and of these only 18 had been resident for one year or less. On the basis of these data, Gordon and Nelson (1993) concluded that less than 1.0 percent of the total inmate population — 18 prisoners out of 1952 — could be described as "newly arrived" immigrants, individuals who had been resident in Canada for one year or less.

Both the study by Thomas (1992) and the census conducted by Gordon and Nelson (1993) examined the kinds of crimes committed by offenders from visible ethnic minorities and those who were immigrants, comparing these with the crimes committed by the rest of the federal and B.C. corrections populations. In the case of immigrants, and regardless of ethnic origin, Gordon and Nelson (1993) analyzed their provincial data by examining, among many other computations, the major offence categories also used by Thomas: break and enter, theft, robbery, murder, assault, sex offences, fraud, conspiracy, extortion, narcotics, prostitution offences, and counselling murder. Separate analyses were conducted for the total provincial inmate population and for all adult inmates not born in Canada.[3]

The data represented in Figure 19.1 provide a comparison of the numbers of adult inmates in provincial facilities in British Columbia who were, and who were not, born in Canada in each primary offence category. The bar for each offence category also shows a line and a number that reflects the expected number of foreign-born offenders in each category, given the proportion of foreign-born individuals in the general population of the province (22.3 percent). This information is not provided in three categories — conspiracy, extortion, and prostitution — because of the small number of offenders in each category. The figures at

Figure 19.1

B.C. Provincial Adult Inmates Held for Selected Offences: Canadian-Born and Foreign-Born

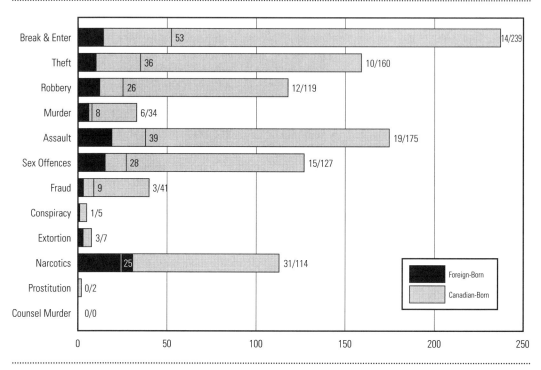

Break & Enter	53	14/239
Theft	36	10/160
Robbery	26	12/119
Murder	8	6/34
Assault	39	19/175
Sex Offences	28	15/127
Fraud	9	3/41
Conspiracy		1/5
Extortion		3/7
Narcotics	25	31/114
Prostitution		0/2
Counsel Murder		0/0

Foreign-Born
Canadian-Born

0   50   100   150   200   250

SOURCE: R.M. Gordon and S. Foley. *Criminal Business Organizations, Street Gangs and Related Groups in Vancouver: The Report of the Greater Vancouver Gang Study.* Victoria: Ministry of the Attorney General, 1998.

the end of each bar are the number of inmates in the offence category who were foreign-born expressed as a fraction of the total number of inmates in that category. So, for example, in the category of break and enter, 14 of the 239 inmates imprisoned for that offence were immigrants. The expected number was 53.

As these data indicate, the actual number of adult inmates who were not born in Canada in each offence category is quite low when compared to the total number of inmates in each category. The numbers are also much lower than the expected number of foreign-born inmates, and especially with respect to the main types of property crime — break and enter, theft, and fraud. Of all the offence categories, the number of foreign-

born inmates convicted of narcotics offences is closest to, and in fact slightly exceeds, the expected number (25), but it should be remembered that the actual number of immigrant offenders in this category (31) is minute when compared to the number of immigrants in the general population of the province (22.3 percent of the population, or approximately 750 000).

The data presented in Figure 19.2 provide a graphic comparison of the findings of the federal (Thomas, 1992) and the provincial (Gordon and Nelson, 1993) research, but by using percentages rather than actual numbers and by including comparisons of the federal data, the total provincial inmate population (i.e., youth and adults), and the provincial adult inmate population.

Figure 19.2

Percent of Those Held for Selected Major Offences Who Are Foreign-Born

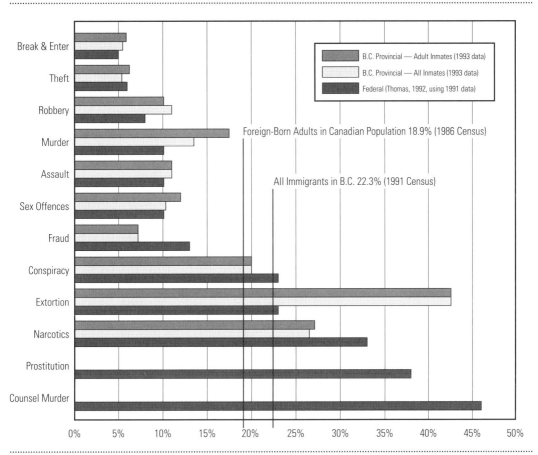

As these data indicate, many of the major offence categories show considerable consistency between the provincial and the federal data. When compared to the percentage of foreign-born people in British Columbia (22.3 percent), adult foreign-born inmates were underrepresented in the categories of break and enter (5.8 percent), theft (6.2 percent), robbery (10.1 percent), murder (17.6 percent), assault (10.8 percent), sex offences (11.8 percent), and fraud (7.8 percent). As with Thomas's data, the percentage of foreign-born adult inmates in provincial correctional facilities for conspiracy (20 percent) was higher than all the offence categories except extortion and narcotics, but unlike the federal data, the percentage did not exceed the percentage of foreign-born people in British Columbia (22.3 percent). It should be noted that the number of inmates serving time for this offence (five) is very small.

In his study of the federal corrections population, Thomas (1992) found an overrepresentation for extortion, and as the data in Figure 19.2 indicate, the percentage of adult provincial inmates who were foreign-born and in this category (42.8 percent) is nearly twice the expected percentage (22.3 percent). However, as is the case with the conspiracy category, the number of inmates affected is very small (seven). Offenders not born in Canada were overrepresented in the narcotics category in both Thomas's analysis and the provincial study by Gordon and Nelson (1993). The latter found that 27.2 percent of inmates in this category were immigrants instead of the expected (and normal) 22.3 percent.

Gordon and Nelson (1993) gathered considerable information about the kinds of crimes for which individuals from different visible ethnic minorities had been convicted and imprisoned, regardless of their place of birth (i.e., regardless of whether or not they were immigrants). These data are set out in Table 19.1, which provides a breakdown of the primary offence for which inmates from the major ethnic groups had been imprisoned, an indication of the size of the group in each offence category against the size of the particular ethnic group in the general provincial population, and in the case of those from visible ethnic minorities, the number (in brackets) in each offence category who were not born in Canada.

The first, and most important, thing to note about these data is that the number of subjects from non-aboriginal, visible ethnic minorities was quite small (124) when compared with the overall provincial prison population (1952). It follows that any conclusions drawn from the data must be tentative. There is a danger of unjustly stereotyping and condemning entire ethnic groups because of the concentrated activities of a handful of offenders (e.g., 29 Indo-Canadians, or 29 blacks). The second point to note is that the majority of the inmates from visible ethnic minorities — 98 out of 124, or 79 percent — were not born in Canada. In the case of those imprisoned for narcotics offences, every inmate from a visible minority was also an immigrant. Again, however, these data should be approached with caution because the actual number of offenders is minute when compared to the numbers of individuals from the different ethnic groups in the general provincial population.

With these important caveats in mind, the data indicate that Indo-Canadian, black, and Asian inmates were more likely to be in prison for crimes of violence or sex-related crimes. Hispanic inmates were more likely to be serving time for narcotics offences. Overall, inmates belonging to visible ethnic minorities were more likely to be in prison for crimes of violence and sex crimes (47.5 percent), followed by property crime (23 percent), and narcotics offences (19.2 percent).

The study by Gordon and Nelson (1993) included a special examination of all inmates — youth and adult — who were identified by police and corrections personnel as being involved with gangs. Of the 41 subjects in this special study, 22 (53.6 percent) were from non-aboriginal, visible ethnic minorities, the largest subgroup of these

Table 19.1

Inmates Incarcerated by Crime Categories: British Columbia, 1993*

Ethnic Group	Property		Violence/Sex		Narcotics		Other		Total	
Aboriginal	122	.72	139	.80	24	.14	67	.39	352	2.00
Caucasian	521	.19	432	.15	74	.03	267	.09	1294	.46
Indo-Canadian	9	.08 (6)	15	.13 (9)	1	.01 (1)	4	.04 (4)	29	.26 (20)
Hispanic	3	.20 (2)	7	.49 (6)	15	1.00 (15)	1	.07 (1)	26	1.79 (24)
Black	9	.37 (6)	14	.57 (8)	2	.32 (2)	4	.16 (3)	29	1.19 (19)
Asian	8	.03 (7)	23	.08 (19)	7	.03 (7)	3	nil (2)	40	.14 (35)

* Frequency and rate per 1000 of ethnic group in general population.
NOTE: Numbers shown in brackets are the numbers of inmates from visible ethnic minorities in each category who were not born in Canada.

subjects being those of Asian ethnic origin (14 of the 41). As a point of comparison, an estimated 13.3 percent of the provincial population are from non-aboriginal visible minorities (Gordon and Nelson, 1993). Clearly, the members of visible ethnic minorities were overrepresented among the gang members in facilities, but no definitive conclusions should be drawn from these data because of the size of the sample. In addition, it is important not to lose sight of the fact that the largest single group of gang-involved inmates were of Caucasian ethnic origin (16/41), the vast majority of whom were born in Canada (Gordon, 1993).

Seventy-four percent (20/27) of those 17 years of age and younger and 50 percent (7/14) of the adults identified as gang-involved were born in Canada, primarily in British Columbia. Overall, however, 32 percent of the gang-involved inmates were not born in Canada. As we have seen, 11 percent of the population of provincial correctional centres were immigrants, compared with approximately 22.3 percent of the B.C. population (Gordon and Nelson, 1993). The percentage of immigrants among young gang members (17 years of age or younger) was 26 percent. This is considerably higher than in the inmate population as a whole, but only slightly higher than might be expected in a normal and equitable distribution. The total percentage of immigrant gang members (32 percent), however, is higher than in both the correctional centres and the provincial populations. Again, these data must be used with caution because of the small number of subjects in the sample. There is also concern that the data may have been a product of the labelling of individuals from visible ethnic minorities as gang members, and especially those who are of Asian ethnic origin, as a consequence of nearly ten years of negative media attention.

CONCLUSIONS

Two relatively recent studies of corrections populations in Canada indicate that, overall, people from non-aboriginal, visible ethnic minorities and immigrants are significantly underrepresented in the federal corrections system and in British Columbia's youth and adult correctional centres. These results are consistent with the results of studies of the relationship among crime, ethnicity, and immigration in Canada in the 1950s, the 1960s, and again in the 1970s (see, e.g., Samuel and Faustino-Santos, 1991). Of particular note in the recent studies is the finding that there are half as many immigrants in the corrections system as one might expect under normal circumstances. Assuming that these findings reflect the situation in the general population of offenders and that there is no massive reverse discrimination in the criminal justice system (a possibility for which there is no supporting evidence), these results invite some interesting new criminological questions. In exploring the relationships among variables such as crime, ethnicity, and immigration, the question "Why criminal activity?" should, perhaps, be rephrased as "Why is there less criminal activity than is found among other groups?"

This requires a significant shift in thinking away from existing bodies of theory, such as strain theories and culture conflict theories, which assume crime is a problem among visible ethnic minorities and immigrants and attempt to explain criminal behaviour, somewhat sympathetically, by reference to the challenges and problems of migration and settlement in a new land. These are theories that have their roots in the work of the Chicago School of sociology as well as famous sociologists such as Robert Merton, and they were constructed in the 1930s and 1940s to account for what were, arguably, quite different immigration practices, policies, and experiences. Since that time, the problems of settlement have been examined and addressed by governments, and an underrepresentation of visible ethnic minorities and immigrants may well be due to effective programming for immigrants, and especially those from ethnic minorities, on their arrival in Canada. It may well be a function of effective screening undertaken by Canadian immigration officials at the place of origin or perhaps simply a product of the type of individuals migrating to Canada.

An examination of the situation in British Columbia helps cast some light on these issues. The province is second only to Ontario in having the highest proportion of its population who are immigrants. Statistics from the 1991 national census indicate that the proportion of immigrants in British Columbia is increasing slightly faster than the increase in the general population. While the province has about 12 percent of the Canadian population, it attracts approximately 16 percent of the immigrants who come to Canada. Of these immigrants, the proportion who are European-born has been declining steadily, and the proportion born in Asia has increased. During the period 1988 to 1991, 71.5 percent of B.C. immigrants were born in Asia, compared with 13.7 percent born in Europe.

While these data suggest an increasing number of immigrants who are members of visible ethnic minorities in British Columbia, there are also indications of "protective factors" that may assist these people in making successful adjustments and possibly avoiding any contact with the criminal justice system. Many of the immigrants who chose British Columbia were investors (46.1 percent of all investor immigrants to Canada landed in the province), retired (45.3 percent of immigrants to Canada), or entrepreneurs (25.1 percent of immigrants to Canada). The number of immigrants in these classes totaled 8941 or approximately one-third of the 27 270 immigrants landing in British Columbia between 1982 and the third quarter of 1992. For Canada as a whole, there were 25 358 of 187 728 or approximately 13.5 percent of immigrants in these classes. This may suggest that, compared with the Canada-wide proportions, British Columbia has a significantly higher proportion of immigrants who are likely to be financially resourceful. If, as Thomas (1992) suggests, it is important to remove barriers to legitimate opportunities for immigrants and individuals from visible ethnic minorities, then it may be that British Columbia's immigrant population is in a particularly favourable position for doing so. This significant protective factor — the relative abundance of legitimate financial resources — is likely to be important, particularly when coupled with the fact that the majority of people who migrate do not do so in order to find a place where they can commit crime.

Ironically, it is possible that the very factors that buffer or protect many immigrants of visible ethnic minorities from any involvement with crime — their financial resources — may also make them prime targets for a variety of predators, including those who are themselves immigrants and members of visible minorities. In Vancouver, for example, there are occasional spates of "home invasions," usually carried out by small groups consisting primarily of offenders of Asian ethnic origin who target wealthy victims with a similar ethnic background. In a similar vein, Thomas (1992) found an overrepresentation of foreign-born people incarcerated for crimes that are considered characteristic of organized crime (e.g., extortion, narcotics offences, counselling murder, and prostitution), while crime categories such as break and enter, theft, and robbery had the lowest representation of foreign-born prisoners.

Gordon and Nelson (1993) have uncovered a similar situation in the provincial system with the evidence that immigrants and people from visible ethnic minorities are more likely to be imprisoned for particular kinds of offences (notably, narcotics and violence) that are conducted in a particular way — in the company of others in a semi-organized and collective manner (i.e., in "gangs"). But the number of inmates convicted of such offences is small when compared to the overall size of the federal and provincial corrections populations.

How might we account for the overrepresentation that occurs in specific offence categories? Unlike their more affluent counterparts — the investor and the entrepreneur — many immigrants lack the financial resources necessary for successful settlement and run into significant difficulties making the transition from their former country to their new home (see, for example, Lee, 1992). These individuals encounter a battery of predictable barriers — the lack of language skills, unemployment or employment in low-paying and low-prestige jobs, social isolation, and so forth —

that limit a person's choices (Gordon and Foley, 1998) and may result in what Henry (1994) refers to as "differential incorporation" of these cultural communities into Canadian society. It may also be noted that the assistance available in the form of human rights legislation, which may ameliorate some of the discriminatory barriers, may be under-used by certain racialized immigrant groups (see, e.g., Kallen, 1995). With such limitations on choice, and with little use of protective legislation, the potential increases for individuals to engage in certain forms of crime as a way of carving out a living. Faced with indigence and a dependence upon charity, and with little hope of improvement, it is perhaps not surprising that some immigrants, and especially those from visible ethnic minorities, seek employment in company with others in illegitimate business ventures and especially, it would seem, in the sale and distribution of narcotics, a commodity for which there is a large market and a seemingly endless supply of ready and enthusiastic consumers (see, e.g., Gordon and Foley, 1998).

Strain theories should not, therefore, be rejected prematurely when attempting to understand the relationships among crime, ethnicity, and immigration. They have their place in the matrix of explanation — but only as possibilities and only as a way of accounting for the activities of what appears to be a relatively small number and proportion of foreign-born individuals who engage in crime. Above all else, strain theories need to be tested in the Canadian context. At this point, the acceptance of such theories is more an act of faith, reinforced by a healthy dose of intuition, than a decision based upon sound research that explores the actual experiences of immigrants (and their families) and especially those from visible ethnic minorities. Hopefully, the discovery that immigrants and members of visible ethnic minorities are underrepresented in corrections systems does not deter researchers from pursuing inquiries in this area. Likewise, it is to be hoped that in this age of problem-focused research the findings of the corrections studies do not contribute to a funding drought as scarce resources are directed to other areas.

NOTES

1. See, volume 36, number 2, of the *Canadian Journal of Criminology* (1994) for various articles addressing the issue of crime and race statistics. These articles contain various references to and comments on the growing interest in the relationships among crime, ethnicity, and immigration in Canada.
2. Unfortunately, Thomas does not specify the degree to which these groups are overrepresented.
3. Young offenders were excluded in order to ensure consistency with Thomas's work: there are no young offenders in federal correctional facilities.

DISCUSSION QUESTIONS

1. What charges of criminal justice bias have been levelled against the Canadian system? What do Gordon and Nelson show in this regard?
2. When studying crime we sometimes utilize prison populations for our sample. Discuss the problems involved in such use.
3. What factors are likely to "protect" immigrants from involvement in crime?
4. How can strain theory be used to help understand the relationships among crime, ethnicity, and imigration?

REFERENCES

Archibald, B. P. (1989). Sentencing and visible minorities: equality and affirmative action in the criminal justice system. *Dalhousie Law Journal* (Nov.), 377–411.

Breton, R. (1964). Institutional completeness of ethnic communities and the personal relations of immigrants. *American Journal of Sociology, 70*(2), 193–205.

Brown, I., & Hullin, R. (1993). Contested bail applications: The treatment of ethnic minority and white offenders. *Criminal Law Review* (Feb.), 107–113

Burtch, B. (1992). *The sociology of law: Critical approaches to social control.* Toronto: Harcourt Brace Jovanovich Canada.

Cheung, Y. W. (1980). Explaining ethnic and racial variations in criminality rates: A review and critique. *Canadian Criminology Forum, 3* (Fall), 1–14.

The Commission on Systemic Racism. (1995). *Report of the commission on systemic racism in the Ontario criminal justice system.* Toronto: Queen's Printer.

Dandurand, Y. (1974). Ethnic group members and the correctional system: A question of human rights. *Canadian Journal of Crime and Corrections, 16* (1), 35–52.

Etherington, B., Bogart, W. A, Irish, M., & Stewart, G. (1991). *Preserving identity by having many identities: A report on multiculturalism and access to justice.* Windsor: University of Windsor.

Frazier, C. E., Bishop, D. M., and Hennelly, J. C. (1992). The social context of race differentials in juvenile justice dispositions. *Sociological Quarterly, 33,* 447–458.

Giffen, P. J. (1976). Official rates of crime and delinquency. In W. T. McGrath (Ed.), *Crime and its treatment in Canada.* Toronto: Macmillan.

Goldenberg, S., & Haines, V. A. (1992). Social networks and institutional completeness: From territory to ties. *Canadian Journal of Sociology, 17* (3), 301–312.

Gordon, R. M. (1993). *Incarcerated gang members in British Columbia: A preliminary study.* Victoria: Ministry of Attorney General.

Gordon, R. M., & Foley, S. (1998). *Criminal business organizations, street gangs and related groups in Vancouver: The report of the Greater Vancouver gang study.* Victoria: Ministry of the Attorney General.

Gordon, R. M., & Nelson, J. (1993). *Census '93: The report of the 1993 census of provincial correctional centres in British Columbia.* Victoria: Ministry of Attorney General.

Gross, S., & Mauro, R. (1984). Patterns of death: An analysis of racial disparities in capital sentencing and homicide victimization. *Stanford Law Review, 37,* 27.

Henry, F. (1994). *The Caribbean diaspora in Toronto: Learning to live with racism.* Toronto: University of Toronto Press.

Jackson, M. (1989). Locking up natives in Canada. *University of British Columbia Law Review, 23,* 215–300.

Jefferson, R., & Walker, M. A. (1992). Ethnic minorities in the criminal justice system. *Criminal Law Review* (Feb.), 81–95.

Johnson, S. L. (1988). Unconscious racism and the criminal law. *Cornell Law Review, 73,* 1016–1037.

Kallen, E. (1995). *Ethnicity and human rights in Canada* (2nd ed.). Toronto: Oxford University Press.

LaPrairie, C. (1990). Aboriginal crime and justice: Explaining the present, exploring the future. *Canadian Journal of Criminology, 32,* 429–440.

LaPrairie, C. (1992). *Dimensions of aboriginal over-representation in correctional institutions and implications for crime prevention.* Ottawa: Ministry of the Solicitor General.

Lee, C. (1992). *The dilemma of new Canadian youth: A discussion paper.* Vancouver: Asian Youth Task Force.

O'Connell, R. M. (1991). The elimination of racism from jury selection: Challenging the peremptory challenge. *Boston College Law Review, 32,* 433–485.

Reiman, J. (1989). *The rich get richer and the poor get prison.* New York: John Wiley and Sons.

Ribordy, F. (1980). Culture conflict and crime among Italian immigrants. In R. Silverman & J. Teevan (Eds.), *Crime in Canadian society* (2nd ed.). Toronto: Butterworths.

Roberts, J. (1994). Crime and race statistics: Toward a Canadian solution. *Canadian Journal of Criminology, 36* (2), 175–186.

Samuel, T. J., & Faustino-Santos, R. (1991). Canadian immigrants and criminality. *International Migration Review, 29* (1), 51–73.

Thomas, D. (1992). *Criminality among the foreign born: Analysis of federal prison population.* Ottawa: Immigration and Employment Canada.

Walmsley, R., Howard, L., & White, S. (1993). *The national prison survey, 1991.* London: Home Office Research Study 128.

Yeager, M. G. (1997). Immigrants and criminality: A cross-national review. *Criminal Justice Abstracts* (March), 143–171.

Woman Killing: Intimate Femicide in Ontario

ROSEMARY GARTNER
MYRNA DAWSON
MARIA CRAWFORD

INTRODUCTION

In March 1988, a young mother of two was killed by her estranged husband in a northern Ontario town. The killer had been visiting his wife, who was staying in a shelter for abused women. Convinced that she was not going to return to him, he shot her twice at close range. Later that year, in a small town outside of Edmonton, a woman was shot dead in her home by her estranged husband, who then shot and killed himself. Miraculously, the woman's three-year-old girl, whom she was holding in her arms when she was shot, was not wounded. These women were two of the 202 female victims of homicide in Canada in 1988. They shared with 68 other female victims a marital relationship with their killers.

A literature review (Women We Honour Action Committee & Gartner, 1990) led to a number of conclusions about the then-existing state of knowledge about intimate femicide. First, obtaining an accurate estimate of the number of such killings in Canada or in Ontario from statistics in official publications was not possible because official publications restricted their classifications to "spouse killings," which excluded killings by estranged common-law partners and current or former boyfriends. Second, information on the nature of intimate femicide — its dynamics as well as its structural and cultural sources — was incomplete.

Third, much of the research had been conducted in the United States, which is atypical in both the quantity and quality of its homicides. That is, spousal homicides make up a much smaller proportion of total homicides in the U.S. compared to many other nations. Moreover, the ratio of female to male victims of spouse killings is more balanced in the U.S. than in other countries (about 1.3:1, compared to about 3:1 in Canada, Australia, Denmark, the U.K. and other countries).[1]

To address these limitations, the Women We Honour Action Committee obtained funding from the Ontario Women's Directorate to conduct a study of intimate femicide in Ontario. The study had three goals: to document for Ontario the incidence of killings of women by intimate partners, including legal spouses, common-law partners, and boyfriends, both current and estranged; to describe the characteristics of the people involved in and the circumstances surrounding these killings; and to present the stories of a small number of women who had been killed by their intimate partners. That study, completed in 1992, compiled and analyzed data on all intimate femicides known to authorities in Ontario from 1974 through 1990 (Crawford et al., 1992). A second study, designed to update the data through 1994, was completed in April 1997 (Crawford et al., 1997).

In this paper, we describe the major findings of these two studies of intimate femicide. Our purpose

Adapted from Woman Killing: Intimate Femicide in Ontario, 1974–94, by Rosemary Gartner, Myrna Dawson, and Maria Crawford (1998). *Resources for Feminist Research*, *26* (3–4): 151–173. Reprinted with permission.

is twofold: first, to provide an overview and statistical picture of intimate femicide in Ontario for the 21 years from 1974 through 1994; and second, to locate this statistical picture in what is now a substantially larger and more sophisticated literature on violence against women by intimate partners. That literature encompasses studies similar in many ways to ours — that is, studies of the incidence and characteristics of relatively large numbers of femicides — as well as work designed to provide a theoretical and conceptual framework for understanding intimate femicide. We draw on that literature below in discussing our findings.

FRAMING THE ISSUE OF INTIMATE FEMICIDE

After completing our literature review in 1989, we concluded that intimate femicide is a phenomenon distinct in important ways both from the killing of men by their intimate partners and from non-lethal violence against women and, hence, that it requires analysis in its own right. This view was in contrast to much of the existing literature, which treated "spousal violence" as a relatively undifferentiated phenomenon arising out of the intense emotions, stresses, and conflicts that often characterize marital relations.[2] These analyses tended to locate the sources of "spousal violence" in patterns of learning early in life, in the disinhibitory effects of alcohol consumption, and in dysfunctional patterns of communication between marital partners. Much of this early work also tended to devote limited attention and analysis to gender differences in spousal violence.

In response to this neglect of gender, a number of analysts have made gender a central feature of their accounts of spousal violence. Sex role theorists highlight gender differences in socialization which teach males to view toughness, power, and control as masculine attributes. The arguments of these more gender-sensitive analyses resonated with the experiences of members of the Women We Honour Action Committee. Power, control, and domination were themes that they encountered daily in

talking with abused women and that they detected in relationships ending in intimate femicide.

In recent work specifically focused on women killed by their intimate partners, these themes have been elaborated and, in the case of feminist analyses, placed in a historical and institutional context.[3] For example, Wilson and Daly cite "male sexual proprietariness" as the predominant motive in the killing of wives across cultures and historical epochs. "Men exhibit a tendency to think of women as sexual and reproductive 'property' that they can own and exchange . . . Proprietary entitlements in people have been conceived and institutionalized as identical to proprietary entitlements in land, chattels, and other economic resources." They go on to note, "[t]hat men take a proprietary view of female sexuality and reproductive capacity is manifested in various cultural practices," including claustration[4] practices, asymmetrical adultery laws, and bride-prices (Wilson & Daly, 1992a: 85). From this perspective, an extreme, if apparently incongruous, manifestation of male proprietariness is intimate femicide. If unable to control or coerce his partner through other means, a man may exert the ultimate control over her by killing her.

Thus, male proprietariness, or male sexual jealousy, has been placed at the centre of many empirical and theoretical analyses of intimate femicide. For example, research on intimate femicide and spousal homicide in Canada, Australia, Great Britain, and the United States[5] has identified a common core in these killings of "masculine control, where women become viewed as the possessions of men, and the violence reflects steps taken by males to assert their domination over 'their' women" (Polk, 1994: 56). This empirical work challenges many of the popular notions about the characteristics of such crimes, for example, the belief that they are explosive, unplanned, and unpredictable acts of passion. At the same time, it contests the validity and coherence of the concept "spousal homicide," with its connotations of sexual symmetry in violence, by revealing distinct differences between intimate partner killings by men and those by women. As Dobash et al. note:

Men often kill wives after lengthy periods of prolonged physical violence accompanied by other forms of abuse and coercion; the roles in such cases are seldom if ever reversed. Men perpetrate familicidal massacres, killing spouses and children together; women do not. Men commonly hunt down and kill wives who have left them; women hardly ever behave similarly. Men kill wives as part of planned murder-suicides; analogous acts by women are almost unheard of. Men kill in response to revelations of wifely infidelity; women almost never respond similarly . . . (1992: 81)

In sum, there have been significant advances in both empirical and conceptual analyses of lethal violence against women by their partners since the literature review that served as the impetus for our research. Those advances have not, however, filled all of the gaps identified in our earlier review. In particular, empirical research in Canada has continued to rely largely on official statistics from police sources, which exclude from their classification of spousal homicides killings by men of their estranged common-law partners and girlfriends. Relying on these official statistics also restricts analyses to the information and coding schemes employed by police agencies and personnel. Because of our concerns about the potential for lost information and for the introduction of unknown biases, we relied on a wider range of information sources than typically used in previous research. In this way, our study is unusual in the comprehensiveness of its data. As we see below, it is not, however, unique in its findings about the nature of intimate femicide.

DATA SOURCES

These files frequently contain copies of police reports as well as medical reports on the condition of the body, the way in which the woman was killed and the violence she suffered, details often not available from other sources. However, coroners' records, like all official sources of information on homicide, are imperfect measures of the actual

number of deaths due to homicide. For example, cases of homicide in which no body has been found will not typically appear in coroners' records. As a consequence, we expect our estimates of the incidence of intimate femicide to undercount the true incidence, an issue we discuss in more depth below.[6] We were able to cross-check and supplement data from coroner's records by reviewing police homicide investigation files for many of our cases.[7] In the second study, we were also able to review data from Crown Attorney files on many of the cases in which charges were laid between 1991 and 1994. In both studies, we supplemented our data from official sources with information from newspaper and magazine articles on some of the killings and on trials of some of the alleged offenders.

We compiled this information so that it could be used in both quantitative and qualitative analyses. Our final data collection instrument was designed to provide codes for approximately 52 variables, as well as space to record a narrative of the case where further information was available.[8]

THE INCIDENCE OF INTIMATE FEMICIDE IN ONTARIO, 1974–1994

Between 1974 and 1994, 1206 women aged 15 and older[9] were killed in Ontario, according to official records. In 1120 (93%) of these cases, the crimes were solved and the killers were identified. In 705 (63%) of the solved cases, the killers were the current or former legal spouses, common-law partners, or boyfriends of their victims. Thus, in Ontario over this 21-year period, intimate partners were responsible for the majority of all woman killings and an average of 34 women were victims of intimate femicide each year. These data indicate that the focus in official publications and some academic research on "spousal homicides" of women provides an incomplete picture of the more general phenomenon of intimate femicide: excluding killings of women by their estranged common-law partners and current and former boyfriends underestimates the total number of intimate femicides by about 25%.

The actual number of intimate femicides in Ontario during these years is undoubtedly higher than this. Intimate partners were certainly responsible for some portion of the cases in which no offender was identified or in which we had too little information to determine the precise nature of the relationship between victim and offender.[10] Adjusting for excluded cases, we estimate that intimate femicides may have accounted for as many as 76% of all femicides in Ontario between 1974 and 1994. However, since it is impossible to know the number and characteristics of excluded cases, the analyses that follow focus only on those 705 cases in which the offender was officially identified as the current or former intimate partner of the victim.

TRENDS IN INTIMATE FEMICIDE

Between 1974 and 1994, the rate of intimate femicide (i.e., the number of victims of intimate femicide per 100 000 women in the general population) ranged from a low of .55 in 1978 to a high of 1.26 in 1991, but appears to follow no particular trend over time. Dividing the 21-year period in half suggests otherwise, however: the average annual rate for the second half of the period (1.02 per 100 000) was slightly higher than the rate for the first half (.92 per 100 000).

On its own, this difference is insignificant statistically and, it might appear, substantively. However, when compared to the statistically significant decreases in other types of lethal violence, the slightly higher rate of intimate femicide in the latter period takes on greater importance. The annual rate at which women were killed by strangers or unknown assailants declined significantly from an average of .27 during 1974–1983 to .16 during 1984–1994. Moreover, the annual rate at which men were killed by their spouses also declined significantly, from an average rate of .31 during 1974–1983 to .18 during 1984–1994. In other words, during a period when women's risks from strangers and men's risks from spouses decreased, women's risks from their intimate partners increased slightly. Put another way, after 1984 — a

period of substantial expansion in services for abused women — men's risks of being killed by intimate partners decreased significantly whereas women's risks did not.

Without further analysis of these patterns — which is beyond the scope of this paper — we can only speculate as to the reasons for this apparently counter-intuitive finding. One possible explanation is that the expansion of services for abused women may have resulted in the protection of men from violence by their intimate partners, but not necessarily the reverse. Research shows that women are most likely to kill their intimate partners after prolonged abuse and when they fear continued or more serious violence against themselves or their children (Browne, 1987). Where services for abused women are available, women in abusive relationships have an alternative to killing their partners. As Browne and Williams (1989) note, "By offering threatened women protection, escape and aid, [legal and extra-legal] resources can engender an awareness that there are alternatives to remaining at risk" and thus prevent "killings that occur in desperation." Their analysis of U.S. data lends support to this interpretation: states with higher levels of services to abused women had lower rates of spouse killings of males, but not lower rates of spouse killings of females.

CHARACTERISTICS OF THE VICTIMS AND THEIR KILLERS

In many respects, the women killed by their intimate partners and the men who killed them[11] are very similar to women and men in the general population of Ontario (see Table 20.1). For example, women killed by their intimate partners were, on average, about 37 years old; 51% were employed; 80% had children; and 76% were born in Canada. These characteristics do not distinguish the victims from other women in Ontario.

In some other respects, however, victims of intimate femicide and their killers differed from women and men in the general population.[12] We can think of these differences as risk markers for

Table 20.1

Characteristics of Victims of Intimate Femicide and Their Killers, Ontario, 1974–1994

Characteristics	Victims	Offenders
Total number	705	705
Average age	37	41
% born in Canada	76%	70%
% with children	80%	77%
Employment Status		
% employed	51%	64%
% unemployed	7%	21%
% homemakers	18%	0%
% students	5%	2%
% retired or on disability pension	9%	13%
Relationship of Victim to Offender		
% legal spouse, cohabiting	39%	
% legal spouse, separated	16%	
% common-law partner, cohabiting	18%	
% common-law partner, separated	7%	
% divorced spouse	<1%	
% current girlfriend	12%	
% estranged girlfriend	8%	
% Aboriginal	6%	6%

SOURCE: Compiled from coroners' records, police records, and newspaper reports.

intimate femicide because they tell us that some types of women and men face disproportionately high risks of intimate victimization or offending.[13] Each of the markers we discuss below has also been associated with increased risks of lethal violence against women in other research.

Relationship Status

Research based on data on spouse killings from Great Britain, Australia, the U.S., and Canada shows that two indicators of the status of the relationship — estrangement and common-law status — are associated with a higher risk of spouse killings of women (Johnson, 1996; Wilson & Daly, 1993; Wallace, 1986; Campbell, 1992). We find similar patterns in our intimate femicide data, although the limited availability of data on marital separation and common-law unions within the general population restricts our analysis somewhat.

Census Canada collects information on marital separations, but only for registered marriages. According to census figures, during the years of our study, 3% of women in Ontario were separated from their legal spouses. According to our data, among the victims of intimate femicide, 16% were separated from their legal spouses. Separation, then, appears to be a risk factor for intimate femicide, since women who were separated from their partners were greatly over-represented among victims of intimate femicide.

Data on the prevalence of common-law unions in the general population have been collected only since 1991, so we can estimate the risks to women living in common-law relationships only for the most recent years of our research. According to census data, 4% of women were living in common-law unions in 1991 in Ontario. According to our data, during 1991–1994 21% of the victims of intimate femicide were killed by common-law partners with whom they were living. Based on our calculations, the rate of intimate femicide for women in common-law unions was approximately six times greater than the average rate of intimate femicide in Ontario in the early 1990s.[14] Clearly, then, women in common-law unions were greatly over-represented among victims of intimate femicide during the early 1990s, and perhaps in earlier years as well.

The higher risks associated with common-law status and estrangement have been interpreted in various ways. Compared to couples in registered marriages, common-law partners are more likely to be poor, young, unemployed, and childless — all factors associated with higher homicide rates. Compared to co-residing couples, estranged couples are more likely to have a history of domestic violence (Johnson & Sacco, 1995; Rodgers, 1994). This violence may be associated both with women's decisions to leave their relationships and with their greater risks of intimate femicide. In other words, "the fact that separated couples constitute a subset of marriages with a history of discord could explain their higher homicide rates" (Wilson & Daly, 1994: 8).

Male sexual proprietariness could also play a role in the higher risks for common-law and estranged relationships. If, as some have speculated, "husbands may be less secure in their proprietary claims over wives in common-law unions" (Wilson et al., 1995: 343), they may be more likely to resort to serious violence to enforce those claims or to lethal violence when those claims are challenged. Echoing a similar theme, several studies that have found elevated risks at separation have cited the male's inability to accept termination of the relationship and obsessional desires to maintain control over his sexual partner: "He would destroy his intimate 'possession' rather than let her fall into the hands of a competitor male" (Polk, 1994: 29).[15]

Ethnicity

Women in certain ethnic groups have risks of intimate femicide disproportionate to their representation in the population, according to several studies. For example, in the United States African-American women face unusually high risks of intimate femicide. In Canada, such research is more difficult to do because of restrictions on the collection of crime statistics by race and ethnicity. However, Statistics Canada has collected data on Aboriginal victims of spousal homicides which indicate that Aboriginal women's rates of spousal homicide are between five and ten times higher than the rates for non-Aboriginal women (Kennedy et al., 1989; Silverman & Kennedy, 1993).

We estimate that at least 6% of the victims of intimate femicide in Ontario between 1974 and 1994 were Aboriginal women. Census data for these years indicate that just under 1% of all women living in Ontario classified themselves as Aboriginal. Thus, Aboriginal women in Ontario appear to be over-represented among the victims of intimate femicide. Conversely, Aboriginal men are over-represented as offenders, since all but four of the Aboriginal victims were killed by Aboriginal men.

A number of factors might explain the disproportionate risks of intimate femicide faced by Aboriginal women. Aboriginal Canadians, similar to African-Americans, are an economically impoverished and politically disenfranchised ethnic minority. Considerable research has shown that economic, social, and political disadvantages are associated with higher homicide rates generally, as well as higher rates of serious spousal violence. In addition, Aboriginal Canadian couples also have disproportionate rates of other risk markers for intimate partner violence, such as common-law marital status, low income, bouts of male unemployment, exposure to violence in childhood, alcohol abuse, overcrowded housing conditions, and social isolation — all of which have been cited as reasons for the higher rates of family violence in Aboriginal communities (Health and Welfare Canada, 1990;

Long, 1995). Some analysts situate these risk factors within a structural approach that views them as consequences of internal colonialism: "the conditions of colonialism [are] directly related to aboriginal acts of political violence as well as rates of suicide, homicide, and family violence among the aboriginal peoples" (Long, 1995: 42).[16]

Employment

Men's unemployment is commonly cited as a risk factor for wife assaults and is also associated with elevated risks of spousal homicide. Women's employment status, on the other hand, does not appear to be consistently associated with their risks of violence from their partners (Johnson, 1996; Macmillan & Gartner, 1996; Hotaling & Sugarman, 1986; Brinkerhoff & Lupri, 1988). The association between men's unemployment and violence against their female partners traditionally has been attributed to the stresses produced by unemployment and limited economic resources. But if this were the case, one would expect to find more evidence that women's unemployment is also associated with spousal violence, which is not the case. For those who see male violence against their partners as one resource for demonstrating power and control, the gender-specificity of the effects of unemployment is not surprising: men who lack more traditional resources (such as economic success) may "forge a particular type of masculinity that centers on ultimate control of the domestic setting through the use of violence" (Messerschmidt, 1993: 149).

Our data on intimate femicide are consistent with this interpretation. For women, employment status is not associated with differential risks of intimate femicide: 51% of women in both the victim population and the general population were employed during the period of our study. For men, however, employment status is associated with differential risks. Among intimate femicide offenders, 64% were employed, whereas among males in the general population, 73% were employed. In Ontario, then, male unemployment

appears to be associated with higher risks of intimate femicide offending.

Offenders' Violent Histories

Several studies have shown that men who kill their spouses frequently have histories of violent behaviour, both in and outside of their marital relationships (see Johnson, 1996). As Johnson notes, "[a]lthough some wife killings are the result of sudden, unforeseeable attacks by depressed or mentally unstable husbands and are unrelated to a history of violence in the family, most do not seem to fit this description" (1996: 183). Because of this, risk assessment tools designed to assess battered women's risk of lethal violence typically include measures of their partners' violence against their children and outside of the home, and threats of serious violence against their wives or others (see Campbell, 1995).

We also found evidence of unusual levels of violence in the backgrounds of the offenders in our sample. At least 31% of them had an arrest record for a violent offense.[17] At least 53% of them were known to have been violent in the past toward the women they ultimately killed. This corresponds to data for Canada as a whole which indicates that in 52% of spousal homicides of women between 1991 and 1993, police were aware of previous violent incidents between the spouses (Canadian Centre for Justice statistics, 1993). In addition, in at least 34% of the cases of intimate femicide, the offenders were known to have previously threatened their victims with violence.[18] At least 10% of the killings occurred while the offender was on probation or parole, or under a restraining order.

It is important to emphasize that these are minimum estimates of the number of offenders with violent and criminal histories. In over 200 of the 705 cases of intimate femicide we did not have enough information to determine if previous violence or police contact had occurred. Nevertheless, the information we were able to find clearly challenges the view that intimate femicides are typically momentary rages or heat-of-passion killings by otherwise non-violent men driven to act out of character by extreme circumstances.

A Summary of Risk Markers for Intimate Femicide

Women killed by their intimate male partners and the men who kill them are drawn from all classes, all age groups, all cultural and ethnic backgrounds. However, the victims of intimate femicide and their killers in our study did differ from other women and men in Ontario in some important respects: they were more likely than women and men in the general population to be separated from their partners, in common-law relationships, and to be Aboriginal. In addition, men who killed their intimate partners were also more likely to be unemployed and to have histories of criminal violence. These risk markers for intimate femicide have been noted in other research on spousal homicides, and have been interpreted from within various theoretical frameworks. We suggest that they are perhaps most consistent with a framework which views intimate femicide as the manifestation of extreme (if ultimately self-defeating) controlling and proprietary attitudes and behaviours by men toward their female partners.

CHARACTERISTICS OF THE KILLINGS

An adequate understanding of the sources of intimate femicide will need to take account of the particular characteristics of these killings. Prior research has devoted much less attention to these characteristics than to the characteristics of the individuals involved in the killings.[19] As a consequence, we are limited in both the comparisons we can draw between our findings and the findings from other research and in the interpretations we can offer of these findings.

Intimate femicides are typically very private acts: three-quarters of the victims were killed in their own homes and, in almost half of these cases,

in their own bedrooms. Less than 20% occurred in public places, such as streets, parks, workplaces, or public buildings. The most typical method was shooting: one-third of the victims were killed with firearms. Virtually all the other methods required direct and often prolonged physical contact between offenders and their victims: about two-thirds of the offenders stabbed, bludgeoned, beat, strangled, or slashed the throats of their victims.

One of the distinguishing features of intimate femicide is the extent and nature of the violence done to the victim. Unlike killings by women of their intimate partners,[20] intimate femicides often involve multiple methods or far more violence than is necessary to kill the victim. For example, in over half of the stabbings, offenders inflicted four or more stab wounds. Beatings and bludgeonings typically involved prolonged violence, leading some coroners to use the term "over-kill" to describe them. In about 20% of the cases, offenders used multiple methods against their victims, such as stabbing and strangling or beating and slashing. In about 10% of the cases, we also found evidence that the victim's body had been mutilated or dismembered.

The violence in these killings is much more likely to be sexualized than when women kill their intimate partners.[21] Records on approximately half of the cases in our study provided sufficient information for us to determine whether sexual violence was present. In 27% of these cases we found evidence that the victims had been raped, sodomized, or sexually mutilated; in another 22% of the cases the victim's body was found partially or completely unclothed.

Consumption of alcohol by offenders and/or victims was no more common in intimate femicides than in other killings: 39% of the offenders and 32% of the victims had been drinking immediately prior to the killing. In only 3% of the cases was there evidence of drug use by offenders or victims immediately prior to the killing.

Establishing the motives in these killings is fraught with difficulties, as suggested earlier. We made our own determination of the motive after reviewing all the information available to us. In about one-fourth of the cases we felt we had insufficient information to make a judgement about the offender's motive. In the remaining cases, one motive clearly predominated: the offender's rage or despair over the actual or impending estrangement from his partner. This motive characterized 45% of the killings in which we identified a motive. In contrast, women who kill their intimate partners only rarely kill out of anger over an estrangement (Browne, 1987; Daly & Wilson, 1988).

Suspected or actual infidelity of the victim was the motive in another 15% of the intimate femicides. In 10% of the cases the killing appears to have been the final act of violence in a relationship characterized by serial abuse.[22] In only 5% of the cases did stressful life circumstances — such as bankruptcy, job loss, or serious illness — appear to motivate the killer; and in only 3% of the cases was there evidence that the killer was mentally ill.

Another feature that distinguishes intimate femicide from intimate partner killings by women is the number of people who die as a result of these crimes. The 705 cases of intimate femicide resulted in the deaths of 977 persons. Most of these additional deaths were suicides by the offenders: 31% of the offenders killed themselves after killing their female partners.[23] But offenders killed an additional 74 persons, most of whom were children of the victims. In addition, over 100 children witnessed their mothers' deaths; thus, while they may have escaped physical harm, they obviously suffered inestimable psychological harm.

Our documentation of these characteristics of intimate femicide cannot sufficiently convey the complexity and context surrounding these crimes. Nevertheless, it serves important purposes. Comparing characteristics of intimate partner killings by males and females shows the distinctiveness of these two types of killings — a distinctiveness that is obscured in studies that treat intimate partner killing by men and women as instances of a single phenomenon. Compared to killings of men by intimate female partners, intimate femicides are much more likely to involve extreme and sexualized vio-

lence, to be motivated by anger over separation, to be followed by suicide of the offender, and to be accomplished by the killing of additional victims. These features highlight the gender-specificity of intimate partner killings and are consistent with a perspective on intimate femicide which views it as based in a larger system of gender[ed] inequality and stratification which perpetuates male control over women's sexuality, labour, and, at times, lives and deaths.

THE GENDER-SPECIFIC NATURE OF INTIMATE FEMICIDE

We have alluded to the gender-specific nature of intimate femicide at various points in our analysis. Here, we develop our ideas about this gender-specificity by considering what is known about gender differences in homicide more generally. We base this discussion on a large body of criminological research on homicide, as well as on data on over 7000 homicides collected by the first author as part of a separate research project.

Among those who study homicide, it is well known that women and men are killed in different numbers, by different types of people, and in different circumstances. Women are less likely to be victims of homicide than men in virtually all societies. Canada and Ontario are no different: men outnumbered women as victims of homicide by a ratio of approximately 2:1 in Canada and in Ontario between 1974 and 1994.

This may appear to indicate that women have a sort of protective advantage over men — that, at least in this sphere of social life, women are not disadvantaged relative to men. However, if we consider gender differences in offending, a different picture emerges. Men accounted for 87% of all homicide offenders in Ontario during these years; and males outnumbered females as offenders by a ratio of almost 7:1. When women were involved in homicides, then, they were almost three times more likely to be victims than offenders; when men were involved in homicides they were more likely to be offenders than victims. In other words, women are over-represented among victims and under-represented among offenders; for men, the opposite is true.

Women were also much more likely than men to be killed by someone of the opposite sex, as these figures imply. Fully 98% of all women killed in Ontario between 1974 and 1994 were killed by men. Only 17% of adult male victims were killed by women. Thus, man killing appears to be primarily a reflection of relations within a gender, whereas woman killing appears to be primarily a matter of relations between the genders. Because women are the majority of victims in cross-sex killings, such killings can be seen as one of the high costs to women of male dominance and desire for control in cross-sex relationships.

It is in intimate relationships between women and men that male dominance and control are most likely to erupt into physical violence. Women accounted for about 75% of all victims of spouse killings in Ontario during the last two decades.[24] So women outnumber men among victims of spouse killings by a ratio of about 3:1. Moreover, spousal homicides accounted for over 50% of all killings of women but less than 10% of all killings of men.

If males, unlike females, are not killed primarily by their intimate partners, who are they killed by and under what circumstances? In Ontario, about 60% of male victims are killed by acquaintances and strangers; another 20% are killed by unknown assailants. Most male-male homicides are the result of arguments or disputes that escalate to killings. In many cases, victim and offender have been drinking, and who becomes the victim and who the offender is a matter of happenstance.[25] One classic study of homicide (Wolfgang, 1958) concluded that male-male homicides, as an instance of the more generally physically aggressive behaviour of males, converge with notions of masculine identity.

When males kill their intimate female partners, their methods of and motives for killing take on a character distinctive from male-male killings — a character that denotes the gender-specificity of intimate femicide. As noted above, a substantial number of intimate femicides involved multiple methods, excessive force, and continued violence even after the woman's death would have been apparent.[26] The violence in intimate femicides also frequently involves some form of sexual assault, a very rare occurrence in killings of men.

The motives in intimate femicide also point to its gender-specificity. The predominance of men's rage over separation as a motive in intimate femicides has no obvious counterpart in killings of men — even killings of men by their intimate female partners. We agree with others who see this motive as a reflection of the sexual proprietariness of males toward their intimate female partners.

In sum, our analysis of intimate femicide and our review of other research and data on gender differences in homicide suggest that woman killing in general and intimate femicide in particular are uniquely gendered acts. By this we mean these killings reflect important dimensions of gender stratification, such as power differences in intimate relations and the construction of women as sexual objects generally, and as sexual property in particular contexts. Intimate femicide — indeed, probably most femicide — is not simply violence against a person who happens to be female. It is violence that occurs and takes particular forms *because* its target is a woman, a woman who has been intimately involved with her killer.

CONCLUSION

Our purpose in this paper has been to document the incidence and provide a description of the phenomenon of intimate femicide. For some, our approach may be unsatisfying, because we have not proposed a systematic explanation of nor outlined a detailed strategy for preventing these killings. Obviously explaining and preventing intimate femicides are critical tasks, but both require comprehensive knowledge of the phenomenon. The statistical data we have gathered and analyzed are intended to contribute to this knowledge.

Nevertheless, we recognize that our overview of the extent and character of intimate femicide in Ontario between 1974 and 1994 has raised at least as many questions as it has answered. Why, for example, did women's risks of intimate femicide increase slightly when public concern over and resources available to abused women were also increasing; when other forms of lethal violence were decreasing; and when criminal justice responses to intimate femicide were becoming more punitive? Why did some women — such as those in common-law relationships and Aboriginal women — face disproportionately high risks of intimate femicide? Were there other types of women with elevated risks of intimate femicide — for example, immigrant women or disabled women — whom we couldn't identify because of the limitations of our data? Why are intimate partner killings by men and women so distinctively different? All of these questions deserve answers, but the answers will require research that goes beyond the data and analysis we have been able to present in this paper.

There are other types of questions raised by our research that are more immediately pressing, questions about how to prevent intimate femicides. Our research has shown that intimate femicides are not the isolated and unpredictable acts of passion they are often believed to be. Most of the killers in our study had acted violently toward their partners or other persons in the past and many had prior contact with the police as a consequence. Many of the victims had sought help from a variety of sources. In a substantial portion of these intimate femicides, then, there were clear signs of danger preceding the killing, signs that were available to people who might have been able to intervene to prevent the crime. We believe this information could be combined with what we know about the risk factors for intimate femicide — such as estrangement — to develop interventions that would save women's lives.

As these and other analyses emphasize, preventing intimate femicides will require that the public as well as those working in fields relevant to the prevention of violence begin to see intimate femicide as a preventable crime. From our own and others' research on intimate violence, it should be apparent that these crimes are patterned and predictable. The

danger lies in maintaining the view that violence is inevitable, unavoidable, and inherent in intimate relationships. Such fatalism must be challenged, so that women's safety in and outside their homes is seen as an achievable and preeminent goal.

NOTES

1. For efforts to analyze the source of these variations in the sex ratio of spouse killings, see Margo Wilson & Martin Daly, 1992b; Regoeczi & Silverman, 1997.
2. See, for example, Peter D. Chimbos, 1978; Martin Blinder, 1985; James Boudoris, 1971; William Goode, 1969.
3. See, for example, Jacquelyn C. Campbell, 1992; Govind Kelkar, 1992; Isabel Marcus, 1994; Martha A. Mahoney, 1994.
4. Claustration means "the act of shutting in a cloister." Claustration practices, then, are any practices that are aimed at keeping women out of the public eye and out of public activity — e.g., wearing of clothes that cover the entire body, face, and head; limits on when and where women can be out in public; limits on whom women can interact with and under what circumstances, etc.
5. See, e.g., Allison Wallace, 1986; Kenneth Polk, 1994; Martin Daly & Margo Wilson, 1988; P. W. Easteal, 1993; R. Emerson Dobash & Russell P. Dobash, 1984.
6. Coroners' records are limited in another obvious and unavoidable way: they are observations removed in time and space from the actual killing. As a consequence, the description in the records will be shaped by the interests and perspectives of the observer. A coroner's perspective is that of an investigator after the fact and his/her primary interest is in determining the cause and means of death. Thus, the information recorded by coroners is intended to serve these purposes, not the interests of researchers.
7. Different procedures were used in the two studies to obtain access to municipal police

and OPP records. These records are not centrally compiled and it was impossible to contact and obtain cooperation from all of the forces around Ontario which investigate and keep records on cases of homicide.

8. Obviously, the coded data provide only a partial and, in some respects, an incomplete portrayal of intimate femicide. The lives and deaths of the women represented in these statistics cannot be sufficiently understood from counts and categorizations. For this reason, we devoted a considerable portion of our first study to reconstructing the stories of some of the women who died through interviews with their families and friends.

9. Our research has looked only at killings of females aged 15 and older because the killing of children differs in distinctive ways from the killing of adults.

10. The number of intimate femicides is undercounted in official records for other reasons as well. For example, in some cases of intimate femicide, the woman's death may be incorrectly classified as due to suicide, accident, or natural causes. Among the intimate femicides in our study, at least eight were not initially classified as homicides and only reclassified after further investigation. Another example of this occurred while this article was being written: the body of a southern Ontario woman who died by hanging was exhumed and an investigation revealed she had not killed herself, as originally determined, but had been killed by her boyfriend.

11. Of the cases of intimate femicide between 1974 and 1994, we found only three in which the offender was a woman.

12. Identifying differences between victims or offenders and women and men in the general population requires establishing the proportion of victims (or offenders) with the particular characteristic and comparing this to the proportion of women (or men) in the general population of Ontario during the years 1974–1994 with the same characteristic. If the former proportion is larger than the latter proportion, this indicates that women with that particular characteristic are over-represented among victims of intimate femicide. Tests for statistically significant differences are not appropriate here because the data are based on populations, not samples. Because we used information from census reports to determine the characteristics of women in the general population of Ontario, we were limited in our search for risk markers of intimate femicide to characteristics which are measured in the census.

13. By highlighting these characteristics, we do not mean to obscure the fact that women from all types of backgrounds and in all types of relationships are victims of intimate femicide; nor do we mean to imply that certain characteristics of women make them likely targets for intimate violence. Rather, we would suggest that certain groups of women may be more vulnerable to intimate violence because they share characteristics that have isolated them, limited their access to resources for protection, or prevented them from obtaining a level of personal security that many Canadians take for granted.

14. The average annual rate of intimate femicide (per 100 000 women aged 15 and older) for the years 1991–1994 was calculated by 1) dividing the number of victims durings those years (159) by the number of women aged 15 and older in the Ontario population in 1991 (4 130 450); 2) multiplying this figure by 100 000; and 3) dividing this figure by four (the number of years). This yields an average annual rate of .96 per 100 000 women aged 15 and older.

The average annual rate of intimate femicides of women living in common-law unions was calculated by 1) dividing the number of victims living common-law during those years (45) by the number of women aged 15 and older in Ontario living in common-law unions in 1991 (182 155); 2) multiplying this figure by 100 000; and 3) dividing this figure by 4.

This yields an annual average rate of 6.18 per 100 000 women aged 15 and older living in common-law unions.

15. See also, Christine Rasche, 1989; Wilson & Daly, 1993; Campbell, 1992.

16. See also Sharlene Frank, 1993; Ronet Bachmann, 1993.

17. Another 30% had been arrested and charged with non-violent criminal offenses.

18. In contrast, in only 6% of the cases were the victims known to have been violent toward their killers in the past; and in only 2% of the cases were the victims known to have previously threatened their partners with violence.

19. What researchers can describe about homicide and femicide is largely determined by the types of information officials collect. This means that many details about the events leading up to the killing, the dynamics of the interaction immediately preceding the killing, or the states of mind of victim and offender are absent or at most only hinted at in official reports. Some characteristics of intimate femicide can be easily and reliably determined, such as where they occurred or whether weapons were involved. Other characteristics — such as the offender's motivation — are more susceptible to post hoc reconstructions that introduce the inevitable biases of observers and officials. When we collected and coded information, we reviewed all the information available to us and made our own best judgements about these characteristics. We recognize, however, that our judgements are necessarily based on limited information about extremely complex events. Our discussion of the characteristics of the killings, therefore, should be viewed with these limitations in mind.

20. We base this and other conclusions about the characteristics of intimate partner killings by women on data from an ongoing study by the first author of over 7000 homicides in two Canadian cities and two U.S. cities over the twentieth century.

21. Indeed, none of the data or research with which we are familiar indicates that women who kill their intimate partners exact sexual violence against their victims.

22. This does not mean that offenders who appeared to act for other motives had not engaged in systematic abuse of the women they killed. Rather, it indicates that, in 10% of the cases, the only motive we could identify was systematic, serial abuse that ultimately led to the woman's death.

23. Other research has noted the high rates at which offenders suicide after intimate femicides, and has contrasted this to the rarity of suicides by women who kill their intimate partners (see, for example, Carolyn R. Block & A. Christakos, 1995). Daly and Wilson (1988) have suggested that this pattern is grounded in males' feelings of possessiveness and ownership over their partners.

24. We use the category "spouse killings" here because we could find no statistics on the number of men killed by intimate partners, only statistics of men killed by spouses. To be comparable, we compare these figures to the number of women killed by spouses — a subset of all intimate femicides.

25. Marvin Wolfgang (1967) has noted that where males are victims of homicide, victim-precipitation of the violence is fairly common.

26. Wolfgang (1967) found a similar pattern in his study of homicides in Philadelphia.

DISCUSSION QUESTIONS

1. Define "intimate femicide." Describe the patterns of intimate femicide in Ontario between 1974 and 1994.

2. What are the "causes" of intimate femicide?

3. Discuss similarities and differences between victims and offenders in intimate femicide.

4. What research needs to be done in this area? What kinds of studies might be designed to answer the critical questions raised by these authors?

REFERENCES

Bachmann, R. (1993). *Death and violence on the reservation: Homicide, family violence, and suicide in American Indian populations.* New York: Auburn House.

Blinder, M. (1985). *Lovers, killers, husbands, and wives.* New York: St. Martin's Press.

Block, C. R., & Christakos, A. (1995). Intimate partner homicide in Chicago over 29 years. *Crime and Delinquency, 41,* 496–526.

Boudoris, J. (1971). Homicide and the family. *Journal of Marriage and the Family, 32,* 667–676.

Brinkerhoff, M., & Lupri, E. (1988). Interspousal violence. *Canadian Journal of Sociology, 13,* 407–434.

Browne, A. (1987). *When battered women kill.* New York: The Free Press.

Browne, A., & Williams, K. (1989). Exploring the effect of resource availability on the likelihood of female-perpetrated homicides. *Law and Society Review, 23,* 75–94.

Campbell, J. C. (1992). "If I can't have you no one else can": Power and control in homicide of female partners. In J. Radford and D. E. H. Russell (Eds.), *Femicide: The politics of woman killing* (pp. 99–113). New York: Twayne.

Campbell, J. (1995). Prediction of homicide of and by battered women. In *Assessing dangerousness: Violence by sexual offenders, batterers, and child abusers* (pp. 96–113). Thousand Oaks, CA: Sage.

Canadian Centre for Justice Statistics. (1993). *Homicide survey.* Unpublished statistics.

Chimbos, P. D. (1978). *Marital violence: A study of interspousal homicide.* San Francisco: R & E Associates.

Crawford, M., Gartner, R., & Dawson, M., in collaboration with the Women We Honour Action Committee. (1997). *Woman killing: Intimate femicide in Ontario, 1991–1994.* Toronto: Women We Honour Action Committee.

Crawford, M., Gartner, R., & Women We Honour Action Committee. (1992). *Woman killing: Intimate femicide in Ontario, 1974–1990.* Toronto: Women We Honour Action Committee.

Daly, M., & Wilson, M. (1988). *Homicide.* New York: Aldine de Gruyter.

Dobash, R. E., & Dobash, R. P. (1984). The nature and antecedents of violent events. *British Journal of Criminology, 24,* 269–288.

Dobash, R. P., Dobash, R. E., Wilson, M., & Daly, M. (1992). The myth of sexual symmetry in marital violence. *Social Problems, 39,* 81.

Easteal, P. W. (1993). *Killing the beloved: Homicide between adult sexual intimates.* Canberra: Australian Institute of Criminology.

Frank, S. (1993). *Family violence in Aboriginal communities: A First Nations report.* British Columbia: Report to the Government of British Columbia.

Goode, W. (1969). Violence among intimates. In D. Mulvihill and M. Tumin (Eds.), *Crimes of Violence, vol. 131* (pp. 941–977). Washington, DC: USGPO.

Health and Welfare Canada. (1990). *Reaching for solutions: Report of the special advisor to the minister of national health and welfare on child sexual abuse in Canada.* Ottawa: Supply and Services.

Hotaling, G., & Sugarman, D. (1986). An analysis of risk markers in husband to wife violence: The current state of knowledge *Violence and victims, 1,* 101–124.

Johnson, H. (1996). *Dangerous domains: Violence against women in Canada.* Toronto: Nelson Canada.

Johnson, H., & Sacco, V. (1995). Researching violence against women: Statistics Canada's national survey. *Canadian Journal of Criminology, 3,* 281–304.

Kelkar, G. (1992). Women and structural violence in India. In J. Radford and D. E. H. Russell (Eds.), *Femicide: The politics of woman killing* (pp. 117–123). New York: Twayne.

Kennedy, L. W., Forde, D. R., & Silverman, R. A. (1989). Understanding homicide trends: Issues in disaggregating for national and cross-national comparisons. *Canadian Journal of Sociology, 14,* 479–486.

Long, D. A. (1995). On violence and healing: Aboriginal experiences, 1960–1993. In J. I. Ross (Ed.), *Violence in Canada: Sociopolitical perspectives* (pp. 40–77). Don Mills: Oxford University Press.

Macmillan, R., & Gartner, R. (1996). Labour force participation and the risk of spousal violence against women. Paper presented at the Annual Meetings of the American Society of Criminology.

Mahoney, M. A. (1994). Victimization or oppression? Women's lives, violence, and agency. In M. A. Fineman & R. Mykitiuk (Eds.), *The public nature of private violence: The discovery of domestic abuse* (pp. 59–92). New York: Routledge.

Marcus, I. (1994). Reframing domestic violence: Terrorism in the home. In M. A. Fineman & R. Mykitiuk (Eds.), *The public nature of private violence: The discovery of domestic abuse* (pp. 11–35). New York: Routledge.

Messerschmidt, J. W. (1993). *Masculinities and crime: Critique and conceptualization of theory.* Lanham, MD: Rowman and Littlefield.

Polk, K. (1994). *When men kill: Scenarios of masculine violence.* Cambridge: Cambridge University Press.

Rasche, C. (1989). Stated and attributed motives for lethal violence in intimate relationships. Paper presented at the Annual Meetings of the American Society of Criminology.

Regoeczi, W., & Silverman, R. (1997). Spousal homicide in Canada: Exploring the issue of racial variations in risk. Paper presented at the Annual Meetings of the American Society of Criminology.

Rodgers, K. (1994). *Wife assault: The findings of a national survey.* Ottawa: Canadian Centre for Justice Statistics.

Schneider, E. (1994). The violence of privacy. In M. Fineman & R. Mykitiuk (Eds.), *The public nature of private violence: The discovery of domestic abuse* (pp. 36–58). New York: Routledge.

Silverman, R., & Kennedy, L. (1993). *Deadly deeds: Murder in Canada.* Toronto: Nelson Canada.

Wallace, A. (1986). *Homicide: The social reality.* New South Wales: NSW Bureau of Crime Statistics and Research.

Wilson, M., & Daly, M. (1992a). Til death do us part. In J. Radford & D. E. H. Russell (Eds.), *Femicide: The politics of woman killing.* New York: Twayne.

Wilson, M., & Daly, M. (1992b). Who kills whom in spouse killings? On the exceptional sex ratio of spousal homicides in the United States. *Criminology, 30,* 189–215

Wilson, M., & Daly, M. (1993). Spousal homicide risk and estrangement. *Violence and Victims, 8,* 3–16

Wilson, M., & Daly, M. (1994). Spousal homicide. *Juristat,* Service Bulletin, *14*(8).

Wilson, M., Johnson, H., & Daly, M. (1995). Lethal and nonlethal violence against wives. *Canadian Journal of Criminology, 37,* 343.

Wolfgang, M. (1958). *Patterns in criminal homicide.* Philadelphia: University of Pennsylvania Press.

Wolfgang, M. (1967). *Studies in homicide.* New York: Harper and Row.

Women We Honour Action Committee, & Gartner, R. (1990). *Annotated bibliography of works reviewed for project on intimate femicide.* Toronto: Women We Honour Action Committee.

Organized Crime and Money Laundering[1]

MARGARET BEARE

INTRODUCTION

Defining Organized Crime

This paper argues that to the extent that the term "organized crime" is useful, the essential, unique, distinguishing characteristic about the concept is that it indicates a *process* or method of committing crimes, not a distinct type of crime in itself nor even a distinct type of criminal. Lupsha and Block argue a similar position when they speak of the organized crime process having certain "attributes and characteristics" (Lupsha, 1986: 33) and involving "the endless weaving of criminal conspiracies" (Block, 1990). There is a distinctive harm that organized criminals can deliver. This distinctive harm stems from the process by which the crimes — often consensual crimes — are committed. The crimes committed for profit are, themselves, often less serious than the fear stemming from the group's reputation. For instance, these groups are known for violence committed in order to eliminate competition or to avoid detection; they corrupt government officials; and they infiltrate legitimate businesses (Pennsylvania Crime Commission, 1991: 3).

A good description of organized crime must capture the essential aspects of the "process" that certain criminals use in carrying out criminal activity, increasingly within an international arena.

Whatever other differences there may be between organized crime activities, the operations should have the following in common (Maltz, 1990; Reuter, 1983):

- a criminal organization with the capability to use political corruption and/or the potential of violence
- a structure that allows the individual criminals to be removed and substituted without jeopardizing the viability of the criminal activity; and
- criminal activity committed via continuing criminal conspiracies (i.e., ongoing, repetitive, rather than one or two criminal acts for profit).

These "requirements" do not include the need for there to be a formal hierarchy as is depicted on the charts of the mob "families." While there usually is a structure, the formal nature of this structure varies considerably. While the governmental and academic debate used to focus on "how organized" and on whether a single omnipotent force or commission controls organized crime,[2] now the issues must focus more on the range of criminal activities to be included in the definition.[3] Organized transnational crimes of all sorts, including international economic crimes, international corporate crimes, drug trafficking, and terrorism funded through organized crime activity, compete with domestic organized crime for "fit" in the defined criteria for an organized crime process.[4]

Written for this volume. Adapted from the article that appeared in the fifth edition of *Crime in Canadian Society*.

The Evolution of Organized Crime

Organized crime is not static. Early forms of organized crime and linkages among criminal activities and criminal groups provide the foundation for current activities. History and economics unique to specific commodities, and political agreements, have all played a role in the creation of distinct criminal organizations. The criminals who operate in this manner evolve as markets change, as public demands change, as technology provides new options, and as law enforcement and regulatory efforts create new opportunities. Illicit activity responds to new legislation, new technology, and new forms of competition. Hence it is not the specific crimes that are key to understanding organized crime, but rather networks of criminal activity that are carried out via a particular process — defined to be an organized crime process.

When you take this approach, you discover that not only are the crimes diverse, but also the groups involved in the organized crime activity are very different from one another — in motivation, sophistication, longevity, and commitment to the criminal behaviour. Theories of organized crime causation and law enforcement strategies for control must take this diversity into account. In contrast, if you begin with a fixed idea of the supposed organized crime groups, the task becomes self-fulfilling. You will be restricted to finding that which you look for, and enforcement efforts will therefore be targeted mainly at the predetermined organized crime "threats."

Indeed, increases in the globalization of markets, financial institutions, and the electronic transfer of data mean that our understanding of organized criminal processes must continually evolve. The one constant is that the objective of organized crime is *profit*, and globally the search is on for profit-making opportunities. Gradually the message is being disseminated that organized criminals may be businessmen, politicians, financiers, bikers, and represent a full range of ethnic and racial backgrounds including First Nations, new immigrants, and born-in-Canada third or fourth generation citizens!

Legal Definitions

In addition to academic accounts of organized crime, the criminal justice systems of countries engaged in law enforcement against the phenomena that we term "organized crime" offer us legal definitions. While the term "organized crime" does not appear in the current English version of the Canadian Criminal Code (CC), the 1989 Proceeds of Crime legislation makes reference to the term "enterprise crime." In the French version of the CC, the phrase used is "*infraction de criminalité organisée.*" The CC reference to enterprise crime/*infraction de criminalité organisée* includes a list of 24 offences that are deemed to be enterprise/organized crimes and designated drug offences to which the Proceeds of Crime Legislation applies. New legislation passed in 1993 has added tobacco smuggling to this list (Bill C-102). In 1997 additional legislation recognized "criminal organizations" (Bill C-95, An Act to Amend the CC (criminal organizations) and to Amend Other Acts in Consequence). This new legislation does not make it a criminal offence to belong to a criminal organization, but if there is evidence of such membership, the legislation allows for enhanced police powers during the investigation and enhanced sentences if the suspect is convicted.

In Canada the following pieces of legislation provide the legal tools against organized crime and money laundering:

- ◆ 1988 — Bill C-58, The Mutual Legal Assistance in Criminal Matters Act (MLAT);
- ◆ 1989 — Bill C-61, The Proceeds of Crime Legislation;
- ◆ 1993 — Bill C-9, The Proceeds of Crime Money Laundering Act (record-keeping legislation);
- ◆ 1993 — Bill C-123, the Seized Property Management Act; and
- ◆ 1997 — Bill C-95, An Act to Amend the CC (criminal organizations) and to Amend Other Acts in Consequence.

Together they acknowledge that much serious crime today is international crime. This type of crime requires that diverse enforcement jurisdictions

Box 21.1

"Enterprise crime offence" (Section 462.3 of the Canadian Criminal Code) means an offence against any of the following provisions, namely:

- bribery of judicial officers;
- bribery of officials;
- frauds upon the government;
- breach of trust by public officer;
- corrupting morals;
- keeping gaming or betting house, betting, pool-selling;
- bookmaking;
- keeping common bawdy-house;
- procuring;
- murder;
- theft, robbery;
- extortion, forgery;
- uttering forged documents;
- fraud, fraudulent manipulation of stock exchange transactions;
- secret commissions;
- arson;
- making, possessing, or uttering counterfeit money;
- laundering proceeds of crime;
- tobacco smuggling;
- possession of property obtained by crime;
- designated drug offence;
- conspiracy or an attempt to commit the above;
- an act or omission anywhere that, if it had occurred in Canada, would have constituted an offence listed above.

Globalization of Markets and Organized Crime

To understand organized crime, one must understand the globalization of financial markets as well as the globalization of certain criminal activities. Organized criminals look for new opportunities, which are being offered by the growing body of facilitating laws and procedures that encourage legitimate cross-jurisdictional financial and business operations.

Contradictory pressures attempt to *facilitate* international trade while *curbing* international crimes. While we used to make a valid distinction between white collar crimes, corporate crimes, and organized crimes, increasingly white collar and corporate crimes are becoming global crimes and are being carried out in an organized crime manner. Likewise, with the recent police and prosecutorial targeting of criminal proceeds, we are more aware of how extensively white collar and corporate crimes are being intertwined into organized crime. Often this is done to move, hide, and increase via legitimate businesses the criminal proceeds. As Edelhertz and Overcast emphasize (1993: 168):

> In our view the data gathered in this study confirm the central importance of investigating and prosecuting white collar crime violations in proceeding against organized crime groups. . . . The body of embezzlement, fraud, breach of trust, and tax cases was truly impressive.[5]

Politics and Organized Crime

An opportunity for profit is synonymous with an opportunity for organized crime. Politics as well as economics can provide these opportunities. A good example of this is the recent fall of political structures in Eastern Europe, where the gaps between old structures and new regimes are being exploited by criminals — organized and otherwise. The opening up of borders, worldwide stock markets, and free-trade agreements occur simultaneously with increased awareness of international criminal

work together in order to deprive criminal operations of their illicit proceeds. In addition, the 1997 legislation acknowledges that it is hard for the police to use traditional police practices to build cases involving "criminal organizations." That enhanced sentences may be attached under this legislation also indicates that an ongoing pattern of criminal activity is perhaps more serious than individual criminal acts.

networks, international corporate and white-collar frauds, and international drug trafficking and money laundering schemes. Nationally and internationally, organized criminals trade in art objects, participate in high seas and highway piracy, operate stolen car networks and international credit card theft/fraud operations, engage in the illicit disposal of dangerous and toxic wastes, and orchestrate the distribution of smuggled cigarettes. All of these illicit activities supplement the more traditional organized crime activity of rackets, protection, prostitution, illegal gambling and criminal operations within legal gambling operations, and the biggest money maker of them all, illegal drugs.

Search for Illicit Markets

In 1993, a Russian mob operating out of New York collaborated with the Gambino organized crime family in New York City in what was claimed by law enforcement to be the largest fuel tax evasion scheme in U.S. history. As U.S. Attorney Michael Chertoff stated as he unsealed a 101 count federal indictment against 13 defendants: "This was a marriage between traditional organized crime and emerging organized crime" (quoted in *CLEU Line*, May 1994: 58).

If there is a greater sense of "danger" from the current organized crime activities, it is due to the *sophistication*, the *violence*, the *diversity*, and the *collaboration* of the operations. Control agencies can no longer treat organized crime groups as separate and competitive ethnic-based operations. Rather, business opportunities — licit or illicit — require market analysis that continually assesses shifting demand for commodities and shifting client groups/markets. To survive in this milieu, the organized crime groups are not only tolerating each other but building the networks required for efficient business operations.

While one may still challenge those analysts who make comparisons between the corporate organizational structure and the organized crime operational structure, the "thinking" of the organized crime operator has definitely become corporate. For example, Colombian cartels are actively changing markets and commodities in order to reach a wider buying public. If there is more money to be made in heroin, they will grow opium. If the image or expense of a particular drug is too restrictive, a different form and a "lower price special" will be arranged. Crack cocaine became the answer to enticing new cocaine users. Lowered introductory pricing of cocaine was correctly deemed important in order to introduce the drug into Russia. If the Eastern European/Russian markets are bigger than the North American market, they will obligingly serve them.

ORGANIZED CRIME ACTIVITIES IN CANADA

Organized crime activities involve all of the major forms plus every lesser profit-making criminal enterprise:

- narcotics
- extortion
- loan sharking
- organized white collar crimes, frauds, and scams
- smuggling of cigarettes, alcohol, guns, and other weapons
- smuggling and other illegal schemes involving the trafficking in aliens
- pornography, prostitution
- credit card theft and frauds
- murder/contract killings
- gambling — illegal operations and organized crime activities in legalized gaming facilities
- environmental crimes — trade in endangered species, hazardous waste
- motor vehicle theft
- money laundering activities

Canadian legislation recognizes the need for criminals to launder their proceeds in order to protect these illicit earnings from law enforcement and taxation. Under the new legislation, money laundering schemes *are* organized crime activities. Criminal sanctions may involve the seizure of legitimate and illegitimate enterprises purchased with criminal assets.[6]

ORGANIZED CRIME GROUPS

The point must be emphasized that, while it is necessary to discuss the involvement of ethnic groups in organized crime activities, literally all ethnic groups are involved to some extent. No ethnic group has shown itself to be immune from the lure of the exploitable illicit profit. The truth of this claim is perhaps best illustrated by the example of organized groups of Mennonites smuggling marijuana between Mexico and Canada. While some groups are of more concern currently than other groups, this fluctuates over time. As Dubro stated in *The Globe and Mail*:

> "Organized crime is not a racial construct, although it is a sad fact that many criminal organizations are restricted to criminals of the same ethnic background . . . just about every ethnic group has participated in a major way in organized crime over the years . . ."(March 25, 1993: A16)

Given the diversity and integrated nature of Canadian organized crime, no creditable analyst would suggest that organized crime is an "alien conspiracy" inflicted upon Canada by foreign "ethnic" enclaves. Therefore, one must clarify why it is important to specify the ethnic connections that run through some organized crime activity. To suggest that ethnic groups are involved in organized crime is not to imply that there is any particular proclivity to criminal activity on the part of these identified groups, but rather to indicate that there are very real advantages gained from creating a *closed and loyal* criminal operation. One way to succeed is to create a group that is difficult to penetrate and has a loyalty or commitment that extends beyond making money. Outlaw motorcycle gangs achieve this unity through their club rules, initiation rites, willingness to retaliate, and lifestyle. Another way to achieve loyalty and cohesion is through ethnicity requirements. The ethnic factor

- ◆ may make it difficult for the police to use undercover operators to penetrate the group;
- ◆ may increase loyalty if actual families or community members are involved;
- ◆ may facilitate international organized crime by enabling the use of intimidation and extortion between countries of origin and the new country; and
- ◆ may result in an ability to control criminal activity from the first stage of production, to importing, and through to the final stage of street selling.

Therefore organized crime represents a marketplace, and *all ethnic and racial groups*, with varying visibility or exclusiveness, are involved. In analyses of current large police investigations, what one sees are relatively stable networks of individuals who are prepared to commit criminal activity and interact with one another in order to most efficiently accomplish the criminal tasks and make the largest amount of profit. In some instances the groups are recent immigrants with ethnic ties but just as often the group is "bonded" by little more than crime and profit.

Groups operating as organized criminals in Canada[7] are often listed according to the following categories (Stamler, 1992; CACP, 1993; Sacco and Kennedy, 1994):

- ◆ "traditional" Italian organized crime families
- ◆ Asian Triads, Vietnamese gangs
- ◆ Aboriginal organized crime groups
- ◆ outlaw motorcycle gangs
- ◆ Colombian cartels
- ◆ Russian organized crime groups
- ◆ Nigerian groups
- ◆ Eastern European groups
- ◆ Jamaican organized crime
- ◆ Japanese Yakuza

With a non-inclusive list that is this long, clearly the merit of even making a list vanishes. The organized crime activity has to do with *profit*, and while individuals make the decision whether or not to participate in these forms of crime, no group is exempt from some degree of participation.

Traditional Italian Organized Crime

The terms typically used in the literature to describe organized crime groups are quite euphemistic in that "traditional" is quickly seen to refer to the Italian groups: Mafia, La Cosa Nostra, and `Ndrangheta. While the term "mafia" is often used quite loosely to refer to "organized crime" in general, the term was originally used to refer to Sicilian-related organized crime. La Cosa Nostra relates to American-based organized crime; and `Ndrangheta is the Calabrian Mafia or Calabrian organized crime.

All of the provinces with active Mafia-related organized crime identify drugs as a major revenue producing commodity, but in no way an exclusive criminal activity. Illegal gaming, stock-market manipulation, frauds, loan-sharking, union racketeering, counterfeiting, extortions, control of aspects of the construction industry and the food supply industry, distribution of illicitly operated video poker machines, and money laundering all contribute to their criminal proceeds. Of concern to law enforcement, in addition to the actual criminal activity, is their extensive investment in legitimate businesses. These operations are used to invest their profits, serve in a money laundering capacity, and function as a cover or front for criminal operations. As indicated by the Edelhertz/Overcast (1993) U.S. study, the connections between criminal operations often weave through legitimate operations. However, in most cases even these legitimate operations will not be run totally legitimately. The resources available to the criminal organizations provide unfair advantage over any competition, and depending on the nature of the business there will likely be "services" that further the criminal operations that the legitimate business can perform.

The willingness for so-called ethnic-based organized criminals to work with other criminals is perhaps most evident in the seemingly compatible working relationships between the Italian Mafia operations and the outlaw motorcycle gangs. Their mutual involvement in the trafficking of drugs forms the basis for this cooperative association. Manitoba, Ontario, and Quebec report these links between the traditional organized crime operations and the outlaw motorcycle gangs and also cooperative relations between the Sicilian and the Calabrian Mafia operations — across Canada, the United

States, and internationally. Specific police projects such as "Green Ice" and "Contrat-Compote-Creditor" (mentioned in some detail later in this chapter) indicate an increasing willingness of the Mafia to work with the Colombian cartels to facilitate international cocaine trafficking.

Asian Triads and Vietnamese Gangs

All provinces have some Asian organized crime, but the centres for this activity seem to be British Columbia, Ontario, and Quebec, with significant activity in Alberta and Manitoba. While the crimes may be similar to those perpetrated by the traditional "Mafia" organizations, law enforcement emphasizes the violence and the automatic weapons that are often connected with the Asian organized crime operations. There was considerable fear leading up to 1997 that there might be an increase of Asian criminals coming into Canada to avoid the Chinese takeover of Hong Kong. This increase has not seemed to materialize; however, the current level of criminal activity and illicit profit generated by these organizations is considerable.

More so than any other category of organized crime groups, the Asian operations are difficult to police. Asian communities are only recently beginning to turn to the police for protection from the crime and extortion perpetrated upon them by Asian criminals. The silence, language, and cultural

---

Box 21.2

Triads originated in the mid-seventeenth century in China. They consisted of secretive societies working to overthrow the ruling Manchu or Ch'ing Dynasty through overt force and subversion. They derive their name, the Triads, from the groups' sacred picture, a triangle whose three sides represent heaven, earth, and man, the three basic forces of nature for the Chinese (CACP, *Organized Crime Committee Report*, 1993: 47).

differences combine with a different orientation toward relying on external public police. These factors have meant that trust has had to be slowly earned before the police could expect assistance from inside some of these communities. Part of this building of trust was a slow process of recruiting Asian police officers onto urban Canadian police forces and in some cases recruiting trained police from Hong Kong for this task. While these criminals do not restrict their operations to within their own ethnic communities, these citizens are particularly victimized. The police have identified a number of schemes that specifically target Asian people. For example, the Big Circle Boys created a shell corporation and advertised for employees in the Chinese daily newspaper. By this means, this gang gathered identification and personal information on over 100 would-be victims and used this data to apply for credit, open bank accounts, and pass forged cheques (CACP, 1993: 52).

Law enforcement officials have identified a number of key Triad operations including the Kung Lok, 14K, Sun Yee On, United Bamboo, and Wo Hop To (CACP, 1993; U.S. Senate "New International Criminal and Asian Organized Crime," 1992; U.S. Senate Hearings, 1992.) Other groups are associated with these main operations — including the Big Circle Boys or Dai Huen Jai gang. In addition to the Chinese/Hong Kong gangs, Vietnamese gangs operate across Canada, and Quebec has recently identified a newer gang made up of members from Cambodia. Utilizing a combination of intimidation and force, these gangs commit a vast array of crimes, including extortion, illegal gambling and legalized gaming frauds, smuggling (aliens, alcohol, and cigarettes), trafficking in cocaine and heroin, prostitution, home invasions,[8] sophisticated frauds including credit card schemes, organized break and enters, and forgery.

Aboriginal Organized Groups

While only a small percentage of Aboriginal reserve members are involved in criminal activities, I am including Aboriginal organized crime since it is such a perfect example of a "manufactured" organized crime problem. As Akwesasne Chief Mike Mitchell stated on CBC Newsworld (July 23, 1991, time 19:30):

> The money — it's unbelievable the money you can make and it's so easy . . . You can buy a pack of cigarettes on the American side of the reservation for $1.58 and you go across here in Cornwall and you have to buy it for close to $7.00 a pack, same pack, within a short distance of each other, so no one is surprised that all this is happening.

Until February 1994, Canadian cigarettes were sold "duty and tax exempt" for export to foreign jurisdictions such as the U.S., St. Pierre and Miquelon, and Europe, where they are subject to foreign taxes, and also to special categories of customers such as through duty-free stores, embassies, and the Aboriginal reserves. As the price differences widened, the tax-exempt status became increasingly valuable and hence vulnerable to exploitation. As with the bootleggers in the 1920s, the public has felt some sympathy for the entrepreneurs who have chosen to turn a "bad" tax into a "good" profit (Stamler, 1992, 1993).

In economic terms, the cigarette trade was comparable to drug trafficking. An automobile crossing into Canada with 10–15 cases of cigarettes had a potential to make, in a single trip, a profit of $14 250. A single tractor trailer loaded with 1200 cases of cigarettes could make a profit of $1 140 000 (RCMP and Customs estimate).

Most of the contraband was Canadian tobacco smuggled back across the 7000 km U.S./Canada border and through the French-owned islands of St. Pierre and Miquelon off the coast of Newfoundland. Of perhaps the greatest concern is the key role played by the three Indian reserves located along the U.S./Canada border — the Akwesasne Reserve that straddles Ontario, Quebec, and New York; Kahnawake Reserve in Quebec; and the St. Regis Reserve in New York. Aboriginal criminals within the Aboriginal community made use of their legitimate group status (location of the reserves, rights accruing to reserve members, jurisdictional disputes regarding policing of reserves) in order to facilitate carrying out specific types of organized crimes. Illegal gaming operations plus smuggling of cigarettes and alcohol, and, in some areas, involvement in alien smuggling are the main organized crimes carried out by these groups. These are "opportunistic" crimes in the sense that a significant profit-making opportunity is taken advantage of, rather than sought out and developed. The ambiguity surrounding the self-government rights of the reserve members added another dimension to these criminal activities and contributes to the justifications for committing these acts and continuing to operate alternative smuggling businesses.

Outlaw Motorcycle Gangs

Belonging to a motorcycle club is a legitimate pastime, and motorbikes appear to be one of the purchases that aging baby boomers are increasingly making. Unfortunately, in addition to the motorbike clubs there are the outlaw clubs that combine riding with committing serious organized crimes. Within the last few years these organized crime operations have changed greatly. Not only have they begun to link into the influence networks controlled by the Mafia organizations with whom they affiliate, but they now have their own connections into the economic and social establishment. In addition to the links forged by the actual club members, police intelligence from Quebec indicates that the Hell's Angels are using their spouses and other close associates to infiltrate and gain information from legitimate businesses and government departments (*RCMP Gazette*, 1994).

Police intelligence indicates that in addition to the crimes that these outlaw members commit independently, they have begun to operate with the Mafia to carry out organized crimes. The large August 1994 RCMP case titled "Contrat-Compote-Creditor" involved the Hell's Angels operating as international drug distributors for the Mafia out of London, England. While initially they were used in secondary roles or as "debt collectors" and hitmen for more sophisticated operations, they have now gained the sophistication to carry out their

own complex organized crimes and to operate in a more equal partnership with other criminal groups. Police believe that these affiliations are being made in jails. Their criminal activities include drug trafficking and manufacturing of narcotics, extortion, prostitution, contract killing, frauds, fencing of stolen property, and money laundering. There are over 41 separate outlaw clubs across Canada; the two main clubs with national and international status are the Hell's Angels and the Outlaws. In some provinces, such as Quebec, the Hell's Angels control all of the exotic dancer clubs and control many other bars through extortion and intimidation.

Policing outlaw motorcycle gangs is problematic for the same sorts of reasons that it is difficult to police ethnic gangs. It is very difficult for the police to gain entry into these clubs due to strict membership and initiation rites and the expectations to commit certain criminal acts. Likewise, informants are rare due to the retaliation that would befall the individual. In addition, police have acknowledged that, organizationally, outlaw clubs have begun to use sophisticated counter-surveillance equipment and security on their premises. Outlaw motorcycle club members have "come a long way." They are no longer the scruffy, brawling gang members, but are increasingly businessmen with the education and specialized skills that enable them to orchestrate financial frauds and complex laundering schemes (CACP, 1993: 10). The "biker war" between the Hell's Angels and the Rock Machine motorcycle gang in Quebec during spring 1997 was instrumental in providing pressure on the government to pass the 1997 "Criminal organizations" (Bill C-95) legislation. This legislation was referred to in the media as the "anti-gang" Bill.

Colombian Cartels and Newer Forms of Organized Crime

Specifically in terms of drug trafficking, mention must be made of the significant role played by Colombian cartel organizations. There is evidence that these criminals — involved mainly in the importation and trafficking of cocaine — are increasingly prepared to work collaboratively with other organized crime groups such as the Mafia and are prepared to broaden their range of criminal commodities to include heroin. Several large police sting operations have revealed the large amounts of illicit proceeds that these organizations must launder on a continual basis, indicating a huge criminal enterprise. Other organized crime groups involved in drug trafficking include Nigerian operations, Japanese Yakuza or Boryokudan groups, and Jamaican trafficking groups known as "posses."

Russian Organized Crime

Russian organized crime is as much of a problem for Canada as for other countries. Police investigations indicate a wide and to some extent unruly range of criminal activity committed by Russian organized criminals. There is a recognition that these criminals use excessive violence, including seemingly haphazard retaliation and murder. Canadian and U.S. law enforcement agencies are still determining the nature of these operations. While some of these criminals appear to be operating in an organized crime manner, others are more independent street criminals who look for and find opportunities to commit frauds or steal. Internationally, authorities are increasingly concerned with the potential for Russian organized criminals, working with criminals from countries including Colombia and Spain, to be involved in the smuggling and sale of nuclear weapons–quality plutonium.

Criminal Activities and Criminal Groups

Looking at organized crime as separate categories makes it appear to operate in far too "insular" a manner. In reality, few organized crime activities are the domain strictly of any one organized crime group, and likewise, any one organized crime group is most likely involved in more than one form of criminal activity. We see, for example, significant overlay and interdependence of one organized crime group on another. Woven between these organized crime operations are some violent

"independent" operations — Russians and other newcomers — who are gradually beginning to fit into the ongoing criminal landscape.

The "Facilitators" of Organized Crime: Professionals as Criminals

There is also a fringe group around the organized criminal activity that involves the "facilitators" of the crimes. As these criminal activities become increasingly sophisticated and extensive, the organizations must recruit or hire the providers of "services" such as money launderers, accounting and legal advisers, computer specialists, and others with professional expertise. When these individuals are knowing participants to the criminal activity, then they are themselves criminals. The most valued segment of this fringe group is of course the public, which agrees to purchase the illegal commodities, consents to participate in laundering schemes, and in numerous ways elevates the position of criminal to that of a respected member of society. An analysis of organized crime must somehow capture these interconnections between the core criminal and the facilitators; the legitimate and the illegitimate activities; the criminal operations and the changing environment (changing government policies, economic conditions, and competing operations).

CRIMINAL JUSTICE RESPONSE: FOCUS ON MONEY LAUNDERING

A current law enforcement focus recognizes the importance of following and seizing the illicit proceeds of the organized crime network. No longer is the emphasis placed on arresting individuals, but rather on "hurting" the organization by taking their proceeds of crime. Ironically, therefore, a major problem for many large-scale organized crime groups is the cash that their crimes generate. They must continually turn their illicit proceeds into some non-suspicious, spendable form that has the appearance of legitimate earnings through a process called *money laundering*. Failure to successfully "process" their criminal proceeds can result in detection, conviction, and the potential seizure and forfeiture of the illicit profits made from criminal activity. While we often dismiss the eventual arrest and conviction of Al Capone as having been merely for income tax evasion, in fact his failure was a failure to adequately launder his illicit proceeds and then, having done this, a failure to put into place the evasive strategies that his legitimate colleagues use to lawfully reduce the amounts owing to Internal Revenue. These are not today mere bookkeeping operations, but rather represent the tasks of financial advisors hired full-time to work for "serious" organized crime groups.

Definition of Money Laundering

Money laundering involves a multi-stage process, and while the term is often used with little precision, a thorough laundering process will culminate in the creation of the *perception* of a legitimate source or legitimate ownership of the illicit proceeds. Based on the U.N. definition, a study on money laundering in Canada (Beare and Schneider, 1990) argues that money laundering usually involves the following:

- the conversion of illicit cash to another asset, often involving the "placement" of the funds into a financial institution;
- the concealment of the true source or ownership of the illegally acquired proceeds, possibly through a technique referred to as "layering" whereby a series of otherwise legitimate transactions are carried out creating a paper-trail that is hard or impossible to follow; and
- the creation of the perception of legitimacy of source and ownership. By this stage the funds may be "integrated" into the legitimate economy.

The greater the volume of proceeds and the more frequent the laundering transactions, the more sophisticated the scheme that must be developed. Similar to experiences in other countries, research in Canada indicates that 80% of the laundering cases had an international dimension (Beare and Schneider, 1990).

Business and Financial Institutions Used in Money Laundering Schemes

A study of the case material from Canada, Australia, and the United States indicates that similar vulnerable financial and business institutions are being used by money launderers. In some instances these are the result of the nature of the legitimate operation, and in other circumstances there is a regulatory or enforcement gap that is exploited by the launderers. The following functions have been identified in the Canadian *Tracing of Illicit Funds* report (Beare and Schneider, 1990), the Australian *Taken to the Cleaners: Money Laundering in Australia* (Australia, NCA, 1991), and separate U.S. reports including the *Assessment of Narcotics Related Money Laundering* (Department of the Treasury, FinCEN):

- deposit-taking institutions
- currency exchange houses
- securities industry
- insurance industry
- real estate
- casino operations
- lawyers and accountants
- travel industry
- luxury goods industries
- incorporation and operation of companies
- gold market/ precious gems/ jewellery stores

Laundering Schemes

Laundering schemes range from the very simple to the professionally created, highly complex international interweaving of illicit and licit funds. A simple laundering vehicle would be a tavern, laundry, vending machine company, pizza parlour — any business that deals in cash and has a "stock" that can be manipulated. Criminals can claim that their legitimate businesses generated a greater profit than was actually the case. The difference between the real profit and the claimed profit is the amount of money that is laundered. Some other types of businesses that have huge budgets and are highly specialized can be used in slightly more complex schemes. For example, dredging, waste, scrap metal, construction, and development are attractive industries for large-scale laundering schemes. The Canadian Hamilton Harbour dredging scandal in the mid-1970s is a perfect example of the use of these large-budget industries to launder funds on an ongoing basis.

This scheme began with a conspiracy among dredging companies to rig their bids and agree among themselves whose turn it was to win the contract. Rindress, vice-president of the J.P. Porter dredging company is quoted as having testified:

> . . . price-fixing has been going on in the dredging industry for at least thirty to forty years. . . . companies maintain "score cards" to keep track of whose turn it is to bid high on a given contract and how much the company awarded the contract must pay as compensation for the others bidding high. (Freeman and Hewitt, 1979: 162)

The funds that were laundered were from fraudulent work-orders, false invoices, and direct pay-offs. The illicit profits were absorbed into the paperwork of operating their dredging companies. Few people, aside from other dredgers, are aware of what are legitimate costs in these operations. The full investigation of this particular conspiracy revealed a more complicated international laundering and corruption scheme than would fall under this category in our typology. However, the basic formula was one of price-fixing and the hiding of these illicit funds in a simple invoice scam.

The really sophisticated launderers and the criminals with a large, ongoing amount of illicit proceeds to launder must resort to international laundering schemes. The focus on money laundering within Canada and other Western countries has progressed beyond the days when a criminal could, with little risk, take frequent gym bags of cash into the bank of his or her choice. One makes this claim a bit hesitantly! However, bank awareness programs and new legislation add a culpability factor to persuade people against knowingly facilitating money laundering. Off-shore laundering havens, shell corporations, legitimate businesses, smuggling, wire-transfers, loan

---

Box 21.3

The invoice to J.P. Porter was from Wm. Seymour, Electrical Contractor, 1223 Gerrard Street East, Toronto. It carried an apparently legitimate work-order number: HAM 224A-70. It was for expected services: overhaul of diesel engine, etc. $3250; rewinding of generator, $4780; replace wiring, $2640; check and clean . . . for a total of $13 500. The work was said to have been completed August 25, 1970. . . . Stamler (Rod T. Stamler, RCMP) had almost passed the invoice by when he realized something about it bothered him: there was no telephone number. How many businesses didn't display telephone numbers on their invoices. . . . Stamler dawdled along behind a Gerrard Street streetcar looking for 1223, expecting to find a business of some sort there. What he found was a typical Toronto semi-detached house. . . . The bogus invoice was a key to a door that led to a criminal mind or two — but whose? (Quoted in Palango, 1994: 114.)

---

scams, and invoice manipulations may all be a part of these international laundering schemes.

Andelman (1994) describes a fairly simple scheme that he refers to as the "equivalent of the eighteenth-century Triangular Trade." In modern times, this triangle involves Colombian drug traffickers who purchase legitimate products such as coffee and leather using Colombian bank loans secured with letters of credit from Panamanian banks backed by drug-generated cash. The legitimate product, i.e., tens of millions of dollars of coffee, is sold in the United States and the proceeds are transferred to shell corporations in Europe. The funds in the bank accounts are at this stage the legitimate proceeds of a coffee transaction.

"Operation Green Ice"

Operation Green Ice may serve to illustrate some of the complexities of current money laundering cases. This 1992 international case illustrates the global reach of criminal operations and the increasing globalization of some policing efforts. This case, headed by the DEA, involved the work of law enforcement officers operating in the United States, Italy, Spain, Costa Rica, Colombia, United Kingdom, Cayman Islands, and Canada. The United States referred to it as being the first operational international task force formed to combat money laundering. At the end of the initial phase of this project, approximately 192 arrests had been made, and approximately $54 million in cash and property was seized worldwide. Perhaps most importantly, this case established the links between Colombian cocaine cartels and the Mafia organizations in Italy (Sicily, Naples, and Calabria) and the United States. In terms of "king-pin" arrests, officials claim to have arrested seven of the top money managers of the Colombian Cali drug cartel. From a Canadian perspective, "Green Ice" represents one of the first tangible results generated by the newly created Integrated Anti-Drug Profiteering Units funded under Canada's Drug Strategy.

The objective of the project was to infiltrate money laundering enterprises of targeted kingpin organizations that were run by leaders of the major Colombian cocaine cartels, particularly the Cali cartel. Undercover agents posed as money laundering facilitators and used informants to identify several major drug money brokers in Colombia. These Colombian brokers acted as intermediaries between Cali cartel kingpins in Colombia and money laundering organizations in the United States. Beginning in San Diego and Los Angeles, the investigations took undercover agents to Houston, Ft. Lauderdale, Miami, Chicago, and New York to pick up money and to establish "fronts," i.e., leather shops which were then used to launder drug money profits by the importation of merchandise that then legitimized the currency held in banks in Colombia. As the case developed, undercover agents were asked to provide money laundering services in Europe, Canada, and the Caribbean. In the United Kingdom, Her Majesty's Customs and Excise service was involved; in Italy, the Servico Centrale Operativo; in

Spain, the National Police; in the United States, the DEA; and in Canada, the Royal Canadian Mounted Police. In order to assist the DEA investigation, the RCMP carried out a parallel operation in Canada to accommodate the transfer of money from a Montreal-based cocaine trafficker. Three deliveries of cash totalling approximately $3 million were made to RCMP undercover operators. On September 24, 1992, $1 075 000 was subject to seizure.

Role of Lawyers as Facilitators of Crime

Most of the notorious organized crime cases have had a lawyer involved in both the creation and implementation of the laundering schemes — and of course at the stage of defending the suspect if charged. Lawyers can operate knowingly as an accomplice in the laundering scheme or as an innocent facilitator. The 1986 U.S. Commission on Organized Crime spoke of the "renegade" or "mob-connected" lawyers. Former U.S. Attorney General Meese equated a professional money launderer to a "fence" utilized by a burglar. At the more extreme end of lawyer corruption is the unique "specialization" within law whereby individuals become intimately involved by choice in the laundering schemes of their clients. A 1998 U.N. report on money laundering titled *Financial Havens, Bank Secrecy and Money Laundering* emphasizes the role of lawyers in the laundering of illicit proceeds, and specifically argues that the lawyer-client privilege of confidentiality ought not to apply in cases where the funds that the lawyer is protecting have resulted from criminal activity.

It becomes an interesting legal question at what point a lawyer assisting criminals to carry out their legal (if not illegal) dealings becomes a mobster. *Time* magazine was sued for libel by Frank Ragano in 1966 after they printed a photograph showing Ragano at a restaurant having dinner with major Mafia bosses. Ragano had by this time been acting as a lawyer for the Mafia for over ten years, and yet he expressed shock at being classified in this manner. At the trial, Robert Blakey, testifying for *Time*, stated that he considered Ragano a "house counsel" and a "functional part" of Cosa Nostra because of his long association and frequent social meetings with Santo Trafficante: "When a lawyer showed up at night to post bail for Mafia figures and defended them at grand jury hearings, you can assume he's in bed with them" (Ragano and Raab, 1994: 247).

The Canadian and the Australian money laundering reports identified the same list of laundering "services" offered by lawyers.[9] While each of these functions is important, the lawyer's ability to act on behalf of, and in the name of, the client in a nominee role is extremely useful:

- providing a nominee function;
- incorporating companies;
- conducting commercial and financial transactions;
- managing and physically handling illicit cash;
- coordinating international transactions; and
- buying and selling real estate.

Gary Hendin represents one of Canada's most famous "professional" money launderers. A disbarred lawyer, Hendin pleaded guilty to charges involving the laundering of $12 000 000 over a three year period (Beare and Schneider, 1990: 318–319). The flow-chart that the police created from this case illustrated the benefits of a multi-focused scheme. Hendin operated under the auspices of a construction company, which in fact was a company owned and controlled by the criminal organization, purchased real estate, made use of a Currency Exchange house, opened law practice trust accounts for the criminal proceeds, registered a mortgage against properties, and used a tax haven country for source of the funds.

"Contrat-Compote-Creditor"

On August 31, 1994, the RCMP out of Montreal announced the culmination of a four year undercover operation — a three part operation called "Contrat-Compote-Creditor." Twenty-six persons with international connections were charged with conspiracy to traffic in cocaine and money laundering over $100 000 000. This case was claimed to be

the largest money laundering Canadian case to date. Over 200 bank accounts in 29 banking institutions were frozen, including all of the records and bank accounts of 34 companies. Of particular interest was the collaborative working arrangement between the Colombian cartels, traditional Italian Mafia, and the Hell's Angels (and their lawyers). Three lawyers were arrested and charged with laundering the proceeds of crime. Criminal operations such as this would be impossible without the knowing assistance of lawyers — or teams of lawyers.[10]

Lawyers are a powerful lobby group who have been granted special privileges argued to be necessary in order to protect the legitimate privileged relationship between lawyers and their clients. In October 1989, the U.S. Internal Revenue Service launched a national operation, titled the "Attorney's Project," that targeted lawyers for failure to provide details about their cash-paying clients. The lawyers claimed that this filing violated their attorney-client privileges (*Money Laundering Alert*, 1989, Vol. 1, No. 3). Similar resistance took place in Canada in relation to protecting the lawyer-client privileges from what was seen to be the intrusiveness of the newly introduced Bill C-89, Money Laundering Act (Resolutions, 1991 CBA Annual Meeting). This legislation was passed, but not without negotiations with the Canadian Bar Association (CBA). The automatic claim of lawyer-client privilege was made, even though the legislation in question required only that records be kept of transactions over $10 000 cash "to be paid or transferred on another's behalf."

Even with appropriate legislation in place, police cases involving lawyers become particularly problematic. The U.S. President's Organized Crime Commission (1985) spoke of the need for "sting" operations, undercover agents, and electronic surveillance in order to break through the attorney-client privilege that otherwise would be "an impenetrable shield protecting lawyers who engage in a wide variety of criminal actions" (quoted in Beare and Schneider, 1990: 331). In Canadian court cases in the early 1990s, there has been increased difficulty for police in building cases against lawyers. For example, the *R. v. Duarte* decision specifies that authorizations are now required for electronic surveillance in evidence-gathering undercover operations involving private communications. The fear is that judges signing the authorizations and other lawyers assisting the police to prepare the authorization requests may be hesitant to target other lawyers. This fear may be unfounded. While police experiences vary across Canada, there is some evidence that the legal profession has reached a point of wanting to "clean out" criminal, compromised, or incompetent lawyers.

In addition to the role of the lawyer as willing or unsuspecting accomplice in the laundering activities, one of the "services" that lawyers provide is legal defence in the often long and complicated trials of charged suspects. Much debate continues as to whether lawyers' fees should be exempt from the seizure and forfeiture provisions of a country's proceeds of crime/anti-organized crime legislation. The United States does not exempt the fees; Australia does (except Queensland); Canada does — amid continuing controversy.

CONCLUSION

Organized crime activity is market driven and socially, politically, and economically defined. No one ethnic group has a monopoly on looking for and finding opportunities to profit by the existence of desirable commodities that have been defined as illegal. The "answers" to combatting organized crime are varied and include looking at the potential legalization of some commodities and raising the risks for criminal operations.

Targeting the "proceeds" is a popular law enforcement focus which must be carefully regulated and monitored by clear policies. The difficulty with any straightforward response to organized crime is that it tends to ignore the complexities — the interwoven nature of organized crime with the political, social, and economic fabric of the society; the resistance of separate police forces to true collaboration on an ongoing basis; and the fact that different nations have very different priorities, and

in some instances organized crime may be seen to serve these priorities rather than diminish them.

NOTES

1. While I am responsible for all errors made, I would like to acknowledge the assistance received from the police community and from ex-police officers, including Inspector Wayne Blackburn, Rodney Stamler, Frederick Martens, and many other people working within the OPP, RCMP, and CACP. This paper resulted from research I completed for *Criminal Conspiracies: Organized Crime in Canada*, published in 1996 by Nelson Canada.

2. It is truly time to move beyond this debate, which has consumed an inordinate amount of energy. Fixating on a monolithic Italian criminal conspiracy has diverted attention away from the diverse alternative forms of organized crime. The court transcripts, sworn testimony, and other evidence have justified the law enforcement targeting of these organized crime groups, but not as the sole target as was perhaps arguably the case for a period of years.

3. While it is important to be inclusive of new forms of organized crime, some definitions are so broad as to render the term somewhat useless. For example, a report completed in 1998 for the federal department of the Solicitor General (Porteous, 1998) omits the requirement that the term "organized crime" must imply an ongoing or repetitive criminal involvement. Once one-time-only criminal operations become "organized crime," the unique aspects of this concept are threatened.

4. The United Nations uses the term "transnational criminality" in some of its documents as an umbrella term that encompasses criminal activity such as "international organized crime," "international economic crime," and "terrorism." While each of these terms has a separate and distinct definition, the three converge. This convergence is of particular interest and of particular threat to governments.

5. Edelhertz (1993: 168) emphasizes the need for the police and prosecutors to be adept at conducting white collar investigations that involve forensic accounting skills to detect irregularities that will reveal "the maintenance of false records, the submission of false claims, collusion between customers and suppliers, commercial bribery, kickbacks, vertical and horizontal monopolies and . . . omnipresent tax violations."

6. The list of organized crime commodities reflects previous Canadian research and the findings of the 1998 Organized Crime Impact Study completed for the Department of the Solicitor General, Canada, by Sam Porteous.

7. A web-site maintained by the Nathanson Centre for the Study of Organized Crime and Corruption at Osgoode Hall Law School (http://www.yorku.ca/nathanson) contains a bibliography of organized crime by group and by commodity.

8. Reported home invasions are more frequent in British Columbia than elsewhere in Canada. Criminals force their way into a person's home, tie up family members, often using violence, and steal the valuables. Asian homes were initially the main targets, but now criminals are broadening their scope to include other people known to have items of value in their homes. In addition to the Asian organized crime gangs, gypsy criminals are also involved in home invasions.

9. For a detailed discussion please see M. Beare and S. Schneider, *Tracing of Illicit Funds: Money Laundering in Canada*; and National Crime Authority, *Taken to the Cleaners: Money Laundering in Australia*, Vol. 1 and 2.

10. It is important to note, however, that since the time of the media coverage of this 1994 RCMP case, there has been considerable controversy surrounding the ethics or policies of the RCMP in their conducting of this case. A series of articles by Andrew McIntosh for *The Ottawa Citizen* ran for a week in June 1998 and outlined the "imaginative" strategies used by the RCMP during this four year undercover operation. The police were particularly criticized for using the commissions earned from laundering the drug proceeds through their undercover Exchange House to finance part of their undercover operation (see McIntosh, 1998).

DISCUSSION QUESTIONS

1. Discuss the components of a definition of organized crime. How does "the mob" fit into such a definition?

2. Compare and contrast the "groups" involved in organized crime in Canada.

3. What is money laundering? Be specific. Show how it has been accomplished in Canada. What is the role of lawyers?

4. Beare claims that organized crime is interwoven with the political, social, and economic fabric of society. Discuss.

REFERENCES

Albini, J. L. (1988). Donald Cressey's contributions to the study of organized crime: An evaluation. *Crime and Delinquency, 34*(3).

Albini, J. L., & Bajon, B. J. (1978). Witches, mafia, mental illness and social reality: A study in the power of mythical belief. *International Journal of Criminology and Penology, 6*(4), 285–294.

Albini, J. L., & Bajon, B. J. (1993). The mafia and the devil: What they have in common. *Journal of Contemporary Criminal Justice, 9*(3), 241.

Andelman, D. A. (1994). The dirty money maze. *Foreign Affairs,* (July/August), 94–108.

Andrieux, J. P. (1983). *Prohibition and St. Pierre.* Canada: W .R. Rannie.

Australia, National Crime Authority (NCA). (1991). *Taken to the Cleaners: Money Laundering in Australia.* 3 volume study.

Beare, M. E. (1996). *Criminal Conspiracies: Organized Crime in Canada.* Toronto: Nelson.

Beare, M. E., & Schneider, S. (1990). *Tracing of illicit funds: Money laundering in Canada.* Solicitor General Canada, User Report No. 1990-05.

Block, A. (1990). Thoughts on the history of organized crime: In praise of revisionist criminology. Paper presented at the American Society of Criminology meetings.

British Columbia, Ministry of the Attorney General, Coordinated Law Enforcement Unit. (1994, May). *CLEU Line.* Policy Analysis Division.

Calder, J. D. (n.d.) Al Capone and state-sanctioned criminology, or government-defined organized crime. Undated paper given at the American Society of Criminology meetings.

Canadian Association of Chiefs of Police (CACP). (1993). *Organized crime committee report.* Produced by the Canadian Intelligence Service Canada.

Canadian Bar Association. (1991). *Resolutions.* 1991 CBA Annual Meeting.

CBC Newsworld. (1991, July 23). Cigarette smuggling at Akwesasne.

Coad, B., & Richardson, D. (1993). Reducing market opportunities for organized crime. Paper delivered at the Australian Academy of Forensic Science, Sydney, Australia, May 20.

Commonwealth Secretariat. (1992). *Basic documents on international efforts to combat money laundering.*

Commonwealth Secretariat. *Action against transnational criminality.* Papers from the 1991 and 1992 Oxford Conference on International and White Collar Crime.

Cressey, D. R. (1967). The functions and structure of criminal syndicates. *Task force report: Organized crime* (annotations and consultant's papers), 25–60.

Cressey, D. R. (1969). *Theft of the nation: The structure and operations of organized crime in America.* New York: Harper and Row.

Dubra, J. (1993, March 25). Organized crime. *The Globe and Mail,* A16.

Edelhertz, H. (Ed.). (1987). Major issues in organized crime control: Symposium proceedings. Washington, DC, September 25–26, 1986. U.S. Department of Justice, National Institute of Justice.

Edelhertz, H., & Overcast, T. D. (1993). *The business of organized crime: An assessment of organized crime business-type activities and their implications for law enforcement.* Loomis, CA: Palmer Press.

Edwards, P. (1991). *The big sting: The true story of the Canadian who betrayed Colombia's drug barons.* Toronto: Key Porter Books.

Freeman, B., & Hewitt, M. (1979). *Their town: The mafia, the media and the party machine.* Toronto: James Lorimer.

Haller, M. H. (1987). Business partnerships in the coordination of illegal enterprise. Paper presented at the American Society of Criminology meetings, Montreal.

Kelly, R. (1987). The nature of organized crime and its operations. In H. Edelhertz (Ed.), *Major issues in organized crime control.* National Institute of Justice Symposium Proceedings, September 25–26, 1986, 5–50.

Kelly, R. J., Chin, K., & Fagan, J. (1993). The structure, activity, and control of Chinese gangs: Law enforcement perspectives. *Journal of Contemporary Criminal Justice, 9*(3), 221–239.

Lacy, R. (1991). *Little man: Meyer Lansky and the gangster life.* New York: Little, Brown and Co.

Stamler, R. T. (1993). *Contraband tobacco estimate,* June 30, 1992; *Contraband tobacco estimate*, released March 1993. Toronto: Linquist Avey Macdonald Baskerville Inc.

Lupsha, P. (1981, May). Individual choice, material culture, and organized crime. *Criminology, 19*(1), 3–24.

Lupsha, P. (1986). Organized crime in the United States. In R. J. Kelly (Ed.), *Organized crime: A global perspective.* Rowman and Littlefield.

Lupsha, P. (1988). Organized crime: Rational choice not ethnic group behaviour: A macro perspective. *Law Enforcement Intelligence Analysis Digest.* International Association of Law Enforcement Intelligence Analysts, Washington (Winter), 1–8.

Maltz, M. (1990). *Measuring the effectiveness of organized crime control efforts.* University of Illinois at Chicago, The Office of International Criminal Justice.

Martens, F. T. (1991). Transnational enterprise crime and the elimination of frontiers. *International Journal of Comparative and Applied Criminal Justice, 15*(1) (Spring), 99–107.

Martens, F. T., & Cunningham-Niederer, M. (1985). Media magic, mafia mania. In *Federal probation* (pp. 60–68). Washington, DC: Government Printing Office.

Martin's Annual Criminal Code. (1975). Agincourt, ON: Canada Law Book Limited.

Martin's Annual Criminal Code. (1993). Agincourt, ON: Canada Law Book Inc.

McIntosh, A. (1998, June 11). How the RCMP helped "push" $2 billion worth of cocaine. *Ottawa Citizen.*

McIntosh, A. (1998, June 12). Agents "reinvested" profits in drug-money business. *Ottawa Citizen.*

McIntosh, A. (1998, June 13). Government defies court order to open files on "illegal" drug sting. *Ottawa Citizen.*

Merton, R. K. (1967). *On theoretical sociology.* New York: Free Press.

Merton, R. K. (1968). *Social theory and social structure.* New York: Free Press.

Money laundering alert. 1991, Vol. 2(5) (February); 1989, Vol. 1(3); 1993, Vol. 4(10) (July); 1993, Vol. 4(11) (August).

Moore, M. (1987). Organized crime as a business enterprise. In H. Edelhertz (Ed.), *Major issues in organized crime control* (pp. 51–64). National Institute of Justice Symposium Proceedings, Washington, September 25–26, 1986.

Nonna, J. M., & Corrado, M. P. (1990). RICO reform: "Weeding out" garden variety disputes under RICO. *St. John's Law Review, 64*(4) (Fall), 825–848.

Palango, P. (1994). *Above the law: The crooks, the politicians, the mounties, and Rod Stamler.* Toronto: McClelland and Stewart.

Pennsylvania Crime Commission. (1991). *Organized crime in Pennsylvania: A decade of change 1990 report.* Commonwealth of Pennsylvania.

Porteous, S. (1998). *Organized crime impact study: Highlights.* Prepared for the Federal Department of the Solicitor General, Canada.

Ragano, F., & Raab, S. (1994). *Mob lawyer.* New York: Charles Scribner's Sons.

Reuter, P. (1983). *Disorganized crime: The economics of the visible hand.* Cambridge, MA: MIT Press.

Rogovin, C., & Martens, F. (1990). The invaluable contributions of Donald Cressey to the study of organized crime. Paper presented at the Academy of Criminal Justice Sciences Annual Conference (March).

Royal Canadian Mounted Police (*RCMP*) *Gazette.* (1994). Outlaw motorcycle gangs. Vol. 56(3 & 4).

Sacco, V., & Kennedy, L. (1994). *The criminal event.* Toronto: Nelson Canada.

Stamler, R. T. (1992). Organized crime. In R. Linden (Ed.), *Criminology: A Canadian perspective.* Toronto: Harcourt Brace Jovanovich.

Sterling, C. (1994). *Crime without frontiers.* Little, Brown.

Sterling, C. (1994). *Thieves' world: The threat of the new global network of organized crime.* New York: Simon and Schuster.

Stier, E. H., & Richards, P. R. (1987). Strategic decision making in organized crime control: The need for a broadened perspective. In *Major Issues in Organized Crime Control.* National Institute of Justice, Symposium Proceedings, Washington, DC, 1986.

United Nations, General Assembly. (1989). Convention against illicit traffic in narcotic drugs and psychotropic substances. Vienna, December 20, 1988, 28 I.L.M. 493.

United Nations, General Assembly. (1992). The strengthening of international cooperation in combatting organized crime: Report to the secretary-general. 47th session, agenda item 93(b), Social development: Crime prevention and criminal justice, September 28.

United Nations, General Assembly. (1998). Financial havens, banking secrecy and money laundering (preliminary draft). Office for Drug Control and Crime Prevention, Global Programme Against Money Laundering. (To be published as a joint publication of the *International Review of Criminal Policy* (#49-50)and *UNDCP Technical Series* (#8).

United States Government. President's Commission on Law Enforcement and Administration of Justice, Task Force on Organized Crime. (1967). *Task force report: Organized crime.* Washington.

United States Government. Department of the Treasury. (1992). *An assessment of narcotics related money laundering.* Financial Crimes Enforcement Network (FinCEN) (July).

United States Government. Senate. (1992). *The new international criminal and Asian organized crime.* Report made by the Permanent Subcommittee on Investigations of the Committee on Governmental Affairs (December).

United States Government. Senate. (1992). Asian organized crime: The new international criminal. Hearings, June 18 to August 4.

Wolf, D. R. (1991). *The rebels: A brotherhood of outlaw bikers.* Toronto: University of Toronto Press.

Zagaris, B. (1993). *Implementation of a world-wide anti-money laundering system: Constructing an international financial regime.* Police Executive Research Forum, Washington, July.

Cases Cited

R. v. Duarte [1990], 53 C.C.C. (3rd) 1 (S.C.C.).

Corporate Crime[1]

CARL KEANE

INTRODUCTION

Every day, individuals holding positions of responsibility, at senior levels in the corporate world, violate the laws of society. The few studies that have investigated corporate crime report that it is not uncommon. Yet, with the exception of well-publicized cases such as the Bre-X mining fraud, few people are aware of the extent of such crime.

It was the ground-breaking work of Sutherland (1949) that first brought corporate crime into the spotlight. Sutherland analysed the life careers of the 70 largest U.S. manufacturing, mining, and mercantile corporations, examining the following legal violations: restraint of trade; misrepresentation in advertising; infringements of patents, trademarks, and copyrights; labour law violations; illegal rebates; financial fraud and violation of trust; violations of war regulations; and finally some miscellaneous offences. He found a total of 980 decisions had been made against the 70 corporations, an average of 14 decisions per corporation (1949:29). Other research shows that his findings are not unusual. For example, focusing on illegal acts such as price-fixing, overcharging, violation of environmental regulations and antitrust laws, bribes, fraud, patent infringements, and violations of other market regulations, a 1984 survey found that approximately two-thirds of the Fortune 500 largest industrial companies had been involved in illegal behaviour since the mid-1970s (Etzioni, 1985).

Perhaps the most extensive examination to date of corporate offending is the study conducted by Clinard and his colleagues (Clinard et al., 1979; Clinard and Yeager, 1980). This research involved the analysis of federal administrative, civil, and criminal actions either initiated or completed by 25 U.S. agencies during 1975–1976 against the 477 largest publicly owned U.S. manufacturing companies and the 105 largest U.S. wholesale, retail, and service companies. Six main types of corporate illegal behaviour were discovered: administrative violations such as noncompliance with an order from a court or government agency; environmental violations such as pollution of the air or water; financial violations including bribery, tax violations, and accounting malpractices; labour violations involving employment discrimination, occupational safety and health hazards, and unfair labour practices; manufacturing violations such as violations of the Consumer Product Safety Act; and unfair trade practices, involving various abuses of competition such as price-fixing as well as acts such as false advertising (Clinard and Yeager, 1980:113–115). The researchers found that of the 582 corporations, approximately 60% had at least one federal action brought against them, and for those companies that had at least one action brought against them, the average was 4.4 cases (1980:113).

Focusing on violations of the Combines Act in Canada, Goff and Reasons (1978) reported that between 1952 and 1972 a total of 157 decisions

Written for this volume. Adapted from the article that appeared in the fifth edition of *Crime in Canadian Society*.

were made against the 50 largest Canadian corporations, an average of three decisions per corporation. Taken together, these studies demonstrate the wide extent of corporate offending, and reveal that individuals in the middle and upper socio-economic classes, contrary to popular stereotypes, quite frequently engage in illegal behaviour.

What causes such crime? Reflecting on Sutherland's (1949) point that corporate offenses cannot be explained by conditions of poverty, nor by individual pathology, any search for the causes of corporate crime should begin with an examination of the context within which such crimes occur — the organization. This approach calls for an analysis of the corporation and its impact on the individuals who work there. As such, it is useful to first examine external and internal factors that affect the organization, followed by those factors that affect the employees of the organization. Let us begin with external factors of influence.

EXTERNAL FACTORS OF INFLUENCE

Any organization both affects, and is affected by, its environment. Organizations are constrained by laws, and at the same time, they may try to influence legislators. Some corporations conduct business in markets with numerous competitors, consumers, and suppliers — others with few. And organizations operate in economies ranging from capitalist to communist. To help us understand the influence of external factors, we can begin with an examination of the economic system.

Capitalism

Some criminologists argue that to understand corporate crime we should adopt a macro-perspective, and focus on the features of our capitalist economy. They suggest that corporate capitalism, with its primary emphasis on the goals of maximizing profitability and minimizing costs, leads to unsafe products, environmental pollution, employee and consumer deception, and unsafe working condi-

tions (see Henry, 1982:85). At the same time, it is argued that the content and enforcement of laws against corporate crime reflect the interests of the economic elite, who through their economic dominance are able to influence the political elite, leading to weakened legislation and lax enforcement of existing laws (Snider and West, 1985; also see Snider, 1993, for a thorough examination of the problems of corporate regulation). However, organizational problems are not restricted to capitalist countries. For example, in an effort to meet productivity goals, former Soviet workers endured one of the worst records of industrial safety and occupational health in the world (Handelman, 1989). Others have reported a variety of economic crimes such as bribery, fraud, property theft, and "black-market" operations that have been widespread in communist countries (Los, 1982). Therefore, the economic system alone cannot provide a comprehensive explanation for organizational deviance. Let us thus look to competition.

Competition

Some see competition, common to both the profit and not-for-profit sectors, as a precipitating factor in the genesis of corporate crime. The infamous case of the Ford Pinto automobile can be cited as an example. Facing increasing competition from foreign small-car imports, the Ford Motor Company attempted to speed up the production process of the Pinto in order to meet the competition. When it was determined that a faulty fuel system could cause the car to explode on impact, Ford executives conducted a cost-benefit analysis, weighing the estimated number of injuries and deaths and resulting lawsuits that would occur against the cost of recalling all the defective cars. In accordance with the results of the cost-benefit analysis, the company decided against recalling the Ford Pinto, a decision that ultimately resulted in numerous deaths and injuries (Cullen et al., 1987; Dowie, 1977). This example is but one manifestation of a "culture of competition" which exists in all industrialized countries. It is related to corporate crime in that it motivates individuals to succeed at virtually any cost (Coleman, 1987; 1989).

In fact, at a session on business ethics at the World Economic Forum, it was reported that "corrupt practices such as bribery are considered inevitable — if not acceptable — in international business, and executives fear they will lose contracts to competitors unless they go along with the corrupt practices" (*Globe and Mail*, February 14, 1994, p. B7). And a World Bank–sponsored survey of 3600 companies in 69 countries found that more than 40% of respondents reported having to pay bribes to get things done (*Globe and Mail*, September 20, 1997, pp. A10, A21). Thus, the quest for success is framed within a competitive global milieu.

Strain Theory

We have seen how companies pitted against each other in a "culture of competition" produce a situation of inter-firm rivalry wherein some firms might violate the law to gain advantage over a competitor. What we have described is a setting where the industry culture promotes competition as a means of attaining corporate goals, but the market structure limits the opportunity for all companies to achieve success. This discrepancy between culture and structure produces a situation of strain which increases the possibility of corporate corruption (see Keane, 1993). A similar process can be seen even internal to the organization. That is, in the planning and budgeting process, companies regularly set internal corporate goals. In this situation competition may exist between two divisions; between plants; and/or between time periods, such as when a company budgets to decrease costs or forecasts to increase sales over the previous year. Again we have a situation where the corporate culture emphasizes competition, but the corporate structure may not provide the opportunity to achieve the corporate goal. According to Merton (1938) this type of situation may lead to illegal behaviour. Merton postulated that if individuals are thwarted in their quest to attain their desired goals, such as the culturally prescribed goal of suc-

cess, they will become frustrated. This frustration, caused by a disjuncture between legal means and desired goals, will produce a situation of strain, and individuals will adapt to alleviate the strain. Some individuals, whom Merton called "innovators," while accepting the goal will reject conventional means and embrace illegal means of attaining the goal. With respect to strain, Clinard (1983) reported on the pressure exerted on middle managers from top management to increase profitability, decrease costs, and meet production and sales quotas, pressure which may result in illegal behaviour. Simply stated, some individuals, faced with a discrepancy between goals and the legal means to achieve them, will become corporate criminals. Competition, however, is a necessary but not sufficient cause of corporate crime. For example, although competition exists in every industry, some industries are more crime prone than others. Also, even within the same industry, some firms violate the law more than others. As researchers of corporate crime we must ask, what is there about particular industries, and particular firms, that produces a higher rate of corporate crime? This question calls for a closer examination of other aspects of the external environment of modern organizations.

Environmental Uncertainty

In examining the external structure of organizations we can identify certain factors that vary among firms and industries. For example, while all organizations place an organizational priority on goal attainment (Finney and Lesieur, 1982), organizations may have a variety of goals, and goals will differ among organizations. Although profitability is often the primary goal, organizations may strive to maximize revenue, earnings per share, market share, growth, or production quotas — or the primary goal may be survival. Organizations, however, do not operate in a vacuum. The external environment of an organization comprises political, sociocultural, economic, physical, and technological factors, and perhaps most importantly, other organizations. These various elements of what has been referred to as an organization's "task environment" (Dill, 1958) produce a high degree of uncertainty. In order to meet corporate goals an organization operating within an uncertain environment may attempt to reduce that uncertainty through illegal behaviour (see Aldrich, 1979). For example, to reduce uncertainty concerning pricing vis-à-vis competitors, as well as to reduce the uncertainty of profitability, an organization may collude with other firms in the same industry to set and maintain prices (see Simpson, 1986). This price-fixing conspiracy serves to reduce uncertainty by providing the company with some control over an important element of its external environment.

In general, as environmental uncertainty increases, thus threatening goal attainment, illegal behaviour may increase in attempts to control or minimize the uncertainty, and to increase the likelihood of goal achievement.

Market Structure

As discussed above, price-fixing reduces uncertainty about profitability and competitive behaviour. However, for a price-fixing conspiracy to be successful there must be agreement among the firms that prices will be maintained. Hence, the greater the number of firms in a particular industry, the harder it may be to coordinate a collusion, and thus the harder it will be for all to agree to maintain prices. Therefore, price-fixing may be more prevalent in concentrated industries dominated by a small number of firms. More specifically, Coleman (1989:225) suggests, "it would seem that industries with many small, highly competitive firms would be characterized by a high rate of crimes that are intended to improve competitive performance, such as fraud, false advertising, and espionage, and that collusion and antitrust activities are most common in more concentrated industries." An example of the relationship between price-fixing and a concentrated market structure can be seen in the case of the compressed gases industry in Canada. In this case, it was found that only five companies supplied 97% of the compressed gases sold in Canada. Representatives of these companies

admitted in a statement of facts read in court that they met and agreed to adopt common prices for the sale of various compressed gases, thereby violating the Competition Act (*Globe and Mail*, September 7, 1991, p. B2; *Globe and Mail*, October 19, 1991, p. B3). So the market structure of the industry is important with respect to the type of illegal activity most likely to occur. In addition, some situations may be particularly conducive to criminal behaviour in that there is an increased opportunity to violate the law. This leads us to a discussion of what can be termed opportunity theory.

Opportunity Theory

The notion of "opportunity" differs slightly from the preceding discussion of industry concentration and corporate deviance by focusing on the increased likelihood of a firm to violate a specific type of law. For example, oil companies in the course of producing and/or shipping oil have a greater likelihood of polluting the environment (Clinard and Yeager, 1980:250–251), while firms that are labour-intensive, placing a heavy reliance upon workers as opposed to equipment, are more likely to violate labour laws (Clinard and Yeager, 1980:131–132). Thus, some industries, and the firms and employees within them, may be more prone to committing certain offences than others.

At the same time, some industries more than others may find themselves the target of various regulatory agencies. That is, some industries such as the pharmaceutical industry, the automobile industry, and the chemical and petroleum industries, because of the potential harm their products can cause, are more regulated than others (Coleman, 1989), and in turn, they have higher crime rates than others (Clinard and Yeager, 1980), if only because of the greater regulation imposed upon them. Also, because some industries may be more stringently regulated than others, it follows that those organizations that are diversified into a number of stringently regulated industries are more likely to face "opportunities" to deviate and/or are more likely to attract regulatory attention (Clinard and Yeager, 1980:131).

To summarize briefly, companies are goal oriented, and with factors such as globalization of business and rapid social change, they may find themselves operating in uncertain environments. And in the process of minimizing uncertainty and maximizing goal attainment, regulations peculiar to the industry may be violated. Nevertheless, differences in the rates of violation exist among companies in the same industry. That is, although some industries tend to violate the law more than others, there is still variation within industries, with some firms more deviant than others (Clinard and Yeager, 1980:58). This being the case, we must ask, what characteristics distinguish criminal from non-criminal firms? Or, put another way, what are the characteristics of those firms that come to the attention of regulatory bodies? An examination of the internal environment of the corporation may provide an answer to these questions.

INTERNAL FACTORS OF INFLUENCE

Internal Control

The modern corporation is a large, diffuse, hierarchical system oriented towards goal(s) attainment through effective use of available resources in an uncertain environment. Employees of the corporation are one resource deployed to meet organizational goals. And just as an organization will attempt to have some influence over its external environment, it must also manage its internal resources, including its employees. However, the internal structure of the corporation may make it difficult to control corporate illegality. For example, conditions associated with larger size may be conducive to corrupt behaviour (Clinard and Yeager, 1980). As companies grow along dimensions such as number of product lines, number of employees, and number of geographically dispersed locations, they become more difficult to manage, more difficult to control, and in short, more complex. Deviant activities can remain hidden in this complex structure. In attempts to control the internal environment in the

midst of this complexity, lines of authority may become decentralized. Stated differently, complexity and diversification, resulting from corporate growth, may call for a decentralized corporate structure as a means of coping with the vast numbers of people and information. And it can be argued that a decentralized corporate structure in turn may be actually more conducive to corruption, rather than less, because visibility is decreased and responsibility is diffused (Finney and Lesieur, 1982; Keane, 1995). That is, when an individual is geographically distant, such as in a branch plant in another country, and/or shielded from senior management by several levels of staff, communication may suffer. So in a decentralized system it is easier to withhold information. In turn, senior management can distance themselves from wrongdoing occurring at the divisional level and/or at a distant location and deny accountability; a tactic referred to by Sutherland (1949:226) as "obfuscation as to responsibility." Pearce and Tombs (1993) provide an example of this process in their study of the Union Carbide disaster in Bhopal, India. They describe how the parent company attempted to shift responsibility for the disaster to the subsidiary, thereby minimizing the accountability of the parent company.

To briefly summarize once more, previously we argued that the organization's external environment is a contributing factor to corporate crime. Now we see that internal corporate factors are also important. But the picture is still incomplete. Although the form of the corporation may provide the setting where control is difficult and the potential for criminal activity is increased, certain individual variables may also be necessary for crime to occur, and we examine these in turn.

INDIVIDUAL LEVEL FACTORS

Control Theory

Theorists advocating control theories of crime argue that individuals who have weak ties to the norms of conventional society are more likely to deviate than those who are (1) emotionally attached to conventional others and therefore reluctant to deviate for fear of displeasing these others; (2) committed to conventional goals acquired through conventional means; (3) involved in conventional/legal activities; and who (4) believe in the validity of the laws of society and the need to obey those laws (Hirschi, 1969). In essence, control theorists argue that the more individuals are integrated into a legal, as opposed to an illegal, culture, the less likely they are to violate society's laws. Thus, at first glance, it appears that social control theory would be deficient in explaining crimes of the privileged, since unlike the stereotypical "street" criminal, the corporate executive appears to be strongly connected to conventional society. If we modify control theory, however, and examine the subculture of the organization, we can hypothesize that corporate offenders may be more tightly bonded to the culture of the organization than they are to the larger society. This suggests a socialization process whereby individuals come to identify closely with the organization and its goals. That is, through work-related activities and social interaction with other company employees, they intensify their bond of loyalty to the organization. This bond to the organization may then be strengthened through social mobility via promotions and/or geographic mobility via transfers (Coleman, 1989:220), both of which may make it difficult for individuals to develop long-term social ties outside the organization. Thus, individuals may come to associate predominantly with other members of the organization for whom they come to care, and from whom they learn the behaviour required to attain corporate goals with which they come to strongly identify.

Differential Association

Continuing with individual level explanations of wrongdoing, Sutherland's (1949) interactionist theory of "differential association" also makes a contribution. A form of learning theory, differential association postulates that deviant behaviour is learned, just like any other type of behaviour. Differential association points to the importance of

learning both the illegal methods as well as the beliefs supporting the use of the methods (Sutherland, 1949:234). Clinard and Yeager (1980:58) have confirmed the validity of differential association theory in explaining economic crimes, arguing that although the corporation is influenced by its external environment, the behaviour of a firm is also a product of cultural norms operating within a given corporation. With respect to corporate crimes, the theory suggests that executives become enmeshed in a corporate or professional subculture, and through association with deviant peers learn illegal behaviour. Two essential components of this theory are that (1) the individual must be exposed to an excess of definitions favourable to crime, and (2) the individual must be isolated from definitions unfavourable to crime. Given the loyalty and feelings of identification with the corporation that some organizations are able to instill in their employees, it is easy to see how an individual could be socialized to commit an unlawful act. For example, the former head of securities lending for Gordon Capital Corporation of Toronto, who was banned from trading for ten years for exposing the firm to improper risks by abusing the regulatory system, argued in his own defence that "the Gordon culture sacrificed compliance for profits." He also argued that "many others were involved in the transactions and . . . no one indicated any concerns or problems to him" (*Globe and Mail*, June 18, 1993, p. B2).

Finney and Lesieur (1982:277) wrote that internal organizational constraints against crime will vary along a continuum, "one end representing moral commitment against law violation, the middle representing a state of neutral receptivity, and the other end representing positive attitudes towards law violation." Accordingly, illegal behaviour is more likely if corporations selectively hire, selectively promote, and socialize a significant number of employees who adopt a stance on the continuum near the neutral or deviant end. Thus, the presence of internal cultural constraints, or their absence, will have an influence on organizational members, and in turn the level of organizational deviance.

Techniques of Neutralization

Finally, how does the corporate criminal justify his or her deviant behaviour? Sykes and Matza (1957:664–670) argued that individuals who periodically "drift" from a basic conformity into illegal behaviour will rationalize their guilt by using various "techniques of neutralization." These techniques, which allow normally law-abiding people, such as corporate executives, to justify illegal behaviour are outlined below.

1. DENIAL OF RESPONSIBILITY

Vandivier (1987:114–115) relates a conversation he had with a senior executive at the B.F. Goodrich Co., who when asked why he was not going to report to senior management that a faulty aircraft brake was being developed replied: "Because it's none of my business, and it's none of yours. I learned a long time ago not to worry about things over which I had no control. I have no control over this." Not satisfied with this answer, Vandivier asked him if his conscience wouldn't bother him if during test flights on the brake, something should happen resulting in death or injury to the test pilot. To this the executive replied: "I have no control over this thing. Why should my conscience bother me?"

2. DENIAL OF INJURY

In 1993 the U.S. government fined the Louisiana-Pacific Corporation $11.1 million (U.S.) for excessive emissions and giving false information to environmental officials. The violations occurred at 14 facilities in 11 states. A spokesperson for the company later insisted that federal officials "aren't charging us with any significant emissions of anything hazardous into the air or any environmental harm. What they're saying is the proper procedures, as they see them, weren't followed" (*Globe and Mail*, May 25, 1993, p. B5). Even more recently, Dow Corning Corporation, the largest manufacturer of silicone-gel breast implants, agreed to pay Quebec and Ontario women up to $35 million (U.S.) to settle a class action suit and to finance a program to assist women in removing their breast implants. According to a report in the *Globe and Mail* newspaper, a spokesperson for the company said that "the settlement does not mean the company admits the implants posed dangers" (*Globe and Mail*, April 3, 1998, p. A11).

3. DENIAL OF THE VICTIM

Continuing with the example given earlier of the Canadian compressed gas industry, in 1991 Union Carbide was fined $1.7 million, while Canadian Oxygen Ltd. was fined $700 000 after pleading guilty to fixing prices. Officials at both companies claimed, however, that because of long-term contracts, no customers were penalized during the period from January to May 1990, when prices were fixed by the conspirators (*Globe and Mail*, September 7, 1991, p. B2).

4. CONDEMNATION OF THE CONDEMNERS

An example of this technique is the case of Charles Keating who was fined in excess of $260 million and sentenced to over 12 years in prison for his involvement in the Lincoln Savings and Loan Association fraud in the United States. Professing his innocence, he claimed that a vendetta by banking regulators caused Lincoln's collapse in 1989 and his ruination (*Globe and Mail*, July 29, 1993, p. B15).

5. APPEAL TO HIGHER LOYALTIES

When the chairman of France's largest private corporation was arrested and charged with fraud, embezzlement, and corruption, the country's minister of industry and trade argued that the country should have more important things to do in a recession than prosecute business leaders. He questioned whether the prosecution of this senior executive should be a priority in a country with 3.4 million people unemployed (*Globe and Mail*, July 6, 1994, p. B10).

To this point we have seen that at the macro level, external factors have an impact on the organization and have some influence on the structure of the organization. Further, these macro-level factors, as well as micro-level influences, are felt at the individual level. Let us now attempt to synthesize these findings.

THEORETICAL INTEGRATION

To gain a clearer picture of corporate crime, a theoretical integration of external, internal, and individual factors related to corporate offending may be useful. To begin, the economic condition of the industry and the extent of task-environment uncertainty are important, as is the degree of industry competition, which may lead to behaviour to reduce uncertainty. Also, the likelihood of a firm violating a particular law varies with the type of industry and the level of industry regulation. Further, large firms may be more likely to be deviant because of the diffusion of responsibility and diminished control. And if the firm is not performing well, the potential for illegal behaviour increases.

So, to this point we can speculate that large firms operating in regulated industries, experiencing economic strain and environmental uncertainty are more at risk of corporate crime. However, although this setting may be conducive to illegal behaviour, individuals must also be exposed to a socialization process whereby they come to identify with the company and its goals, learn the illegal behaviour required to meet the objectives perceived to be unattainable through legal means, and rationalize their actions through various techniques. Hence, the external culture and the internal corporate culture interact to either promote or inhibit law violation.

An element of strain exists in both cultures of an offending corporation. At the external level, the strain may be caused by forces such as competitors, suppliers, or government legislation posing a threat to the corporation's objectives. At the internal level, the strain may also be caused by the potential failure to meet corporate objectives, but the pressure is imposed by internal rather than external actors. And if cultural restraints such as values and regulations opposing and thus inhibiting corporate criminal behaviour are lacking or weak, both externally,

in society in general, and internally, within the organization, corruption is more likely to occur. This being the case, can we control corporate crime?

CONTROLLING CORPORATE OFFENDING

Braithwaite (1989:40) argued that "in modern capitalist societies there are many more statutes that criminalize the behaviour of corporations (anti-pollution laws, occupational health and safety laws, consumer protection laws, antitrust laws, laws to enforce compliance with standards) than there are laws that criminalize the behaviour of the poor." However, application of the law is another matter. That is, evidence suggests that crimes of the powerful are punished differently than crimes of the powerless. For example, focusing on Canadian securities violations, Hagan (1989; Hagan and Parker, 1985) examined all cases referred for prosecution under the Criminal Code or the Securities Act from 1966 to 1983. After categorizing offenders in terms of their class position, the researchers found that those offenders in positions of power committed crimes larger in scope than those with less power, but they received proportionately less severe sanctions because the powerful were less likely to be charged under the Criminal Code, and more likely to be charged under the Securities Act, which carries lesser sanctions.

Also considering the element of power is research by Goff and Reasons (1978). Their research involved an investigation of the major Canadian corporations which have violated the Combines Act and have been investigated by the Combines Branch from 1952 to 1973. Concentrating on the illegal acts of combinations, mergers, monopolies, resale price maintenance, misleading price advertising, predatory pricing, price discrimination, and violations of patents, they concluded that the "Combines Branch has centred its attentions upon the investigation, prosecution, and conviction of small- and medium-sized companies and corporations leaving the very largest corporations free to engage in their monopolistic practices" (Goff and

Reason, 1978:86). Again, they suggested that this occurs because large corporations operating in oligopolistic industries have the ability to obscure their illegal practices. Only very recently have we seen governments taking a more aggressive stance against those illegal cartels that are discovered. For example, the food giant Archer-Daniels-Midland Co. was fined a record $100 million (U.S.) in the United States, and $16 million in Canada, for taking part in a conspiracy to fix prices. The significance of those record fines is lessened, however, when we consider that in 1997 the company had worldwide sales of $13.8 billion and a profit of $377 million. In fact, a spokesperson for the company reported that the fine would be covered under current reserves and "does not have an impact on earnings" (*Globe and Mail*, May 28, 1998, pp. B1, B6).

From another perspective, Snider (1982) compared the punishments given to those offenders who commit traditional non-violent economic offences with those offenders who commit what she terms "upperworld" non-violent economic offences. Examples of upperworld non-violent economic offences are acts such as false advertising, misleading price representation, and violations of Acts such as the Food and Drug Act, the Packaging and Labelling Act, the Weights and Measures Act, the Hazardous Products Act, and the Combines Investigation Act. Examples of traditional underworld non-violent economic offenses are theft, possession of stolen goods, breaking and entering, and taking a motor vehicle without consent. In brief, she found that over a considerable period of time more traditional offenders were charged, and the sanctions for the traditional economic crimes were much heavier than for the upperworld economic crimes. Others have similarly argued that corporate criminals enjoy a legal advantage because of the types and combinations of legal sanctions that they experience (see Hagan and Nagel, 1982). For example, although New York state had originally sued Occidental Chemical Corporation for almost $700 million in costs and damages toward the cleanup of Love Canal, the company agreed to pay only $98 million (U.S.) to settle a 14 year liability lawsuit over the toxic disaster that forced hundreds of families from their homes (*Globe and Mail*, June 22, 1994, p. B2).

CONCLUSIONS

In summary, corporate criminals have been spared the stigma of criminalization often imposed on those less privileged. Furthermore, given the evidence of recidivism reported by researchers such as Goff and Reasons (1978) and Clinard and Yeager (1980), the existing sanctions appear to have little deterrent effect. This being the case, to control corporate corruption perhaps we should recall that the roots of unethical behaviour are embedded in the organizational and cultural contexts.

Sanctions which have been suggested to inhibit organizational deviance include stiffer penalties for corporations and executives, negative publicity, nationalization of firms that are habitual offenders, and forced deconcentration and divestiture of offending firms, to name a few (Braithwaite, 1984; Clinard and Yeager, 1980; Coleman, 1989). These sanctions are similar in that they are imposed by others external to the organization, and they are imposed after the criminal act. It may also be possible to control corporate crime at the internal corporate level.

Internal corporate control can be increased by actions such as improving and strengthening the firm's self-regulatory systems (Braithwaite, 1984) and providing for public and/or union representation on corporate boards of directors (Clinard and Yeager, 1980). These internal corporate mechanisms would serve to control the actions of executives prior to any offence. Another method of controlling corporate crime which has received increased attention is the development of a stronger business ethic (Clinard and Yeager, 1980; Coleman, 1989). This proposal is directed at the culture of the organization and is preventive in its orientation. An increasing number of companies are finding that "business does well by doing good" (*Globe and Mail*, October 2, 1997, p. B2). Unethical corporate behaviour may destroy a company's reputation, and given the increase in foreign competition experienced by many industries, a loss of customers may accompany the loss of reputation. In addition, failure to follow ethical business practices may result not only in consumer protest, but also in government intervention (Hilts, 1989). Many companies are taking steps to avoid this possibility. A survey conducted in 1997 by KPMG found that 66% of Canada's largest corporations now have a code of ethics. In the United States, however, this figure is more than 90% (*Globe and Mail*, November 27, 1997, p. B2).

Whether the institutionalization of ethics is successful in decreasing corporate crime remains to be seen. However, it will be a step in creating a culture in which corporate crime is, at least publicly, not tolerated. On a broader scale, Braithwaite (1989) has argued that what society needs "is punishment for organizational crime that maximizes the sense of shame and sends a message to executives that corporate crime is as despicable to society as street crime." He further asserted that "once members of the organization internalize this abhorrence of corporate wrongdoing, then the self-regulation of executive consciences and corporate ethics and compliance policies will do most of the work for the government" (1989:143).

NOTE

1. The author would like to thank Krysia Mossakowski for her research assistance.

DISCUSSION QUESTIONS

1. Outline the internal, external, and individual factors related to corporate offending.
2. Which theories does Keane find useful in trying to understand corporate crime? How does each of them help our understanding?
3. You were introduced to the theories that Keane uses to explain corporate crime in Part 2 of this volume. Show how the same theories are used to understand "street crime" and crime in the boardroom.
4. Discuss the role of ethics in corporate crime.

REFERENCES

Aldrich, H. E. (1979). *Organizations and environments.* Englewood Cliffs, NJ: Prentice-Hall.

Braithwaite, J. (1984). *Corporate crime in the pharmaceutical industry.* London: Routledge & Kegan Paul.

Braithwaite, J. (1989). *Crime, shame and reintegration.* Cambridge: Cambridge University Press.

Clinard, M. B. (1983). *Corporate ethics and crime: The role of middle management.* Beverly Hills: Sage.

Clinard, M. B., & Yeager, P. C. (1980). *Corporate crime.* New York: The Free Press.

Clinard, M. B., Yeager, P. C., Brissette, J., Petrashek, D., & Harries, E. (1979). *Illegal corporate behavior.* Washington, DC: U.S. Department of Justice.

Coleman, J. W. (1987). Toward an integrated theory of white-collar crime. *American Journal of Sociology, 93*(2), 406–439.

Coleman, J. W. (1989). *The criminal elite: The sociology of white-collar crime* (2nd ed.). New York: St. Martin's Press.

Cullen, F. T., Maakestad, W. J., & Cavender, G. (1987). *Corporate crime under attack: The Ford Pinto case and beyond.* Cincinnati: Anderson Publishing Co.

Dill, W. R. (1958). Environment as an influence on managerial autonomy. *Administrative Science Quarterly, 2*(Mar.), 409–443.

Dowie, M. (1977). Pinto madness. *Mother Jones* (Sept.-Oct.), 18–32.

Etzioni, A. (1985). Will a few bad apples spoil the core of big business? *Business and Society Review, 55*(Fall), 4–5.

Finney, H. C., & Lesieur, H. R. (1982). A contingency theory of organizational crime. In S. B. Bacharach (Ed.), *Research in the sociology of organizations,* vol. 1. Greenwich, CT: JAI Press.

The Globe and Mail (Toronto). (1991). Union Carbide fined $1.7-million for price fixing. (September 7).

The Globe and Mail (Toronto). (1991). Pair fined $75,000 each for price-fixing role. (October 19).

The Globe and Mail (Toronto). (1993). Louisiana-Pacific fined. (May 25).

The Globe and Mail (Toronto). (1993). OSC slaps Gordon players. (June 18).

The Globe and Mail (Toronto). (1993). Keating fined $265-million for fraud. (July 29).

The Globe and Mail (Toronto). (1994). To bribe or not to bribe. (February 14).

The Globe and Mail (Toronto). (1994). Love Canal settlement. (June 22).

The Globe and Mail (Toronto). (1994). Alcatel boss rejects fraud charges. (July 6).

The Globe and Mail (Toronto). (1997). Aid donors vow war on graft. (September 20).

The Globe and Mail (Toronto). (1997). Business does well by doing good. (October 2).

The Globe and Mail (Toronto). (1997). Heat's on to get an effective code. (November 27).

The Globe and Mail (Toronto). (1998). Breast implant lawsuit settled. (April 3).

The Globe and Mail (Toronto). (1998). ADM fined $16-million in price-fix case. (May 28).

Goff, C. H., & Reasons, C. E. (1978). *Corporate crime in Canada.* Scarborough, ON: Prentice-Hall.

Hagan, J. (1989). *Structural criminology.* New Brunswick, NJ: Rutgers University Press.

Hagan, J., & Nagel, I. (1982). White collar crime, white collar time: The sentencing of white collar criminals in the southern district of New York. *American Criminal Law Review, 20*(2), 259–301.

Hagan, J., & Parker, P. (1985). White-collar crime and punishment: The class structure and legal sanctioning of securities violations. *American Sociological Review, 50*, 302–316.

Handelman, S. (1989). Fighting to put people before production. *The Toronto Star* (July 16), H1–H2.

Henry, F. (1982). Capitalism, capital accumulation, and crime. *Crime and Social Justice, 18*, 79–87.

Hilts, P. J. (1989). Wave of protests developing on profits from AIDS drug. *The New York Times* (September 16), 1.

Hirschi, T. (1969). *Causes of delinquency.* Berkeley: University of California Press.

Keane, C. (1993). The impact of financial performance on frequency of corporate crime: A latent variable test of strain theory. *Canadian Journal of Criminology, 35*(3), 293–308.

Keane, C. (1995). Loosely coupled systems and unlawful behaviour: Organization theory and corporate crime. In F. Pearce & L. Snider (Eds.), *Corporate crime: Ethics, law and the state.* Toronto: University of Toronto Press.

Los, M. (1982). Crime and economy in the communist countries. In P. Wickman & T. Dailey (Eds.), *White-collar and economic crime.* Toronto: D.C. Heath and Company.

Merton, R. K. (1938). Social structure and anomie. *American Sociological Review, 3*, 672–682.

Pearce, F., & Tombs, S. (1993). US capital versus the third world: Union Carbide and Bhopal. In F. Pearce & M. Woodiwiss (Eds.), *Global crime connections: Dynamics and control.* Toronto: University of Toronto Press.

Simpson, S. (1986). The decomposition of antitrust: Testing a multi-level, longitudinal model of profit-squeeze. *American Sociological Review, 51*, 859–875.

Snider, D. L. (1982). Traditional and corporate theft: A comparison of sanctions. In P. Wickman & T. Dailey (Eds.), *White-collar and economic crime.* Toronto: D.C. Heath and Company.

Snider, D. L. (1993). *Bad business: Corporate crime in Canada.* Scarborough: Nelson Canada.

Snider, D. L., & West, W. G. (1985). A critical perspective on law in the Canadian state: Delinquency and corporate crime. In T. Fleming (Ed.), *The new criminologies in Canada: Crime, state and control.* Toronto: Oxford University Press.

Sutherland, E. H. (1949). *White collar crime.* New York: Holt, Rinehart and Winston.

Sykes, G. M., & Matza, D. (1957). Techniques of neutralization: A theory of delinquency. *American Sociological Review, 22*, 664–670.

Vandivier, K. (1987). Why should my conscience bother me? In M. D. Ermann & R. J. Lundman (Eds.), *Corporate and governmental deviance.* New York: Oxford University Press.

READER REPLY CARD

We are interested in your reaction to *Crime in Canadian Society*, Sixth Edition, by Robert A. Silverman, James J. Teevan, and Vincent F. Sacco. You can help us to improve this book in future editions by completing this questionnaire.

1. What was your reason for using this book?

   ❏ university course   ❏ college course   ❏ continuing education course

   ❏ professional   ❏ personal   ❏ other (please specify)_____
   development   interest   _____

2. If you are a student, please identify your school and the course in which you used this book.

3. Which chapters or parts of this book did you use? Which did you omit?

4. What did you like best about this book?

5. What did you like least about this book?

6. Please identify any topics you think should be added to future editions.

7. Please add any comments or suggestions.

8. May we contact you for further information?

Name: _____

Address: _____

_____

Phone: _____

(fold here and tape shut)

0116870399-M8Z4X6-BR01

Larry Gillevet
Director of Product Development
HARCOURT BRACE & COMPANY, CANADA
55 HORNER AVENUE
TORONTO, ONTARIO
M8Z 9Z9